The Official Visitor's Guide of the National Park Foundation Comprehensive Information on all 358 of America's National Park Areas

The Complete Guide to *America's National Parks*

1992-1993 Edition:

Published by:
National Park Foundation
1101 17th Street, N.W.
Washington, D.C. 20036

Distributed by:
Prentice Hall Trade
A division of Simon & Shuster Inc.
15 Columbus Circle
New York, New York 10023

Share the parks with a friend
To order additional copies of the Guide,
turn to the handy order form in the back of this book.

Message from the President

DEAR VISITOR:

I hope the National Park Foundation's *Complete Guide To America's National Parks* will be a useful companion for you on many visits to the areas of the National Park System—the crown jewels of this country's most spectacular lands, and a vast network of national monuments, historic sites, seashores, battlefields and recreation areas.

The 1992-1993 *Guide* is completely revised to include a system-wide map, photographs, and new sections on special interest parks, regional touring, and rivers and trails. The task of obtaining and verifying the quantity of information needed for the *Guide* from the more than 350 national park areas, was made possible by the excellent cooperation of the superintendents and staffs of each area. In addition, the NPS in Washington and at Harpers Ferry Center provided much useful information and welcome advice as we revised and changed the *Guide*.

Weather information is a unique feature of the *Guide*. Each of the climatables for the 50 great parks is organized to provide you with very useful information on the weather conditions you can expect when you visit these Parks. It was compiled by Climadate Corporation of Philadelphia, Pennsylvania.

The 7th Edition of the *Guide* includes expanded accessibility information for disabled persons for many of the National Parks. The National Park System is committed to providing the highest level of accessibility possible and feasible for persons with visual, hearing, mobility, and mental impairments, consistent with the obligation to conserve park resources and preserve the quality of the park experience for everyone.

Our National Park System, with its diversity, beauty, and breadth of visitor activities has become an integral part of our way of life. It has evolved through the hard work, the vision, the tenacity and the generosity of the people of the United States. It is unique and embodies the commitment that we as a nation have made to preserve the best of our natural, scenic, recreational and historic heritage for the use and enjoyment of all.

As the events in celebration of the NPS 75th Anniversary year come to a close, the National Park Service faces a broad range of challenges to its mission to manage the park system. The Park Service is responding by building the national park system as a model of conservation and preservation—a model that can teach valuable lessons to a world increasingly concerned with environmental threats, as well as with rapid cultural and historical changes. This is the park system that we introduce you to in the new *Guide*, the parks that will lead us in the 21st century. It carries the values and virtues of our rich cultural and scenic heritage.

For the National Parks to flourish, commitment must be on-going. The National Park Foundation was chartered by the United States Congress 25 years ago as a non-profit organization to provide a means for all people to directly support the improvement and enhancement of the National Parks. Donated funds are crucial to achieving the Foundation's mission—to support the overall enhancement of the National Park System, and to foster public awareness, appreciation, understanding of and involvement with the national parks. This *Guide* is unique in that proceeds from its sale are directed to National Park Service programs. If you would like to contribute for the benefit of the National Parks, send funds, or write to me at the National Park Foundation, Department CG, 1101 17th Street, NW, Washington, D.C. 20036.

Have many enjoyable visits to the National Parks—they belong to you!

Alan A. Rubin
President
National Park Foundation

Library of Congress Catalog Card No. 89-063985

ISBN: 0-13-157686-0

The Complete Guide to America's National Parks—1992-1993 Edition Production Manager: Mary D. Hewes. Research assistance provided by National Park Service: Division of History; Division of Long Distance Trails; Division of Park Planning and Protection; Office of Tourism; and Harpers Ferry Center Publications Division. Text design and typesetting: Chase, Fitzgerald, Inc., Warrenton, Virginia. Regional maps designed, drawn and produced by Rapidesign, Inc., Waco, Kentucky.

Cover photograph of Canyonlands National Park and photograph of Cuyahoga Valley National Recreation Area by Robert Glenn Ketchum ©Copyright 1991 the National Park Foundation. All other photographs courtesy of the National Park Service, Historic Photographic Collections. Back Cover: *Twelve Pound Hailstorm* oil painting by Grant Kanies, 1990 Arts for the Parks winner, from National Park Foundation Art Collection.

Introduction

USING THE GUIDE

The 1992-1993 Seventh Edition of *The Complete Guide To America's National Parks* has been made as accurate as possible. The entry for each park has been submitted for review by the park's superintendent and staff and checked again for accuracy by the staff of the National Park Foundation. **Although every effort has been made to provide accurate and authoritative information in the 7th Edition of the *Guide*, the National Park Foundation can assume no responsibility for any inconvenience, delay, or damage that may arise from any inaccuracy or omission. You should verify the accuracy and completeness of important details before beginning a trip. While information on accommodations, campgrounds, and other facilities has been included for the convenience of our readers, no attempt has been made to evaluate these facilities, and no endorsement of any of them should be inferred from their inclusion.**

You will find information in the *Guide* on more than 350 areas of the National Park System, including those areas that, while not part of the System, receive administrative, technical, or financial support from the National Park Service.

WEATHER INFORMATION

The Climatables™

The 7th Edition of the *Guide* contains useful weather information on park areas in the form of "Climatables™" beginning at page 353. These are referenced in each park area entry in the book. The Climatables™ presented are compilations of official National Oceanic and Atmospheric Administration (NOAA) data from individual National Weather Service Offices, cooperative observation stations, and from several publications on the National Climatic Data Center.

Each Climatable™ is intended to represent or characterize the normal and extreme weather conditions that might be expected to be encountered in the specified National Park area. **The Climatables™ do not in any way represent a forecast of weather conditions, but simply indicate to the Park visitor the type and range of weather conditions that have occurred in the past. The Climatables™ should not be read as predictions of the weather you will actually encounter in your park visit.**

In some National Parks, where the area represented is quite large and there are extensive variations in topography and elevation, a single table of values cannot possibly characterize the weather at every location in the park. **The Climatables™ are not a definitive and detailed climatology of the entire park area, but they present the park visitor with a good understanding of the general types and intensity of weather conditions that have occurred in the past in each area and a reasonable indication of the possible range of weather conditions that could occur throughout the year.** The weather information in the *Guide* ought to be considered when planning a visit to park areas, recognizing that during any particular visit, near-normal weather conditions could be encountered or new weather records could be set.

The weather normals and extremes given in the Climatables™ are not, for the most part, taken from any one observation site. Since each Climatable™ is intended to typify or characterize the weather and climate over the entire area represented, in almost all cases the data have been assembled from a number of observation sites applicable to the designated area. In only a few cases, the area represented was sufficiently limited to permit the data record from a single major National Weather Service office to be used for the Climatable™.

Using The Climatables™

Each Climatable™ contains information in tabular form typifying the temperature, precipitation, and sunshine/cloudiness for all of the National Park sites listed at the top of the table. Two graphs to assist in visualization of some of the temperature and cloudiness information are also included. Other climate or weather information, important or unique to the area covered, is inserted in the box entitled "ETC . . ."

TEMPERATURE: The values for *Normal Daily Maximum* and *Normal Daily Minimum* together indicate the normal daily range of temperature that might be expected to occur during each month of the year. Of course, on any given day, temperatures may be warmer or colder than normal. The values given for *Extreme High* and *Extreme Low* Temperature indicate the full range of temperatures that have occurred in the past. In planning your visit, it would be advisable to consider the possibility of encountering temperatures anywhere between these monthly extremes. Once again, remember, the given values are generally typical or characteristic of the entire area and do not necessarily reflect the absolute record high or low temperature that may have been recorded at any specific location within the area covered.

The number of days each month on which it can normally be expected that the temperature will reach or exceed 90°F or will fall to or below freezing are the last two parameters given under the temperature section. In any given year, these numbers can be exceeded or many fewer days with temperatures reaching these levels might occur. The values presented simply indicate over what portion of each month these temperatures might normally be expected.

PRECIPITATION: The *Normal* and *Maximum* monthly precipitation values together are an indication of how much total precipitation, that is rain and snow combined, is apt to be encountered under normal and extremely wet conditions. At the opposite extreme, it should be noted that at some time in the past, every part of the country has experienced very dry or drought conditions in all months of the year. The values given for *Maximum 24-Hour Precipitation* suggest the wettest day that could be expected to be encountered.

The occurrence of snow can be a delight to the eye and at the same time an inconvenience or even a hazard to the park visitor. In those areas and times of year when the precipitation is primarily in the form of snow, as evidenced by normal daily maximum temperatures being near or below freezing, multiplying the normal precipitation by 10 provides a fairly good estimate of the normal monthly snowfall in inches. The values for *Maximum Snowfall* shown in the Climatable™ indicate how much snow has fallen in the past; but remember these are extreme values.

How often it can be expected to rain or snow is also of importance to the traveler. *Days With Measurable Precipitation* indicates the normal number of days each month on which a measurable amount of precipitation (one-one hundredth inch) can be expected to fall. Of course, a day is counted as a "precipitation day" whether it rains all day or the precipitation is recorded in just one brief shower. To further indicate the nature of the precipitation in each area, the *Average Number of Thunderstorms* that occur each month is given. Those months when the average number of thunderstorms is relatively high are the times of year when the precipitation, even in the absence of thunderstorms, might be expected to be showery or intermittent in nature. It should always be remembered that any thunderstorm can bring with it locally heavy rain, hail, high winds, and electrical activity; treat them with respect.

SUNSHINE/CLOUDINESS: This section of the Climatable™ presents a simple tabulation of the average number of days each month when the period between sunrise and sunset can be characterized as being *Clear, Partly Cloudy* or *Cloudy. The normal Percentage of Possible Sunshine* that can be expected each month expresses the number of daytime hours each month during which sunshine will be seen. This entire section of the Climatables™ together with the number of precipitation days is also helpful in further understanding whether the precipitation indicated for the area is most likely to be in the form of intermittent showers or extended periods of rain.

GRAPHS: The two graphs that are part of each Climatable™ are included to help visualize the temperature and cloudiness information that are in the accompanying table. The bars in the upper graph indicate the extremes in temperature for each month. The two curves through the center of the graph show the normal daily range of temperature. In the lower graph, the number of clear, partly cloudy and cloudy days are expressed as a percentage. Thus, it is relatively easy to see the proportion of each month throughout the year when these sky cover conditions may be expected to be encountered.

"ETC . . .": The information included as "ETC . . ." is intended to both emphasize important weather information and to highlight unique and interesting weather and climate information not brought out by the accompanying tabulation. Where relevant, some cautionary notes are included relative to severe or extreme weather typical of the area.

BEFORE YOU START YOUR TRIP

When you are planning your trip, consult the *Guide* to find out what parks are near your primary destination. You may be close to a fascinating site that you haven't heard about, and may be able to plan a side trip for a day or an afternoon.

To orient you with the locations of park sites, we have included state maps marking the major roads and relative positions of park areas. **These maps are meant only to show you what parks are located in the immediate vicinity of your destination. In order to keep the maps simple we have not made them to exact scale, and have eliminated some smaller roads which might be necessary to reach the parks. So, the maps in this book cannot substitute for detailed road maps.** Additional location information is given in the *DIRECTIONS* section of each park listing.

We have included as much specific information as possible, such as hours, fees, holiday closings and weather information to help you plan your park visit. We have made every attempt to be accurate; however, **you should verify in advance any details of importance to you.** Handicapped accessibility is being improved throughout the National Park System. Likewise, every effort has been made to obtain accurate information on hospital and first aid facilities. **Persons traveling who are concerned about possible health problems, or who have been ad-** **vised to restrict their activities because of known health problems, should investigate the specific nature of the hospital and first aid facilities available in the area of planned travel.** You should also carry a first aid kit with you while you travel.

ENTRANCE FEES

Legislation passed in the United States Congress mandated entrance fees for several areas within the National Park System starting in 1987. The fees vary at each park, while most remain free to those under 16 and over 62 years of age. Please be aware that fees may change from those quoted in the *Guide* as decisions concerning entrance fees were still being made at the time of printing of this 7th Edition. Call ahead to the park if fees are a concern to you.

An annual entrance permit, the ***Golden Eagle Pass,*** is issued for $25 at all parks charging entrance fees and other park related locations. Persons 62 years of age and older are entitled to a free lifetime entrance permit, the ***Golden Age Passport.*** Handicapped persons who are eligible for Federal benefits as a result of disability may obtain the ***Golden Access Passport.*** Admission fees at all areas collecting fees are waived to holders of the Golden Eagle Pass and the Golden Age and Golden Access Passports and those persons accompanying the holder in a non-commercial vehicle. You can obtain more information on these annual passports by contacting the National Park Service in Washington, D.C. (202) 208-4747 or any of the National Park Service regional offices: Alaska (907) 451-7352 (Alaska Public Lands Information Center); Mid-Atlantic (215) 597-7013; Midwest (402) 221-3431; National Capital (202) 619-7005; North Atlantic (617) 565-8800; Pacific Northwest (206) 553-5565; Rocky Mountain (303) 969-2500; Southeast (404) 331-5185; Southwest (505) 988-6387; and Western (415) 744-3876. Campsite fees are not waived for holders of any of the Pass/Passport series, although holders of the Golden Age Passport are generally given a reduced rate.

RESERVATION INFORMATION

Generally, most campgrounds in National Parks are on a "first come-first served" basis.

Concessioner operated lodges are to be found in the National Park System's more visited parks. These hotels and lodges are extremely popular and usually require advanced reservations. You are advised to call the particular park you intend to visit to obtain the name and number of the concessioner or reservation system in use in that park. We also suggest that you obtain official government brochures on the areas you intend to visit since they contain detailed maps of the parks themselves. They are generally available without charge by writing to: National Park Service, Office of Public Information, Department of Interior, Washington, D.C. 20240.

HISTORIC STRUCTURES IN THE NATIONAL PARKS

Among the most interesting, though less known features of our national parks are the cultural resources that the National Park Service has been mandated to protect and interpret: the man-made places, structures, and objects that reflect our history as a nation.

As part of its responsibility for cultural resources, the Park Service manages thousands of structures of historical importance throughout the United States. They are an important part of the park system because they tell us something about who we are as a culture and how we live. Many are directly associated with historic individuals or events; others illustrate ways of life or cultural developments. Some, like the Statue of Liberty, and the Abraham Lincoln Birthplace—are powerful symbols of American ideals.

In the continuing celebration of the 75 years of the National Park Service, remember that the parks are more than the well known and famous Yellowstone and Yosemite; enjoy and experience the historic structures that contribute so richly to our country's heritage.

DISABILITY ACCESS

Throughout the United States, accessibility for people with disabilities is an increasingly important issue. With the passage of the Americans with Disabilities Act (ADA) in 1990, barriers and obstacles to persons with disabilities are being removed from employ-ment, education, housing, and public recreational opportunities.

Long before the ADA, the National Park Service became a leader in developing accessible recreation and interpretation for people with disabilities. The National Park Foundation and the National Park Service are working together to ensure that many parks have fully accessible features. But much remains to be done before park trails, facilities and programs are accessible for everyone. Where there are accessible features and programs in the parks, they are noted in the *Guide* as **Handicapped Accessibility** in bold face type.

Two fine examples of accessibility are found at Everglades National Park, Florida, and Carlsbad Caverns National Park, New Mexico. The level, half-mile asphalt and boardwalk Anhinga Trail at Everglades allows visitors to experience the wildlife which abounds in ponds along the Taylor Slough.

Alligators, turtles and many varieties of birds provide a spectacular show around the Anhinga Trail. Blind visitors can take advantage of an audio taped interpretive tour of the trail. The cassettes and player, available from the park, are keyed to textured cue pads on the trail.

Carlsbad Caverns offers an underground tour that is wheelchair accessible. Visitors can descend into the cavern by a 750 foot elevator ride. Handheld radio receivers in several languages, including "child English" and amplified for hearing-impaired visitors, relay interpretive information in the cave. A major portion of the accessible trail is through the Big Room and all visitors can experience the cavern's famous stalagmites, stalactites and unusual limestone formations. Carlsbad Cavern's visitor center has accessible exhibits, restrooms and a theatre.

Many other parks have similar unique features and opportunities for all visitors to enjoy. Whether they have disabilities or not, everyone can benefit from our national park teasures. See for yourself in the **Easy Access National Parks** video for sale through the National Park Foundation: an easy ordering coupon is in the back of this *Guide*.

Officers and Board Members of the National Park Foundation

Emeritus Board Members

Regional Tours of the National Parks

There are many wonderful opportunities to visit parks within easy driving distance of each other in different states. This *Guide* includes 4 regions in which there are two or more park sites located within a days' drive of each other. The parks selected are included to help in planning regional trips and tours.

The national parks, battlefields, memorials, monuments, and historic sites listed below are grouped by region and are conveniently cross-indexed.

Touring Region I
See map on page xii.

Acadia NP .... ME   p.-133

Saint-Gaudens NHS .... NH   p.-197

Boston African American
    NHS .... MA   p.-149

Boston NHP .... MA   p.-150

Cape Cod NS .... MA   p.-152

Frederick Law Olmsted
    NHS .... MA   p.-156

John F. Kennedy NHS .... MA   p.-156

Longfellow NHS .... MA   p.-157

Lowell NHP .... MA   p.-158

Minute Man NHP .... MA   p.-159

Salem Maritime NHS .... MA   p.-163

Saugus Iron Works NHS ..... MA   p.-164

Roger Williams National
    Memorial .... RI   p.-262

Touro Synagogue NHS ...... RI   p.-263

Weir Farm NHS .... CT   p.- 88

Eleanor Roosevelt NHS ...... NY   p.-213

Home of Franklin D.
    Roosevelt NHS .... NY   p.-219

Martin Van Buren NHS ...... NY   p.-220

Vanderbilt Mansion NHS .... NY   p.-226

Touring Region II
See map on page xiii.

Antietam NB .... MD   p.-137

Catoctin Mountain Park ...... MD   p.-139

Chesapeake and Ohio Canal
    NHP .... MD   p.-140

Monocacy NB .... MD   p.-146

Allegheny Portage Railroad
    NHS .... PA   p.-251

Eisenhower NHS .... PA   p.-254

Fort Necessity NB .... PA   p.-255

Friendship Hill NHS .... PA   p.-255

Gettysburg NMP .... PA   p.-256

Johnstown Flood National
    Memorial .... PA   p.-259

Harpers Ferry NHP .... WVA   p.-329

Appomattox Court House
    NHS .... VA   p.-303

Fredericksburg and
    Spotsylvania County
    Battlefields Memorial
    NMP .... VA   p.-307

George Washington Memorial
    Parkway .... VA   p.-308

Manassas NBP .... VA   p.-311

Prince William Forest Park .. VA   p.-313

Wolf Trap Farm Park for the
    Performing Arts .... VA   p.-317

Touring Region III
See map on page xiv.

Abraham Lincoln Birthplace
    NHS .... KY   p.-128

Mammoth Cave NP .... KY   p.-130

Andrew Johnson NHS .... TN   p.-273

Fort Donelson NB .... TN   p.-275

Shiloh NMP .... TN   p.-277

Martin Luther King, Jr.
    NHS .... GA   p.-106

Ninety Six NHS .... SC   p.-267

Brices Cross Roads NBS ..... MS   p.-174

Tupelo NB .... MS   p.-176

Russell Cave NM .... AL   p.- 2

Tuskegee Institute NHS ...... AL   p.- 3

Touring Region IV

See map on page xv.

Arches NP .... UT   p.-292

Bryce Canyon NP .... UT   p.-293

Canyonlands NP .... UT   p.-294

Capitol Reef NP .... UT   p.-295

Cedar Breaks NM .... UT   p.-296

Natural Bridges NM .... UT   p.-298

Rainbow Bridge NM .... UT   p.-299

Aztec Ruins NM .... NM   p.-201

Capulin Volcano NM .... NM   p.-203

Chaco Culture NHP .... NM   p.-205

Fort Union NM .... NM   p.-207

Curecanti NRA .... CO   p.- 67

Mesa Verde NP .... CO   p.- 72

Hovenweep NM .... CO   p.- 71

Canyon de Chelly NM .... AR   p.- 20

Glen Canyon NRA .... AR   p.- 25

Grand Canyon NP .... AR   p.- 26

Lake Mead NRA .... NV   p.-196

Navajo NM .... AR   p.- 29

Pipe Spring NM .... AR   p.- 33

NB   = National Battlefield

NBS   = National Battlefield Site

NMP = National Military Park

NHS   = National Historic Site

NHP   = National Historical Park

NM   = National Monument

NRA = National Recreation Area

NS   = National Seashore

NP   = National Park

Consult the full park entries for complete, current information on park fees and facilities, as well as actual distances and suggested routes.

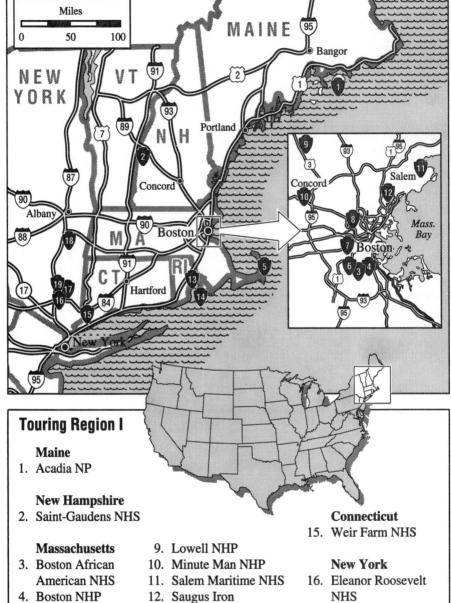

Touring Region I

Maine
1. Acadia NP

New Hampshire
2. Saint-Gaudens NHS

Massachusetts
3. Boston African
   American NHS
4. Boston NHP
5. Cape Cod NS
6. Frederick Law
   Olmsted NHS
7. John F. Kennedy
   NHS
8. Longfellow NHS

9. Lowell NHP
10. Minute Man NHP
11. Salem Maritime NHS
12. Saugus Iron
    Works NHS

Rhode Island
13. Roger Williams
    National Memorial
14. Touro Synagogue NHS

Connecticut
15. Weir Farm NHS

New York
16. Eleanor Roosevelt
    NHS
17. Home of Franklin D.
    Roosevelt NHS
18. Martin Van Buren
    NHS
19. Vanderbilt Mansion
    NHS

Touring Region II

Maryland
1. Antietam NB
2. Catoctin Mountain Park
3. Chesapeake & Ohio Canal NHP
4. Monocacy NB

Pennsylvania
5. Alleghany Portage Railroad NHS
6. Eisenhower NHS
7. Fort Necessity NB
8. Friendship Hill NHS
9. Gettysburg NMP
10. Johnstown Flood Nat'l. Memorial

West Virginia
11. Harpers Ferry NHP

Virginia
12. Appomattox Courthouse NHS
13. Fredericksburg and Spotsylvania County Battlefields Memorial NMP
14. George Washington Memorial Parkway
15. Manassas NBP
16. Prince William Forest Park
17. Wolf Trap Farm Park for the Performing Arts

Touring Region III

Kentucky
1. Abraham Lincoln Birthplace NHS
2. Mammoth Cave NP

Tennessee
3. Andrew Johnson NHS
4. Fort Donelson NB
5. Shiloh NMP

Georgia
6. Martin Luther King, Jr. NHS

South Carolina
7. Ninety Six NHS

Mississippi
8. Brices Cross Roads NBS
9. Tupelo NB

Alabama
10. Russell Cave NM
11. Tuskegee Institute NHS

Touring Region IV

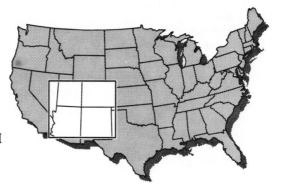

Utah
1. Arches NP
2. Bryce Canyon NP
3. Canyonlands NP
4. Capitol Reef NP
5. Cedar Breaks NM
6. Natural Bridges NM
7. Rainbow Bridge NM

New Mexico
8. Aztec Ruins NM
9. Capulin Volcano NM
10. Chaco Culture NHP
11. Fort Union NM

Colorado
12. Curecanti NRA
13. Hovenweep NM
14. MesaVerde NP

Arizona
15. Canyon de Chelly NM
16. Glen Canyon NRA
17. Grand Canyon NP
18. Lake Mead NRA
19. Navajo NM
20. Pipe Spring NM

Special Interest Parks

America's national parks provide diverse experiences for visitors of all ages. They range from the wonders of our dramatic scenic heritage and natures' unique botanical and geological features, to historic houses, military battlefields and the landmarks and monuments recognizing the accomplishments of our country's cultural and social leaders.

The categories of parks listed below include those parks noted for their outstanding features or unique characteristics and are included for visitors who have specific interests to pursue. These categories may also suggest other special interest parks for visitors to investigate.

African American history sites
Archeological and paleontological sites
Battlefields
Hispanic heritage sites, and sites that relate to the 500th anniversary of America's discovery
Presidential history sites
Volcanoes, caves, and hot springs
Womens' history sites

NB   = National Battlefield
NBS = National Battlefield Site
NMP = National Military Park
NHS = National Historic Site
NHP = National Historical Park
NM   = National Monument
NP   = National Park

African American History Sites

Booker T. Washington NM	VA	p.-305
Boston African American NHS	MA	p.-149
Frederick Douglass NHS	DC	p.- 79
George Washington Carver NM	MO	p.-178
Maggie L. Walker NHS	VA	p.-311
Martin Luther King, Jr. NHS	GA	p.-106
Tuskegee Institute NHS	AL	p.- 3

Archeological and paleontological sites

Agate Fossil Beds NM	NE	p.-190
Aztec Ruins NM	NM	p.-201
Bandelier NM	NM	p.-202
Canyon de Chelly NM	AR	p.- 20
Casa Grande NM	AZ	p.- 22
Chaco Culture	NM	p.-205
Dinosaur NM	CO & UT	p.- 68
Florissant Fossil Beds NM	CO	p.- 69
Fossil Butte NM	WY	p.-338
Gila Cliff Dwellings NM	NM	p.-207
Hovenweep NM	CO & UT	p.- 71
Mesa Verde NP	CO	p.- 72
Montezuma Castle NM	AZ	p.- 29
Navajo NM	AR	p.- 29
Tonto NM	AZ	p.- 35
Tuzigoot NM	AZ	p.- 37
Walnut Canyon NM	AZ	p.- 38
Wupatki NM	AZ	p.- 39
Yucca House NM	CO	p.- 76

Battlefields

Antietam NB	MD	p.-137
Big Hole NB	MT	p.-184
Brices Cross Roads NBS	MS	p.-174

Chickamauga & GA &
  Chattanooga NMP .... TN p.-101
Colonial NHP–Yorktown
  Battlefield .... VA p.-318
Cowpens NB .... SC p.-265
Custer Battlefield NM .... MT p.-185
Fort Donelson NB .... TN p.-275
Fort Necessity NB .... PA p.-255
Fredericksburg & Spotsylvania
  County Battlefields
  Memorial NMP .... VA p.-307
Gettysburg NMP .... PA p.-256
Guilford Courthouse NMP .. NC p.-234
Horseshoe Bend NMP .... AL p.- 1
Jean Lafitte NHP–Chalmette
  Battlefield .... LA p.-131
Kennesaw Mountain NBP ... GA p.-105
Kings Mountain NMP .... SC p.-266
Manassas NBP .... VA p.-311
Minute Man NHP .... MA p.-159
Monacacy NB .... MD p.-146
Moores Creek NB .... NC p.-235
Palo Alto Battlefield NHS ... TX p.-290
Pea Ridge NMP .... AR p.- 43
Petersburg NB .... VA p.-312
Richmond NBP .... VA p.-314
Saratoga NHP .... NY p.-224
Shiloh NMP .... TN p.-277
Stones River NB .... TN p.-278
Tupelo NB .... MS p.-176
Vicksburg NMP .... MS p.-177
War in the Pacific NHP ......Guam p.-346
Wilson's Creek NB .... MO p.-183

Hispanic heritage sites, and NPS sites that
relate to the 500th anniversary of America's
discovery:
Amistad NRA .... TX p.-280
Arkansas Post N Mem .... AR p.- 40
Big Bend NP .... TX p.-281
Biscayne NP .... FL p.- 90
Cabrillo NM .... CA p.- 45
Canyon de Chelly NM .... AZ p.- 20

Castillo de San Marcos
  NM .... FL p.- 92
Chamizal N Mem .... TX p.-284
Channel Islands NP .... CA p.- 45
Christiansted NHS .... VI p.-351
Coronado N Mem .... AZ p.- 23
Cumberland Island NS .... GA p.-102
De Soto N Mem .... FL p.- 93
El Morro NM .... NM p.-206
Fort Caroline N Mem .... FL p.- 95
Fort Frederica NM .... GA p.-103
Fort Matanzas NM .... FL p.- 96
Fort Jefferson NM .... FL p.- 95
Fort Point NHS .... CA p.- 49
Golden Gate NRA .... CA p.- 50
Gulf Islands NS (Bateria de FL &
  San Antonio) .... MS p.- 97
Jean Lafitte NHP .... LA p.-131
Jefferson National Expansion
  Mem .... MO p.-180
John Muir NHS .... CA p.- 51
Natchez NHP .... MS p.-175
Natchez Trace Parkway ...... AL,
                          MS &
                          TN p.-175
Padre Island NS .... TX p.-289
Palo Alto Battlefield NHS ... TX p.-290
Pecos NM .... NM p.-208
Point Reyes NS .... CA p.- 57
Salinas Pueblo Missions
  NM .... NM p.-209
San Antonio Missions
  NHP .... TX p.-291
San Juan National HS .... PR p.-349
Santa Monica Mountains
  NRA .... CA p.- 59
Sitka NHP .... AK p.- 17
Timucuan Ecological &
  Historic Preserve .... FL p.- 98
Tumacacori NM .... AZ p.- 36
Wrangell-St. Elias NP &
  PRES .... AK p.- 17

Presidential history sites

Abraham Lincoln Birthplace
NHS .... KY   p.-128

Adams NHS .... MA   p.-148

Andrew Johnson NHS .... TN   p.-273

Eisenhower NHS .... PA   p.-254

Ford's Theatre NHS .... DC   p.- 77

George Washington
Birthplace NM .... VA   p.-308

Harry S. Truman NHS .... MO   p.-179

Herbert Hoover NHS .... IA   p.-125

Home of Franklin D.
Roosevelt NHS .... NY   p.-219

James A. Garfield NHS ...... OH   p.-242

Jimmy Carter NHS .... GA   p.-105

John Fitzgerald Kennedy
NHS .... MA   p.-156

John F. Kennedy Center for
the Performing Arts .... DC   p.- 79

Lyndon Baines Johnson
Memorial Grove
on the Potomac .... DC   p.- 81

Lyndon B. Johnson NHP .... TX   p.-288

Lincoln Boyhood NM .... IN   p.-123

Lincoln Home NHS IL   p.-119

Lincoln Memorial .... DC   p.- 80

Martin Van Buren NHS ...... NY   p.-220

Sagamore Hill NHS .... NY   p.-223

Theodore Roosevelt
Birthplace NHS .... NY   p.-222

Thomas Jefferson
Memorial .... DC   p.- 86

Theodore Roosevelt Inaugural
NHS .... NY   p.-222

Theodore Roosevelt Island .. DC   p.- 85

Ulysses S. Grant NHS .... MO   p.-182

Washington Monument ...... DC   p.- 87

White House .... DC   p.- 88

William Howard Taft NHS .. OH   p.-244

Volcanoes, caves, and hot springs

Capulin Volcano NM .... NM   p.-203

Carlsbad Caverns NP .... NM   p.-204

Crater Lake NP .... OR   p.-246

Craters of the Moon NM ..... ID   p.-116

Hawaii Volcanoes NP .... HI   p.-110

Hot Springs NP .... AR   p.- 42

Jewel Cave NM .... SD   p.-269

Lassen Volcanic NP .... CA   p.- 52

Lava Beds NM .... CA   p.- 54

Lehman Caves NM
(Great Basin NP) .... NV   p.-194

Mammoth Cave NP .... KY   p.-130

Oregon Caves NM .... OR   p.-250

Sunset Crater Volcano NM .. AZ   p.- 35

Timpanogos Cave NM .... UT   p.-305

Wind Cave NP .... SD   p.-271

Yellowstone NP .... WY   p.-341

Women's history sites

Clara Barton NHS .... MD   p.-142

Eleanor Roosevelt NHS ...... NY   p.-213

Maggie L. Walker NHS ...... VA   p.-311

Whitman Mission NHS ...... WA   p.-327

Women's Rights NHP .... NY   p.-227

National Trails System

The National Trails System is made up of four types of trails established under the authority of the National Trails System Act:

National Scenic Trails are continuous extended routes of outdoor recreation within protected corridors.

National Historic Trails recognize past routes of exploration, migration, and military action. These are not necessarily continuous, but feature outstanding "high potential" trail sites and segments.

National Recreation Trails are existing Federal, State, or local trails recognized as components of the National Trails System. (Some 780, totalling 9,000 miles, have been registered.)

Side and Connecting Trails provide additional access to components of the National Trails System. (Two have been registered to date.)

Management of the 17 national scenic and national historic trails established to date is an inter-agency effort: The 12 administered by the National Park Service are included in the *Guide*. For further information about the National Trails System contact:

National Trails System Branch
National Park Service – 782
P.O. Box 37127, Wash., D.C. 20013-7127
202-343-3780

Appalachian National Scenic Trail

Maine, New Hampshire, Vermont, Massachusetts, Connecticut, New York, New Jersey, Pennsylvania, Maryland, West Virginia, Virginia, Tennessee, North Carolina, and Georgia

MAILING ADDRESS: Appalachian Trail Conference, P.O. Box 807, Harpers Ferry, WV 25425 **Telephone:** 304-535-6331

DIRECTIONS: Contact the Appalachian Trail Conference for detailed information on directions to the Trail.

Approximately 2,144 miles (3,430 km) of this scenic trail follow the Appalachian Mountains from Katahdin, ME, through to Springer Mountain, GA. The trail is one of the two initial units of the National Trail System. Designated by act of Congress on Oct. 2, 1968; completed by volunteers, Aug. 14, 1937.

VISITOR ACTIVITIES: Short- and long-term hiking, camping, bird- and wildlife-watching, backcountry; **Permits:** A permit is not required to hike the Trail, but camping permits are necessary in the Shenandoah National Park and Great Smoky Mountains National Park. These permits are available at Ranger Stations upon arrival. See listings on these parks in this book for information on facilities and reservations. Camping facilities are also available at Green Mountain National Forest, VT; White Mountain National Forest, NH; and Baxter State Park, ME; **Fees:** At certain Northeast campsites, a $2-4 fee per site; **Visitor facilities:** Lean-to shelters, fire pits, picnic tables; **Any limitations on vehicle usage:** Motor vehicles are prohibited on hiking trails; **Hiking trails:** Yes, some circuit hikes (blue blazed). Guide books with maps may be ordered from address above; **Backcountry:** Yes, Contact the Appalachian Trail Conference, P.O. Box 807, Harpers Ferry, WV 25425, phone 304-535-6331; **Camping:** Yes, no reservations available for campsites; **Other overnight accommodations on site:** There are youth hostels, church-related hostels, and other sleeping accommodations along certain sections of the Appalachian Trail. Guidebooks describe. **Meals served in the park:** Only in some national parks along the trail. Hikers have regular food drop points at post offices near the trail; **Food and supplies obtainable in the park:** No; **Food and supplies obtainable nearby:** Yes, stores are often located near major road crossings. Hut system operates in White Mountains, providing shelter and food at higher fee; **Overnight accommodations:** Accommodations are generally available at nearby towns; **First Aid available on trail:** Yes; **Nearest Hospital:** In most of the larger nearby towns; **Days/Hours:** Trail never closes.

GENERAL INFORMATION: Most long-distance hikers start in March or April and take 5 to 6 months to hike the entire trail, mostly from south to north. Primary use of trail is by weekend or short-distance hikers.

Appalachian National Scenic Trail

Ice Age National Scenic Trail
Wisconsin

MAILING ADDRESS: National Park Service, Ice Age National Scenic Trail, 700 Rayovac Drive, Suite 100, Madison, WI 53711 **Telephone:** 608-264-5610. Additional guidebook and background materials available from the Ice Age Park and Trail Foundation, P.O. Box 422, Sheboygan, WI 53082-0422.

DIRECTIONS: When completed, this scenic Trail will meander approximately 1,000 miles (1,600 km) across Wisconsin following a chain of glacial landscape features—moraines, eskers, kames, kettles, potholes, and erratics. Six of the nine units of the Ice Age National Scientific Reserve are linked together by the trail. Four hundred fifty miles (720 km) of the trail are presently available for public use.

Designated by an act of Congress on October 3, 1980.

VISITOR ACTIVITIES: Hiking, backpacking, camping, nature study. Some trail segments are open to bicycling, cross-country skiing, and limited snowmobiling; **Permits:** Yes, for a few trail segments; **Fees:** Yes, for some developed campgrounds within the National Forest and State Parks along the trail; **Visitor facilities:** Various, as provided by the managing authority for a particular segment; **HANDICAPPED ACCESSIBILITY:** Restrooms, Visitor Centers, and other facilities are accessible in *some* park and forest areas along the trail. Few segments of the trail itself are accessible. **Any limitations on vehicle usage:** Except for certain segments open to snowmobiling, use of motorized vehicles by the public is prohibited along the trail; **Hiking trails:** Yes; **Backcountry:** Yes, for information, write to the above address; **Camping:** As permitted; **Other overnight accommodations on site:** No; **Meals served in the park:** No; **Food and supplies obtainable in the park:** Yes, in some parks along the trail; **Food and supplies obtainable nearby:** Yes, in many communities along the trail; **Overnight accommodations:** In many communities along/near the trail; **First Aid available on trail:** No; **Days/Hours:** Open at all times, except as limited by regulations governing individual parks/forests or private lands through which the trail passes.

TRAVEL ACCESS: Many points on or near the trail are accessible by bus, rail, or air.

NEARBY FACILITIES & POINTS OF INTEREST: Scenic, historic, natural, and cultural interests are located along the trail. The main theme of the trail is Wisconsin's glacial features. **Campsites:** Reservation systems in use for some public and private campgrounds.

Wisconsin

209

79

208

179

181

Ice Age National Scenic Trail

Juan Bautista De Anza National Historic Trail
Arizona and California

MAILING ADDRESS: NPS Western Region, Planning, Grants, and Environmental Quality, 600 Harrison St., Suite 600, San Francisco, CA 94107-1372 **Telephone:** 415-744-3968

DIRECTIONS: This 1,200-mile route commemorates the 1775 expedition of Spanish colonization from Mexico to San Francisco's Presidio. After determining that the California coast could be reached overland from Mexico, Colonel Juan Bautista De Anza led an expedition north along Arizona's Santa Cruz valley, past the site of today's Tucson, and then west to follow the Gila River to Yuma. In southern California they followed a northwest route past the Salton Sea, through the Los Angeles basin to the coast, and up the California coast, visiting Spanish missions as they went, to San Luis Obispo. There they went inland behind the coastal mountains to the south end of San Francisco Bay and on to the Golden Gate. A side route to explore the bay runs north along the east side of the bay to the Sacramento River delta and returns behind the East Bay Hills to the bay. An expedition re-enactment from Mexico took place in 1975 and 1976.

VISITOR ACTIVITIES: This trail was established by Congress on August 15, 1990. The trail's comprehensive management plan has not yet been started, so precise management and route marking programs have yet to begin. Many sites along the way include historic and commemorative information about the De Anza expedition. Small portions of the trail can be hiked near Tucson and in California's Anza-Borrego State Park west of the Salton Sea.

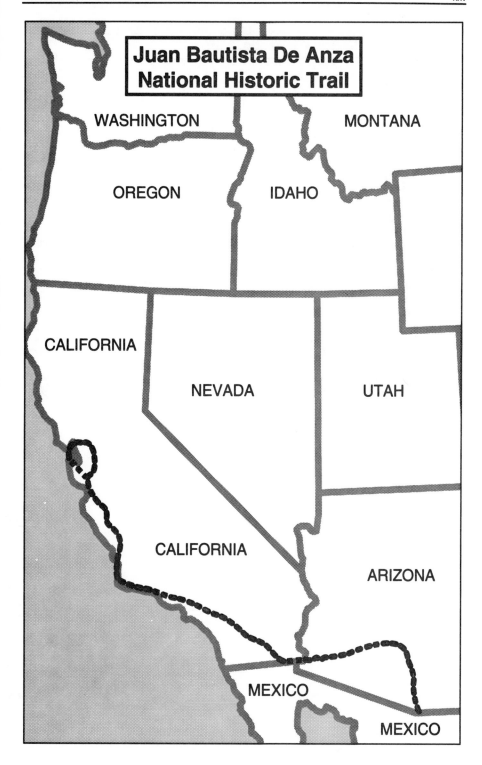

Juan Bautista De Anza
National Historic Trail

Lewis and Clark National Historic Trail

Illinois (also in Missouri, Kansas, Nebraska, Iowa, South Dakota, North Dakota, Montana, Idaho, Oregon, Washington)

MAILING ADDRESS: Lewis and Clark Trail Heritage Foundation, P.O. Box 3434, Great Falls, MT 59403 or National Park Service, Lewis and Clark National Historic Trail, 700 Rayovac Drive, Suite 100, Madison, WI 53711 **Telephone:** 608-264-5610

DIRECTIONS: The designation of the 3,700-mile (5,920-km) Lewis and Clark National Historic Trail by Congress on Nov. 10, 1978, included both the outbound and inbound routes of the 1804-06 expedition. A comprehensive management plan, completed in Jan. 1982, calls for the development of water-based trails (along the Missouri and Columbia Rivers and tributaries), land-based trails (for travel on foot), and marked motor routes for public retracement of the Trail.

Over 500 recreation and historic sites provide or have potential to provide access to the route and interpretation of the expedition. These sites are or will be owned and managed as part of the trail by cooperating Federal, State, and local agencies and private organizations. Efforts have begun to officially certify and mark these sites as part of the national historic trail. NPS areas which provide interpretation of the expedition are Jefferson National Expansion Memorial Historic Site (MO), Knife River Indian Villages National Historic Site (ND), Nez Perce National Historical Park (ID), and Fort Clatsop National Memorial (OR). The Lewis and Clark Trail highways marked and maintained by State highway departments are not part of the national historic trail, but complementary to it.

VISITOR ACTIVITIES: HANDICAPPED ACCESSIBILITY: Restrooms, Visitors Centers, and other facilities are accessible in *some* park and forest areas along the trail. Few segments of the trail itself are accessible.

Lewis and Clark National Historic Trail

Mormon Pioneer National Historic Trail
Illinois (also in Iowa, Nebraska, Wyoming, and Utah)

MAILING ADDRESS: National Park Service, Rocky Mountain Regional Office, Planning and Compliance Division, 12795 W. Alameda Parkway, Lakewood, CO 80225 **Telephone:** 303-969-2830

DIRECTIONS: It is still possible to closely follow this 1,300-mile (2,080 km)-long trail of history. Where wagons once rolled and teams traveled now highways, railroads, and bridges allow for modern-day travel. An auto route has been designated to go from the Mississippi River across the midwest plains and through the Rocky Mountains to descend into the Great Salt Lake Basin. Visitors are invited to retrace the route. While nearly two-thirds of the trail is now in private ownership, many of the places and events associated with the trail can be seen or visited. It is suggested that visitors send for the Mormon Pioneer Trail brochure and use the Primary Route Map to guide them.

VISITOR ACTIVITIES: The eastern end of the trail begins in west central Illinois at the Nauvoo National Historic District. The town of Nauvoo sits on the east bank of the Mississippi River and contains authentically restored buildings, shops, and homes of historic interest. Along the trail, 73 historic sites have been selected to commemorate and interpret important events and landmarks. There are also 6 cross-country trail segments totaling 47 miles (75.2 km) on Federal lands, chosen to offer excellent opportunities for hiking, horseback riding, and other appropriate recreational activities. Note: The National Park Service provides no facilities (restrooms, etc.) specifically for trail users. These sites and cross-country segments are identified on the Primary Route Map in the brochure. The western terminus of the trail is at Pioneer Trail State Park in Salt Lake City, UT. The area includes "This is the Place" monument and exhibits structures from temporary dug-outs to substantial public buildings.

Natchez Trace National Scenic Trail
Mississippi, Alabama and Tennessee

MAILING ADDRESS: Natchez Trace Parkway, Rural Route 1, NT-143, Tupelo, MS 38801 **Telephone:** 601-842-1572 or Natchez Trace Trail Conference, P.O. Box 6579, Jackson, MS 39282

DIRECTIONS: The Natchez Trace National Scenic Trail follows some existing portions of the old Natchez Trace which lie within the boundaries of the Natchez Trace Parkway. See pp. xx-xx for additional access and activity information along the Parkway. Three principal segments of the trace near Nashville, Tennessee, and Jackson and Natchez, Mississippi, totalling 110 miles have been identified for restoration and public trail use—some of these segments are open to the public.

VISITOR ACTIVITIES: The Natchez Trace commemorates an ancient path that began as a series of animal tracks and Native American trails and was later used by early explorers, "Kaintuck" boatmen, post riders, and military men. The trail was established as a national scenic trail by Congress in 1983. The portions of the trace open to the public will be limited to walking and horseback. Bicycling is permitted the entire length of the Parkway. Other visitor activities are the same as for the Parkway.

North Country National Scenic Trail
New York, Pennsylvania, Ohio, Michigan, Wisconsin, Minnesota,
North Dakota

MAILING ADDRESS: North Country Trail Association, P.O. Box 311, White Cloud, MI 49349 **Telephone:** 616-689-1912 or National Park Service, North Country National Scenic Trail, 700 Rayovac Drive, Suite 100, Madison, WI 53711 **Telephone:** 608-264-5610

DIRECTIONS: When completed, the Scenic Trail will extend approximately 3,200 miles from the vicinity of Crown Point, New York, to Lake Sakakawea State Park on the Missouri River in North Dakota, the route of the Lewis and Clark National Historic Trail. Approximately 1,400 miles are presently available for public use. Established by an act of Congress on Mar. 5, 1980.

VISITOR ACTIVITIES: Hiking, backpacking, camping, nature study. Some trail segments are open to horseback riding, bicycling, cross-country skiing; **Permits:** Yes, for a few trail segments; **Fees:** Yes, for some developed campgrounds within the National Forests, State Parks, and similar areas along the trail; **Visitor facilities:** Various, as provided by the managing authority for a particular segment; **HANDICAPPED ACCESSIBILITY:** A few sections of the trail are accessible to the handicapped (wheelchair use). Restroom and other facilities at developed areas in many Federal and State parks along the trail are accessible. **Any limitations on vehicle usage:** Use of motorized vehicles by the public is prohibited along the trail; **Hiking trails:** Yes; **Backcountry:** Yes, for information, write to the above address; **Camping:** As permitted; **Other overnight accommodations on site:** No; **Meals served on the trail:** Yes; **Food and supplies obtainable on the trail:** Yes; **Food and supplies obtainable nearby:** Yes, in many communities along or near the trail; **Overnight accommodations:** In many communities along or near the trail; **First Aid available on the trail:** Yes; **Days/Hours:** Open at all times, except as limited by regulations governing individual parks/ forests through which the trail passes.

TRAVEL ACCESS: Many points on or near the trail are accessible by bus, rail, or air.

NEARBY FACILITIES & POINTS OF INTEREST: Scenic, historic, natural, and cultural interests are located along the trail. **Campsites:** Reservation system in use for some public and private campgrounds.

North Country National Scenic Trail

Oregon National Historic Trail
Missouri (also in Kansas, Nebraska, Wyoming,
Idaho, Oregon, and Washington)

MAILING ADDRESS: Oregon-California Trails Association, P.O. Box 1019, Independence, MO 64051-0519 **Telephone:** 816-252-2276 or National Park Service, Pacific Northwest Regional Office, Oregon National Historic Trail, 83 S. King St., Suite 212, Seattle, WA 98104 **Telephone:** 206-553-5366

GENERAL INFORMATION: The Oregon Trail was the most important transportation route used by western emigrants during the years 1841-1848. These pioneers traveled 2,170 miles (3,200 km) from Independence, MO, across the plains and mountains of Kansas, Nebraska, Wyoming, Idaho, and Washington to Oregon's Willamette River Valley. The National Park Service Comprehensive Management and Use Plan describes the official Oregon National Historic Trail route, lists 125 historic sites and 7 cross-country segments, and makes recommendations for resource protection, trail management, and marking. Many of the sites and segments are on public lands and open to visitation. Others are located on private lands; please check with landowners before entry. For information about access and travel conditions along the cross-country segments, contact local offices of the Bureau of Land Management or the Forest Service. Agency addresses and phone numbers are listed in the trail brochure. General information and trail brochures are available from the National Park Service Pacific Northwest Regional Office.

Oregon National Historic Trail

Overmountain Victory National Historic Trail
Virginia, Tennessee, North Carolina and
South Carolina

MAILING ADDRESS: National Park Service, Southeast Regional Office, Planning, Design and Compliance Division, 75 Spring St., SW, Atlanta, GA 30303 **Telephone:** 404-331-5465 or Overmountain Victory Trail Association (OVTA), PO Box 632, Manassas Park, VA 22111

DIRECTIONS: In 1780 upcountry patriots from Virginia, Tennessee, and North Carolina marched across the Southern Appalachians where they defeated British troops at the Battle of Kings Mountain, setting in motion events which led to the British surrender and the end of the American Revolutionary War at Yorktown. This 310-mile trail was established by Congress in 1980. Today the route can be accessed from the towns of Abingdon, VA, Elizabethton, TN, North Wilkesboro, Lenoir, Morganton, and Rutherfordton, NC, and Gaffney, SC. It crosses the Blue Ridge Parkway at Heffner Gap, NC, and the Appalachian National Scenic Trail at Yellow Mountain Gap, and passes through Cowpens National Battlefield and Kings Mountain National Military Park.

VISITOR ACTIVITIES: The entire route is commemorated each fall by a 14-day re-enactment with period costumes and equipment (contact OVTA—address above—for more information). Most of the Overmountain Victory National Historic Trail is now marked on state highways. Hiking opportunities along the trail route are available at Sycamore Shoal State Historic Area, Carter County, TN; Roan Mountain State Park, Carter County, TN; Yellow Mountain Gap in the Cherokee National Forest, TN; North Cover/Linville Mountain in the Nantahala National Forest, NC; the W. Kerr Scott Reservoir, Wilkes County, NC; Cowpens National Battlefield, SC; and Kings Mountain National Military Park, SC.

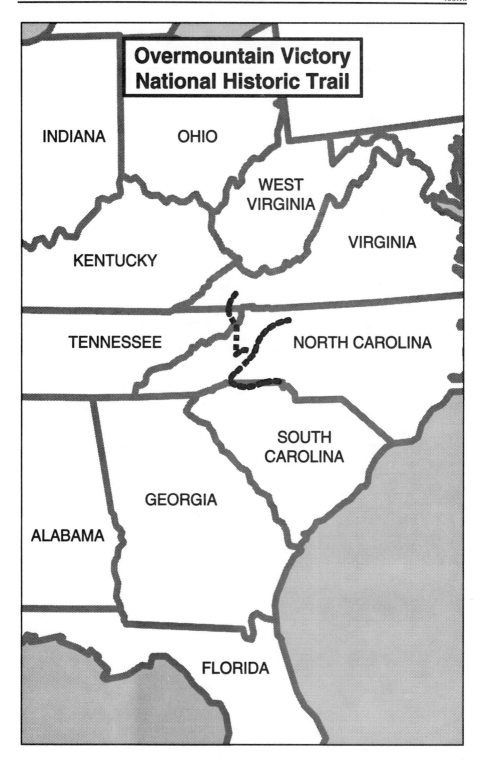

Overmountain Victory National Historic Trail

Potomac Heritage National Scenic Trail
Virginia, Maryland and Pennsylvania

MAILING ADDRESS: Potomac Heritage Trail Association, c/o Potomac Appalachian Trail Club, 1718 N St., NW, Washington, D.C. 20036 **Telephone:** 202-638-5306 or NPS, National Capital Region—LUCE, 1100 Ohio Drive, SW, Washington, DC 20242 **Telephone:** 202-485-9880

DIRECTIONS: The Potomac Heritage National Scenic Trail was authorized to be included in the National Park System on March 28, 1983. The trail route has not yet been formally designated and, therefore, is not generally available for public use. A planning effort is underway which will result in a comprehensive management plan leading to ultimate designation of trail segments. The trail segments can only be designated upon application to the Secretary of the Interior by state or local governments.

The 700-mile (1,120 km) -long trail will extend through the Potomac River Valley linking sites that commemorate a rich blend of historical events, natural scenes, and recreational opportunities. The general trail corridor will extend from the Chesapeake Bay at Smith Point, VA, and Point Lookout, MD, to Washington, DC, and west through Virginia hunt country to Harpers Ferry where it crosses to Maryland and joins the Chesapeake and Ohio Canal towpath to Cumberland. The entire 184-mile (294.4-km) length of the Cheaspeake and Ohio Canal is included as a segment of the trail from Georgetown in the District of Columbia to Cumberland, MD. From Cumberland, the trail would continue through Maryland into Pennsylvania to Conemaugh Gorge, just west of Johnstown.

VISITOR ACTIVITIES: For activities within the Chesapeake and Ohio Canal National Historical Park, see that listing for details or write to Superintendent, C&O Canal National Historical Park, P.O. Box 4, Sharpsburg, MD 21782, and the Supt., George Washington Memorial Parkway for information about the Mount Vernon Trail. In addition, directions for following a 55-mile hiking trail from the western end of the C&O Canal at Cumberland, MD, to Pennsylvania's Laurel highlands can be obtained by written request from the Potomac Heritage Trail Association, address above.

GENERAL INFORMATION: By law only those portions of the Potomac Heritage NST already on Federal land may be Federally owned. These include (but are not yet so marked) the 184-mile (294.4-km) towpath of the Chesapeake and Ohio Canal National Historic Site in Maryland and the District of Columbia and the 17-mile (27.3-km) Mount Vernon Trail within the George Washington Memorial Parkway in Virginia.

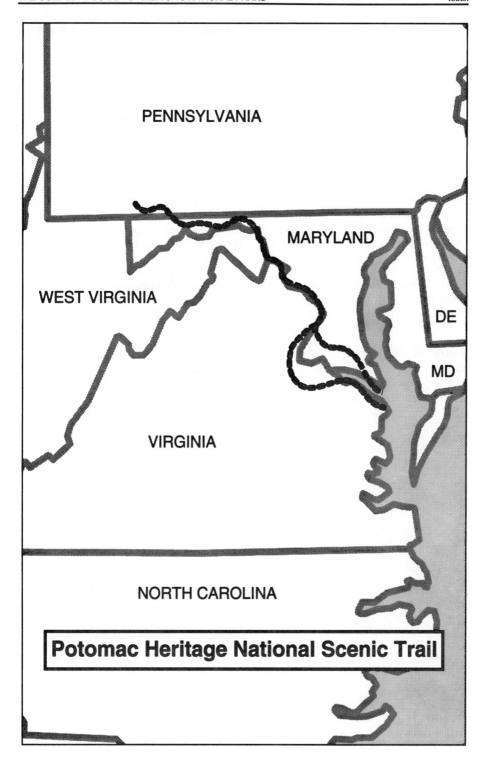

PENNSYLVANIA

MARYLAND

WEST VIRGINIA

DE

MD

VIRGINIA

NORTH CAROLINA

Potomac Heritage National Scenic Trail

Santa Fe National Historic Trail

Missouri, Kansas, Colorado, Oklahoma and
New Mexico

MAILING ADDRESS: Santa Fe Trail Association, Santa Fe Trail Center, Route 3, Larned, KS 67550 **Telephone:** 316-285-2054 or National Park Service, Southwest Region, Branch of Long Distance Trails, P.O. Box 728, Santa Fe, NM 87504-0728 **Telephone:** 505-988-6888

DIRECTIONS: In 1821 U.S. and Mexican traders developed the Santa Fe Trail which quickly became the principal commercial and cultural link between the two countries. Starting on the shores of the Missouri River, it became a route of conquest during the Mexican and Civil Wars, and was made obsolete by the railroad in 1880. The 1,203-mile route was established as a national historic trail by Congress in 1987, and the comprehensive management and use plan was completed in 1990. Much of the route can be traced from nearby highways. Moving east to west, major cities and highways include: Boonville and Independence, MO (via US routes 65 and 24), Kansas City, Council Grove, Larned, Dodge City, and Cimarron, KS (via US route 56), Lamarr, La Junta, and Trinidad, CO (via US routes 50 and 350 along the Mountain Branch), Boise City, OK and Clayton, NM (via US route 56 along the Cimarron Cut-off), and Cimarron, Watrous, Las Vegas, and Santa Fe, NM (along US route 64 and NM route 25).

VISITOR ACTIVITIES: Only a few sites and segments have so far been certified for public access along the trail. Interpretive services are available at Fort Osage, MO; the National Frontier Trails Center, Independence, MO; Fort Larned National Historical Site and the Santa Fe Trail Center both in Larned, KS; Bent's Old Fort National Historic Site, La Junta, CO; and Fort Union National Monument and Pecos National Historic Site, both in New Mexico. Historic ruts may be accessed at a variety of sites along the trail, especially at the Cimarron National Grassland in southwest Kansas and the Comanche National Grassland in Colorado.

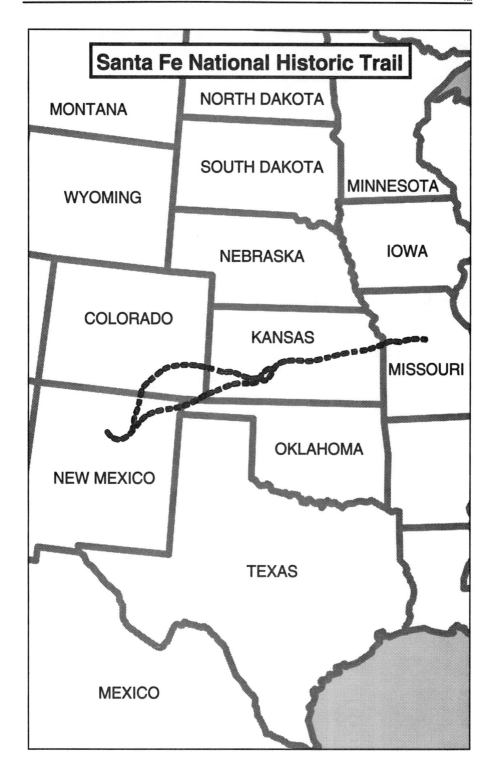

Santa Fe National Historic Trail

MONTANA

NORTH DAKOTA

SOUTH DAKOTA

MINNESOTA

WYOMING

NEBRASKA

IOWA

COLORADO

KANSAS

MISSOURI

OKLAHOMA

NEW MEXICO

TEXAS

MEXICO

Trail of Tears National Historic Trail

North Carolina, Georgia, Tennessee, Alabama, Kentucky, Illinois, Missouri, Arkansas and Oklahoma

MAILING ADDRESS: NPS Southwest Region, Branch of Long Distance Trails, P.O. Box 728, Santa Fe, NM 87504-0728 **Telephone:** 505-988-6888

DIRECTIONS: In 1838-9 16,000 Cherokee Indians from the southeastern states were moved by the U.S. Army to lands west of the Mississippi River. Various detachments followed different routes west to Oklahoma. Thousands died along the way. The trail was established by Congress in 1987 and follows two of these routes: 1,226 miles by water and 826 miles by land. The water route begins at Ross's Landing in downtown Chattanooga, TN, and follows the Tennessee River all the way to the Ohio River, down the Ohio to the Mississippi, and down the Mississippi, past Memphis, to the mouth of the Arkansas River, and up to Arkansas past Little Rock and Fort Smith, AR, to a point due south of Tahlequah, OK, where the trail ends. The overland route will be marked as an auto tour route connecting near the towns of Cleveland, Dayton, McMinnville, and Nashville, TN; Hopkinsville, KY; Golconda and Vienna, IL; Cape Girardeau, Farmington, Rolla, Springfield, and Cassville, MO, through Fayetteville, AR on US 60 to Tahlequah, OK.

VISITOR ACTIVITIES: Until the trail's comprehensive management and use plan is completed, exact development sites, themes, and programs have not been determined. Significant interpretive facilities associated with the trail story can be found at the Museum of the Cherokee Indian, Cherokee, NC; Red Clay and Port Royal State Historic Areas, TN; Trail of Tears Park, Hopkinsville, KY; Trail of Tears State Park, MO; and the Cherokee National Museum, Tahlequah, OK.

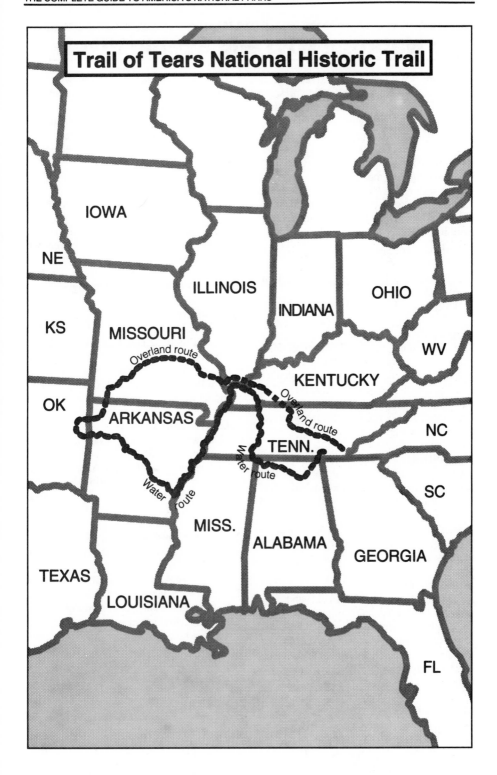

Trail of Tears National Historic Trail

The National Wild and Scenic Rivers

The National Wild and Scenic Rivers System was created by Congress in 1968 to preserve certain rivers with outstanding natural, cultural or recreational features in a free-flowing condition for the enjoyment of present and future generations. As of December 1990, the National System had grown from its initial eight components to a 123-river system with representation in 33 states. The 22 rivers managed by the National Park Service are described below. For additional information contact:

National Park Service
U.S. Department of the Interior
Division of Park Planning and Protection
Room 3230
Washington, D.C. 20013-7127

Alagnak River
Katmai National Park and Preserve, P.O. Box 7, King Salmon, AK 99613
The Alagnak River flows from Kukaklek Lake in Katmai National Preserve and offers outstanding wilderness recreation and fishing opportunities. The river is also noted for abundant wildlife.

Alatna River
Gates of the Arctic National Park and Preserve, P.O. Box 74680, Fairbanks, AK 99707
The stream lies partially within Gates of the Arctic National Park and Preserve, Alaska, in the Central Brooks Range. Wildlife, scenery, and interesting geologic features abound in the river corridor.

Aniakchak River
Aniakchak National Monument and Preserve, P.O. Box 7, King Salmon, AK 99613
The river, which lies within Aniakchak National Monument and Preserve, Alaska, flows out of Aniakchak Caldera and plunges spectacularly through "The Gates" on its way to the Pacific Ocean.

Bluestone River
c/o New River Gorge National River, P.O. Box 246, Glen Jean , WV 25846

The lower 17 miles of the river, which are designated, offer excellent warm water fishing, hiking, boating and scenic views. Pipestem and Bluestone State Parks and Bluestone Public Hunting and Fishing Area are located along the river and provide diverse recreation opportunities.

Charley River
Yukon-Charley Rivers National Preserve, P.O. Box 64, Eagle, AK 99738
Lying within Yukon-Charley Rivers National Preserve, Alaska, this stream is known for the exceptional clarity of its water. For the experienced canoer or kayaker, it offers many miles of whitewater challenges.

Chilikadrotna River
Lake Clark National Park and Preserve, 701 C Street, Box 61, Anchorage, AK 99513
The river lies within Lake Clark National Park and Preserve, Alaska. Long stretches of swift water and outstanding fishing are exceptional features.

Delaware (Middle) River
c/o Delaware Water Gap National Recreation Area, Bushkill, PA 18324
This river flows through the Delaware Water Gap National Recreation Area. The rivers offers swimming, boating and fishing opportunities.

Delaware (Upper) River
National Park Service, P.O. Box C, Narrowsburg, NY 12764
This is a 73.4-mile stretch of free-flowing river between Hancock and Sparrow Bush, N.Y., along the Pennsylvania border. Public fishing and boating access are provided. The area also is home to the Roebling Bridge, believed to be the oldest existing wire cable suspension bridge. The Zane Grey House and museum are here also.

Flathead River
Flathead National Forest, P.O. Box 147, Kalispell, MT 59901

Glacier National Park, West Glacier, MT 59901

This designation includes the North Fork, Middle Fork and South Fork above Hungry Horse Reservoir. The river is the boundary with Glacier National Park and flows through the Bob Marshall and Great Bear Wilderness areas.

John River
Gates of the Arctic National Park and Preserve, P.O. Box 64680, Fairbanks, AK 99707

The river flows south from Anaktuvuk Pass in Alaska's Brooks Range. The valley is an important migration route for the Arctic caribou herd.

Kobuk River
Gates of the Arctic National Park and Preserve, P.O. Box 74680, Fairbanks, AK 99707

From its headwaters in the Endicott Mountains and Walker Lake, the river courses south and west through a wide valley and passes through two scenic canyons.

Koyukuk River, North Fork
Gates of the Arctic National Park and Preserve, P.O. Box 74680, Fairbanks, AK 99707

The river flows from the south flank of the Arctic Divide through broad, glacially-carved valleys through the rugged Endicott Mountains in Alaska's Central Brooks Range. It passes between the "Gates of the Arctic" at Boreal Mountain and Frigid Crags.

Lower Saint Croix River
National Park Service, P.O. Box 708, St. Croix Falls, WI 54024

Recreational opportunities for much of the upper Midwest are provided along this 27-mile stretch of the St. Croix.

Merced River
Bureau of Land Management, 800 Truxtun Ave., Bakersfield, CA 93301
Sierra National Forest, 1600 Tollhouse Road, Clovis, CA 93612
Yosemite National Park, P.O. Box 577, Yosemite National Park, CA 95389

Including the South Fork, the Merced flows through superlative scenery—glaciated peaks, lakes, alpine and subalpine meadows-in alternating pools and cascades. Wildflower displays are also spectacular. The South Fork possesses one of the few remaining pristine Sierra fisheries with self-sustaining populations of rainbow, eastern brook, and brown trout. Archeological and wildlife features are also noteworthy.

Missouri River
c/o Midwest Region, National Park Service, 1709 Jackson Street, Omaha, NE 68102

One of the last free-flowing stretches of the Missouri, this reach from Gavins Point Dam near Yankton, South Dakota, to Ponca State Park, Nebraska, still exhibits the river's dynamic character in its islands, bars, chutes and snags.

Mulchatna River
Lake Clark National Park and Preserve, 701 C Street, Box 61, Anchorage, AK 99513

The Mulchatna River, which lies within Lake Clark National Park and Preserve, Alaska, is exceptionally scenic as it flows out of Turquoise Lake with the glacier-clad Chigmit Mountains to the east. Both moose and caribou inhabit the area.

Noatak River
Gates of the Arctic National Park and Preserve, P.O. Box 74680, Fairbanks, AK 99707
Noatak National Preserve, P.O. Box 1029, Kotzebue, AK 99752

The Noatak is situated in Gates of the Arctic National Park and Preserve and Noatak National Preserve in Alaska. The Noatak drains the largest mountain-ringed basin in America that is still virtually unaffected by human activities.

Rio Grande River
Big Bend National Park, Big Bend National Park, TX 79834

A 191.2 mile strip of the American shore of the Rio Grande in the Chihuahuan Desert protects the river. It begins in Big Bend National Park and continues downstream to the Terrell-Val Verde county line.

Saint Croix River

National Park Service, P.O. Box 708, St. Croix Falls, WI 54024

About 200 miles of the beautiful St. Croix River and Namekagon tributary make up this area.

Tinayguk River

Gates of the Artic National Park and Preserve, P.O. Box 75680, Fairbanks, AK 99707

Alaska's Tinayguk River is the largest tributary of the North Fork of the Koyukuk. Both lie entirely within the pristine environment of Gates of the Arctic National Park.

Tlikakila River

Lake Clark National Park and Preserve, 701 C Street, Box 61, Anchorage, AK 99513

Located about 100 air miles west of Anchorage in Lake Clark National Park, Alaska, the Tlikakila River is closely flanked by glaciers, 10,000-foot high rock-and-snow-capped mountains, and perpendicular cliffs.

Tuolumne River

Bureau of Land Management, 2800 Cottage Way, Sacramento, CA 95825-1889
Stanislaus National Forest, 19777 Greenley Road, Sonora, CA 95370
Yosemite National Park, P.O. Box 577, Yosemite National Park, CA 95389

The Tuolumne originates from snowmelt off Mounts Dana and Lyell in Yosemite National Park and courses 54 miles before crossing into Stanislaus National Forest and BLM public land. This river contains some of the most noted whitewater in the high Sierras and is an extremely popular rafting stream. The park segment provides views of some of America's most spectacular scenery.

For additional information on park sites associated with the wild and scenic rivers see park listings in the *Guide*.

Table of Contents

ALABAMA
Horseshoe Bend National Military Park 1
Russell Cave National Monument 2
Tuskegee Institute National Historic Site 3
ALASKA
The Alagnak Wild River 4
Aniakchak National Monument
  and Preserve 5
Bering Land Bridge National Preserve 6
Cape Krusenstern National Monument 7
Denali National Park and Preserve 7
Gates of the Arctic National Park
  and Preserve 8
Glacier Bay National Park and Preserve 10
Katmai National Park and Preserve 11
Kenai Fjords National Park 12
Klondike Gold Rush National Historical
  Park 13
Kobuk Valley National Park 14
Lake Clark National Park and Preserve 15
Noatak National Preserve 16
Sitka National Historical Park 17
Wrangell-St. Elias National Park and
  Preserve 17
Yukon-Charley Rivers National Preserve 19
ARIZONA
Canyon de Chelly National Monument 20
Casa Grande National Monument 22
Chiricahua National Monument 22
Coronado National Memorial 23
Fort Bowie National Historic Site 24
Glen Canyon National Recreation Area 25
Grand Canyon National Park 26
Hohokam Pima National Monument 28
Hubbell Trading Post National Historic
  Site 28
Montezuma Castle National Monument 29
Navajo National Monument 29
Organ Pipe Cactus National Monument 31
Petrified Forest National Park 32
Pipe Spring National Monument 33
Saguaro National Monument 33
Sunset Crater National Monument 35
Tonto National Monument 35
Tumacacori National Monument 36
Tuzigoot National Monument 37
Walnut Canyon National Monument 38
Wupatki National Monument 39

ARKANSAS
Arkansas Post National Memorial 40
Buffalo National River 41
Fort Smith National Historic Site 42
Hot Springs National Park 42
Pea Ridge National Military Park 43
CALIFORNIA
Cabrillo National Monument 45
Channel Islands National Park 45
Death Valley National Monument 47
Devils Postpile National Monument 48
Eugene O'Neill National Historic Site 48
Fort Point National Historic Site 49
Golden Gate National Recreation Area 50
John Muir National Historic Site 51
Joshua Tree National Monument 52
Lassen Volcanic National Park 52
Lava Beds National Monument 54
Muir Woods National Monument 55
Pinnacles National Monument 55
Point Reyes National Seashore 57
Redwood National Park 58
San Francisco Maritime National
  Historical Park 59
Santa Monica Mountains National
  Recreation Area 59
Sequoia Kings Canyon National Parks 60
Whiskeytown-Shasta-Trinity National
  Recreation Area 61
Yosemite National Park 62
COLORADO
Bent's Old Fort National Historic Site 64
Black Canyon of the Gunnison National
  Monument 65
Colorado National Monument 66
Curecanti National Recreation Area 67
Dinosaur National Monument 68
Florissant Fossil Beds National
  Monument 69
Great Sand Dunes National Monument 70
Hovenweep National Monument 71
Mesa Verde National Park 72
Rocky Mountain National Park 73
Yucca House National Monument 76
CONNECTICUT
The J. Alden Weir Home 88
DISTRICT OF COLUMBIA
Constitution Gardens 76

Ford's Theatre National Historic Site   77
Fort Dupont Park and Activity Center   78
Frederick Douglass National Historic
    Site   79
John F. Kennedy Center for the
    Performing Arts   79
Lincoln Memorial   80
Lyndon Baines Johnson Memorial Grove
    on the Potomac   81
National Capital Region   81
National Mall   82
Old Stone House   82
Pennsylvania Avenue National Historic
    Site   82
Potomac Heritage National Scenic Trail   83
Rock Creek Park   84
Sewall-Belmont House National
    Historic Site   85
Theodore Roosevelt Island   85
Thomas Jefferson Memorial   86
Vietnam Veterans Memorial   86
Washington Monument   87
The White House   88
FLORIDA
Big Cypress National Preserve   89
Biscayne National Park   90
Canaveral National Seashore   91
Castillo de San Marcos National
    Monument   92
DeSoto National Memorial   93
Everglades National Park   93
Fort Caroline National Memorial   95
Fort Jefferson National Monument   95
Fort Matanzas National Monument   96
Gulf Islands National Seashore   97
Timucuan Ecological Historic Preserve   98
GEORGIA
Andersonville National Historic Site   99
Chattahoochee River National
    Recreation Area   100
Chickamauga & Chattanooga National
    Military Park   101
Cumberland Island National Seashore   102
Fort Frederica National Monument   103
Fort Pulaski National Monument   104
Jimmy Carter National Historic Site   105
Kennesaw Mountain National
    Battlefield Park   105
Martin Luther King, Jr. National Historic
    Site and Preservation District   106
Ocmulgee National Monument   107

HAWAII
Haleakala National Park   108
Hawaii Volcanoes National Park   110
Kalaupapa National Historical Park   111
Kaloko-Honokohau National Historical
    Park   111
Pu'uhonua o Honaunau National
    Historical Park   112
Puukohola Heioau National Historic
    Site   113
U.S.S. Arizona Memorial   114
IDAHO
City of Rocks National Reserve   115
Craters of the Moon National
    Monument   116
Hagerman Fossil Beds National
    Monument   116
Nez Perce National Historical Park   117
ILLINOIS
Chicago Portage National Historic Site   118
Lewis and Clark National Historic Trail   119
Lincoln Home National Historic Site   119
Mormon Pioneer National Historic
    Trail   120
INDIANA
George Rogers Clark National Historical
    Park   121
Indiana Dunes National Lakeshore   122
Lincoln Boyhood National Memorial   123
IOWA
Effigy Mounds National Monument   124
Herbert Hoover National Historic Site   125
KANSAS
Fort Larned National Historic Site   126
Fort Scott National Historic Site   127
KENTUCKY
Abraham Lincoln Birthplace National
    Historic Site   128
Cumberland Gap National Historical
    Park   129
Mammoth Cave National Park   130
LOUISIANA
Jean Lafitte National Historical Park   131
Poverty Point National Monument   132
MAINE
Acadia National Park   133
Appalachian National Scenic Trail   135
Saint Croix Island Intl Historic Site   136
MARYLAND
Antietam National Battlefield   137
Assateague Island National Seashore   138
Catoctin Mountain Park   139

Chesapeake and Ohio Canal National
  Historical Park   140
Clara Barton National Historic Site   142
Fort McHenry National Monument and
  Historic Shrine   142
Fort Washington Park   143
Glen Echo Park   144
Greenbelt Park   144
Hampton National Historic Site   145
Monocacy National Battlefield Park   146
Oxon Hill Farm   146
Piscataway Park   147
Thomas Stone National Historic Site   147

MASSACHUSETTS
Adams National Historic Site   148
Boston African-American National
  Historic Site   149
Boston National Historical Park   150
Bunker Hill Battlefield and Monument   151
Cape Cod National Seashore   152
Charlestown Navy Yard   153
Dorchester Heights   154
Faneuil Hall   155
Frederick Law Olmsted National
  Historic Site   156
John F. Kennedy National Historic Site   156
Longfellow National Historic Site   157
Lowell National Historical Park   158
Minute Man National Historical Park   159
Old North Church   159
Old South Meeting House   160
Old State House   161
Paul Revere House   162
Salem Maritime National Historic Site   163
Saugus Iron Works National Historic
  Site   164
Springfield Armory National Historic
  Site   164
USS Constitution   165
Visitor Center   165

MICHIGAN
Father Marquette National Memorial
  and Museum   166
Isle Royale National Park   166
Pictured Rocks National Lakeshore   168
Sleeping Bear Dunes National
  Lakeshore   169

MINNESOTA
Grand Portage National Monument   170
Mississippi National River   170
Pipestone National Monument   172
Voyageurs National Park   172

MISSISSIPPI
Brices Cross Roads National Battlefield
  Site   174
Natchez National Historical Park   175
Natchez Trace Parkway   175
Tupelo National Battlefield   176
Vicksburg National Military Park   177

MISSOURI
George Washington Carver National
  Monument   178
Harry S Truman National Historic Site   179
Jefferson National Expansion
  Memorial   180
Oregon National Historical Trail   181
Ozark National Scenic Riverways   181
Ulysses S. Grant National Historic
  Site   182
Wilson's Creek National Battlefield   183

MONTANA
Big Hole National Battlefield   184
Bighorn Canyon National Recreation
  Area   185
Custer Battlefield National Monument   185
Fort Benton   186
Glacier National Park   187
Grant-Kohrs Ranch National Historic
  Site   188

NEBRASKA
Agate Fossil Beds National Monument   190
Chimney Rock National Historic Site   191
Homestead National Monument of
  America   191
Missouri National Recreational River   192
Scott's Bluff National Monument   193

NEVADA
Great Basin National Park   194
Lake Mead National Recreation Area   196

NEW HAMPSHIRE
Saint-Gaudens National Historic Site   197

NEW JERSEY
Edison National Historic Site   199
Morristown National Historical Park   199
Pinelands National Reserve   200

NEW MEXICO
Aztec Ruins National Monument   201
Bandelier National Monument   202
Capulin Volcano National Monument   203
Carlsbad Caverns National Park   204
Chaco Culture National Historical Park   205
El Malpais National Monument   206
El Morro National Monument   206
Fort Union National Monument   207

Gila Cliff Dwellings National
  Monument 207
Pecos National Monument 208
Salinas Pueblo Missions National
  Monument 209
White Sands National Monument 210
Zuni-Cibola National Historical Park 211
NEW YORK
Castle Clinton National Monument 212
Eleanor Roosevelt National Historic
  Site 213
Ellis Island 214
Federal Hall National Memorial 215
Fire Island National Seashore 216
Fort Stanwix National Monument 216
Gateway National Recreation Area 217
General Grant National Memorial 218
Hamilton Grange National Memorial 219
Home of Franklin D. Roosevelt
  National Historic Site 219
Martin Van Buren National Historic
  Site 220
North Country National Scenic Trail 221
Theodore Roosevelt Birthplace
  National Historic Site 222
Theodore Roosevelt Inaugural National
  Historic Site 222
Sagamore Hill National Historic Site 223
Saint Paul's National Historic Site 223
Saratoga National Historical Park 224
Statue of Liberty National Monument 225
Upper Delaware Wild and Scenic River 225
Vanderbilt Mansion National Historic
  Site 226
Women's Rights National Historical
  Park 227
NORTH CAROLINA
Blue Ridge Parkway 228
Cape Hatteras National Seashore 230
Cape Lookout National Seashore 232
Carl Sandburg Home National Historic
  Site 232
Fort Raleigh National Historic Site 233
Guilford Courthouse National Military
  Park 234
Moores Creek National Battlefield 235
Wright Brothers National Memorial 235
NORTH DAKOTA
Fort Union Trading Post National
  Historic Site 237
International Peace Garden 238

Knife River Indian Villages National
  Historic Site 238
Theodore Roosevelt National Park 239
OHIO
Cuyahoga Valley National Recreation
  Area 240
James A. Garfield National Historic
  Site 242
Mound City Group National Monument 242
Perry's Victory and International Peace
  Memorial 243
William Howard Taft National Historic
  Site 244
OKLAHOMA
Chickasaw National Recreation Area 245
OREGON
Crater Lake National Park 246
Fort Clatsop National Memorial 247
John Day Fossil Beds National
  Monument 248
McLoughlin House National Historic
  Site 249
Oregon Caves National Monument 250
PENNSYLVANIA
Allegheny Portage Railroad National
  Historic Site 251
Benjamin Franklin National Memorial 252
Delaware Water Gap National
  Recreation Area 253
Edgar Allan Poe National Historic Site 254
Eisenhower National Historic Site 254
Fort Necessity National Battlefield 255
Friendship Hill National Historic Site 255
Gettysburg National Military Park 256
Gloria Dei (Old Swedes') Church
  National Historic Site 257
Hopewell Furnace National Historic
  Site 257
Independence National Historical Park 258
Johnstown Flood National Memorial 259
Steamtown National Historic Site 260
Thaddeus Kosiuszko National
  Memorial 260
Valley Forge National Historical Park 261
RHODE ISLAND
Roger Williams National Memorial 262
Touro Synagogue National Historic
  Site 263
SOUTH CAROLINA
Charles Pinckney National Historic
  Site 264

Congaree Swamp National Monument 264
Cowpens National Battlefield 265
Fort Sumter National Monument 266
Kings Mountain National Military Park 266
Ninety Six National Historic Site 267
SOUTH DAKOTA
Badlands National Park 268
Jewel Cave National Monument 269
Mount Rushmore National Memorial 270
Wind Cave National Park 271

TENNESSEE
Andrew Johnson National Historic Site 273
Big South Fork National River and
    Recreation Area 274
Fort Donelson National Battlefield Park 275
Great Smoky Mountains National Park 275
Obed Wild and Scenic River 277
Shiloh National Military Park 277
Stones River National Battlefield and
    Cemetery 278
TEXAS
Alibates National Monument 280
Amistad National Recreation Area 280
Big Bend National Park 281
Big Thicket National Preserve 282
Chamizal National Memorial 284
Fort Davis National Historic Site 285
Guadalupe Mountains National Park 286
Lake Meredith National Recreation
    Area 287
Lyndon B. Johnson National Historical
    Park 288
Padre Island National Seashore 289
Palo Alto Battlefield National Historic
    Site 290
Rio Grande Wild and Scenic River 290
San Antonio Missions National
    Historical Park 291
UTAH
Arches National Park 292
Bryce Canyon National Park 293
Canyonlands National Park 294
Capitol Reef National Park 295
Cedar Breaks National Monument 296
Golden Spike National Historic Site 297
Natural Bridges National Monument 298
Rainbow Bridge National Monument 299
Timpanogos Cave National Monument 300
Zion National Park 301
VIRGINIA
Appomattox Court House National
    Historical Park 303

Arlington House, The Robert E. Lee
    Memorial 304
Booker T. Washington National
    Monument 305
Colonial National Historical Park 306
Fredericksburg and Spotsylvania County
    Battlefields Memorial National
    Military Park 307
George Washington Birthplace National
    Monument 308
George Washington Memorial Parkway 308
Great Falls Park 309
Jamestown National Historic Site 310
Maggie L. Walker National Historic
    Site 311
Manassas National Battlefield Park 311
Petersburg National Battlefield 312
Prince William Forest Park 313
Richmond National Battlefield Park 314
Shenandoah National Park 315
The Claude Moore Colonial Farm at
    Turkey Run 316
U.S. Marine Corps War Memorial and
    Netherlands Carillon 316
Wolf Trap Farm Park 317
Yorktown Battlefield 318
WASHINGTON
Coulee Dam National Recreation Area 319
Fort Vancouver National Historic Site 320
Lake Chelan National Recreation Area 321
Mount Ranier National Park 322
North Cascades National Park 323
Olympic National Park 324
Ross Lake National Recreation Area 325
San Juan Island National Historical
    Park 326
Whitman Mission National Historic
    Site 327
WEST VIRGINIA
Bluestone National Scenic River 328
Gauley River National Recreation Area 328
Harpers Ferry National Historical Park 329
New River Gorge National River 330
WISCONSIN
Apostle Islands National Lakeshore 331
Ice Age National Scientific Reserve 332
Ice Age National Scenic Trail 333
Lower St. Croix National Scenic
    Riverway 334
Saint Croix National Scenic Riverway 335
WYOMING
Devils Tower National Monument 336

Fort Laramie National Historic Site   337
Fossil Butte National Monument   338
Grand Teton National Park   338
John D. Rockefeller, Jr. Memorial
   Parkway   340
Yellowstone National Park   341
CANADA
Roosevelt Campobello International
   Park   344
NORTHERN MARIANA ISLANDS
American Memorial Park   345

GUAM
War in the Pacific National Historical
   Park   346
AMERICAN SAMOA
The National Park of American Samoa   348
PUERTO RICO
San Juan National Historic Site   349
VIRGIN ISLANDS
Buck Island Reef National Monument   350
Christiansted National Historic Site   351
Virgin Islands National Park   351

Alabama

NATCHEZ TRACE
PARKWAY

RUSSELL CAVE
NATIONAL MONUMENT

Birmingham

Montgomery

HORSESHOE BEND
NATIONAL MILITARY PARK

TUSKEGEE INSTITUTE
NATIONAL HISTORIC SITE

Horseshoe Bend National Military Park
Daviston, Alabama

MAILING ADDRESS: Superintendent, Horseshoe Bend National Military Park, Route 1, Box 103, Daviston, AL 36256 **Telephone:** 205-234-7111

DIRECTIONS: The Park, on AL-49, is 12 miles (19 km) north of Dadeville and 18 miles (29 km) east of Alexander City via New Site.

General Andrew Jackson's forces broke the power of the Creek Indian Confederacy and opened Alabama and other parts of the Old Southwest to settlement after fierce fighting here on Mar. 27, 1814, on the "horseshoe bend" of the Tallapoosa River. Authorized for addition to the National Park System on July 25, 1956. Proclaimed Aug. 11, 1959.

VISITOR ACTIVITIES: Interpretive and audiovisual exhibits, auto and walking tours, picnicking, boating, hiking, fishing, flintlock fire arm demonstrations given when staffing permits; **Permits:** No; **Fees:** Only for special uses; **Visitor facilities:** Visitor Center, museum, hiking trails, boat launching ramp, picnic area; **Any limitations on vehicle usage:** Vehicles are restricted to paved roads; **Hiking trails:** Yes, the park contains nature trails which vary from 3 to 7 miles (4.5 to 11 km) in length; **Backcountry:** No; **Camping:** No; **Other overnight accommodations on site:** No; **Meals served in the park:** No; **Food and supplies obtainable in the park:** No; **Food and supplies obtainable nearby:** Yes; **Overnight accommodations:** Dadeville 12 miles (19 km), and Alexander City 18 miles, (29 km), both on US 280; **First Aid available in park:** Yes; **Nearest Hospital:** Dadeville, 12 miles (19 km) and Alexander City, 18 miles (29 km), both on US 280; **Days/Hours:** Museum and grounds open daily from 8 a.m. to 4:30 p.m; **Holiday Closings:** Dec. 25.

GENERAL INFORMATION: Be alert to hazards such as poisonous snakes, poison ivy, and fire ants. Exercise caution while boating and walking along the river bank.

Russell Cave National Monument
Bridgeport, Alabama

MAILING ADDRESS: Russell Cave National Monument, Rte. 1, Box 175, Bridgeport, AL 35740 **Telephone:** 205-495-2672

DIRECTIONS: The park is best approached by US 72 leading to Bridgeport, Alabama. Turn north on County Road 91 to the community of Mt. Carmel, then turn right on County Road 75 to the Park entrance. The distance from Bridgeport to the Park is about 8 miles (12 km) over paved road.

An almost continuous archaeological record of human habitation from at least 7000 B.C. to about 1650 A.D. is revealed in this cave, which was "discovered" in 1953. Created by Presidential Proclamation on May 11, 1961.

VISITOR ACTIVITIES: Interpretive films and slide programs available for showing upon request in park's audiovisual room. Slide program in cave shelter area. Interpretive exhibits and talks, demonstrations of ancient Indian life, guided tours of the cave shelter for groups; **Permits:** No; **Fees:** No; **Visitor facilities:** Picnic area, hiking trails, restrooms; **HANDICAPPED ACCESSIBILITY:** Parking, restrooms with limited accessibility; audiovisual programs, audio description of exhibits for sight-impaired, printed cave program text for hearing impaired; **Any limitations on vehicle usage:** No; **Hiking trails:** Yes, a 1.2 mile (.8 km) hiking trail; nature trail extends to a hiking trail; **Backcountry:** No; **Camping:** No; **Other overnight accommodations on site:** No; **Meals served in the park:** No; **Food and supplies obtainable in the park:** No; **Food and supplies obtainable nearby:** Yes, in Bridgeport, South Pittsburg, Stevenson; **Overnight accommodations:** Kimball, TN, Junction of US 72 and I-24, 18 miles (29 km), Stevenson, Alabama, on U.S. 72, approximately 13 miles (20.8 km) from the park; **First Aid available in park:** Yes; **Nearest Hospital:** Bridgeport, County 75 to 91 to US 72, 10 miles (16 km); **Days/Hours:** Open daily from 8 a.m. to 5 p.m., C.S.T.; **Holiday Closings:** Dec. 25; **Visitor attractions closed for seasons:** No; **Weather:** Summers are hot and humid, winters are relatively mild, with occasional near-zero temperatures and snow.

GENERAL INFORMATION: You are advised not to run on the trails and not to wander from them or to take short cuts. The hiking trail is steep and arduous and you are urged to walk it with care.

Tuskegee Institute National Historic Site
Tuskegee Institute, Alabama

MAILING ADDRESS: Superintendent, Tuskegee Institute National Historic Site, P.O. Drawer 10, Tuskegee Institute, AL 36088 **Telephone:** 205-727-6390

DIRECTIONS: The site is located on Old Montgomery Road and is adjacent to the city of Tuskegee, AL. When approaching via Interstate 85, exit onto AL 81 South. Turn right at the intersection of 81 and Old Montgomery Road. Follow signs to Visitor Center located in Carver Museum.

Booker T. Washington founded this college for black Americans in 1881. Preserved here are the student-made brick buildings, Washington's home, and the George Washington Carver Museum. Authorized for addition to the National Park System on Oct. 26, 1974.

VISITOR ACTIVITIES: Informal interpretive talks at Carver Museum, formal tours at The Oaks, special activities intermittently throughout the year; **Permits:** No; **Fees:** No; **Visitor facilities:** Museum, restored home; **HANDICAPPED ACCESSIBILITY:** Rear of Carver Museum; parking available in front of Carver Museum and rear of The Oaks; restrooms at Carver Museum; **Any limitations on vehicle usage:** No; **Hiking trails:** No; **Backcountry:** No; **Camping:** No; **Other overnight accommodations on site:** Yes, for reservations at Dorothy Hall Guest House, contact Tuskegee Institute, Tuskegee Institute, AL 36088, phone 205-727-8753; **Meals served in the park:** No; **Food and supplies obtainable in the park:** No; **Food and supplies obtainable nearby:** Yes, Tuskegee Institute campus or downtown Tuskegee; **Overnight accommodations:** I-85 and Notasulga Highway, 5 miles (8 km); **First Aid available in park:** Yes; **Nearest Hospital:** East Alabama Medical Center, Opelika, AL, 25 miles (40 km) north; **Days/Hours:** Open daily from 9 a.m.-5 p.m.; **Holiday Closings:** Dec. 25 & Jan. 1; **Visitor attractions closed for seasons:** No; **Weather:** Summer is humid, with high temperatures in mid-90s from July-Sept.; winter is cold, with lows in the 20s from Dec.-Feb.; spring and fall have moderate rainfall, with temperatures from 75-85°F.

GENERAL INFORMATION: *For your safety*—Be especially careful on old walkways and steps. Natural areas have steep slopes, poisonous or spiny vegetation, and animals that sting or bite. Pedestrians have the right-of-way on campus roads.

TRAVEL ACCESS: Bus: Greyhound offers daily service to downtown Tuskegee, AL; **Rail:** No; **Air:** Delta, Southeastern service Montgomery/Auburn, AL.

NEARBY FACILITIES & POINTS OF INTEREST: Hotel/Motel: Tuskegee Inn, I-85 & Notasulga Hwy, 205-727-5400 5 miles; **Campgrounds:** Tuskegee National Forest; **Parks, other points of interest:** Tuskegee National Forest, Chewacla State Park.

Alaska

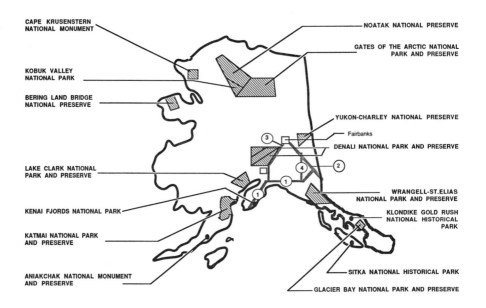

CAPE KRUSENSTERN
NATIONAL MONUMENT

NOATAK NATIONAL PRESERVE

GATES OF THE ARCTIC NATIONAL
PARK AND PRESERVE

KOBUK VALLEY
NATIONAL PARK

BERING LAND BRIDGE
NATIONAL PRESERVE

YUKON-CHARLEY NATIONAL PRESERVE

Fairbanks

DENALI NATIONAL PARK AND PRESERVE

LAKE CLARK NATIONAL
PARK AND PRESERVE

WRANGELL-ST.ELIAS
NATIONAL PARK AND PRESERVE

KENAI FJORDS NATIONAL PARK

KLONDIKE GOLD RUSH
NATIONAL HISTORICAL
PARK

KATMAI NATIONAL PARK
AND PRESERVE

ANIAKCHAK NATIONAL MONUMENT
AND PRESERVE

SITKA NATIONAL HISTORICAL PARK

GLACIER BAY NATIONAL PARK AND PRESERVE

The Alagnak Wild River
Alaska

MAILING ADDRESS: Superintendent, Katmai National Park & Preserve, P.O. Box 7, King Salmon, AK 99613-0007 **Telephone:** 907-246-3305

DIRECTIONS: Accessible by scheduled airlines to King Salmon, charter flights available to Kukaklek Lake, the source of the Alagnak.

VISITOR ACTIVITIES: Fishing and recreational river floating; **Permits:** Yes, backcountry permits are available from the Superintendent, Katmai N.P. at the above address; **Fees:** No; **Visitor facilities:** No; **Any limitations on vehicle usage:** N.A. (no roads); **Hiking trails:** No; **Backcountry:** cross-country hiking only; **Camping:** Wilderness camping only; **Other overnight accommodations on site:** No; **Meals served in the park:** No; **Food and supplies obtainable in the park:** No; **Food and supplies obtainable nearby:** King Salmon; **Overnight accommodations:** No; **First Aid available in park:** No; **Nearest Hospital:** Dillingham, AK; **Days/Hours:** N.A. **Holiday Closings:** N.A. **Visitor attractions closed for seasons:** N.A. **Weather:** Be prepared for cool, rainy weather in summer; for snow, wind, and freezing temperatures in other seasons. Good rain gear and wool clothing are advised.

GENERAL INFORMATION: This is a wilderness area used primarily by recreational river floaters and fishermen. There are several allotments (private property) along the river.

TRAVEL ACCESS: Bus: No; **Rail:** No; **Air:** Charter aircraft from King Salmon, AK.

Aniakchak National Monument and Preserve
Alaska

MAILING ADDRESS: Aniakchak National Monument and Preserve, Box 7, King Salmon, AK 99613-0007 **Telephone:** 907-246-3305

DIRECTIONS: To visit Aniakchak is no simple task. Reeve Aleutian Airways, Inc., has scheduled flights between Anchorage and Port Heiden Airfield. The cost of a round trip ticket is around $400. From Port Heiden Airfield a person could walk to the monument, which is a distance of about 10 miles (16 km), and quite a difficult job. The terrain is tundra meadow, interspersed with scattered thickets of willow, alder, and birch. Very few people have tried to make this walk. A person can also charter an aircraft and fly into the monument. This cost is about $200 per hour. Mark Air and Peninsula Airways all have twice daily flights from Anchorage to King Salmon for $330 round trip. From King Salmon, one can charter an airplane for approximately $200 per hour. As evidenced by the methods available, this is quite an expensive place to visit.

Thirty square-mile Aniakchak Crater, one of the world's largest, contains a lake and a river, and a volcano which erupted in 1931. Aniakchak River flows through the caldera wall to the Pacific. Established as a national monument and preserve through the Alaska National Interest Lands Conservation Act, Dec. 2, 1980.

VISITOR ACTIVITIES: Wildlife-watching, float trips, primitive camping, fishing; **Permits:** Alaska fishing license, available in Anchorage and King Salmon, is required; **Fees:** No; **Visitor facilities:** No; **Any limitations on vehicle usage:** No roads; **Hiking trails:** No; **Backcountry trails:** Yes, information can be obtained from Alaska Regional Office of the National Park Service or Superintendent, Katmai National Park/Preserve in King Salmon; **Camping:** Yes, primitive camping available; **Other overnight accommodations on site:** No; **Meals served in the park:** No; **Food and supplies obtainable in the park:** No; **Food and supplies obtainable nearby:** No, should be obtained in Anchorage or King Salmon; **Overnight accommodations:** King Salmon, about 150 miles (240 km); **First Aid available in the park:** No; **Nearest Hospital:** Kodiak, Dillingham; **Days/Hours:** Monument never closes; **Holiday Closings:** No; **Visitor attractions closed for seasons:** No; **Weather:** The weather will vary a great deal. For winter, the maximum may be in the low 30°s F to -30°. Summer temperatures range from the mid and upper 40°s to a high of 70°. The caldera is subject to violent wind storms which can make camping inside the caldera very difficult. In June and July, 1973, an individual had his camp destroyed twice during a six-week period and his boat blown away. Local pilots who have flown into the caldera have reported bad experiences with strong turbulent winds.

GENERAL INFORMATION: Visitors in the area should have wool clothing, rubber boots, and good rain gear. Bring your own food if camping and be sure that the tent can withstand bad weather conditions. One of the most experienced air taxi services for this area is Peninsula Airways, Inc., P.O. Box 36, King Salmon, AK 99613, phone 907-246-3372. Other charter aircraft are available in Anchorage, Port Heiden Airfield, and King Salmon.

Bering Land Bridge National Preserve
Alaska

MAILING ADDRESS: Box 220, Nome, AK 99762-0220 **Telephone:** 907-443-2522

DIRECTIONS: The Preserve is quite isolated. No roads lead to the area, and airports at Nome and Kotzebue that handle jets are rather distant from the Preserve's boundaries. Nonetheless, Nome and Kotzebue are for most visitors the intermediate points from which to fly into the Preserve or to Native villages in close proximity to the boundaries. Round-trip air fare from Anchorage to either Kotzebue or Nome is $426. It is possible to charter flights out of Nome and Kotzebue into Serpentine Hot Springs and onto beaches of the Preserve. Charter fares run about $200 per hour.

This area on the north side of Seward Peninsula 50 miles (80 km) from Siberia contains remains of land bridge once connecting Asia and North America. The promising archaeological site is also the habitat of polar bear, grizzly bear, wolves, 21 other mammals, and 112 bird species. Established by Alaska National Interest Lands Conservation Act, Dec. 2, 1980.

VISITOR ACTIVITIES: Wilderness hiking and camping, photography, fishing, river floating, boating, canoeing, walking, wildlife- and wildflower-watching. Part of the attraction of the Preserve is the lifestyle of Eskimos from the neighboring villages, their reindeer herds, and arts and crafts; **Permits:** Alaska fishing license, available locally, is required; **Fees:** No; **Visitor facilities:** No; **Any limitations on vehicle usage:** No roads; **Hiking trails:** No; **Backcountry:** Yes, information available from Superintendent; **Camping:** Only primitive camping—no reservations; **Other overnight accommodations on site:** No; **Meals served in the park:** No; **Food and supplies obtainable in the park:** No; **Food and supplies obtainable nearby:** Yes, certain items—food, clothing, beverages, and some gear—may be purchased from merchants in Nome and Kotzebue, but supplies in village stores are generally limited; **Overnight accommodations:** Lodging and eating facilities are available at the intermediate points of Nome and Kotzebue. Room reservations are suggested because touring groups book much of the touring space. Rooms average about $85 per day, and meals are proportionately as expensive. Transportation costs for goods and services in "bush" Alaska raise prices considerably in such places as Nome and Kotzebue. Visitors planning to stay in the Preserve should plan to arrive self-sufficient. **First Aid available in park:** No; **Nearest Hospital:** Nome and Kotzebue; **Days/Hours:** Preserve never closes; **Holiday Closings:** No; **Visitor attractions closed for seasons:** No; **Weather:** Most visitors come into the area between mid-June and mid-Sept. when the temperatures average in the mid-40s F along the coast and mid-60s F inland. During the ice-free periods along the coasts (late May to late Oct.), cloudy skies prevail, fog occurs, daily temperatures remain fairly constant in the long hours of daylight, and the relative humidity is high.

GENERAL INFORMATION: Visitors to the Preserve must arrive self-sufficient with their food, clothing, and shelter, and in some cases with fuel. There is some driftwood along the beaches, but inland wood is scarce and should be used chiefly for cooking. You should possess skills, talents, and stamina to survive some difficult conditions. In other words, you should have hiking, backpacking, and camping experience, and be knowledgeable about food, clothing, and gear. Since visitors carry everything on their backs once they've arrived in the Preserve, they bring only the *essentials*: good tents with rain flies, sleeping bags and pads, insect repellents and head nets, cooking and eating utensils, first aid items, maps, knife, food, warm clothing and rain gear, calf-high boots with waterproof lowers, fishing tackle, extra socks, and possibly some camera equipment. In parties of two or more it is advisable to always travel with others in the Preserve—many of the above items can be shared, reducing the weight one must carry.

Cape Krusenstern National Monument
Alaska

MAILING ADDRESS: National Park Service, Cape Krusenstern National Monument, P.O. Box 1029, Kotzebue, AK 99752 **Telephone:** 907-442-3890

DIRECTIONS: The Monument is in northwestern Alaska. Access is from Kotzebue via charter airplane.

The 114 beach ridges on this Chukchi Sea area, 600 miles (960 km) northwest of Anchorage, tell of successive Eskimo communities living here for 400 years. Created by act of Congress Dec. 2, 1980.

VISITOR ACTIVITIES: Wildlife-watching, beach walking, fishing, primitive camping; **Permits:** Alaska fishing license, available locally, is required; **Fees:** No; **Visitor facilities:** Information can be obtained from Superintendent Cape Krusenstern National Monument, Kotzebue, AK 99752; **Camping:** Yes, primitive camping only; **Other overnight accommodations on site:** No; **Meals served in the park:** No; **Food and supplies obtainable in the park:** No; **Food and supplies obtainable nearby:** Yes, at Kotzebue; **Overnight accommodations:** Kotzebue; **First Aid available in park:** No; **Nearest Hospital:** Kotzebue; **Days/ Hours:** Monument never closes; **Holiday Closings:** No; **Visitor attractions closed for seasons:** No.

GENERAL INFORMATION: Because of rugged terrain and harsh climate visitors should contact NPS visitor information office in Kotzebue prior to visiting the area.

TRAVEL ACCESS: Bus: No; **Rail:** No; **Air:** Alaska Airlines provides daily service to Kotzebue; **Other:** Air charter available in Kotzebue. A few charter boats available intermittently in Kotzebue.

NEARBY FACILITIES & POINTS OF INTEREST: Hotel/Motel: Nullugvik, Kotzebue, AK 99752, 907-442-3331, 20 miles (32 km) by air or boat to the Monument; **Parks, other points of interest:** Noatak National Preserve, Kobuk Valley National Park, Bering Land Bridge National Preserve, Nana Museum of the Arctic; **Reservation systems in use for campsites, other facilities:** No.

Denali National Park & Preserve
Denali, Alaska   **SEE CLIMATABLE NO. 4**

MAILING ADDRESS: Superintendent, Denali National Park & Preserve P.O. Box 9, Denali Park, AK 99755-0009 **Telephone:** 907-683-2294

DIRECTIONS: The park is 238 miles (386 km) north of Anchorage and 126 miles (193 km) south of Fairbanks, on Alaska Highway 3. Buses run regularly from both cities, summer only. The Alaska Railroad provides passenger and freight service to the park; 8 hours from Anchorage and 4 hours from Fairbanks. For information write to Alaska Railroad, Traffic Division, P.O. Box 7-2111, Anchorage, AK 99510.

Mount McKinley, at 20,320 feet, is the highest mountain in North America. Large glaciers of the Alaska Range, caribou, sheep, moose, grizzly bears, wolves, and other wildlife are highlights of this national park. Originally established as Mount McKinley National Park by act of Congress on Feb. 26, 1917, and expanded and renamed Denali National Park & Preserve in 1980.

VISITOR ACTIVITIES: Camping, wildlife-watching, interpretive talks and walks, hiking, backcountry use, fishing, dog sledding, cross-country skiing; **Permits:** For backcountry, required all year, in summer, at Visitor Access Center and in winter, at Park Headquarters dispatch office; **Fees:** Admission fee $3/person or $5/family. Campground fees $12 per night; **Visitor facilities:** Stop at the Visitor Access Center for campsite registration, bus coupons, backcountry permits, books, maps, etc. Lodging, food service, groceries, supplies and gas can be obtained a short distance from the Visitor Access Center. Minor auto repairs are available in Healy, 12 miles (19 km) north. After you leave the entrance area for the park interior, gasoline and food service are not available. **HANDICAPPED ACCESSIBILITY:** The Visitor Access Center, the free shuttle, the wildlife tour, 5 of the seven campgrounds, ARA Denali Park Hotels, Park Headquarters and Eielson Visitor Center are handicap accessible; **Any limitations on vehicle usage:** Maximum speed limit is 35 mph. During the visitor season, private vehicles are not permitted beyond Savage River. All motorized and non-motorized vehicles must not leave the park road. Other campgrounds are accessed by camper bus only. Snowmobiles are prohibited.

Since private vehicles are not allowed, there is *free transportation*. Buses regularly run from the Visitor Access Center (VAC) to Eielson Visitor Center and on to Wonder Lake. The buses make regularly scheduled stops at key points along the park road for your convenience, but you should feel free to get on and off and to change buses as many times as you please. Remember during peak season buses run full and several may pass by before space is available. Bring all the food you will need, because there is no food service beyond the entrance area; **Hiking trails:** Yes, most hiking is cross-country. Both long- and short-range trips are available; **Backcountry:** Yes, a permit is required for backcountry use. Obtain information from the Visitor Access Center upon arrival or by contacting the Park in advance; **Camping:** Yes, if you plan to camp in the park you must first register for it at the Visitor Access Center in the Headquarters-entrance area. All campsites are available on first-come first-served basis. Register at Visitor Access Center for sites in all campgrounds. After you have registered, in some instances, you will be allowed to drive your own vehicle just to the campsite. Once there you must hike or use the free public transportation system to get to other points of interest in the park. Sanctuary Igloo and Wonder Lake campgrounds are accessible only by shuttle bus. Too many new campgrounds to mention them individually. Same for areas further away. There are privately-owned campgrounds around the McKinley Park entrance; **Other overnight accommodations on site:** Yes, for information and reservations at Denali National Park Hotel contact ARA Outdoor World Ltd., Denali Park, AK 99755, or you may call (number noted below). Wildlife tour buses available through ARA Denali Park Hotels; **Meals served in the park:** Yes, at Denali National Park Hotel; **Food and supplies obtainable in the park:** Yes, near Denali National Park Hotel. For detailed information on this concessioner's services, contact ARA Outdoor World Ltd., from May, at 825 W. 8th Ave., #240, Anchorage, AK 99501, phone 907-276-7234.

Gates of the Arctic National Park & Preserve
Alaska   **SEE CLIMATABLE NO. 3**

MAILING ADDRESS: Gates of the Arctic National Park & Preserve, P.O. Box 74680 Fairbanks, AK, 99707-4680 **Telephone:** 907-456-0281

DIRECTIONS: Most visitors to the central Brooks Range fly via scheduled flights from Fairbanks to Bettles (about $83 one-way) and then charter small aircraft in Bettles for flights into the Park ($125-$185 per hour). Charter flights into the Brooks Range can also begin in Fairbanks (air-time is generally paid to and from the destination). Additionally, scheduled flights from Fairbanks and Bettles to Anaktuvuk Pass (within Park boundaries) are available several times a week.

It is best for the visitor to write directly to the park for a list of licensed air taxi operators.

This vast tundra wilderness contains 7 designated wild rivers and many lakes and rivers yet unnamed. Broad valleys contrast with razor-like Arrigetch Peaks and turreted Mt. Igikpak, high point of the central and western Brooks Range. Here, 200 miles (320 km) northwest of Fairbanks, is habitat vital to the arctic caribou, grizzly bear, sheep, moose, wolves, and raptors. Created by U.S. Congress on Dec. 2, 1980.

VISITOR ACTIVITIES: Hiking, backpacking, rock and mountain climbing, limited fishing, wildlife-watching, canoeing; **Permits:** Alaska fishing and hunting licenses, available in Fairbanks at Alaska Dept. of Fish and Game, are required. Hunting is allowed only in the Preserve (⅛ of the Park area—no hunting in the parklands); Though state regulations apply to fishing, Park encourages catch-and-release fishing because cold waters and very short seasons limit productivity; **Fees:** No; **Visitor facilities:** No; **Any limitations on vehicle usage:** No roads or off-road vehicles; **Hiking trails:** No; **Backcountry:** Yes, information can be obtained from Park Office in Fairbanks; U.S.G.S. quadrangle maps available in Fairbanks at U.S.G.S. and in Bettles; **Camping:** Allowed, but there are no designated campsites; **Other overnight accommodations on site:** Yes. A few very small private lodges are located within or adjacent to the Park. **Meals served in the park:** No; **Food and supplies obtainable in the park:** No; **Food and supplies obtainable nearby:** Yes, Bettles (very limited) Anaktuvuk Pass, Fairbanks; **Overnight accommodations:** Coldfoot, 6 miles (9.6 km) east, and Bettles, 20 miles (32 km) south; **First Aid available in park:** No; **Nearest Hospital:** Fairbanks; **Days/Hours:** Park never closes; **Holiday Closings:** No; **Visitor attractions closed for seasons:** No; **Weather:** Long, cold winters and short, mild summers are the rule. Along the south slopes of the Brooks Range, particularly in the lowlands, mid-summer temperatures may occasionally rise into the 80s and rarely into the 90s. Temperatures in the highlands are generally cooler, and on the northern slopes temperatures range from 30°F to 60°F. In the highlands and on the north slopes freezing temperatures may occur in mid-Aug. and definitely occur in early Sept. August is often a rainy month. Frost may occur in any month, especially at higher elevations.

GENERAL INFORMATION: This Park/Preserve is extremely remote. Visitors must come prepared to be totally self-sufficient. Because nearly all visitors to the Park will be backpacking or canoeing/rafting for extended periods, it is essential that clothing, camping gear, and food are of good quality and are light in weight. Clothing should include enough "layers" even during the summer months to provide warmth in sub-freezing temperatures; and rain gear is essential. Visitors should treat water and should not rely on wood fires for heat source—take a gas or propane stove. Tents should be strong, light, and have a rainfly. Food will have to consist primarily of dried and freeze-dried items, and should be in greater quantities than what is expected to be consumed during the planned trip since Air Charter delays often occur in bad weather. Visitors should be well familiar with their gear before starting a backpacking or river trip in this area, and should additionally be competent at hiking, camping, and survival skills. Winter travel requires special skills and hardiness, and should only be undertaken after careful planning.

The land and its resources must be used lightly, according to Park guidelines, in order to preserve the wilderness for future generations.

Mosquitoes usually come out in mid-June and begin to disappear in early or mid-Aug. Gnats and whitesocks hatch in Aug. Insects are most bothersome in wet lowlands and areas of heavy vegetation, and are not as numerous on dry highlands where breezes are frequent. Carry good mosquito repellent and a headnet.

Glacier Bay National Park and Preserve
Gustavus, Alaska   **SEE CLIMATABLE NO. 5**

MAILING ADDRESS: Superintendent, Glacier Bay National Park and Preserve, Gustavus, AK 99826 **Telephone:** 907-697-2230

DIRECTIONS: The Park is located at the northwest end of the Alexander Archipelago in southeastern Alaska. There are no roads to the Park, and access is by various types of commercial transport, including regularly scheduled and charter air services, cruise ships and charter boats, private boats, and tours via kayak. By boat, the distance from Juneau is about 100 miles (161 km). Flying time from Juneau is about 30 minutes. An airfield is at Gustavus, just outside the park.

Great tidewater glaciers, a dramatic range of plant communities, and several species of wildlife can be found in this unit of the National Park System. Created by Presidential Proclamation on Feb. 25, 1925.

VISITOR ACTIVITIES: Glacier-viewing, boating, camping, hiking, fishing, wildlife- and bird-watching, evening programs; **Permits:** Required for fishing; **Fees:** Only for concession-operated and commercial transportation to tidewater glaciers; **Visitor facilities:** Restrooms, lodge, interpretive programs and hikes, hiking trails, food service, campground. Boaters may obtain gasoline, diesel fuel, and water, permits required for boating and use limited during humpback whale season, June 1-August 30. No other public facilities for boats are available at the Park. **HANDICAPPED ACCESSIBILITY:** Lodge has two accessible rooms, ramp, and elevator; restrooms are accessible; one section of forest trail accessible via boardwalk; **Any limitations on vehicle usage:** No; **Hiking trails:** Two in Bartlett Cove area; the Park's several hundred miles of shoreline, numerous islands (several closed during nesting season) and alpine meadows offer nearly unlimited camping and hiking opportunities; **Backcountry:** Yes, a hikers' guide with many suggestions for backcountry use and topographical maps covering the Park can be obtained at Bartlett Cove; **Camping:** Yes, campers should bring food and supplies to Glacier Bay. There are no camping services locally. **Other overnight accommodations on site:** Yes, concessioner-operated Glacier Bay Lodge at Bartlett Cove is open from about mid-May to mid-Sept. Rooms and meals are available. For reservations, write to Glacier Bay Lodge, Glacier Bay National Park, Gustavus, AK 99826, during the operating season, and Glacier Bay Lodge, Inc., 520 Pike Street, Suite 1610, Seattle, WA 98101, phone 800-622-2042 for reservations, 206-623-7110 other, the remainder of the year. A tour boat makes daily cruises from the lodge to the glaciers. For campers and hikers, rain gear, a tent fly, and water-resistant boots are often essential items for a successful trip. **Meals served in the park:** Yes, at Glacier Bay Lodge, in season; **Food and supplies obtainable in the park:** A limited amount of food and supplies is available at Gustavus general store; **Food and supplies obtainable nearby:** No, at Juneau, AK, 100 miles (161 km) distant; **Overnight accommodations:** Gustavus, 10 miles (16 km) distant. Otherwise Juneau, 100 miles (161 km); **First Aid available in park:** Yes, at Park Headquarters; **Nearest Hospital:** Juneau, 100 miles (161 km) by air; **Days/Hours:** Park always open, concession facilities are open from late May to mid-September; **Holiday Closings:** No; **Visitor attractions closed for seasons:** Only concession facilities are closed from mid-Sept. to mid-May; **Weather:** Warm clothing and rain gear are essential when visiting the Park. Summer temperatures seldom exceed 72°F and extended periods of wet weather are to be expected. The ground is usually moist and footwear should be selected accordingly.

Katmai National Park & Preserve
Alaska   **SEE CLIMATABLE NO. 1**

MAILING ADDRESS: Superintendent, Katmai National Park & Preserve, P.O. Box 7, King Salmon, AK 99613-0007 **Telephone:** 907-246-3305

DIRECTIONS: Katmai is 290 air miles (467 km) southwest of Anchorage. Daily commercial jet flights connect Anchorage with King Salmon. Travel from King Salmon to Brooks Camp is by amphibious bush aircraft. Visitor information is available at the Brooks Camp Visitor Contact Station and at Park Headquarters in King Salmon.

Variety marks this vast land: lakes, forests, mountains, and marshlands all abound in wildlife—including the Alaska brown bear, the world's largest carnivore. Here, in one of the largest areas in the National Park System, Novarupta Volcano erupted violently in 1912, forming the ash-filled "Valley of Ten Thousand Smokes." Today, only a few active vents remain. Created by Presidential Proclamation on Sept. 24, 1918. Katmai National Monument was greatly enlarged in 1978 and became the 4,093,214 acre Katmai National Park and Preserve by Congressional Action on Dec. 2, 1980.

VISITOR ACTIVITIES: Hiking, walking, wildlife-watching, fishing, camping, backcountry travel, bird-watching, boating, mountain climbing, kayaking and canoeing; **Permits:** Fishing licenses can be obtained at Brooks Lodge; backcountry permits available without charge at Brooks Camp Visitor Contact Station or at Headquarters in King Salmon; **Fees:** Yes, for Alaska State fishing licenses; **Visitor facilities:** Concession boats, bus tours, interpretive talks, charter aircraft, cabins, lodge, dining room, campgrounds, fuel, fishing equipment rental, concession boats are available with guide, canoes can be rented; **Any limitations on vehicle usage:** 80% of Katmai's visitors are recorded at Lake Camp (just inside boundary), which is 10 miles (16 km) from King Salmon by dirt road. Brooks camp and other areas are not accessible by any road system—access is by aircraft or boat; **Hiking trails:** Yes, detailed information on hiking is provided in a free publication, available by mail or at Brooks Camp Visitor Contact Station or from Headquarters in King Salmon; **Backcountry:** Yes, permit required; check at Brooks Camp Visitor Contact Station or at Headquarters in King Salmon; **Camping:** Yes; Camping at Brooks Camp requires reservations; **Other overnight accommodations on site:** Yes, a lodge is at Brooks Camp. Katmailand, Inc., 4700 Aircraft Dr., Suite 2, Anchorage, AK 99502, 907-243-5448 or 1-800-544-0551, provides accommodations and services at Brooks Camp and Grosvenor Lake. Katmailand also operates Kulik Lodge—a 16 bed lodge on private land within the Park extensions, Katmailand also operates wilderness camps at Nonvianuk and Battle Lakes. All serve meals, provide guide service and beds; **Meals served in the park:** Yes, at Brooks Camp and Grosvenor Lake Camp; **Food and supplies obtainable in the park:** Yes, camping supplies and groceries should be obtained before visiting the park. Limited freeze-dried food items and stove fuel available at the park. **Food and supplies obtainable nearby:** Yes, a small general store in King Salmon; **Overnight accommodations:** Motel in King Salmon; **First Aid available in park:** Yes, or nearby medical facilities in Naknak, Dr. on duty in summer; **Nearest Hospital:** Anchorage, 290 miles (467 km) by air; **Days/Hours:** It is accessible by private aircraft or charter anytime; but is accessible by commercial aircraft only June-Sept. The Park is never actually closed; **Visitor attractions closed for seasons:** Lodge and concession facilities closed from Sept. 11 to June 1. **Weather:** Summer high temperatures average 63°F and low temperatures average 44°F. Strong winds and sudden, gusty rainstorms known as williwawes periodically sweep the area. The sky is clear about 20% of the summer.

GENERAL INFORMATION: Day hikers should have sturdy hiking boots with good support, good rain gear, and warm clothing. Come prepared for some sunshine and some stormy weather. Clothing that may be useful includes comfortable sport clothes, avoid cotton, a warm sweater or windbreaker, walking shoes or boots with thick soles and good support, wool socks and a rain coat or hat. You will need insect repellent.

Katmai is a wildlife sanctuary. Keep your distance from and do not feed the animals. Keep all food sealed to reduce odors; use food caches. Make lots of noise when you walk.

NEARBY FACILITIES & POINTS OF INTEREST: Hotel/Motel: King Ko Inn, King Salmon, 907-246-3377; Quinnat Landing Hotel, King Salmon, 907-246-3000. **Food/ Supplies:** King Salmon Commercial, King Salmon, 907-246-3411; **Other points of interest:** Salmon fishing activities in Naknek in July; **New information:** The Park, as expanded, now includes three other lodges (operated by Katmailand) in the northern extension. City Market, King Salmon, AK 99613 907-246-6109.

Kenai Fjords National Park
Alaska

MAILING ADDRESS: Kenai Fjords National Park Box 1727, Seward, AK 99664-1727 **Telephone:** 907-224-3175

DIRECTIONS: The gateway community of Seward, AK, is 127 miles (203.2 km) from Anchorage. Air transportation from Anchorage is available via commercial and charter flights. In addition, Seward has bus service. Exit Glacier is the only area of the park accessible by autos and RVs on an 8½-mile (13.6-km) gravel road. Scheduled commercial charter boat services provide opportunities to see and enjoy the coast on half- and full-day trips. Air charters are also available for access to the Fjords as well as the icefield.

Within a few miles of Seward, this 580,000-acre National Park is a portion of the southern Kenai Mountains, two interrelated icefields and a coastal Fjord system where abundant marine mammals, seabirds, and mountain goats are found. Created by Congressional Action on Dec. 2, 1980.

VISITOR ACTIVITIES: Fishing, sailing, sea kayaking, hiking, skiing, snowmachining, dog sledding, snowshoeing, visiting a glacier, wildlife-watching, flightseeing, and charter boats. Ranger-led nature walks and hikes leave from Exit Glacier Ranger Station; **Permits:** Alaska fishing licenses required, available in Seward or Anchorage; **Fees:** No; **Visitor facilities:** Visitor Center in Seward, open 8 a.m.-7 p.m., 7 days a week May-Sept. and 8 a.m.-5 p.m. Mon.-Fri. rest of the year. Evening programs, films, and a regularly scheduled park slide show. Ranger Station at Exit Glacier. A State Ferry System links Seward with Prince William Sound, Homer, and Kodiak Island. Flightseeing chartered tours leave from Seward and Homer. Hotels, motels, and campgrounds, food and services are available in Seward. **HANDICAPPED ACCESSIBILITY:** 2 parking lots at the glacier for cars and motorhomes. Restrooms at glacier. Maintained ½-mile (.8-km) paved trail leads to view of glacier and nature display; **Any limitations on vehicle usage:** 8½-mile (13.6-km) gravel road to Exit Glacier; **Hiking trails:** Yes, trails to Exit Glacier, Harding Icefield, and other areas in the park as well as on adjacent federal and state lands; 700-sq. mile (1,120-km) Harding Icefield is accessible by a 3.5-mile (5.6-km) trail that begins at Exit Glacier. Strenuous 3,000-ft. gain in elevation; **Backcountry:** Yes, information can be obtained from the Park Service Office in Seward; **Camping:** Yes, 10-site walk in campground at Exit Glacier; **Other overnight accommodations on site:** Public use cabin in Aialik Bay, fee and reservations required. No reservations required for campgrounds in Seward and within adjacent national forest land. Winter public use cabin at Exit Glacier, fee and reservations required. Contact the Seward Chamber of Commerce Information Center, phone 907-224-8051, or Homer information, phone 907-235-5300; **Meals served in the park:** No; **Food and supplies obtainable in the**

park: No; **Food and supplies obtainable nearby:** Yes, at Seward; **Overnight accommodations:** Seward; **First Aid available in park:** Yes; **Nearest Hospital:** Seward; **Days/Hours:** Park always open; **Holiday Closings:** No; **Visitor attractions closed for season:** Exit Glacier may be closed to vehicle traffic from Nov.-Apr. dependent on snowfall. Charterboats operate from late May to Labor Day; **Weather:** A coastal maritime climate influences the area.

GENERAL INFORMATION: Nights are cool along the coast and high humidity and rainfall can be expected. Comfortable wool clothing and appropriate rain gear are important considerations.

Klondike Gold Rush National Historical Park
Skagway, Alaska and Seattle, Washington

MAILING ADDRESS: Superintendent, Klondike Gold Rush National Historical Park, P.O. Box 517, Skagway, AK 99840 *OR* Superintendent, Klondike Gold Rush National Historical Park, 117 S. Main St., Seattle, WA 98104 **Telephone:** AK: 907-983-2921, WA: 206-553-7220

DIRECTIONS: Access to Skagway is by auto, plane, bus, cruise ship, or by State of Alaska ferry. For further information, contact your travel agent or the City of Skagway, Box 415, Skagway, AK 99840. The City of Skagway Visitor Center is located in the Arctic Brotherhood Building on the west side of Broadway, south of the alley between Second and Third Avenue. National Park Service Visitor Center is located at 2nd and Broadway. The Seattle Visitor Center is at 117 S. Main Street in the Pioneer Square area.

The Park is a memorial to the thousands of miners who followed trails from Skagway, AK, to the Yukon Territory of Canada during the 1898 gold rush. It preserves historic structures in Skagway, Chilkoot Trail (from Dyea to the Canadian Border), and part of the White Pass Trail. Authorized for addition to the National Park System on June 30, 1976. Established May 14, 1980.

VISITOR ACTIVITIES: Skagway: wildlife-watching, camping, foot, bus, and chartered aircraft tours. Information on films, displays, interpretive programs and guided walks available at the Skagway Visitor Center, Alaska; Seattle: interpretive displays, films, special tours and other events; **Permits:** No; **Fees:** No; **Visitor facilities:** Seattle: Visitor Center, restrooms, exhibits; Alaska: Visitor Center, campground, groceries and other limited supplies, and restrooms; **Any limitations on vehicle usage:** Vehicles are restricted to designated roadways; **Hiking trails:** In Alaska, the 40-mile (64-km) Chilkoot Trail is accessible only on foot. You must be properly outfitted before embarking on a hike over the Chilkoot Trail. Weather conditions may change rapidly from hour to hour, especially in the summit area. You must be prepared for cold temperatures, snow or rain, fog, and travel through swampy areas and snow fields. Proper equipment includes warm clothing (preferably wool), sturdy rain gear (not plastic), a tent with waterproof fly, campstove, and adequate fuel (there is no wood in the summit area and campfires are not allowed at all in the Canadian portion), good hiking boots, adequate food plus emergency rations, and first-aid kit. Current trail information available at the Visitor Center in Skagway or the Area Superintendent, Yukon National Historic Sites, Canadian Parks Service, P.O. Box 5540, Whitehorse, Yukon, YIA5H4 Canada, 403-668-2116. Hiking the trail north from Dyea is recommended because it is the historic route. Traveling the trail in reverse is not recommended because descending the steep summit scree, the "Gold Stairs" of the gold rush days, is dangerous.

For Your Safety—Be alert for symptoms of hypothermia, a lowering of body temperature that results in uncontrollable shivering, disorientation, weariness, and possibly death. Never feed wild animals. Make noise when you hike, announcing your presence, since bears are most dangerous when startled or cornered. Never approach a potentially dangerous animal. Keep your campsite and equipment clean. Food should be sealed in airtight containers and hung from trees so that animals will not be attracted by the food odors. You are advised not to take pets on the Chilkoot Trail. It is a difficult hike. **Backcountry:** Yes; **Camping:** In Alaska, no reservations available for primitive campsites; **Other overnight accommodations on site:** Yes; **Meals served in the park:** Not within either section of the park, but meals are available nearby; **Food and supplies obtainable in the park:** Yes, groceries and limited supplies in Alaska; **Food and supplies obtainable nearby:** Yes, Seattle: 2 blocks north, Alaska: Skagway Historic District; **Overnight accommodations:** Seattle and Skagway; **First Aid available in park:** Yes; **Nearest Hospital:** Seattle, 1 mile (1.6 km) away for Skagway; Whitehorse 112, Juneau 90 airm.; **Days/Hours:** Seattle: 9 a.m. to 7 p.m. in summer; shorter hours during the off-season, Skagway: Visitor Center open from 8 a.m. to 6 p.m., only in summer; **Holiday Closings:** Seattle Visitor Center holiday closings have not yet been determined. **Visitor attractions closed for season:** Skagway Visitor Center open only in summer.

GENERAL INFORMATION: International Regulations: Customs and Immigration laws require that anyone travelling to Canada must report to Canadian Customs. Canadian Customs Offices are located in Fraser, B.C., and Whitehorse, YT. Anyone proceeding to Skagway from Canada must report to U.S. Customs and Immigration authorities in Skagway.

TRAVEL ACCESS: Bus: Gray Line of Alaska, Alaskan Pass and Alaskan motorcoaches have scheduled bus service in the region, phone 1-800-544-2206; (Alaska Sightseeing Company) from Skagway to Dyea. Weekly service from Skagway to Anchorage; **Air:** Scheduled and charter small aircraft (single engine) operate daily service.

Kobuk Valley National Park
Alaska

MAILING ADDRESS: National Park Service, Kobuk Valley National Park, Box 1029, Kotzebue, AK 99752. **Telephone:** 907-442-3890

DIRECTIONS: Access is via charter aircraft from Kotzebue.

The Kobuk River, flowing west across this area to the Chukchi Sea, has been a major transportation route for centuries. Archaeological resources are extensive. Other features in this area between the Baird Mountains on the north and Waring Mountains are the Salmon River, caribou migrating routes of moose, grizzly bear, black bear and wolves; and the Great Kobuk Sand Dunes. Created by Act of Congress, Dec. 2, 1980.

VISITOR ACTIVITIES: Float trips, fishing, hiking, photography, primitive camping; **Permits:** Alaska fishing license, available in Anchorage or Kotzebue is required; **Fees:** No; **Visitor facilities:** No; **Any limitations on vehicle usage:** No roads; **Hiking trails:** No; **Backcountry:** Yes, information can be obtained from The National Park Service Information Office in Kotzebue; **Camping:** Yes, primitive camping only; **Other overnight accommodations on site:** No; **Meals served in the park:** No; **Food and supplies obtainable in the park:** No; **Food and supplies obtainable nearby:** Yes, in Kotzebue, Ambler, or Kiana; **Overnight accommodations:** No; **First Aid available in park:** No; **Nearest Hospital:** Kotzebue; **Days/Hours:** Park never closes.

GENERAL INFORMATION: Visitor Contact facility now available in Kotzebue. Because of rugged terrain and harsh climate visitors should contact NPS office prior to visiting the area.

TRAVEL ACCESS Bus: No; **Rail:** No; **Air:** Alaska Airlines provides daily service to Kotzebue; scheduled flights also serve nearby villages of Ambler and Kiana; **Other:** Air charter available in Kotzebue. A few charter boats available intermittently in Kotzebue or other nearby villages.

NEARBY FACILITIES & POINTS OF INTEREST: Hotel/Motel: Nul-Luk-Vik, Kotzebue, AK 99752, 907-442-3331, 120 miles (192 km) from the park by air, Kobuk river lodge in Ambler 907-455-2150 or 907-455-2166, and Blankenship Trading Post in Kiana 907-475-2177; **Parks, other points of interest:** Cape Krusenstern National Monument, Noatak National Preserve, Bering Bridge National Preserve, NANA Museum of the Arctic.

Lake Clark National Park & Preserve
Alaska

MAILING ADDRESS: Lake Clark National Park and Preserve, 4230 University Drive, Suite 311, Anchorage, AK 99508 **Telephone:** 907-271-3751

DIRECTIONS: Most visitors charter an aircraft from Anchorage to the Lake Clark area at a cost of $180 an hour depending on the weight load, number of passengers, and type of aircraft. Most places in the Park and Preserve are within 1½ hours flight time from Anchorage. There is commercial air service available from Anchorage to Iliamna, costing about $160-$210 round trip. Points within the Park and Preserve from Iliamna are visited via air charter, at the same cost per hour as Anchorage's air charter services.

Already popular with summer hikers and fishermen, this 3.7-million acre area across Cook Inlet from Anchorage provides major recreational potential. Among the wildlife to be viewed in this rugged country are caribou, grizzly bear, black bear, sheep at the southern limit of its range, wolves, wolverine, mink, marten, lynx, and other fur bearers. The coastal mountains contain two steaming volcanoes. The Park and Preserve preserves major red salmon spawning waters. This area was set aside by Presidential Proclamation on Dec. 1, 1978. Later on Dec. 2, 1980, the Park and Preserve was established by federal law.

VISITOR ACTIVITIES: Hiking, wildlife, birdwatching, fishing, hunting in Preserve, boating, river trips, primitive camping; **Permits:** Alaska fishing licenses are required and are available in Anchorage; **Fees:** No; **Visitor facilities:** Boat rental, fishing tackle, guide services on the coast shores of Lake Clark, and lodging and Guide Services at Silver Salmon Coast and Crescent Lake; **Any limitations on vehicle usage:** No roads; aircraft landing permitted. **Hiking trails:** Yes, several primitive and unmarked trails; **Backcountry:** Yes, information can be obtained from Park Headquarters; **Camping:** Yes, primitive camping only; **Other overnight accommodations on site:** Yes, 4 lodges are located within the boundaries of the Preserve along the shores of Lake Clark. Other lodging is available through commercial and air charter services in Anchorage to points on the periphery of the area. Lodging ranges from primitive cabins to modern lodges with plumbing; **Meals served in the park:** Yes, but generally for guests at lodging facilities; **Food and supplies obtainable in the park:** Yes, limited food and supplies at nearby Nondalton and Iliamna; **Overnight accommodations:** No; **First Aid available in park:** Yes, limited. Clinic in Iliamna; **Nearest Hospital:** Kenai, Anchorage; **Days/Hours:** Park and Preserve never close; **Holiday Closings:** No; **Visitor attractions closed for season:** No; **Weather:** Most visitors arrive between mid-June and early Sept., when high temperatures average between 60°F and 75°F, with an occasional 80° day in the interior. Coastline areas are cooler with temperatures between 50° and 65°. Wind and rainfall are present on the coastal areas, with mostly sunny and milder temperatures in the interior.

GENERAL INFORMATION: Insects may be numerous and precautions should be taken by obtaining adequate tents for camping on open river and lake bars. Having an ample supply of insect repellent is suggested. One should plan on wearing clothing that will ward off the extremes of possible freezing temperatures, wet weather, and warm sunny days. Extra socks and tennis shoes are practical for river running travel, plus a rainsuit, wool shirts and pants. Campers should travel light by carrying freeze-dried and high-energy foods, dried fruit, powdered milk, and packaged soups. Ordinary camping gear such as a warm sleeping bag, tent with rain fly and mosquito-proof webbing, knife, small hatchet or saw, insect repellent, sturdy hat, matches in waterproof container, and maps with protective casing are suggested.

TRAVEL ACCESS: Bus: No; **Rail:** No; **Air:** Yes, unscheduled air service to Anchorage, Kenai/Soldotna, Homer, Iliamna.

NEARBY FACILITIES & POINTS OF INTEREST: Parks, other points of interest: Lake Iliamna, Katmai, Denali.

Noatak National Preserve
Alaska

MAILING ADDRESS: National Park Service Noatak National Preserve, Box 1029, Kotzebue, AK 99752 **Telephone:** 907-442-3890

DIRECTIONS: Access is via charter aircraft from Kotzebue.
    The Noatak River has the country's largest mountain-ringed basin unaffected by man's technology, a 65-mile (104-km) Grand Canyon of the Noatak, a transition zone for diverse plant and animal life and a vital caribou migration route. Some of its 200 archaeological sites date back 5000 years. Created by act of Congress on Dec. 2, 1980.

VISITOR ACTIVITIES: Float trips, fishing, primitive camping; **Permits:** Alaska fishing license, available in Anchorage or Kotzebue is required; **Fees:** No; **Visitor facilities:** No; **Any limitations on vehicle usage:** No roads; **Hiking trails:** No; **Backcountry:** Yes, information can be obtained from The National Park Service Information Office in Kotzebue; **Camping:** Yes, primitive camping only; **Other overnight accommodations on site:** No; **Meals served in the park:** No; **Food and supplies obtainable in the park:** No; **Food and supplies obtainable nearby:** Yes, at Kotzebue; **Overnight accommodations:** No; **First Aid available in park:** No; **Nearest Hospital:** Kotzebue; **Days/Hours:** Preserve never closes; **Holiday Closings:** No; **Visitor attractions closed for season:** No.

GENERAL INFORMATION: Visitor contact facility available in Kotzebue. Because of rugged terrain and harsh climate visitors should contact NPS office prior to visiting the area.

TRAVEL ACCESS: Bus: No; **Rail:** No; **Air:** Alaska Airlines offers regular service to Kotzebue; **Other:** Air charter available in Kotzebue. A few charter boats available intermittently in Kotzebue or other nearby villages.

NEARBY FACILITIES & POINTS OF INTEREST: Hotel/Motel: Nul-Luk-Vik, Kotzebue, AK 99752, 907-442-3331, 70 miles (112 km) from the Preserve by air; **Parks, other points of interest:** Cape Krusenstern National Monument, Kobuk Valley National Park, Bering Land Bridge National Preserve, NANA Museum of the Arctic.

Sitka National Historical Park
Sitka, Alaska

MAILING ADDRESS: Sitka National Historical Park, Box 738, Sitka, AK 99835
Telephone: 907-747-6281

DIRECTIONS: Sitka is in Alaska's southeastern panhandle. It can be reached by com-
merical airline direct from Seattle, Juneau, and Anchorage, and is port of call for cruise
ships and ferries on the Alaska Marine Highway System.

The site of the 1804 fort and battle which marked the last major Tlingit Indian resistance to Russian colonization is preserved here. Native artists demonstrate crafts and dis-
cuss their culture. The Park features totem pole exhibits and the restoration of one of the
oldest Russian buildings in Alaska, the Russian Bishop's House. Created March 23, 1910.

VISITOR ACTIVITIES: Interpretive talks, audiovisual exhibits, and craft demonstrations at the Visitor Center, picnicking, walking tours; **Permits:** No; **Fees:** No; **Visitor
facilities:** Parking and restrooms, picnic tables, fireplaces, Indian Cultural Center, trails,
beach; **Any limitations on vehicle usage:** No bicycle riding on park trails; No off-road
vehicle use; **Hiking trails:** Yes, almost 2 miles (3 km) of walkways thread the park;
Backcountry: No; **Camping:** No; **Other overnight accommodations on site:** No;
Meals served in the park: No; **Food and supplies obtainable in the park:** No; **Food
and supplies obtainable nearby:** Yes, in Sitka, ½ mile (.8 km); **Overnight accommodations:** Sitka, ½ mile (.8 km); **First Aid available in park:** Yes; **Nearest Hospital:**
Sitka, ½ mile (.8 km); **Days/Hours:** Open daily from 8 a.m. to 5 p.m. with extended
hours in summer, closed Sundays in winter; **Holiday Closings:** Thanksgiving, Dec. 25,
and Jan. 1; **Visitor attractions closed for seasons:** No native craft demonstrations from
Oct. 1 to June 1. Russian Bishop's House has reduced and limited access in winter.
Phone Visitor Center for information; **Weather:** Summer has frequent rain, temperatures range from the high 50s°-mid 60s°F. Winter is rainy and snowy; temperatures from
high teens to the 30s.

GENERAL INFORMATION: Visitors should also see nearby landmarks: St.
Michael's Cathedral, Castle Hill, the Russian Memorial, and Old Sitka.

TRAVEL ACCESS: Bus: No; **Rail:** No; **Air:** Yes, Alaska Airlines provides daily
service to Sitka Airport; **Other:** Alaska Marine Highway Ferry System.

**NEARBY FACILITIES & POINTS OF INTEREST: Parks, other points of
interest:** Castle Hill, St. Michael's Cathedral, Sheldon Jackson Museum, Isabel Miller
Museum.

Wrangell-St. Elias National Park & Preserve
Alaska   **SEE CLIMATABLE NO. 2**

MAILING ADDRESS: P.O. Box 29, Glennallen, AK 99588 **Telephone:** 909-822-5234

DIRECTIONS: Access into the central portion of the park by road is available from
the community of Chitina via the state maintained Chitina-McCarthy road, passable by
conventional vehicle with good clearance, which is generally passable during the summer

months, and extends some 61 miles (97.6 km) up the Chitina River Valley following the historic route of the Copper River and Northwestern Railroad to the Kennicott River. Road access into the northern section of the Park/Preserve is from Slana (on the Tok cutoff) along a state-maintained route passable by conventional vehicle which extends some 45 miles (72 km) into the abandoned mining community of Nabesna. (Nabesna is private land.) Access to the remaining interior portions of the Park/Preserve is by air. Charter air service is available from the Gulkana and Tok airports to a number of interior landing strips. Costs vary but an average round-trip cost from Gulkana to McCarthy with pick-up at a later point in time would cost about $700/plane with 3 people and gear for a Cessna 185. The community of Glennallen is some 200 miles (320 km) by paved highway from Anchorage and is reached by regularly scheduled bus service (seasonal). Air access to the southern coastal sections including the beaches is available from Yakutat, Cordova, and Valdez. Costs are about the same as above. At present there are no charter boats available out of Yakutat.

A day's drive east of Anchorage, this Park/Preserve contains a vast mountain wilderness that receives only light visitation. Here is the country's largest collection of glaciers and of peaks over 14,000 feet in North America, 9 of which are among the 16 highest; 4 of the 9 are over 16,000 feet. Caribou, dall sheep, and grizzly and black bears, wolves, wolverine, moose, and mountain goats are among the wildlife. Created by the Alaska National Interest Lands Conservation Act P.L. 96-487, Dec. 2, 1980.

VISITOR ACTIVITIES: Backpacking, lake fishing, camping, river rafting, cross-country skiing, mountain climbing, hiking, rafting, air tours; **Permits:** Alaska fishing licenses required, available in communities surrounding the park; **Fees:** No; **Visitor facilities:** Lodging and meals available in McCarthy and Kennecott and along the Nabesna Road; Surface transportation available between McCarthy and Kennecott, 5 miles (8 km); **Any limitations on vehicle usage:** Both roads are passable to conventional vehicle with good ground clearance; **Hiking trails:** Yes, trails are primitive. Contact the Park Office for further information; **Backcountry:** Yes; **Camping:** Yes; **Other overnight accommodations on site:** Yes; There are scattered remote cabins located throughout the region that will accommodate backcountry parties. Standard accommodations are available in motels and cabins in and around the communities of Chitina and Glennallen, on the Glenn and Richardson highways, and along the Tok cutoff. State campgrounds are found at Liberty Creek near Chitina and along the major highways. **Food and supplies obtainable near the park:** Yes, Glennallen has a good supermarket, and limited supplies are available in McCarthy, but all visitors to the backcountry must of necessity be self-sufficient and carry sufficient food to cover unexpected delays in getting picked up; **First Aid available in park:** No; **Nearest Clinic:** Glennallen; **Days/ Hours:** Park/Preserve never closes; **Holiday Closings:** No; **Visitor attractions closed for season:** Check locally for conditions and services; **Weather:** Summer weather can be cool, or warm; sunny days are not uncommon in July and August. Weather conditions can interfere with scheduled air pickups, resulting in trips longer than scheduled. Clear, hot days are not uncommon, particularly in July, which has the best weather. August is cooler and wetter but generally more mosquito free. The fall is excellent but of short duration. Winters are cold and dark, but clear weather is common. Average snow cover is about 2 feet.

GENERAL INFORMATION: Good rain gear and wool clothing are a must. Road conditions can change on very short notice making the road impassable to all but 4-wheel-drive vehicles.

TRAVEL ACCESS: Air: No scheduled Airline, Charters available to Park from fixed base operators. Charges for charter fares vary. Yakutat, Cordova, Valdez, Anchorage, Gulkana, Northway, Tok, Fairbanks, and McCarthy; **Bus:** Bus companies serving Glennallen will drop people off at any point along their routes.

NEARBY FACILITIES & POINTS OF INTEREST: Campgrounds: Liberty Falls (near Chitina), Sourdough (north of Gulkana), Porcupine Creek (near Tonsina); **Attractions:** Glennallen, Valdez (about 100 miles), King Salmon fishing and the Alaska pipeline.

Yukon-Charley Rivers National Preserve
Alaska

MAILING ADDRESS: Superintendent, Yukon-Charley Rivers National Preserve, P.O. Box 167, Eagle, AK 99738 **Telephone:** 907-547-2233

DIRECTIONS: Eagle and Circle are the gateway cities to the Preserve. Take either the Taylor Highway to Eagle (the highway connects with the Alaska Highway at Tetlin Junction near Tok, Alaska) or the Steese Highway from Fairbanks to Circle. There are scheduled flights from Fairbanks to both Eagle and Circle. Round trip fare to Eagle is $183 and to Circle $140. (1987 prices)

This Preserve encompasses a 130-mile (209 km) stretch of the 1800-mile (2900 km) Yukon river and the 118 mile (190 km) scenic Charley River which drains a million-acre watershed near the Canadian border. Also protected are one of the largest nesting concentrations of the endangered peregrine falcon, arctic steppe communities and historic resources of the gold rush days. Created by Alaska National Interest Lands Conservation Act, December 2, 1980.

VISITOR ACTIVITIES: Wildlife- and bird-watching, river floating, hiking, camping, photography, backcountry, picnicking, kayaking, canoeing; **Permits:** Alaska fishing and hunting licenses, available at local sporting goods stores, are required; **Fees:** No; **Visitor facilities:** Eagle; NPS visitor center, BLM campground, grocery and hardware stores, cafe, motel, fuel. Circle; Trading Post, motels, cafe/bar, liquor store, fuel and campground; **Any limitations on vehicle usage:** no roads within preserve; **Hiking trails:** No; **Backcountry:** Information can be obtained from the Superintendent's office in Eagle; topographic maps are available from the Alaska National History Association outlet at the visitor center, and there is also a small reference library for visitor use. **Camping:** Yes; no reservations needed at Eagle or Circle campgrounds; **Other overnight accommodations on site:** No; **Meals served in the park:** No; **Food and supplies obtainable in the park:** No; **Food and supplies obtainable nearby:** Yes, Eagle and Circle; **Overnight accommodations:** Circle Hot Springs or along the Alaska Highway and Eagle, Circle; **First Aid available in park:** No; **Nearest Hospital:** Fairbanks (180 air-miles); **Days/Hours:** Preserve never closes; **Holiday Closings:** No; **Visitor attractions closed for seasons:** Many highways closed in winter; **Weather:** Most visitors come into the Preserve between mid-June and mid-September when the temperatures average between 40° and 70°F and water conditions are most conducive to travel. Thunderstorms with strong winds can arise suddenly. They can become violent, pose dangers, and raise whitecaps on the wider stretches on the Yukon. Water may also rise on the Charley River.

GENERAL INFORMATION: If you intend to be out in the backcountry for a few days or longer in summer, carry clothing for all seasons. Within a span of a few hours on the Yukon River temperatures may vary greatly. Wear layered clothing. Tennis shoes are practical for river travel because they dry easily, but you'll need additional footwear. Extra socks and a rain suit or poncho are essential. Your choice of food items will depend upon a number of variables: length of planned visit, activities planned, weight you can carry, and kinds of meals planned. Plan to protect your food from bears with containers or by hanging it. The minimum impact traveler such as the backpacker or kayaker or the person wishing to abandon some of the amenities of civilization for a while will travel lightly and simply: freeze-dried and high-energy foods, packaged soups, dried fruit, powdered milk, etc. Ordinary camping gear is sufficient for summer visitors: a good sleeping bag that will dry, a tent with rain fly, knife, hatchet, insect repellent and head net, matches in waterproof container, cooking and eating utensils, water container, good maps, fishing tackle, and photographic equipment. Insects are numerous and irritating from early summer to early August when they diminish. To avoid some of the irritation from insects, most travelers camp on bars and open shorelines where winds are most likely to prevail. Yukon river currents are strong and swift and deceptive in that they may not be readily apparent. The Charley River and other floatable side streams are subject to rapid rise in water levels due to up-river thunderstorms.

Arizona

Canyon de Chelly National Monument
Chinle, Arizona

MAILING ADDRESS: Superintendent, Canyon De Chelly National Monument, P.O. Box 588, Chinle, AZ 86503 **Telephone:** 602-674-5436

DIRECTIONS: The Visitor Center is 3 miles (4.8 km) from Route 191 in Chinle. From Gallup, NM, follow Routes 666, 264 to 191, 99 miles (159 km) to Chinle. From Grand Canyon, AZ, Routes 64, 89, 160, 264 to 191, 270 miles (370 km). From Holbrook-Petrified Forest, I-40, to 191. From Kayenta, Routes 160, 59 to 191, 82 miles (131.2 km). From Mesa Verde, Routes 789, 160 to 191, 158 miles (254 km). From Monument Valley, Routes 163, 160 to 191, 128 miles (206 km). From Page-Lake Powell, Routes 98, 160, 59 to 191, 208 miles (334.7 km). From Tuba City, Route 160, 59 to 191, 176 miles (283 km).

Ruins of Indian villages built between A.D. 350 and 1300 are at the base of sheer red cliffs and in caves in canyon walls. Modern Navajo Indians live and farm here. Authorized for addition to the National Park System on Feb. 14, 1931.

VISITOR ACTIVITIES: Auto tours, hiking, pictograph-viewing, ruin tours, interpretive exhibits and talks, horseback riding (by prior arrangement with the horse operators), picnicking, photography; **Permits:** Yes, you must have a tribal permit to fish on the reservation. Concession jeep tours available from Thunderbird Lodge, P.O. Box 548, Chinle, AZ 86503. Phone 602-674-5841 or -5842. Hiking within the canyon, requires a Park Service permit plus an authorized Navajo guide, except along the White House Ruins Trail. Hiking with a guide—one guide may take up to 15 people. A $7.50 per hour fee for up to 10 people is paid directly to the guide. To drive on the canyon bottom, you must have your own 4x4 and obtain a Park Service permit and be accompanied by an authorized Navajo guide. Fee is $7.50 per hour for 1 vehicle, $.50/hour for each additional vehicle up to 5 vehicles, with a 5 vehicle maximum per guide; **Fees:** For concession jeep tours and guided tours; **Visitor facilities:** Hiking and auto trails, parking, restrooms, exhibits, concession canyon trips, rental horses (by prior arrangement), campgrounds; **HANDICAPPED ACCESSIBILITY:** Some overlook areas are accessible, as well as some areas of the Thunderbird Lodge; **Any limitations on vehicle usage:** Autos should use paved highways only, 4-wheel drive vehicles must be used to travel to the bottom of the canyon; **Hiking trails:** Yes, a 2.5 mile (4 km) hiking trail leads to White House Ruin; **Backcountry:** Yes, backcountry and backcountry camping with an authorized guide; **Camping:** Yes, no reservations for individual campsites, which are free of charge and are open year-round. Reservations for group sites, of 15 or more people, may be made by contacting the park; no reservations accepted for RV groups; **Other overnight accommodations on site:** Yes, lodging is available at Thunderbird Lodge. Make reservations in advance by writing Thunderbird Lodge, Box 548, Chinle, AZ 86503, phone 602-674-5841 or -5842; **Meals served in the park:** Yes, at Thunderbird Lodge; **Food and supplies obtainable in the park:** No; **Food and supplies obtainable nearby:** Yes; **Overnight accommodations:** Window Rock, AZ 66 miles (106.2 km) away, Monument Valley, Hwy 191 and 160 to 163, 128 miles (206 km); and Gallup, NM Hwy 191 and 264 to 666, 99 miles (159 km), which has over 50 motels; **First Aid available in park:** Yes; **Nearest Hospital:** Chinle Hospital, 3 miles (4.8 km), 602-674-5281. Other hospitals in Gallup, NM, 99 miles (159 km), Ganado, AZ, 36 miles (56 km) 607-753-3411; **Days/Hours:** Visitor Center open daily 8 a.m. to 5 p.m. Oct.-April, 8 a.m. to 6 p.m. May-Sept. **Holiday Closings:** None, open all year; **Visitor attractions closed for seasons:** The inner canyons become impassable in winter and at certain other times of the year; **Weather:** Hot summers and cold winters, with little precipitation all year.

GENERAL INFORMATION: Quicksand, deep dry sand, cliffs, loose rocks and flash floods make the canyons hazardous.

NEARBY FACILITIES & POINTS OF INTEREST: Parks, other points of interest: Hubbell Trading Post National Historic Site.

Casa Grande Ruins National Monument
Coolidge, Arizona

MAILING ADDRESS: Superintendent, Casa Grande Ruins National Monument, 1100 Ruins Drive, Coolidge, AZ 85228 **Telephone:** 602-723-3172

DIRECTIONS: The monument is located in North Coolidge on AZ 87, about halfway between Phoenix and Tucson.

Perplexing ruins of a massive four-story building, constructed of high-lime desert soil by Indians who farmed the Gila Valley 600 years ago, raise many unanswered questions for modern man. The first archeological park established and the fourth area protected overall. The Casa Grande Ruin Reservation was authorized by Congress in 1889, and proclaimed a national monument on June 22, 1892, at which time the National Park Service assumed administration of the area.

VISITOR ACTIVITIES: Interpretive talks and exhibits, walking tours, picnicking; **Permits:** No; **Fees:** Entrance fee is $1 per person. Golden Eagle, Golden Age, and Golden Access Passports accepted and available; **Visitor facilities:** Parking and restrooms at Visitor Center, drinking water, picnic area; **HANDICAPPED ACCESSIBILITY:** Yes; **Any limitations on vehicle usage:** No; **Hiking trails:** Yes, a 400-yard round trip self-guiding walking trail leads through the ruins area; **Backcountry:** No; **Camping:** No; **Other overnight accommodations on site:** No; **Meals served in the park:** No; **Food and supplies obtainable in the park:** No; **Food and supplies obtainable nearby:** Yes, in Coolidge; **Overnight accommodations:** Coolidge, AZ 87, Florence, AZ 287, 12 miles (19 km) east; Casa Grande, AZ 287, 22 miles (33 km) southwest; **First Aid available in park:** Yes, or nearby in Coolidge, AZ 87; **Nearest Hospital:** Florence, AZ 287, 12 miles (19 km) east; **Days/Hours:** Open from 7 a.m. to 6 p.m., 365 days a year; **Holiday Closings:** No; **Weather:** The most comfortable time for visiting is between early October and early May, because summer temperatures approach 120°F.

GENERAL INFORMATION: WARNING: You are in harsh desert area. Beware of the cactus. Intense heat can cause varying degrees of discomfort. Be cautious of poisonous snakes, centipedes, and scorpions.

Chiricahua National Monument
Willcox, Arizona

MAILING ADDRESS: Superintendent, Chiricahua National Monument, Dos Cabezas Route, Box 6500, Willcox, AZ 85643 **Telephone:** 602-824-3560

DIRECTIONS: The Visitor Center is 36 miles (57.6 km) south of Willcox on AZ 186 and 181. Elevations range from approximately 5,100 feet at the park entrance to just over 7,310 feet. The monument is located in the northern portion of the Chiricahua mountains, which rise over 5,000 feet from the surrounding high desert grasslands to nearly 10,000 feet in elevation.

The varied rock formation here were created millions of years ago by volcanic activity, aided by erosion. Established by Presidential Proclamation.

VISITOR ACTIVITIES: Camping, hiking, auto tours, bird watching, interpretive exhibits, campfire programs in spring and summer, picnicking; **Permits:** No; **Fees:** $3 per car entrance fee; $6 per night per site camping fee, with Golden Eagle Passport, free admission, camping $6; Golden Age Passport, free admission, camping $3. Camping and entrance fees are subject to change. **Visitor facilities:** Parking and restrooms at Visitor Center, campgrounds, drinking water, fireplaces, tables, picnic areas; **Any limitations on vehicle usage:** No wheeled vehicles are permitted on the trails; **Hiking trails:** Yes, more than 20 miles (32 km) of trails provide views of all the park's features; **Backcountry:** No; **Camping:** Yes, no reservations for campsites maximum trailer length of 26 feet; **Other overnight accommodations on site:** No; **Meals served in the park:** No; **Food and supplies obtainable in the park:** No; **Food and supplies obtainable nearby:** Yes, in Willcox; **Overnight accommodations:** Willcox, AZ, 36 miles (57.6 km) north, has motels, restaurants, commercial campgrounds and trailer parks; **First Aid available in park:** Generally; **Nearest Hospital:** Willcox, AZ, 36 miles (57.6 km); **Days/Hours:** Open daily 8 a.m. to 5 p.m.; **Holiday Closings:** Dec. 25; **Visitor attractions closed for seasons:** Road occasionally closed in winter; **Weather:** Temperatures are generally moderate. The mean daily temperature in Jan. is 40°F and in July, 74°F. Chiricahua National Monument is a year-round park with distinct seasons of winter, spring, summer, and fall. Winter typically has snowfall, spring and fall are generally dry, and thunderstorms dominate the summer.

GENERAL INFORMATION: *For Your Safety*—Be alert for an occasional rattlesnake during warm weather. The scenic drive is winding and mountainous; watch for fallen rocks on the road, and ice in the winter.

TRAVEL ACCESS: Bus: several buses from Tucson—120 miles (192 km) from park.

NEARBY FACILITIES & POINTS OF INTEREST: Hotel/Motel: Willcox, AZ, 36 miles (57.6 km) from park; **Food/Supplies:** Willcox, AZ, 36 miles (57.6 km) from park; **Campgrounds:** U.S. Forest Service, Coronado National Forest; **Parks, other points of interest:** Cochise Visitor Center; Chiricahua Wilderness area, and nearby Fort Bowie National Historic Site; tremendous birding opportunities. Recently, the National Park Service purchased a 420 acre national register site for inclusion within Chiricahua National Monument. Faraway Ranch is open daily with conducted tours of the ranch house during the busy spring and summer seasons. Conducted tours of the house are provided at other times of the year on weekends or by arrangement with the park staff. Contact the park interpretive office at (602) 824-3560 to arrange for off-season tours of the house. This once-working cattle and guest ranch is open throughout the year and may be toured by a self-guiding tour booklet available at the monument's bookstore.

Coronado National Memorial
Hereford, Arizona

MAILING ADDRESS: Superintendent, Coronado National Memorial, Rural Route 2, Box 126, Hereford, AZ 85615 **Telephone:** 602-366-5515 — 458-9333

DIRECTIONS: The Memorial is about 22 miles (35 km) south of Sierra Vista, AZ, and 30 miles (48 km) west of Bisbee, AZ. The headquarters/Visitor Center is located 5 miles (8 km) off AZ 92 in Montezuma Canyon.

Francisco Vasquez de Coronado, who explored what is now the American Southwest in 1540-42, is commemorated here. A higher point in the park, Coronado Peak, overlooks the area where the expedition entered into our country. Emphasis on our Hispanic culture and heritage is shown in the museum. Coronado National Memorial was established by an act of Congress on Nov. 5, 1952.

VISITOR ACTIVITIES: Interpretive exhibits, picnicking, self-guided walking tours, hiking, and cave exploring; **Permits:** No; **Fees:** No; **Visitor facilities:** Parking, restrooms, wayside exhibits, picnic area, foot trails, trailside benches; **HANDICAPPED ACCESSI-**

BILITY: Yes, for parking, Visitor Center, restrooms, and picnic sites; **Any limitations on vehicle usage:** No off-road travel, no motorized vehicles on trails; **Hiking trails:** Yes, scenic foot trails begin at the parking area and Visitor Center, and at Montezuma Pass area; **Backcountry:** No; **Camping:** No; **Other overnight accommodations on site:** No, a U.S. Forest Service campground is at Parker Lake 18 miles (29 km) west of the Memorial; **Meals served in the park:** No; **Food and supplies obtainable in the park:** No; **Food and supplies obtainable nearby:** Yes, at Sierra Vista, Bisbee; **Overnight accommodations:** Sierra Vista, AZ 92 North, 22 miles (35 km); Bisbee, AZ 92 East, 30 miles (48 km); **First Aid available in park:** Yes; **Nearest Hospital:** Sierra Vista, AZ 92 North, 22 miles (35 km), Bisbee, AZ 92 East, 30 miles (48 km); **Days/Hours:** Park open daily from dawn to dusk, Visitor Center open daily from 8 a.m. to 5 p.m.; **Holiday Closings:** Visitor Center closed Thanksgiving, Dec. 25, and Jan. 1; **Visitor attractions closed for seasons:** No; **Weather:** Rainy periods are July through Oct. and Dec. through March. Temperatures are generally in the 70s to 90s in summer and into the 20s in winter. There are light snowfalls in winter.

GENERAL INFORMATION: *For Your Safety*—Watch out for unexpected steps, low branches, cactus, poison ivy, black widow spiders, scorpions, and rattlesnakes.

Fort Bowie National Historic Site
Bowie, Arizona

MAILING ADDRESS: Superintendent, Fort Bowie National Historic Site, P.O. Box 158, Bowie, AZ 85605 **Telephone:** 602-847-2500

DIRECTIONS: There is no road to the ruins proper. They can be reached only by a 1.5 mile (2.4 km) foot trail that begins midway in Apache Pass. The trailhead may be reached from two directions: from the town of Willcox, located on Int. 10, drive 22 miles (35.4 km) south on AZ 186 to the graded road leading east into Apache Pass; from the town of Bowie, also on Int. 10, drive southerly 12 miles (19.3 km) on a graded dirt road that then bears westerly into Apache Pass.

Established in 1862, this fort was the focal point of military operations against Geronimo, Cochise and their band of Chiricachua Apaches. Authorized for addition to the National Park System on Aug. 30, 1964.

VISITOR ACTIVITIES: Walking tours, exhibits, wildflower- and wildlife-watching, hiking; **Permits:** No; **Fees:** No; **Visitor facilities:** Small museum in the ranger station, parking area, pit toilets. **HANDICAPPED ACCESSIBILITY:** Available for Fort ruins, but requires advance notice. To make arrangements or obtain further information, write or call Fort Bowie National Historic Site, P.O. Box 158, Bowie, AZ 85605, 602-847-2500; **Any limitations on vehicle usage:** No vehicle access beyond the parking lot at the trailhead; **Hiking trails:** Yes, 1.5 mile (2.4 km) foot trail to ruins; 1.5 mile alternate return trail via Overlook Ridge to main trail and parking area; **Backcountry:** Yes, write the Site for information; **Camping:** No; **Other overnight accommodations on site:** No; **Meals served in the park:** No; **Food and supplies obtainable in the park:** No; **Food and supplies obtainable nearby:** Yes, at Willcox and Bowie; **Overnight accommodations:** Willcox and Bowie, Int. 10, 22 miles (35.4 km) and 12 miles (19.3 km); **First Aid available in park:** Yes, at the contact station in the ruins; **Nearest Hospital:** Willcox, 12 miles (19.2 km) to Bowie and 25 miles (40 km) more by I-10; **Days/Hours:** A ranger is usually on duty at the contact station from 8 a.m. to 5 p.m. daily; **Holiday Closings:** Dec. 25; **Visitor attractions closed for seasons:** No; **Weather:** Drizzling rain in winter, heavy rains in July and August, with flash flood warnings. Beware of muddy roads for short period of time after major storms.

GENERAL INFORMATION: Water is available at the fort. However, the summer hiker should consider a canteen since temperatures may climb above 100°. Summer storms may suddenly and briefly flood the washes. Simply wait out high water. Be alert for an occasional rattlesnake or Gila monster.

Glen Canyon National Recreation Area
Page, Arizona (also in Utah)

MAILING ADDRESS: Superintendent, Glen Canyon National Recreation Area, P.O. Box 1507, Page, AZ 86040 **Telephone:** 602-645-2471

DIRECTIONS: Park Headquarters is at 337 North Navajo Drive in Page, AZ, off US 89. There is a Visitor Center by Glen Canyon Dam, about 2 miles (3.2 km) from Page on US 89.

Glen Canyon National Recreation Area includes Lake Powell, which is formed by the Colorado River and stretches for 186 miles (297.6 km) behind one of the highest dams in the world. Established by act of Congress on Oct. 27, 1972.

VISITOR ACTIVITIES: Camping, swimming, boating, fishing, water skiing, hunting, driving, hiking, dam tours, photography, interpretive exhibits, picnicking; **Permits:** Fishing permits are available at sporting goods stores in Page or at the park's marina. Licenses vary in length of validity and cost; **Fees:** Camping fee is $7 per night per site; **Visitor facilities:** Restrooms, marinas, launching ramps, beaches, campgrounds, trailer villages, restaurants, lodging, boat rentals and tours, picnic areas; **Any limitations on vehicle usage:** Drive only on designated roads. Boaters should be familiar with boating regulations; see pamphlet available at the Visitor Center; **Hiking trails:** Yes, Rangers can suggest good routes; **Backcountry:** Yes, nearly 90 percent of the area is wilderness proposed backcountry. Write for information; **Camping:** Yes, no reservations; **Other overnight accommodations on site:** Yes, lodging at Wahweap, Bullfrog, Hite, and Halls Crossing. R.V. hookups available at Wahweap, Bullfrog, Halls Crossing. Houseboats available at Wahweap, Bullfrog, Halls Crossing, San Juan, and Hite. Write: Reservations, Del Webb Recreational Properties, Box 29040, Phoenix, AZ 85038 or call 1-800-528-6154 (in AZ 1-800-352-6508) or San Juan Marina, 356 South Main Street, Blanding, Utah 84511, 801-678-2217; **Meals served in the park:** Yes, Wahweap and Bullfrog; **Food and supplies obtainable in the park:** Yes, Wahweap, Bullfrog, Halls Crossing, Dangling Rope, Hite, and San Juan; **Overnight accommodations:** Page, 2 miles (3.2 km) from the Park on US 89; **First Aid available in park:** Yes, at Dangling Rope Marina and Ranger Stations at Wahweap, Bullfrog, Halls Crossing, and Hite; **Nearest Hospital:** Page, about 6½ miles (10.4 km) from Wahweap, Samaritan Health Clinic at Bullfrog; Clinic in Green River, Hospital in Grand Junction, CO; **Days/Hours:** Park never closes; **Holiday Closings:** Visitor Center closes on Dec. 25, and Jan. 1; **Visitor attractions closed for seasons:** No; **Weather:** July and Aug. are the hottest months, but the weather is mild through the middle of Nov. Winters are short with spring arriving in March.

GENERAL INFORMATION: An all-day and ½-day cruise takes boaters to Rainbow Bridge National Monument (see listing in this book). If you are camping, be sure to pick a campsite on flat or gently sloping terrain, not on talus slopes or underneath ledges where you can see that rock has fallen.

Grand Canyon National Park
Grand Canyon, Arizona   **SEE CLIMATABLE NO. 6**

MAILING ADDRESS: Superintendent, Grand Canyon National Park, P.O. Box 129, Grand Canyon, AZ 86023 **Telephone:** 602-638-7888

DIRECTIONS: There are three separate areas in the park— the South Rim, the North Rim (open approximately mid-May to late Oct. only), and the Inner Canyon. Each has different facilities, different activities, and even different climates. The South Rim Visitor Center is 5 miles (8 km) north of the South Entrance Station, in Grand Canyon Village, 60 miles (96 km) north of Williams and 57 miles (91.2 km) west of Cameron, both on AZ 64. The North Rim Ranger Station and developed area is on State Hwy 67, 45 miles (72 km) south of Jacob Lake (at intersection with Hwy 89).

The park, focusing on the world-famous Grand Canyon of the Colorado River, encompasses 277 miles (443.2 km) of the 1,400-mile (2,240-km) river and adjacent uplands from the southern terminus of Glen Canyon National Recreation Area to the eastern boundary of Lake Mead National Recreation Area. The forces of erosion have exposed an immense variety of formations that illustrate vast periods of geological history. National Park established by act of Congress on Feb. 26, 1919.

VISITOR ACTIVITIES: Interpretive exhibits, guided and self-guiding tours, picnicking, camping, backcountry hiking, horseback riding (outside the Park only, on the South Rim), white water rafting, kayaking, fishing, biking, bus tours, mule trips, river tours. Some trails open to stock use in park; **Permits:** Required for backcountry camping, stock use and river running. For fishing, licenses and trout stamps are available at Babbitt's Store in Grand Canyon Village; **Fees:** $10 entrance fee; $8 camping fee at Desert View, $10 at Mather, and $8 at North Rim Campgrounds. Golden Eagle, Golden Age, and Golden Access Passports accepted and available; **Visitor facilities:** Picnic areas, campgrounds, hiking trails, bus, taxi, guided hikes, river float trips, religious services, post office, bank, backpacking equipment rentals, food and lodging facilities, air tours from outside the park; **HANDICAPPED ACCESSIBILITY:** Parking; wheelchairs available (free) at Visitor Center; some West Rim and Village shuttle buses equipped with lifts and ramps. Scripts available for the hearing impaired; Park has prepared Accessibility Guide; **Any limitations on vehicle usage:** No vehicles may be operated outside of established public roads and designated areas (includes cars, pickups, trucks, motorcycles, trail bikes, etc.); **Hiking trails:** Yes, 38 maintained trails of nearly 400 miles (640 km), 400 non-maintained trails. Check at Information Centers for details; **Backcountry:** Yes, backcountry reservations and permits are required and issued by mail or in person. Contact Backcountry Reservations Office, Grand Canyon National Park, P.O. Box 129, Grand Canyon, AZ 86023, phone 602-638-7888 for recorded information; **Camping:** Desert View, no reservations required; closed in winter; Trailer Village (hookups available—open year-round) is operated by concessioner on South Rim, phone 602-638-2401; Reservations are taken for Mather Campground (South Rim) sites for the period between May 15-Sept. 30. North Rim Campground open mid-May to late Oct.: Contact Ticketron Reservation Office, P.O. Box 2715, San Francisco, CA 94126. Any unreserved campsites will be assigned on a first-come, first-served basis. Most in-park campsites fill by noon, May through Sept. No reservations are available for other campsites at Grand Canyon. Other sites are available near the Park; contact Grand Canyon for further information; **Other overnight accommodations on site:** On South Rim: Bright Angel Lodge, El Tovar Hotel, Kachina Lodge, Thunderbird Lodge, Maswick Lodge, Yavapai Lodge. For reservations phone 602-638-2401; On the North Rim: Grand Lodge, phone 801-586-7686; **Meals served in the park:** Yes, at North Rim, Grand Canyon Village, Desert View, Phantom Ranch, and Tusayan; **Food and supplies obtainable in the park:** Yes, Grand Canyon Village, Desert View, and the North Rim; **Food and supplies obtainable nearby:** Yes, Tusayan, AZ, 1 mile (1.6 km) south of the park; **Overnight accommodations:** Tusayan, Cameron, Gray Mountain, Flagstaff, Williams, Kaibab Lake, Jacob Lake, Fredonia, Marble Canyon, and Page, AZ; Kanab, UT; **First Aid available in park:** Yes, at the Information Desk in Grand Lodge (North Rim) or at Grand Canyon Clinic, Center Road between South Entrance Station and Grand Canyon Village. In case of emergency, telephone 911; **Nearest Hospital:** For South Rim, Flagstaff, I-40 and AZ 180, 80 miles (128 km)—Williams has daytime clinic only. For North Rim, Kanab, UT, via UT 89, 81 miles (129.6 km); **Days/Hours:** South Rim never closes; North Rim open 24 hours a day from mid-May to late-Oct.; **Holiday Closings:** No; **Visitor attractions closed for seasons:** North Rim closed in winter, from about late Oct. to mid-May; **Weather:** Temperature ranges—South Rim: 51°-82°F in summer, 20°-43°F in winter; North Rim: 43°-75°F in summer, 18°-39°F in winter; Inner Canyon: 76°-115°F in summer, 39°-59°F in winter.

GENERAL INFORMATION: For up-to-date recorded information about weather, road conditions, phone 602-638-7888, 24 hours a day. For information (recorded daily) about interpretive activities phone 602-638-7888. *For Your Safety*—Do not climb in the canyon; most of the rock is too crumbly for safety. Avoid overexertion. The South Rim averages 7000 feet and the North Rim over 8000 feet in elevation. Cardiac and respiratory patients should take care. Temperatures within the Inner Canyon can reach extremes. Take enough water and food, dress for the weather, and know your own physical limitations. If you are hiking, carry plenty of water. Be careful near the canyon rim.

TRAVEL ACCESS: Bus: Nava-Hopi provides regular service between Flagstaff, AZ, and Bright Angel Lodge in the park; **Rail:** Amtrak to Flagstaff (AZ), 80 miles (128 km) south of Park. **Air:** Scenic Airlines, Las Vegas Airlines, Air Nevada, and others provide service to Grand Canyon National Park Airport Tusayan, AZ 8 miles (12.8 km) south of Grand Canyon Village; **Other:** Taxi available in park and from airport to Grand Canyon Village.

NEARBY FACILITIES & POINTS OF INTEREST: Hotel/Motel: South Rim: Red Feather Lodge, 602-638-2414, and Canyon Squire Motel, 602-638-2681, Tusayan, AZ, 8 miles (12.8 km) south of Grand Canyon Village. For North Rim: Kaibab Lodge, 602-638-2389; Jacob Lake Lodge, 602-643-7232; Moqui Lodge, 602-638-2424; Quality Inn, 602-

638-2673; Seven Mile Lodge, 602-638-2291; **Food/Supplies:** Canyon Food Mart in Tusayan, AZ; **Camping:** Grand Canyon Camper Village (private), Tusayan, AZ, 602-638-2887, and Ten X (U.S.F.S.—closed in winter), 5 miles (8 km) south of Tusayan, AZ, 602-638-2443.

Hohokam Pima National Monument
Sacaton, Arizona

MAILING ADDRESS: Superintendent, Hohokam Pima National Monument, c/o Casa Grande Ruins National Monument, P.O. Box 518, Coolidge, AZ 85228 **Telephone:** 602-723-3172

DIRECTIONS: NOT OPEN TO THE PUBLIC.
The Monument will preserve the Snaketown archeological site, which contains the remains of a large Hohokam Indian village occupied between 300 A.D. and 1100 A.D. Although the Monument was authorized by Congress for addition to the National Park System on Oct. 21, 1972, it has not yet been established. The area remains closed to the public pending completion of land exchanges necessary to bring the site under National Park Service administration.

Hubbell Trading Post National Historic Site
Ganado, Arizona

MAILING ADDRESS: Superintendent, Hubbell Trading Post National Historic Site, P.O. Box 150, Ganado, AZ 86505 **Telephone:** 602-755-3475/3477

DIRECTIONS: The site is on the Navajo Indian Reservation, 1 mile (1.6 km) west of Ganado and 55 miles (89 km) northwest of Gallup, NM. It can be reached by AZ 264 (Navajo Route 3) from the east and west by US 191 from the north and south.
This still-active 100 year-old trading post illustrates the influence of reservation traders on the Indians' way of life. Authorized for addition to the National Park System on August 28, 1965.

VISITOR ACTIVITIES: Walking tours, exhibits, weaving and silversmithing demonstrations, picnicking, tours of the Hubbell home, watching the ongoing trading operation and craft demonstrations; **Fees:** No; **Visitor facilities:** Parking and restrooms at Visitor Center, picnic area; **HANDICAPPED ACCESSIBILITY:** Parking and restrooms; portable wheelchair ramps available; **Any limitations on vehicle usage:** Off-road vehicle travel is prohibited; **Hiking trails:** No; **Backcountry:** No; **Camping:** No; **Other overnight accommodations on site:** No; **Meals served in the park:** No, restaurant in Ganado; **Food and supplies obtainable in the park:** Yes, groceries; **Food and supplies obtainable nearby:** Yes, at Chinle or Window Rock; **Overnight accommodations:** Chinle, 37 miles (56 km) north on US 191; Window Rock, 28 miles (48 km) east on AZ 264; Chambers, 38 miles (61 km) south on US 191; Second Mesa, 67 miles (92 km) west on AZ 264; **First Aid available in park:** Yes; **Nearest Hospital:** Ganado, 1 mile (1.6 km) east; **Days/Hours:** Open daily from 8 a.m. to 5 p.m., until 6 p.m. in summer; **Holiday Closings:** Thanksgiving, Dec. 25, and Jan. 1; **Visitor attractions closed for seasons:** No; **Weather:** Elevation is 6300 feet. Climate is mild. Record extremes are -50°F and 102°F. High winds blow the sand in spring. Fall and early spring may bring snow flurries.

GENERAL INFORMATION: You will find Hubbell Trading Post on the way to Grand Canyon National Park, Canyon de Chelly National Monument (see listings in this book), and the Hopi Mesas. *For your safety*—Be cautious when walking around the grounds as burrs and bits of metal and glass have been left over the years. In many cases the floors are uneven in the buildings, and there is usually a step between rooms.

Montezuma Castle National Monument
Camp Verde, Arizona

MAILING ADDRESS: Superintendent, Montezuma Castle National Monument, P.O. Box 219, Camp Verde, AZ 86322 **Telephone:** 602-567-3322

DIRECTIONS: The Visitor Center is 2½ miles (3.8 km) off Interstate 17, 5 miles (8 km) north of Camp Verde.
   One of the best-preserved cliff dwellings in the United States, this 5-story, 20-room pueblo was built by prehistoric farmers over 700 years ago. Montezuma Well, a separate section of the Monument, is 10 miles (17 km) north of the Castle. This natural sinkhole is continually fed by spring water at the rate of 1½ million gallons a day. Archaeological sites include pueblo ruins, cliff dwellings, and an excavated pithouse. Created by Presidential Proclamation on Dec. 8, 1906.

VISITOR ACTIVITIES: Picnicking, photography, self-guiding walking tours, exhibits; **Permits:** No; **Fees:** Yes, entrance fee is $1 per person. No charge to US residents age 62 and older. Golden Eagle and Golden Age Passports accepted and available; **Visitor facilities:** Restrooms, picnic areas, interpretive trails, museum; **HANDICAPPED ACCESSIBILITY:** At Montezuma Castle, restrooms, Visitor Center, and trail are accessible; at Montezuma Well, only the picnic area, not trail; **Any limitations on vehicle usage:** Visitors should arrive before 10 a.m. or after 3 p.m. during the summer months because of limited parking; **Hiking trails:** Yes, a ⅓ mile (.6 km) self-guiding trail leads to the ruins; **Backcountry:** No; **Camping:** No; **Other overnight accommodations on site:** No; **Meals served in the park:** No; **Food and supplies obtainable in the park:** No; **Food and supplies obtainable nearby:** Yes, at Camp Verde; **Overnight accommodations:** Camp Verde, 5 miles (8 km) south; **First Aid available in park:** Yes, or nearby at Camp Verde; **Nearest Hospital:** Cottonwood, Int. 17 to AZ 279 to by pass road to Jerome, 20 miles (32.2 km); **Days/Hours:** Open daily from 8 a.m. to 5 p.m., and from 7 a.m. through 7 p.m. from June to September.

GENERAL INFORMATION: Visitors may wish to explore other nearby monuments, including Tuzigoot, Walnut Canyon, Wupatki, and Sunset Crater (see listings in this book). Nearby points of interest include Fort Verde and Jerome State Historical Parks.

Navajo National Monument
Tonalea, Arizona

MAILING ADDRESS: Superintendent, Navajo National Monument, HC 71 Box 3, Tonalea, AZ 86044-9704 **Telephone:** 602-672-2366/2367

DIRECTIONS: The monument is in northeastern Arizona, south to southeast of Lake Powell and the Glen Canyon Recreation Area. It is reached from US 160 which diagonals through the Navajo Reservation. At Black Mesa 50 miles (80.5 km) northeast of Tuba City, 22 miles (35.4 km) southwest of Kayenta, you turn north onto Route 564. Route 564 dead-ends at the

Monument Headquarters, 9 miles (14.5 km) from US 160.

Betatakin, Keet Seel, and Inscription House are three of the best-preserved and most elaborate cliff dwellings known. Created by Presidential Proclamation Mar. 20, 1909.

VISITOR ACTIVITIES: Hiking, interpretive exhibits and trails, guided tours during visitor season, evening campfire programs in summer, camping, picnicking, horseback riding; **Permits:** required for tours to Keet Seel only, apply by mail, phone, or in person; **Fees:** No; **Visitor facilities:** Visitor Center, exhibits, craft shop in summer, hiking trails, picnic area, campgrounds; **HANDICAPPED ACCESSIBILITY:** Restrooms, Visitor Center, and one campsite; **Any limitations on vehicle usage:** Vehicles are limited to paved and graded roads; **Hiking trails:** Yes, Sandal Trail is 1 mile (1.6 km) long roundtrip and leads to the Betatakin Point Overlook. May-Oct., weather permitting, tours of not more than 24 people leave from the Visitor Center to Betatakin Ruin down into the canyon. It is only about 5 miles (8 km), roundtrip but it's not easy. You climb down and back up a 700-foot steep incline, equivalent to a 70-story building! The tour takes about 5-6 hours and is Ranger-led. *You may enter the canyon or the ruin only with a Ranger!* Keet Seel, the largest cliff dwelling in Arizona, is about 8 miles (12.8 km) north of the Visitor Center. It can be reached only on foot or horseback; the trail is rugged and the elevation change is over a thousand feet. *You can enter Keet Seel only with a Park Ranger.* All travel is by reservation and there is a limit of 20 people per day. So write or phone ahead up to 2 months in advance if you want to make this trip; **Backcountry:** Yes, for information write or phone Headquarters; **Camping:** Yes, no reservations available for campsites. The Monument maintains a campground of 30 sites at the Headquarters area. Trailers up to 25 feet in length can be accommodated. The campground is closed from Oct. 15 to April 15. There is a group campground and overflow camping about ¼ mile (.4 km) from the Visitor Center, open when weather permits; **Other overnight accommodations on site:** No; **Meals served in the park:** No; **Food and supplies obtainable in the park:** No; **Food and supplies obtainable nearby:** Off US 160 to get to the Monument; **Overnight accommodations:** Kayenta, US 160, 31 miles (50 km) northeast of the Monument; Tuba City, US 160, 59 miles (95 km) southwest; Tsegi, 20 miles (32 km) east; **First Aid available in park:** Yes; **Nearest Hospital:** Flagstaff, AZ, 150 miles (241.4 km) or Tuba City, AZ. **Days/Hours:** The Visitor Center is open year-round from 8 a.m. to 5 p.m. daily, until 6 p.m. in summer; **Holiday Closings:** Thanksgiving, Dec. 25, Jan 1; **Visitor attractions closed for seasons:** Sandal Trail to the overlook is closed when snow and ice is severe, Betatakin Cliff dwelling approx. Nov.-Apr., Keet Seel from Labor Day to Memorial Day weekend, Inscription House is closed indefinitely to the public; **Weather:** The Monument is at an elevation of over 7,280 feet. Winter comes early and stays late. Snow accumulation is heavy, especially in the small canyons which provide access to the cliff dwellings. Trails into the canyon are closed after the first snowfall and remain closed until all snow melts in spring.

GENERAL INFORMATION: While you hike, remember that the altitude is 7280 feet. The air is thin. You may find that walking can tire you out faster than you might expect if you are not used to the elevation. Pace yourself, eat well, and don't try to rush. None of the more strenuous trips are recommended for anyone who has heart or respiratory ailments. The formations are sandstone and natural rockfalls are common. When traveling the Navajo Reservation you should always watch out for livestock wandering on or about the highway, and respect the privacy and land of the Navajo People. Hiking in the Tsegi Canyon outside the Monument is strictly prohibited by both park service and tribal law.

Organ Pipe Cactus National Monument
Ajo, Arizona

MAILING ADDRESS: Superintendent, Organ Pipe Cactus National Monument, Route 1, Box 100, Ajo, AZ 85321 **Telephone:** 602-387-6849

DIRECTIONS: The monument lies on the border of the United States and Mexico, 140 miles (224 km) south of Phoenix via Arizona 85, and 142 miles (227 km) west of Tucson via AZ 86 and AZ 85. Access to the park from Mexico is via Mexico Route 2 from the west and Mexico Routes 2 and 8 from the south. The Visitor Center is 17 miles (27 km) south of the park entrance.

Sonoran Desert plants and animals found nowhere else in the United States are protected here. Established by Presidential Proclamation on Apr. 13, 1937.

VISITOR ACTIVITIES: Interpretive talks and walks, scenic drives, hiking, backpacking, photography, wildlife- and bird-watching, camping, picnicking; **Permits:** For backcountry, available at Visitor Center; **Fees:** $3 entrance fee; Camping fee is $8 per night per site; **Visitor facilities:** Visitor Center, museum, campgrounds, picnic areas, mail drop, trails, restrooms. General store, cafe, and gas station in Lukeville, 5 miles (8 km) south of Visitor Center; **HANDICAPPED ACCESSIBILITY:** Parking, restrooms; audiovisual programs with volume control, captioned slide programs, and scripts are available for the hearing impaired; hard-surfaced trail, campsites, scenic drives with accessible restrooms; **Any limitations on vehicle usage:** Drive only on established roads and turnouts, large recreational vehicles not recommended on graded dirt roads. Visitors should be prepared for driving on desert roads. In summer carry a gallon of water per person in the car. If water is flowing across the road, do not try to drive through it. Wait until the water goes down—usually this takes about an hour. During the summer storm season (July and August), check at the Visitor Center for possible park road closures. When driving at night, be alert for wildlife on the road; **Hiking trails:** Yes, check at Visitor Center for information on the trails; **Backcountry:** Yes, permit is required, check at Visitor Center. Most backpacking is cross-country (few trails); **Camping:** Yes, no reservations for the 208-site campground except for organized groups using the group campsites, RVs not to exceed 35 feet in length; **Other overnight accommodations on site:** Yes; **Meals served in the park:** Yes; **Food and supplies obtainable in the park:** No; **Food and supplies obtainable nearby:** Yes, at Lukeville; **Overnight accommodations:** Lukeville, 5 miles (8 km) south of the Visitor Center, Why, 22 miles (35.2 km) north, and Ajo, 35 miles (56 km) north; **First Aid available in park:** Yes; **Nearest Hospital:** Tucson or Phoenix 145 miles (232 km); **Days/Hours:** Visitor Center is open 7 days a week from 8 a.m. to 5 p.m., year-round; **Holiday Closings:** No; **Visitor attractions closed for seasons:** Interpretive programs during winter months only; **Weather:** Nov.-Apr. is mild and usually sunny, May-Oct. is hot, with daytime temperatures over 100°F.

GENERAL INFORMATION: The Monument is a good stopoff point while traveling to Mexico via Tucson or Phoenix. *Beware of the cactus!* The spines of these plants and many other trees and shrubs can cause you painful injury. Visitors should be prepared for desert walking. For protection from the sun, rough terrain, and the weather, you should have a hat and wear clothing and shoes that are comfortable and sturdy. Carry enough drinking water (4 liters or 1 gallon per day per person when hiking). At night, walk carefully and use a flashlight to look for rattlesnakes in your path; five species are found in the monument. Snakes play an important role in the ecology of the desert and should not be harmed. Poisonous creatures such as rattlesnakes are common.

Traveling in Mexico: There is free access into Sonoyta and westward on Mexico Route 2. However, if you continue into the interior or go to Puerto Peñasco, you must have a tourist permit. A car entry permit is required for trips into the interior. Permits may be obtained from Mexican officials at the border. To get a tourist permit, you must have proof of citizenship (birth certificate, voter's registration card, or passport), and to get a car permit, you will need your automobile registration. To re-enter the United States with pets, you must carry proof of valid pet vaccinations. Transportation of firearms into Mexico is a violation of Mexican law.

Petrified Forest National Park
Petrified Forest National Park, Arizona

MAILING ADDRESS: Superintendent, Petrified Forest National Park, Petrified Forest National Park, AZ 86028 **Telephone:** 602-524-6228

DIRECTIONS: The Painted Desert Visitor Center is 26 miles (42 km) east of Holbrook on Interstate 40. The Rainbow Forest Entrance is 19 miles (30.6 km) east of Holbrook on US 180.

Features of the park include a large section of the colorful Painted Desert, Prehistoric Indian ruins and petroglyphs, high desert, "shortgrass prairie" ecosystem, petrified trees, and the remains of Triassic-age prehistoric animals, a museum, and the Painted Desert Inn National Historic Landmark. Created by Presidential Proclamation on December 8, 1906, established as a National Park, December 9, 1962.

VISITOR ACTIVITIES: Paved trails and wilderness hiking, interpretive walks and talks in summer, film, picnicking, self-guiding auto tours; **Permits:** Required for overnight backcountry, can be obtained at Rainbow Forest Museum and Painted Desert Visitor Center; **Fees:** $5 entrance fee, Golden Eagle, Golden Age and Golden Access Passports accepted and available; **Visitor facilities:** Picnic areas, restrooms, film about the Park at Painted Desert Visitor Center, interpretive exhibits including specimens of petrified wood. A guide map of the 28-mile (48-km) park road is available at the entrance stations; **HANDICAPPED ACCESSIBILITY:** All major facilities, including concession; Park supplies detailed guide covering floor conditions, steps, curbs, availability of sign-language trained personnel; **Any limitations on vehicle usage:** No off-road vehicular use permitted. Park only in designated parking areas; **Hiking trails:** Yes, walking trails at Giant Logs (behind Rainbow Forest Museum), Long Logs, Agate House, Crystal Forest, Blue Mesa, and Kachina Point to Tawa Point. Trails vary in length from ½-¾ mile (.8 km-1.2 km); **Backcountry:** Yes, approximately 50,000 acres of wilderness area are open for camping and hiking; **Camping:** Yes, camping is limited to the wilderness area, required permits available at either the museum or Visitor Center; **Other overnight accommodations on site:** No; **Meals served in the park:** Yes, at Painted Desert Oasis; **Food and supplies obtainable in the park:** No; **Food and supplies obtainable nearby:** Yes, at Holbrook, AZ, 26 miles (42 km) west on I-40; Sanders, AZ, 30 miles (48.3 km) east; Gallup, NM, 70 miles (113 km) east; **Overnight accommodations:** Holbrook, 26 miles (42 km) west on I-40; Chambers, AZ, 20 miles (33 km) east on I-40; Gallup, NM, 70 miles (113 km) east; **First Aid available in park:** Yes; **Nearest Hospital:** Holbrook, AZ, just off I-40, 26 miles (42 km) from the Park; **Days/Hours:** The Park is open during daylight hours all year, with occasional closings due to heavy snow and icy roads; **Holiday Closings:** Park closed on Dec. 25; **Weather:** Summer days may be quite warm, and clear weather may be broken by sudden thundershowers. In winter, cold and snowy days are not uncommon. High winds may be expected in any season.

GENERAL INFORMATION: Have sufficient water and notify park personnel if you plan an extended hike. Park elevations range from 5100 to 6235 feet; beware of overexertion in the high altitude. Do not climb on petrified logs; petrified wood can be extremely sharp. Federal law prohibits removal of any petrified wood or any other object from this park.

TRAVEL ACCESS: Bus: Greyhound Tours, Flagstaff, AZ, offers tours from Flagstaff, AZ, to Park, no direct access via Greyhound from Holbrook, AZ (closest bus service); **Rail:** No, closest rail service by Amtrak to Winslow, AZ; service may be cut back; **Air:** No, closest air service to Gallup, NM or Flagstaff, AZ.

NEARBY FACILITIES & POINTS OF INTEREST: Campgrounds: KOA: Holbrook Hilltop KOA, 102 Hermosa Drive, Holbrook, AZ, 602-524-6689, 26 miles (42 km) west; OK RV Park, Roadrunner Lane, Holbrook, AZ, 602-524-3226, 26 miles (42 km) west.

Pipe Spring National Monument
Moccasin, Arizona

MAILING ADDRESS: Superintendent, Pipe Spring National Monument, Moccasin, AZ 86022 **Telephone:** 602-643-7105

DIRECTIONS: Pipe Spring is 14 miles (22.5 km) west of Fredonia, AZ, and can be reached from US 89A via AZ 389; from I-15, UT 9 and 17 connect with UT 59 at Hurricane, UT, from which a paved road leads to the Monument.

This historic fort and other structures, built here by pioneers in the 1870s, commemorate the struggle for exploration and settlement of the southwest. Created by Presidential Proclamation on May 31, 1923.

VISITOR ACTIVITIES: Walking tours; **Permits:** No; **Fees:** $1.00 per person 17 through 62. Golden Age, Access, and Eagle Passports accepted and available; **Visitor facilities:** Self-guiding tours around the fort; conducted tours, exhibits, and visual interpretation within; **HANDICAPPED ACCESSIBILITY:** At the visitor center, and on grounds, but, limited inside the fort; **Any limitations on vehicle usage:** Vehicles must park in the lot at the Visitor Center; **Hiking trails:** Yes, self-guiding ½-mile (.8 km) loop trail; **Backcountry:** No; **Camping:** No; **Other overnight accommodations on site:** No; **Meals served in the park:** A frontier kitchen is located in the Visitor Center complex; **Food and supplies obtainable in the park:** No; **Food and supplies obtainable nearby:** Yes, at Kanab or Fredonia; **Overnight accommodations:** Kanab, 21 miles (33.8 km) east on US 89 or Fredonia, 14 miles (22.5 km) east on AZ 389; **First Aid available in park:** Yes, or nearby in Fredonia, 14 miles (22.5 km) east on AZ 389; **Nearest Hospital:** Kanab via AZ 389 & US 89; **Days/Hours:** Monument open daily from 8 a.m. to 4:30 p.m. historic buildings closed at 4 p.m., the Visitor Center is open until 4:30 p.m. Park operates on Mountain Standard Time year-round; **Holiday Closings:** Thanksgiving, Dec. 25, and Jan. 1; **Weather:** Dry and sunny with some summer storms; temperatures range from 85° to 100°F.

GENERAL INFORMATION: Be especially careful of the steep, narrow stairways and low doorways in the buildings. Watch children around ponds and livestock.

Saguaro National Monument
Tucson, Arizona

MAILING ADDRESS: Superintendent, 3693 South Old Spanish Trail, Saguaro National Monument, Tucson, AZ 85730-5699 **Telephone:** 602-296-8576

DIRECTIONS: The Visitor Center and Park Headquarters in the Rincon Mountain District are located on Old Spanish Trail at Freeman Road, 2 miles (3.2 km) east of Tucson City limit.

The Visitor Information Center in the Tucson Mountain District is on Kinney Road, 2 miles (3.2 km) west of the Arizona-Sonora Desert Museum.

Giant Saguaro cactus, unique to the Sonoran Desert of southern Arizona and northwestern Mexico, sometimes reach a height of 40 feet (10 m) in this cactus forest. Created by Presidential Proclamation on Mar. 1, 1933.

VISITOR ACTIVITIES: Wildlife- and bird-watching, hiking, picnicking, photography, wilderness backcountry, overnight hiking (Rincon Mtn. District only), horseback riding, scenic pleasure driving; Tucson Mtn. and Rincon Mtn. Districts; **Permits:** Required for overnight backcountry, can be obtained at Visitor Center; **Fees:** Rincon Mtn. District $3 per car entrance fee; $1 walk-in fee per person; $1 per bicyclist; No fees TMD. Golden Eagle, Golden Age, and Golden Access Passports accepted and available; **Visitor facilities:** Rincon Mtn. District audiovisual program and exhibits in the Visitor Center. Naturalist walks both units, self-guiding walks and picnic areas in both districts; **HANDICAPPED ACCESSIBILITY:** Visitor Centers, restrooms, modified latrines at some picnic areas, wheelchairs available, program scripts for hearing impaired; **Any limitations on vehicle usage:** Drive only on established roadways; **Hiking trails:** Yes, both districts; **Backcountry:** Yes, information from Visitor Center in the Rincon Mtn. District and Information Center in the Tucson Mtn. District; **Camping:** Backcountry only, Rincon Mtn. District; **Other overnight accommodations on site:** No; **Meals served in the park:** No, but meals are available nearby (1-3 miles) **Food and supplies obtainable in the park:** No; **Food and supplies obtainable nearby:** Yes, in Tucson; **Overnight accommodations:** Downtown Tucson, 16 miles (26 km) east of the Rincon Mtn. District and 15 miles (24 km) east of the Tucson Mtn. District along Int. 10 and at Gilbert Ray Campground 2 miles from TMD information center. **First Aid available in park:** Yes; **Nearest Hospital:** 10 miles (16 km) west of the park via Broadway Blvd., at Wilmot and 5th Streets; St. Mary's Hospital 16½ miles (26.4 km) east of Tucson Mtn. District, corner of St. Mary's and Silverbell. **Days/Hours:** Rincon Mtn. District is open from 7 a.m. to 6 p.m. April 1-Oct., 8 a.m. to 5 p.m. Nov.-March, Visitor Center 8 a.m.-5 p.m. Tucson Mtn. District open all year, Information Center from 8 a.m. to 5 p.m.; **Holiday Closings:** No; **Visitor attractions closed for seasons:** No; **Weather:** Winter and summer have rainy periods. Spring and fall are dry. Annual rainfall is 11″. Temperatures at Tucson Mtn. District may reach 115°F in summer.

GENERAL INFORMATION: On the way to Tucson Mtn. District, visit the adjacent Arizona-Sonora Desert Museum to see a presentation of living plants and animals of the desert in simulated natural habitats.

TRAVEL ACCESS: Bus: Greyhound and Trailways provide regular service into Tucson; **Rail:** No; **Air:** Major airlines service Tucson; **Other:** Taxi service from Tucson, Bicycle trail from Tucson to Rincon Mountain District alongside Old Spanish Trail (road).

NEARBY FACILITIES & POINTS OF INTEREST: Campgrounds: Gilbert Ray Campground, Pima County Parks and Recreation, 602-883-4200, 2 miles (3.2 km) south of Tucson Mt. District; **Parks, other points of interest:** Sabino Canyon-Coronado National Forest, N. Sabino Rd., 602-749-3223, 13 miles (20.8 km) from Rincon Mt. District; Arizona-Sonoran Desert Museum—Kinney Rd., 602-883-1380, 2 miles (3.2 km) from Tucson Mt. District.

Sunset Crater Volcano National Monument
Flagstaff, Arizona

MAILING ADDRESS: Superintendent, Sunset Crater National Monument, 2717 N. Steves Blvd. #3, Flagstaff, AZ 86004 **Telephone:** 602-527-7042 (Park), 602-527-7134 (HQ)

DIRECTIONS: Drive north of Flagstaff on US Hwy 89 approximately 13 miles (21 km). Turn right on the Sunset Crater-Wupatki Loop Road and continue 2 miles (3.2 km) to the Visitor Center.

This colorful volcanic cinder cone with summit crater was formed in 1064-65 A.D. and looks as if it has barely cooled. Created by Presidential Proclamation on May 26, 1930.

VISITOR ACTIVITIES: Naturalist activities, campfire programs in summer, exhibits, picnicking; **Permits:** No; **Fees:** Yes; **Visitor facilities:** Information and drinking water at the Visitor Center, picnic areas, restrooms; **Any limitations on vehicle usage:** You should stay strictly on the road, due to soft shoulders; **Hiking trails:** Yes, one foottrail, self-guiding Lava Flow Nature Trail; fee: $3 per car load, summer only; **Backcountry:** No; **Camping:** Yes, first-come basis located in U.S. Forest Service campground next to Sunset Crater Visitor Center. Fee charged per night. Camping season: May 15 to Oct. 15; **Other overnight accommodations on site:** No; **Meals served in the park:** No; **Food and supplies obtainable in the park:** No; **Food and supplies obtainable nearby:** Yes, in Flagstaff; **Overnight accommodations:** Flagstaff, Hwy 89, 15 miles (24 km); **First Aid available in park:** Yes; **Nearest Hospital:** Flagstaff, 15 miles (24 km) south on Hwy 89; **Days/Hours:** Open daily from 8 a.m. to 5 p.m.; **Holiday Closings:** Dec. 25 and Jan. 1; **Visitor attractions closed for seasons:** At times, roads are icy and snowy during the winter, but rarely closed.

GENERAL INFORMATION: Sunset Crater is an interesting stopoff while driving to the Grand Canyon. Wupatki National Monument (see listing in this book), containing pre-historic Indian ruins, is located 20 miles (32 km) distant. Both Monuments are located on a scenic 36-mile loop drive. The most prominent hazards in the parks are deep, narrow earth cracks and razor-sharp lava, and unstable backcountry ruins. Do not walk on pre-historic walls or disturb plants, animals, and geological and archeological features. Sunset Crater is closed to hiking but other nearby craters may be climbed.

Tonto National Monument
Roosevelt, Arizona

MAILING ADDRESS: Superintendent, Tonto National Monument, P.O. Box 707, Roosevelt, AZ 85545 **Telephone:** 602-467-2241

DIRECTIONS: The park is located near Roosevelt Lake, 5 miles (8 km) east of Roosevelt Dam. From Globe, take AZ 88 about 30 miles (48 km) to the park entrance. Travelers coming from the north can take AZ 87 south of Payson, then turn onto AZ 188 to Roosevelt Dam. A third alternative is the scenic Apache Trail that starts at Apache Junction. The last 22 miles (35.2 km) of this drive is unpaved mountain road. Allow 2½ to 3 hours driving time from Phoenix, regardless of the route selected.

These well-preserved cliff dwellings were occupied during the 14th century by Salado Indians, who farmed in the Salt River Valley. Created by Presidential Proclamation on December 19, 1907.

VISITOR ACTIVITIES: Interpretive exhibits, guided tours, slide program; **Fees:** Entrance fee is $3 per vehicle; Golden Eagle and Golden Age Passports accepted and available; **Visitor facilities:** Museum, observation deck, parking, restrooms, picnic area; **HANDICAPPED ACCESSIBILITY:** Parking lot, restrooms, museum; because of stairs and steep trails, slide program and ruins are not accessible; a video is available; **Any limitations on vehicle usage:** Vehicles must stay on the paved road; 30 ft. limit on vehicles traveling the Apache Trail; **Hiking trails:** Yes, A self-guiding ½-mile (.8-km) trail leads to the Lower Ruin. Tours of the 40-room Upper Ruin are available from mid-Oct. through April on a reservation only basis. This trail climbs 600 vertical feet in one and one-half miles and requires three hours to complete. Call Park for details and reservations; **Backcountry:** No; **Camping:** No, Numerous primitive non-reserved campsites can be found at nearby Roosevelt Lake. For further information contact the U.S. Forest Service at P.O. Box 648, Roosevelt, AZ, phone 602-467-2236; **Other overnight accommodations on site:** No; **Meals served in the park:** No; **Food and supplies obtainable in the park:** No; **Food and supplies obtainable nearby:** Yes, immediate area and in the Globe-Miami and Payson areas; **Overnight accommodations:** Roosevelt Lake Resort, 8 miles (14.5 km), at Globe, 30 miles (48 km), and at Payson, 55 miles (88 km); **First Aid available in park:** Yes, aid station located at Roosevelt; **Nearest Hospital:** Globe-Miami area, 30 miles (48 km); **Days/Hours:** Open year-round from 8 a.m. to 5 p.m. Hours may be extended during summer. The trail to the Lower Ruin closes one hour before the park closes; **Holiday Closings:** Dec. 25; **Visitor attractions closed for seasons:** No; **Weather:** The most comfortable weather occurs between late October and early June.

GENERAL INFORMATION: *For Your Safety*—Natural features here could be hazardous. Be on the lookout for steep slopes, falling rocks, spiny vegetation, rattlesnakes and Gila monsters. Stay on the trails. To avoid traffic delays visit early in the day.

TRAVEL ACCESS: Bus: Grayline/Sun Valley Bus provides a weekly tour from Phoenix, Arizona Bus Lines provides charter service from Phoenix; **Rail:** No; **Air:** No.

NEARBY FACILITIES & POINTS OF INTEREST: Hotel/Motel: Roosevelt Lake Resort, HC02, Box 901, Roosevelt, AZ 85545, 602-467-2276, 9 miles (14½ km) from Monument; **Food/Supplies:** Spring Creek Store, 602-467-2468, 8 miles (12.8 km) from Monument and Roosevelt Lake Marina, Roosevelt, AZ, 602-467-2245, 3 miles; **Parks, other points of interest:** Roosevelt Dam (Highest Masonry; 1st Bureau of Reclamation Dam), 5 miles (8 km). Besh-Ba-Gowah Indian Ruins, in Globe, AZ, 35 miles (56 km). Boyce Thompson Southwestern Arboretum, near Superior, AZ, 55 miles (88 km).

Tumacacori National Historical Park
Tumacacori, Arizona

MAILING ADDRESS: Superintendent, Tumacacori National Historical Park, P.O. Box 67, Tumacacori, AZ 85640 **Telephone:** 602-398-2341

DIRECTIONS: Tumacacori is 45 miles (72.4 km) south of Tucson on I-19, 18 miles (28.97 km) north of Nogales and the Mexican border.
This historic Spanish Catholic mission building stands near the site first visited by Jesuit Father Kino in 1691. Created by Presidential Proclamation on Sept. 15, 1908.

VISITOR ACTIVITIES: Interpretive exhibits, self-guiding walks, living history demonstrations, picnicking; **Permits:** No; **Fees:** Entrance fee is $1 per person on bus tours, $1 per person, maximum $3 per carload; Golden Eagle, Golden Age, and Golden Access Passports accepted and available; **Visitor facilities:** Parking, picnic area; **HANDICAPPED ACCES-SIBILITY:** Parking area, museum, restrooms, trails; **Any limitations on vehicle usage:** No; **Hiking trails:** No; **Backcountry:** No; **Camping:** No; **Other overnight accommodations on site:** No; **Meals served in the park:** No; **Food and supplies obtainable in the park:** No; **Food and supplies obtainable nearby:** Yes, in Tucson or Nogales; **Overnight accommodations:** Tucson, 45 miles (72.42 km) north and Nogales, 18 miles (29 km) south; **First Aid available in park:** Yes; **Nearest Hospital:** Nogales, 18 miles (29 km) south; **Days/Hours:** Open year-round from 8 a.m. to 5 p.m.; **Holiday Closings:** Thanksgiving and Dec. 25; **Weather:** Summers are very hot.

GENERAL INFORMATION: A fiesta is held the first Sunday in December, featuring an outdoor Mariachi Mass, continuous entertainment, and craft and native food sales.

TRAVEL ACCESS: Bus: Citizen Auto Stage provides regular service to Nogales, AZ; **Rail:** No; **Air:** No.

NEARBY FACILITIES & POINTS OF INTEREST: Hotel/Motel: Rancho Santa Cruz, Tumacacori, AZ 85640, 602-281-8383, 3 miles (4.8 km); Rio Rico Resort, Rio Rico AZ 85621, 602-281-1901, 8 miles (12.8 km); Tubac Golf Resort, Tubac, AZ 85646, 602-398-2211, 3 miles (4.8 km); **Food/Supplies:** Carmen Store, Carmen, AZ, 1 mile (1.6 km); **Campgrounds:** Rio Rico Campground, Rio Rico, AZ 85621, 8 miles (12.8 km); **Parks, other points of interest:** Tubac State Historic Park, 3 miles (4.8 km); Pena Blanca Lake, 20 miles (32 km).

Tuzigoot National Monument
Clarkdale, Arizona

MAILING ADDRESS: Superintendent, Tuzigoot National Monument, P.O. Box 219, Camp Verde, AZ 86322 **Telephone:** 602-634-5564

DIRECTIONS: The Visitor Center is 2 miles (3 km) east of Clarkdale, 3 miles (4.8 km) west of Cottonwood.
　　　Ruins of a large Indian pueblo which flourished in the Verde Valley between A.D. 1000 and 1450 have been excavated here. Created by Presidential Proclamation on July 25, 1939.

VISITOR ACTIVITIES: Interpretive exhibits in the museum, walking tours; **Permits:** No; **Fees:** Entrance fee is $1 per person, Golden Eagle and Golden Age Passports accepted and available; **Visitor facilities:** Parking and restrooms at Visitor Center; **Any limitations on vehicle usage:** No; **Hiking trails:** Yes, from the Visitor Center to the ruin and overlook; **Backcountry:** No; **Camping:** No; **Other overnight accommodations on site:** No; **Meals served in the park:** No; **Food and supplies obtainable in the park:** No; **Food and supplies obtainable nearby:** Yes, in Cottonwood, AZ, 3 miles (4.8 km); **Overnight accommodations:** Cottonwood, AZ, 3 miles (4.8 km); **First Aid available in park:** Yes; **Nearest Hospital:** Cottonwood, AZ, 3 miles (4.8 km); **Days/Hours:** Open daily from 8 a.m. to 5 p.m. winter, 8 a.m. to 7 p.m. summer; **Holiday Closings:** No; **Weather:** Summer is very hot. Spring and fall are pleasant, winter is mild.

GENERAL INFORMATION: 27 miles (40 km) from Tuzigoot is Montezuma Castle National Monument, one of the best preserved cliff dwellings in the United States. It can be reached from a good road branching from US 89A. If you plan to continue north on US 89A to Flagstaff, you can easily reach other national monuments: Walnut Canyon, Wupatki, and Sunset Crater (see listings in this book).

NEARBY FACILITIES & POINTS OF INTEREST: Parks, other points of interest: Jerome State Park, Dead Horse Ranch State Park.

Walnut Canyon National Monument
Flagstaff, Arizona

MAILING ADDRESS: Superintendent, Walnut Canyon National Monument, Walnut Canyon Road, Flagstaff, AZ 86004-9705 **Telephone:** 602-526-3367

DIRECTIONS: The entrance road to Walnut Canyon is a 2.8 mile (4.5 km) highway connecting with Int. 40 at a point 7.5 miles (12 km) east of Flagstaff.

These cliff dwellings were built in shallow caves under ledges of limestone by Sinagua Indians about 800 years ago. Created by Presidential Proclamation on Nov. 30, 1915.

VISITOR ACTIVITIES: Interpretive exhibits, hiking, picnicking, interpretive walks in summer; **Permits:** No; **Fees:** Entrance fee is $1 per person, maximum $3 per carload in a noncommercial vehicle, Golden Eagle, Golden Age, or Golden Access Passports accepted and available; **Visitor facilities:** Parking, museum, picnic area, hiking trails; **HANDICAPPED ACCESSIBILITY:** Parking, restrooms; Rim Trail accessible to wheelchairs except during snow periods; picnic tables, videos; **Any limitations on vehicle usage:** Vehicles are restricted to designated roadways; **Hiking trails:** Yes, a paved foot trail leads to 25 of the cliff dwelling rooms; you can see several others from the trail. There is also a short rim trail; **Backcountry:** No; **Camping:** No; **Other overnight accommodations on site:** No; **Meals served in the park:** No, meals and lodging may be obtained at Flagstaff and Winslow and along major highways: I-40, I-17, Hwy. 89N and 89A; **Food and supplies obtainable in the park:** No; **Food and supplies obtainable nearby:** Yes, at Flagstaff, 10 miles (16 km); **Overnight accommodations:** Flagstaff, 10 miles (16 km) west of the Monument; **First Aid available in park:** Yes; **Nearest Hospital:** Flagstaff, 12 miles (19 km); **Days/Hours:** Open all year, from 7 a.m. to 6 p.m. Memorial Day through Labor Day; 8 a.m. to 5 p.m. the rest of the year; **Holiday Closings:** Thanksgiving and Dec. 25; **Visitor attractions closed for seasons:** No, except during snowstorms.

GENERAL INFORMATION: *For your safety*—and to adequately protect archeological features, it is prohibited to walk off designated trails. Those with heart ailments or other infirmities should realize that the Island Trail includes a 185-foot (55 meter) climb at an altitude of nearly 7000 feet (2134 meters). These conditions can tax the heart and lungs.

NEARBY FACILITIES & POINTS OF INTEREST: Campgrounds: USFS Campground 23 miles (36.8 km) north at Sunset Crater National Monument, KOA and other private campgrounds in Flagstaff area; **Parks, other points of interest:** North, Sunset Crater National Monument, 20 miles (32 km), Wupatki National Monument 35 miles (56 km), Grand Canyon National Park 90 miles, (144 km); east, Petrified Forest National Park, 117 miles (187.2 km); south, Montezuma Well National Monument, 50 miles (80 km), Montezuma Castle National Monument, 56 miles (89.6 km), Tuzigoot National Monument, 80 miles (128 km), Oak Creek Canyon USFS, 27 miles (43.2 km).

Wupatki National Monument
Flagstaff, Arizona

MAILING ADDRESS: Superintendent, Wupatki National Monument, 2717 N. Steves Blvd., Suite #3, Flagstaff, AZ 86004 **Telephone:** Headquarters 602-527-7134, Monument 602-527-7040

DIRECTIONS: The Visitor Center is on the 35 mile (55 km) loop road which connects Wupatki with Sunset Crater National Monument. Drive 15 miles (24 km) north of Flagstaff on Hwy 89, then east on the loop road 22 miles (35 km) to Wupatki Visitor Center.

Ruins of red sandstone pueblos built by farming Indians about A.D. 1120 are preserved here. The modern Hopi Indians are believed by some to be descendants of these people. Created by Presidential Proclamation on Dec. 9, 1924.

VISITOR ACTIVITIES: Interpretive exhibits, hiking, walking, auto tours; **Permits:** No; **Fees:** Yes, $3 per car; **Visitor facilities:** Parking and restrooms at Visitor Center, hiking trails; **Any limitations on vehicle usage:** Due to soft shoulders, drivers should stay strictly on the road; **Hiking trails:** Yes, self-guiding trails to Nalakihu-Citadel Ruins, to Wupatki Ruin; Lomaki Ruin; Doney Crater Trail; **Backcountry:** No; **Camping:** No; **Other overnight accommodations on site:** No, no reservations are accepted for U.S. Forest Service campsites which are located across from Sunset Crater Visitor Center. For further information, contact Sunset Crater at 2717 N. Steves Blvd., Suite #3, Flagstaff, AZ 86004, phone 602-527-7134; **Meals served in the park:** No; **Food and supplies obtainable in the park:** No; **Food and supplies obtainable nearby:** Yes, at Flagstaff, 37 miles (59 km) south on Hwy 89; **Overnight accommodations:** Flagstaff, 37 miles (59 km) south on Hwy 89; **First Aid available in park:** Yes; **Nearest Hospital:** Flagstaff, 37 miles (59 km) south on Hwy 89; **Days/Hours:** Visitor Centers open from 8 a.m. to 5 p.m. daily; 7 a.m. to 7 p.m. in summer; **Holiday Closings:** Dec. 25 and Jan. 1; **Visitor attractions closed for seasons:** No. The campground Sunset Crater is open from April 15 to Nov. 15; **Weather:** Summer is moderate to hot; Winter is cold, with snow common at Sunset Crater.

GENERAL INFORMATION: The most common hazards in the park are deep, narrow earth cracks, razor-sharp lava, and unstable backcountry ruins. Drinking water is available at Headquarters of Wupatki and Sunset Crater.

Arkansas

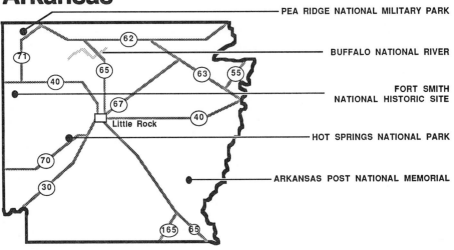

PEA RIDGE NATIONAL MILITARY PARK

BUFFALO NATIONAL RIVER

FORT SMITH
NATIONAL HISTORIC SITE

HOT SPRINGS NATIONAL PARK

ARKANSAS POST NATIONAL MEMORIAL

Arkansas Post National Memorial
Gillett, Arkansas

MAILING ADDRESS: Superintendent, Arkansas Post National Memorial, Route 1, Box 16, Gillett, AR 72055 **Telephone:** 501-548-2432

DIRECTIONS: The memorial is on AR 169, 7 miles (11 km) south of Gillett via U.S. 165 (The Great River Road) and about 20 miles (32 km) northeast of Dumas via U.S. 165.

The first semi-permanent French settlement in the lower Mississippi Valley was founded near this site in 1686. Authorized for addition to the National Park System on July 6, 1960.

VISITOR ACTIVITIES: Indoor and outdoor exhibits, audiovisual program, walking, picnicking, fishing, biking; **Permits:** An Arkansas fishing license required, available locally; **Fees:** No; **Visitor facilities:** Visitor Center, picnic area, restrooms; **HANDICAPPED ACCESSIBILITY:** Parking, restrooms at Visitor Center; hiking trails are paved; picnic area is accessible; **Any limitations on vehicle usage:** Off-road vehicle use is prohibited; **Hiking trails:** Yes, a 2 mile (1.6 km) nature-history trail; **Backcountry:** No; **Camping:** No; **Other overnight accommodations on site:** No; No reservations are needed for campsites at Moore's Bayou, ½ mile (.8 km) away. This is a developed Corps of Engineers recreation area, with no hook-ups for trailers. Contact Arkansas Post for further information. **Meals served in the park:** No; **Food and supplies obtainable in the park:** No; **Food and supplies obtainable nearby:** Yes, in Gillett, AR, 7 miles (11 km) north on U.S. 165; **Overnight accommodations:** Dewitt, 20 miles (32 km) north or Dumas, 20 miles (32 km) southwest on U.S. 165; **First Aid available in park:** Yes (minor injuries); **Nearest Hospital:** Dewitt, 20 miles (32 km) north or Dumas, 20 miles (32 km) southwest; **Days/Hours:** Visitor Center open daily from 8 a.m. to 5 p.m., park open until dark; **Holiday Closings:** Dec. 25; **Visitor attractions closed for seasons:** No.

GENERAL INFORMATION: Be on the lookout for snakes, ticks, and poison ivy as you walk through the area. Watch your step and stay on the trails. The best time to visit the area is Sept. through May because of the extreme heat, humidity, and insects in summer.

Buffalo National River
Harrison, Arkansas

MAILING ADDRESS: Superintendent, Buffalo National River, P.O. Box 1173, Harrison, AR 72602-1173 **Telephone:** 501-741-5443

DIRECTIONS: Buffalo Point, off AR 14, 17 miles (27.4 km) south of Yellville, is the major center for visitor activities at the river. Information centers are operated at the Buffalo Point off Hwy. 14, Tyler Bend, off Hwy. 65, Pruitt District Ranger Station off Hwy. 7 and at Buffalo National River Headquarters, Federal Building, Walnut and Erie Streets, Harrison.

Offering both swift-running and placid stretches, the Buffalo is one of the few remaining unpolluted, free-flowing rivers in the lower 48 states. It courses through multicolored bluffs and past numerous caves and springs along its 137-mile (219.2 km) length. Authorized for addition to the National Park System on March 1, 1972.

VISITOR ACTIVITIES: Interpretive exhibits, camping, picnicking, canoeing, swimming, hiking, fishing, campfire programs, guided walks, guided canoe trips; **Permits:** An Arkansas fishing or hunting license is required, available locally for a nominal fee; **Fees:** $8 ($5 for walk-in tent sites) per site per night camping fee at Buffalo Point Campground and Tyler Bend. Twelve less developed campgrounds are free of charge; **Visitor facilities:** Year-round campground, picnic areas, day-use pavilions, canoe launch areas, hiking trails, food service, boat and canoe rentals, restrooms, cabin rentals; **HANDICAPPED ACCESSIBILITY:** Erbie, Tyler Bend and Buffalo Point Campgrounds have accessible campsites, and restrooms. Accessible campsites are held open until all other sites are filled and then made available for general use; Buffalo Point restaurant is accessible but its restrooms thus far are too small for wheelchairs; **Any limitations on vehicle usage:** Motor vehicles are restricted to open roadways; **Hiking trails:** Yes, self-guiding hiking trails; **Backcountry:** Yes, information can be obtained by writing Park Headquarters in Harrison; **Camping:** Yes, arrive early in the day in summer, since all campgrounds are available on a first-come, first-served basis; **Other overnight accommodations on site:** Yes, for cabin information and reservations write to Buffalo Point Concessions, HCR#66, Box 388, Yellville, AR 72687; **Meals served in the park:** Yes, at Buffalo Point; **Food and supplies obtainable in the park:** No; **Food and supplies obtainable nearby:** Yes, in Yellville, Harrison, Jasper, Marshall, Mountain Home and Gilbert; **Overnight accommodations:** Yellville, Harrison, Jasper, Marshall and Mountain Home; **First Aid available in park:** Yes, at Buffalo Point and Tyler Bend Ranger Stations; **Nearest Hospital:** Harrison, AR Hwy 62, approx. 50 miles (80 km); Yellville, Hwy 14, 17 miles (27 km) north of Hwy #14; **Days/Hours:** Open 24 hours a day, 7 days a week; **Holiday Closings:** No; **Visitor attractions closed for seasons:** No; **Weather:** Summer is hot and humid; fall and winter are pleasant.

GENERAL INFORMATION: *For Your Safety*—Stay off the bluffs, don't dive into the river, keep alert to river conditions and avoid the river during high water. Be advised that this is "tick" country and there have been cases of lyme disease and rocky mountain spotted fever reported. Remove all ticks immediately.

Fort Smith National Historic Site
Fort Smith, Arkansas

MAILING ADDRESS: Superintendent, Fort Smith National Historic Site, P.O. Box 1406, Fort Smith, AR 72902 **Telephone:** 501-783-3961

DIRECTIONS: The site is in downtown Fort Smith. It can be reached from Garrison Ave. (US 64) by turning south on 4th Street to Parker Avenue then right on Parker. A Visitor Center is in the old Barracks Building.
   The story from 1817 to 1896 of the two Fort Smiths and federal court of Isaac Parker revolve around the forced relocation of southeastern tribes to Indian Territory. Authorized for addition to the National Park System on Sept. 13, 1961.

VISITOR ACTIVITIES: Interpretive exhibits and walks; **Permits:** No; **Fees:** $1.00 for adults, children 16 and under and adults 62 and over are free; **Visitor facilities:** Parking and restrooms at Visitor Center; **HANDICAPPED ACCESSIBILITY:** Parking lot and trails mostly accessible; wheelchair lifts available in the Visitor Center; restrooms are accessible. **Any limitations on vehicle usage:** No; **Hiking trails:** No; **Backcountry:** No; **Camping:** No; **Other overnight accommodations on site:** No; **Meals served in the park:** No; **Food and supplies obtainable in the park:** No; **Food and supplies obtainable nearby:** Yes, in Fort Smith; **Overnight accommodations:** Fort Smith; **First Aid available in park:** Yes; **Nearest Hospital:** Sparks South I Street, 1 mile (1.6 km) from the park; **Days/Hours:** Open daily from 9 a.m. to 5 p.m.; **Holiday Closings:** Dec. 25; **Visitor attractions closed for seasons:** No; **Weather:** Summer is hot and humid, winter is generally mild and humid. Strong winds occur often in the spring.

TRAVEL ACCESS: Bus: Trailways, Greyhound, and Jefferson provide frequent service into Fort Smith; **Rail:** Passenger service is at Little Rock, AR; **Air:** American Eagle, Air Midwest, Atlantic Southeast Airlines provide service to Fort Smith.

NEARBY FACILITIES & POINTS OF INTEREST: Parks, other points of interest: Old Fort Museum.

Hot Springs National Park
Hot Springs, Arkansas   **SEE CLIMATABLE NO. 7**

MAILING ADDRESS: Superintendent, Hot Springs National Park, P.O. Box 1860, Hot Springs, AR 71902 **Telephone:** 501-624-3383

DIRECTIONS: The park can be reached by auto via US 70 and 270, and AR 7. The Visitor Center is in the rehabilitated Fordyce Bathhouse in the middle of Bathhouse Row.
   Approximately one million gallons of water a day flow from 47 hot springs here, unaffected by climate or seasonal temperatures. Persons suffering from illness or injury often seek relief in the ancient tradition of thermal bathing. Also used by persons who simply want to soak and relax in the soothing, naturally heated water. Set aside as Hot Springs Reservation on Apr. 20, 1832; designated a national park on Mar. 4, 1921.

VISITOR ACTIVITIES: Thermal water baths and Swedish massages, audiovisual and interpretive exhibits at Visitor Center, campfire programs and exhibits at campground Ranger Station, hiking, auto tours, picnicking, scenic overlooks. **Permits:** No; **Fees:** Campground: $6 per night; Observation Tower, Hot Springs MT: Adults-$2.75, Children $1.75. Fees are charged by bathhouses. Rate schedules available from the Superintendent; **Visitor facilities:** The 6 bathing establishments—2 in the park (including the Hot Springs Health Spa) and 4 in the hotels in the city—use thermal waters of the park. All are concessions or permittees of the Federal Government, subject to regulation and inspection. The baths (full immersion type) may be taken by direct application to the bathhouses. Bathing in the thermal water is not recommended for persons who suffer from certain ailments. When in doubt, consult a Registered Physician. All bathhouses have facilities for whirlpool baths, showers, massages, and alcohol rubs. The Libbey Memorial Physical Medicine Center offers hydrotherapy treatments by registered physical therapists under physician prescriptions; **Any limitations on vehicle usage:** Bicycles, motorcycles, and similar vehicles are not allowed on the park trails; **Hiking trails:** Yes, many wooded trails; **Backcountry:** Yes; **Camping:** Yes, the campground is at Gulpha Gorge, 2 miles (3.2 km) northeast of the center of the city. Campers must first register at the campground ranger station; Camping is on a first-come basis. Contact the park for further information; **Other overnight accommodations on site:** No; **Meals served in the park:** No; **Food and supplies obtainable in the park:** No; **Food and supplies obtainable nearby:** Yes, in city of Hot Springs, adjacent to the Park; **Overnight accommodations:** Yes, the city of Hot Springs, a separate municipality not under National Park Service jurisdiction, nearly surrounds the park. The city has many large hotels offering a choice of American or European plans, smaller hotels, motels, boardinghouses, housekeeping quarters, and furnished or unfurnished cottages. Lists of accommodations and general information are available from the Hot Springs Chamber of Commerce, P.O. Box 1500, Hot Springs, AR 71902, phone 501-321-1700; **First Aid available in park:** Yes; **Nearest Hospital:** Hot Springs, AR, adjacent to the park; **Days/Hours:** Park open 24 hours daily. Visitor Center; Open daily 9:00 a.m. to 5:00 p.m.; **Holiday Closings:** Dec. 25 and Jan. 1; **Visitor attractions closed for seasons:** No; **Weather:** Hot Springs enjoys a favorable climate all year. The winters are mild and, except for infrequent short intervals, are conducive to outdoor recreation. The mild weather and sunshine are often decided aids to the bath treatments. Summers are usually hot and humid.

GENERAL INFORMATION: *Fires* are one of the park's greatest perils. Campfires are permitted only in designated sites. Cigars and cigarettes should be completely extinguished.

Pea Ridge National Military Park
Pea Ridge, Arkansas

MAILING ADDRESS: Superintendent, Pea Ridge National Military Park, Pea Ridge, AR 72751 **Telephone:** 501-451-8122

DIRECTIONS: The Visitor Center is 10 miles (16 km) north of Rogers off US Hwy 62.
The Union victory here on March 7-8, 1862, led to the Union's total control of Missouri. The battle was one of the major engagements of the Civil War west of the Mississippi. Authorized for addition to the National Park System on July 20, 1956.

VISITOR ACTIVITIES: Interpretive exhibits, biking, self-guiding auto tours; **Permits:** Yes; Entrance Permit required. Entrance fee $1 per person (under 17 and over 62 free.) $3 maximum charge for family; **Visitor facilities:** Parking, restrooms, drinking water, picnic area, fireplaces, observation deck, bicycle and nature trails, 7 mile (11 km) self-guiding auto tour; **HANDICAPPED ACCESSIBILITY:** Yes; **Any limitations on vehicle usage:** Drive only on paved roads; **Hiking trails:** Yes, ½-mile (.8 km) nature trail and 10-mile (16 km) Boy Scout trail; **Backcountry:** No; **Camping:** No; **Other overnight accommodations on site:** No, camping is permitted at Beaver Lake, 10 miles (16 km) away. **Meals served in the park:** No; **Food and supplies obtainable in the park:** No; **Food and supplies obtainable nearby:** Yes, in Garfield, Pea Ridge, and Rogers; **Overnight accommodations:** Rogers, US 71S, 10 miles (16 km) from the park; **First Aid available in park:** Yes; **Nearest Hospital:** Rogers, US 62, 10 miles (16 km); Bentonville, US 62 to AR 102, 15 miles (24 km); **Days/Hours:** Open daily from 8 a.m. to 5 p.m.; **Holiday Closings:** Thanksgiving Day, Dec. 25, and Jan. 1; **Weather:** Relatively mild winters and warm, humid summers.

TRAVEL ACCESS: Air: Nearest service into Joplin, MO, 80 miles (128 km), Fayetteville, AR 35 miles (56 km).

NEARBY FACILITIES & POINTS OF INTEREST: Hotel/Motel: Battle Field Inn, Garfield, 501-451-1188, 2 miles (3.2 km); **Parks, other points of interest:** Prairie Grove State Park, 42 miles (67.2 km); Beaver Lake, 12 miles, Eureka Springs, 25 miles, Buffalo National River, 65 miles.

California

Cabrillo National Monument
San Diego, California

MAILING ADDRESS: Superintendent, Cabrillo National Monument, P.O. Box 6670, San Diego, CA 92166 **Telephone:** 619-557-5450

DIRECTIONS: To reach the Monument, follow Rosecrans Street south to Canon Street (State Route 209), turn right on Canon, follow to Catalina Boulevard. Turn left on Catalina, proceed through U.S. Navy Ocean Systems Center, past Fort Rosecrans National Cemetery to Cabrillo National Monument, near tip of Point Loma. Stop at entrance station first. Proceed to parking area, go to Visitor Center.

Juan Rodriquez Cabrillo, who claimed the west coast of the United States for Spain in 1542, is memorialized here. Momument also contains historic 1855 Old Point Loma Lighthouse. Pacific gray whales migrate from Alaska offshore Dec.-Feb. Also contains pristine examples of Pacific Coast tidepools, and examples of WWI and WWII coastal fortifications. Monument created by Presidential Proclamation on Oct. 14, 1913. Contains 147 acres.

VISITOR ACTIVITIES: Interpretive exhibits, guided walks, self-guided tours, lighthouse tours, audio-visual programs, tidepools, whale-watching, birding; **Permits:** No; **Fees:** $3/vehicle; **Visitor Facilities:** Visitor Center, restrooms, museum, bookstore, auditorium, parking; **HANDICAPPED ACCESSIBILITY:** All of the above are accessible; **Any limitations on vehicle usage:** Vehicles not permitted lighthouse area; **Hiking trails:** Yes, 1-mile (1.6-km) Bayside Trail; **Backcountry:** No; **Camping:** No; **Other overnight accommodations on site:** No; **Meals served in the park:** No; **Food and supplies obtainable in the park:** Vending machines for snacks and beverages are available; **Food and supplies obtainable nearby:** Yes, 10 minutes by car in Point Loma area; **Overnight accommodations nearby:** Point Loma/San Diego, 5 miles (8 km) by car; **First Aid available in park:** Yes; **Nearest Hospital:** Sharp Cabrillo Medical Center, 5 miles (8 km); **Days/Hours:** Open 9:00 a.m. to 5:15 p.m. throughout the year (may be open 9:00 a.m. to sunset, June through Sept., subject to change without notice); **Holiday Closings:** No; **Visitor attractions closed for seasons:** No; **Weather:** Mediterranean-type climate; cooler weather in winter, night and morning fog in early summer.

GENERAL INFORMATION: *For Your Safety*—Stay back from cliff edges and on trails. Rattlesnakes common in brushy areas. Tidepool rocks are sharp and slippery. Wear rubber-soled shoes in tidepools. Tidepool animals cannot be removed from the park.

TRAVEL ACCESS: **Bus:** San Diego Transit provides daily service hourly. Commercial tours available. **Rail:** AMTRAK daily to San Diego; **Air:** San Diego.

NEARBY FACILITIES & POINTS OF INTEREST: Parks, other points of interest: San Diego Zoo and Wild Animal Park, Sea World, Balboa Park museum complex, whale-watching cruises, Old Town State Park, many other state and county parks.

Channel Islands National Park
Ventura, California   **SEE CLIMATABLE NO. 8**

MAILING ADDRESS: Superintendent, Channel Islands National Park, 1901 Spinnaker Drive, Ventura, CA 93001 **Telephone:** 805-644-8262

DIRECTIONS: Southbound on U.S. Highway 101 take Seaward offramp in Ventura, then take Harbor Blvd. south to Spinnaker Drive, turn right and proceed to Visitor's Center at the end of the drive. Northbound on U.S. Highway 101 take Victoria offramp in Ventura, follow Channel Islands signs.

The Park includes Anacapa, Santa Barbara, San Miguel, Santa Rosa, and Santa Cruz Islands. Each island hosts a variety of cultural and natural resources including Indian middens, large rookeries of sea lions, nesting sea birds, and unique plants and animals. Created by an act of Congress March 5, 1980.

VISITOR ACTIVITIES: Hiking, camping, exhibits and audiovisual programs, scuba diving, picnicking, wildlife- and bird-watching, fishing, snorkeling, swimming, boating; **Permits:** For camping and island landing permits, call or write Park Superintendent; **Fees:** For concession-operated boat trips. Inquire with The Island Packers (see below); **Visitor facilities:** New Visitor Center with "hands-on" exhibits, films, videotape programs and regularly scheduled evening programs; boat service to and from the islands, campgrounds, comfort facilities, picnic area. For public transportation and tour information write or call: The Island Packers, 1867 Spinnaker Drive, Ventura, CA 93001, phone 805-642-1393; For transportation by air: Channel Islands Adventures, 305 Durley Ave., Canarillo, CA 93010; **Any limitations on vehicle usage:** No vehicles are allowed on the islands; **Hiking trails:** Yes, self-guiding trails; **Backcountry:** Yes, call or write Park Superintendent; **Camping:** Yes, on Anacapa, Santa Rosa, San Miguel, and Santa Barbara Islands. Write or call Park Headquarters. You will need to bring water, camping gear, food, and cooking equipment. No fires permitted. Bring warm clothing, for the nights are cool. You will want a tent as shelter from the ever-present winds. If you are camping on Anacapa, keep in mind that everything must be carried up a steep stairway (152 steps) and then ¼ mile (.4 km) to the camping area; **Other overnight accommodations on site:** No; **Meals served in the park:** No; **Food and supplies obtainable in the park:** No; **Food and supplies obtainable nearby:** Yes, in Ventura, Oxnard; **Overnight accommodations:** Ventura, Oxnard have hotels and motels; **First Aid available in park:** Yes; **Nearest Hospital:** Ventura, 4 miles (6.4 km) from Headquarters, 18 miles (28.8 km) from Anacapa; **Days/Hours:** Islands: daylight hours and overnight camping available on Anacapa and Santa Barbara Islands. Visitor Center—8:00 a.m.-5 p.m. with extended hours in summer, 7 days a week; **Holiday Closings:** Visitor Center closed Thanksgiving, Dec. 25, and Jan. 1; **Visitor attractions closed for seasons:** No.

GENERAL INFORMATION: *For Your Safety*—Hike only on beaches and established trails when on Anacapa and Santa Barbara Islands. Landing permit required for San Miguel, Santa Rosa Islands.

TRAVEL ACCESS: Bus: Greyhound Bus Service to Ventura, CA, several times a day, also Southcoast Area Transit (city bus) goes from Ventura to Pierpont Bus Terminal, near the park headquarters several times a day; **Rail:** Amtrak provides daily service to Oxnard; **Air:** Several daily flights to Oxnard Airport. Area airports include Los Angeles International 70 miles (112 km) south and Santa Barbara 40 miles (64 km) north.

NEARBY FACILITIES & POINTS OF INTEREST: Hotel/Motel: Several in nearby area; **Campgrounds:** McGrath State Beach Park, about 3 miles (4.8 km) south off Harbor Blvd. **Reservation systems in use for campsites, other facilities;** Camping on the Islands by permit only; Day use on San Miguel and Santa Rosa Islands by permit only. The Ventura Visitors and Convention Bureau (785 S. Seaward Avenue, Ventura, CA 93001) offers more extensive details on accommodations and activities in "Recreation Guide" and "Motel and Restaurant Guide."

Death Valley National Monument
Death Valley, California and Nevada

MAILING ADDRESS: Superintendent, Death Valley National Monument, Death Valley, CA 92328 **Telephone:** 619-786-2331

DIRECTIONS: US 395 passes west of Death Valley and connects with State Routes 190 and 136 or by an unnumbered county road from Trona, CA, to the park. US 95 passes east of the park and connects with NV 267, 374, and 373 to the park. Interstate 15 passes southeast of the park and connects with State Route 127 to the park.
This large desert, nearly surrounded by high mountains, contains the lowest point in the Western Hemisphere. The area includes Scotty's Castle, the palatial home of a famous prospector, and other remnants of gold and borax mining activity. Created by Presidential Proclamation on Feb. 11, 1933.

VISITOR ACTIVITIES: Driving, hiking, jeep riding, camping, photography, biking, interpretive exhibits, guided tours, picnicking, backcountry, horseback riding; **Permits:** Backcountry permits are encouraged, available at Ranger Stations; **Fees:** Yes, $5 entrance fee, campground fees at major campgrounds, Guided Castle tours are $6 per person and $3 for Golden Age passport holders; **Visitor facilities:** Visitor Center, campgrounds, hiking trails, parking, restrooms, lodging, picnic areas, interpretive programs, post office, bicycle rentals; **HANDICAPPED ACCESSIBILITY:** Salt Creek Nature Trail is accessible; **Any limitations on vehicle usage:** Drive only on existing roads, only on main roads in summer, and always carry water for your car. In case of breakdown, remain with your car until help arrives; **Hiking trails:** Yes, self-guiding walking trails; **Backcountry:** Yes, contact the park for further information; **Camping:** Yes, reservations taken for group campsites only. For further information, write for a copy of the folder *Camping in Death Valley* or pick up a copy at the Visitor Center or any Ranger Station; **Other overnight accommodations on site:** Yes, resorts provide lodging and other commercial services at two locations within the Monument. Facilities at Furnace Creek and Stove Pipe Wells are operated by Fred Harvey, Inc., P.O. Box 187, Death Valley, CA 92328, phone 619-786-2345. Services at these locations are limited from May through Oct. Call or write for details; **Meals served in the park:** Yes, at Furnace Creek, Stove Pipe Wells, Scotty's Castle; **Food and supplies obtainable in the park:** Yes, at Stove Pipe Wells, Furnace Creek, and Scotty's Castle; **Food and supplies obtainable nearby:** Yes, in Beatty, Shoshone; **Overnight accommodations:** Beatty, 45 miles (72 km) from park HQ or Furnace Creek; Shoshone, 60 miles (96 km) from park HQ or Furnace Creek; Trona, 40 miles (64 km) from Wildrose; **First Aid available in park:** Yes, or nearby in Beatty, US 95; Trona, State Route 178; Shoshone, CA 127; **Nearest Hospital:** Lone Pine, 100 miles (61 km) west; Las Vegas, 140 miles (225 km) east, Tonopah, 90 miles (145 km) northeast; **Days/Hours:** Park never closes. Visitor Center open 8 a.m. to 8 p.m. from Nov. 1 to Easter; 8-5 the rest of the year. **Holiday Closings:** No; **Visitor attractions closed for seasons:** Some jeep roads closed in summer; **Weather:** Summer has extreme heat and low humidity; winter is cooler with snow at high elevations. Flash-flooding and desert rainstorms can close roads temporarily in both winter and summer.

GENERAL INFORMATION: *For Your Safety—the desert can be dangerously hot in summer.* Always carry water for you and your car. *Never enter mines or tunnels;* abandoned shafts are often deep and old timbers rotten. *Forgotten caches of explosives* are occasionally found in mine areas. Do not touch them, but report them to a park ranger as soon as possible. Be alert for *flash floods* when it looks stormy. Do not ford low places when water is running. Flood waters can undercut pavement or sweep a car from the road. *All animals in the park are wild.* They can bite and/or carry diseases. Never feed or touch them. *Never travel alone.* Always tell someone where you are going and when you expect to return. Be extremely cautious in this wild area. If you travel in Death Valley in summer, pick up a copy of the folder *Hot Weather Hints* at distribution boxes at any entrance to the Monument, at the Visitor Center, or any Ranger Station.

TRAVEL ACCESS: Bus: No; **Rail:** No; **Air:** Service available; **Other:** Bicycle rental available at Furnace Creek.

Devils Postpile National Monument
Mammoth Lakes, California

MAILING ADDRESS: Park Manager, Devils Postpile National Monument, P.O. Box 501, Mammoth Lakes, CA 93546. **Telephone:** 619-934-2289 summer and fall, 209-565-3341 winter and spring.

DIRECTIONS: The Monument is reached by a 10-mile (16-km) drive to Minaret Summit on a paved road from US 395, then by 7 miles (11.2 km) of mountain road.

Hot lava cooled and cracked some 100,000 years ago to form basalt columns 40 to 60 feet high resembling a giant pipe organ. The John Muir Trail between Yosemite and Kings Canyon National Parks crosses the Monument. Created by Presidential Proclamation on July 6, 1911.

VISITOR ACTIVITIES: Guided walks, picnicking, evening campfire programs, fishing, camping; **Permits:** California fishing license, available locally for a nominal fee is required; **Fees:** $7 camping fee; **Visitor facilities:** Restrooms near Ranger Station, picnic area, campground, shuttle bus; **Any limitations on vehicle usage:** Restricted use mid-day during heavy-use season; visitors will be required to use a shuttle bus to reach the Monument. Contact the park for further information; **Hiking trails:** Yes, trips may be made north or south along the John Muir Trail and west on the King Creek Trail. Devils Postpile also has several short trails; **Backcountry:** No; **Camping:** Yes, no reservations are available for the campground, which is open from about June 20 to Oct. 1, depending on the weather; **Other overnight accommodations on site:** No; **Meals served in the park:** No; **Food and supplies obtainable in the park:** No; **Food and supplies obtainable nearby:** Yes, at Mammoth Lakes or Reds Meadow; **Overnight accommodations:** Mammoth Lakes, 14 miles (22.4 km), Reds Meadow, 1.5 miles (2.4 km); **First Aid available in park:** Yes; **Nearest Hospital:** Complete 24 hours a day emergency services at Centinela Mammoth Hospital, 14 miles (22.4 km); **Days/Hours:** Open 24 hours a day, 7 days a week in season; **Holiday Closings:** No; **Visitor attractions closed for seasons:** The Monument is open from approximately mid-June through Oct.; **Weather:** Summer thundershowers occur frequently in the afternoon.

GENERAL INFORMATION: Warning: Bears inhabit the Monument; proper food storage is required by Federal law. Stay on the regular designated trails since these are the safest places to hike. Stay back when viewing features from near the edge of a cliff or gorge. Footing is hazardous.

Eugene O'Neill National Historic Site
Danville, California

MAILING ADDRESS: Superintendent, National Park Service, P.O. Box 280, Danville, CA 94526 **Telephone:** 415-838-0249

DIRECTIONS: Limited public access is available for Ranger-guided tours of the site via a National Park Service operated van. Reservations are required and can be arranged by contacting the address above or by phoning. Tours are offered twice daily, Wednesday through Sunday.

Tao House, near Danville, CA, was built for Eugene O'Neill, who lived here from 1937 to 1944. Several of his best-known plays, including *The Iceman Cometh* and *Long Day's Journey into Night* were written here—now a memorial to the playwright. Authorized for addition to the National Park System on Oct. 12, 1976. Title transferred to the National Park Service on July 29, 1980.

VISITOR ACTIVITIES: Park Ranger guided tours; **HANDICAPPED ACCESSIBILITY:** Van has no wheelchair lift; wheelchair can be transported if person can transfer to van seat; only first floor of house is accessible to wheelchairs; restroom not accessible.

JOHN MUIR NATIONAL HISTORIC SITE

GOLDEN GATE NATIONAL RECREATION AREA

POINT REYES NATIONAL SEASHORE

MUIR WOODS NATIONAL MONUMENT

ALCATRAZ

FORT POINT NATIONAL HISTORIC SITE

EUGENE O'NEILL NATIONAL HISTORIC SITE

Fort Point National Historic Site
Presidio of San Francisco, California

MAILING ADDRESS: Site Manager, Fort Point National Historic Site, P.O. Box 29333, Presidio of San Francisco, CA 94129 **Telephone:** 415-556-1693 or 556-2857

DIRECTIONS: Fort Point is located under the south end of the Golden Gate Bridge. Turn off Hwy 101 at the bridge to reach the fort.

This classic brick and granite mid-19th-Century coastal fortification is the only one of its type on the west coast of North America. Established by act of Congress on Oct. 16, 1970.

VISITOR ACTIVITIES: Interpretive exhibits and guided tours, cannon drills, picnicking, fishing; **Permits:** No; **Fees:** No; **Visitor facilities:** Parking and restrooms; **Any limitations on vehicle usage:** All motor vehicles are restricted to developed, paved roadways and parking areas; **Hiking trails:** Yes, short scenic trails through the area; **Backcountry:** No; **Camping:** No; **Other overnight accommodations on site:** No; **Meals served in the park:** No; **Food and supplies obtainable in the park:** No; **Food and supplies obtainable nearby:** Yes, in the immediate area; **Overnight accommodations:** San Francisco—reservations are advisable;

First Aid available in park: Yes; **Nearest Hospital:** Letterman Army Medical Center, Lincoln Blvd., 1 mile (1.6 km); **Days/Hours:** Park open sunrise to sunset. Fort open daily from 10 a.m. to 5 p.m.; **Holiday Closings:** Thanksgiving, Dec. 25, and Jan. 1; **Weather:** Average temperature is 58°F with winds 5-10 mph. Wear warm clothes when you visit the area.

GENERAL INFORMATION: Use caution while climbing or descending stairs, which are steep and narrow. Stay on established roadways and off walls, which can be dangerous if climbed.

TRAVEL ACCESS: Bus: Municipal buses from San Francisco provide access to park area; **Rail:** Amtrak and Southern Pacific Railroads provide service to the Oakland/San Francisco area; **Air:** Major airlines serve San Francisco and Oakland airports.

Golden Gate National Recreation Area
San Francisco, California

MAILING ADDRESS: General Superintendent, Golden Gate National Recreation Area, Fort Mason, San Francisco, CA 94123 **Telephone:** 415-556-0560

DIRECTIONS: In San Francisco, Golden Gate National Recreation Area follows the city's northern and western shoreline. These areas are accessible by the Municipal Railway (MUNI) bus system and can easily be reached by car. Ferries provide access to Alcatraz. Across the Golden Gate Bridge in Marin County, the park is reached by various access roads off Hwy 101: Alexander Avenue, Shoreline Highway, and Sir Francis Drake Boulevard. MUNI serves Rodeo Beach in Marin on Sundays. Visitor information is available at Fort Mason, the Cliff House, Ft. Point, The National Maritime Museum, Rodeo Beach, and Muir Woods.

Golden Gate National Recreation Area offers a variety of recreational, scenic, natural, and historic areas on the doorstep of San Francisco. The beauty of the city, the Bay, the ocean, and coastal landscape are brought together in one park which contains about 31,000 acres of open space on both sides of the Golden Gate. The park was established in 1972 and represents an effort to bring parks closer to people in urban areas.

VISITOR ACTIVITIES: An endless variety of recreational, cultural, and educational activities are available here, including tours of Alcatraz, the National Maritime Museum at the San Francisco Maritime National Historical Park, picnicking, fishing, camping, swimming, short walks and sightseeing, hiking, and cultural programs at Fort Mason Center; **Permits:** Needed for special use only; **Fees:** Hyde Street Pier, $2 for adults (includes the Balclutha) children under 17, free; Alcatraz boat, $5, audio tour, $2.50; **Visitor facilities:** Picnic sites, fishing piers, beaches, tours of historic areas, campgrounds, snack bars, restrooms, parking, recreational equipment is not available; **Any limitations on vehicle usage:** No off-road vehicles; **Hiking trails:** Yes, trails vary in length and difficulty. Major trailheads are in the Marin Headlands, Muir Woods, and Tennessee Valley; **Backcountry:** No; **Camping:** Yes, American Youth Hostels offer overnight accommodations in the Marin Headlands Area of the park and at Fort Mason. Hike-in and group camping available in the Marin Headlands; **Other overnight accommodations on site:** No; **Meals served in the park:** Yes, food service facilities are available at the Fort Mason Center, The Cliff House, and Muir Woods. **Food and supplies obtainable in the park:** No; **Food and supplies obtainable nearby:** Yes, in the nearby urban community; **Overnight accommodations:** The San Francisco Area offers a wide variety of overnight accommodations, many within walking distance of the park; **First Aid available in park:** Yes, at most Visitor Centers and in the surrounding community; **Nearest Hospital:** Letterman, San Francisco General Hospital, and many others in the vicinity; **Days/Hours:** Most of the park is open all day, all year. Hours for individual facilities vary, but 10 a.m.-5 p.m. are the most common hours of operation; **Holiday Closings:** Alcatraz, Hyde Street Pier, Maritime Museum, and Fort Point are closed on Thanksgiving Day, Dec. 25, and Jan. 1; **Visitor attractions closed for seasons:** No; **Weather:** Weather at the park is variable. Wind and fog are common from June to Sept., especially near the Golden Gate. Fall generally brings the warmest weather. Most rainfall occurs from Nov. to April. Bring a sweater or light jacket that you can carry easily if it warms up.

TRAVEL ACCESS: Bus: MUNI System in San Francisco, Greyhound provides services to San Francisco; **Rail:** Amtrak service to Oakland, and Southern Pacific has passenger service into San Francisco; **Air:** Major airlines service San Francisco International Airport and Oakland International Airport.

NEARBY FACILITIES & POINTS OF INTEREST: The Presidio: The Presidio of San Francisco is a 1440 acre U.S. Army base which will become part of the Golden Gate National Recreation Area in September 1995. It contains a unique 200 year history of continuous occupation and use reflected in buildings, grounds, and artifacts including some of the best military architecture in the country. Its urban parkland includes one of the oldest golf courses on the west coast, 21 listed rare plant species, and San Francisco's last free-flowing stream.

John Muir National Historic Site
Martinez, California

MAILING ADDRESS: Superintendent, John Muir National Historic Site, 4202 Alhambra Ave., Martinez, CA 94553 **Telephone:** 415-228-8860

DIRECTIONS: The site is located at the foot of the off ramp of the Alhambra Ave. exit of State Route 4, 10 miles (16 km) east of Interstate 80, 5 miles (8 km) west of State Route 680. Access is also available via Bay Area Rapid Transit (BART). Call 415-933-2278 for information on connecting schedules between BART trains and bus service to Martinez.

This 9-acre site preserves the 17-room Victorian home and orchard fragment of the great American writer, naturalist, and defender of the national parks, John Muir. Authorized for addition to the National Park System on Aug. 31, 1964.

VISITOR ACTIVITIES: Guided and self-guiding tours are available. A film about Muir's life and philosophy is shown hourly. Picnicking is available. Guided tours are available for groups over 10 by reservation. Please notify park 2 weeks in advance. Self-guided tours are available daily from 10 a.m. to 4:30 p.m.; **Permits:** No; **Fees:** $1 for adults 17-61, seniors free. Golden Eagle and Golden Age Passports are available; **Visitor facilities:** Visitor Center, parking, restrooms, picnic area; **HANDICAPPED ACCESSIBILITY:** One parking space, restrooms in Visitor Center, easy access trail to Muir House, wheelchair lift to first floor Muir House, electric cart for rides to Muir House from Visitor Center. **Any limitations on vehicle usage:** No vehicles are allowed in the park, access cart available for handicapped visitors; **Hiking trails:** Yes, short trails around the grounds; **Backcountry:** No; **Camping:** No; **Other overnight accommodations on site:** No; **Meals served in the park:** No; **Food and supplies obtainable in the park:** No; **Food and supplies obtainable nearby:** Yes, in Martinez; **Overnight accommodations:** Yes, overnight accommodations are available a few blocks away and also in Martinez, ½ mile (.8 km); **First Aid available in park:** Yes; **Nearest Hospital:** Martinez, 1 mile (1.6 km); **Days/Hours:** Open Wed.-Sun. from 10:00 a.m. to 4:30 p.m.; **Holiday Closings:** Thanksgiving, Dec. 25, and Jan. 1; **Visitor attractions closed for seasons:** No; **Weather:** Moderate climate; warm summers.

Joshua Tree National Monument
Twentynine Palms, California

MAILING ADDRESS: Superintendent, Joshua Tree National Monument, 74485 National Monument Drive, Twentynine Palms, CA 92277 **Telephone:** 619-367-7511

DIRECTIONS: The Monument is 140 miles (225 km) east of Los Angeles; from the west it is approached via I-10 (US 60) and Twentynine Palms Hwy (Hwy 62) to the north entrances at the town of Joshua Tree and Twentynine Palms. The Cottonwood Spring (south) entrance is 25 miles (40 km) east of Indio, CA, via I-10 (US 60).

The Monument is a desert area of great diversity encompassing the unique ecosystems of both the Joshua Tree-defined Mojave and lower Colorado deserts. Rich in ecological, historical, and recreational resources, the Monument was established Aug. 10, 1936.

VISITOR ACTIVITIES: Hiking, interpretive walks and talks, picnicking, wildlife-watching, camping; **Permits:** For backcountry; **Fees:** Not for backcountry use. General entrance fee is $5 for 1-7 days; $15 for year pass; $25 Golden Eagle (all park pass)—campground use fee at two campgrounds is $6 and $10 per night; Cottonwood fees are $6 a night and free during the summer months; Fees for Black Rock are $10 a night but it closes during summer months; **Visitor facilities:** Campgrounds, tables, fireplaces, toilets, picnic area; **HANDICAPPED ACCESSIBILITY:** Cottonwood and Black Rock Campgrounds, Cap Rock Nature Trail and Twentynine Palms Oasis Nature Trail; **Any limitations on vehicle usage:** Vehicles must be operated only on established roads; **Hiking trails:** Yes, trails vary in length and difficulty; **Backcountry:** Yes, there is a self registration system used throughout the monument. Contact the park or inquire at the Visitor Center; **Camping:** Yes, first-come, first-served except Black Rock is available only through Ticketron reservations. Campers must bring their own water and firewood and be prepared for wide fluctuations in temperature. Three group camping sites available, reservations required through Ticketron. **Other overnight accommodations on site:** No; **Meals served in the park:** No; **Food and supplies obtainable in the park:** No; **Food and supplies obtainable nearby:** Yes, in Twentynine Palms, Yucca Valley, Joshua Tree; **Overnight accommodations:** Twentynine Palms, 3 miles (5 km) from North Park Entrance; in Joshua Tree, 5 miles (8 km) from West Park Entrance; Yucca Valley, 11 miles (17.7 km) from West Park entrance; **First Aid available in park:** Yes; **Nearest Hospital:** Joshua Tree, 8 miles (13 km) from West Park entrance; **Days/Hours:** Open all year, 24 hours a day. Visitor Center open daily from 8 a.m. to 4:30 p.m.; **Holiday Closings:** Visitor Center closed Dec. 25; **Visitor attractions closed for seasons:** Guided walks and talks in spring and fall only; **Weather:** It is cold from Dec. through mid-Feb., July and Aug. temperatures range from 100°F to 115°F.

GENERAL INFORMATION: When hiking, biking, or driving in Joshua Tree, during hot weather drink at least one gallon (4 liters) of water per day. Stay clear of mine shafts. Beware of rattlesnakes.

Lassen Volcanic National Park
Mineral, California   **SEE CLIMATABLE NO. 10**

MAILING ADDRESS: Superintendent, Lassen Volcanic National Park, P.O. Box 100, Mineral, CA 96063-0100 **Telephone:** 916-595-4444

DIRECTIONS: From the north and south, the park is reached via Hwy 89. From the east and west, via State Route 36 and 44. Route 36 is to the south of the park, Route 44 to the north.

Redding is 48 miles (76.8 km) west of the Park on State Route 44.

The park contains examples of volcanic phenomena, including Lassen Peak, a recently active volcano that erupted intermittently from 1914 to 1921. Created by an act of Congress on August 9, 1916.

VISITOR ACTIVITIES: Interpretive programs, nature walks, hiking, self-guiding auto tours, camping, cross-country and downhill skiing, picnicking, boating, backpacking, swimming, winter sports; **Permits:** Wilderness permits are required for overnight stays in the backcountry. Permits are available at Park Headquarters and all Ranger Stations. They should be requested by mail or telephone at least 2 weeks in advance; **Fees:** Yes, entrance fee is $5 per car; campground fee is $6 to $8 per campsite, depending on facilities. Golden Eagle, Golden Access, and Golden Age Passports are accepted and available; **Visitor facilities:** Campgrounds, hiking trails, fast food service, picnic areas, boat ramp, supplies, and ski trails, tows, and equipment rental; **HANDICAPPED ACCESSIBILITY:** Manzanita Lake: Visitor Center, restrooms, Indian Ways Program and amphitheater (with assistance), campsite restrooms. Summit Lake: Campsite, restrooms, picnic area (with assistance). Southwest Entrance: Information Station, and campground restrooms. Butte Lake: Campsite, restrooms. Park HQ: Restrooms. Portable restrooms (with assistance) at Bumpass Hill, Lassen Peak, Lupine picnic area. Restrooms open during summer operation period only. Chalet restroom open most of year; **Any limitations on vehicle usage:** Motorized boats are not allowed on any park waters. Some campgrounds will accommodate trailers up to 35 feet; **Hiking trails:** Yes, there are 150 miles (240 km) of foot trails in the park; **Backcountry:** Yes, permit is required for overnight stays. Check at Park Headquarters, any Ranger Station, or send for information; **Camping:** Yes, 4 campgrounds are located along Lassen Trans-park Road. The campgrounds at Manzanita Lake, Crags Summit Lake, and Butte Lake have chemical or flush toilets and spaces for trailers (no hookups for electricity, water, or sewage). The Southwest Campground also has modern facilities. This is a walk-in tent campground. The Juniper Lake and Warner Valley Campgrounds have primitive facilities and are not recommended for trailers because of the rough road. Campgrounds are open from June to Oct., depending on the weather and the location of the campground. Group campgrounds are also available, and reservations must be made in advance. Complete campground information is provided on request. Call 916-595-4444 for information on lodging facilities; **Other overnight accommodations on site:** Yes, at Drakesbad Guest Ranch, call the Susanville operator and ask for Drakesbad Toll Station No. 2; **Meals served in the park:** Yes, fast food services are available at the Manzanita Lake Camper Service Store and Chalet; **Food and supplies obtainable in the park:** Yes, Manzanita Lake Campground; **Food and supplies obtainable nearby:** Yes, in Mineral, 10 miles (16 km) southwest; Old Station, 15 miles (24 km) northeast and Shingletown, 17 miles (27.2 km) northwest; **Overnight accommodations:** Mineral, 10 miles (16 km) south; Hat Creek, 14 miles (22.4 km) north; **First Aid available in park:** Yes; **Nearest Hospital:** Burney, State Route 44, 45 miles (72 km) west of the north end; Chester, State Route 36, 35 miles (56 km) from the south end; **Days/Hours:** Park is always open; **Holiday Closings:** No; **Visitor attractions closed for seasons:** Trans-park Road is closed during winter; **Weather:** Most of the 30-mile (48-km) Lassen Park Road is closed by snow from the end of Oct. until early June, although the park is open all year. Winter sports are centered in an area near the southwest entrance.

GENERAL INFORMATION: *For Your Safety*—Stay on established trails at all times in hot springs or steaming areas. Keep small children under strict physical control to avoid burns or accidents. Ground crusts that appear to be safe may be dangerously thin. Hot lunches, and ski-rental equipment and accessories are available on weekends and holidays. Ski lifts are operated 3 days a week. Overnight accommodations are available at Mineral and Chester.

The terrain and snow conditions are usually excellent for cross-country skiing. For safety reasons, Park Rangers should be notified of all trips. Wilderness permits are required for all overnight stays.

The road is kept open from the northwest entrance to the Manzanita Lake District Office. Many people visit this section of the Park to enjoy the scenery and winter sports.

TRAVEL ACCESS: Bus: Mt. Lassen Motor Transit stops at Mineral, CA, and Red Bluff daily, except Sundays and holidays.

NEARBY FACILITIES & POINTS OF INTEREST: Hotel/Motel: South of park; Mineral, Mill Creek, Paynes Creek, and Chester, CA; North of park; Old Station, and Shingletown, CA; **Food/Supplies:** Chalet, Mineral, Manzanita, Old Station, and Shingletown, CA.

Lava Beds National Monument
Tulelake, California

MAILING ADDRESS: Superintendent, Lava Beds National Monument, P.O. Box 867, Tulelake, CA 96134 **Telephone:** 916-667-2282

DIRECTIONS: Monument Headquarters is 30 miles (48 km) from Tulelake, CA, and 58 miles (93 km) from Klamath Falls, OR, off State Route 139, 5 miles (8 km) south of Tulelake and 26 miles (42 km) north of Canby.

Volcanic activity spewed forth molten rock and lava here creating an incredibly rugged landscape—a natural fortress used by the Indians in the Modoc Indian War, 1872-73. Created by Presidential Proclamation on Nov. 21, 1925.

VISITOR ACTIVITIES: Camping, walking, picnicking, interpretive talks, campfire programs, cave exploration, bird- and animal-watching; **Permits:** No; **Fees:** Entrance fees $3, campground fees are $6 per day per site from mid-May–mid-Oct.; **Visitor facilities:** Picnic areas, campgrounds, drinking water, toilets; **HANDICAPPED ACCESSIBILITY:** Visitor Center, Visitor Center comfort station, Fleener Chimneys picnic area (table and restrooms); Campground—site reserved until 4 p.m., comfort station; guidebooks and program scripts for hearing impaired; guidebooks for assistants and tours of historic area for seeing impaired; **Any limitations on vehicle usage:** Vehicles are restricted to maintained roads; **Hiking trails:** Yes, moderate to rugged both in and outside the wilderness areas; **Backcountry:** Yes, information available by writing or calling the Monument, or from Visitor Center; **Camping:** Yes, no reservations for campsites, which are near Visitor Center and are open all year. The 40-unit campground has sites suitable for tents, pickup campers, and small trailers and has water and toilets. From Oct. 15 through May 15 water must be carried from Headquarters. Fleener Chimneys picnic area has no water, and fires may not be built there; **Other overnight accommodations on site:** No; **Meals served in the park:** No; **Food and supplies obtainable in the park:** No; **Food and supplies obtainable nearby:** Yes, at Tulelake and Klamath Falls; **Overnight accommodations:** Tulelake, State Route 139, 30 miles (48 km); Klamath Falls, OR, State Route 139, 58 miles (93 km), and Merrill, OR; **First Aid available in park:** Yes, or nearby in Tulelake, State Route 139, 30 miles (48 km); **Nearest Hospital:** Klamath Falls, OR, State Route 139, 58 miles (93 km); **Days/Hours:** Monument never closes, Visitor Center open daily from 8 a.m. to 5 p.m.; 9 a.m.-6 p.m. in summer; **Holiday Closings:** Thanksgiving and Christmas days; **Visitor attractions closed for seasons:** No; **Weather:** At these elevations, cold weather is possible anytime; snow has been recorded in all months. Winter daily high temperatures average around the 40s F; lows are in the 20s. Fog is frequent. Summers are moderate; with daytime highs averaging from 80° to 90° F, lows are in the 40s and 50s F. Precipitation in this area averages 1.08 inches or less per month.

GENERAL INFORMATION: Hunting, gathering specimens, and collecting souvenirs are prohibited. Among the potential hazards you may encounter in the lava tubes are low ceilings, steep trails and stairways, and uneven footing. Take more than one light source. Wear protective headgear. Wear adequate clothing—cave temperatures are cool. Notify a Park Ranger before exploring caves other than those listed in the brochure, or if you plan to use your own lighting equipment. Be aware that rattlesnakes are found throughout the Monument; children should be cautioned never to put their hands and feet in places they cannot see.

TRAVEL ACCESS: Bus: No; **Rail:** Amtrak provides daily service into Klamath Falls, OR; **Air:** Horizon Air, American Eagle provide daily services to Klamath Falls, OR.

Muir Woods National Monument
Mill Valley, California

MAILING ADDRESS: Site Manager, Muir Woods National Monument, Mill Valley, CA 94941 **Telephone:** 415-388-2595

DIRECTIONS: The Monument is 17 miles (27 km) north of San Francisco and is reached by US 101 and CA 1. Tour van service is available from downtown San Francisco.

This virgin stand of coastal redwoods was named for John Muir, conservationist and co-founder of the Sierra Club. Created by Presidential Proclamation on Jan. 9, 1908.

VISITOR ACTIVITIES: Walking, hiking; **Permits:** No; **Fees:** No; **Visitor facilities:** Visitor Center, parking, restrooms, souvenir stand, trailside markers, signs, and exhibits; **HANDICAPPED ACCESSIBILITY:** All facilities and main park trails are accessible to wheelchairs and strollers. Parking, restrooms, telephones, and most special programs are also accessible. Jr. Ranger Discovery Packs are available for families to use while visiting; **Any limitations on vehicle usage:** No motorized equipment, horses, or bicycles are permitted; **Hiking trails:** Yes, 6 miles (10 km) of trails join those of other public lands. Bridges along Redwood Creek make short loops possible; **Backcountry:** No; **Camping:** No; **Other overnight accommodations on site:** No; **Meals served in the park:** Yes, snacks are available at the concession shop near the Visitor Center; **Food and supplies obtainable in the park:** No; **Food and supplies obtainable nearby:** Yes; **Overnight accommodations:** Mill Valley, 4 miles (6.4 km); **First Aid available in park:** Yes; **Nearest Hospital:** San Rafael, 12 miles (19.3 km); **Days/Hours:** Open daily from 8 a.m. to sunset; **Holiday Closings:** No; **Visitor attractions closed for seasons:** No; **Weather:** 40 inches of rain per year, mostly between Nov. and May.

GENERAL INFORMATION: Weather is often cool and wet, so jackets are advisable. Stay on trails, which can become slippery when wet. Poison oak and nettles are common. Do not pick berries, roots, or mushrooms. Several plants found in Muir Woods are poisonous. No picnicking or dogs allowed at the Monument.

Pinnacles National Monument
Paicines, California

MAILING ADDRESS: Superintendent, Pinnacles National Monument, Paicines, CA 95043 **Telephone:** 408-389-4485

DIRECTIONS: The Monument is separated into an east and west district with Visitor Service facilities located in both districts. Park Headquarters and the Bear Gulch Visitor Center are on the east side of the Monument and are reached via CA 25 and Highway 146 from Hollister. The Chaparral Ranger Station and campground are on the west side and can be reached via CA 146 from Soledad. The road from Soledad to West Pinnacles is steep and narrow. Visitors driving large campers and towing trailers should use extreme caution. There is no road connecting the east and west sides of the Monument.

Spirelike rock formations 1200 to 3300 feet high, with caves and a variety of organic features, rise above the smooth contours of the surrounding countryside. Created by Presidential Proclamation on Jan. 16, 1908.

VISITOR ACTIVITIES: Hiking, climbing, picnicking, camping, evening talks on spring and fall weekends, wildlife-, wildflower-, and bird-watching; **Permits:** None required, but climbers may register with a Park Ranger before and after a climb; **Fees:** $3 per vehicle entrance fee. Golden Eagle and Golden Age Passports accepted and available. $10 per night per site camping fee; **Visitor facilities:** Picnic areas, campsites, drinking water, comfort stations, self-guiding trails, hiking trails; **Any limitations on vehicle usage:** Motor vehicles and mountain bikes are not allowed on any of the trails; **Hiking trails:** Yes, trails vary in length and difficulty. Pets are not allowed on the trails. For further information, inquire at Visitor Center; **Backcountry:** No; **Camping:** Yes, West Side Chapparal campground is reached from Highway 101, 11 miles (17.6 km) east from the turnoff at Soledad with sites available on a first- come, first-served basis for *individuals* only. Organized groups are permitted from June 1 to Jan. 31. Requests for reservations must be received by mail or telephone 7 days prior to arrival date. Reservations *for group sites only* can be made by calling 408-389-4526. Picnic tables, fireplaces, water, and chemical toilets are provided. No gasoline, food, or supplies are available. Pinnacles Campground Inc., a private campground, is adjacent to the park's east boundary on CA 146. It offers individual and group campsites with tables and grills and modern restrooms. It has showers, a camper store, gas pump, swimming pool, recreation vehicle utility hookups, and an amphitheater. Call for fee information. The campground operates on a first-come, first-served basis. Reservations are required for groups of 10 or more. For further information call 408-389-4462 or write 2400 Highway 146, Paicines, CA 95043; **Other overnight accommodations on site:** No; **Meals served in the park:** No; **Food and supplies obtainable in the park:** No; **Food and supplies obtainable nearby:** Yes, stores at Pinnacles Campground and in Paicines, 23 miles (36.8 km) to the north; **Overnight accommodations:** Soledad, Hollister, and King City; **First Aid available in park:** Yes; **Nearest Hospital:** Hollister and King City; **Days/Hours:** Park never closes; **Holiday Closings:** No; **Visitor attractions closed for seasons:** No; **Weather:** Fall and spring are the Park's busiest seasons. Spring is one of the best times to enjoy the Park. Summer daytime temperatures can exceed 100°F.

GENERAL INFORMATION: *For Your Safety*—Caves have low ceilings and very slippery rocks. Use flashlights. Only experienced climbers and persons under competent leadership should attempt rock climbs in the park. *Stay on regular designated trails*. Rock faces off the trails are unstable and likely to flake off beneath you. *Poison oak* abounds; stay on the trails and in developed areas, which are kept reasonably free of this plant. *Rattlesnakes* may be on the trails in the spring and fall. *Water* is not always as pure as it seems, so drink only from hydrants and fountains on the Park's water supply. Be sure to *wear stout, comfortable shoes*, loose-fitting clothing, and in the summer, a hat. CARRY WATER!!!

TRAVEL ACCESS: Bus: Greyhound provides daily service to Gilroy or King City; **Rail:** No; **Air:** No.

Point Reyes National Seashore
Point Reyes Station, California

MAILING ADDRESS: Superintendent, Point Reyes National Seashore, Point Reyes, CA 94956 **Telephone:** 415-663-1092

DIRECTIONS: The Seashore is one hour or 40-45 miles (65-70 km) north of San Francisco via US 101 and Sir Francis Drake Blvd., or via US 1 near Mill Valley.

This peninsula, near San Francisco, is noted for its long beaches backed by tall cliffs, lagoons and esteros, forested ridges and offshore bird and sea lion colonies. Part of the area remains in pastoral use. Authorized for addition to the National Park System on Sept. 13, 1962.

VISITOR ACTIVITIES: Hiking, biking, picnicking, guided tours, surf fishing, horseback riding, bird watching, backcountry; **Permits:** Required for camping, obtained by registering at the Bear Valley Visitor Center; **Fees:** No; **Visitor facilities:** Beaches, hiking trails, horse trails, picnic areas, three Visitor Centers, self-guiding trails, four hike-in campgrounds with 50 sites total; **HANDICAPPED ACCESSIBILITY:** Visitor Centers, restrooms; Earthquake Trail, ½-mile (.8 km) self-guided loop trail, is paved; hands-on exhibits can be arranged for visually impaired; large print handouts available; TDD and cassettes for hearing impaired; **Any limitations on vehicle usage:** All motor vehicles are restricted to developed, paved roadways and parking areas; **Hiking trails:** Yes, Bear Valley Trailhead is a gateway to more than 140 miles (273.6 km) of trails. The 4.1 mile (6.5 km) Bear Valley Trail is the most popular route, winding through grassy meadows and forests to the sea. Other trails branch from it and ascend steeply into the high country of the Inverness Ridge and the southern portion of the Seashore. Stay on designated trails; wandering off may result in losing your way or being exposed to poison oak, which abounds here. Carry a canteen—stream water is not potable; **Backcountry:** Yes, information can be obtained from the Superintendent; **Camping:** Yes, to obtain a permit or reservation call Mon.-Fri. 9 a.m.-12 noon, 415-663-1092. Register at Bear Valley Visitor Center; **Other overnight accommodations on site:** No; **Meals served in the park:** Yes, at Drakes Beach; **Food and supplies obtainable in the park:** No; **Food and supplies obtainable nearby:** Yes, at Point Reyes Station, Inverness, Olema; **Overnight accommodations:** Olema, US 1, 1 mile (1.6 km); Inverness, Sir Francis Drake Highway, 5 miles (8 km); **First Aid available in park:** Yes, or nearby in Point Reyes Station, Inverness, Olema; **Nearest Hospital:** San Rafael and Petaluma, both 20 miles (32 km) away; **Days/ Hours:** Park is always open; Visitor Center is generally open from 9 a.m. to 5 p.m.; **Holiday Closings:** Some facilities closed on Dec. 25; **Visitor attractions closed for seasons:** No; **Weather:** The ocean strongly influences the weather at Point Reyes. The ocean beaches are frequently foggy and windy enough to make warm clothing welcome. Throughout the summer these beaches experience more days of fog than sunshine, but spring and autumn can be mild and pleasant. The country east of Inverness Ridge, accessible by hiking trails, is free of summer fog, but it has heavy rains in winter and spring.

GENERAL INFORMATION: A privately operated tent and trailer campground is ½ mile (0.8 km) from Seashore Headquarters. Horses can be rented nearby. *Caution*! Pounding surf and rip currents make some Point Reyes beaches too dangerous for swimming, surfing, and wading. Steep cliffs are dangerous; walking near the edge or below invites catastrophe. No sleeping on beaches. No pets. Store food properly as raccoons and foxes are plentiful.

TRAVEL ACCESS: Bus: Golden Gate Transit provides regular service to Inverness and Point Reyes, CA; **Rail:** Amtrak provides service into Oakland, CA; **Air:** Major Airlines offer service into San Mateo Co., CA; **Other:** Taxi service available in San Rafael, CA, 20 miles

(32 km) distant. Bicycling is possible, but not recommended because of hazardous road conditions.

NEARBY FACILITIES & POINTS OF INTEREST: Hotel/Motel: Inverness Valley Inn, Inverness, CA, 415-669-7250 about 6 miles (10 km); Golden Hinde Boatel, Inverness, CA, 415-699-1389 about 6 miles (10 km); **Campgrounds:** Olema Ranch Campground, Olema, CA, 415-663-8001, 0.6 mile (1 km); Samuel P. Taylor State Park, Lagunitas, CA, 415-448-9897, 6 miles (10 km); Seashore Lodge, Olema, CA, 415-663-9000; **Parks, other points of interest:** Muir Woods National Monument, Audubon Canyon Ranch, Golden Gate National Recreation Area, Samuel P. Taylor State Park, Tomales Bay, and Mt. Tamalpais State Parks.

Redwood National Park
Crescent City, California   **SEE CLIMATABLE NO. 11**

MAILING ADDRESS: Superintendent, Redwood National Park, 1111 Second St., Crescent City, CA 95531 **Telephone:** 707-464-6101

DIRECTIONS: The Park can be reached by private auto and scheduled bus lines on US 101 south from the Oregon coast, north from Eureka and Arcata, and east via US 199 from Grants Pass and Medford, OR, and east via US 299 from Redding. Visitor Centers are in Hiouchi, Crescent City, and Orick.

The park contains coastal redwood forests with virgin groves of ancient trees, including the world's tallest. It includes 40 miles (64 km) of scenic Pacific coastline. Established by act of Congress on Oct. 2, 1968.

VISITOR ACTIVITIES: Driving, hiking, shoreline walks, photography, fishing, picnicking, bird- and wildflower-watching, interpretive services, camping; **Permits:** For fishing and backcountry; backcountry permits issued without charge at trailhead; Fishing license may be purchased at hardware and tackle shops. Licenses vary in length of validity and cost; **Fees:** $14 per night at campgrounds, $5 per vehicle for day-use picnic areas in State Parks; **Visitor facilities:** Hiking trails, exhibits, campgrounds, picnicking facilities are at a number of locations, including Enderts Beach Road, Lagoon Creek, and the State parks; **HANDICAPPED ACCESSIBILITY:** Some parts of Redwood Creek Trailhead, and Bald Hills Road are accessible. Wayside exhibits viewable from autos. Accessible restrooms at Lady Bird Johnson Grove, Lost Man Creek Picnic Area (assistance needed with wood-chip path), Requa Road, Lagoon Creek Picnic Area. Wheelchair accessible picnic tables at Vista Point (no restrooms). Crescent Beach is accessible; Overlook has no restrooms. Restrooms accessible at HQ, Redwood Information Center, Redwood Creek Trailhead. Hiouchi Ranger Station has ramps; **Any limitations on vehicle usage:** Trailers should not be taken off main roads because of weather, general road conditions, and steep grades; **Hiking trails:** Yes, on the shore and through redwood forests; **Backcountry:** Yes, inquire at any Ranger Station or write the above address. Redwood National Park has 3 primitive campsites located at Nickel Creek, DeMartin, and Flint Ridge (see map and guide); all are located along Coastal Trail; **Camping:** No, the National Park does not have developed campgrounds, but camping is available in the state parks and national forests. Each state park has a developed campground suitable for tents, campers, and small trailers up to 26 feet long. There are 349 campsites in the 3 state parks. Sites may be reserved through MISTIX, P.O. Box 85705, San Diego, CA 92138-5705, or call 800-444-7275. A reservation fee of $3.95 is charged. Information and forms are available at any California State Park Office. Reservations are helpful from July 1 to after Labor Day. Campsites not filled by reservation are assigned on a first-come, first-served basis. State Parks have fees for camping and day-use picnic areas. Interpretive programs are presented daily in the summer. National forests: Four campgrounds are off US 199 in Six Rivers National Forest. They contain 87 campsites, developed for tents, campers, and small trailers, and are about a 45-minute drive from US 101. Other campgrounds are also on CA 299 and 96 in Six Rivers, Klamath, and Trinity National Forests. These are 1- to 4-hour drives from US 101; **Other overnight accommodations on site:** No; **Meals served in the park:** No; **Food and supplies obtainable in the park:** No; **Food and supplies obtainable nearby:** Yes, at Crescent City, Eureka, Klamath, Orick; **Overnight accommodations:** A number of motels, private trailer parks, and campgrounds are along US 101 from Eureka, CA, to the Oregon line and on CA 299 and 96 and US 199 to the east; **First Aid available in park:** Yes; **Nearest Hospital:** Nearest hospital from Orick is Mad River Hospital, 300 Janes Road, Arcata, 30 miles (48 km) south of Orick on US 101. Hospital in Crescent City is Sutter Coast Hospital, 100A Crescent City; **Days/Hours:** Open 24 hours a day year-round; **Holiday Closings:** Ranger Stations closed on Dec. 25 and Jan. 1; **Visitor attractions closed for seasons:** Mill Creek Campground closes in winter; **Weather:** Summer, spring and fall visits are recommended. Winter is windy and rainy.

GENERAL INFORMATION: For current information on access to park lands, inquire at a Ranger Station or ask a Park Ranger. Shuttle bus service June-Sept. from Orick to Tall Trees Grove Trail, 2.7 miles (4.3 km). Grove includes tallest known tree in world. Fee: Adult: $3, children (15 and under) $1, Senior (62 and over) $1.50. See map and guide info on the new Redwood Information Center.

TRAVEL ACCESS: Bus: Greyhound provides daily service to Crescent City, Arcata; **Rail:** No; **Air:** Commuter and scheduled air lines to Crescent City and Arcata/Eureka. Rental cars available Medford, OR, and Arcata/Eureka, CA.

San Francisco Maritime National Historical Park
San Francisco, California

MAILING ADDRESS: San Francisco Maritime National Historical Park, Fort Mason, Building 201, San Francisco, CA 94123. Contact: Bill Thomas, Superintendent **Telephone:** 415-556-1659

Is now open to visitors.
The square-rigged sailing ship Balclutha, steam schooner Wapama, three-mastered schooner C.A. Thayer, walking-beam ferry Eureka, scow schooner Alma, steam tug Hercules, paddle wheel tug Eppleton Hall, and numerous smaller craft are preserved. Many of the ships are at the Hyde Street Pier in San Francisco. Not far from the pier is the National Maritime Museum with displays of ship models and historic artifacts. The J. Porter Shaw Library and extensive collections of ship plans and photographs are at the nearby Fort Mason Center, as is the World War II Liberty Ship SS Jeremiah O'Brien.
Established: June 27, 1988. Acreage: 29 total acres.

Santa Monica Mountains National Recreation Area
California

MAILING ADDRESS: Superintendent, Santa Monica Mountains National Recreation Area, Suite 140, 22900 Ventura Blvd., Woodland Hills, CA 91364 **Telephone:** 818-888-3770

DIRECTIONS: The Santa Monica Mountains National Recreation Area is bordered by

Griffith Park on the east and Los Posas Road on the west, Pacific Coast Hwy. to the south and the 101 Frwy. to the north. The area has many roads which allow accessibility. Some of the roads that run north-south are Topanga Canyon Blvd., Malibu Canyon Road, and Kanan-Dume Road. The main east-west roadway is Mulholland Highway. Set in a 155,000-acre boundary, there are 65,000 acres of federal, state, and local parklands. The Santa Monica Mountains National Recreation Area encompasses rolling hills, oak forests, canyons, streams, waterfalls, and beaches. The recreation area preserves Mediterranean chaparral ecosystems through cooperative land management between government agencies and the private sector. Bird watching, hiking, riding trails, picnicking, festivals, nature centers, and evening programs are available year round. Some of the parks are minutes away from Los Angeles, while others are more remote, providing isolated habitat for hawks, eagles, cougars, and bobcats. March and April are the best months to enjoy the colorful displays of wildflowers.

Many sites are handicapped accessible. To check on the degree of accessibility at each site call 818-888-3770.

Sequoia and Kings Canyon National Parks
Three Rivers, California   **SEE CLIMATABLE NO. 12**

MAILING ADDRESS: Superintendent, Sequoia and Kings Canyon National Parks, Three Rivers, CA 93271 **Telephone:** 209-565-3341

DIRECTIONS: Proceed east on CA 198 from CA 99 to the south entrance of Sequoia Park. To reach Kings Canyon Park, go east on CA 180 from CA 99 to the entrance. Generals Highway connects CA 198 and 180, and passes through Sequoia Park to the Grant Grove area, Kings Canyon Park, a 2-hour drive.

Two enormous canyons of the Kings River and the summit peaks of the High Sierra dominate Kings Canyon. Grant Grove, with its giant sequoias, is a detached section of the Park. Attractions at Sequoia include Mount Whitney, the highest mountain in the U.S. outside of Alaska, and giant sequoia groves. Kings Canyon established by act of Congress on Mar. 4, 1940; Sequoia established on Sept. 25, 1890.

VISITOR ACTIVITIES: Sightseeing, photography, camping, hiking, fishing, Nordic and downhill skiing, horseback riding, exhibits, campfire programs, guided nature walks; **Permits:** For wilderness use, (including wilderness camping); obtain permit at Park Headquarters or Visitor Centers. Fishing licenses from local stores; **Fees:** $5 entrance fee per car. Camping is $8 per night. Golden Eagle and Golden Age Passports accepted and available; **Visitor facilities:** Campgrounds, lodges, and cabins, cafeteria, dining rooms, camper supply stores, post offices, rental pack and saddle stock, ski trails; **HANDICAPPED ACCESSIBILITY:** Visitor Centers, campgrounds, restrooms, several paved trails, modified fountains, picnic tables, telephones; Chart available indicating curb cuts, steep grades, surfaces; **Any limitations on vehicle usage:** All vehicles are restricted to developed roadways. No vehicles are permitted on trails. Park roads are paved and steep with many turns; drive slowly, keep to the right, and use lower gears to avoid overheating the brakes and transmissions. Generals Hwy. between Hospital Rock and Giant Forest, 50 foot limit on vehicle/combination of vehicles. Trailers are limited to specific campgrounds; **Hiking trails:** Yes, 700 miles (1,190 km) of hiking from relatively easy to steep mountain trails. Elevations range from 2,000 to 14,495 feet; **Backcountry:** Yes, information available by contacting the Superintendent; **Camping:** Yes, campground reservations are required at Lodgepole campground only; other campgrounds are operated on a first-come, first-served basis. Reservations can be made at 1-800-452-1111 with Visa or MasterCard. Reservations at Lodgepole available Memorial Day to Labor Day. They can be made no more than 8 weeks in advance of day of visit. Most campgrounds and picnic areas have at least one campsite accessible to physically disabled; **Other overnight accom-**

modations on site: Yes, for reservations at cabins, contact Sequoia and Kings Canyon Guest Services, Sequoia National Park, CA 93262, phone 209-561-3314; **Meals served in the park:** Yes, at Giant Forest, Grant Grove, and Cedar Grove; **Food and supplies obtainable in the park:** Yes, at Giant Forest, Lodgepole, Grant Grove, and Cedar Grove; **Food and supplies obtainable nearby:** Yes, in Three Rivers, Visalia, Fresno; **Overnight accommodations:** Kings Canyon: Fresno, CA 180, 55 miles (88.5 km) from Grant Grove. Sequoia: Three Rivers, CA 198, 22 miles (35.2 km) from Giant Forest; Visalia, CA 198, 55 miles (88.5 km) from Giant Forest; **First Aid available in park:** Yes; **Nearest Hospital:** Kings Canyon: Fresno, CA, CA 180, 55 miles (88.5 km) from Grant Grove. Sequoia: Exeter, CA, CA 198, 46 miles (73.6 km) from Giant Forest; **Days/Hours:** Parks open all year; **Holiday Closings:** No; **Visitor attractions closed for seasons:** Some activities are closed during the winter snow period. The Generals Highway between Lodgepole and Grant Grove is open year-round, but may be closed during winter months for several days at a time due to heavy snow; **Weather:** Warm mountain climate with cool nights in summer; snow and relatively severe mountain winters.

GENERAL INFORMATION: *For Your Safety—Drowning* is the leading cause of fatalities. Extreme caution is advised around rivers, especially in the spring and early summer when they are swift, deep, and very cold. *Lightning* is dangerous on exposed peaks. *Injuries from falling* are best prevented by staying away from steep places, wearing proper footgear, and hiking in the company of others. *Respiratory or circulatory problems* may be aggravated at higher elevations. *Bears and other wildlife,* though sometimes tame in appearance, are wild and could be dangerous. Regulations that prohibit feeding or aggravating animals are enforced for your safety, as well as for the benefit of the animals.

TRAVEL ACCESS: Bus: Tulare County Transit operates twice-weekly service between Three Rivers and Visalia (Does not enter the park); **Rail:** Amtrak service into Hanford; **Air:** Nearest access to Fresno and Visalia.

Whiskeytown-Shasta-Trinity National Recreation Area
Whiskeytown, California

MAILING ADDRESS: Superintendent, Whiskeytown-Shasta-Trinity National Recreation Area, P.O. Box 188, Whiskeytown, CA 96095 **Telephone:** 916-241-6584

DIRECTIONS: The main Visitor Center is Overlook Information Station, located at the intersection of CA 299 and Kennedy Memorial Drive.
Whiskeytown Lake, formed by a dam on Clear Creek in a scenic mountain region, is an excellent resource for water-related recreation. The other two units are administered by the U.S. Forest Service. Created by an act of Congress on Nov. 8, 1965.

VISITOR ACTIVITIES: Whiskeytown Lake is excellent for most water-related activities, including swimming, scuba diving, water skiing, boating, and fishing. Picnicking, camping backcountry, hunting, interpretive programs, and horseback riding are also popular; **Permits:** Free backcountry permits are available at headquarters; **Fees:** Camping fee at Oak Bottom for tent sites or recreational vehicles, year round; **Visitor facilities:** Historical museum at Shasta, self-guiding trail, picnic area, campground, bathhouse, boat ramp and rentals, food and supplies, hiking and horse trails; **HANDICAPPED ACCESSIBILITY:** Most of the Park is accessible; **Any limitations on vehicle usage:** Vehicles are restricted to designated roadways; **Hiking trails:** Yes, 3.7 miles (5.9 km) of frontcountry hiking trails; **Backcountry:** Yes, information can be obtained from Visitor Center and headquarters;

Camping: Yes, reservations available for campsites through Ticketron (fees vary according to seasons and vehicles); **Other overnight accommodations on site:** No; **Meals served in the park:** Yes, snack bars at Oak Bottom and Brandy Creek during summer season; **Food and supplies obtainable in the park:** Yes, snack bars at Oak Bottom Marina and Whiskeytown Store, ¼ mile (.4 km) off CA 299 during summer season; **Food and supplies obtainable nearby:** Yes, at Redding, CA, 8 miles (12.9 km) east of Overlook Information Station; **Overnight accommodations:** Redding, CA 299, 8 miles (12.9 km) east of Overlook Information Station; **First Aid available in park:** Yes; **Nearest Hospital:** Redding, CA 299, 8 miles (12.9 km) east; **Days/Hours:** Open all year, camping and boating hours are unlimited, swimming beaches close at 11 p.m. during the summer; **Holiday Closings:** No; **Visitor attractions closed for seasons:** No.

GENERAL INFORMATION: Visitors should inquire at Overlook Information Station or Headquarters for information about the recreation area and programs. The most prominent landmark of the region is 6,209-foot Shasta Bally, rising in the midst of rolling woodlands and clear-flowing streams. The summit may be reached on foot and by four-wheel drive auto.

NEARBY FACILITIES & POINTS OF INTEREST: Parks, other points of interest: Redwoods National Park, Lassen Volcanic National Park, Lava Beds National Monument, Shasta State Historic Park.

Yosemite National Park
Yosemite National Park, California   **SEE CLIMATABLE NO. 9**

MAILING ADDRESS: Superintendent, P.O. Box 577, Yosemite National Park, CA 95389 **Telephone:** 209-372-0200

DIRECTIONS: Access to Yosemite is via State Route 140 and 120 eastbound from Merced and Manteca; State Route 41 northbound from Fresno; State Route 120 westbound from Lee

Vining (closed in winter).

Granite peaks and domes rise high above broad meadows in the heart of the Sierra Nevada Mountains; groves of giant sequoias dwarf other trees and wildflowers; and mountains, lakes, and waterfalls, including the Nation's highest, are found here. Established by act of Congress on Oct. 1, 1890.

VISITOR ACTIVITIES: Camping, hiking, climbing, horseback riding, fishing, swimming, rafting, boating (no motors), alpine and cross-country skiing, rock climbing, backpacking, bus tours, walks, talks, cultural demonstrations, self-guiding tours, interpretive exhibits, natural history seminars; **Permits:** Backcountry wilderness permits can be obtained by written application to Backcountry Office between Feb. 1 and May 31, or in person at Wawona, Yosemite Valley, Big Oak Flat Entrance, or Tuolomne Meadows; fishing licenses available in person only; **Fees:** Daily vehicle entrance fee is $5; daily campground use fee varies from $2 to $12, depending on facilities; Golden Eagle and Golden Age Passports accepted and available; **Visitor facilities:** Individual and group campgrounds, picnic areas, Visitor Centers, showers, laundromat, repair garage, service stations, food service, accommodations, alpine and nordic ski schools, mountaineering school, recreational equipment rental, scheduled transportation and interpretive bus tours; **HANDICAPPED ACCESSIBILITY:** Facilities and activities available to and usable by the disabled upon request; **Any limitations on vehicle usage:** All vehicles are required to stay on surfaced roads. Commercial vehicles are allowed only on Park business; commercial buses require authorization from NPS concessions management office; **Hiking trails:** Yes, 800 miles (1,280 km) of trails; **Backcountry:** Yes, information can be obtained at all Ranger Stations, Visitor Centers, and wilderness permit kiosks. Visitors planning trips during summer holiday weekends should reserve wilderness permits in advance. Contact the Park's Backcountry Office well in advance; **Camping:** Yes, camping is available year-round on a first-come, first-served basis. The 5 Yosemite Valley Campgrounds are on the Ticketron reservation system year-round. Reservations can be made 8 weeks in advance at Ticketron outlets nationwide, or by writing to Ticketron Reservations Offices. Group campsites are available during the summer season and must be reserved in advance; the Yosemite Valley Group Camp is reservable through Ticketron up to 12 weeks in advance. Telephone reservations made at (800) 452-1111 for U.S. callers; (312) 902-1919 for foreign callers; **Other overnight accommodations on site:** Yes, at Yosemite Valley, White Wolf, Wawona, Tuolumne Meadows, and the 5 High Sierra Camps. Reservations are advised at all times for accommodations in hotels, lodges, and cabins. Contact Yosemite Park and Curry Company, 5410 E. Home, Fresno, CA 93727, phone 209-252-4848; **Meals served in the park:** Yes, at Yosemite Valley, Wawona, White Wolf, Tuolumne Meadows, and the 5 High Sierra Camps; **Food and supplies obtainable in the park:** Yes, Yosemite Valley, Wawona, White Wolf, Tuolumne Meadows, and the 5 High Sierra Camps; **Food and supplies obtainable nearby:** Yes, in Lee Vining, Groveland, El Portal, Wawona, Oakhurst, Fish Camp, Mariposa; **Overnight accommodations:** Lee Vining, Groveland, El Portal, Oakhurst, Fish Camp, Mariposa; **First Aid available in park:** Yes, Yosemite Medical Group provides 24-hour emergency outpatient care; **Nearest Hospital:** Merced, Fresno, Sonora, Bridgeport, and Mariposa; **Days/Hours:** Open 24 hours a day year-round; **Holiday Closings:** No; **Visitor attractions closed for seasons:** Mariposa Grove road open all year except for intermittent winter closures, Tuolumne Grove, Glacier Point Road, Tioga Road closed from mid-Nov. to late May; **Weather:** Cool summers above 5000 feet, periodic late summer thunderstorms and snow flurries in high elevations.

GENERAL INFORMATION: Life and death emergency only telephone 9-1-1. For weather and road conditions, telephone 209-372-4605. For general park information, call 209-372-0264. To report structural and wildland fires, telephone: Yosemite Valley— 9-1-1; Wawona—9-1-1; El Portal—209-379-2333. To report emergencies within the Park, dial toll-free "9-1-1." Shuttlebus service is available year-round in Yosemite Valley. For illustrated publications describing natural features write to Yosemite Association, P.O. Box 230, El Portal, CA 95318, or stop at a Visitor Center.

TRAVEL ACCESS: Bus: VIA and Yosemite Grey Line Tours provides daily service from Merced; **Rail:** Amtrak provides daily service to Merced, Fresno, and Madera. Connecting bus service by Yosemite Grey Line Tours also provides connecting service from Fresno airport, Amtrak and Greyhound station to Yosemite, Parlor Car, and Yosemite Express and Greyhound to Merced (all year); **Air:** West Air Commuter, United, Pacific Southwest Airlines (PSA), Western provide daily service to Fresno. West Air serves Merced. Connecting bus service by VIA and California Yosemite Tours; **Other:** Rental cars are available in Fresno and Merced.

Colorado

ROCKY MOUNTAIN NATIONAL PARK

DINOSAUR NATIONAL MONUMENT

FLORISSANT FOSSIL BEDS NATIONAL MONUMENT

COLORADO NATIONAL MONUMENT

BLACK CANYON OF THE GUNNISON NATIONAL MONUMENT

CURECANTI NATIONAL RECREATION AREA

HOVENWEEP NATIONAL MONUMENT

YUCCA HOUSE NATIONAL MONUMENT

MESA VERDE NATIONAL PARK

Denver

BENT'S OLD FORT NATIONAL HISTORIC SITE

GREAT SAND DUNES NATIONAL MONUMENT

Bent's Old Fort National Historic Site
La Junta, Colorado

MAILING ADDRESS: Superintendent, Bent's Old Fort National Historic Site, 35110 Highway 194 East, La Junta, CO 81050 **Telephone:** 719-384-2596

DIRECTIONS: The site is 8 miles (13 km) east of La Junta and 15 miles (24 km) west of Las Animas on CO 194.

As a principal crossroads of civilization on the Santa Fe Trail in the early 1800s and a trading post for Indians, the Fort became the center of a vast fur-trading empire in the west. Authorized for addition to the National Park System on June 3, 1960. Fort reconstructed in 1975-76.

VISITOR ACTIVITIES: Interpretive and audiovisual program, guided tours, living history program; **Permits:** No; **Fees:** Yes; Visitor entrance fee $3 per vehicle; pedestrian, bicycle, and commercial bus passengers $1; **Visitor facilities:** Parking area is 600 yards from the fort. Transportation available for the elderly and handicapped, 8 a.m. to 4:30 p.m. daily. Restrooms are available, picnic area (reservations for groups over 15); **HANDICAPPED ACCESSIBILITY:** 2 parking spaces available, paved trail of 600 yds from parking area to the Fort; transportation available from parking area to the Fort; closed-captioned film; restrooms and drinking fountain; special tours available upon request; **Any limitations on vehicle usage:** Visitor vehicles are restricted to the parking lot; **Hiking trails:** No; **Backcountry:** No; **Camping:** No; **Other overnight accommodations on site:** No; **Meals served in the park:** No; **Food and supplies obtainable in the park:** No; **Food and supplies obtainable nearby:** Yes, in La Junta; **Overnight accommodations:** La Junta, CO 194, 8 miles (13 km) west; **First Aid available in park:** Yes; **Nearest Hospital:** La Junta, CO 194, 8 miles (13 km) west; **Days/Hours:** Open daily 8 a.m. to 4:30 p.m. from Sept. through May; 8 a.m. to 6 p.m. Memorial Day through Labor Day; **Holiday Closings:** Thanksgiving, Dec. 25, Jan. 1; **Visitor attractions closed for seasons:** No.

GENERAL INFORMATION: *For Your Safety*—Watch your step on the steep stairways. Don't let children climb on the walls or run on the upper gallery; there are no handrails. Please do not annoy the animals.

TRAVEL ACCESS: Bus: Trailways provides daily service to La Junta, CO; Daily East & West; **Rail:** Amtrak provides daily service to La Junta, CO; **Air:** Charter and Private aircraft accommodated at La Junta, CO.

NEARBY FACILITIES & POINTS OF INTEREST: Campgrounds: KOA, 26680 Highway 50 W. La Junta, CO, 303-384-9817, 10 miles (16 km) from Park; **Parks, other points of interest:** Koshare Indian Museum, 18th & Santa Fe, La Junta, CO, 303-384-4801, 8 miles (12.8 km) from Park.

Black Canyon of the Gunnison National Monument
Montrose, Colorado

MAILING ADDRESS: Superintendent, Black Canyon of the Gunnison National Monument, 2233 East Main, Montrose, CO 81401 **Telephone:** 303-249-7036

DIRECTIONS: You can drive both rims of the Canyon. The South Rim is open to traffic all year; the North is closed to traffic in winter. From Montrose, CO, the distance to the South Rim entrance is 11 miles (18 km)—6 miles (9.7 km) east via US 50 and 5 miles (8 km) north over a hard-surfaced road. You can reach the North Rim from CO 92, just east of Crawford over a 14-mile (22.5 km) graded road. Information is available at Park Headquarters on Highway 50 East at 2233 East Main, or during the season, at the South Rim Visitor Center or North Rim Ranger Office.
　　Shadowed depths of this sheer-walled canyon accentuate the darkness of ancient rocks of obscure origin. Created by President Proclamation on Mar. 2, 1933.

VISITOR ACTIVITIES: Camping, fishing, hiking, wildlife- and bird-watching, interpretive exhibits; **Permits:** State fishing license, free backcountry permit are required. Fishing license available from any sporting goods store in Montrose, backcountry permit from a Park Ranger no more than 24 hours in advance of the trip; **Fees:** Yes, camping fee is $6 per site, 7 people per site. Golden Eagle and Golden Age Passports accepted and available. $3 per car entrance fee; **Visitor facilities:** Campgrounds, snack bar, souvenir stand, picnic areas, restrooms and overlooks (all closed in winter); **Any limitations on vehicle usage:** All vehicles must stay on established roadways; **Hiking trails:** Yes, trails to overlooks and nature trails; **Backcountry:** Yes, you should register at the Ranger Station before starting any inner canyon activity; **Camping:** Yes, no reservations for the two campgrounds/one on each rim; **Other overnight accommodations on site:** No; **Meals served in the park:** Light snacks are available on the South Rim; **Food and supplies obtainable in the park:** Yes; **Food and supplies obtainable nearby:** Yes, in Montrose, US 50, 11 miles (18 km); **Overnight accommodations:** US 50, 11 miles (18 km); **First Aid available in park:** Yes, but only in season; **Nearest Hospital:** Montrose, US 50 11 miles (18 km); **Days/Hours:** Open 24 hours a day, but occasionally closed in winter due to heavy snow; **Visitor attractions closed for season:** Gunnison Point Visitor Center open intermittently in winter. Rim House open only from mid-May through Sept.; **Weather:** Extremely low temperatures and heavy snows in winter; travel not advised.

GENERAL INFORMATION: *For Your Safety*—Stay on the trails! View the canyon from behind the railings at the designated overlooks. *Fire* is Black Canyon's greatest peril. Fires are permitted only in the fireplaces in the campground. Be sure your fire is out. All pets must be kept on a leash. No pets are permitted in the inner canyon or in the wilderness areas.

TRAVEL ACCESS: Bus: No bus service of any kind to the monument but regular service to Montrose from other Colorado towns; **Rail:** No; **Air:** United Express and Continental Express Airlines provide daily service to town of Montrose—12 miles (19.2 km) from Park.

Colorado National Monument
Fruita, Colorado

MAILING ADDRESS: Superintendent, Colorado National Monument, Fruita, CO 81521 **Telephone:** 303-858-3617

DIRECTIONS: The Monument is easily accessible by highway: US 6, 50, and I-70 to Grand Junction; and US 6, 50, and I-70 to Fruita. The Monument is 4 miles (6.4 km) west of Grand Junction and 2.5 miles (4 km) south of Fruita, CO. Both entrances directly accessible via Colorado Hwy 340.

Sheer-walled canyons, towering monoliths, and strange formations reflect the action of time and weather on colorful sandstone. Created by Presidential Proclamation on May 24, 1911.

VISITOR ACTIVITIES: Exhibits, audiovisual programs, auto tours, interpretive talks, nature walks, campfire programs, camping, picnicking, backcountry, hiking, climbing, horseback riding, cycling, cross-country skiing; **Permits:** Suggested for backcountry, can be obtained at Ranger Stations; **Fees:** $3 entrance fee per single-visit carload, $1 per person for commercial tours. Golden Age, Golden Access, and Golden Eagle Passports accepted and available. Camping is $7 per night per site or $3.50 for Golden Age and Golden Access; **Visitor facilities:** Visitor Center, parking, campground, picnic areas, hiking trails, new self-guiding nature trail begins at Visitor Center; **HANDICAPPED ACCESSIBILITY:** Restrooms, Visitor Center; 3 of 16 overlooks along 23-mile (36.8-km) scenic drive have now been modified to permit wheelchair access; **Any limitations on vehicle usage:** No off-road use, including mountain bikes; **Hiking trails:** Yes, 21 miles (34 km) of constructed trails, self-guiding nature walks; **Backcountry:** Yes, write or call for more information; **Camping:** Yes, no reservations for campgrounds; **Other overnight accommodations on site:** No; **Meals served in the park:** No; **Food and supplies obtainable in the park:** No; **Food and supplies obtaina-**

ble nearby: Yes, Grand Junction, Fruita, and Glade Park Store; **Overnight accommodations:** Grand Junction 4 miles (6.4 km) east; Fruita, 3 miles (5.6 km) north; **First Aid available in park:** Yes; **Nearest Hospital:** Fruita, 2.5 miles (4 km) north; Grand Junction, 4 miles (6.4 km) east; **Days/Hours:** Park is open 24 hours a day. Visitor Center open from 8 a.m. to 4:30 p.m., with extended hours in summer; **Holiday Closings:** Reduced hours at the Visitor Center on Dec. 25; **Visitor attractions closed for seasons;** No, but snow may hamper access; **Weather:** Summers are hot and dry; winters are generally cool and snowy.

GENERAL INFORMATION: *For Your Safety*—Do not touch, feed, or harm the animals. Do not hike or climb alone. Register for difficult and technical climbs.

TRAVEL ACCESS: Bus: Continental Trailways and Greyhound provide daily service to Grand Junction/Fruita; **Rail:** Amtrak provides service to Grand Junction every other day; **Air:** American West, Continental, United Express, and Sky West Airlines have daily service to Grand Junction.

NEARBY FACILITIES & POINTS OF INTEREST: Campgrounds: Fruita Junction RV Park, 607 Highway 340, Fruita, CO 303-858-3155.

Curecanti National Recreation Area
Gunnison, Colorado

MAILING ADDRESS: Superintendent, Curecanti National Recreation Area, 102 Elk Creek, Gunnison, CO 81230 **Telephone:** 303-641-2337

DIRECTIONS: The Elk Creek Visitor Center is 16 miles (25 km) west of Gunnison via US 50, on Blue Mesa Lake. A Visitor Center and Narrow Gauge Railroad exhibit is also available at the Cimarron Area, 20 miles (32 km) east of Montrose.

Beautiful fiord-like Crystal Lake and Morrow Point Lake are encompassed by this 42,000-acre Colorado High Country recreation area as well as Blue Mesa Lake, the largest lake in CO. Eleven miles (17.6 km) of the Gunnison River and numerous tributary streams provide many additional recreational opportunities.

VISITOR ACTIVITIES: Boating, fishing, swimming, water skiing, windsurfing, campfire programs, camping, picnicking, hunting, snowmobiling, naturalist activities, backcountry camping, ice fishing, interpretive exhibits, boat tours of Morrow Point Lake (call 303-641-0406 for information, fees, and schedules); **Permits:** Fishing requires a Colorado license available from the Colorado Division of Wildlife Office or local sporting goods stores. Licenses vary in length of validity and cost; **Fees:** Elk Creek, Lake Fork, Cimarron $8 night/site; Red Creek, Dry Gulch, Ponderosa, East Portal and Stevens Creek $7 night/site; **Visitor facilities:** Parking, campgrounds, launching ramps, scenic overlooks, two marinas, restaurant, showers, boat and slip rentals, grocery store, fish observation pond, restrooms, hiking trails, cross-country ski routes, amphitheater, telephones, snowmobile route; **HANDICAPPED ACCESSIBILITY:** Parking, camping, Visitor Centers, restrooms and amphitheaters; **Any limitations on vehicle usage:** Vehicles are restricted to designated roadways; **Hiking trails:** Yes; **Backcountry:** Yes, boat in campsites on Blue Mesa, Morrow Pt., and Crystal Lakes; **Camping:** Yes, no reservations available for campgrounds except for East Elk Creek group camping area. **Other overnight accommodations on site:** No; **Meals served in the park:** Yes, restaurant at Elk Creek Marina; **Food and supplies obtainable in the park:** Yes, some groceries available at the Elk Creek and Lake Fork Marinas; **Food and supplies obtainable nearby:** Yes, in Gunnison and Montrose; **Overnight accommodations:** Gunnison and Montrose area; **First Aid available in park:** Yes; **Nearest Hospital:** Gunnison, US 50, 16 miles (25.7 km) east of the Elk Creek Headquarters Area; Montrose, US 50, 20 miles (32.2 km) west of Cimarron; **Days/Hours:** Open 24 hours a day, year-round; **Holiday Closings:** No; **Visitor attractions closed for seasons:** Campgrounds with limited facilities are kept open until closed by snow; **Weather:** Winter temperatures drop as low as $-35°F$ at night. Summer daytime highs may reach the mid 90s, (average temperature 83°F) with around upper 30s to 40s at night.

GENERAL INFORMATION: There are no designated areas for swimming and no lifeguards. Watch out for precipitous shorelines, submerged rocks, and cold water. Summer afternoon winds are common.

TRAVEL ACCESS: Bus: Continental Trailways stops in Gunnison 16 miles (25.6 km) east of Park Headquarters—No bus service to Park; **Rail:** No; **Air:** Airport is in Gunnison. Continental and United Express have regular daily flights. Charter service is available to other areas.

NEARBY FACILITIES & POINTS OF INTEREST: Parks, other points of interest: Black Canyon of the Gunnison National Monument, Rocky Mountain National Park, Dinosaur National Monument, Mesa Verde National Park, Great Sand Dunes National Monument, Florissant Fossil Beds National Monument.

Dinosaur National Monument
Dinosaur, Colorado

MAILING ADDRESS: Superintendent, Dinosaur National Monument, P.O. Box 210, Dinosaur, CO 81610 **Telephone:** 303-374-2216

DIRECTIONS: The Dinosaur Quarry Visitor Center: 13 miles (21 km) east of Vernal, UT, to Jensen, UT, on US 40; then 7 miles (11.3 km) north to Quarry on UT 149. Headquarters is 2 miles (3 km) east of Dinosaur, CO on US 40 37 miles (60 km) east of Vernal, UT, on US 40.
   The quarry contains fossil remains of dinosaurs and other ancient animals. Spectacular canyons were cut by the Green and Yampa Rivers through upfolded mountains. Created by Presidential Proclamation on Oct. 4, 1915.

VISITOR ACTIVITIES: Dinosaur fossil displays, talks, programs (summers only), walking, hiking, picnicking, camping, backcountry driving, fishing, white-water boating, wildflower-watching; **Permits:** For fishing, white-water boating, and backcountry hiking. For boating apply between Dec. 1 and Jan. 15 for the following season; **Fees:** $5 fee to enter park on Quarry Road; $6 per night camping fee; **Visitor facilities:** Campgrounds, nature walks, and trails, concession-operated boat trips, interpretive programs, parking and restrooms at Visitor Center, telephones, boat ramp; **HANDICAPPED ACCESSIBILITY:** Monument Headquarters Visitor Center is accessible. Dinosaur Quarry is not accessible (very steep ramp, restrooms not accessible); **Any limitations on vehicle usage:** Some backcountry roads require a high clearance vehicle and are impassable when wet, inquire at the Visitor Center. All visitors use a shuttlebus to the quarry from Memorial Day to Labor Day; **Hiking trails:** Yes, short nature walks at Monument Headquarters, Plug Hat and Harpers Corner and self-guided nature trails at Split Mountain Campground and Lodore; **Backcountry:** Yes, write Park Superintendent in advance, or see any Ranger on arrival. Drinking water in the backcountry is scarce; **Camping:** Yes, no reservations available for campsites; **Other overnight accommodations on site:** No; **Meals served in the park:** No; **Food and supplies ob-**

tainable in the park: No; **Food and supplies obtainable nearby:** Yes, in Dinosaur, Rangely, and Craig, CO; Vernal and Jensen, UT; **Overnight accommodations:** Dinosaur, Rangely, and Craig, CO; Vernal and Jensen, UT; **First Aid available in park:** In emergency; **Nearest Hospital:** Vernal, US 40, 21 miles (33.8 km); Rangely, CO, via CO 64; **Days/ Hours:** Visitor Center open 8 a.m.-4:30 p.m. Oct. through May, 8 a.m.-7 p.m. Memorial Day through Labor Day; **Holiday Closings:** Thanksgiving, Dec. 25, and Jan. 1; **Visitor attractions closed for seasons:** Backcountry and canyon road closed by snow; **Weather:** Summer days 90°, nights 60°; spring and fall are mild with cool nights. Winters are cold with 60 days of snow on ground. Low humidity all year.

GENERAL INFORMATION: *For Your Safety*—Most of the accidents at Dinosaur occur while people are boating the rivers or while climbing or hiking in the rugged canyon areas. For your benefit, it is suggested that you check with a Park Ranger about your plans and about local road conditions.

TRAVEL ACCESS: Bus: Greyhound Lines provides service to Dinosaur, CO, and to Jensen and Vernal, UT; **Rail:** No; **Air:** Sky West from Salt Lake City, UT; **Other:** Hertz Rent-A-Car available in Vernal, UT.

NEARBY FACILITIES & POINTS OF INTEREST: Parks, other points of interest: Ashley National Forest/Flaming Gorge National Recreation Area 50 miles (80 km) north of Vernal on UT 44. Utah Field House of Natural History State Park in Vernal, UT.

Florissant Fossil Beds National Monument
Florissant, Colorado

MAILING ADDRESS: Superintendent, Florissant Fossil Beds National Monument, P.O. Box 185, Florissant, CO 80816 **Telephone:** 719-748-3253 or 748-3051

DIRECTIONS: The Park can be reached by taking US 24 west from Colorado Springs to the small village of Florissant, 35 miles (56 km) away. At the Village Center, turn south toward Cripple Creek on the unpaved Teller County Road #1. The Visitor Center is 2½ miles (4 km) from Florissant.
　　The finest of fossil insects, seeds, and leaves of the eocene epoch are preserved here in remarkable detail. An unusual display of standing petrified Sequoia stumps is also here. Authorized for addition to the National Park System on Aug. 20, 1969.

VISITOR ACTIVITIES: Interpretive exhibits and walks, hiking, picnicking, horseback riding, cross-country skiing; **Permits:** No; **Fees:** $1 per person; **Visitor facilities:** Parking and restrooms at Visitor Center, picnic areas, trails, exhibits; **HANDICAPPED ACCESSIBILITY:** Parking, restroom, 1 trail; **Any limitations on vehicle usage:** Motor vehicles are restricted to designated roadways; **Hiking trails:** Yes, a one-half mile (.8 km) and one mile (1.6 km) self-guided nature walk around some of the largest petrified Sequoia stumps in the world, plus 10 additional miles (16 km) of backcountry trails; **Camping:** No; **Other overnight accommodations on site:** No, there are several well-marked public campgrounds in the surrounding Pike National Forest; **Meals served in the park:** No; **Food and supplies obtainable in the park:** No; **Food and supplies obtainable nearby:** Yes, in Woodland Park, Divide, Florissant, Lake George, and Cripple Creek; **Overnight accommodations:** Woodland Park, Divide, Florissant, Lake George, and Cripple Creek; **First Aid available in park:** Yes; **Nearest Hospital:** Colorado Springs, 35 miles (56 km) east on US 24; **Days/Hours:** Open daily from 8 a.m. to 4:30 p.m., until 7 p.m. in summer; **Holiday Closings:** Thanksgiving, Dec. 25, and Jan. 1; **Weather:** Heavy snow in winter may occasionally cause hazardous driving.

GENERAL INFORMATION: *WARNING:* Ticks spreading Colorado tick fever and Rocky Mountain spotted fever are here in spring and early summer. If you are hiking, tuck your pant legs inside your socks and check yourself for ticks periodically. If you have any imbedded ticks, contact a Ranger or physician.

TRAVEL ACCESS: Bus: No; **Rail:** No; **Air:** Major airlines provide daily service through Colo. Springs Municipal Airport.

NEARBY FACILITIES & POINTS OF INTEREST: Campgrounds: Lake George, Pikes Peak National Forest; **Parks, other points of interest:** Cripple Creek Historic District, Pikes Peak, Air Force Academy, Garden of the Gods, Bear Creek Nature Center, White House Ranch.

Great Sand Dunes National Monument
Mosca, Colorado

MAILING ADDRESS: Superintendent, 11500 Highway 160, Great Sand Dunes National Monument, Mosca, CO 81146 **Telephone:** 719-378-2312

DIRECTIONS: The Visitor Center is on Hwy 150, 38 miles (60.8 km) northeast of Alamosa, CO. Write or phone ahead for detailed information on facilities and activities.
The tallest dunes in North America, these dunes were deposited over thousands of years by southwesterly winds blowing toward the passes of the lofty Sangre de Cristo Mountains. Established by Executive Proclamation on Mar. 17, 1932.

VISITOR ACTIVITIES: Hiking, nature walks, dune climbing, camping, picnicking, 4-wheel drive auto tours, snowshoeing, cross-country skiing, interpretive exhibits, naturalist activities from June through Aug.; **Permits:** Yes, free backcountry permits available at the Visitor Center; **Fees:** $3 per vehicle entrance fee; hikers, bikers, and bus passengers are admitted for $1 per day. Golden Age and Golden Eagle Passports are accepted and available. $8 per vehicle per night charge for developed campsites in the summer. Campground open all year. Entrance fees are collected from May through Sept.; **Visitor facilities:** Visitor Center, air pump, drinking water, picnic area, campground with restrooms, fire grates, picnic tables, 4-wheel drive road, group campsites; **HANDICAPPED ACCESSIBILITY:** Parking at Visitor Center, Dunes, and campground; all restrooms; **Any limitations on vehicle usage:** All motor vehicles and their operators must be licensed on all roads within the Monument. The Medano Pass Primitive Road is restricted to 4-wheel drive vehicles and licensed trail bikes. Off-road travel or driving on the dunes is prohibited; **Hiking trails:** Yes, trails vary in length and degree of difficulty; **Backcountry:** Yes, contact the Park for information. Permits and maps are available at the Visitor Center; **Camping:** Yes, no reservations available for individual campsites. Group camping may be arranged in advance by calling or writing; **Other overnight accommodations on site:** No; **Meals served in the park:** No; **Food and supplies obtainable in the park:** No; **Food and supplies obtainable nearby:** Yes, groceries, snacks, gasoline, showers, campground, gifts, and hookups are located 4 miles (6.4 km) south of the entrance station, food and supplies open most months with reduced winter services; **Overnight accommodations:** Alamosa, 38 miles (60.8 km); Salida, 90 miles (145 km); and Ft. Garland, 29 miles (46.7 km); **First Aid available in park:** Yes; **Nearest Hospital:** Alamosa, Hwy 160, 38 miles (60.8 km); **Days/Hours:** Open 24 hours a day year-round; **Holiday Closings:** Visitor Center closed federal holidays in winter.

GENERAL INFORMATION: Hiking on the dunes is most pleasant early and late in the day. Surface temperatures in the summer can reach 140°F at midday—hot enough to blister your feet. Shoes should be worn or carried. Most visitors begin their walk on the dunes from the picnic area, choosing their own routes because there are no trails on the dunes. A walk to the top and back requires about 1½ hours.

Hovenweep National Monument
(near) Cortez, Colorado

MAILING ADDRESS: Superintendent, Hovenweep National Monument, McElmo Rt., Cortez, CO 81321 **Telephone:** 303-529-4465

DIRECTIONS: 45 miles (72 km) from Cortez: travel south on US 666/160 to County Road G (the airport road), then follow the Hovenweep signs; includes approximately 19 miles (30.4 km) of graded gravel road.

Pre-Columbian Indians built these pueblos, remarkable for the numerous standing towers and preserved in six separate units in Colorado and Utah as a national monument. Authorized for addition to the National Park System on Mar. 2, 1923.

VISITOR ACTIVITIES: Self-guiding trails, camping, picnicking, hiking; **Permits:** No; **Fees:** No entrance fee. Camping fee is $5 per night, $2.50 with Golden Age/Access Passport; **Visitor facilities:** Visitor Center, picnic area, campground, trails, comfort station; **HANDICAPPED ACCESSIBILITY:** Visitor Center, restrooms, picnic tables. Trails to the ruins are not accessible; **Any limitations on vehicle usage:** Vehicles (including bicycles) are restricted to roadways. The graded dirt roads can become muddy and sometimes impassable during or following storms. Inquire locally during stormy weather regarding road conditions; **Hiking trails:** Yes, self-guiding trails lead through the prehistoric ruins of Square Tower Group; **Backcountry:** No; **Camping:** Yes, no reservations available for the modern campground near the Ranger Station, which is open all year (limited facilities in winter). Camping supplies, firewood, and gasoline are not available at the Monument; **Other overnight accommodations on site:** No; **Meals served in the park:** No; **Food and supplies obtainable in the park:** No; **Food and supplies obtainable nearby:** Yes, Hatch Trading Post, 16 miles (26 km) west, Ismay Trading Post, 14 miles (22.5 km) southeast, and Aneth, 20 miles (32 km) southwest; **Overnight accommodations:** Cortez, CO, 46 miles (73.6 km), Bluff, UT, 40 miles (64 km), Blanding, UT, 45 miles (72 km); **First Aid available in park:** Yes; **Nearest Hospital:** Cortez, CO, 46 miles (73.6 km); **Days/Hours:** The Monument is open from 8 a.m. to 5 p.m. year-round; **Holiday Closings:** No; **Weather:** Winter temperatures average in the mid 30's and 40's during the day and the teens overnight. Summer temperatures are in the mid 90's with night time lows in the mid 50's and 60's.

GENERAL INFORMATION: During late May and June biting gnats are plentiful. The trails are primitive, so wear good hiking shoes.

TRAVEL ACCESS: Bus: No; **Rail:** No; **Air:** Mesa Airlines/United Express provides daily service to Cortez from Denver.

NEARBY FACILITIES & POINTS OF INTEREST: Parks, other points of interest: Mesa Verde National Park, Natural Bridges National Monument, Anasazi Heritage Center.

Mesa Verde National Park
Mesa Verde National Park, CO   **SEE CLIMATABLE NO. 13**

MAILING ADDRESS: Superintendent, Mesa Verda National Park, Mesa Verde National Park, CO 81330 **Telephone:** 303-529-4465

DIRECTIONS: To get the most out of your visit, you should go first to either the Far View Visitor Center (open only in summer from 8 a.m. to 5 p.m.) or the Chapin Mesa Museum (open from 8 a.m. to 6:30 p.m. in summer and 8 a.m. to 5 p.m. the rest of the year). The Park entrance is midway between Cortez and Mancos on US 160. It is 21 miles (33.6 km) from the entrance to the museum and the Chapin Mesa ruins area. The Morefield Campground is 4 miles (6.4 km) from the entrance. The Far View Visitor Center is 15 miles (24 km) away. The narrow, mountainous road has sharp curves and steep grades. Depending on traffic and weather conditions, allow at least 45 minutes to make this drive. Park roads are generally designed as scenic drives with reduced speed limits. The average speed limit in the Park is 35 miles (56 km) per hour.

These pre-Columbian cliff dwellings and other works of early humans are among the most notable and best preserved in the United States. Established by act of Congress on June 29, 1906.

VISITOR ACTIVITIES: Photography, interpretive exhibits and talks, camping, picnicking, auto tours, guided tours, hiking, and campfire programs in summer. **Permits:** Yes, for hiking only, available at Chief Ranger's Office; **Fees:** $5 per vehicle entrance fee, $2 for bus passengers. Golden Access, Golden Age, and Golden Eagle Passports are accepted and available. Camping fee is $8 per night, $4 with Golden Age. Organized groups are $20 or $1 per person, whichever is greater. Full hookup fee is $14.50 per day plus $2 per person for 3 or more in party (camping rates are subject to changes); **Visitor facilities:** Campground, gas stations, stores, showers, picnic areas, post office, laundry, hiking trails, restaurants, telephones, lodging; **HANDICAPPED ACCESSIBILITY:** Scenic Overlooks accessible with assistance. Morefield Campground has parking, restrooms, paved walks, and graveled trails. Visitor Center has parking, ramps. Wetherill Mesa has accessible restrooms. Persons in wheelchairs must be able to be lifted into and from bus and mini-train. Long House Ruin not accessible. Step House Ruin accessible with assistance (steep trail). Spruce Tree House Ruin has paved trail (steep trail). Archeological Museum has restrooms, ramp. Other Cliff Dwellings not accessible (ladders, tunnel). Some steps at Ruins Road Drive accessible. Programs scripts, Braille transcriptions available; **Any limitations on vehicle usage:** Motor vehicles are allowed only on roadways, turnouts, or parking areas. Weight and length restrictions for vehicles using Wetherill Mesa Road. Check with Rangers; **Hiking trails:** Hiking is restricted to only 5 trails within the Park. Register at the Chief Ranger's Office; **Backcountry:** No; **Camping:** Yes, Morefield campground is open from mid-Apr. through mid-Oct. for tents and trailers. It has restrooms and single and group campsites. Reservations cannot be made. Each campsite has a table, benches, and grills for which fuel can be bought at the store. There are 15 sites with utility hookups (higher fee), and the campground has a disposal system for dumping trailer holding tanks. Groceries, souvenirs, carry-out food, a gasoline station, showers, and laundry facilities are also available. All services and facilities are closed from approximately mid-Oct. to early-May; **Other overnight accommodations on site:** Yes, at Far View, which has lodging, dining room, cafeteria, gift shops, and gas station. Concessioner-operated commercial bus tours of Chapin Mesa leave from this point. *Lodging* is available from mid-May to mid-Oct. From June 1 to Labor Day it is advisable to make reservations with the Mesa Verde Co., P.O. Box 227, Mancos, CO 81328, phone 303-529-4421; **Meals served in the park:** Yes, at Morefield, Far View, and Chapin Mesa, and snacks at Wetherill Mesa; **Food and supplies obtainable in the park:** Yes, at Morefield; **Food and supplies obtainable**

nearby: Yes, at Cortez and Mancos, CO; **Overnight accommodations:** Cortez, Hwy 160, 7 miles (11.2 km) west; Mancos, Hwy 160, 8 miles (12.8 km) east; **First Aid available in park:** Yes, emergency first aid is provided at the Chief Ranger's Office and the Morefield Campground Ranger Station; **Nearest Hospital:** Cortez, 7 miles (11.2 km) west of the Park entrance; **Days/Hours:** Accommodations, facilities, and services are available from mid-May to mid-Oct. Maximum interpretive services begin mid-June and last until Labor Day; **Holiday Closings:** No; **Visitor attractions closed for seasons:** The Museum and Spruce Tree House cliff dwelling are open all year. Ruins Road may be closed in winter by snowfall. Cliff Palace and Balcony House ruins are closed from approximately mid-Oct. to mid-Apr. Wetherill Mesa ruins (Long House, Step House, and Badger House Community complex) open from early June through Labor Day only, closed the rest of the year. From mid-Oct. to mid-Apr. most concession facilities, including gasoline, food, and lodging are closed. In winter the Spruce Tree Terrace cafeteria and restaurant are open with limited food services; **Weather:** In summer, daytime temperatures are comfortably warm with highs ranging from 85°F to 100°F. Evening temperatures are cool with lows ranging from 55°F to 65°F. Winter highs range from 40°F to 50°F with lows of 25°F to 15°F. Snow-covered ground is predominant.

GENERAL INFORMATION: *For Your Safety*—Visits to cliff dwellings, whether on a Ranger-guided tour or a self-guided walk, tend to be quite strenuous. Adequate footwear, such as hiking boots or sturdy shoes, is recommended for these trips. Strenuous activity at the high elevations (7,000-8,500 ft.) of the Park may adversely affect those persons who experience heart or respiratory ailments. You may wish to reconsider climbing into and out of the cliff dwellings. With the exception of Balcony House, all major cliff dwellings can be viewed from overlooks on the canyon rims. Parents should be especially alert for their childrens' safety when nearing the canyon rim cliff areas. Do not throw rocks or other objects, for other visitors may be below. Be on the lookout for bicycles on the narrow roads. Contact a Ranger if you are involved in an accident or are injured.

TRAVEL ACCESS: **Bus:** Mesa Verde bus service, Cortez, CO, 6:45 a.m. and 4:30 p.m.; **Rail:** No; **Air:** Mesa Air serves Cortez, CO, from Denver. Rental cars available at airport.

NEARBY FACILITIES & POINTS OF INTEREST: **Hotel/Motel:** Cortez or Mancos 7 (11.2 km) and 8 miles (12.8 km) from Park; **Food/Supplies:** Cortez or Mancos; **Campgrounds:** Cortez or Mancos, and within 1 mile (1.6 km) of the Park. McPhee Reservoir (boating and fishing), second largest lake in Colorado, 10 miles (16 km) north of Cortez.

Rocky Mountain National Park
Estes Park, Colorado   **SEE CLIMATABLE NO. 14**

MAILING ADDRESS: Superintendent, Rocky Mountain National Park, Estes Park, CO 80517 **Telephone:** 303-586-2371; Telecommunications Device for the Deaf (TDD) 303-586-8506

DIRECTIONS: The Park is accessible by Trail Ridge Road, which crosses the Continental Divide. Access from the east is by US 34/36 to Estes Park, from the southwest by US 34 to Grand Lake. Trail Ridge Road is usually closed from mid-Oct. until Memorial Day. Opening and closing dates vary depending on weather conditions.
    The Park's rich scenery typifies the grandeur of the Rocky Mountains. Peaks towering over 13,000 feet shadow wildlife and wildflowers in 414 square miles (662.4 km) of the Rockies' Front Range. Established by act of Congress on Jan. 26, 1915.

VISITOR ACTIVITIES: Interpretive programs, auto touring, camping, picnicking, hiking, mountain climbing, fishing, horseback riding, downhill and cross-country skiing, snowshoeing, snowmobiling (west side only), bird and animal watching; **Permits:** A Colorado fishing license, available locally, is required. Backcountry use permits for overnight stays available from Park Headquarters or the Kawuneeche Visitor Center; **Fees:** Entrance fees, subject to change, are $5 per noncommercial vehicle and $2 per person for commercial vehicles or bus passengers. Golden Age, Golden Access, and Golden Eagle Passports are accepted and available. Entrance fees are waived for persons under 16 years of age. Campground fees are, per night per site, $7 when first-come, first-served, $9 when on reservation. Holders of Golden Age and Golden Access Passports will be given a 50% discount; **Visitor facilities:** Schedules for guided walks, campfire programs, and other activities are available at Information Centers in summer. Be sure to see the orientation program at Headquarters. Interpretive programs offered daily in summer. Contact the Park for a detailed list of camping facilities and picnic areas; **HANDICAPPED ACCESSIBILITY:** Braille and cassette tapes of publications available at Visitor Centers. Parking, restrooms at Vistor Center, comfort stations at Rock Cut and Rainbow Curve; Campgrounds have at least one fully accessible restroom. Handicapped Campsite is available for backcountry type camping for wheelchaired and other handicapped visitors. Reservations required. Contact Backcountry Office, Rocky MT National Park, CO 80517, telephone 303-586-4459 for complete information on these programs; **Any limitations on vehicle usage:** Vehicles must remain on established roads and parking areas; No vehicles or combination rigs (i.e. trailers, RVs, mobile homes) over 50 ft. maximum length over Trail Ridge Road. No trailers allowed up Old Fall River Road maximum length 25 ft. **Hiking trails:** Yes, more than 355.6 miles (572.5 km) of trails provide access to remote sections of the Park; **Backcountry:** Day use requires no permit. A permit for bivouac and overnight stays is required, and can be obtained without charge on a first-come basis at Park Headquarters or the Kawuneeche Visitor Center or by writing no earlier than 30 days ahead of the visit. The number of permits issued is limited. Contact the Park for detailed information on backcountry; **Camping:** Yes, Rocky Mountain has 5 roadside campgrounds: Moraine Park, Glacier Basin, Aspenglen, Longs Peak, and Timber Creek. Camping is limited to 3 days at Longs Peak and 7 days parkwide at the other sites. In summer campgrounds usually fill to capacity early each day. Group sites at Glacier Basin can be reserved. Longs Peak is restricted to tent camping. There are no showers, electrical, water, or sewage connections at any campsite. Three campgrounds are kept open all year. Reservations for the Moraine Park and Glacier Basin Campgrounds are available through Ticketron during the summer months. Wood fires are permitted in fire grates at campgrounds and picnic areas. A written permit is required for fires outside of those areas. Wood gathering is prohibited parkwide except in designated backcountry campsites with valid permit. Warm clothing and rain gear are advised. Contact the Park for detailed information on camping and campsites. Privately owned facilities are available in the vicinity. For information about facilities adjacent to the Park, write to the Chamber of Commerce at either Estes Park, CO 80517 or Grand Lake, CO 80447; **Other overnight accommodations on site:** No; **Meals served in the park:** No, but light lunches at Trail Ridge Store (Fall River Pass) in summer; **Food and supplies obtainable in the park:** No; **Food and supplies obtainable nearby:** Yes, at Estes Park and Grand Lake; **Overnight accommodations:** Estes Park, US 34 or 36, 2-4 miles (3.2-6.4 km) from the Park and Grand Lake, US 34, 1 mile (1.6 km); **First Aid available in park:** Yes, or nearby in Estes Park and Grand Lake; **Nearest Hospital:** Granby, 14 miles (22.5 km) southwest of the Grand Lake Entrance, just beyond the junction of US 40 with US 34; and Estes Park, US 34 or 36, 2-4 miles (3.2-6.4 km) from the Park; **Days/Hours:** Open 24 hours a day year-round; **Holiday Closings:** Park Headquarters-Visitor Center closed Dec. 25; **Visitor attractions closed for seasons:** Trail Ridge Road and Old Fall River Road usually close in Oct. **Weather:** The high country produces a variable weather pattern primarily due to differences in altitude, slope, and exposure. Elevation plays a most important role. Contact the Park for detailed seasonal and monthly weather information.

GENERAL INFORMATION: There are several hazards which you should be aware of. Many serious accidents have occurred on *snow and ice fields* in the summer. Stay away from the edge of steep snow slopes and avoid sliding on snow and/or ice. Know and obey park regulations.

Remember, *mountain climbing* is a technical sport requiring extensive training, skill, conditioning, and proper equipment. Registration with a Park Ranger is required for all bivouac climbs.

Although they appear small, *streams and waterfalls* can be deceptively dangerous, especially in the spring when they are high and turbulent from melting snow. During *thunderstorms*, stay off ridges and peaks and avoid exposed lone objects such as large rocks, trees, or telephone lines. If you are riding horseback, dismount and get away from your horse.

Trail Ridge Road reaches elevations of more than 2 miles (3.2 km) above sea level (max. 12,183 feet) and could be dangerous to persons with heart conditions and respiratory ailments. Even healthy persons are normally winded by the slightest exertion at these levels.

TRAVEL ACCESS: Bus: Charles Limousine and Grayline, provide service between Estes Park and Stapleton Airport in Denver. Within the park, Bear Lake Shuttle System provides shuttle service along Bear Lake Road during the summer; Several companies provide tour service into the Park. **Rail:** No; **Air:** Access through Denver.

NEARBY FACILITIES & POINTS OF INTEREST: Contact Chamber of Commerce for information on accommodations and camping; Estes Park CO 80517, Grand Lake, CO 80447.

Yucca House National Monument
Cortez, Colorado

MAILING ADDRESS: Yucca House National Monument, c/o Mesa Verde National Park, Mesa Verde National Park, CO 81330 **Telephone:** 303-529-4465

DIRECTIONS: Lands surrounding Yucca House are in private ownership. The approach road is almost impassable in wet weather. Visitors should seek directions from the Chief Ranger's Office, Mesa Verde National Park. Created by Presidential Proclamation on Dec. 19, 1919.

VISITOR ACTIVITIES: None. This large prehistoric Indian pueblo ruin west of Mesa Verde is not yet excavated and there is little to see.

TRAVEL ACCESS: Bus: No; **Rail:** No; **Air:** Mesa Airlines/United Express provides daily service to Cortez from Denver.

NEARBY FACILITIES & POINTS OF INTEREST: Parks, other points of interest: Mesa Verde National Park, Hovenweep National Monument, Anasazi Heritage Center.

Constitution Gardens
Washington, D.C.   **SEE CLIMATABLE NO. 15**

MAILING ADDRESS: Superintendent, National Capital Parks-Central, 900 Ohio Drive, SW, Washington, DC 20242 **Telephone:** 202-485-9880

DIRECTIONS: Located between Washington Monument and the Lincoln Memorial, bordered by Constitution Ave., 17th St., and the Reflecting Pool.

VISITOR ACTIVITIES: Sightseeing and to be enjoyed for scenic beauty; **Permits:** Needed for special events, First Amendment Activities; **Fees:** No; **Visitor facilities:** Food Kiosk, restrooms; **Any limitations on vehicle usage:** Yes, bikes only; **Hiking trails:** No; **Backcountry:** No; **Camping:** No; **Other overnight accommodations on site:** No; **Meals served in the park:** Snack bar open approximately Apr.-Oct.; **Food and supplies obtainable in the park:** No; **Food and supplies obtainable nearby:** Metropolitan area; **Overnight accommodations:** Hotels in Washington, DC, and nearby Maryland and Virginia; **First Aid available in park:** Yes, at nearby Lincoln Memorial; **Nearest Hospital:** George Washington Hospital; **Days/Hours:** Dawn to dusk; **Holiday Closings:** No; **Visitor attractions closed for seasons:** No; **Weather:** Summer is hot and humid, with an average temperature of 88° and occasional thundershowers. Winter can be cold; average temperature is 30°.

District of Columbia

ROCK CREEK PARK

SEWALL-BELMONT HOUSE
NATIONAL HISTORIC SITE

FORD'S THEATRE
NATIONAL HISTORICAL SITE

THE WHITE HOUSE

WASHINGTON MONUMENT

OLD STONE HOUSE

LINCOLN MEMORIAL

VIETNAM VET. MEMORIAL/
CONSTITUTION GARDEN

JOHN F. KENNEDY CENTER
FOR THE PERFORMING ARTS

GEORGE WASHINGTON
MEMORIAL PARKWAY

THEODORE ROOSEVELT ISLAND

U.S. MARINE MEMORIAL
AND NETHERLANDS CARILLON

ARLINGTON HOUSE,
THE ROBERT E. LEE MEMORIAL

LYNDON BAINES JOHNSON MEMORIAL
GROVE ON THE POTOMAC

THOMAS JEFFERSON MEMORIAL

NATIONAL MALL

PENNSYLVANIA AVENUE NATIONAL HISTORIC SITE

NATIONAL CAPITAL PARKS

FREDERICK DOUGLASS MEMORIAL HOME

FORT DUPONT PARK AND ACTIVITY CENTER

GENERAL INFORMATION: This 40-acre manmade park includes a 7-acre lake, 56 Signers of the Declaration of Independence, and the Vietnam Veterans Memorial.

TRAVEL ACCESS: Bus: Tourmobile sightseeing bus, Metro bus; **Rail:** Smithsonian stop plus 5 blocks; **Air:** No.

Ford's Theatre National Historic Site
Washington, D.C.

MAILING ADDRESS: Site Manager, Ford's Theatre National Historic Site, 511 Tenth Street, NW, Washington, DC 20004 **Telephone:** 202-426-6924 (TDD) 202-426-1749

DIRECTIONS: Ford's Theatre and the Lincoln Museum are located at 511 Tenth Street, N.W., between "E" and "F" Streets, in the heart of downtown Washington, D.C. The House

Where Lincoln Died is situated across the street from the theatre at 516 Tenth Street. The site is convenient to the Metro Center subway (1½ blocks from the 11th St. exit) and to other public transportation.

VISITOR ACTIVITIES: Fifteen-minute talks on the history of the theatre and the assassination are presented daily, except when the theatre is closed for stage work, rehearsals, or matinee performances. No reservations necessary, but recommend calling ahead to confirm theatre schedule. **Permits:** No; **Fees:** Admission to Ford's Theatre, the House Where Lincoln Died, and the Lincoln Museum is free during National Park Service operating hours. Admission to theatrical performances sponsored by the Ford's Theatre Society is by paid ticket only, call box office (202-347-4833) for ticket information; **Visitor facilities:** Bookstore is located in museum. Pay parking is adjacent to the theatre; **HANDICAPPED ACCESSIBILITY:** A handicapped accessible bathroom is located next door to the theatre at 517 10th St., N.W. The orchestra level of the theatre is wheelchair accessible. The Presidential Box, where Lincoln was shot is not accessible, but may be viewed from the orchestra level. The Museum and the House Where Lincoln Died are not wheelchair accessible. Ranger in the lobby will show a video featuring museum exhibits. Call ahead to arrange sign-language and visually-impaired tours; **Food and supplies obtainable nearby:** Yes, many within one block of the site; **Overnight accommodations:** Washington, DC; **First Aid available:** Yes; **Nearest Hospital:** Washington, DC; **Days/Hours:** Open daily from 9 a.m. to 5 p.m. Theatre closes for matinee performances and rehearsals; **Holiday Closings:** Dec. 25.

GENERAL INFORMATION: On April 14, 1865, President Abraham Lincoln was shot while attending a play at Ford's Theatre. He was carried across the street to a boarding house where he died 9 hours later. The Lincoln Museum, located downstairs in the theatre, contains an exhibit on the assassination. Ford's Theatre operates as a legitimate theatre with productions throughout the year. *For information on performances*, call 202-347-4833.

TRAVEL ACCESS: Bus: Local subway and Metrobus information, 202-637-2437; **Rail:** Amtrak provides regular service to Washington's Union Station; **Air:** Major airlines service National Airport, Dulles International Airport, and the Baltimore-Washington International Airport.

NEARBY FACILITIES & POINTS OF INTEREST: Washington Convention Center, National Archives, Smithsonian Museums, F.B.I., and many shops and restaurants.

Fort Dupont Park and Activity Center
Washington, D.C.

MAILING ADDRESS: Site Manager, Fort Dupont Park and Activity Center, 1900 Anacostia Dr., S.E., Washington, D.C. 20020 **Telephone:** 202-426-7723. Site Location is Minnesota Avenue and Randle Circle, S.E., Washington, D.C. 20019.

DIRECTIONS: The Park is located just north of Alabama Ave. between Massachusetts Ave. Extension and Ridge Rd., S.W., at Randle Circle. It may be reached by heading east on Pennsylvania Avenue, crossing the Anacostia River, and proceeding to the second traffic light, Minnesota Ave. Turn left onto Minnesota; go 10 blocks to Randle Circle and follow signs.

The 375-acre Park is designed for many types of recreational and community activities. Authorized for addition to the National Park System in 1949.

VISITOR ACTIVITIES: Basketball, arts and crafts programs, day camp, football, baseball, tennis, walking, ice skating, picknicking, guided talks, nature walks, film programs. Free summer concerts; **Permits:** Yes, for picnic areas, call 673-7647; **Fees:** No; **Visitor facilities:** Basketball courts and football, baseball and soccer fields, year-round ice skating rink, picnic areas, Visitor Center, tennis courts, nature trails; **Any limitations on vehicle usage:** No; **Hiking trails:** Yes; **Backcountry:** No; **Camping:** No; **Other overnight accommodations on site:** No; **Meals served in the park:** No; **Food and supplies obtainable in the park:** No; **Food and supplies obtainable nearby:** Yes, in Washington; **Overnight accommodations:** Washington, D.C., or suburban Maryland; **Nearest Hospital:** Greater Southeast Community Hospital, D.C. General Hospital; **Days/Hours:** Park open from dawn to dusk; Activity Center open Mon.-Fri. from 7:45 a.m. to 4:15 p.m.; **Holiday Closings:** Visitor Center closed on all holidays.

Frederick Douglass Memorial
Washington, D.C.

MAILING ADDRESS: Site Manager, Frederick Douglass Memorial, 1411 W Street, SE, Washington, D.C. 20020 **Telephone:** 202-426-5961

DIRECTIONS: The Home can be best reached by crossing the 11th Street (Anacostia) Bridge to Good Hope Road, turning left on Good Hope Road to 14th Street and right on 14th Street. Make a left onto W Street. The Home is on top of the hill at 14th and W Streets, SE. Visitors arriving from the north or south on Int. 295 (Anacostia Freeway) should use the "Pennsylvania Avenue East" exit. Proceed east on Pennsylvania Avenue 2 blocks to Minnesota Avenue. Turn right on Minnesota to Good Hope Road. Turn right on Good Hope Road, proceed one-half block, and turn left on 14th Street. Public transportation is available within a short distance of the site.

This was the home of the Nation's leading 19th-century Black spokesman from 1877 to 1895. He was U.S. minister to Haiti, 1889. Authorized for addition to the National Park System on Sept. 5, 1962.

VISITOR ACTIVITIES: Guided house tours, interpretive talks, a film of Frederick Douglass' life shown on the hour while tours are given on the half-hour; **Permits:** No; **Fees:** No; **Visitor facilities:** Parking area; **HANDICAPPED ACCESSIBILITY:** Yes, except accessibility of the second floor by wheelchair is not possible; **Any limitations on vehicle usage:** No; **Hiking trails:** No; **Meals served in the park:** No; **Food and supplies obtainable in the park:** No; **Food and supplies obtainable nearby:** Yes, in Washington, D.C.; **Overnight accommodations:** Washington, D.C., or vicinity; **First Aid available in park:** Yes; **Nearest Hospital:** Washington (Southeast Community), Martin Luther King Jr. Ave. to South Capitol Street to Southern Ave., 5 miles (8 km); **Days/Hours:** Summer hours 9 a.m.-5 p.m., fall/winter hours 9 a.m.-4 p.m., 7 days a week. **Holiday Closings:** Thanksgiving, Dec. 25, and Jan 1.

GENERAL INFORMATION: *For Your Safety*—Be extra careful when climbing steps and walking on the hilly grounds. Visitor Center and off-street parking are available.

John F. Kennedy Center for the Performing Arts
Washington, D.C.

MAILING ADDRESS: General Manager, National Park Service, John F. Kennedy Center for the Performing Arts, Washington, DC 20566 **Telephone:** 202-416-7910

DIRECTIONS: The Center is at New Hampshire Ave. and F Street, N.W. overlooking the Potomac River.

The marble structure, designed by Edward Durell Stone, is the sole official memorial in Washington, DC, to the 35th President. It culminates an interest in a National Cultural Center dating back to George Washington. The Center houses 5½ auditoriums—the Opera House, the Concert Hall, the Eisenhower Theatre, the rooftop Terrace Theatre, The Theater Lab, and the American Film Institute Theatre. Authorized for addition to the National Park System on Sept. 3, 1972.

VISITOR ACTIVITIES: Interpretive tours, exhibits, cultural events; **Permits:** No; **Fees:** Tickets are required for many of the cultural events held at the Center; **Visitor facilities:** Restrooms, exhibits, restaurants, telephones; **Any limitations on vehicle usage:** Parking is available in a garage underneath the Center; **Meals served in the park:** Yes, restaurants are on the rooftop level; **Food and supplies obtainable in the park:** No; **Food and supplies obtainable nearby:** Yes, in Washington, DC; **Overnight accommodations:** Washington, DC, or vicinity; **First Aid available in park:** Yes; **Nearest Hospital:** George Washington Hospital within ¼ mile (.4 km); **Days/Hours:** The building is open daily from 10 a.m. to midnight. Tours are given every day from 10 a.m. to 1 p.m.; **Holiday Closings:** No; **Visitor attractions closed for seasons:** No.

GENERAL INFORMATION: The Center is furnished with gifts from 30 foreign governments. Visitors should consult the Center's calendar of events for specific offerings or call Friends of the Kennedy Center at 202-416-8340, TDD 202-416-8524.

TRAVEL ACCESS: Bus: D.C. Metrobus provides service to Kennedy Center; subway stops nearby at Foggy Bottom; **Rail:** Amtrak and others provide daily service into Union Station, Washington, DC; **Air:** Major airlines service National Airport, Dulles Airport, and Baltimore-Washington International Airport.

Lincoln Memorial
Washington, D.C.

MAILING ADDRESS: Superintendent, National Capital Parks—Central, 900 Ohio Drive, SW, Washington, DC 20242 **Telephone:** 202-485-9880

DIRECTIONS: The Memorial is in downtown Washington at the beginning of 23rd St., NW, between Constitution and Independence Avenues. From Virginia, follow Rte. 50 west to Washington and turn right on 23rd St. or take George Washington Parkway to Memorial Bridge.

This classical structure contains Daniel Chester French's monumental sculpture of the 16th President of the United States. Lincoln's Gettysburg Address and Second Inaugural Address are carved on the marble walls. Authorized for addition to the National Park System on Feb. 9, 1911.

VISITOR ACTIVITIES: Interpretive talks are given upon request daily from 8 a.m. to 11:30 p.m.; **Permits:** Yes, for special events and First Amendment activities; **Fees:** No; **Visitor facilities:** Telephones and restrooms, parking on nearby Ohio Drive, drinking water, snack bar, bookstore, souvenir stand; **HANDICAPPED ACCESSIBILITY:** Elevator available; **Any limitations on vehicle usage:** Lincoln Memorial Circle is closed to vehicles; **Meals served in the park:** Yes, concessioner snack bar on Lincoln Memorial Circle; **Food and supplies obtainable in the park:** No; **Food and supplies obtainable nearby:** Yes, in

Washington, DC; **Overnight accommodations:** Washington, DC, or vicinity; **First Aid available in park:** Yes; **Nearest Hospital:** George Washington University Hospital, 6 blocks from the Memorial; **Days/Hours:** Open daily from 8 a.m. to midnight all year; **Holiday Closings:** No interpretive talks on Dec. 25; **Weather:** Summer is hot and humid, with an average temperature of 88° and occasional thundershowers. Winter can be cold; average temperature is 30°.

Lyndon Baines Johnson Memorial Grove on the Potomac
Washington, D.C.

MAILING ADDRESS: Superintendent, George Washington Memorial Parkway, % Turkey Run Park, McLean, VA 22101 **Telephone:** 703-285-2598

DIRECTIONS: The Grove is in Lady Bird Johnson Park on the George Washington Memorial Parkway, west of I-95 and the 14th Street Bridge. Parking is at nearby Columbia Island Marina.

A living memorial to the 36th President, the Park overlooks the Potomac River, providing a vista of the Capital. The design features 500 white pines and engravings on Texas granite. Authorized for addition to the National Park System on Dec. 28, 1973.

VISITOR ACTIVITIES: Picnicking, strolling, fishing; **Permits:** Yes, fishing permits required; **Fees:** No; **Visitor facilities:** Restrooms, water, picnic tables, parking area; **HANDICAPPED ACCESSIBILITY:** Parking, restrooms, trails; **Any limitations on vehicle usage:** Vehicles are restricted to parking lots; **Trails:** Yes, 1 mile (1.6 km) of woodland walkways; **Meals served in the park:** No, but nearby at Columbia Island Marina; **Food and supplies obtainable in the park:** No; **Food and supplies obtainable nearby:** Yes, in Washington, DC, area; **Overnight accommodations:** Washington, DC, and vicinity; **First Aid available in park:** No; **Nearest Hospital:** Arlington, VA; **Days/Hours:** Open during daylight hours year-round; **Visitor attractions closed for seasons:** No; **Weather:** Hot, humid summers; cold winters.

National Capital Region
Washington, D.C. (also in Maryland, Virginia and West Virginia)

MAILING ADDRESS: National Capital Region, 1100 Ohio Drive SW, Washington, DC 20242 **Telephone:** 202-485-9880

DIRECTIONS: For information about or directions to any of the more than 300 park units in the Washington metropolitan area, call 202-485-9666. For a recorded message of daily events in metropolitan Washington park areas, call 202-485-PARK.

This park system in the Nation's Capital includes parks, parkways, and reservations in the Washington metropolitan area, including such properties as the National Mall, Vietnam Memorial, Old Post Office tower, the President's Parks (Lafayette Park north of the White House and the Ellipse south of the White House), the parks flanking the Great Falls of the Potomac, and a variety of military fortifications and greenswards. Authorized for addition to the National Park System on Aug. 10, 1933.

The Headquarters has handicapped parking, ramps, and handicapped restrooms.

National Mall
Washington, D.C.

MAILING ADDRESS: Superintendent, National Capital Parks-Central, 900 Ohio Drive, SW, Washington, DC 20242 **Telephone:** 202-426-6720

DIRECTIONS: For general information on the Mall, call the management office at 202-426-6841.

Rows of stately elms mark the sweep of the greensward from the U.S. Capitol to the Washington Monument, a key feature of Pierre Charles L'Enfant's plan for the city of Washington in 1790. The Mall today includes many buildings of the Smithsonian Institution. For further information on the Smithsonian, contact: Information and Reception Center, Smithsonian Institution, Washington, DC 20560, phone 202-381-6264.

TRAVEL ACCESS: Bus: Trailways, Greyhound, Tourmobile Service provide regular services to terminal 3 blocks from Mall; **Rail:** Amtrak offers inter-city service into Union Station 2 blocks from Mall, local transportation via Metro (subway) stops in the Mall; **Air:** Major airlines service Washington, DC and nearby airports.

Old Stone House
Washington, D.C.

MAILING ADDRESS: Old Stone House, 3051 M Street, N.W., Washington, DC 20007 **Telephone:** 202-426-6851 voice or TDD (TDD is a phone device for the hearing impaired.)

DIRECTIONS: The house is located at 3051 M Street, N.W., in Georgetown.

Built in 1765, Old Stone House is a fine example of pre-Revolutionary architecture and the oldest existing house in the Nation's Capital. Administered by the National Park Service since 1953.

VISITOR ACTIVITIES: Guided and self-guiding tours, living history demonstrations, interpretive exhibits, walking through the garden, candlelight evening program with 18th century music on the second Wednesday of each month 7-9:30 p.m. Oct.-June, Christmas Program Wed. of the 3rd week in Dec. 7-9:30 p.m.; **Permits:** No; **Fees:** No; **HANDICAPPED ACCESSIBILITY:** There is a sign language interpreter for the hearing-impaired. The first floor is accessible for the physically impaired; a slide projector of the upper floors available for those who cannot go upstairs. **Any limitations on vehicle usage:** Only commercial or on-street parking is available; **Hiking trails:** No; **Meals served in the park:** No; **Food and supplies obtainable in the park:** No; **Food and supplies obtainable nearby:** Yes, Georgetown or Washington, DC; **Overnight accommodations:** Within several blocks or anywhere in metropolitan Washington; **First Aid available in park:** Yes; **Nearest Hospital:** Washington, D.C., Pennsylvania Ave., 8 blocks; **Days/Hours:** Open from 9:30 a.m. to 5 p.m. Wednesday through Sunday. Closed Monday and Tuesday; **Holiday Closings:** All legal holidays.

Pennsylvania Avenue National Historic Site
Washington, D.C.

MAILING ADDRESS: Pennsylvania Avenue Development Corporation, 331 Pennsylvania Ave., N.W., Suite 1220 North, Washington, DC 20004-1703 **Telephone:** 202-426-6720

DIRECTIONS: The Site includes the architecturally and historically significant area between the Capitol and The White House in Washington, DC.

The Site includes a portion of Pennsylvania Avenue and the area adjacent to it between the Capitol and the White House encompassing Ford's Theatre National Historic Site, several blocks of the Washington commercial district, and a number of Federal structures. Existing park areas are listed separately in this book. Designated Sept. 30, 1965.

VISITOR ACTIVITIES: Walking tours, theatrical performances, shopping, ice skating and cafe in Pershing Park, 14th and Pennsylvania; Noon-time activities in Western Plaza, 13th and Pennsylvania, tours of the National Archives, FBI, National Museum of American Art, and National Gallery of Arts buildings; **Permits:** No; **Fees:** Only for admission to performances at the National Theatre and Ford's Theatre; **Visitor facilities:** Museums, theaters, stores, restaurants, lodging; **Any limitations on vehicle usage:** No trucks; **Meals served in the park:** Yes, there are numerous restaurants in the downtown area; **Food and supplies obtainable in the park:** Yes, a grocery store at 12th and F Streets, N.W.; **Food and supplies obtainable nearby:** Yes, Washington and vicinity; **Overnight accommodations:** Washington and vicinity; **First Aid available in park:** Yes, at museums and theaters within the Historic Site; **Nearest Hospital:** George Washington University Hospital, 23rd and Pennsylvania Ave., N.W.; **Days/Hours:** Site always open; **Visitor attractions closed for seasons:** No.

GENERAL INFORMATION: Architour, a non-profit educational organization, is offering regularly scheduled architectural tours of the Pennsylvania Avenue National Historic Site. For information, call 202-265-6454.

TRAVEL ACCESS: Bus: DC Metro (subway) stops at Federal Triangle and Metro Center.

NEARBY FACILITIES & POINTS OF INTEREST: Hotel/Motel: Harrington Hotel, E. St. and 1st Street, N.W.; Hotel Washington, 15th Street and Pennsylvania Ave., N.W., JW Marriott Hotel 14th and Pennsylvania Ave., Willard Hotel. Numerous hotels are located in this vicinity.

Potomac Heritage National Scenic Trail
Virginia, Maryland and Pennsylvania

MAILING ADDRESS: Potomac Heritage Trail Association, c/o Potomac Appalachian Trail Club, 1718 N St., NW, Washington, D.C. 20036 **Telephone:** 202-638-5306 or NPS, National Capital Region—LUCE, 1100 Ohio Drive, SW, Washington, DC 20242 **Telephone:** 202-485-9880

DIRECTIONS: The Potomac Heritage National Scenic Trail was authorized to be included in the National Park System on March 28, 1983. The trail route has not yet been formally designated and, therefore, is not generally available for public use. A planning effort is underway which will result in a comprehensive management plan leading to ultimate designation of trail segments. The trail segments can only be designated upon application to the Secretary of the Interior by state or local governments.

The 700-mile (1,120 km) -long trail will extend through the Potomac River Valley linking sites that commemorate a rich blend of historical events, natural scenes, and recreational opportunities. The general trail corridor will extend from the Chesapeake Bay at Smith Point, VA, and Point Lookout, MD, through tidewater Maryland and Virginia, along the George Washington Memorial Parkway's Mount Vernon Trail, to Washington, DC, and west through Virginia hunt country to Harpers Ferry where it crosses to Maryland and joins the Chesapeake and Ohio Canal towpath to Cumberland. The entire 184-mile (294.4-km) length of the Cheaspeake and Ohio Canal is included as a segment of the trail from Georgetown in the District of Columbia to Cumberland, MD. From Cumberland, the trail would continue through Maryland into Pennsylvania to Conemaugh Gorge, just west of Johnstown.

VISITOR ACTIVITIES: For activities within the Chesapeake and Ohio Canal National Historical Park, see that listing for details or write to Superintendent, C&O Canal National Historical Park, P.O. Box 4, Sharpsburg, MD 21782, and the Supt., George Washington Memorial Parkway for information about the Mount Vernon Trail. In addition, directions for following a 55-mile hiking trail from the western end of the C&O Canal at Cumberland, MD, to Pennsylvania's Laurel highlands can be obtained by written request from the Potomac Heritage Trail Association, address above.

GENERAL INFORMATION: By law only those portions of the Potomac Heritage NST already on Federal land may be Federally owned. These include (but are not yet so marked) the 184-mile (294.4-km) towpath of the Chesapeake and Ohio Canal National Historic Site in Maryland and the District of Columbia and the 17-mile (27.3-km) Mount Vernon Trail within the George Washington Memorial Parkway in Virginia.

Rock Creek Park
Washington, D.C.

MAILING ADDRESS: Superintendent, Rock Creek Park, 5000 Glover Road, N.W., Washington, DC 20015 **Telephone:** 202-426-6832

DIRECTIONS: The Nature (Visitor) Center is located south of Military Road and Oregon Avenue at 5200 Glover Road, N.W., Washington, DC Telephone: 202-426-6829.
    Rock Creek Park is the largest Natural Park in an urban area. The wooded preserve contains a wide range of natural, historical, cultural, and recreational resources in the midst of metropolitan Washington, D.C. Authorized for addition to the National Park System on Sept. 27, 1890.

VISITOR ACTIVITIES: Nature walks and hikes, horseback riding, picnicking, planetarium, golf, tennis, recreation fields, exercise trails, running and jogging; **Permits:** Required for large picnic areas. To reserve call D.C. Recreation Dept.: 202-673-7647; **Fees:** For rental horses, Rock Creek Horse Centre, near the Nature Center on Glover Road, offers rental horses and riding instruction. Telephone: 202-362-0117. There is an 18-hole public golf course with a greens fee, golf cart and golf club rental, entrance 16th and Rittenhouse Streets, NW. Telephone: 202-882-7332. Tennis: 17 soft- and 5 hard-surface tennis courts at 16th and Kennedy Streets, NW, 6 soft-surface courts located off Park Road, east of Pierce Mill. Reservations. Telephone: 202-722-5949. **Visitor facilities:** Nature Center and planetarium, operating grist mill, Pierce Mill; Art Barn, Old Stone House, Carter Barron Amphitheatre for summer events, 1 able-bodied and 1 handicapped-able-bodied exercise trail; **HANDICAPPED ACCESSIBILITY:** Nature Center has accessible restrooms, planetarium, exhibit hall, auditorium; first floor of Old Stone House is wheelchair accessible; Exercise Course at 16th and Kennedy Sts. Recreation area is accessible including water fountain and restrooms; Carter Barron Amphitheater is accessible including water fountains, restrooms, and parking lot; Picnic Groves #1, #6, #23, and #24 are accessible with picnic tables and parking lot; **Any limitations on vehicle usage:** Vehicles must stay on road and park in designated areas; **Bike trails:** Bicycles are prohibited on hiking and horse trails (off road); 7.5 miles (12 km) bike trails. 2.5-mile (4-km) section of Beach Drive between Joyce Road and Broad Branch Roads and a 1-mile (1.6-km) section of Beach Drive at Picnic Grove #10, located just north of Sherill Drive, to Wise Drive, is closed from 7 a.m. Saturdays thru 7 p.m. Sundays and holidays for recreation activities; **Hiking Trails:** Yes, there are about 20 miles (35 km) of trails, with footbridges across Rock Creek. Hikers may also use 11 miles (17.6 km) of bridle trails; **Backcountry:** No; **Camping:** No; **Other overnight accommodations on site:** No; **Meals served in the park:** Yes, snacks are available at the golf and tennis courts; **Food and supplies obtainable in the park:** No; **Food and supplies obtainable nearby:** Yes, in Washington, D.C.; **Overnight accommodations:** Washington and vicinity; **First Aid available in park:** No, obtain local assistance by telephoning 911; **Nearest Hospital:** Washington— George Washington University Hospital; **Days/Hours:** Open dawn to dusk. Nature Center closed on Mondays. Parking areas closed at dark. No overnight camping or parking allowed. Pierce Mill, Art Barn, and Old Stone House are closed on Monday and Tuesday; **Holiday Closings:** All sites are closed on all federal holidays; **Visitor attractions closed for seasons:** No.

GENERAL INFORMATION: Wading and swimming are not recommended in Rock Creek Park or its tributaries because of polluted water.

Sewall-Belmont House National Historic Site
Washington, D.C.

MAILING ADDRESS: Superintendent, Sewall-Belmont House National Historic Site, 144 Constitution Ave., N.E., Washington, D.C. 20002 **Telephone:** 202-546-3989 or 546-1210

DIRECTIONS: The house is located near the U.S. Capitol at 144 Constitution Ave., N.E. (corner of 2nd St. N.E.)
　　Rebuilt after fire damage from the War of 1812, this red brick house is one of the oldest on Capitol Hill. It has been the National Woman's Party headquarters since 1929 and commemorates the party's founder and suffrage leader, Alice Paul, and associates. Authorized for addition to the National Park System on Oct. 26, 1974.

VISITOR ACTIVITIES: Guided tours, exhibits; **Permits:** No; **Fees:** No; **Visitor facilities:** Memorabilia of suffrage and equal rights campaigns including busts and portraits of suffrage and equal rights leaders and valuable antique furniture, garden; **Any limitations on vehicle usage:** On-street parking can be scarce during the week, plentiful spaces on weekends and holidays; **Meals served in the park:** No; **Food and supplies obtainable in the park:** No; **Food and supplies obtainable nearby:** Yes; **Overnight accommodations:** Washington, D.C.; **First Aid available in park:** No; **Nearest Hospital:** Capitol Hill Hospital, 7 blocks; **Days/Hours:** Guided tours offered from 10 a.m. to 3 p.m. on weekdays (closed Mondays) and from noon to 4 p.m. on weekends and holidays; **Holiday Closings:** Thanksgiving, Dec. 25, and Jan. 1; **Visitor attractions closed for seasons:** No.

Theodore Roosevelt Island
Washington, D.C.   **SEE CLIMATABLE NO. 38**

MAILING ADDRESS: Superintendent, George Washington Memorial Parkway, Turkey Run Park, McLean, VA. **Telephone:** 703-285-2598

DIRECTIONS: The parking area is accessible from the northbound lane of the George Washington Memorial Parkway, on the Virginia side of the Potomac River. A footbridge connects the Island to the Virginia shore.

Wooded trails lead to an imposing statue and memorial to Roosevelt, the 26th President, on this island sanctuary in the Potomac River. Authorized for addition to the National Park System on May 21, 1932.

VISITOR ACTIVITIES: Guided tours, hiking, fishing, wayside exhibits; **Permits:** Yes, fishing permits are required for persons over 16 years; **Fees:** No; **Visitor facilities:** Restrooms, drinking water, hiking trails; **HANDICAPPED ACCESSIBILITY:** Parking; restrooms not accessible; trails in poor condition for wheelchairs, having gravel/dirt surface, difficult grade in some areas. Assistance required. **Any limitations on vehicle usage:** No vehicles are permitted on the Island; **Hiking trails:** Yes, 2½ miles (4 km) of wooded trails; **Backcountry:** No; **Camping:** No; **Other overnight accommodations on site:** No; **Meals served in the park:** No; **Food and supplies obtainable in the park:** No; **Food and supplies obtainable nearby:** Yes, Arlington, VA, or the Washington area; **Overnight accommodations:** Arlington, VA, or the Washington metropolitan area; **First Aid available in park:** Yes; **Nearest Hospital:** Arlington, VA, or Washington, D.C.; **Days/Hours:** Open year round during daylight hours; **Holiday Closings:** No; **Visitor attractions closed for seasons:** No; **Weather:** Hot, humid summers. **Note:** A footbridge connects the island parking lot with nearby Rosslyn, VA, allowing easy pedestrian access to the island. **Closest Metro stop:** Rosslyn.

Thomas Jefferson Memorial
Washington, D.C.

MAILING ADDRESS: Superintendent, National Capital Parks—Central, 900 Ohio Drive, SW, Washington, DC 20242 **Telephone:** 202-485-9880

DIRECTIONS: The Memorial is on the south bank of the Tidal Basin, near downtown Washington. From Virginia, take the George Washington Parkway to Memorial Bridge, cross the bridge, and follow Ohio Drive to the Memorial.

The circular, colonnaded Memorial to the 3rd President of the United States contains a bronze statue and is surrounded by Japanese cherry trees. Dedicated Apr. 13, 1943.

VISITOR ACTIVITIES: Interpretive talks given upon request by Park Rangers, paddle boating on the Tidal Basin, Cherry Blossom Festival about the first week of April; **Permits:** For special events and First Amendment activities; **Fees:** Only for paddle boat rentals; **Visitor facilities:** Parking, paddle boat rentals, telephones, restrooms, drinking water, books and gifts; **HANDICAPPED ACCESSIBILITY:** Parking, elevator; **Any limitations on vehicle usage:** No; **Meals served in the Park:** No; **Food and supplies obtainable in the park:** No; **Food and supplies obtainable nearby:** Yes, in Washington, DC, and vicinity; **Overnight accommodations:** Washington and vicinity; **First Aid available in park:** Yes; **Nearest Hospital:** George Washington Hospital, 2 miles (3.2 km) from the Memorial; **Days/Hours:** Open 7 days a week from 8 a.m. to Midnight year-round; **Holiday Closings:** No interpretive talks offered on Dec. 25; **Visitor attractions closed for seasons:** No.

Vietnam Veterans Memorial
Washington, DC

MAILING ADDRESS: Superintendent, National Capital Parks-Central, 900 Ohio Dr., SW, Washington, DC 20242 **Telephone:** 202-485-9880

DIRECTIONS: Constitution Avenue and 23rd Street, NW, Washington, DC, Constitution Gardens, a part of West Potomac Park, built in 1982.

The memorial is composed of two black granite walls 246.75* feet long which intersect at a 125°* angle (*figure stated in official brochure). Inscribed on these tablets are the names of over 58,000 men and women who were killed or remain missing as a result of the Vietnam conflict. A bronze statue of three servicemen is located near the wall.

VISITOR ACTIVITIES: Permits: For First Amendment activities, Yes, contact Office of Public Affairs, NCR, 1100 Ohio Drive, SW, Washington, DC 20242; **Fees:** No; **Visitor facilities:** Restrooms, bookstores located in nearby park areas and memorials; **Any limitations on vehicle usage:** No vehicles or bikes are permitted; **Hiking trails:** No; **Backcountry:** No; **Camping:** No; **Other overnight accommodations on site:** No; **Meals served in the park:** No; **Food and supplies obtainable in the park:** No; **Food and supplies obtainable nearby:** Yes, Washington, DC; **Overnight accommodations:** Numerous hotels in the Washington area; **First Aid available in park:** Yes; **Days/Hours:** Open daily; **Holiday Closings:** No; **Visitor attractions closed for seasons:** No.

TRAVEL ACCESS: All major transportation available; **Rail:** Union Station, Washington, DC; **Air:** National Airport, Dulles Airport, Baltimore-Washington International Airport.

NEARBY FACILITIES & POINTS OF INTEREST: Contact Washington Convention & Visitor Association, 1575 Eye Street, NW, Washington, DC 20005, for general information; **Parks, other points of interest:** Contact Office of Public Affairs address above or telephone weekdays 202-619-7222.

Washington Monument
Washington, D.C.

MAILING ADDRESS: Superintendent, National Capital Parks-Central, 900 Ohio Drive, SW, Washington, DC 20242 **Telephone:** 202-485-9880

DIRECTIONS: The Monument is located on the National Mall between 15th and 17th Streets and Independence and Constitution Avenues. From Virginia follow Rte. 50 east or Int. 395 north to Washington.

This 555-foot obelisk honors the country's first President and is a dominant feature of the Nation's Capital. Construction began in 1848, and the monument was dedicated on Feb. 21, 1885.

VISITOR ACTIVITIES: Visitors can ascend to the top by elevator and view the city through 8 windows; **Permits:** No; **Fees:** No; **Visitor facilities:** Restrooms, snack bar, parking lot, information booths; **HANDICAPPED ACCESSIBILITY:** Parking, elevator; **Any limitations on vehicle usage:** Parking is limited to 1 hour, but there is limited free parking along nearby Ohio Drive; **Hiking trails:** No, but the Mall is suitable for short and long walks; **Meals served in the park:** Snacks at Kiosk on 15th Street; **Food and supplies obtainable in the park:** No; **Food and supplies obtainable nearby:** Yes, in downtown Washington or the metropolitan area; **Overnight accommodations:** Washington or the metropolitan area; **First Aid available in park:** Yes, or nearby in Washington; **Nearest Hospital:** George Washington University Hospital 1½ miles (2.4 km) from the Monument; **Days/Hours:** Open daily from 9 a.m. to 5 p.m. from Oct.-Mar. and 8 a.m. to Midnight from Apr. through Labor Day; **Holiday Closings:** Dec. 25; **Visitor attractions closed for seasons:** No; **Weather:** Summers are hot; average temperature 88°F, with very high humidity and occasional thunderstorms. Winter is mild, with average temperatures of 30° and some snow.

GENERAL INFORMATION: Tickets are not required for entry to monument. In spring and summer, waiting lines often exceed 1 hour.

The White House
Washington, D.C.

MAILING ADDRESS: The White House, c/o National Park Service, 1100 Ohio Drive, SW, Washington, DC 20242 **Telephone:** 202-755-7798. For current tour schedules, telephone 202-456-7041 (recorded message).

DIRECTIONS: The White House is at 1600 Pennsylvania Ave., NW, in downtown Washington, DC. Visitors should use the East Gate, on East Executive Park, to enter for tours.

The White House has been the official residence of every American President since November 1800. The cornerstone was laid on Oct. 13, 1792, on the site selected by George Washington and included in the L'Enfant Plan. The building was renovated between 1949-52. Administration transferred to the National Park Service on June 10, 1933.

VISITOR ACTIVITIES: Free public tours year-round Tuesdays through Saturdays, 10 a.m. until 12 noon. **November 1 to February 28** - no tickets required. **March 1 to October 31** - tickets may be picked up on the Ellipse, the park area south of the White House grounds, beginning at 8 a.m. on the day of the tour. These limited tickets are available until they are gone for the day or at 12:00 noon, whichever comes first. One person may pick up tickets for one or more people. Tickets will have a time on them for the tour. **Special Events Open to the Public:** Easter Egg Roll on Easter Monday; Spring and Fall Garden Tours, one weekend in April and Oct., respectively; Candlelight Tours in late Dec.; **Permits:** No; **Fees:** No admission is ever charged; beware of people attempting to sell White House Tours; **Meals served in the park:** No; **Food obtainable in the park:** On the Ellipse; **Food and supplies obtainable nearby:** Yes, in Washington, within several blocks; **Overnight accommodations:** Washington, DC; **First Aid available in park:** On the Ellipse; **Nearest Hospital:** George Washington University Hospital, 23rd Street, NW; **Visitor attractions closed for seasons:** No. The White House is closed for tours on Thanksgiving, Dec. 25, and Jan. 1, and for official functions.

GENERAL INFORMATION: More detailed information about The White House may be found in "The President's House," "The White House, An Historic Guide," "The Living White House," "The Presidents," and "First Ladies of The White House," published by The White House Historical Association, 740 Jackson Place, NW, Washington, DC 20506, phone 202-737-8292.

Connecticut

The J. Alden Weir House
Wilton, Connecticut

MAILING ADDRESS: 735 Nod Hill Road, Wilton, CT 06897 **Telephone:** 203-761-9945

DIRECTIONS: The Weir Home is located 1 mile (1.6 km) off Route 7 in western Connecticut.

This site was enacted into law as a National Park Service Historic Site by the 51st Congress, but as of August 1, 1991 appropriations are pending for its acquisition. It is currently administered by the Weir Farm Heritage Trust.

The Weir Home is Connecticut's first National Historic Site and the first park in the nation to commemorate an American Painter.

Florida

FORT CAROLINE
NATIONAL MEMORIAL

CASTILLO DE SAN MARCOS
NATIONAL MONUMENT

FORT MATANZAS
NATIONAL MONUMENT

GULF ISLANDS NATIONAL SEASHORE

CANAVERAL NATIONAL SEASHORE

DE SOTO NATIONAL MEMORIAL

BIG CYPRESS NATIONAL PRESERVE

EVERGLADES NATIONAL PARK

BISCAYNE NATIONAL PARK

FORT JEFFERSON NATIONAL MONUMENT

Big Cypress National Preserve
Ochopee, Florida

MAILING ADDRESS: Superintendent, Big Cypress National Preserve, S.R. Box 110, Ochopee, FL 33943 **Telephone:** 813-695-2000 or 813-262-1066

DIRECTIONS: The Superintendent's Office (Preserve Headquarters) is approximately 35 miles (56 km) east of Naples, FL, on U.S. 41. The west boundary of the Preserve is 30 miles (48 km) from Naples, via US 41 and Alligator Alley. The east boundary is 30 miles (48 km) from Miami, FL.

The Preserve comprises 716,000 acres of watershed which provide a natural freshwater supply to the northwest portion of Everglades National Park. It is the ancestral home of the Seminole and Miccosukee Indians, and contains abundant subtropical plant and animal life. Authorized for addition to the National Park System on Oct. 11, 1974.

VISITOR ACTIVITIES: Camping, hiking, backpacking, picnicking, sightseeing, canoeing, fishing, hunting; **Permits:** For hunting and fishing from the Florida Game and Fresh Water Fish Commission, Tallahassee, FL 32301, phone 904-488-1960; **Fees:** For fresh water fishing; for more information, write Florida Game and Fish Commission, Tallahassee,

FL 32301. Licenses vary in cost and in length of validity; **Visitor facilities:** The only facility is Oasis Ranger Station, the field operational base. Staff is available from 8 a.m.-4:30 p.m. daily; **HANDICAPPED ACCESSIBILITY:** Parking, restrooms, Visitor Center at Oasis Ranger Station. **Any limitations on vehicle usage:** Permits required; Off-road vehicle use is restricted; **Hiking trails:** Yes, developed hiking trails can be located on private lands; **Backcountry:** Yes, information available from Florida Trail Association, P.O. Box 13708, Gainesville, FL 32604; **Developed Camping:** No, camping facilities are at Collier Seminole State Park and Everglades National Park, and at privately owned campgrounds in the vicinity; **Other undeveloped RV and tent camping sites:** Yes; **Food and supplies obtainable in the park:** Yes, along US 41; **Food and supplies obtainable nearby:** Yes, in Miami and Naples; **Overnight accommodations:** Miami and Naples, approx. 50 miles (80 km) from Oasis Ranger Station; All nearby areas are on US 41; **First Aid available in park:** Yes, at Oasis Ranger Station; **Nearest Hospital:** Naples Community Hospital, US 41 west, approx. 58 miles (93 km) from the Oasis Ranger Station; **Days/Hours:** Open year-round; **Holiday Closings:** Oasis Ranger Station closed Dec. 25; **Visitor attractions closed for seasons:** No.

Biscayne National Park
Homestead, Florida   **SEE CLIMATABLE NO. 17**

MAILING ADDRESS: Superintendent, Biscayne National Park, P.O. Box 1369, Homestead, FL 33090-1369 **Telephone:** 305-247-PARK.

DIRECTIONS: Limited public boat transportation is available by concession. For information, call 305-247-2400. Otherwise you must have your own boat or a hired boat to explore the keys and to swim and dive. You should stop at Park Headquarters on Convoy Point, 9 miles (14.5 km) east of Homestead, or at the Ranger Station on Elliott Key (open weekends only). Park personnel can answer your questions and help you plan your visit.

Most of the Park is reef and water, but within its boundaries about 42 keys, or islands, form a north-south chain, with Biscayne Bay on the west and the Atlantic Ocean on the east. The Park contains a significant example of living coral reef. Most of the shoreline on both mainland and keys is exposed, rough coral rock. This occurs during low tide. Authorized for addition to the National Park System on Oct. 18, 1968.

VISITOR ACTIVITIES: Boating, fishing, swimming, snorkeling, scuba diving, camping, picnicking, hiking, interpretive exhibits, bird-watching; **Permits:** Backcountry permits can be obtained from a Park Ranger; **Fees:** No; **Visitor facilities:** At Elliott Key Harbor Ranger Station: 64-slip harbor, primitive campground, picnic area, grills, interpretive trail, restrooms, and cold water showers. At Convoy Point: Picnic area, restrooms, Ranger-led activities, and Visitor Center. At Boca Chita Key: Docking facilities, primitive campground, restrooms, picnic tables, grills. At Adams Key: Day-use only, docking facilities, picnic tables, grills, restrooms. Gasoline is not available at the Park but it can be obtained near the Headquarters at Homestead Bayfront Park or Black Point Park. Meals, lodging, campgrounds, gasoline, and other supplies are available in Homestead. Many well-supplied marinas are located along the mainland coast and in the Florida Keys. Check your charts or ask a Park Ranger; **HANDICAPPED ACCESSIBILITY:** The Visitor Center, restroom facilities, and Headquarter building at Convoy Point are accessible to the mobility impaired visitor, as are restroom facilities at Elliott Key, Adams Key, and Boca Chita Key. **Any limitations on vehicle usage:** Be familiar with boating rules. Obtain a copy of them at Headquarters or the Ranger Station; **Hiking trails:** Yes; **Backcountry:** Yes; **Camping:** Yes, at keys or islands (none at Convoy Point), no reservations for campsites; **Other overnight accommodations on site:** No; **Meals served in the park:** No; **Food and supplies obtainable in the park:** No; **Food**

and supplies obtainable nearby: Yes, limited food and supplies at Homestead Bayfront Park and Black Point Park; **Overnight accommodations:** Homestead, US 1, 9 miles (14.5 km); **First Aid available in park:** Yes, at Elliott Key and Convoy Pt. Visitor Centers; **Nearest Hospital:** Homestead, US 1, 15 miles (24 km); **Days/Hours:** Open 24 hours a day, 365 days per year. Headquarters: Convoy Point Visitor Center is open from 8:30 a.m. to 5:00 p.m. all year-round; Elliott Key Visitor Center open only on weekends, year-round; **Holiday Closings:** No; **Visitor attractions closed for seasons:** No; **Weather:** Summers are humid with frequent afternoon rain showers; winters are cool and clear.

GENERAL INFORMATION: No trash or garbage pick-up in any of our keys or islands. Pack it out. Be sure to read the safety precautions published in the pamphlet on Biscayne available from Headquarters or the Ranger Station. Nearby points of interest include Everglades National Park (see listing in this book) and John Pennekamp Coral Reef State Park.

Canaveral National Seashore
Titusville, Florida

MAILING ADDRESS: Superintendent, Canaveral National Seashore, 2532 Garden Street, Titusville, FL 32796 **Telephone:** 407-267-1110

DIRECTIONS: Located midway down the Florida east coast between Jacksonville and West Palm Beach, the Seashore is readily accessible via such major arteries as US 1 and Int. I-95, I-4, and I-75. New Smyrna Beach provides access via FL A1A into the Seashore in the vicinity of Turtle Mound, a shell midden made by native Indians. Titusville, the southern Gateway City, provides access via FL 402. Playalinda Beach on the Seashore's southern end is now the principal visitor use area. It is accessible via FL 402 from Titusville and FL 3, which cuts off to the south from U.S. 1 between Titusville and Oak Hill. In addition, the Intercoastal Waterway linking Florida with the north skirts the western edge of Mosquito Lagoon before entering the Indian River via the Haulover Canal.

The Seashore offers a great variety of wildlife, including many species of birds, on a segment of largely undeveloped land. Established by act of Congress Jan. 3, 1975. Merritt Island National Wildlife Refuge, administered by Fish and Wildlife Service, U.S. Dept. of the Interior is located next to the seashore.

VISITOR ACTIVITIES: Bird-watching, boating, swimming, surfing, sun bathing, shell collecting, surf fishing, wildlife observation, photography, wildland hiking, waterfowl hunting, picnicking, walking; **Permits:** Backcountry camping, horse use; no others except hunting, but hunting in season is subject to U.S. Fish and Wildlife Service and state regulations; **Fees:** No fees to enter the beach at this time; **Visitor facilities:** Exhibits and slide program; toilets at beaches; picnic tables; **HANDICAPPED ACCESSIBILITY:** Restrooms and beach access at designated areas; designated parking places; **Any limitations on vehicle usage:** Vehicles are restricted to established roads and are prohibited on the beach; **Hiking trails:** Yes, Turtle Mound, ¼ mile (.4 km), Castle Windy Trail, ½ mile (.8 km), Eldora Hammock, ½ mile (.8 km), and Old Eldora, ¼ mile (.4 km), all self-guiding; **Backcountry:** Yes, camping is permitted on the north beach and islands in the north end of Mosquito Lagoon; There is a closed period when space vehicles are on launch pad or during launching; **Camping:** Beach backcountry camping closed May 15-Sept. 30; **Other overnight accommodations on site:** No, there are private campgrounds in nearby communities; **Meals served in the park:** No; **Food and supplies obtainable in the park:** No; **Food and supplies obtainable nearby:** Yes, at Titusville, 12 miles (19.2 km); New Smyrna Beach 10 miles (16 km); **Overnight accommodations:** Titusville, 12 miles (19.2 km); New Smyrna Beach, 10 miles (16 km);

First Aid available in park: Limited; **Nearest Hospital:** Titusville, 12 miles (19.2 km); New Smyrna Beach, 10 miles (16 km); **Days/Hours:** Open 6:30 a.m.-8 p.m. (Eastern Standard) to 6 p.m. (Daylight Savings) 7 days a week; **Holiday Closings:** Visitor Center closed Christmas Day and New Years Day; **Visitor attractions closed for seasons:** No; **Weather:** The climate is sub-tropical, with short, mild winters and hot, humid summers. Ocean temperatures remain relatively warm all year.

GENERAL INFORMATION: Swimming can be dangerous due to strong ocean currents. Lifeguards are not provided. Visitors to inland areas away from the influence of off-shore breezes should carry a repellent to protect themselves from mosquitoes and other biting insects. Space operations at Kennedy Space Center require closing of Playalinda Beach for safety and security prior to and during launch of the space shuttle. Pets and glass containers are not allowed on the beaches.

TRAVEL ACCESS: Bus: Greyhound provides daily service to Titusville and New Smyrna Beach, FL; **Rail:** No; **Air:** Daily commuter air service into Tico Airport, Titusville, FL, Daytona Beach, FL.

NEARBY FACILITIES & POINTS OF INTEREST: Campgrounds: KOA campgrounds in Mims and New Smyrna Beach, FL, Jetty Park, Cape Canaveral, FL— campground; **Parks, other points of interest:** Kennedy Space Center, Merritt Island National Wildlife Refuge.

Castillo de San Marcos National Monument
St. Augustine, Florida

MAILING ADDRESS: Superintendent, Castillo de San Marcos National Monument, 1 Castillo Drive, St. Augustine, FL 32084 **Telephone:** 904-829-6506

DIRECTIONS: The Monument is at 1 Castillo Drive in downtown St. Augustine.

This oldest masonry fortification in the continental United States, constructed in 1672-95 "modernized" by 1756, replaced the last of nine wooden forts built in succession since the founding of St. Augustine in 1565. These structures affirmed the Spanish title to Florida, and Castillo eventually became the principal fortification in a regional defense system that preserved Spanish dominion during 235 years.

VISITOR ACTIVITIES: Interpretive exhibits, ranger talks, living history demonstration, self-guiding tours; **Permits:** No; **Fees:** $1 per person fee for those 17 and older. U.S. Senior Citizens are free. Golden Age and Golden Eagle Passports accepted and available; **Visitor facilities:** Parking, restrooms; **Any limitations on vehicle usage:** No; **Hiking trails:** No; **Meals served in the park:** No; **Food and supplies obtainable in the park:** No; **Food and supplies obtainable nearby:** Yes, adjacent to the Park in St. Augustine; **Overnight accommodations:** St. Augustine; **First Aid available in park:** Yes; **Nearest Hospital:** 2 major hospitals in St. Augustine; **Days/Hours:** 9:00 a.m.-5:15 p.m. winter; Call for summer hours, generally 8:30 a.m.-7:45 p.m.; **Holiday Closings:** Dec. 25.

GENERAL INFORMATION: *For Your Safety*—Watch out for rough and uneven floors, fragile walls, and steep drops.

TRAVEL ACCESS: Bus: Greyhound/Trailways provides daily service to within ½ mile (.8 km) of Park; **Rail:** No; **Air:** Not direct; **Other:** Two "tour" trains operate in St. Augustine stopping at the Park.

NEARBY FACILITIES & POINTS OF INTEREST: **Campgrounds:** Anastasia St. Park, Anastasia Island, St. Augustine, FL, 904-829-2668, 3 miles (4.8 km) from Park.

DeSoto National Memorial
Bradenton, FL

MAILING ADDRESS: Superintendent, DeSoto National Memorial, P.O. Box 15390, Bradenton, Florida 34280-5390 **Telephone:** 813-792-0458

DIRECTIONS: The Park is on Tampa Bay 5 miles (8 km) west of Brandenton, FL, on 75th Street, NW, 2 miles (3.2 km) north of SR 64 W.
    The landing of Spanish explorer Hernando de Soto in Florida in 1539 and the first extensive organized exploration of what is now the southern United States by Europeans are commemorated here. Authorized for addition to the National Park System on Mar. 11, 1948.

VISITOR ACTIVITIES: Interpretive film, exhibits, trail, fishing, living history demonstration in season, special films and programs with prior approval; **Permits:** Yes, for weddings and other special uses; **Fees:** No entrance fees; **Visitor facilities:** Parking and restrooms at Visitor Center; **HANDICAPPED ACCESSIBILITY:** Parking, portable handicapped toilet, trail, boardwalk, living history program, Visitor Center; **Any limitations on vehicle usage:** No vehicles allowed on the trails or outside roads and parking areas; **Hiking trails:** Yes, a ½ mile (.8 km) nature trail; **Backcountry:** No; **Camping:** No; **Other overnight accommodations on site:** No; **Meals served in the park:** No; **Food and supplies obtainable in the park:** No; **Food and supplies obtainable nearby:** Yes, in Bradenton; **Overnight accommodations:** Bradenton; Palmetto 10 miles (16 km); **First Aid available in park:** Yes; **Nearest Hospital:** Bradenton, 59th Street, 5 miles (8 km); **Days/Hours:** Open daily from 8 a.m. to 5:30 p.m.; **Holiday Closings:** No; **Visitor attractions closed for seasons:** Living history program closed from Apr. through Nov.; **Weather:** Temperatures are in the mid 90°s F in summer, with high humidity. Winter highs range from the 70°s to the mid 50°s with moderate humidity. Winter days are characterized by strong breezes and blue skies.

TRAVEL ACCESS: **Bus:** Greyhound provides daily service to Bradenton; **Rail:** No; **Air:** American, Continental, Delta, Northwest, Republic, TWA, USAir, United, and others provide daily service to Sarasota/Bradenton.

NEARBY FACILITIES & POINTS OF INTEREST: **Hotel/Motel:** Found in Bradenton; **Food/Supplies:** Found in Bradenton; **Campgrounds:** Found in Bradenton; **Parks, other points of interest:** Gamble Mansion, Lake Manatee State Park, Myakka River State Park, South Florida Museum/Bishop Planetarium, Manatee County Tourist Information Center, Manatee Village Historic Park, Mote Marine.

Everglades National Park
Homestead, Florida   **SEE CLIMATABLE NO. 16**

MAILING ADDRESS: Superintendent, Everglades National Park, P.O. Box 279, Homestead, FL 33030 **Telephone:** 305-247-6211

DIRECTIONS: The main Visitor Center is near the Park entrance, 12 miles (20 km) southwest of Homestead on Route 9336. Other Visitor Centers are at Royal Palm, Shark Valley, Flamingo, and Everglades City.
    This largest remaining subtropical wilderness in the conterminous United States has

extensive fresh- and salt-water areas, open prairies, and mangrove forests. Abundant wildlife includes rare birds. Park dedicated on Dec. 6, 1947.

VISITOR ACTIVITIES: Boating, camping, picnicking, wildlife- and bird-watching, photography, hiking, interpretive talks and exhibits, fishing, backcountry, canoeing, open-air tram and sightseeing boat rides; **Permits:** Florida fishing license, available at local bait and tackle shops, is required for fresh water fishing. The state of Florida requires a salt water fishing license as of Jan. 1, 1990. Licenses vary in length of validity and cost. Free backcountry use permits available at Everglades City and Flaming Ranger stations. The May-Oct. off season has a self-registration system; **Fees:** $5 per vehicle or $3 per person at main entrance; $3 per vehicle or $2 per person at Shark Valley entrance. Overnight camping in developed sites is $8 per night and $4 for walk-in tent sites, from Nov. 1-Apr. 30, free the remainder of the year. Shark Valley tram tours are concession fee-operated. Golden Age, Golden Eagle, and Golden Access Passports available. It is suggested that frequent visitors to the park purchase the Everglades National Park Pass for $15, good for unlimited entrances on a calendar year basis; **Visitor facilities:** Bookstore, parking, restrooms, and telephones at Visitor Center; boat rentals and ramp, marina, nature trails, campgrounds, picnic areas, environmental study area, restaurant, houseboat rentals; **HANDICAPPED ACCESSIBILITY:** A handicapped accessibility guide is available at park Visitor Centers. Most walking trails and boat tours are accessible by wheelchair; **Any limitations on vehicle usage:** No off-road vehicles are permitted in the park. No private vehicles permitted on Shark Valley Road; all vehicles restricted to designated roadways; **Hiking trails:** Yes, many short trails lead off the main park road; **Backcountry:** Yes, required permit available from Ranger stations at Everglades City and Flamingo. Most backcountry campsites are accessible by boat only. Insect repellent is needed on all backcountry trails throughout the year; **Camping:** Yes, individual campsites cannot be reserved. Group campsites can be reserved by contacting Chief Ranger, ENP, P.O. Box 279, Homestead, FL 33030; **Other overnight accommodations on site:** Yes, there is a motor lodge at Flamingo. Reservations should be made well in advance to Flamingo Lodge, Marina & Outpost, Flamingo, FL 33030; 24-hour phone 813-695-3101. Additional camping near Everglades City can be found at Copeland, 7 miles (11 km) north on FL 29, and at Collier-Seminole State Park, 19 miles (30.5 km) west on US 41; **Meals served in the park:** Yes, at Flamingo; The restaurant at Flamingo is closed during the summer season; **Food and supplies obtainable in the park:** Yes, at Flamingo Marina; **Food and supplies obtainable nearby:** Yes, at Homestead, Key Largo, Everglades City; **Overnight accommodations:** Homestead, Florida City, 12 miles (19.3 km); Florida Keys, 40 miles (64.4 km); Everglades City, 90 miles (144.8 km); **First Aid available in park:** Yes, at Ranger stations; **Nearest Hospital:** Homestead, 48 miles (77 km) from Flamingo; **Days/Hours:** Open 24 hours a day year-round; **Holiday Closings:** No; **Visitor attractions closed for seasons:** Services reduced at Flamingo during the summer; **Weather:** Winters are dry and clear; summers are rainy with torrential local downpours and lightning storms. Temperatures range in the 80s and 90s during the summer and on rare occasions drop to the 30s in winter.

GENERAL INFORMATION: Rates for overnight accommodations are considerably higher throughout South Florida during the winter season (Dec. 15-Apr. 15.) Mosquitoes and other biting insects make camping and backcountry use during the summer rainy season virtually unbearable by all but the most dedicated outdoorsperson.

NEARBY FACILITIES & POINTS OF INTEREST: Hotel/Motel: All services available in Homestead, FL, 12 miles (19.2 km) from main entrance; **Parks, other points of interest:** Biscayne National Park, Big Cypress National Preserve.

Fort Caroline National Memorial
Jacksonville, Florida

MAILING ADDRESS: Superintendent, Fort Caroline National Memorial, 12713 Fort Caroline Road, Jacksonville, FL 32225 **Telephone:** 904-641-7155

DIRECTIONS: The Memorial is about 13 "driving" miles (20.8 km) east of downtown Jacksonville and 17 miles (27.2 km) west of Mayport. It can be reached by FL 10: Turn north on St. Johns Bluff Road or Monument Road, then proceed east on Fort Caroline Road. Travelers heading south on I-95 should take FL Rt. 9A, across the St. Johns River on the Broward Bridge, then to Merrill Rd., turn left (east); follow to Ft. Caroline Rd. Park is 4 miles (6.4 km) ahead.

The model fort overlooks the site of a French Huguenot colony of 1564-65, the second French attempt at settlement within the present United States. Here the French and Spanish began two centuries of European colonial rivalry in North America. Authorized for addition to the National Park System on Sept. 21, 1950.

VISITOR ACTIVITIES: Interpretive exhibits, walking tours; **Permits:** No; **Fees:** No; **Visitor facilities:** Visitor Center, museum, sales outlet, walking trails, picnic area (no fires); **HANDICAPPED ACCESSIBILITY:** Visitor facilities and programs are handicapped accessible; **Any limitations on vehicle usage:** No; **Hiking trails:** Yes, three trails; the longest is 1 mile (1.6 km); **Backcountry:** No; **Camping:** No; **Other overnight accommodations on site:** No; **Meals served in the park:** No; **Food and supplies obtainable in the park:** No; **Food and supplies obtainable nearby:** Yes, in Jacksonville and Jax Beaches; **Overnight accommodations:** Jacksonville, FL, 9 miles (14.4 km) and Jax Beaches, 12 miles (19 km); **First Aid available in park:** Yes; **Nearest Hospital:** Jacksonville, 12 miles (19 km); **Days/ Hours:** 9 a.m.-5 p.m., year around; **Holiday Closings:** Dec. 25.

GENERAL INFORMATION: The proximity of the river to the Fort requires additional caution. Visitors are advised to bring mosquito repellent.

Fort Jefferson National Monument
70 miles (112 km) west of Key West, Florida

MAILING ADDRESS: Superintendent, Everglades National Park, P.O. Box 279, Homestead, FL 33030 **Telephone:** 305-247-6211

DIRECTIONS: The Monument can be reached only by boat or seaplane. Currently, several operators of boat and air taxi services offer trips to the Dry Tortugas from Key West, and the Lower Keys, as well as from the Naples and Fort Meyers area of southwest Florida. Specific information regarding these services may be obtained from the Chambers of Commerce located at 3330 Overseas Highway, Marathon, FL 33052, phone 305-743-5417; Old Mallory Square, Key West, FL 33040, phone 305-294-2587; and 1700 N. Tamiami Trail, Naples, FL 33940, 813-262-6141.

VISITOR ACTIVITIES: Interpretive exhibits, self-guiding tours, Ranger-lead activities, bird- and wildlife-watching, picnicking, salt-water sport fishing (Florida Salt Water Fishing License required), snorkeling, swimming, and scuba diving; **Permits:** Required for overnight camping groups of 10 or more; **Fees:** No; **Visitor facilities:** Visitor Center, picnic area, small camping area, salt-water toilets; **HANDICAPPED ACCESSIBILITY:** Restrooms, main tour route; **Any limitations on vehicle usage:** The island is roadless; Personal watercraft, i.e., jetskis are not permitted; **Hiking trails:** Half mile moat walk; **Backcountry:** No; **Camping:** Yes, permitted on Garden Key only where small number of primitive campsites are available on first-come basis, camping groups of 10 or more must obtain Special Permit in advance; **Other overnight accommodations on site:** No; **Meals served in the park:** No; **Food and supplies obtainable in the park:** No; **Food and supplies obtainable nearby:** Key West, 70 miles (112 km) by water; **Overnight accommodations:** Key West, 70 miles (112 km) by water; **First Aid available in park:** Yes; **Nearest Hospital:** Key West, 70 miles (112 km) by water; **Days/Hours:** Open daily year-round from sunrise to sunset; **Holiday Closings:** No; **Visitor attractions closed for seasons:** Bush Key is closed to visitors from Apr. to Sept. to protect nesting Sooty and Noddy Terns, day use only on all keys except Garden Key; **Weather:** Generally sunny and warm; occasional squalls are common, breezy conditions during fall, winter and spring. Boaters should be prepared for the possibility of extremely rough seas. Hurricane season is June 1 to November 30.

GENERAL INFORMATION: The Monument's central feature is Fort Jefferson, the largest all-masonry fortification in the Western hemisphere. Construction was begun in 1846, but was never fully completed. The cluster of seven islands known as the Dry Tortugas and the 100 square miles (160 km) of pristine coral reefs and seagrass beds provide outstanding opportunities for viewing seabirds and marine life. Created by Presidential Proclamation on January 4, 1935.

Since the Monument is isolated, visitors must provide for their own independent existence. All food, water, and supplies must be brought from the mainland. All trash generated must be removed with you. Fishing requires a Florida Salt Water License, which must be obtained on the mainland. *For Your Safety*—Do not stand near wall edges. Mortar in historic structures may be loose or weakened. Watch for uneven walking surfaces, spiral stairways, sudden drop-offs, and darkened areas. Never swim alone. Be cautious in areas of strong currents. Cuts from coral and punctures from the sea urchins may be painful and slow to heal.

Fort Matanzas National Monument
Saint Augustine, Florida

MAILING ADDRESS: Superintendent, Castillo de San Marcos National Monument, 1 Castillo Drive, St. Augustine, FL 32084 **Telephone:** 904-471-0116

DIRECTIONS: The Park is 14 miles (22 km) south of St. Augustine and can be reached by FL A1A on Anastasia Island. The Park consists of 298 acres on Rattlesnake Island, where the fort is located, and on Anastasia Island, where the Visitor Center is located. The Fort is accessible only by boat. A ferry crosses to Rattlesnake Island daily between 9 a.m. and 4:30 p.m. daily year-round, weather permitting.

This Spanish fort was built between 1740 and 1742 to protect St. Augustine from attack via Matanzas Inlet. Created by Presidential Proclamation on Oct. 15, 1924.

VISITOR ACTIVITIES: Interpretive walks and talks, ferry boat rides, fishing; **Permits:** No; **Fees:** No; **Visitor facilities:** Restrooms and parking at Visitor Center (handicap accessible); **Any limitations on vehicle usage:** Vehicles are restricted to designated roadways; **Hiking trails:** Nature trail ½-mile (.8-km) boardwalk, handicap accessible; **Backcountry:** No; **Camping:** No; **Other overnight accommodations on site:** No; **Meals served in the park:** No; **Food and supplies obtainable in the park:** No; **Food and supplies obtainable nearby:** Yes, in St. Augustine Beach, 10 miles (16 km); **Overnight accommodations:** St. Augustine Beach, 10 miles (16 km), St. Augustine, 15 miles (24 km); **First Aid available in park:** Yes; **Nearest Hospital:** St. Augustine, 15 miles (24 km); **Days/Hours:** Open daily from 8:30 a.m.

to 5:30 p.m.; **Holiday Closings:** Dec. 25; **Visitor attractions closed for seasons:** No; **Weather:** A wide variety of weather conditions.

GENERAL INFORMATION: *For Your Safety*—Do not swim in the treacherous waters near the inlet or climb on the fort walls. Be wary of sharp oyster shells.

NEARBY FACILITIES & POINTS OF INTEREST: Campgrounds: Anastasia State Recreation Area 12 miles (19.2 km) north; Flagler Beach State Recreation Area 18 miles (28.8 km) south; several private campgrounds nearby; **Parks, other points of interest:** Historic sites in St. Augustine 15 miles (24 km) north, Marineland 5 miles (8 km) south.

Gulf Islands National Seashore
Florida and Mississippi

MAILING ADDRESS: Superintendent, Gulf Islands National Seashore, 1801 Gulf Breeze Parkway, Gulf Breeze, FL 32561. **Telephone:** FL: 904-934-2600, MS: 601-875-0821

DIRECTIONS: Access to Ship Island in the Mississippi District is provided by concession boats from Gulfport MS, March through October and from Biloxi, MS, Memorial Day weekend through Labor Day. Consult the concessioners' printed schedules for frequency and times. Private boats may dock near Fort Massachusetts on West Ship Island in the daytime. Horn, Petit Bois and East Ship Islands are reached by chartered or private boats. Davis Bayou can be reached by following the signs on U.S. 90 for Gulf Islands National Seashore. Recommended routes for reaching the major visitor areas within the Florida District are Johnson Beach (Perdido Key)—take FL 292 southwest from Pensacola; historic mainland forts and Naval Museum—use the main entrance of Pensacola Naval Air Station off Barrancas. (FL 295); Naval Live Oaks and the Fort Pickens and Santa Rosa Areas—take US 98 from downtown Pensacola across the Pensacola Bay Bridge.

This series of offshore islands and mainland areas has both historic forts and sparkling white sand beaches near Pensacola, FL, and Pascagoula and Biloxi, MS, with mainland facilities in Ocean Springs, MS. Authorized for addition to the National Park System on Jan. 8, 1971.

VISITOR ACTIVITIES: Interpretive exhibits and programs, picnicking, camping, hiking, sunbathing, swimming, boating, fishing, auto tours, scuba diving, guided fort tours; **Permits:** No; **Fees:** $10 fee for campgrounds without electricity, $12 with; entrance fee of $3 per vehicle for 7-day permit or $10 annual permit; **Visitor facilities:** Picnic areas, campgrounds, bathhouses, boat dock and ramp, laundry, boat charters, campground store, restrooms, snack shops, visitor centers, guarded beaches, souvenirs and bookstore, fishing pier, hiking and bicycle trails, playground, ball field, ball court, wilderness area; **HANDICAPPED ACCESSIBILITY:** William M. Colmer Visitor Center, Davis Bayou, Ocean Springs, MS; West Ship Island, MS; Santa Rosa Day Use Facility; Santa Rosa Island, FL; Fort Barrancas Visitor Center, onboard NAS, Pensacola, FL; Visitor Center and Picnic Area, Naval Live Oaks; Johnson Beach, Perdido Key Area; Fort Pickens and visitor center, museum and auditorium at Fort Pickens Area; Accessible programs at the following locations: William M. Colmer Visitor Center, Davis Bayou, Ocean Springs, MS, Fort Barrancas Visitor Center, onboard NAS, Pensacola, FL; Visitor Center, Naval Live Oaks; Santa Rosa Exhibit Room; Fort Pickens and interpretive facilities; **Any limitations on vehicle usage:** Motor vehicles are not allowed on sand dunes and beaches. **Hiking trails:** Yes, interpretive trails are in each state; **Backcountry:** Yes, Horn and Petit Bois Islands are wilderness areas, and can be reached by private or charter boat. **Camping:** Yes, no reservations available for campsites. Long tent stakes for use in the sand and mosquito netting are a must; **Other overnight accommoda-**

tions on site: No; **Meals served in the park:** Yes, snacks at Santa Rosa Area, Perdido Key Area, Fort Pickens Area, Okaloosa Area, Ship Island; **Food and supplies obtainable in the park:** Yes, at Ft. Pickens Area campground store; **Food and supplies obtainable nearby:** Yes, in major urban centers along the entire 175-mile (280-km) overland route from Gulfport, MS to Fort Walton Beach, FL, from Ship Island, MS, to Santa Rosa Island, FL; **Overnight accommodations:** In urban centers: Gulfport, Biloxi, Ocean Springs, and Pascagoula, MS; Pensacola and Ft. Walton Beach, FL; **First Aid available in park:** Yes; **Nearest Hospital:** Ocean Springs, MS, Highway 90, 5 miles (8 km); Pensacola, FL, Baptist Hosp., 12 miles (20 km); Gulf Breeze, FL, Gulf Breeze Hospital, 2 miles (3.2 km); **Days/Hours:** Open 24 hours a day, except Naval Live Oaks, Fort Barrancas, Santa Rosa, Perdido Key, Ship Island, and Okaloosa Areas; **Holiday Closings:** No; **Visitor attractions closed for seasons:** Guarded beaches closed from Sept.-May, Redoubt closed from Sept.-May; **Weather:** Hot, humid summer; cool, moderate winter; comfortable spring and fall.

GENERAL INFORMATION: *For Your Safety*—Be extremely careful of strong currents in heavy surf, and avoid stinging jellyfish and Portuguese man-of-war. Do not swim alone in unguarded waters. Watch your step while exploring the forts and batteries. You should carry a flashlight since the passageways are dimly lighted.

TRAVEL ACCESS: Bus: Greyhound-Trailways provide service to Biloxi, and Pensacola; **Rail:** No; **Air:** Continental, USAir, Northwest and Delta services into Pensacola, Continental, Northwest and ASA service into Gulfport.

NEARBY FACILITIES & POINTS OF INTEREST: Parks, other points of interest: Naval Air Museum (Pensacola), Home of Jefferson Davis (Biloxi).

Timucuan Ecological and Historic Preserve
Jacksonville, Florida

MAILING ADDRESS: Timucuan Ecological and Historic Preserve, c/o Fort Caroline National Memorial, 12713 Fort Caroline Road, Jacksonville, FL 32225 **Telephone:** 904-641-7111

Preserve headquarters are located with Fort Caroline National Memorial, the core unit of this new park. The Park Service is engaged presently in the necessary and required land use planning and acquisition phases. Information on these activities may be obtained by contacting the Superintendent.

This 46,000-acre preserve encompasses the coastal marshes, islands, mudflats and meandering tidal creeks of north Jacksonville. Cultural sites within the preserve cover a time span beginning with the prehistoric Timucuan Indians, believed to have roamed the area more than 2,000 years before Columbus' New World Discovery, and ending with the Spanish-American War in 1898.

Authorized: Feb. 16, 1988. Acreage: 46,000; 1,000 federal.

The Theodore Roosevelt Area, immediately adjacent to the southeast corner of Fort Caroline National Memorial, is the only new Preserve acquisition presently open to the public.

VISITOR ACTIVITIES: Walking tours, bicycling, fishing; **Permits:** No; **Fees:** No; **Visitor facilities:** Restrooms, picnic (no fires, pack out all refuse); **Any limitations on vehicle use:** No vehicles or motorbikes on trail/road system; **Hiking trails:** Yes, 2 trails, the longest is 2.5 miles (4 km); **Backcountry:** No; **Camping:** No; **Other overnight accommodations on site:** No; **Meals served in the park:** No; **Food and supplies obtainable in the park:** No; **Food and supplies obtainable nearby:** Yes, in Jacksonville and Jax Beaches; **Overnight**

accommodations: Jacksonville, FL, 9 miles (14.4 km) and Jax Beaches, 12 miles (19 km); **First Aid available in park:** Yes; **Nearest Hospital:** Jacksonville, 12 miles (19 km); **Days/ Hours:** 8 a.m. to dusk, year round; **Holiday Closings:** No.

GENERAL INFORMATION: The density of this 544-acre woodland and its proximity to saltwater marshes and freshwater ponds/streams requires additional caution concerning mosquitoes, snakes, and poisonous plants.

As new areas are added to the Preserve visitor facilities and activities will follow. Contact Preserve headquarters for information.

Georgia

CHICKAMAUGA AND CHATTANOOGA
NATIONAL MILITARY PARK

APPALACHIAN NATIONAL SCENIC TRAIL

CHATTAHOOCHEE RIVER
NATIONAL RECREATION AREA

KENNESAW MOUNTAIN
NATIONAL BATTLEFIELD PARK

MARTIN LUTHER KING, JR.
NATIONAL HISTORIC SITE

OCMULGEE NATIONAL MONUMENT

FORT PULASKI
NATIONAL MONUMENT

ANDERSONVILLE
NATIONAL HISTORIC SITE

JIMMY CARTER NATIONAL HISTORIC SITE

FORT FREDERICA
NATIONAL MONUMENT

CUMBERLAND ISLAND
NATIONAL SEASHORE

Andersonville National Historic Site
Andersonville, Georgia

MAILING ADDRESS: Superintendent, Andersonville National Historic Site, Rt. 1, Box 85, Andersonville, GA 31711 **Telephone:** 912-924-0343

DIRECTIONS: The Site is northeast of Americus, GA, on Route 49, in Macon County. Interstate 75 south of Macon, GA, intersects Route 49, north of the Park. Routes 224 and 27 and U.S. 280 at Cordele also connect I-75 with Route 49.

Established by act of Congress on July 1, 1971, this 500-acre Site includes a national cemetery and the site of the Civil War prison camp where 45,000 Union soldiers were imprisoned and 12,912 of them died. Andersonville was mandated by Congress on Oct. 16, 1970, to commemorate the sacrifices of American POWs throughout the history of our country.

VISITOR ACTIVITIES: Picnicking, auto tape tours, walking, commemorative Monuments, interpretive exhibits, Visitor Center and Museum, and POW Museum; **Permits:** No; **Fees:** No; **Visitor facilities:** Parking and restrooms at Visitor Center; **Any limitations on vehicle usage:** Vehicles are confined to parking area and auto tour roads; **Hiking trails:** No; **Backcountry:** No; **Camping:** No; **Other overnight accommodations on site:** No; **Meals served in the park:** No; **Food and supplies obtainable in the park:** No; **Food and supplies obtainable nearby:** Yes, Andersonville, .5 mile (.8 km), Americus, 10 miles (16 km), Montezuma, 10 miles (16 km); **Overnight accommodations:** Americus, Highway 49, 10 miles (16 km), Montezuma, 10 miles (16 km); **First Aid available in park:** Yes; **Nearest Hospital:** Americus, Hwy 49, 10 miles (16 km); **Days/Hours:** Open 7 days a week: 8 a.m. to 5 p.m., until 7 p.m. on Memorial Day; **Holiday Closings:** No; **Visitor attractions closed for season:** No.

GENERAL INFORMATION: *For Your Safety*—Wear shoes to protect yourself from sandspurs which grow wild in the grass. Also be aware of snakes, poison ivy, and fire ants (characterized by red sandy mounds), which have a painful sting. Do not climb on Monuments, fences, or earthworks.

TRAVEL ACCESS: Bus: Continental Trailways will stop at the Park entrance upon request to Bus Driver.

NEARBY FACILITIES & POINTS OF INTEREST: Campgrounds: GA Veterans State Park, 30 miles (48 km), Andersonville, .5 mile (.8 km), and Whitewater Park, 10 miles (16 km); **Other points of interest:** American Camelia Society Gardens, Antebellum Homes, Jimmy Carter National Historic Site, Plains, GA.

Appalachian National Scenic Trail
For details see listing in Maine

Chattahoochee River National Recreation Area
Atlanta, Georgia

MAILING ADDRESS: Chattachoochee River National Recreation Area, 1978 Island Ford Parkway, Dunwoody, GA 30350 **Telephone:** 404-394-7912

DIRECTIONS: Sixteen separate land units along a 48-mile (77-km) stretch of the Chattahoochee River, extending into northwest Atlanta, are preserved "for public enjoyment" for their scenic, recreational, natural, and cultural features. Authorized for addition to the National Park System on Aug. 15, 1978. Land units and river access points are readily accessible via the Interstate and major road systems.

VISITOR ACTIVITIES: Fishing, picnicking, jogging, hiking, bird-watching, photography, horseback riding and various river paddling (floating) activities; **Permits:** No; **Fees:** No; **Visitor facilities:** Watercraft rentals and bus shuttling service (mid-May through Sept.), limited picnic areas, parking and restroom facilities; **HANDICAPPED ACCESSIBILITY:** Some facilities and trails (improved) are handicapped accessible. **Any limitations on vehicle**

usage: All vehicle use is restricted to park-established roadways and designated parking areas; **Hiking trails:** Yes, most are unimproved trails; **Backcountry:** No; **Camping:** No; **Other overnight accommodations on site:** No; **Meals served in the park:** No; **Food and supplies obtainable in the park:** No; **Food and supplies obtainable nearby:** Yes, within the nearby communities; **Overnight accommodations:** Metro-Atlanta area; **First Aid available in park:** Yes; **Nearest Hospital:** Hospitals are located in close proximity to most park units; **Days/Hours:** Open 7 days a week, closing hours posted; **Holiday Closings:** Dec. 25; **Visitor attractions closed for seasons:** No.

GENERAL INFORMATION: *For Your Safety*—Please respect the river corridor and private property rights. Only self-contained fires are permitted. Only non glass containers permitted on river.

Chickamauga and Chattanooga National Military Park
Fort Oglethorpe, Georgia

MAILING ADDRESS: Superintendent, Chickamauga and Chattanooga National Military Park, P.O. Box 2128, Fort Oglethorpe, GA 30742 **Telephone:** 404-866-9241

DIRECTIONS: The Chickamauga Visitor Center is on US 27, off I-75, south of Chattanooga, TN. The Lookout Mountain Visitor Center is at entrance to Point Park.
   The Park includes the Civil War Battlefields of Chickamauga, Orchard Knob, Lookout Mountain, Signal Point, and Missionary Ridge. Established by act of Congress on Aug. 19, 1890.

VISITOR ACTIVITIES: Interpretive exhibits, auto tours, living history demonstrations, hiking, horseback riding; A new multi-media presentation on the Battle of Chickamauga available at Chickamauga Battlefield, adults $2.25, seniors and children under 16, $1.00, 26 minutes in length; **Permits:** No; **Fees:** Yes, admission fee for Cravens House in the Lookout Mountain Unit is $1, not to exceed $3 per family. Golden Age and Golden Eagle Passports accepted and available; **Visitor facilities:** Parking and restrooms at Visitor Center, museum, hiking trails; **HANDICAPPED ACCESSIBILITY:** In both Chickamauga Visitor Center and Lookout Mountain Visitor Center, and designated parking spaces. Point Park is accessible, but not the trails. All restrooms in the Visitor Centers and the Lookout Mountain picnic area have handicap facilities; **Any limitations on vehicle usage:** No overnight parking is allowed; **Hiking trails:** Yes, self-guiding trails; **Backcountry:** No; **Camping:** Group sites only BSA/ GSA, etc., $8 per site per nite Chickamauga Battlefield only; **Other overnight accommodations on site:** No; **Meals served in the park:** No; **Food and supplies obtainable in the park:** No; **Food and supplies obtainable nearby:** Yes, Fort Oglethorpe and Chattanooga; **Overnight accommodations:** Fort Oglethorpe, Ga, US 27, continues to Chickamauga Battlefield; Chattanooga, TN (surrounds park areas); **First Aid available in park:** Yes; **Nearest Hospital:** Fort Oglethorpe, GA, US 27, several blocks from the Visitor Center; **Days/Hours:** Park open 24 hours a day, except Lookout Mountain Unit, which is closed at night; **Holiday Closings:** Dec. 25; **Visitor attractions closed for seasons:** No, except Cravens House, which closes Dec. 1 till March 1; **Weather:** Summer is hot and humid; Winter is cold, with a few days below freezing; early spring is rainy.

NEARBY FACILITIES & POINTS OF INTEREST: **Hotels/Motels:** Cluster of motels located within 10 miles (16 km) of area; Ramada Inn, Holiday Inn, Howard Johnson, Days Inn, Quality Inn, Scottish Inn, etc.; **Campgrounds:** Cloudland Canyon, GA; Harrison Bay, TN, KOA-Chattanooga, TN; **Parks, other points of interest:** Fort Mountain, Chatsworth, GA; Russell Cave, Bridgeport, AL; Rock City, Ruby Falls, Lookout Mountain, TN.

Cumberland Island National Seashore
Saint Marys, Georgia

MAILING ADDRESS: Superintendent, Cumberland Island National Seashore, P.O. Box 806, Saint Marys, GA 31558 **Telephone:** 912-882-4335—Reservations only, and 912-882-4336—Information.

DIRECTIONS: The temporary Park Headquarters and Visitor Center are on US 40, which ends at the St. Marys River. To reach St. Marys, take GA 40 east from I-95 near Kingsland. A National Park Service concession passenger ferry provides off-season access to the Seashore from St. Marys, GA, daily except Tuesday and Wednesday. 7 days a week service starts March 15 and runs through Sept. Mainland departure times are 9 a.m. and 11:45 a.m. Island departure times are 10:15 a.m. and 4:45 p.m. The trip takes 45 minutes. Ferry reservations are advisable and can be made by calling 912-882-4335. No written reservations. *Don't miss the ferry from the island.* It leaves as scheduled. If you miss the boat, you must charter a boat to take you to the mainland. The ferry does not transport cars, bicycles, or pets.

Magnificent beaches and dunes, marshes, maritime forest, and freshwater lakes make up this largest of Georgia's Golden Isles, one of the finest remaining natural areas on the East Coast. Established by act of Congress on Oct. 23, 1972.

VISITOR ACTIVITIES: Naturalist programs, walking tours, bird- and wildlife-watching, swimming, fishing, photography, hiking, camping, backcountry; **Permits:** Required for camping, available at Island debarkation point; **Fees:** Fee for roundtrip ferry tickets, $7.50 plus tax—adult 13 to 64; $6.25 plus tax—65 and older; $3.85 plus tax—12 and under; **Visitor facilities:** Restrooms, campgrounds, bath house, beaches, hiking trails; **HANDICAPPED ACCESSIBILITY:** Handicapped parking is reserved on the mainland (2 spaces). Wheelchairs must be carried on and off boats and docks on the island and mainland presently. All park restrooms are accessible to wheelchair users. The beach is accessible but the sandy foredune area poses problems to wheelchair users. (Plastic mats, used leap frog fashion, are available on request to aid the handicapped in loose sandy areas. Users must provide own attendants.) There are no paved roads or trails on the island. Handicapped visitors have negotiated the Dungeness interpretive trail with little difficulty. **Any limitations on vehicle usage:** No transportation on the island; **Hiking trails:** Yes, a 2-mile (3-km) nature trail leads to the Dungeness Ruins complex, plus another 30 miles (48.0 km) of nature trails. Maps for other trails are available; **Backcountry:** Yes, backpackers should make reservations with headquarters. Campfires are prohibited so a portable stove is necessary; **Camping:** Yes, campers should make reservations with Headquarters and be sure to carry adequate equipment and supplies. All camping equipment must be hand carried ½ mile (.8 km) from the boat dock to campground; **Other overnight accommodations on site:** No; **Meals served in the park:** No; **Food and supplies obtainable in the park:** No; **Food and supplies obtainable nearby:** Yes, at St. Marys; **Overnight accommodations:** Motel accommodations are available in nearby communities. Camping facilities may be found at private commercial campgrounds and 10 miles (16 km) away at Crooked River State Park, Route 1, Box 207, Kingsland, GA 31548, phone 912-882-5256; **First Aid available in park:** Yes; **Nearest Hospital:** St. Marys, GA, via emergency boat from the Island; **Days/Hours:** Seashore closed to public for managed hunts. Check with Headquarters for dates. Sea Camp Visitor Center is open from 8:30 a.m. to 4:30 p.m. daily; **Holiday Closings:** Dec. 25; **Visitor attractions closed for seasons:** No; **Weather:** Cumberland's climate is moderate with short, mild winters. Summer temperatures range from 80s to low 90°sF with some humidity.

GENERAL INFORMATION: Before leaving St. Marys, day and overnight visitors should carefully consider what supplies—food, drinks, suntan lotion, film, sunglasses, and insect repellent—they will need, for there are no stores on the Island. Casual dress, comfortable walking shoes, and rain gear are also recommended.

For Your Safety—Dungeness ruins and most of its outbuildings are unstable. For your protection, these structures are closed. The Island is home to several species of poisonous snakes. Visitors are advised to take normal precautions when venturing into areas where vegetation is thick. Lifeguards are not provided; Be careful while swimming. Be alert for possible hunting activity on adjacent private lands.

TRAVEL ACCESS: **Bus:** Greyhound provides daily service to Kingsland, GA; **Rail:** Seaboard Coast line provides service to Jacksonville, FL; **Air:** Major airlines service Jacksonville International Airport; **Other:** Kings Bay Shuttle/(Taxi) 912-673-6900.

NEARBY FACILITIES & POINTS OF INTEREST: **Hotel/Motel:** Riverview Hotel, St. Marys, GA, 912-882-3242, across street from Visitor Center; **Food/Supplies:** Downtown St. Marys; **Campgrounds:** Crooken River St. Park—St. Marys, 912-882-5256, 10 miles (16 km) from Visitor Center; **Parks, other points of interest:** Okefenokee Swamp, Fort Frederica, Jekyll Island; **Reservation system in use for campsites:** Reservations only 11 months in advance.

Fort Frederica National Monument
St. Simons Island, Georgia

MAILING ADDRESS: Superintendent, Fort Frederica National Monument, Route 9, Box 286-C, St. Simons Island, GA 31522 **Telephone:** 912-638-3639

DIRECTIONS: The Monument is 12 miles (19.3 km) from Brunswick, GA, on St. Simons Island. It can be reached by taking the Brunswick-St. Simons toll causeway which connects with US 17 at Brunswick.

Gen. James E. Oglethorpe built this British fort in 1736-48, during the Anglo-Spanish struggle for control of what is now southeastern United States. Authorized for addition to the National Park System on May 26, 1936.

VISITOR ACTIVITIES: Archaeological site including interpretive exhibits and film, walking tours, living history demonstrations in summer; **Permits:** No; **Fees:** $3 per vehicle; Golden Age Passports are honored (U.S. citizens age 62 and older); No charge for children 16 and younger; **Visitor facilities:** Parking and restrooms at Visitor Center, interpretive publications and sales items. Picnicking is available at several points on St. Simons Island; **HANDICAPPED ACCESSIBILITY:** Ramp to Visitors Center, parking spaces, restroom, wheelchair with wider tires for use on grounds, theater access; movie script for hearing impaired; **Any limitations on vehicle usage:** Vehicles are restricted to the entrance road and parking lot; **Hiking trails:** No; **Backcountry:** No; **Camping:** No; **Other overnight accommodations on site:** No; **Meals served in the park:** No; **Food and supplies obtainable in the park:** No; **Food and supplies obtainable nearby:** Yes, St. Simons Island has restaurants, grocery stores, and convenience stores; **Overnight accommodations:** Several motels are on St. Simons Island; **First Aid available in park:** Yes, there is an emergency squad on St. Simons Island; **Nearest Hospital:** Brunswick, GA, 12.5 miles (20 km); **Days/Hours:** Open daily from 8 a.m. to 5 p.m. Hours may be extended in summer. Contact the Superintendent for further information; **Holiday Closings:** Dec. 25; **Visitor attractions closed for seasons:** No; **Weather:** Spring and fall are mild; winter has occasional cold temperatures. Summers are hot and humid with numerous afternoon thundershowers.

GENERAL INFORMATION: Do not touch the ruins, which are old and fragile and can easily be destroyed. The water is deep and the banks are slippery at the fort. Do not take shelter under the trees during high winds and thunderstorms. Bring an insect repellent in spring and summer.

TRAVEL ACCESS: Bus: Greyhound provides daily service to Brunswick, GA, 12.5 miles (20 km) from park; **Rail:** Amtrak provides daily service to Jessup, GA, 52 miles (83.2 km) from Park; **Air:** Major airlines provide daily service to Jacksonville, FL, 75 miles (120 km) from Park. Atlantic SE Airlines provides daily service to Brunswick; **Other:** Bicycles and mopeds available for rent on St. Simons Island.

NEARBY FACILITIES & POINTS OF INTEREST: Parks, other points of interest: Museum of Coastal History and St. Simons Lighthouse, 6 miles (9.6 km) at the southern tip of St. Simons Island, Jekyll Island Resort Area, 10 miles (16 km) south of Brunswick.

Fort Pulaski National Monument
Tybee Island, Georgia

MAILING ADDRESS: Superintendent, Fort Pulaski National Monument, P.O. Box 30757, Savannah, GA 31410 **Telephone:** 912-786-5787

DIRECTIONS: The Visitor Center is in the delta area of the Savannah River, 15 miles (24 km) east of Savannah on US 80.
Bombardment of this early 19th-century Fort by Federal rifled cannon in 1862 first demonstrated the ineffectiveness of old-style masonry fortifications. Created by Presidential Proclamation on Oct. 15, 1924.

VISITOR ACTIVITIES: Interpretive talks, walks, tours (guided and self-guided), exhibits, wildlife- and bird-watching, picnicking, fishing; **Permits:** No; **Fees:** Entrance fee is $1 per person, $3 max per vehicle. Golden Age, Golden Access, and Golden Eagle Passports accepted and available; **Visitor facilities:** Parking and restrooms at Visitor Center, picnic area; **HANDICAPPED ACCESSIBILITY:** Visitor Center, picnic area, picnic area restrooms, ground level of Fort, Fort restrooms, parking lots, ¼-mile (.4-km) nature trail; **Any limitations on vehicle usage:** Vehicles are confined to designated roadways; **Hiking trails:** Yes, hiking and nature trails lead around the Fort ¼-mile (.4-km) to 2 miles (3.2 km) in length; **Backcountry:** No; **Camping:** No; **Other overnight accommodations on site:** No; **Meals served in the park:** No; **Food and supplies obtainable in the park:** No; **Food and supplies obtainable nearby:** Yes, Tybee Island 4 miles (6 km); Savannah 15 miles (24 km); **Overnight accommodations:** Tybee Island, 4 miles (6 km) east of Park, Savannah, 15 miles (24 km) west of the Monument on US 80; **First Aid available in park:** Yes; **Nearest Hospital:** Savannah, Abercorn, Waters, and Reynolds, about 20 miles (32 km); **Days/Hours:** Open daily from 8:30 a.m. to 5:30 p.m. with extended hours in late spring and summer; **Holiday Closings:** Dec. 25; **Weather:** Temperatures range from 20°F in winter to 100° in summer.

GENERAL INFORMATION: *For Your Safety*—Stay off mounds and top-most walls of the Fort. Don't run on the terreplein (upper level) of the Fort. Come down when there is lightning. Mosquitoes and horseflies are present in spring and summer; use a repellent and wear protective clothing. Watch your step in the Fort, and stay on the trails when walking or hiking. Beware of poisonous snakes.

TRAVEL ACCESS: Bus: C & H Bus Lines, Inc., provides service from Savannah, 8:15 a.m. and 3:35 p.m. daily to Highway 80 within 1 mile (1.6 km) of Fort; **Rail:** Amtrak provides service to Savannah; **Air:** Delta, Eastern, and American Airlines.

NEARBY FACILITIES & POINTS OF INTEREST: Parks, other points of interest: Savannah National Historic Landmark District, Old Fort Jackson, Wormsloe State Historic Site, Fort McAllister and Richmond Hill State Park, Tybee Island: public beach, museum, lighthouse, historic Fort Screven area.

Jimmy Carter National Historic Site
Plains, Georgia

MAILING ADDRESS: Superintendent, Jimmy Carter National Historic Site, c/o Route 1, Box 85, Andersonville, GA 31711 **Telephone:** 912-924-0343

DIRECTIONS: The site is 10 miles (16 km) west of Americus, GA, on U.S. 280 in the town of Plains. Interstate access would be I-75 exit onto U.S. 280 at Cordele, GA, or I-85 exit U.S. 280 at Columbus, GA.

Established by act of Congress on Dec. 23, 1987, as the Jimmy Carter National Historic Site and Plains Historic District. It interprets the life and presidency of President and Mrs. Carter and the rural southern life style of Plains.

VISITOR ACTIVITIES: Visitor Center and Museum, Boyhood Home, Carter Home (home is closed to public.) Driving tape tour, walking and self-guided tours and picnicking; **Permits:** No; **Fees:** No; **Visitor facilities:** Restrooms and picnicking at city park; **Any limitations on vehicle usages:** Governed by State of Georgia Department of Transportation; **Hiking Trails:** No; **Backcountry:** No; **Camping:** No; **Overnight accommodations on site:** Bed and Breakfast in town; **Meals served in the park:** 2 restaurants in town; **Food and supplies obtainable in the park:** Small grocery store; **Food and supplies obtainable nearby:** Yes, Americus, 10 miles (16 km); **Overnight accommodations:** Yes, Plains Bed and Breakfast, Americus, 10 miles (16 km); **First aid available in the park:** Yes, at Railroad Depot; **Nearest Hospital:** Americus, 10 miles (16 km) on Forsyth Street; **Days/Hours:** Open 7 days a week 9 a.m. to 5 p.m.; **Holiday Closing:** Dec. 25; **Visitor attractions closed for season:** No.

GENERAL INFORMATION: Plains is an active rural farm community. You may visit the Presidential Campaign headquarters, walk through and shop in the Historic District; and tour past the Boyhood Home and Carter Home (houses are not open to public).

TRAVEL ACCESS: Private vehicle, no bus service.

NEARBY FACILITIES AND POINTS OF INTEREST: Campgrounds: Shady Acres 5 miles (8 km) east on U.S. 280; Georgia Veterans State Park is 30 miles (48 km) east on U.S. 280; Andersonville National Historic Site, Antebellium Homes, Westville 1850 Village, Providence Canyon State Park, Historic Homes in Americus.

Kennesaw Mountain National Battlefield Park
Marietta, Georgia

MAILING ADDRESS: Superintendent, Kennesaw Mountain National Battlefield Park, P.O. Box 1610, Marietta, GA 30061 **Telephone:** 404-427-4686

DIRECTIONS: The Park is 3 miles (5 km) north of Marietta, GA, a short distance off US 41, and 20 miles (33 km) northwest of Atlanta, off I-75.

Two engagements took place here between Union and Confederate forces during the

Atlanta Campaign, June 20-July 2, 1864. Authorized for addition to the National Park System on Feb. 8, 1917.

VISITOR ACTIVITIES: Exhibits and audiovisual programs at Visitor Center, walking and auto tours of the Park, hiking; **Permits:** No; **Fees:** No; **Visitor facilities:** Picnic areas, restrooms, and hiking trails; **HANDICAPPED ACCESSIBILITY:** Yes, except for trails; **Any limitations on vehicle usage:** All vehicles are restricted to designated roadways; **Hiking trails:** Yes, the Park trails, which start at the Visitor Center, can be used for short walks or long hikes; **Backcountry:** No; **Camping:** No; **Other overnight accommodations on site:** No; **Meals served in the park:** No; **Food and supplies obtainable in the park:** No; **Food and supplies obtainable nearby:** Yes, in Marietta or Atlanta; **Overnight accommodations:** Marietta, 2 miles (3.2 km) south, or Atlanta, 15 miles (24 km) southeast; **First Aid available in park:** Yes; **Nearest Hospital:** Marietta, 2 miles (3.2 km); **Days/Hours:** Open daily from 8:30 a.m. to 5 p.m. year-round; **Holiday Closings:** Dec. 25 and Jan. 1; **Weather:** Moderate temperatures year round. Daytime temperatures are usually in the 40°F range in winter and 90° range in summer.

Martin Luther King, Jr., National Historic Site and Preservation District
Atlanta, Georgia

MAILING ADDRESS: Superintendent, Martin Luther King, Jr., National Historic Site and Preservation District, 526 Auburn Avenue, N.E., Atlanta, GA 30312

DIRECTIONS: Visitors traveling to the Historic Site on southbound I-75/85 should take the Butler Street exit; northbound visitors should take the Edgewood/Auburn Avenue exit. Turn east on Auburn Avenue and proceed approximately .6 miles (1 km) to the Historic Site.
   Established Oct. 10, 1980, to honor the Civil Rights leader, Dr. Martin Luther King, Jr., the Historic Site (23.5 acres) includes the home in which he was born, his spiritual home of Ebenezer Baptist Church, and his grave site. The Site also includes The Martin Luther King, Jr., Center for Nonviolent Social Change, Inc., victorian homes, row (shotgun) houses, an 1894 fire station, and a Catholic missionary school. The surrounding Preservation District (80.1 acres) includes "Sweet Auburn," the economic and cultural center of Atlanta's African-American community during most of the 20th century, and the residential areas surrounding the Historic Site.

VISITOR ACTIVITIES: At present the Park Service owns nineteen historical structures within the Historic Site. Twelve have been restored to their 1930 appearance with plans for restoration of the remaining structures as funds become available. Several structures are used for administrative purposes by the Park Service with the rest of them rented for residential purposes. Ranger guided tours of the Birth Home are conducted every half hour, seven days a week. The tours are limited to 15 people per tour on a first-come first-served basis. The first tour of the day begins at 10:00 a.m. with the last tour beginning at 5:30 p.m. Additional visitor activities are provided by the Park Service on a seasonal basis and by private oganizations at key sites including Ebenezer Baptist Church, Martin Luther King, Jr., Center for Nonviolent Social Change, Inc., and the African-American Panoramic Experience (APEX). **Permits:** Free tour tickets required; **Fees:** No; **Visitor facilities:** Visitor Contact Station and Birth Home; **HANDICAPPED ACCESSIBILITY:** The first floor of the Birth Home is accessible to wheelchairs with a photo album showing the second floor. The Historic Site's Video, "Sweet Auburn," shown at the Visitor Contact Station is captioned for the hearing impaired. The Historic Sites official brochure is available in braille and on cassette tape for use by the visually impaired visitor. The King Center and Ebenezer Baptist Church are both handicapped accessible, including restrooms; **Any limitations on vehicle usage:** Bus parking is allowed along Irwin Street and in the Park's parking lot on Edgewood Avenue; **Hiking trails:** No; **Backcountry:** No; **Camping:** No; **Other overnight accommodations on site:** No; **Meals served in the park:** There is a restaurant located at The King Center and several others located along Auburn Avenue within the Historic Site and Preservation District; **Food and supplies obtainable in the park:** Several stores are located along Edgewood and Auburn Avenues in the Historic Site and Preservation District; **Food and supplies obtainable nearby:** Yes, in downtown Atlanta and the Little 5 Points area; **Overnight accommodations:** Yes, available in downtown Atlanta; **First Aid available in park:** No; **Nearest Hospital:** Georgia Baptist Medical Center is located .5 miles (.8 km) north of the Historic Site on Boulevard Avenue; **Park open to visitors:** Yes, however, many homes are occupied, so please respect the privacy of the occupants; **Holiday Closings:** Dec. 25 and Jan. 1; **Visitor attractions closed for seasons:** No.

TRAVEL ACCESS: Bus: Metropolitan Atlanta Rapid Transit Authority (MARTA) provides city bus service to the Historic Site via route #3 from downtown Atlanta; **Rail:** MARTA also provides rail service to the King Memorial Station (E2) which is within walking distance of the Historic site; AMTRAK serves Atlanta; **Air:** Most major air carriers serve the Atlanta-Hartsfield Airport.

NEARBY FACILITIES & POINTS OF INTEREST: Hotel/Motel: Most major chains and numerous other hotels/motels are available in the Atlanta area; **Campgrounds:** Some private campgrounds are available outside of the Atlanta area; **Parks, other points of interest:** Chattahoochee River National Recreation Area, Kennesaw Mountain National Battlefield Park, Atlanta Historical Society, Carter Presidential Center, Cyclorama, Herndon Home, and Wrens Nest.

Ocmulgee National Monument
Macon, Georgia

MAILING ADDRESS: Superintendent, Ocmulgee National Monument, 1207 Emery Highway, Macon, GA 31201 **Telephone:** 912-752-8257

DIRECTIONS: The Monument is on the east edge of Macon, GA, on US 80 east. Main access is from Int. 75 to Int. 16 east, at the north end of Macon. Take exit #4 from Int. 16 and follow the signs 2 miles (3.2 km) to the Park entrance.
     The cultural evolution of the Indian civilizations in the southern United States are represented in the remains of mounds and villages here. Established by Presidential Proclamation on Dec. 23, 1936, and administered by the National Park Service.

VISITOR ACTIVITIES: Auto tours, interpretive exhibits, picnicking, nature walks, hiking, fishing; **Permits:** No; **Fees:** No; **Visitor facilities:** Parking and restrooms at Visitor Center, picnic area, nature trail; A variety of special events occur throughout the year; **HANDICAPPED ACCESSIBILITY:** Parking, restrooms, water fountain, the Earthlodge, a 1000-year-old ceremonial structure used by the Mississippian Indians; **Any limitations on vehicle usage:** Vehicles must be parked only in designated parking areas; **Hiking trails:** Yes, 5 miles (8 km) of nature and historical trails; **Backcountry:** No; **Camping:** No; **Other overnight accommodations on site:** No, the closest camping area is Lake Tobesofkee Recreation Area, 8 miles (13 km) west of Macon. No reservations available for campsites. For further information, contact the lake at 6600 Mosley-Dixon Road, Macon, GA 31210, phone 912-474-8770;

Meals served in the park: No; **Food and supplies obtainable in the park:** No; **Food and supplies obtainable nearby:** Yes, at Macon; **Overnight accommodations:** Macon; **First Aid available in park:** Yes; **Nearest Hospital:** Macon, Highway 80, ½-mile (.8-km); **Days/ Hours:** Open daily from 9 a.m. to 5 p.m.; **Holiday Closings:** Dec. 25, and Jan. 1; **Visitor attractions closed for seasons:** No; **Weather:** Summers are hot and humid; winters are mostly mild.

GENERAL INFORMATION: *For Your Safety*—Mound slopes and steep banks are dangerous. Please use the marked trails. Drivers of camping vehicles and school buses should be aware of the 8'9" clearance of the tunnel leading to Greater Temple Mound.

TRAVEL ACCESS: **Bus:** Greyhound provides service to Macon; **Air:** ASA Airlines (Delta connector) provides service to Lewis B. Wilson Airport.

NEARBY FACILITIES & POINTS OF INTEREST: **Campgrounds:** Lake Tobesofkee Recreation Area, 8 miles (12.8 km) west of Macon; **Tours:** Macon Historic District. For more area information contact the Macon-Bibb County Convention and Visitors Bureau at 912-743-3401.

Hawaii

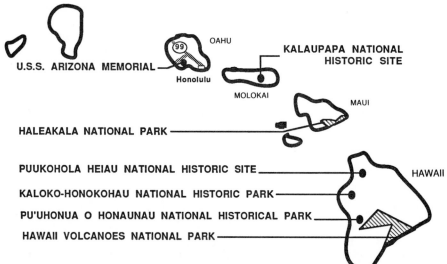

Haleakala National Park
Makawao, Maui, Hawaii

MAILING ADDRESS: Superintendent, Haleakala National Park, P.O. Box 369, Makawao, Maui, HI 96768 **Telephone:** 808-572-9306

DIRECTIONS: The Park extends from the 10,023-foot (3,055 meter) summit of Mt. Haleakala down the southeast flank to the Kipahulu coast near Hana. These two sections of the Park are not directly connected by road, but can be reached by auto from Kahului, as follows: Haleakala Crater is a 3-hour round-trip drive from Kahului via HI 36, 37, 377, and 378.

The Kipahulu District of the Park is a 6-to-7 hour round-trip drive from Kahului via HI 360 to Hana, then via HI 31 towards Kipahulu. The road around East Maui, which is narrow, winding, and slow, is for the adventurous only; it offers roadside state parks, frequent overlooks, and views of rain forests, black lava shores, and rugged coastal cliffs. West of Kipahulu, HI 31 becomes an unpaved road.

The Park preserves the outstanding features of Haleakala Crater on the Island of Maui and protects the unique and fragile ecosystems of Kipahulu Valley, the scenic pools along 'Ohe'o Stream, and many rare and endangered species. Authorized for addition to the National Park System on Aug. 1, 1916.

VISITOR ACTIVITIES: Kipahulu: Hiking, camping, walking, picnicking, swimming. No drinking water at Kipahulu. Haleakala Crater: Interpretive exhibits and talks, walking, hiking, camping, picnicking. Park Headquarters, where information, permits, and publications are furnished, is 1 mile (1.6 km) from the entrance to the Park. The Visitor Center, which contains exhibits, is about 10 miles (16 km) from the park entrance. Summit Exhibit Shelter, about 11 miles (17.6 km) from Park entrance, has displays and is where interpretive talks are held. For detailed information on both areas, contact the Superintendent; **Permits:** For backcountry camping at Haleakala Crater. Permits available from Headquarters or from a Park Ranger; **Fees:** Yes, for backcountry cabin rental; Park entrance fee $3; **Visitor facilities:** Picnic areas, campgrounds, scenic overlooks, interpretive programs, backcountry cabins; **HANDICAPPED ACCESSIBILITY:** Restrooms and exhibit areas are accessible at Park headquarters and Haleakala Visitor Center. The Summit Exhibit Shelter is also accessible via a smooth ramp. The grade at the summit is challenging but the ramp is well maintained. Parking areas at these three locations are ramped and smooth paved access exists into the buildings; **Any limitations on vehicle usage:** Watch out for traffic on narrow roads; **Hiking trails:** Yes, trails vary in difficulty and length; there are several short nature trails; **Backcountry:** Yes, contact the Superintendent for a free brochure; **Camping:** Yes, campsites cannot be reserved ahead and are operated on a first-come first-served basis. These are primitive campsites with only pit toilets and drinking water. Campers should have equipment appropriate for possible cold, wet weather, and must bring a sleeping bag, tent, and cooking stove with fuel (because of the prohibition against open fires). Three crater cabins are maintained by the National Park Service for visitor use on an advance reservation basis only. Each cabin is allocated to one party at a time, with a capacity of 12 people per night; at least one member of the group must be 18 years of age or older. Each cabin has bunks, limited water and firewood, cookstove, and eating and cooking utensils. To reserve cabins, write to the Superintendent at least 90 days in advance of your trip. Include your first and alternate choices of dates and cabins preferred. The less restrictive your choices, the better your chance of confirmation. Reservations are limited to 3 nights per month, with no more than 2 consecutive nights at any one cabin. A fee is charged; **Other overnight accommodations on site:** No; **Meals served in the park:** No; **Food and supplies obtainable in the park:** No; **Food and supplies obtainable nearby:** Yes, at Pukalani, Maui, HI; **Overnight accommodations:** From Kipahulu, 10 miles (16 km) on Rt. 31 to Hana. From Haleakala Crater, 12 miles (19 km) on Rt. 377; **First Aid available in park:** Yes; **Nearest Hospital:** Kahului, 30 miles (48 km); **Days/Hours:** Open 24 hours a day, 365 days a year, Visitor Center open daily from sunrise to 3 p.m.; **Holiday Closings:** No; **Visitor attractions closed for seasons:** No; **Weather:** Weather near the summit varies considerably; summers are generally dry and moderately warm, but you should come prepared for occasionally cold, windy, damp weather. Winters tend to be cold, wet, foggy, and windy. Generally in the spring and fall there is a mixture of all kinds of weather. Kipahulu, being coastal, has a less extreme pattern. Summers are generally warm and humid. Winter temperatures are usually comfortable, but rain, varying from a light mist to torrential tropical down pours is common. Call the National Weather Service at 808-871-5054 for current weather conditions before beginning your trip.

GENERAL INFORMATION: *For Your Safety*—Hikers should bring comfortable, durable hiking shoes, canteen, light raincoat, sun hat, and suntan lotion. Do not travel alone. Swimmers should never swim during high water. If you notice the water rising, GET OUT FAST! 'Ohe'o Stream can become a raging torrent in minutes. Be careful on wet rocks; they are slippery. Check before diving or jumping. In some places there are submerged ledges near the pool's edge.

Hawaii Volcanoes National Park
Hawaii Volcanoes National Park, Hawaii   **SEE CLIMATABLE NO. 18**

MAILING ADDRESS: Superintendent, Hawaii Volcanoes National Park, HI 96718 **Telephone:** 808-967-7311

DIRECTIONS: Visitor Center at Kilauea. Park Headquarters area, including Kilauea Visitor Center, is located 29 miles (46.4 km) southwest of Hilo, off HI 11. The coastal section of the park presently is not accessible from Keaau and Hwy. 130. Lava flows have blocked road since Feb. 1987 and flows continue to this date with no anticipated reopening date. Accessible from the Chain of Craters Road from Park Headquarters. A new visitor facility was dedicated in Jan., 1987, located on the rim of Kilauea Caldera adjacent to the new Hawaiian Volcano Observatory. The new facility is known as "Jaggar Museum." New Visitor Center interpreting volcanic story of park.

Active volcanism continues here on the Island of Hawaii. Rare and luxuriant vegetation provides food and shelter for a variety of native birds. Established by act of Congress on Aug. 1, 1916.

VISITOR ACTIVITIES: Auto tours, walking, hiking, camping, backcountry, picnicking, interpretive programs. Schedule of events available from either Visitor Center or by contacting the Park; **Permits:** For backcountry use can be obtained at Headquarters; **Fees:** Entrance fee of $5 per car or $2 per person on foot, bike, or bus; **Visitor facilities:** Parking, restrooms and museums at Visitor Centers, lodging, cabins, picnic areas; **HANDICAPPED ACCESSIBILITY:** Visitor Center, Jagger Museum; **Any limitations on vehicle usage:** All vehicles are restricted to designated roadways; **Hiking trails:** Yes, check at Visitor Center or write for information on the 150 miles (241 km) of trails; **Backcountry:** Yes, hiker shelters and cabins are available, but you must register at Park Headquarters for overnight stays. Detailed maps are available at Park Headquarters and are highly recommended. Check on trail conditions and water supplies before you start; **Camping:** Yes, no reservations available for individual campsites; **Other overnight accommodations on site:** Yes, Volcano House on the rim of Kilauea Crater is open all year. Reservations are advised year round. Cabins with the use of showers are operated at Namakani Paio by the Volcano House. For reservations contact The Volcano House, Hawaii Volcanoes National Park, HI 96718, phone 808-967-7321. Kilauea Military Camp, a rest and recreation camp for active and retired military personnel, is 1 mile (1.6 km) west of Park Headquarters; **Meals served in the park:** Yes, at Volcano House Restaurant; **Food and supplies obtainable in the park:** No; **Food and supplies obtainable nearby:** Yes, groceries, gasoline, and camping supplies are available in the community of Volcano, 1 mile (1.6 km) north of the park on HI 11. Stores there are open all year. Groceries and meals are also available in the village of Kalapana, 4 miles (6 km) east of the coastal section of the park but are not accessible at this time from the park; **Overnight accommodations:** Hilo, Highway 11, 29 miles (47 km) from the park; **First Aid available in park:** Yes; **Nearest Hospital:** Hilo, Highway 11, 29 miles (47 km); **Days/Hours:** Park open 24 hours a day year-round; **Holiday Closings:** No; **Visitor attractions closed for seasons:** No; **Weather:** The northern side of Kilauea's summit is 4000 feet (1200 meters) above sea level, so the climate can be cool and rain can fall at any time of year. At the same time, Kilauea's leeward side is usually dry and warm. There are few records of freezing at Kilauea, but in winter the snow can extend down to 10,000 feet (3000 meters) on Mauna Loa.

GENERAL INFORMATION: *For Your Safety*—Stay on trails. The surface of Kilauea is laced with deep cracks, and many of these are hidden by vegetation. Recent lava flows are shelly and collapse easily. Fumes from volcanoes can compound respiratory and heart problems. Heed the warning signs. A number of trails lie along the edges of cliff tops, so be sure of your footing.

Eruption Bulletins: You can get up-to-date information about on-going eruptions or potential activity by calling 808-967-7977 anytime. The automatic answering service is updated whenever Kilauea or Mauna Loa shows signs of change. Because eruptions are the most exciting events at Hawaii Volcanoes, temporary road signs will direct you to access or vantage points where you can confront the power of these events when conditions are safe.

Special publications on the geology, human history, and natural history of Hawaii Volcanoes are published by the Hawaii Natural History Association to help you enjoy the park. For a price list write to the Association, Hawaii Volcanoes National Park, HI 96718. An award-winning videotape on the Mauna Loa eruption of 1984 is now available. Funded entirely by the Hawaii Natural History Association "River of Fire" was presented the "Eastman Kodak Award" and an "Indy" Award from the Industrial Film and Video Competition in New York City, 1985 Awards.

Kalaupapa National Historic Park
Molokai, Hawaii

MAILING ADDRESS: Kalaupapa National Historical Park, Kalaupapa, HI 96742

DIRECTIONS: On the windward coast of the Island of Molokai this Historic Park is open to the public on a limited basis. All visitors are required to first obtain permission from the State of Hawaii, Department of Health.

Kalaupapa, unlike many other National Park areas, has a living community as one of the prime resources of the Park. The residents of Kalaupapa are those people that were banished here for committing no crime, but for contracting a much misunderstood and greatly feared disease. The disease, now called Hansen's Disease, is more widely known throughout the world as leprosy. These people with Hansen's Disease were banished here to protect the health and safety of the public. Today this once-dreaded disease is curable with treatment, and there is no longer any medical reason to isolate people with leprosy. Those people who remain here, do so out of choice.

Kalaupapa is jointly managed by the State of Hawaii, Department of Health, and the National Park Service. To protect the privacy of the community, access to Kalaupapa is still quite limited. You must obtain a visitor permit from the Department of Health to enter the settlement. This may be done through a tour company that is owned, and operated by patients. You may write for information to Damien Tours, c/o Kalaupapa Settlement, Kalaupapa, HI 96742. There are no public facilities (camping, restaurants, or stores). Overnight stays are limited to invited guests of residents.

Kaloko-Honokohau National Historical Park
On the Kona coast of the Island of Hawaii

MAILING ADDRESS: P.O. Box 129, Honaunau, HI 96726.

DIRECTIONS: Newly opened to the public. Printed fact sheets available; Pacific Area Office, National Park Service, 300 Ala Moana Blvd., Honolulu, HI 96850. Four miles (6.4 km) south of Keahole Airport, 2 miles (3.2 km) north of Kailua-Kona on Highway 11.

VISITOR ACTIVITIES: The Park contains a great number of Hawaiian archaeological sites and features. According to legend, the first Hawaiian King, Kamehameha I, is buried somewhere in the park. The park also provides important habitat for three endangered species of Hawaiian waterbirds. **HANDICAPPED ACCESSIBILITY:** Yes, all park restrooms are handicap accessible; **Days/Hours:** Park opens 8:00 a.m.-3:30 p.m. (7 days); office opens 7:30 a.m.-4:00 p.m. (Mon.-Fri.).

TRAVEL ACCESS: 0.8 miles (.128 km) unimproved entrance road.

Pu'uhonua o Honaunau National Historical Park
Honaunau, Kona, Hawaii

MAILING ADDRESS: Superintendent, Pu'uhonua o Honaunau National Historical Park, P.O. Box 129, Honaunau, Kona, HI 96726 **Telephone:** 808-328-2326

DIRECTIONS: The Park is located 30 miles (48 km) south of Keahole Airport on HI 160. Take HI 19 to Kailua, thence HI 11 to Honaunau, thence HI 160 to the park.

Until 1819, vanquished Hawaiian warriors, noncombatants, and taboo breakers could escape death by reaching this sacred ground. Prehistoric house sites, royal fishponds, coconut groves, and spectacular shore scenery comprise the park. Authorized for addition to the National Park System on June 26, 1955.

VISITOR ACTIVITIES: Picnicking, snorkeling, swimming, walking tours, craft demonstrations, interpretive exhibits, hiking, fishing; **Permits:** Yes, for picnicking by groups of over 30 people; **Fees:** Yes; **Visitor facilities:** Parking and restrooms at Visitor Center, picnic area; **HANDICAPPED ACCESSIBILITY:** Wheelchair available to loan. Ask at Visitor Center about wheelchair route. Sign language capability among staff. Handicap accessible restrooms; **Any limitations on vehicle usage:** Vehicles are restricted to designated roadways; **Hiking trails:** Yes, self-guiding walking trail through the park; **Backcountry:** No; **Camping:** No; **Other overnight accommodations on site:** No; **Meals served in the park:** No, the nearest restaurant is 10 miles (16 km) away; **Food and supplies obtainable in the park:** No; **Food and supplies obtainable nearby:** No, limited supplies on HI 11, grocery stores at Captain Cook; **Overnight accommodations:** Captain Cook, HI 11, 10 miles (16 km) away; **First Aid available in park:** Yes; **Nearest Hospital:** Kona, 12 miles (19 km); **Days/Hours:** Open daily from 6 a.m. to midnight; **Holiday Closings:** No; **Visitor attractions closed for seasons:** No; **Weather:** The Park is sunny 95% of the time. Summer is the rainy season; average rainfall is 25 inches per year.

GENERAL INFORMATION: *For Your Safety*—Be alert for unexpected high waves when you are on the shore; don't turn your back on the ocean. Do not climb on the stone walls or on the framework of the house models. If you leave the trail, watch for falling coconuts and coconut fronds. Do not climb the coconut trees. Visitors to the area can also see Puukohola Heiau National Historic Site (see listing in this book), at Kawaihae Bay, on the island's northwestern shore.

TRAVEL ACCESS: Bus: ½-day bus tours operate from Kailua, Kona, 20 miles (32 km); **Rail:** No; **Air:** No.

NEARBY FACILITIES & POINTS OF INTEREST: **Hotel/Motel:** Manago Hotel, Capt. Cook, HI 96704, 808-323-2642, 12 miles (19.2 km); **Food/Supplies:** Morihara Grocery

Store at intersection of 11 and 160, 3 miles (4.8 km); **Campgrounds:** None nearby; **Parks, other points of interest:** Kealakekua Bay, 4 miles (6.4 km) north, Site of Cooks Landing, painted church, 3 miles (4.8 km) east.

Puukohola Heiau National Historic Site
Kawaihae, Hawaii

MAILING ADDRESS: Superintendent, Puukohola Heiau National Historic Site, P.O. Box 4963, Kawaihae, HI 96743 **Telephone:** 808-882-7218

DIRECTIONS: Puukohola Heiau is on the northwestern shore of the Island of Hawaii. Airlines make scheduled flights several times daily from Honolulu to airports at Hilo, Keahole, and Waimea-Kohala, which is about 12 miles (19 km) from the park. Taxis and car rentals are available at all airports, except Waimea-Kohala Airport.

Ruins of Puukohola Heiau ("Temple on the Hill of the Whale"), built by King Kamehameha the Great (1753-1819) in 1791 during his rise to power, are preserved here. Authorized for addition to the National Park System on Aug. 17, 1972.

VISITOR ACTIVITIES: Hiking, guided and self-guiding tours. Swimming and picnicking are permitted at nearby Spencer Beach Park; **Permits:** No; **Fees:** No; **Visitor facilities:** Informal interpretive talks are given at the Visitor Center; **Any limitations on vehicle usage:** If you park in front of Puukohola Heiau on the Spencer Beach Road, use caution while entering and leaving the road, due to heavy traffic; **Hiking trails:** Yes, all points of interest in the park can be visited on foot; **Backcountry:** No; the Hawaii Visitors Bureau, a non-profit organization with offices in Honolulu, Hilo, Kona, Waikiki, Lihu, and 209 Post Street, San Francisco, CA 94108, phone 415-392-8273, will supply information on trips to and through the Hawaiian Islands; **Camping:** No, information on camping at nearby Spencer Beach Park may be obtained from Hawaii Visitors Bureau, 209 Post Street, San Francisco, CA 94108, phone 415-392-8173; **Other overnight accommodations on site:** No; **Meals served in the park:** No; **Food and supplies obtainable in the park:** No; **Food and supplies obtainable nearby:** Yes, at Kawaihae, 1 mile (1.6 km) away; **Overnight accommodations:** Waimea, 12 miles (19.2 km) southeast; **First Aid available in park:** Yes; **Nearest Hospital:** Honokaa, 29 miles (46.4 km); **Days/Hours:** Visitor Center open from 7:30 a.m. to 4 p.m.; **Holiday Closings:** No; **Visitor attractions closed for seasons:** No; **Weather:** Nine inches of rainfall per year; occasional 90°F temperatures.

GENERAL INFORMATION: *For Your Safety*—Stay on the designated trails, and do not climb on the walls of the temple. The trail from the Visitor Center is long, hot, and rugged. If you are not physically fit and attired in proper clothing or footwear, do not attempt the hike. You may view the area from the Spencer Beach Park road. To prevent grass fires, do not smoke. The beach fronting Puukohola is unsuitable for swimming, due to silt and coral collections.

TRAVEL ACCESS: Bus: No; **Rail:** No; **Air:** Nearest airport is Waimea-Kohala, 12 miles (19.2 km).

NEARBY FACILITIES & POINTS OF INTEREST: Hotel/Motel: Mauna Kea Beach Hotel, P.O. Box 218, Kamuela, HI 96743, (808) 882-7222, 1.5 miles (2.4 km); **Food/ Supplies:** Jin Ho's, 7/11 Complex and Blue Dolphin .5-1 mile (.8-1.6 km); **Campgrounds:** Spencer Beach Park (County facility) adjoining the Park; **Parks, other points of interest:** Puako Petroglyphs, 6 miles (9.6 km); **Reservation system in use for campsites, other facilities:** Information may be obtained by calling or writing to the following: Superintendent,

Puukohola Heiau NHS (see above for address). Permits are necessary for camping in most parks. A Cultural Festival for two days is held annually in August to celebrate the establishment of Puukohola Heiau as a National Historic Site.

U.S.S. Arizona Memorial
Honolulu, Hawaii

MAILING ADDRESS: USS Arizona Memorial, National Park Service, 1 Arizona Memorial Place, Honolulu, HI 96818. **Telephone:** 808-422-2771. Recorded Information 808-422-0561 or 422-0562

DIRECTIONS: The Memorial is a ½-hour drive from Waikiki. From Waikiki take H-1 west past the airport to the "Stadium-Arizona" exit. Take "Stadium-Arizona" exit off freeway. Turn left at 4th traffic light at sign to USS Arizona Memorial. Public transportation is available from Waikiki (1 hour by bus) and downtown Honolulu to USS Arizona Memorial Visitor Center. For information, call 808-531-1611.

The Memorial is supported by pilings on either side of the Battleship USS *Arizona*, sunk in Pearl Harbor on Dec. 7, 1941. Owned by U.S. Navy, administered by National Park Service.

VISITOR ACTIVITIES: Free tour with Park Ranger, (includes Ranger talk, movie, and shuttle boat, ½ mile, to and from Memorial). Periodic Ranger and Pearl Harbor Survivor talks. Museum with permanent exhibits; **Permits:** No; **Fees:** No; **Visitor facilities:** Restrooms and limited parking available at the Visitor Center. Museum bookshop (film, slides, videotapes, books, and photos.) **Meals served in the park:** No, snacks only; **Food and supplies obtainable in the park:** No; **Food and supplies obtainable nearby:** Yes, at Pearl Ridge Shopping Center; **Overnight accommodations:** At the Airport or Waikiki; **First Aid available in park:** Yes; **Nearest Hospital:** Fronk Clinic, Aiea. **Days/Hours:** Visitor Center open daily 7:30 a.m.-5 p.m., Boat tours 8 a.m.-3 p.m. daily; **Holiday Closings:** Thanksgiving, Dec. 25, and Jan. 1; **Visitor attractions closed for seasons:** No.

TRAVEL ACCESS: Bus: The Bus (City/County of Honolulu) provides frequent service #20 from Waikiki to Kamehameha Highway; Private, Shuttle Bus Co. and organized tours serve Memorial from Waikiki; **Rail:** No; **Air:** Major airlines service to Honolulu.

NEARBY FACILITIES & POINTS OF INTEREST: Hotel/Motel: at Airport; Pearlridge Shopping Center, Kamehameha Highway, 1½ miles (2.4 km) west; **Campgrounds:** No; **Parks, other points of interest:** USS Bowfin Museum, World War II Fleet Submarine— 150 yards west, fee area; U.S. Navy open ship at Pearl Harbor Naval Station first Saturday of each month.

Idaho

City of Rocks National Reserve
Twin Falls, Idaho

MAILING ADDRESS: City of Rocks National Reserve, P.O. Box 169, Almo, ID 83312. Contact: Manager **Telephone:** 208-824-5519, or Superintendent, National Park Service, 963 Blue Lakes Blvd., Twin Falls, ID 83301. **Telephone:** 208-733-8398

    This new addition to the National Park System is an area of scenic granite spires and sculptured rock formations. Remnants of the California Trail are still visible in the area. The Reserve includes camping, hiking, rock-climbing and outstanding scenery. Facilities are limited and primitive.

    Authorized: Nov. 18, 1988. Acreage: 14,407.19; Federal: 7001.18; Nonfederal: 7406.01.

Craters of the Moon National Monument
Arco, Idaho

MAILING ADDRESS: Superintendent, Craters of the Moon National Monument, P.O. Box 29, Arco, ID 83213 **Telephone:** 208-527-3257

DIRECTIONS: The Monument is 18 miles (28.8 km) west of Arco on US 20, 26, and 93.
Volcanic cones, craters, lava flows, and caves make this an astonishing landscape. Established by act of Congress on May 2, 1924.

VISITOR ACTIVITIES: Interpretive exhibits, audiovisual programs, naturalist trips, camping, cross-country skiing; **Permits:** required for backcountry, available at Visitor Center; **Fees:** $3 entrance fee, $8 camping fee, $2 x/c ski track fee; **Visitor facilities:** Restrooms, campground, drinking water, nature trails, picnic area, amphitheater, scenic overlooks; **HANDICAPPED ACCESSIBILITY:** Visitor Center restrooms and drinking fountains; **Any limitations on vehicle usage:** Vehicles must remain on paved roads; **Hiking trails:** Yes, self-guided trails lead to points of interest; **Backcountry:** Yes, write to Superintendent for information; **Camping:** Yes, no reservations for campsites, which have charcoal grills, tables, drinking water, and flush toilets; **Other overnight accommodations on site:** No; **Meals served in the park:** No; **Food and supplies obtainable in the park:** No; **Food and supplies obtainable nearby:** Yes, in Arco, ID; **Overnight accommodations:** Arco, US 20, 26, and 93, 18 miles (28.8 km) northeast; **First Aid available in park:** Yes; **Nearest Hospital:** Arco, US 93, 26, and 20, 18 miles (28.8 km) northeast; **Days/Hours:** Open Sept. to mid-June from 8 a.m. to 4:30 p.m., until 6 p.m. from mid-June to Sept. Visitor Center open year-round; **Holiday Closings:** Thanksgiving, Dec. 25, Jan. 1, Washington's and Martin Luther King, Jr.'s birthdays; **Visitor attractions closed for season:** The road through the Monument is closed by snow from late Nov. to mid-April; **Weather:** Dry, warm, windy summers; cold snowy winters.

Hagerman Fossil Beds National Monument
Twin Falls, Idaho

MAILING ADDRESS: Hagerman Fossil Beds National Monument, P.O. Box 570 Hagerman, ID 83332. Contact: Manager **Telephone:** 205-837-4793 or Superintendent, National Park Service, 963 Blue Lakes Blvd., Twin Falls, ID 83301. **Telephone:** 208-733-8398

Now open to visitors.
Extraordinary fossils are found in the bluffs above the Snake River. This new Monument was added to the National Park System to preserve the outstanding paleontological sites, known as the Hagerman Valley fossil sites, to provide a center for continuing paleontological research, and to provide for the display and interpretation of scientific specimens. NO FEDERAL FACILITIES.
Authorized: Nov. 18, 1988. Acreage: 4,307.08; Federal: 3814.21; Nonfederal: 492.87.

Nez Perce National Historical Park
Spalding, Idaho

MAILING ADDRESS: Superintendent, Nez Perce National Historical Park, P.O. Box 93, Spalding, ID 83551 **Telephone:** 208-843-2261

DIRECTIONS: The Visitor Center is in Spalding, 11 miles (17.6 km) east of Lewiston on US 95.
   The history and culture of the Nez Perce Indian country are preserved, commemorated, and interpreted here. Four federally owned Sites are administered by the National Park Service and twenty sites through cooperative agreements; the 24 Sites are located in an area of about 12,000 square miles. Authorized for addition to the National Park System on May 15, 1965.

VISITOR ACTIVITIES: Intepretive exhibits, cultural demonstrations, self-guiding walks, picnicking, fishing in the Clearwater River adjacent to the park; **Permits:** Idaho fishing license, available locally; **Fees:** No; **Visitor facilities:** Parking at Visitor Center, restrooms, overlooks, and pullouts throughout the park, picnic area; **HANDICAPPED ACCESSIBILITY:** Restrooms: Visitor Center and picnic area; Spalding Visitor Center and picnic area barrier free. Interpretive shelter at White Bird Battlefield, 80 miles (128 km) south or Rt. US 95 is barrier free. **Any limitations on vehicle usage:** Vehicles are restricted to paved roads; **Hiking trails:** No; **Backcountry:** No; **Camping:** No; **Other overnight accommodations on site:** No, camping is available in nearby Clearwater and Nez Perce National Forests, 3 state parks, and private campgrounds. Contact the park for further information; **Meals served in the park:** No; **Food and supplies obtainable in the park:** No; **Food and supplies obtainable nearby:** Yes, Lewiston, Lapwai, Orofino, Kamiah, and Grangeville; **Overnight accommodations:** Lewiston, Orofino, Kamiah, and Grangeville; **First Aid available in park:** Yes; **Nearest Hospital:** Lewiston, US 95, 12 miles (19.2 km); **Days/Hours:** Visitor Center at Spalding is open 8 a.m.-4:30 p.m. Sept. 1-May 31, until 6 p.m. Memorial Day-Labor Day; **Holiday Closings:** Thanksgiving, Dec. 25, and Jan. 1; **Visitor attractions closed for seasons:** Cultural demonstrations offered only in summer.

TRAVEL ACCESS: **Bus:** Greyhound provides daily service into Lewiston; **Air:** Horizon, United Express, Empire Air offer daily service to Lewiston; **Other:** A bicycle path extends along the Clearwater River to within 6 miles (9.6 km) of the Spalding Site from Lewiston.

NEARBY FACILITIES & POINTS OF INTEREST: **Campgrounds:** Hellsgate, Winchester & Chief Timothy State Parks; National Forest Campgrounds area also nearby; **Parks, other points of interest:** Dworshak Dam, Hell's Canyon, River of No Return Wilderness.

Illinois

CHICAGO PORTAGE
NATIONAL HISTORIC SITE

MORMON PIONEER
NATIONAL HISTORIC TRAIL

LINCOLN HOME
NATIONAL HISTORIC SITE

LEWIS AND CLARK
NATIONAL HISTORIC TRAIL

Chicago Portage National Historic Site
River Forest, Illinois

MAILING ADDRESS: Superintendent, Chicago Portage National Historic Site, c/o Forest Preserve District of Cook County, Cummings Square, River Forest, IL 60305 **Telephone:** 708-366-9420

DIRECTIONS: Site is located on the west side of Harlem Ave. (IL 42A), approximately ½-mile (.8-km) north of Stevenson Expressway (I-55).

A portion of the portage discovered by French explorers Jacques Marquette and Louis Joliet is preserved here. Used by pioneers as a link between the Great Lakes and the Mississippi, the portage was one of the economic foundations of Chicago. Designated Jan. 3, 1952. Owned and administered by Forest Preserve District of Cook County.

VISITOR ACTIVITIES: Interpretive story board, historical statue, picnicking; **Permits:** No; **Fees:** No; **Visitor facilities:** Parking, water; **HANDICAPPED ACCESSIBILITY:** Yes; **Any limitations on vehicle usage:** Vehicles are restricted to the parking area; **Hiking trails:** No; **Backcountry:** No; **Camping:** No; **Other overnight accommodations on site:** No; **Meals served in the park:** No; **Food and supplies obtainable in the park:** No; **Food and supplies obtainable nearby:** Yes, Lyons, IL; **Overnight accommodations:** Lyons, Highway 34 (Ogden Ave.), 2 miles (3.2 km); **First Aid available in park:** No; **Nearest Hos-**

pital: LaGrange, Willow Springs Road, approximately 4 miles (6.4 km); **Days/Hours:** 9 a.m. to sunset; **Visitor attractions closed for season:** Site closed in winter.

Lewis and Clark National Historic Trail
Illinois (also in Missouri, Kansas, Nebraska, Iowa, South Dakota, North Dakota, Montana, Idaho, Oregon, Washington)

MAILING ADDRESS: National Park Service, 700 Rayovac Drive, Suite 100, Madison, WI 53711 **Telephone:** 608-264-5610

DIRECTIONS: The designation of the 4,500-mile (7,200-km) Lewis and Clark National Historic Trail by Congress on Nov. 10, 1978, included both the outbound and inbound routes of the 1804-06 expedition. A comprehensive management plan, completed in Jan. 1982, calls for the development of water-based trails (along the Missouri and Columbia Rivers and tributaries), land-based trails (for travel on foot), and marked motor routes for public retracement of the Trail.

Over 500 recreation and historic sites provide or have potential to provide access to the route and interpretation of the expedition. These sites are or will be owned and managed as part of the trail by cooperating Federal, State, and local agencies and private organizations. Efforts have begun to officially certify and mark these sites as part of the national historic trail. NPS areas which provide interpretation of the expedition are Jefferson National Expansion Memorial Historic Site (MO), Knife River Indian Villages National Historic Site (ND), Nez Perce National Historical Park (ID), and Fort Clatsop National Memorial (OR). The Lewis and Clark Trail highways marked and maintained by State highway departments are not part of the national historic trail, but complementary to it.

VISITOR ACTIVITIES: HANDICAPPED ACCESSIBILITY: Restrooms, Visitors Centers, and other facilities are accessible in *some* park and forest areas along the trail. Few segments of the trail itself are accessible.

Lincoln Home National Historic Site
Springfield, Illinois

MAILING ADDRESS: Superintendent, Lincoln Home National Historic Site, 413 South Eighth Street, Springfield, IL 62701-1905 **Telephone:** 217-492-4150

DIRECTIONS: The Site is in downtown Springfield. The Visitor Center is 426 South Seventh Street, one block west of the Lincoln Home.

While living in this home—now the focal point of a four block historic area—Abraham Lincoln rose from the practice of a small-town lawyer to become the 16th President of the United States, 1861-65. The two-story structure, built in 1839, was the only home he ever owned and his residence for 17 years. Authorized for addition to the National Park System on Aug. 18, 1971.

VISITOR ACTIVITIES: Interpretive exhibits and film, house tours; **Permits:** No; **Fees:** Parking fee is $1 per hour; **Visitor facilities:** Visitor Center, restrooms; **Any limitations on vehicle usage:** Vehicle traffic is not allowed within the park; **Hiking trails:** No; **Backcountry:** No; **Camping:** No; **Other overnight accommodations on site:** No; **Meals served in the park:** No; **Food and supplies obtainable in the park:** No; **Food and supplies obtainable nearby:** Yes, in Springfield; **Overnight accommodations:** Springfield, surrounding the

Site; **First Aid available in park:** Yes; **Nearest Hospital:** 7 blocks north of the Home; **Days/ Hours:** Open daily from 8:30 a.m. to 5 p.m. with extended hours in summer; **Holiday Closings:** Thanksgiving, Dec. 25, and Jan. 1; **Weather:** Winters are cold and snowy; summers are hot and humid.

GENERAL INFORMATION: Watch out for uneven, slippery boardwalks and steep, narrow staircases. Tours of the Home are given throughout the day. Free tickets for a specific tour time are distributed at the Visitor Center. Waiting times vary depending on season and time of day.

Mormon Pioneer National Historic Trail
Illinois (also in Iowa, Nebraska, Wyoming, and Utah)

MAILING ADDRESS: Rocky Mountain Regional Office, National Park Service, 12795 W. Alameda Parkway, P.O. Box 25287, Denver, CO 80225 **Telephone:** 303-969-2828

DIRECTIONS: It is still possible to closely follow this 1,300-mile (2,080 km)-long trail of history. Where wagons once rolled and teams traveled now highways, railroads, and bridges allow for modern-day travel. An auto route has been designated to go from the Mississippi River across the midwest plains and through the Rocky Mountains to descend into the Great Salt Lake Basin. Visitors are invited to retrace the route. While nearly two-thirds of the trail is now in private ownership, many of the places and events associated with the trail can be seen or visited. It is suggested that visitors send for the Mormon Pioneer Trail brochure and use the Primary Route Map to guide them.

VISITOR ACTIVITIES: The eastern end of the trail begins in west central Illinois at the Nauvoo National Historic District. The town of Nauvoo sits on the east bank of the Mississippi River and contains authentically restored buildings, shops, and homes of historic interest. Along the trail, 73 historic sites have been selected to commemorate and interpret important events and landmarks. There are also 6 cross-country trail segments totaling 47 miles (75.2 km) on Federal lands, chosen to offer excellent opportunities for hiking, horseback riding, and other appropriate recreational activities. Note: The National Park Service provides no facilities (restrooms, etc.) specifically for trail users. These sites and cross-country segments are identified on the Primary Route Map in the brochure. The western terminus of the trail is at Pioneer Trail State Park in Salt Lake City, UT. The area includes "This is the Place" monument and exhibits structures from temporary dug-outs to substantial public buildings.

Indiana

INDIANA DUNES
NATIONAL LAKESHORE

GEORGE ROGERS CLARK
NATIONAL HISTORICAL PARK

LINCOLN BOYHOOD NATIONAL MEMORIAL

George Rogers Clark National Historical Park
Vincennes, Indiana

MAILING ADDRESS: Superintendent, George Rogers Clark National Historical Park, 401 South Second Street, Vincennes, IN 47591 **Telephone:** 812-882-1776

DIRECTIONS: Follow US 50 (east and west) which intersects with US 41 (north and south) at Vincennes; Park can be reached by 6th Street on US 50 or Willow Street exit on US 41. The entrance to the Park is on Second Street.

On the site of old Fort Sackville, the Park commemorates the capture of the fort from the British by Lt. Col. George Rogers Clark on Feb. 25, 1779. Authorized for addition to the National Park System on July 23, 1966.

VISITOR ACTIVITIES: Interpretive exhibits and film, living history weapon demonstrations and talks on Sunday afternoons in summer; **Permits:** No; **Fees:** $1 fee at Clark Memorial, April thru November, ages 17-61, Visitor Center free; **Visitor facilities:** Memorial building, Visitor Center, parking. In summer, a "Trailblazer" train operated by Vincennes University tours points of interest in Vincennes; **Any limitations on vehicle usage:** Motorcycles are not permitted on sidewalks; **Hiking trails:** No; **Backcountry:** No; **Camping:** No; **Other overnight accommodations on site:** No; **Meals served in the park:** No; **Food and supplies obtainable in the park:** No; **Food and supplies obtainable nearby:** Yes, close to the Park in downtown Vincennes; **Overnight accommodations:** Vincennes; **First Aid available in park:** Yes; **Nearest Hospital:** Vincennes, 7th Street, 6 blocks; **Days/Hours:** Open daily from 9 a.m. to 5 p.m.; **Holiday Closings:** Thanksgiving, Dec. 25, and Jan. 1; **Visitor attractions closed for season:** The Park may be closed for a day or two in severe winter weather; **Weather:** Snow possible from Dec. through Mar.; the annual temperature range is from -10 to 100°F.

TRAVEL ACCESS: Bus: Greyhound provides daily service to Vincennes.

NEARBY FACILITIES & POINTS OF INTEREST: Hotel/Motel: Travelodge, 1411 Willow St., 812-882-1282, 1 mile (1.6 km); Holiday Inn, 600 Wheatland Rd., 812-886-9900, 3 miles (4.8 km); Executive Inn, 1 Executive Blvd., 812-886-5000, 3 miles (4.8 km); **Campgrounds:** Ouabache Trails Park, Fort Knox Road, 6 miles (9.6 km), 812-882-4316; Kimmel Park, Oliphant Street, 812-882-1140, 2 miles (3.2 km); **Parks, other points of interest;** William Henry Harrison Home, Old Cathedral, Old French House, Fort Knox II, Indiana Territory Capitol State Historic Site, Western Sun Print Shop, Maurice Thompson Birthplace, and Old State Bank and Art Gallery.

Indiana Dunes National Lakeshore
Porter, Indiana

MAILING ADDRESS: Superintendent, Indiana Dunes National Lakeshore, 1100 N. Mineral Springs Road, Porter, IN 46304 **Telephone:** 219-926-7561

DIRECTIONS: The lakeshore runs between Gary and Michigan City along the southern shore of Lake Michigan, about 60 miles (96 km) east of Chicago. US 12 and 20, Interstate 94, IN 49, and Indiana Toll Road (I-80 and I-90) pass through the area and connect with roads which lead directly to the lakeshore. The Visitor Center is 3 miles (4.8 km) east of Indiana 49 on US 12 at the Intersection of US 12 and Kemil Road.

Along the southern shore of Lake Michigan between Gary and Michigan City are several sections of clean, sandy beaches backed by huge sand dunes. Many dunes are covered with dense forests, others are continually reshaped by the wind. The parkland, totaling about 14,000 acres, preserves some of these remaining dunes and their associated bogs and marshes and provides recreational opportunities along the beaches and interior lands. Authorized for addition to the National Park System on Nov. 5, 1966.

VISITOR ACTIVITIES: Biking, hiking, horseback riding, cross-country skiing, auto tours, swimming, fishing, photography, interpretive talks, films and programs; **Permits:** An Indiana fishing license available locally; **Fees:** Parking fee at West Beach area, $2.50 per vehicle ($1.25 with Golden Age or Golden Access Passport); **Visitor facilities:** Horse trail, parking lots, restrooms, drinking water, food service, bathhouse, interpretive hikes, trails, talks and films; **HANDICAPPED ACCESSIBILITY:** Call 219-926-7561; **Any limitations on vehicle usage:** Dune buggies, motor bikes, and other motorized vehicles must remain on public roadways; **Hiking trails:** Yes, check at Visitor Center for information on hiking trails in each area; **Backcountry:** No; **Camping:** None available in the National Lakeshore. Private and state campgrounds are nearby. Camping facilities will become available in the National Lakeshore in 1992. Reservations are accepted for campsites at Indiana Dunes State Park, Chesterton, IN 46304, phone 219-926-4520; **Other overnight accommodations on site:** No; **Meals served in the park:** Yes, West Beach area (summer only); **Food and supplies obtainable in the park:** Yes, food at West Beach area (summer); **Food and supplies obtainable nearby:** Yes, Porter, Chesterton, Pines, Michigan City, Gary, Portage; **Overnight accommodations:** Many motels available in neighboring communitites; Michigan City, 6 miles (9.6 km); Pines, 3 miles (4.8 km); Portage, 8 miles (12.8 km); Gary, 12 miles (19.2 km) from the park; **First Aid available in park:** Yes; **Nearest Hospital:** Michigan City, 6 miles (9.6 km), Gary, 12 miles (19.2 km); **Days/Hours:** Visitor Center is open from 8 a.m. to 5 p.m. daily, and until 6 p.m. in summer; **Holiday Closings:** Thanksgiving, Dec. 25, Jan. 1; **Weather:** 75°-90° temperatures in summer, 0°-35° and snowy in winter.

GENERAL INFORMATION: Hunting and open fires are prohibited. Grills and portable stoves using charcoal, gas or liquid fuels are permitted. Private property rights must be respected.

TRAVEL ACCESS: Bus: No; **Rail:** South Shore Line runs regularly to the nearby Dune Park Terminal; **Air:** No.

NEARBY FACILITIES & POINTS OF INTEREST: Parks, other points of inter-
est: Indiana Dunes State Park, Chesterton, IN 46304 219-926-4520; Maple Sugar Festival held in March. Duneland Harvest Festival held in Sept.

Lincoln Boyhood National Memorial
Lincoln City, Indiana

MAILING ADDRESS: Superintendent, Lincoln Boyhood National Memorial, Lincoln City, IN 47552 **Telephone:** 812-937-4541

DIRECTIONS: The Park is on IN 162, 2 miles (3.2 km) east of Gentryville, 4 miles (6.4 km) south of Dale, IN, and 4 miles (6.4 km) west of Santa Claus, IN. Exit I-64 at Dale (exit 57) south on US 231 to IN 162 east, or Santa Claus (exit 63) to IN 162 west.

On this southern Indiana farm Abraham Lincoln grew from youth to manhood. His mother is buried here. Authorized for addition to the National Park System on Feb. 19, 1962.

VISITOR ACTIVITIES: Visitor Center with memorial halls, museum, and film; burial site of Nancy Hanks Lincoln; Lincoln Living Historical Farm, a working pioneer farm with costumed interpretation; walking trails; group tours available by reservation; **Permits:** No; **Fees:** Yes, $1 per person, maximum of $3 per family, no charge for children age 16 and under or for senior citizens age 62 or over; **Visitor facilities:** Memorial Visitor Center with parking, information services, book sales, restrooms, telephone; **HANDICAPPED ACCESSIBIL-ITY:** Visitor Center and Living Historical Farm; **Any limitations on vehicle usage:** Parking is at the Visitor Center and Living Historical Farm parking area. Drivers should be alert for hikers, bikers, and the handicapped; **Hiking trails:** Yes, 2 miles (3.2 km) self-guiding trails, including the Lincoln Boyhood Trail, Trail of Twelve Stones, and the Boyhood Nature Trail; **Backcountry:** No, but adjacent is the 1747-acre Lincoln State Park with 10 miles (16 km) of connecting hiking trails; **Camping:** No, but available at adjacent Lincoln State Park; facilities for picnicking, swimming, boating and fishing; **Other overnight accommodations on site:** No; **Meals served in the park:** No; **Food and supplies obtainable in the park:** No; **Food and supplies obtainable nearby:** Yes, in Dale and Santa Claus, IN; **Overnight accommo-dations:** Dale, 4 miles (6.4 km) north on US 231, Huntingburg, 15 miles (24 km) north and Jasper, 20 miles (32 km) north on US 231; **First Aid available in park:** Yes; **Nearest Hospi-tal:** Huntingburg, 15 miles (24 km) north on US 231; **Days/Hours:** 8:00 a.m.-5:00 p.m. daily (CDT-CST), Grounds open daily during daylight hours, year-round; **Holiday Closings:** Thanksgiving, Dec. 25, Jan. 1; **Visitor attractions closed for seasons:** Farm cabin is open on a limited basis in winter; **Weather:** Summer is humid with temperatures to 95°; winter is mod-erate, but snow and ice storms occur in Jan. and Feb., and roads can be slippery.

GENERAL INFORMATION: The Memorial is on the "Lincoln Heritage Trail," an auto tour route which connects sites relating to Lincoln's life in Kentucky, Indiana, and Illinois. *For Your Safety*—Stay on established trails. Beware of insects, poison ivy, snakes and farm animals that bite. Pets must be leashed or carried.

NEARBY FACILITIES & POINTS OF INTEREST: Hotel/Motel/Restaurants/
Campgrounds: Available nearby, contact park for list; **Parks, other points of interest:** Lin-

coln State Park (Lincoln-related sites), Col. William Jones House, St. Meinrad Archabbey, Ferdinand State Forest, Hoosier National Forest, Patoka Lake.

Iowa

Effigy Mounds National Monument
McGregor, Iowa

MAILING ADDRESS: Superintendent, Effigy Mounds National Monument, Rural Route 1, Box 25A, Harpers Ferry, IA 52146 **Telephone:** 319-873-3491

DIRECTIONS: The Monument is 3 miles (4.8 km) north of Marquette on IA 76.
The Monument contains outstanding examples of prehistoric burial mounds, some in the shapes of birds and bears. Created by Presidential Proclamation on Oct. 25, 1949.

VISITOR ACTIVITIES: Interpretive exhibits, self-guiding and guided walks; **Permits:** No; **Fees:** Federal Entrance Fee Area $1 per visit, 16 years and under free; **Visitor facilities:** Parking and restrooms at Visitor Center, walking trail, exhibits and markers, guided walks 4 times daily from Memorial Day through Labor Day; **HANDICAPPED ACCESSIBILITY:** Visitor Center, restrooms, audiovisual displays, first three mounds are wheelchair accessible. Other trails are very steep for wheelchairs; **Any limitations on vehicle usage:** There are no roads; **Hiking trails:** Yes, 1-3-hour self-guiding trail; **Backcountry:** No; **Camping:** No; **Other overnight accommodations on site:** No; **Meals served in the park:** No; **Food and supplies obtainable in the park:** No; **Food and supplies obtainable nearby:** Yes, in Waukon and McGregor and Prairie du Chien; **Overnight accommodations:** Waukon, 20 miles (32 km), McGregor, 4 miles (6.4 km), and Prairie du Chien, WI, 4 miles (6.4 km); **First Aid available in park:** Yes; **Nearest Hospital:** Prairie du Chien, WI, 4 miles (6.4 km); **Days/Hours:** Visitor Center open daily from 8 a.m. until 5 p.m. and remains open until 7 p.m. in summer; **Holiday Closings:** Dec. 25; **Weather:** Summers are warm to hot with moderate-to-high humidity; winters are cold and snowy with temperatures in the 15°-30° range.

GENERAL INFORMATION: When hiking, stay on trails and do not venture too close to cliff edges. Be alert for poison ivy and stinging nettles.

TRAVEL ACCESS: Bus: No; **Air:** Northwest, United, American Eagle, and Mississippi Valley provide daily service to Dubuque, IA, and Mid State Airlines provide daily service to LaCross, WI; **Other:** Taxi available from Prairie du Chien, WI, to park. Rental cars available at Dubuque, IA, and LaCross, WI, airports.

NEARBY FACILITIES & POINTS OF INTEREST: Campgrounds: Yellow River State Forest; Pikes Peak State Park within 10 miles (16 km); **Parks, other points of interest:** Yellow River State Forest, IA; Pikes Peak State Park, IA; Villa Louis, WI (State Historical Society); Stonefield Village, Wisconsin State Historical Society; Governor Dewey State Park, WI; Montauk House, Iowa State Historical Society; Wyalusing State Park, WI.

Herbert Hoover National Historic Site
West Branch, Iowa

MAILING ADDRESS: Superintendent, Herbert Hoover National Historic Site, P.O. Box 607, West Branch, IA 52358 **Telephone:** 319-643-2541

DIRECTIONS: West Branch is 10 miles (16 km) east of Iowa City on I-80 and 40 miles (65 km) west of Davenport on I-80. The Visitor Center is on Parkside Drive at the intersection with Main Street.

The birthplace home, and 19th century (1874-84) boyhood neighborhood of the 31st President, 1929-33, the gravesites of President and Mrs. Hoover, a restored native prairie, and the Hoover Presidential Library-Museum, are within the Park. Authorized for addition to the National Park System on Aug. 12, 1965.

VISITOR ACTIVITIES: Interpretive talks and exhibits, picnicking, walking tours, cross-country skiing; **Permits:** No; **Fees:** National Park Service fee $1 adults, over 61 free. National Park Service Passports accepted. The Hoover Presidential Library-Museum is administered by the National Archives and Records Administration, and a $1 adults entrance fee is charged; **Visitor facilities:** Parking and restrooms at Visitor Center, picnic areas, walking trails, interpretive exhibits, operating blacksmith in summer; **HANDICAPPED ACCESSIBILITY:** Restrooms at Visitor Center, ramps at most historic buildings on request, parking spaces available, special wheelchair-accommodating picnic tables; **Any limitations on vehicle usage:** Vehicles are restricted to designated roadways; **Hiking trails:** Yes, self-guiding trails; **Backcountry:** No; **Camping:** No; **Other overnight accommodations on site:** No; **Meals served in the park:** No; **Food and supplies obtainable in the park:** No; **Food and supplies obtainable nearby:** Yes, at West Branch; **Overnight accommodations:** West Branch, ½-mile (.8-km); **First Aid available in park:** Yes; **Nearest Hospital:** Iowa City, IA, 10 miles (16 km) via I-80; **Days/Hours:** Open 24 hours a day every day, with exception of Thanksgiving, Dec. 25, and Jan. 1. Visitor Center and Birthplace Cottage are open daily from 9 a.m. to 5 p.m. The Hoover Presidential Library-Museum is open daily from 9 a.m. to 5 p.m. with the exception of Thanksgiving, Dec. 25, and Jan. 1; **Holiday Closings:** Thanksgiving, Dec. 25, and Jan. 1.

GENERAL INFORMATION: Please note the historic walkway surfaces. Boardwalks are especially slippery in frost or wet weather.

Lewis and Clark Trail
For details see listing in Illinois

Kansas

Fort Larned National Historic Site
Larned, Kansas

MAILING ADDRESS: Superintendent, Fort Larned National Historic Site, Route 3, Larned, KS 67550 **Telephone:** 316-285-6911

DIRECTIONS: The Site is 6 miles (9.6 km) west of the city of Larned, KS, on KS 156.

A military fort from 1859 to 1878, Fort Larned was used for protection of mail and travelers on the eastern leg of the Santa Fe Trail. It served as an Indian Agency from 1861 to 1868 and a base for military operations against the Southern Plains Indians. Authorized for addition to the National Park System on Aug. 31, 1964; established in 1966.

VISITOR ACTIVITIES: Guided tours upon request and daily during summer, Living history programs on weekends during summer; **Permits:** No; **Fees:** $1 per adult; 16 and under, free; **Visitor facilities:** Parking, restrooms, exhibits, sales area, and audiovisual facilities at Visitor Center; historic military buildings; interpretive signs; **HANDICAPPED ACCESSIBILITY:** Visitor Center, museum and restrooms are accessible; **Any limitations on vehicle usage:** Vehicles are only allowed in the parking area, separate picnic area; **Hiking trails:** Yes, 1; **Backcountry:** No; **Camping:** No; **Other overnight accommodations on site:** No. Commercial campgrounds are available in Larned. Contact Fort Larned for further information; **Meals served in the park:** No; **Food and supplies obtainable in the park:** Soft drinks only; **Food and supplies obtainable nearby:** Yes, at Larned; **Overnight accommodations:** Larned, 7 miles (11.2 km) on KS 156; **First Aid available in park:** Yes; **Nearest Hospital:** Larned, 7 miles (11.2 km) East on KS 156; **Days/Hours:** Open year-round. From early June through Labor Day from 8 a.m. to 6 p.m.; the rest of the year from 9 a.m. to 5 p.m.; **Holiday Closings:** Thanksgiving, Dec. 25, and Jan. 1; **Visitor attractions closed for seasons:** Living history programs are offered regularly in summer, irregularly the remainder of the year; **Weather:** Summer is warm to hot and often windy. Winter is moderately cold; snow possible between late Dec. and early March.

TRAVEL ACCESS: Rail: Amtrak provides daily service to Dodge City; **Air:** Regular service connects Great Bend to Denver, Kansas City, and Wichita and Oklahoma City.

NEARBY FACILITIES & POINTS OF INTEREST: Hotel/Motel: Townsman Inn, 123 E. 14th Larned, KS, 316-285-3216, 7 miles (11.2 km) from park; Country Inn-Motel, 135 E. 14th Larned KS, 316-285-3216, 7 miles (11.2 km) from park; **Food/Supplies:** Dillon's Family Center, 423 Main, Larned, KS, 316-285-3171, 7 miles (11.2 km) from park; Several other stores available (some 24 hrs); **Parks, other points of interest:** Santa Fe Trail Center, KS 156, 316-285-2054, 4 miles (6.4 km) from park.

Fort Scott National Historic Site
Fort Scott, Kansas

MAILING ADDRESS: Superintendent, Fort Scott National Historic Site, Old Fort Boulevard, Fort Scott, KS 66701 **Telephone:** 316-223-0310

DIRECTIONS: The Fort is near the intersection of US 69 and US 54 in Fort Scott, which is 90 miles (144 km) south of Kansas City and 60 miles (96 km) northwest of Joplin, MO.
    The Fort commemorates the national significance of the "Permanent Indian Frontier" of 1842-1853; Bleeding Kansas 1854-1860; the Civil War 1861-1865; and the Railroad Years of 1869-1873. This area was authorized for addition to the National Park System on Oct. 19, 1978.

VISITOR ACTIVITIES: Self-guided tours of reconstructed and restored historic buildings, including 33 furnished rooms, interpretive exhibits, living interpretive demonstrations and special events as scheduled; **Permits:** No; **Fees:** Yes, $1 admission for ages 17 through 61, others free; **Visitor facilities:** Restrooms, book store, museum; **HANDICAPPED ACCESSIBILITY:** A 25-minute videotape tour of the Fort is available for handicapped visitors; **Any limitations on vehicle usage:** No vehicles are allowed on historic grounds; **Hiking trails:** No; **Backcountry:** No; **Camping:** No; **Other overnight accommodations on site:** No, KOA campground is 2 miles (3.2 km) from the Site; **Meals served in the park:** No; **Food and supplies obtainable in the park:** No; **Food and supplies obtainable nearby:** Yes, at Fort Scott; **Overnight accommodations:** Fort Scott, 2 blocks to 1 mile (1.6 km) from the Site; **First Aid available in park:** Yes; **Nearest Hospital:** Fort Scott, 1 mile (1.6 km); **Days/Hours:** Open daily from 8 a.m. to 5 p.m. extended hours of operation 8 a.m.-6 p.m. Memorial Day through Labor Day; **Holiday Closings:** Thanksgiving, Dec. 25, and Jan. 1; **Visitor attractions closed for seasons:** No; **Weather:** Summers are hot and humid with an average high temperature of 85°. Winters are cool; average high temperature is 40°.

GENERAL INFORMATION: Restored and furnished buildings open to public include post headquarters, barracks, post hospital, bakery, guardhouse, officer's quarters, dragoon stables, quartermaster storehouse and powder magazine. Introductory audiovisual program available at Visitor Center. A wide range of interpretive activities and special events is scheduled from May through September. Write for details.

TRAVEL ACCESS: Bus: Jefferson Bus System provides daily service to/from Kansas City, MO; **Rail:** No; **Air:** Small aircraft only, no commercial service; **Other:** No.

NEARBY FACILITIES & POINTS OF INTEREST: Hotel/Motel: Best Western-Fort Scott Inn, 101 State Street 316-223-0100, ¼ mile (.4 km) from park; Downtowner Motor Hotel, 2 South National, 316-223-3500, ⅛ mile (.2 km) from park; **Parks, other points of**

interest: National Cemetery, Ralph Richards Museum, Gunn Park (picnic areas and fishing), Victorian homes auto tour, restored downtown, trolley tours.

Oregon National Scenic Trail
For details see listing in Missouri

Kentucky

MAMMOTH CAVE NATIONAL PARK

Louisville

CUMBERLAND GAP
NATIONAL HISTORIC PARK

BIG SOUTH FORK NATIONAL
RIVER AND RECREATION AREA

ABRAHAM LINCOLN BIRTHPLACE NATIONAL HISTORIC SITE

Abraham Lincoln Birthplace National Historic Site
Hodgenville, Kentucky

MAILING ADDRESS: Superintendent, Abraham Lincoln Birthplace National Historic Site, 2995 Lincoln Farm Rd., Hodgenville, KY 42748 **Telephone:** 502-358-3874

DIRECTIONS: The Site is 3 miles (4.8 km) south of Hodgenville on US 31E and KY 61, 60 miles (96 km) south of Louisville.

Established by act of Congress on July 17, 1916, this 116.50-acre historic site preserves in its Memorial Building an early 19th-century Kentucky cabin, symbolic of the one in which Lincoln was born.

VISITOR ACTIVITIES: Interpretive talks, exhibits and films, hiking, picnicking; **Permits:** No; **Fees:** No; **Visitor facilities:** Parking at Visitor Center, parking and restrooms at picnic area, environmental study area; **HANDICAPPED ACCESSIBILITY:** Restrooms, picnic grounds, and Memorial Bldg.; **Any limitations on vehicle usage:** Restricted to designated roadways and parking areas; **Hiking trails:** Yes, through forest land; **Backcountry:** No; **Camping:** No; **Other overnight accommodations on site:** No; **Meals served in the park:** No, but available in Hodgenville; **Food and supplies obtainable in the park:** No; **Food and supplies obtainable nearby:** Yes, in Hodgenville; **Overnight accommodations:** Motels are adjacent to the park; **First Aid available in park:** Yes, and nearby in Hodgenville, US 31E; **Nearest Hospital:** Elizabethtown, KY 61, 12 miles (19.2 km); **Days/Hours:** Open daily from 8 a.m. to 6:45 p.m. from Early June-Labor Day, Sept., Oct., April, May, 8 a.m.-5:45 p.m.; 8 a.m. to 4:45 p.m. remainder of the year; Schedule subject to change. **Holiday Closings:** Dec. 25; **Visitor attractions closed for seasons:** No; **Weather:** Warm summers with frequent rain; moderate winters with light snow.

GENERAL INFORMATION: *For Your Safety*—Watch for exposed roots and uneven ground along trails. Poison ivy and briars are abundant in woodland.

Big South Fork National River and Recreation Area
For details see listing in Tennessee

Cumberland Gap National Historical Park
Middlesboro, Kentucky
(also in Tennessee and Virginia)

MAILING ADDRESS: Superintendent, Cumberland Gap National Historical Park, P.O. Box 1848, Middlesboro, KY 40965 **Telephone:** 606-248-2817

DIRECTIONS: The Park can be reached by taking US 25E from Kentucky and Tennessee or US 58 from Virginia. The Visitor Center is ¼ mile (.4 km) south of Middlesboro on US 25E.

The mountain pass in the wilderness, explored by Daniel Boone, developed into a main artery of the great trans-Allegheny migration for settlement of "the Old West" and an important military objective in the Civil War. Authorized for addition to the National Park System on June 11, 1940.

VISITOR ACTIVITIES: Interpretive and audiovisual exhibits, hiking, camping, picnicking, campfire programs, walking, music and craft demonstrations, living history programs, fishing; **Permits:** For backcountry, available from the Superintendent; **Fees:** $8 camping fee, warm showers, Wilderness Road Campground; **Visitor facilities:** Primitive and developed campgrounds, hiking trails, restrooms, picnic areas, drinking water, museum; **Any limitations on vehicle usage:** Off-road vehicle use is not permitted; 20-foot maximum vehicle length on Pinnacle Road; **Hiking trails:** Yes, there are about 50 miles (80 km) of hiking trails in the Park. Trail guides and information are available at the Visitor Center; **Backcountry:** Yes, get information from the Superintendent; **Camping:** Yes, organized group camping area and primitive campsites are reserved by contacting the Superintendent. No other reservations are available; **Other overnight accommodations on site:** No; **Meals served in the park:** No; **Food and supplies obtainable in the park:** No; **Food and supplies obtainable nearby:** Yes, in Middlesboro, KY, Cumberland Gap, TN, Gibson Station and Ewing, VA; **Overnight accommodations:** Middlesboro, KY, US 25E, several blocks; Cumberland Gap, TN, US 25E 2¼ miles (4 km); Harrogate, TN, US 25E, 4 miles (6.4 km); **First Aid available in park:** Yes; **Nearest Hospital:** Middlesboro, KY, US 25E to Hwy 74, 1 mile (1.6 km); **Days/Hours:** Park gates are open from 8 a.m. to dusk year-round. The Visitor Center is open 9 a.m. to 5 p.m. Labor Day to mid-June; 8:00 a.m. to 6:00 p.m. summer months; **Holiday Closings:** Dec. 25; **Visitor attractions closed for seasons:** Pinnacle can be closed temporarily due to snow; **Weather:** Summer is hot and humid; winter is cold to moderate.

GENERAL INFORMATION: *For Your Safety*—Never hike alone. Beware of snakes, poison ivy and poison oak. Nearby points of interest include Cudjo's Cave; the June Tolliver House at Big Stone Gap, VA; Lincoln Memorial University in Harrogate, TN; Pine Mountain State Park, KY; and Dr. Thomas Walker State Park, near Barbourville, KY. Directions and further information on these sites are available at the Middlesboro Visitor Center.

TRAVEL ACCESS: **Bus:** Greyhound provides daily service within 2 miles (3.2 km) of park; **Rail:** No; **Air:** Airport at Knoxville, TN 60 miles (96 km) south.

NEARBY FACILITIES & POINTS OF INTEREST: Hotel/Motel: Holiday Inn, Cumberland Gap, TN 615-869-3631, 3 miles (4.8 km) from Park; **Campgrounds:** Pine Mountain State Park Campground; **Parks, other points of interest:** Pine Mountain State Park.

Mammoth Cave National Park
Mammoth Cave, Kentucky   **SEE CLIMATABLE NO. 19**

MAILING ADDRESS: Superintendent, Mammoth Cave National Park, Mammoth Cave, KY 42259 **Telephone:** 502-758-2328

DIRECTIONS: Visitor Center (which includes cave and surface tour information and ticket sales) is 9 miles (14.4 km) northwest of Park City off Interstate 65 via KY 255 and 70, and 10 miles (16 km) west of Cave City off Interstate 65 via Highway 70 and 255.

Mammoth Cave is a series of underground passageways containing travertine and gypsum formations, deep pits and high domes, and an underground river. Over 330 miles (532 km) of interconnected passageways have been surveyed and mapped, making it the longest cave system in the world. Authorized for addition to the National Park System on May 25, 1926. Selected as a world heritage site Oct. 27, 1981. Became part of an International Biosphere Reserve in 1990.

VISITOR ACTIVITIES: Guided cave trips, guided nature walks and evening programs in summer, self-guiding walking trails, camping, picnicking, boating, fishing, backcountry hiking, and Green River boat trip; **Permits:** For backcountry camping, inquire at Visitor Center or Park Headquarters Campground station; **Fees:** For cave tours, Green River boat trip, and camping in the main campground. Cave tours vary in length (1 ¼ to 6 ½ hours), season offered, and time of departure. Green River boat trip available Apr.-Oct. For a description of tours available, current tour schedule, and prices, contact the Superintendent or Ticketmaster agent; **Visitor facilities:** Visitor Center, hiking trails, picnic area, boat ramps, post office, service station, campgrounds, groceries and camping supplies, coin-operated laundry, showers, lodging, dining room and coffee shop, souvenirs and Green River boat trip; **HANDICAPPED ACCESSIBILITY:** Visitor Center, Tour for the Disabled, Loop D of Main Campground, Amphitheater, Heritage Trail. Picnic area, minimally accessible, does not have accessible restrooms; **Any limitations on vehicle usage:** Off-road vehicles prohibited; mountain bikes permitted only on public roads; **Hiking trails:** Yes, 70 miles (112 km) of hiking tails. Variety of hiking trails available ranging from short to long, easy to strenuous, nature trails to miles of hiking trails. Trail maps and information at Visitor Center; **Backcountry:** Yes, information available at Visitor Center or by contacting the Superintendent. Backcountry camping permit required and may be obtained at the Park Headquarters Campground station, 12 backcountry campsites are designated; **Camping:** Yes, no reservations accepted for the 108 individual campsites (2 sites modified to accommodate handicapped). Camping fee is $6 per night per site. A free campground with 12 sites is at Hounchins Ferry. Dennison Ferry Campground with 4 sites, is also free. A group campsite available by reservation through Chief Ranger's office; **Other overnight accommodations on site:** Yes, Mammoth Cave Hotel is open all year. For reservations, contact National Park Concessions, Inc., Mammoth Cave, KY 42259, phone 502-758-2225; **Meals served in the park:** Yes, at Mammoth Cave Hotel; **Food and supplies obtainable in the park:** Yes, at the service center located next to the main campground. The store is closed from Thanksgiving to Easter Week and is only open on weekends, including Fridays in the spring and fall; **Food and supplies obtainable nearby:** Yes, at Bowling Green, Glasgow, Horse Cave, Park City, Brownsville, and Cave City; **Overnight**

accommodations: Numerous overnight accommodations are available within a 15-45-minute drive of the park, which includes the communities of Bowling Green, Glasgow, Horse Cave, Park City, and Cave City. For information on areas outside the park write the Department of Public Information, Capitol Annex Building, Frankfort, KY 40601; **First Aid available in park:** Yes; **Nearest Hospital:** Caverna Hospital at Horse Cave, US 31W, 15 miles (24 km); **Days/Hours:** Open year-round; Visitor Center open 7:30 a.m.-7 p.m. in summer; 8 a.m.-5:30 p.m. the rest of the year; **Holiday Closings:** Cave tours available year-round except Dec. 25; **Visitor attractions closed for season:** None closed, main campground open year-round.

GENERAL INFORMATION: In the caves the temperature remains near 54°F and the humidity can reach 100%. Bring along a sweater or light jacket. In winter, strong winds near the cave entrance may demand warmer clothing. Some cave tours are strenuous, requiring stooping, ascending and descending steps, and walking over unlevel terrain. Be sure to select the tour that best meets your physical ability. Portions of cave and surface trails are uneven and wet and slippery, so wear sturdy walking shoes—not sandals. Children under 16 years of age must be accompanied by an adult except on the Explorer and Trog Tours, designed specially for children. Tours are available for the disabled. While driving, be on the alert for deer crossing the roadway, particularly at night. Poisonous snakes and poison ivy may be present even around the most heavily visited areas.

TRAVEL ACCESS: Bus: Greyhound provides service to Cave City, KY, 10 miles (16 km) away; **Rail:** No: **Air:** Access to Nashville and Louisville, both about 90 miles (144 km) away. Local airports at Glasgow 18 miles (28.8 km); Bowling Green 35 miles (56 km)—private aircraft.

Jean Lafitte National Historical Park
New Orleans, Louisiana

MAILING ADDRESS: Jean Lafitte National Historical Park, U.S. Customs House, 423 Canal Street, Room 210, New Orleans, LA 70130-2341

DIRECTIONS: Please note that the park consists of 3 different units located in separate sectors of the Greater New Orleans area.

French Quarter Unit: Visitor and Folklife Center is located in the French Market on Decatur Street.

Chalmette Unit: Located 6 miles (9.6 km) from downtown; follow N. Rampart Street east until it merges with St. Claude Avenue. Continue until St. Claude merges with the St. Bernard Highway (LA 46), which passes directly in front of the park.

America won a brilliant victory here in the Battle of New Orleans in the War of 1812. The Park also includes Chalmette National Cemetery, dating back to 1864, Chalmette Monument, Rene Beauregard House, Visitor Center.

Barataria Unit: Located on the West Bank of the Mississippi River, 40 minutes from downtown. Take Route 90 across the Greater New Orleans Bridge, now called Crescent City Connection, then continue on 90 (which becomes the West Bank Expressway) to Barataria Boulevard (LA highway 45). Turn left (south) on 45, and continue 7½ miles (12 km) until you see signs for Barataria.

The Park was established to preserve and interpret the cultural diversity of the Mississippi Delta region. Authorized for addition to the National Park Service on Nov. 10, 1978.

VISITOR ACTIVITIES: *French Quarter Unit:* Ranger-guided walking tours, audiovisual and interpretive exhibits. New Visitor and Folklife Center features performances and demonstrations by traditional artists, craftspeople, and musicians of the Mississippi Delta region. *Chalmette Unit:* Interpretive talks presented by Rangers, audiovisual and interpretive exhibits, 1 self-guiding tour road. *Barataria Unit:* Visitor Center containing audiovisual and interpretive exhibits. Guided and self-guided walking tours, canoeing, fishing. **Permits:** Barataria Unit requires Park permit and State License for hunting and State License for fishing. **Fees:** No; **Visitor facilities:** French Quarter: Exhibits and audiovisual programs. Chalmette: Exhibits and audiovisual programs, parking, restrooms, and picnic tables. Barataria: Parking, restroom, and picnic tables, Palmetto Trail, Plantation Trail, and Marsh Overlook Trail; **HANDICAPPED ACCESSIBILITY:** Parking and restrooms at Barataria and Chalmette Units; Barataria and Coquille Trails are accessible; **Any limitations on vehicle usage:** Vehicles are restricted to designated roadways; **Hiking trails:** Yes, Bayou Coquille Trail and Ring Levee Trail are open in the Barataria Unit; **Backcountry:** No; **Camping:** No; **Other overnight accommodations on site:** No; **Meals served in the park:** No; **Food and supplies obtainable nearby:** Yes, there are many excellent restaurants in the French Quarter and throughout New Orleans; **Overnight accommodations:** Yes, throughout the Greater New Orleans area; **First Aid available in park:** Yes; **Nearest Hospitals:** French Quarter Unit: Charity, Hotel Dieu, Touro. Chalmette Unit: De La Ronde and Chalmette General. Barataria Unit: West Jefferson Medical Center, in Marrero; **Days/Hours:** French Quarter Unit is open from 9 a.m. to 5 p.m. daily, closed Dec. 25 and Mardi Gras days. Chalmette Unit is open daily, with extended summer hours. Barataria Unit is open daily, with extended summer hours; **Holiday Closings:** French Quarter and Chalmette Units only, Dec. 25, Jan. 1, and Mardi Gras; **Visitor attractions closed for seasons:** No.

GENERAL INFORMATION: Summers are hot and humid; winters are mild. Heavy rain showers can occur through the year.

Poverty Point National Monument
Epps, Louisiana

MAILING ADDRESS: Poverty Point National Monument, c/o Poverty Point State Commemorative Area, Post Office Box 248, Epps, LA 71237

Located in northeastern Louisiana, this national monument commemorates a culture that thrived during the first and second millennia, B.C., and which constructed an intricate pattern of mounds and ridges that is the largest and most complex geometrical earthwork created by the early people of North America. Today the ridges are greatly reduced by erosion and more than a century of agriculture. The monument consists of an existing state commemorative area and private land, neither of which is yet acquired by the National Park Service. The monument will be established when the state transfers the commemorative area to the National Park Service.

Established: Oct. 31, 1988. Acreage: 910.85, all nonfederal.

Acadia National Park
Bar Harbor, Maine   **SEE CLIMATABLE NO. 20**

MAILING ADDRESS: Superintendent, Acadia National Park, Box 177, Bar Harbor, ME 04609 **Telephone:** 207-288-3338/TDD 207-288-3338

DIRECTIONS: The Park is located on ME 3, 47 miles (75.2 km) southeast of Bangor, ME. Schoodic Penninsula, the only part of the Park on the mainland, is accessible via ME 186.

Set aside in 1916 and declared a national park in 1919, it combines unusual ocean and mountain scenery over 40 square miles (64 km) of Mount Desert Island, the mainland Schoodic Peninsula, Isle au Haut, and several smaller islands.

VISITOR ACTIVITIES: 27-mile scenic drive connects lakes, mountains, and seashore; carriage paths open to hikers, bicycles, and horses; foot trails; museums on mainland and Little Cranberry Island; frequent showing of a film at the Visitor Center; naturalist programs; boat cruises; **Permits:** No; **Fees:** Park entrance fee collected approximately May 1-Nov. 1, $5/car/week; boat cruise fares: $10-14/adult, $7-9/child(ren) under 12. Prices are subject to change; **Visitor facilities:** Beaches, 2 campgrounds, museums, nature walks, campfire programs, audiovisual and interpretive programs, cassette auto tape tour, picnic areas; **HANDI-CAPPED ACCESSIBILITY:** Thompson Island, Visitor Center, Nature Center, Head-quarters: parking and restrooms. Museums: College of the Atlantic Natural History Museum has accessible parking, restrooms. Wendell Gilley Museum has restrooms. Other museums have various limitations. Picnic Areas: Fabbri; other areas have various limitations; Beaches: various limitations. Campgrounds: Blackwoods, Seawall. Gift shops and restaurant at Cadillac Mt. and Jordan Pond are accessible. Slide presentations, some cruises and trails; **Any limitations on vehicle usage:** Vehicles are confined to established roadways; no motorized vehicles on carriage roads; **Hiking trails:** Yes, there are more than 120 miles (192 km) of hiking trails; **Backcountry:** No backcountry camping; day use only; **Camping:** Yes, 2 campgrounds are available in the Park, and there are numerous private campgrounds in the area. Camping at park campgrounds is limited to 14 days; **Other overnight accommodations on site:** No; **Meals served in the park:** Yes, seasonally; **Food and supplies obtainable in the park:** No; **Food and supplies obtainable nearby:** Yes, Bar Harbor, Northeast Harbor, Southwest Habor, Ellsworth; **Overnight accommodations:** Bar Harbor, ME, 3 miles (4.8 km); Northeast Harbor, ME, 14 miles (22.4 km); Ellsworth, ME 3, 20 miles (32 km); Southwest Harbor, ME, 18 miles (28.8 km); **First Aid available in park:** Yes; **Nearest Hospital:** Bar Harbor, ME 3, 3 miles (4.8 km); **Days/Hours:** Open year-round. Visitor Center is open from May 1-Oct. 31, 7 days; 8 a.m. to 4:30 p.m. in spring/fall; 8 a.m. to 6 p.m. in summer. Visitor Center hours subject to change; **Holiday Closings:** The park is always open, but the Park Headquarters building closes on Thanksgiving, Dec. 24, 25, and Jan. 1; **Visitor attractions closed for seasons:** Visitor Center, Nature Center, Museum, major portions of Park Loop Road not plowed in winter; **Weather:** Cool summers and fog are common, low temperature 55°-60°, high temperature 68°-75°.

GENERAL INFORMATION: *For Your Safety*—Be particularly careful on the rugged shores of Acadia. Ledges and rocks below high tide are slippery with algae, so walk carefully. Watch out for storm waves, particulary in spring and autumn. Occasionally an unusually large wave reaches far up on the ledge or beach—it could knock you down and sweep you into the sea. Watch the trail when hiking, to avoid poison ivy or falling loose stones. If you find one trail too steep or precarious, choose another.

TRAVEL ACCESS: **Bus:** Greyhound may operate between Bangor and Bar Harbor during the summer months. Call 617-423-5810 for current information; **Rail:** No; **Air:** Bar Harbor Airlines daily service to Bar Harbor Airport 10 miles (16 km) from Bar Harbor; **Other:** Downeast Transportation, Inc., operates local public transportation, Taxi services available in Bar Harbor, and Ralph Savage, Summer Taxi of Northeast Harbor also service the Park. Bike rentals in Bar Harbor, Northeast Harbor and Southwest Harbor. Bus tours from Bar Harbor.

NEARBY FACILITIES & POINTS OF INTEREST: **Hotel/Motel:** Contact Chamber of Commerce, Bar Harbor, ME 04069; Southwest Harbor, ME 04679; Northeast Harbor, ME 04662; **Campgrounds:** 12 private campgrounds outside the park. **Reservation system in use for campsites, other facilities:** Seawall open from late May to late Sept. on a first-come basis. Blackwoods open year-round. Operates on a Ticketron reservation system from mid-June to mid-Sept. (subject to change). Reservations made no more than 56 days in advance—by phone or mail to *Ticketron* (no reservations made over the phone through park). Contact headquarters for reservation changes.

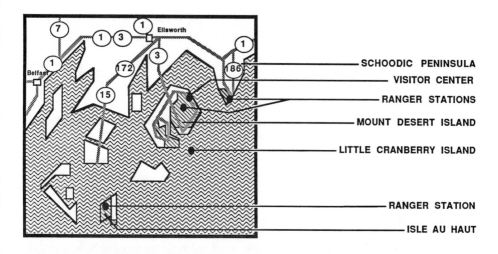

Appalachian National Scenic Trail

Maine, New Hampshire, Vermont, Massachusetts, Connecticut, New York, New Jersey, Pennsylvania, Maryland, West Virginia, Virginia, Tennessee, North Carolina, and Georgia

MAILING ADDRESS: Appalachian Trail Conference, P.O. Box 807, Harpers Ferry, WV 25425 **Telephone:** 304-535-6331

DIRECTIONS: Contact the Appalachian Trail Conference for detailed information on directions to the Trail.

Approximately 2,144 miles (3,430 km) of this scenic trail follow the Appalachian Mountains from Katahdin, ME, through to Springer Mountain, GA. The trail is one of the two initial units of the National Trail System. Designated by act of Congress on Oct. 2, 1968; completed by volunteers, Aug. 14, 1937.

VISITOR ACTIVITIES: Short- and long-term hiking, camping, bird- and wildlife-watching, backcountry; **Permits:** A permit is not required to hike the Trail, but camping permits are necessary in the Shenandoah National Park and Great Smoky Mountains National Park. These permits are available at Ranger Stations upon arrival. See listings on these parks in this book for information on facilities and reservations. Camping facilities are also available at Green Mountain National Forest, VT; White Mountain National Forest, NH; and Baxter State Park, ME; **Fees:** At certain Northeast campsites, a $2-4 fee per site; **Visitor facilities:** Lean-to shelters, fire pits, picnic tables; **Any limitations on vehicle usage:** Motor vehicles are prohibited on hiking trails; **Hiking trails:** Yes, some circuit hikes (blue blazed). Guide books with maps may be ordered from address above; **Backcountry:** Yes, Contact the Appalachian Trail Conference, P.O. Box 807, Harpers Ferry, WV 25425, phone 304-535-6331; **Camping:** Yes, no reservations available for campsites; **Other overnight accommodations on site:** There are youth hostels, church-related hostels, and other sleeping accommodations along certain sections of the Appalachian Trail. Guidebooks describe. **Meals served in the park:** Only in some national parks along the trail. Hikers have regular food drop points at post offices near the trail; **Food and supplies obtainable in the park:** No; **Food and supplies obtainable nearby:** Yes, stores are often located near major road crossings. Hut system operates in White Mountains, providing shelter and food at higher fee; **Overnight accommodations:** Accommodations are generally available at nearby towns; **First Aid available in**

park: No; **Nearest Hospital:** In most of the larger nearby towns; **Days/Hours:** Park never closes, except northernmost 7 miles (11.2 km) (closed Sept. 15-May 15).

GENERAL INFORMATION: Most long-distance hikers start in March or April and take 5 to 6 months to hike the entire trail, mostly from south to north. Primary use of trail is by weekend or short-distance hikers.

Saint Croix Island International Historic Site
Red Beach, Maine

MAILING ADDRESS: Superintendent, Saint Croix Island International Historic Site, c/o Acadia National Park, Box 177, Bar Harbor, ME 04609 **Telephone:** 207-288-3338

DIRECTIONS: The site is 120 miles (192 km) north of Bar Harbor. It is 8 miles (12.8 km) south of Calais, ME, along US 1. There is currently no ferry service to the island.

The attempted French settlement of 1604, which led to the founding of New France, is commemorated on Saint Croix Island, located on the Saint Croix River at the Canadian border. Authorized for addition to the National Park System on June 8, 1949.

VISITOR ACTIVITIES: Walking, picnicking; **Permits:** No; **Fees:** No; **Visitor facilities:** There are no facilities on the island at this time. The mainland has a picnic area and pit toilets. No water is available. A small interpretive shelter located on the mainland explains the historic significance of St. Croix; **Any limitations on vehicle usage:** There are no vehicles allowed on the island. It is reached only by boat; **Hiking trails:** No; **Backcountry:** No; **Camping:** No; **Other overnight accommodations on site:** No; **Meals served in the park:** No; **Food and supplies obtainable in the park:** No; **Food and supplies obtainable nearby:** No; **Overnight accommodations:** Calais, US 1, 12 miles (19.2 km); **First Aid available in park:** No; **Nearest Hospital:** Calais, US 1, 8 miles (12.8 km); **Days/Hours:** Persons having a boat can visit the island anytime, weather permitting; **Weather:** Summers have cool maritime air; winters are cold and wet with frequent snowfall.

TRAVEL ACCESS: Bus: Greyhound provides service to Calais; **Rail:** No; **Air:** No.

NEARBY FACILITIES & POINTS OF INTEREST: Hotel/Motel: Contact Chamber of Commerce, Calais, ME 04619.

Maryland

CATOCTIN MOUNTAIN PARK

APPALACHIAN NATIONAL SCENIC TRAIL

CHESAPEAKE AND OHIO CANAL NATIONAL HISTORICAL PARK

FORT McHENRY NATIONAL MONUMENT AND HISTORIC SHRINE

HAMPTON NATIONAL HISTORIC SITE

ANTIETAM NATIONAL BATTLEFIELD

HARPERS FERRY NATIONAL HISTORICAL PARK

MONOCACY NATIONAL BATTLEFIELD

CLARA BARTON NATIONAL HISTORIC SITE GLEN ECHO PARK

GREENBELT PARK

OXON HILL FARM

FORT WASHINGTON PARK

PISCATAWAY PARK

THOMAS STONE NATIONAL HISTORIC SITE

ASSATEAGUE ISLAND NATIONAL SEASHORE

Antietam National Battlefield
Sharpsburg, Maryland

MAILING ADDRESS: Superintendent, Antietam National Battlefield, P.O. Box 158, Sharpsburg, MD 21782 **Telephone:** 301-432-5124

DIRECTIONS: The Site is 11 miles (17.6 km) south of Hagerstown off MD 65.
    Established by act of Congress on Aug. 30, 1890, this site marks the end of General Robert E. Lee's first invasion of the north in Sept. 1862, a battle which claimed over 23,000 casualties in one single day, Sept. 17, 1862.

VISITOR ACTIVITIES: 26-minute film shown on the hour, Civil War exhibits, self-conducted auto tours (rental taped tours available), hike or bike the 8½ mile (13.6 km) tour road; **Permits:** No; **Fees:** $1 per person (No fee under age 13 or 62 and over); **Visitor facilities:** Visitor Center with museum, Hope panoramic paintings of battle, and award winning film depicting battle and Lincoln's visit. Special programs such as living history, torchlight tour, concerts and lecture series throughout the year. Write for schedule of events; **Any limitations on vehicle usage:** Vehicles are confined to parking area and park roads; **Hiking trails:** Nature and historic; **Backcountry:** No; **Camping:** No; **Other overnight accommodations on site:** Bed & Breakfast (commercial) nearby; **Meals served in the park:** No; **Food and supplies obtainable in the park:** No; **Food and supplies obtainable nearby:** Yes, in Sharpsburg, 1 mile (1.6 km); **Nearest Hospital:** Hagerstown, MD, 12 miles (19.2 km); **Days/Hours:** Park open dawn to dusk year-round. Visitor Center open daily 8:30 a.m. to 5 p.m.; Summer hours are 8 a.m. to 6 p.m.; **Holiday Closings:** Thanksgiving, Dec. 25, Jan. 1; **Visitor attractions closed for season:** Historic church and wayside audio stations not open in winter (Nov.-Mar.).

GENERAL INFORMATION: *For your Safety*—Motorists should be aware of speed limits, one-way roads, pedestrians, and bicyclists. Motor vehicle drivers: stop and pull to road shoulder or designated parking area while reading interpretive signs along the tour road.

Appalachian National Scenic Trail
For details see listing in Maine

Assateague Island National Seashore
Maryland and Virginia

MAILING ADDRESS: Superintendent, Assateague Island National Seashore, Berlin, MD 21811 **Telephone:** 401-641-3030 (MD Campground), 401-641-1441 (MD Visitor Center), or 804-336-6577 (VA District Office).

DIRECTIONS: Via US 50, the Seashore is about 150 miles (240 km) from Baltimore or Washington, DC. Via US 13 and 113, it is about 144 miles (224 km) from Philadelphia and 90 miles (144 km) from Norfolk. Visitor facilities are located at the extreme ends of Assateague Island—on the north end near Ocean City, MD, and on the south opposite Chincoteague, VA. More than 22 miles (35.2 km) of roadless barrier island beach and marsh lie between these developed areas. To get from one end of the island to the other, visitors must drive back onto the mainland.

This 37-mile (59.2-km) barrier island has a sandy beach, pine forests, salt marsh, many kinds of waterfowl and other birds, and a variety of mammals including wild ponies. Most of the Virginia portion consists of the Chincoteague Island National Wildlife Refuge, which was established in 1943. Most of the Maryland section was authorized for addition to the National Park System on Sept. 21, 1965.

VISITOR ACTIVITIES: Surf fishing, clamming, crabbing, canoeing, hiking, birdwatching, camping, swimming, interpretive programs in summer, shell collecting, hunting, pony round-up and auction on the last Wednesday and Thursday of July; **Permits:** Oversand vehicle permits required for oversand use. Backcountry permits required; permits for night surf fishing required in Virginia; **Fees:** For camping, entrance and oversand vehicle permits. Camping is $10 per night May 15-Sept. 30; $8 when sites are reserved and $7 the rest of the year. Entrance fee in Maryland is $3 per vehicle, good for 7 days. Entrance fee in Virginia is $3 per vehicle, 7 days. Golden Eagle/Age/Access passports apply in both states. Oversand vehicle permits are $30 each year. Assateague State Park camping fees are $18, but the facilities are more modern; **Visitor facilities:** Campgrounds and canoe launch in Maryland, picnic areas, bathhouses, lifeguarded beaches in summer, wildlife refuge, self-guided nature trails, crabbing, Visitor Centers with exhibits; **HANDICAPPED ACCESSIBILITY:** Visitor centers in both districts are accessible. Bathhouses in VA are models of accessibility; older MD bathhouse has made most modifications. Ramps provide access to top of oceanfront dunes in both districts; contact lifeguards for assistance to water's edge. VA features two hard-surface nature trails. One campsite in MD has been modified for handicapped and may be reserved. Many Ranger-conducted activities are accessible; contact district naturalists in advance for services to group situations; **Any limitations on vehicle usage:** Vehicles must be registered and licensed; all vehicles must stay on marked routes; motorcycles are restricted to hard-surfaced roads. Oversand vehicles must have a permit. Potential users of oversand routes should contact the park for information on required equipment; **Hiking trails:** Yes, short self-guiding nature trails in both state sections; **Backcountry:** Yes, both hike-in and canoe-in are available. Contact the park or the Visitor Center; **Camping:** Yes, primitive campsites only in Maryland. Reservations for campsites from May 15 to Sept. 30. Some state park campsites may be reserved in summer for a full week only; **Other overnight accommodations on site:** No; **Meals served in the park:** No, but at Assateague State Park, only in summer; **Food and supplies obtainable in the park:** No; **Food and supplies obtainable nearby:** Yes, Berlin, MD, and Chincoteague, VA; **Overnight accommodations:** Chincoteague, VA, 5 miles (8 km); Ocean City, MD, Rte 611, 7 miles (11.2 km); **First Aid available in park:** Yes, or nearby in Chincoteague, VA, Berlin and Ocean City, MD; **Nearest Hospital:** Salisbury, MD, Rte 50 or US 13, approximately 35 miles (56 km) from each end of the island; **Days/Hours:** Virginia section open from 4 a.m.-10 p.m. with shorter hours in winter. Maryland section open 24 hours with certain exceptions. Contact the seashore for details on hours of operation; **Holiday Closings:** Visitor Center closed Thanksgiving, Dec. 25, and Jan. 1; **Visitor attractions closed for seasons:** Assateague State Park campground closed from Nov. to mid-Apr.; **Weather:** Summers can be hot and humid with many biting insects. Spring and autumn offer brisk nights and placid days, allowing a chance to avoid the crowds.

GENERAL INFORMATION: *For Your Safety*—Swim where there are lifeguards; avoid swimming in heavy surf and do not use air mattresses or flotation devices. Seek shelter during lightning. Beware of sunburn and wear shoes in the campgrounds; do not approach ponies; guard against mosquitoes, ticks, and poison ivy. Backcountry canoeing and hiking has its own set of hazards; review the backcountry folders.

Visitors are discouraged from bringing pets, which are prohibited in most areas of the Seashore. The hot, blowing sand and saltwater are hard on dogs' feet and eyes.

TRAVEL ACCESS: Bus: Trailways provides daily service to Ocean City, MD, and T's Corner, VA; **Rail:** No; **Air:** U.S. Air Commuter service daily to Salisbury, MD. **Other:** Bicycles may be rented in Chincoteague, VA, and Ocean City, MD.

NEARBY FACILITIES & POINTS OF INTEREST: For commercial information on hotels and campgrounds contact: Ocean City Chamber of Commerce, 12320 Ocean Gateway, Ocean City, MD 21842, 301-289-8559; Chincoteague Chamber of Commerce, Chincoteague, VA 23336, 804-336-6161; **Parks, other points of interest:** Pocomoke River State Park, MD; Trap Pond State Park, DE; **Reservations system in use for campsites, other facilities:** Reserve sites for 7-day periods only in Assateague State Park, 7307 Stephen Decatur Highway, Berlin, MD 21811; **New park programs:** Canoeing, surf-fishing, clamming and crabbing interpretive demonstrations done during summer.

Catoctin Mountain Park
Thurmont, Maryland

MAILING ADDRESS: Superintendent, Catoctin Mountain Park, 6602 Foxville Road, Thurmont, MD 21788 **Telephone:** 301-663-9330

DIRECTIONS: Catoctin is located in the foothills of the Blue Ridge Mountains. From Rte 15 take Rte 77 west for approximately 3 miles (4.8 km). The Visitor Center is on the right.

In 1936 more than 10,000 acres were acquired by the Federal Government and developed to demonstrate the possibilities of creating parks from wornout land. In 1954 the area was divided into two parts, separated by Rte 77. The Federal Government retained the area to the north (Catoctin Mountain Park) and the remaining acreage was deeded to the State of Maryland to be managed for recreational use (Cunningham Falls State Park).

VISITOR ACTIVITIES: Hiking, camping, picnicking, exhibits, interpretive programs, campfire programs, fishing, horseback riding (only trails are provided—you must supply the horse; there are no rentals in the area), rock climbing, cross-country skiing; **Permits:** For the use of Adirondack (hike-in) shelters and for rock-climbing. Both permits available free of charge at the Visitor Center; **Fees:** $6 per night camping fee at Owen's Creek campground; **Visitor facilities:** Self-guiding trails, picnic areas, bridle trail, hike-in camp shelters; **HANDI-CAPPED ACCESSIBILITY:** Camp Greentop is completely accessible. Chestnut picnic area has some tables designed for wheelchairs, accessible restrooms and the ½-mile (.8-km) Spicebush Nature Trail. This ½-mile (.8-km) loop features a paved surface, resting benches, and interpretive signs. Owen's Creek Campground: Restrooms are accessible with assistance. Camp Misty Mount: Several rental cabins, showers, and restroom are accessible: Visitor Center: Accessible; Handicapped parking spaces available at Visitor Center, picnic areas, and Owen's Creek Campground. Most trail brochures provided in large print upon request. Cunningham Falls State Park provides handicapped parking and an accessible trail to the Falls off Rt. 77. **Any limitations on vehicle usage:** Motorized vehicles and bicycles are restricted to roads; **Hiking trails:** Yes, hiking is permitted on over 30 miles (48 km) of trails; **Backcountry:** Backcountry camping is restricted to 2 Adirondack shelters. Information can be obtained from the Visitor Center; **Camping:** Yes, no reservations accepted for individual campsites; **Other overnight accommodations on site:** Yes, 2 large Environmental Education Cabin Camps are rented to groups of 60 or more people. They are reserved through applications taken between Dec. 1 and Dec. 15 for Long Term Groups, between Jan. 1 and Jan. 30 for Spring Weekend Groups, and between May 1 and May 30 for Fall Weekend Groups. Individual family cabins are also for rent at Camp Misty Mount Apr.-Oct.; **Meals served in the park:** No; **Food and supplies obtainable in the park:** No; **Food and supplies obtainable nearby:** Yes, Cunningham Falls State Park has a concession at the William Houck Lake Area which is open Memorial Day through Labor Day and also in nearby Thurmont; **Overnight accommodations:** Motels in Thurmont. Camping is also available in Cunningham Falls State Park and in 4 privately owned campgrounds within a 15-mile (24-km) radius of the Visitor Center; **First Aid available in park:** Yes, or nearby in Thurmont; **Nearest Hospital:** Frederick and Hagerstown Hospitals are within 20 miles (32 km); **Days/Hours:** The park is open from dawn to dusk. No overnight parking is permitted. Visitor Center hours 10-4:30 weekdays and 8:30-5:00 weekends. **Holiday Closings:** Visitor Center closed Thanksgiving, Dec. 25, and Jan. 1; **Visitor attractions closed for seasons:** Owen's Creek Campground is open Apr. 15 through the third Sunday in Nov. Visitor Center may be closed for other holidays, Nov. through Apr. Visitor Center may limit operations in the winter season due to staffing limitations. Owen's Creek picnic area closed in winter season.

GENERAL INFORMATION: Activities at Cunningham Falls State Park include camping, picnicking, hiking, swimming, boating and fishing. Big Hunting Creek offers the opportunity to fly fish for trout; regulations require a Maryland license, trout stamp, and "Catch and Return" of all trout.

Chesapeake and Ohio Canal National Historical Park
Maryland, District of Columbia

MAILING ADDRESS: Superintendent, C&O Canal National Historical Park, P.O. Box 4, Sharpsburg, MD 21782 **Telephone:** 301-739-4200; **Park Emergency:** 301-739-4206

DIRECTIONS: Park Headquarters Ferry Hill House 8 a.m. to 4:30 p.m. Mon.-Fri. is 4 miles (6.4 km) west of Sharpsburg, MD, on MD 34. Visitor Centers are: Great Falls Canal Tavern Museum, 11710 MacArthur Blvd., Potomac, MD 20854, 301-299-3613; Hancock, MD, 326 E. Main St., 301-678-5463; Western Maryland Railroad Station Center, Canal Street, Cumberland, MD, 301-722-8226.

The Park follows the route of the 184½-mile (295.2-km) canal along the Potomac River between Washington, DC, and Cumberland, MD. The canal was built between 1828 and 1850, ceased operation in 1924, transferred to the National Park Service in 1938, became a National Park in 1971.

VISITOR ACTIVITIES: Hiking, biking, camping, limited horseback riding, canoeing, boating, fishing, picnicking, conducted walks, canal museum at Great Falls, MD, mule-drawn boat ride at Georgetown and Great Falls Tavern mid-Apr. through mid-Oct. weather permitting; phone in advance 301-299-3613 (Great Falls) or 202-653-5844 (Georgetown); **Permits:** For camping at Marsden Tract 11½ miles (18.4 km) from Georgetown (Washington, DC); Permit may be obtained from the Park Ranger at Great Falls Tavern, 11710 MacArthur Boulevard, Potomac, MD 20854, 9 a.m. to 5 p.m., 301-299-3613; **Fees:** No; **Visitor facilities:** Picnic areas, campgrounds, museum, boat rentals, boat ramps, bicycles: hiking/biking on towpath; **Handicapped accessibility:** Palisades District: Georgetown—water fountain at 30th Street, N.W.; Canal Boat Towpath (ramps in some areas, curbs in other areas); Fletchers—water fountain near concession stand; comfort station has a ramp, but the stalls are not designed for wheelchair access; Marsden Tract—one wheelchair accessible pit toilet; Great Falls area—Tavern (downstairs is generally wheelchair accessible), comfort station (1 wheelchair accessible stall on women's side and 1 on men's side); parking lot (2 spaces near the Tavern); canal boat (the crew will carry a wheelchair onto the boat if it is not motorized); Canal Towpath—generally passible but accesses to the towpath are generally poor. Almost all of the bridges that cross the locks are raised up 4″ to 6″ above the grade. In certain areas, it is difficult to go around a cable or gate with a wheelchair. The upper end of widewater is impassible. Sections of the towpath in the area of Edwards Ferry are too deeply rutted to pass in a wheelchair, as are certain sections of level 14; Remainder of Park: Access to towpath poor in most places; towpath passable in many places by wheelchair; no handicapped facilities in restrooms; **Any limitations on vehicle usage:** Parking available in designated areas along canal; **Hiking trails:** Yes, the towpath follows the canal's entire length; **Backcountry:** No; **Camping:** Yes, no reservations for ''Hiker-Biker'' campsites. A Campsite 11½ miles (18.4 km) from Georgetown (Washington, DC), Marsden Tract is primitive, permit only (see permits above); **Other overnight accommodations on site:** No; **Meals served in the park:** No; **Food and supplies obtainable in the park:** Yes, fast food and drink available from concessioners spring through fall at Great Falls, MD., Swains Lock and Fletchers Boat House. Fishing supplies available from Swains Boat House and Fletchers Boat House; **Food and supplies obtainable nearby:** Yes, in stores along the various adjacent access routes; **Overnight accommodations:** In major urban areas, near I-70; **First Aid available in park:** Yes, at all Visitor Centers and Park Headquarters; **Nearest Hospital:** Along the route of the canal, in or near Potomac, Seneca, Poolesville, Brunswick, Sharpsburg, Williamsport, Hancock, Old-town, and Cumberland; **Days/Hours:** Towpath open year around—museum and visitor centers closed Christmas Day; **Holiday Closings:** Selected closings. Call in advance; **Visitor attractions closed for seasons:** Boat ride operations closed from mid-Oct.-Apr. Mule-drawn canal boats operate mid-Apr. through mid-Oct., weather permitting.

GENERAL INFORMATION: *For Your Safety* —Help prevent drownings by keeping your family or group together. Stay on the trail and out of the water. Be prepared to deal with such annoyances as insects, polluted river water, and adverse weather conditions.

Clara Barton National Historic Site
Glen Echo, Maryland

MAILING ADDRESS: Superintendent, George Washington Memorial Parkway, Turkey Run Park, McLean, VA 22101 **Telephone:** 301-492-6246

DIRECTIONS: The Park is just north of Washington, DC. Take MacArthur Boulevard from Washington or Exit 40 or 41 from the Capital Beltway (I-495) to Glen Echo, MD. Turn left at Oxford Road just past Glen Echo Park.

This 38-room home of the founder of the American Red Cross was for 7 years the headquarters of that organization. Authorized for addition to the National Park System on Oct. 26, 1974.

VISITOR ACTIVITIES: Guided tours and exhibits; "interpretive programs and demonstrations on turn-of-the-century lifestyles." **Permits:** No; **Fees:** No; **Visitor facilities:** Restrooms, parking; **Any limitations on vehicle usage:** Vehicles are restricted to the parking lot; **Hiking trails:** No, but hiking is available on the nearby C&O Canal towpath; **Backcountry:** No; **Camping:** No; **Other overnight accommodations on site:** No; **Meals served in the park:** No; **Food and supplies obtainable in the park:** No; **Food and supplies obtainable nearby:** Yes, limited food and supplies in Glen Echo, MD; wider range in Bethesda, MD, and Washington, DC; **Overnight accommodations:** Washington, DC, or vicinity; **First Aid available in park:** Yes, or nearby at Glen Echo Fire Dept., Massachusetts Ave.; **Nearest Hospital:** Sibley Hospital, Washington, DC, 4 miles (6.4 km); **Days/Hours:** Open daily 10 a.m. to 5 p.m.; **Holiday Closings:** Thanksgiving, Dec. 25, and Jan. 1; **Visitor attractions closed for seasons:** Site is open year-round; **Weather:** Hot, humid summer.

GENERAL INFORMATION: Visitors can see the adjacent Glen Echo Park (see listing in this book). Group tours (10 or more), by reservation.

TRAVEL ACCESS: Bus: Washington Metro bus runs limited schedule from downtown Washington to about 2 blocks from Park; **Rail:** Amtrak provides service to Washington, DC; **Air:** Major airlines provide service to Washington, DC.

Fort McHenry National Monument and Historic Shrine
Baltimore, Maryland

MAILING ADDRESS: Superintendent, Fort McHenry National Monument and Historic Shrine, Baltimore, MD 21230-5393 **Telephone:** 301-962-4299

DIRECTIONS: From Interstate 95 Northbound or Southbound, take Exit 55 Key Highway/Fort McHenry National Monument and follow the BLUE and GREEN signs on Key Highway to Lawrence St. Turn left on Lawrence St. and left on Fort Ave. Proceed to Fort McHenry National Monument. From the Inner Harbor take Light St. south to Key Highway. Turn left and follow the BLUE and GREEN signs to Lawrence St. Turn right on Lawrence St. and left on Fort Ave. Proceed to Fort McHenry National Monument.

Successful defense of this fort in the War of 1812, Sept. 13-14, 1814, inspired Francis Scott Key to write "The Star-Spangled Banner." Authorized for addition to the National Park System on Aug. 10, 1933.

VISITOR ACTIVITIES: Interpretive exhibits and film, walking self-guided tours, picnicking, guided activities during summer months and by reservation to groups, also on weekend afternoons in summer, activities by Fort McHenry Guard (volunteers uniformed as 1814 defenders of Baltimore); **Permits:** No; **Fees:** Yes, $1 persons age 17 through 61; all others free; **Visitor facilities:** Parking and restrooms at Visitor Center, picnic area, seawall walking-jogging path; **HANDICAPPED ACCESSIBILITY:** Parking, restrooms, ramps (with exception of guardhouse at Fort); written materials, scripts, and induction loop system in Visitor Center auditorium for hearing impaired, 16-minute film is captioned for hearing impaired; taped narratives and personally conducted tours for those with sight impairments; **Any limitations on vehicle usage:** Vehicles must stay on designated roadways; **Hiking trails:** Yes, a 1-mile (1.6-km) paved foot trail leads around the seawall; **Backcountry:** No; **Camping:** No; **Other overnight accommodations on site:** No; **Meals served in the park:** No; **Food and supplies obtainable in the park:** No; **Food and supplies obtainable nearby:** Yes, in Baltimore; **Overnight accommodations:** Baltimore **First Aid available in park:** Yes, paramedic ambulance service on call; **Nearest Hospital:** Harbor Hospital Center, Hanover St., 2 miles (3.2 km); **Days/Hours:** Open 7 days a week, 8 a.m. to 5 p.m. Please call regarding extended hours from Mid-June through Labor Day; **Holiday Closings:** Dec. 25 and Jan. 1; **Weather:** Summer is hot and humid; air quality is often poor. Winter is cold, damp, and windy; spring and autumn are mild.

GENERAL INFORMATION: *For Your Safety* —Do not climb on monuments, trees, cannons, or the seawall. Stay away from the edge of the fort walls.

TRAVEL ACCESS: Bus: Greyhound, Trailways provide daily service to Baltimore City, local transportation runs to park entrance approx. every ½ hour; Shuttle boat to and from Inner Harbor, Memorial Day through Labor Day, 301-685-4288; **Rail:** Regular Amtrak service to Pennsylvania Station; **Air:** Major airlines provide service into Baltimore-Washington International Airport.

NEARBY FACILITIES & POINTS OF INTEREST: Hotel/Motel: Baltimore; **Campgrounds:** Patapsco State Park, Route 40, West of Baltimore, 301-461-5005, 20 miles (32 km).

Fort Washington Park
Fort Washington, Maryland

MAILING ADDRESS: Superintendent, National Capital Parks East, 1900 Anacostia Drive S.E. Washington, DC 20020 **Telephone:** 202-433-1185 or 301-763-4600

DIRECTIONS: The Park is on the Maryland side of the Potomac River. To reach the Park from the Capital Beltway, take MD 210 (Indian Head Hwy.) south approximately 4 miles (6.4 km). Turn right onto Fort Washington Road, go 3 miles (4.8 km) to park entrance. The old fort is ½ mile (.8 km) inside the Park.

This fort, situated across the Potomac from Mount Vernon and built to protect Washington, DC, was begun in 1814 to replace an earlier fort destroyed that same year. Recreational facilities are included in the Park. Authorized for addition to the National Park System on May 29, 1930.

VISITOR ACTIVITIES: Interpretive tours and living history demonstrations, auto tours, picnicking, hiking; **Permits:** Yes, reserved picnic areas available for groups of 50 or more; **Fees:** Yes; **Visitor facilities:** Picnic areas, parking, restrooms, museum; **Any limitations on vehicle usage:** No trucks are allowed in the Park; **Hiking trails:** Yes, a short trail along the Potomac River and Piscataway Creek; **Backcountry:** No; **Camping:** No; **Other overnight accommodations on site:** No; **Meals served in the park:** No; **Food and supplies obtain-

able in the park: No; **Food and supplies obtainable nearby:** Yes, 3.5 miles (5.6 km) from the Park on Fort Washington Road; **Overnight accommodations:** in the Washington metropolitan area; **First Aid available in park:** Yes, or nearby in Oxon Hill, 12 miles (19.2 km), on Oxon Hill Road; **Nearest Hospital:** Washington, DC, Southern Avenue, 20 miles (32 km); **Days/Hours:** Fort open from 9 a.m. to 5 p.m. daily. Park open from 7:30 a.m. to dark everyday; **Holiday Closings:** Dec. 25 and Jan. 1; **Weather:** Winters are cool and wet, with light snow; Summers are hot and humid. This is a fee area.

George Washington Memorial Parkway
For details see listing in Virginia

Glen Echo Park
Glen Echo, Maryland

MAILING ADDRESS: Site Manager, Glen Echo Park, MacArthur Blvd., Glen Echo, MD 20812 **Telephone:** 301-492-6282 or 301-492-6229

DIRECTIONS: The Park is just north of Washington, DC, at MacArthur Boulevard and Oxford Road. Take MacArthur Boulevard from Washington, Capital Beltway Exit 40 or 41, or Clara Barton Parkway from Maryland. Information on facilities and activities may be obtained at the Park office.

Located on Maryland's Potomac Palisades, the Park was formerly a 19th-century Chautauqua assembly center and then an amusement park. It is now a cultural arts center. Authorized for addition to the National Park System in 1976.

VISITOR ACTIVITIES: Walking tours, carousel rides May-Sept., arts and crafts courses, special programs, free concerts and festivals, picnicking; **Permits:** No; **Fees:** Carousel rides are $.50, tuition fees are charged for courses and admission fees for some performances; **Visitor facilities:** Restrooms, parking, art gallery, picnic areas; **Any limitations on vehicle usage:** Vehicles are restricted to the parking lot; **Hiking trails:** No; **Backcountry:** No; **Camping:** No; **Other overnight accommodations on site:** No; **Meals served in the park:** Yes, food service during carousel hours only, from May-Sept.; **Food and supplies obtainable in the park:** No; **Food and supplies obtainable nearby:** Yes, in town of Glen Echo; **Overnight accommodations:** Suburban Maryland or Washington, DC; **First Aid available in park:** Yes; **Nearest Hospital:** Sibley Hospital, MacArthur Blvd. and Loughboro Rd., Washington, DC; **Days/Hours:** Grounds open 24 hours a day 7 days a week; **Holiday Closings:** Thanksgiving, Dec. 25, and Jan. 1; **Visitor attractions closed for seasons:** Most festivals are held between May and Oct.; **Weather:** Hot, humid summers; cold, snowy winters.

GENERAL INFORMATION: Visitors can also see the adjacent Clara Barton National Historic Site (see listing in this book).

Greenbelt Park
Greenbelt, Maryland

MAILING ADDRESS: Superintendent, Greenbelt Park, 6565 Greenbelt Road, Greenbelt, MD 20770 **Telephone:** 301-344-3948

DIRECTIONS: From the Capital Beltway (Int. 95), take Exit 23 at Kenilworth Avenue

(MD 201), proceed south toward Bladensburg, and follow the signs into the Park. From the Baltimore-Washington Parkway, exit at Greenbelt Road (MD 193) and follow signs.

Just 12 miles (19.2 km) from Washington, DC, this woodland Park offers urban dwellers access to many forms of outdoor recreation. Established by act of Congress in 1950.

VISITOR ACTIVITIES: Picnicking, camping, nature walks, horse trails, biking, hiking; **Permits:** No; **Fees:** Camping fee is $6 per night, $3 if camper has a Golden Age Passport; **Visitor facilities:** Picnic areas, campgrounds, nature trails, interpretive walks, and evening programs, fireplaces (charcoal and wood is permitted), restrooms; **HANDICAPPED ACCESSIBILITY:** 2 wheelchair accessible campsites are available; **Any limitations on vehicle usage:** Park only in designated areas. All vehicles, including bicycles, are restricted to paved roads. Their use on any trail is strictly prohibited; **Hiking trails:** Yes, nearly 12 miles (19.2 km) of well-marked trails lead through the Park. A 6-mile (9.6 km) loop, also designated a bridle trail, circles the Park's western half (no horses available in Park); **Backcountry:** No; **Camping:** Yes, no reservations for the 174-site family campground, which is open all year. There are no showers or hookups; **Other overnight accommodations on site:** No; **Meals served in the park:** No; **Food and supplies obtainable in the park:** No; **Food and supplies obtainable nearby:** Yes, Greenbelt or vicinity; **Overnight accommodations:** Greenbelt; **First Aid available in park:** Yes, but only for emergencies, or nearby in Lanham, MD; **Nearest Hospital:** Doctors Hospital, New Carrollton, Good Luck Road, 4 miles (6.4 km); **Days/Hours:** Open dawn until dark. Campers have access at all times; **Holiday Closings:** Thanksgiving, Dec. 25, and Jan. 1; **Visitor attractions closed for seasons:** No; **Weather:** High heat and humidity in summer, cold in winter with some snow.

Hampton National Historic Site
Towson, Maryland

MAILING ADDRESS: Site Manager, Hampton National Historic Site, 535 Hampton Lane, Towson, MD 21204 **Telephone:** 301-962-0688

DIRECTIONS: To reach Hampton from Baltimore, follow the Jones Falls Expressway, the York Road (MD 45), or Charles Street north to Towson. In Towson, take Dulaney Valley Road (MD 146) across the Beltway (I-695) and immediately thereafter turn right into Hampton Lane, which leads to the Site. This is a dangerous intersection; make sure that you do not enter the Beltway exit ramp. The Site can also be reached from Beltway exit 27, Providence Road. Take exit 27B off Baltimore, Route 695. Turn right onto Hampton Lane, proceed ¾ of a mile (1.2 km) to the Park.

Hampton is a late Georgian style mansion completed in 1790 with formal gardens and landscaped grounds. The estate was owned by the same family for over 200 years. Hundreds of pieces of original furnishings and twenty-seven structures and dependencies remain from a once vast (over 24,000 acres) agricultural and industrial estate. Designated June 22, 1948.

VISITOR ACTIVITIES: Tours of mansion offered every hour from 9:00 a.m. to 4:00 p.m. Self-guiding tours of grounds, stables, gardens and farm site; **Permits:** No; **Fees:** No; **Visitor facilities:** Parking, restrooms, tea room, gift shop; **HANDICAPPED ACCESSIBILITY:** No; **Any limitations on vehicle usage:** No; **Hiking trails:** Yes, a 1-mile (1.6-km) walking tour of the grounds; **Meals served in the park:** Yes, in tea room; **Food and supplies obtainable in the park:** No; **Food and supplies obtainable nearby:** Yes, in Towson; **Overnight accommodations:** Yes, in Towson, MD, approximately 1 mile (1.6 km) south; **First Aid available in park:** Yes, **Nearest Hospital:** Towson, MD, approximately 2 miles (3.2 km); **Days/Hours:** Grounds open daily 9 a.m. to 5 p.m.; Mansion tours daily 9 a.m. to 4 p.m. given on the hour; **Holiday Closings:** Thanksgiving, Dec. 25, and Jan. 1; **Visitor attractions**

closed for seasons: No.

GENERAL INFORMATION: Please be careful on the earthen ramps leading into the gardens; they are steeper than they appear. The cobblestone walks are slippery when wet.

Harpers Ferry National Historical Park
For details see listing in West Virginia

Monocacy National Battlefield Park
Frederick County, Maryland

MAILING ADDRESS: Superintendent, Antietam National Battlefield, P.O. Box 158, Sharpsburg, MD 21782 **Telephone:** 301-432-5124

DIRECTIONS: The Battlefield Visitor Center is located approximately 1 mile (1.6 km) south of the Monocacy River on State Highway 355.

VISITORS ACTIVITIES: Visitor contact station which will open to the public at 1:00 p.m. on July 13, 1991. Beginning July 14, 1991, the Visitor Center will be open seven days a week from 8:00 a.m. to 4:30 p.m. This facility is handicap accessible.

Oxon Hill Farm
Oxon Hill, Maryland

MAILING ADDRESS: Superintendent, National Capital Parks East, 1900 Anacostia Drive, S.E., Washington, DC 20020 **Telephone:** 301-839-1177

DIRECTIONS: From southbound Indian Head Highway (MD 210) at the Capital Beltway (Interstate Rt. 95) exit 3-A, bear right onto Oxon Hill Road. Turn right approximately 200 yards down Oxon Hill Road to the farm parking lot.

The Farm is like many of those found in the Maryland and Virginia countryside around Washington at the end of the 19th Century. It includes pasture lands, woodland, typical farm buildings, animals, and equipment. In operation as a Park since 1967, the Farm is especially attractive for children.

VISITOR ACTIVITIES: Picnicking, machinery and equipment displays, live animal exhibits, daily demonstrations of 1900 era farm chores, educational programs for children, seasonal farming and craft demonstrations, recreational activities; **Permits:** No, but large groups should make advance arrangments; **Fees:** No; **Visitor facilities:** Picnic areas, nature trail, restrooms, Visitor Center, exhibits, farm buildings; **HANDICAPPED ACCESSIBIL-ITY:** Parking, restrooms, most buildings accessible except office and feed-tack building; no trails adapted for handicapped; no special features but special programs for handicapped groups can be arranged; **Any limitations on vehicle usage:** All vehicles must use the designated parking area; **Hiking trails:** Yes, ½ mile (.8 km) self-guiding woodlot nature trail; **Backcountry:** No; **Camping:** No; **Other overnight accommodations on site:** No; **Meals served in the park:** No, many fast-food facilities are ½ mile (.8 km) east on Oxon Hill Road; **Food and supplies obtainable in the park:** No; **Food and supplies obtainable nearby:** Yes, ½ mile (.8 km) east on Oxon Hill Road; **Overnight accommodations:** In the Washington metropolitan area; **First Aid available in park:** Yes; **Nearest Hospital:** Washington,

DC—Southeast Community Hosp.—take Indian Head Highway (MD 201) north 1 mile (1.6 km) to Southern Ave., turn right on Southern Ave. 2 miles (3.2 km) to hospital on left; **Days/ Hours:** Open daily all year from 9:00 a.m.-5 p.m.; **Holiday Closings:** Thanksgiving, Dec. 25, and Jan. 1; **Visitor attractions closed for seasons:** Activities, programs, and demonstrations are curtailed from Dec. to Mar. due to weather; Weather: Spring and fall are temperate, pleasant (60°F) and usually sunny. Summer is warm to hot (70-95°F) and humid. Winter is moderately cold and windy.

GENERAL INFORMATION: *For Your Safety* —Do not smoke in any of the buildings. Be cautious around animals and all machines, which can be dangerous and have heavy moving parts and sharp edges. Be alert for moving equipment such as wagons and tractors. Large groups should call in advance to arrange for visits.

TRAVEL ACCESS: Bus: Washington Metro buses (Routes D-12 and W-12) stop at Oxon Hill and Livingston Roads.

Appalachian National Scenic Trail
For details see listing in Maine

Piscataway Park
Accokeek, Maryland

MAILING ADDRESS: Piscataway Park, Superintendent, National Capital Parks East, 1900 Anacostia Drive S.E., Washington, DC 20020 **Park Telephone:** 301-763-4600

DIRECTIONS: Take Exit 3A from the Capital Beltway (Int. 95) to Route 210S (Indian Head Highway) 10 miles (16 km) to the intersection in Accokeek. Turn right onto Bryan's Point Road and go 4 miles (6.4 km) to the Potomac River.
    The tranquil view of the Maryland shore of the Potomac from Mount Vernon is preserved as a pilot project in the use of easements to protect Parklands from obtrusive urban expansion. Authorized for addition to the National Park System on Oct. 4, 1961.

VISITOR ACTIVITIES: Picnicking, fishing, bird-watching, farm tours; **Permits:** No; **Fees:** A fee is charged for tours of the National Colonial Farm, which is located at Piscataway; **Visitor facilities:** Picnic area, boat dock, National Colonial Farm; **Any limitations on vehicle usage:** No; **Hiking trails:** No; **Backcountry:** No; **Camping:** No; **Other overnight accommodations on site:** No; **Meals served in the park:** No; **Food and supplies obtainable in the park:** No; **Food and supplies obtainable nearby:** Yes, shopping centers are along Route 210; **Overnight accommodations:** Suburban Maryland or metropolitan Washington, DC; **First Aid available in park:** No; **Nearest Hospital:** Washington, D.C., Route 210 to Southern Ave., 20 miles (32 km); **Days/Hours:** Open daily during daylight hours; **Holiday Closings:** No; **Weather:** Hot, humid summers and cold, wet winters.

Thomas Stone National Historic Site
Port Tobacco, Maryland

MAILING ADDRESS: Superintendent, George Washington Birthplace National Monument, RR #1, P.O. Box 717, Washington's Birthplace, VA 22443 **Telephone:** 804-224-1732

DIRECTIONS: The National Historic Site is 6 miles (9.6 km) west of LaPlata, Maryland and is accessible over either Maryland 6 or Maryland 225 and Rose Hill Road.

The Georgian home of Thomas Stone, a signer of the Declaration of Independence, was built by him in 1771. Authorized for addition to the National Park System on Nov. 10, 1978.

VISITOR ACTIVITIES: The Site is open to the public part time only while restoration and development is in progress. Call 804-224-1732 for a schedule of operation hours.

Massachusetts

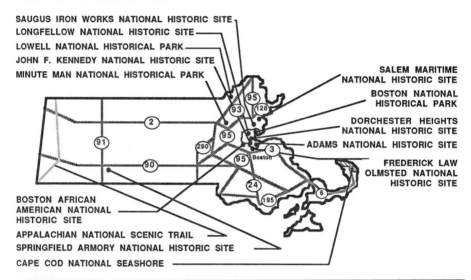

SAUGUS IRON WORKS NATIONAL HISTORIC SITE
LONGFELLOW NATIONAL HISTORIC SITE
LOWELL NATIONAL HISTORICAL PARK
JOHN F. KENNEDY NATIONAL HISTORIC SITE
MINUTE MAN NATIONAL HISTORICAL PARK

SALEM MARITIME NATIONAL HISTORIC SITE
BOSTON NATIONAL HISTORICAL PARK
DORCHESTER HEIGHTS NATIONAL HISTORIC SITE
ADAMS NATIONAL HISTORIC SITE
FREDERICK LAW OLMSTED NATIONAL HISTORIC SITE

BOSTON AFRICAN AMERICAN NATIONAL HISTORIC SITE
APPALACHIAN NATIONAL SCENIC TRAIL
SPRINGFIELD ARMORY NATIONAL HISTORIC SITE
CAPE COD NATIONAL SEASHORE

Adams National Historic Site
Quincy, Massachusetts

MAILING ADDRESS: Superintendent, Adams National Historic Site, P.O. Box 531, Quincy, MA 02269 **Telephone:** 617-773-1177

DIRECTIONS: 8 miles (12.8 km) south of Boston. Take Route 93 South (Southeast Expressway) to Exit 8 (formerly Exit 24) (Furnace Brook Parkway). Once on Furnace Brook Pkwy. at third set of traffic lights turn right onto Adams Street. Site is 1 mile (1.6 km) ahead on left at the corner of Adams Street and Newport Avenue.

Established by act of Congress on Dec. 9, 1946, the Site contains 8.45 acres and includes the house, library, garden, and stables of Presidents John Adams and John Quincy Adams, and statesman Ambassador Charles Francis Adams and his literary sons Henry and Brooks Adams.

The John Adams and John Quincy Adams Birthplaces: Approximately 9 miles (14.4 km) south of Boston. Take Exit 8 (formerly Exit 24) (Furnace Brook Parkway interchange) of the Southest Expressway (Route 3) to Adams Street East to Hancock Street through Quincy Center to School Street. Turn right onto School Street then left on Franklin Street. The Adams Birthplaces are on your right at 133 and 141 Franklin Street.

VISITOR ACTIVITIES: Historic Site tours; **Permits:** No; **Fees:** $2 admission fee for adults, children 16 and under admitted free when accompanied by an adult. Entrance fee includes all three homes. Golden Eagle, Golden Age, Annual Park Pass, and Golden Access Passports accepted and available; **Visitor facilities:** No; **Any limitations on vehicle usage:** Parking for visitors is available on the public street in front of the house; **Other overnight accommodations on site:** No; **Meals served in the park:** No; **Food and supplies obtainable in the park:** No; **Food and supplies obtainable nearby:** Yes, Quincy, about ¼ mile (.4 km) south of the Site; **Overnight accommodations:** Boston area along Route 3; **First Aid available in park:** No; **Nearest Hospital:** Quincy City Hospital, less than ¼ mile (.4 km) from the site; **Days/Hours:** Open 9 a.m.-5.p.m. daily Apr. 19 through Nov. 10, Adams Birthplaces are open daily Apr. 19 through Nov. 10; **Holiday Closings:** No; **Visitor attractions closed for seasons:** Closed Nov. 11 through Apr. 18.

TRAVEL ACCESS: Bus: Mass Bay Trans. Authority service to nearby Quincy Center; **Rail:** Mass Bay Trans. Authority hourly service to nearby Quincy Center; **Air:** All major airlines provide daily service to Logan Airport.

NEARBY FACILITIES & POINTS OF INTEREST: Hotel/Motel: President's City Motel, Hancock Street, about ½ mile (.8 km); **Food/Supplies:** Many stores in Quincy Center ¼ mile (.4 km) from Site; **Campgrounds:** None nearby; **Parks, other points of interest:** First Parish Church and other historic Sites in Quincy.

Appalachian National Scenic Trail
For details see listing in Maine

Boston African American National Historic Site
Boston, Massachusetts

MAILING ADDRESS: Site Manager, Boston African American National Historic Site, National Park Service, 46 Joy Street, Boston, MA 02114 **Telephone:** 617-742-5415.

DIRECTIONS: As parking is difficult in downtown Boston, visitors are advised to park and take mass transit (MBTA Green or Red Lines to Park Street Station). Parking is available at the Boston Common. If driving from the Massachusetts Turnpike, take the Prudential-Copley Square Exit to Stuart Street, then left onto Route 28 to the Boston Common. From Route 93, take Storrow Drive to Copley Square Exit. Turn left onto Beacon, right onto Arlington, left onto Boylston, left onto Charles Street (Route 28).

Established in 1980, Boston African American comprises the largest concentration of pre-Civil War black history sites in the U.S.

VISITOR ACTIVITIES: Self-guided walking tours. Guided tours are offered daily Memorial Day to Labor Day and by special request at other times. **Permits:** Required for special use and obtained by contacting the site manager; **Fees:** No; **Visitor facilities:** Restrooms and information are located at the Boston African American NH Site's Office, 46 Joy St., Boston, MA 02114; **Any limitations on vehicle usage:** No; one-way streets make driving on Beacon Hill difficult; **Hiking trails:** Yes, the 1.6-mile (2.6-km) Black Heritage Trail connects the 16 sites; **Backcountry:** No; **Camping:** No; **Other overnight accommodations on site:** No; **Food and supplies obtainable in the park:** No; **Food and supplies obtainable nearby:** Yes, on Charles and Cambridge Streets; **Overnight accommodations:** Boston. List available at Site Office, 46 Joy Street, Boston, MA 02114; **First Aid available in park:** No; **Nearest Hospital:** Boston Hospitals—Massachusetts General, Tufts University Clinic;

Days/Hours: 5 days a week in the winter, spring, and fall, 9 a.m.-4 p.m., summer 9 a.m.-5 p.m.; **Holiday Closings:** Thanksgiving, Dec. 25, and Jan. 1; **Visitor attractions closed for seasons:** No; **Weather:** Spring, summer are best times to visit. Winter is icy.

GENERAL INFORMATION: The visitor experience here is an outdoor walking tour. The African Meeting House is open to the public on weekdays during the winter, spring, and fall, and daily during the summer.

TRAVEL ACCESS: Bus: Major companies, daily; **Rail:** Amtrak, Boston, North and South Stations, daily; **Air:** Major Airlines serve Boston (Logan), daily; **Other:** Bay State Lines (boats from Provincetown), Boston, daily.

NEARBY FACILITIES & POINTS OF INTEREST: Boston Harbor Islands State Park offers primitive camping. Contact 617-727-5250 for information.

Boston National Historical Park
Boston, Massachusetts

MAILING ADDRESS: Superintendent, Boston National Historical Park, Charlestown Navy Yard, Boston, MA 02129 **Telephone:** 617-242-5644

DIRECTIONS: We recommend that you don't drive in downtown Boston; mass transit provides a good option. If you do drive, from Route 1 south and Route 93 north or south, follow signs to the Charlestown Navy Yard (berth of USS Constitution). Further directions into downtown Boston can be obtained here.

The Park consists of 7 historic sites and a Visitor Center along Boston's Freedom Trail plus Dorchester Heights and the Boston African American National Historic Site. The Park was founded in 1974. The Freedom Trail is a red line painted on the sidewalks of Boston.

VISITOR ACTIVITIES: During the peak season (summer), the sites provide historic information in a variety of ways: tours, lectures, living history, exhibits, and publications. Park Service rangers are at the Charlestown Navy Yard, Bunker Hill and the downtown Visitor Center daily. At Dorchester Heights, a ranger is on duty from 10 a.m.-4 p.m. weekends from June 15 to Labor Day and on Wednesday evenings from 4 p.m.-8 p.m. during July and August. Faneuil Hall and the Old State House are closed for rehabilitation and are scheduled to reopen in spring 1992. At the Navy Yard, the Commandant's House is open for tours upon request at the Information Desk in Building 5. The USS Constitution Museum with exhibits, gift shop and special programs is open from 9 a.m.-6 p.m. from June to September, 9 a.m.-5 p.m. from September to December, 10 a.m.-4 p.m. during the winter months and closed Thanksgiving, Christmas and New Year's Day; **Permits:** Only for special use; **Fees:** Yes, entrance fees are collected at the privately owned and operated Sites, by self-supporting associations working cooperatively with the Park; **Visitor facilities:** Restrooms at the Visitor Center, Navy Yard, and Faneuil Hall; **HANDICAPPED ACCESSIBILITY:** Restrooms currently at the Visitor Center and Navy Yard with handicapped access. When Faneuil Hall and the Old State House reopen, they will be handicapped accessible in exhibit areas and restrooms. USS Constitution Museum is handicapped accessible; **Any limitations on vehicle usage:** Commercial parking lot and very limited free parking is available at the Navy Yard outside the National Park. Commercial parking rates at fairly high costs are available in the city convenient to the Freedom Trail and public transportation; **Hiking trails:** Yes, the Freedom Trail follows an urban route; **Camping:** No; **Meals served in the park:** No restaurant with wait staff, full meal menu; **Food and supplies obtainable in the park:** Yes, in summer season, snack bar with inside and outside seating, counter service. Handicapped accessible; **Food and supplies obtainable nearby:** Yes, in Quincy Market, North End, and Charlestown. There are many restaurants in the vicinity; **Overnight accommodations:** Hotels and motels throughout the city; **First Aid available in park:** Yes; **Nearest Hospital:** Hospitals near Sites include Massachusetts General, Bunker Hill Community Health Center, Tufts University, and University Hospital; **Days/Hours:** Summer: 7 days per week, 9 a.m.-6 p.m.; Winter: 7 days per week, 9 a.m.-5 p.m. or 10 a.m.-5 p.m., depending on Site; **Holiday Closings:** Thanksgiving, Dec. 25, and Jan. 1; **Visitor attractions closed for seasons:** No; **Weather:** Summer is usually hot and humid with a sea breeze; winter is windy and usually cold.

TRAVEL ACCESS: **Bus:** Major bus companies; **Rail:** Daily service into Boston's South Station and North Station; **Air:** Major airlines service into Boston Logan Airport.

NEARBY FACILITIES & POINTS OF INTEREST: Parks, other points of interest: Adams National Historic Site, Saugus Ironworks, Kennedy Birthplace, Longfellow, Frederick Law Olmsted, and Salem Maritime National Historical Sites; Lowell and Minuteman National Historical Parks.

Bunker Hill Battlefield and Monument
Boston National Historical Park, Boston, MA

MAILING ADDRESS: Superintendent, Boston National Historical Park, Charlestown Navy Yard, Boston, MA 02129 **Telephone:** 617-242-5644

DIRECTIONS: The Monument is located in residential Charlestown, where street parking is limited. We recommend Mass transit. It is a 10-minute walk to the Monument from the Community College subway station (Orange subway line).

The Bunker Hill Monument is constructed on the site of the famous Battle of Bunker Hill fought on June 17, 1775. Though the British won the battle, the colonials gained new-found respect by their determined resistance to the Redcoats.

VISITOR ACTIVITIES: Bunker Hill Monument is a unit of Boston National Historical Park. The Bunker Hill Lodge is open daily and features exhibits on the battle. A climb to the top of the Monument will provide a spectacular view of Boston and the surrounding area. Park Rangers on duty provide 15-minute talks on the battle every hour; **Permits:** Only for special usage. Special programs for children or visiting groups can be arranged by contacting the site in advance; **Fees:** No; **Visitor facilities:** Restrooms are available at the lodge. **HANDICAPPED ACCESSIBILITY:** The restrooms and exhibits in the lodge are accessible by wheelchair; **Any limitations on vehicle usage:** There is limited street parking in Charlestown near the Monument; **Hiking trails:** Bunker Hill Monument is located along Boston's historic Freedom Trail; **Camping:** No; **Food Service:** Restaurants located along Main Street in Charlestown and throughout Boston; **Overnight accommodations:** Hotels and motels are located throughout Boston; **First Aid available in park:** Yes; **Nearest Hospitals:** Massachusetts General, Bunker Hill Community Clinic; **Days/Hours:** Open daily from 9 a.m. until 5 p.m. Visitors may climb the Monument until 4:30 p.m; **Holiday Closings:** Thanksgiving, Dec. 25, and Jan. 1; **Visitor attractions closed for seasons:** No; **Weather:** Summer temperatures generally in the 80s; winter is windy with temperatures down to the teens.

NEARBY FACILITIES & POINTS OF INTEREST: Adams, Saugus Iron Works, John F. Kennedy, Longfellow, Frederick Law Olmsted, and Salem Maritime National Historic Sites, Lowell and Minuteman National Historical Parks.

Cape Cod National Seashore
South Wellfleet, Massachusetts

MAILING ADDRESS: Superintendent, Cape Cod National Seashore, South Wellfleet, MA 02663 **Telephone:** 508-349-3785

DIRECTIONS: Visitor Centers are at Salt Pond (in Eastham on Route 6) and Province Lands (in Provincetown on Race Point Road). Headquarters is at the Marconi Station Area in Wellfleet.

Ocean and bay beaches, dunes, woodlands, freshwater ponds, and marshes make up this Park on outer Cape Cod. The area preserves notable examples of Cape Cod houses, an architectural style founded in America. Authorized for addition to the National Park System on Aug. 7, 1961.

VISITOR ACTIVITIES: Interpretive exhibits and talks, swimming, surfing, driving, horseback riding, camping, picnicking, fishing, hiking, shellfishing, biking; **Permits:** Shellfishing from local towns, fresh water fishing, state license applicable; oversand vehicles from Race Point Ranger Station, subject to inspection and annual fee; **Fees:** Beach parking lot $5 per carload entrance fee late June through Labor Day. Golden Eagle, Golden Age, and Golden Access Passports accepted and available. Park pass for season also available for $15. Annual oversand vehicle fees are $45 for regular ORVs and $75 for self-contained; **Visitor facilities:** Bicycle trails, nature trails, bridle paths and beaches, lifeguard services and other swimming facilities, picnic areas; bicycle rentals in adjoining communities, horse rentals, restaurants, lodging, gift stores; **HANDICAPPED ACCESSIBILITY:** Parking, restrooms, specially designed shower for wheelchairs at Herring Cove Beach, paved or portable ramps for beach access; large-print park folder available for visually impaired as well as ¼-mile (.4 km) guide-rope. Buttonbush Trail, adjacent to Salt Pond Visitor's Center, which has trail-side labels in Braille and large type; audio program available; touch and feel boxes at Visitor Centers; Other Ranger talks, guided walks, and other accessible programs may be available at the time of your visit; self-guided nature trails have labeled exhibits for the hearing impaired; **Any limitations on vehicle usage:** Summer traffic is very heavy—roads are narrow. Motorized vehicles including mopeds are not allowed on paved bicycle trails; **Hiking trails:** Yes, day use only; outer beach is also good for day hiking; **Camping:** Camping not permitted on National Seashore property, however, various private campgrounds are available locally. Reservations are essential for summer season. A large state-owned campground is in Nickerson State Park in nearby Brewster. Reservations cannot be made for this campground. Sleeping and campground accommodations, restaurants, gift shops, grocery and other stores, and gas stations are in towns adjoining the seashore. For information and reservations, write to Cape Cod Chamber of Commerce, Hyannis, MA 02601; **Other overnight accommodations on site:** No; **Meals served in the park:** No; **Food and supplies obtainable in the park:** No; **Food and supplies obtainable nearby:** Yes, along Route 6 and in local towns; **Overnight accommodations:** Available in areas serving the seashore. Contact Chamber of Commerce as noted above; **First Aid available in park:** Yes, emergency only; all towns have rescue squads; **Nearest Hospital:** Hyannis, 30 miles (48 km) away; **Days/Hours:** Open from 6 a.m. to midnight year-round; **Holiday Closings:** Salt Pond Visitor Center closed Jan. and Feb. Province Lands Visitor Center closed Dec. to mid-Apr.; **Visitor attractions closed for seasons:** Interpretive services, walks, talks, etc., are offered from Apr.-Nov.; **Weather:** Summer and fall are the best times to visit; spring is often damp; winter is mild and potentially stormy.

GENERAL INFORMATION: *Caution*—Swim only where lifeguards are on duty. The ocean can be dangerous. Be alert for riptides and underwater obstacles. For your safety, do not take glass containers, rafts, rubber tubes, snorkels, or masks to any beach. Watch out for painful sunburn. Do not leave valuables in vehicles. Sand collapses easily. Climbing slopes or digging deep holes is hazardous.

TRAVEL ACCESS: Bus: Plymouth & Brockton Bus Lines, Boston to Hyannis. Bonanza Bus Lines, Providence to Hyannis, Cape Cod Bus Co., Via Route 6, Hyannis to Province-town; **Rail:** Amtrak, Providence and Boston; **Air:** New York Air; Continental Express, Hyannis, Provincetown. **Other:** Paved bicycle trail from Nickerson State Park in Brewster to Salt Pond Visitor Center, Eastham.

Charlestown Navy Yard
Boston National Historical Park, Boston, MA

MAILING ADDRESS: Superintendent, Boston National Historical Park, Charlestown Navy Yard, Boston, MA 02129 **Telephone:** 617-242-5644

DIRECTIONS: The Charlestown Navy Yard can be reached by following the signs from Route 1 south and Route 93 north or south. Limited parking is available outside the Yard. The site is a 15-minute walk from either the Bunker Hill Community College subway station (Orange subway line) or North Station (Orange or Green subway lines). Water transportation including a harbor cruise is available from Long Wharf near the Aquarium.

The Charlestown Navy Yard is a unit of Boston National Historical Park. The Navy Yard, established in 1800, continued in operation until 1974. It is best known as home port of the USS Constitution, and for the developments in shipbuilding and repair technology that took place there.

VISITOR ACTIVITIES: Park Rangers operate an information center and lead tours of the Navy Yard, the Commandant's House, and the World War II destroyer, Cassin Young. Other cooperative attractions in the Navy Yard include USS Constitution, operated by the U.S. Navy, the Constitution Museum, and the Museum of the Boston Marine Society, which fea-tures exhibits on Boston's maritime past. Special programs for school and other visiting groups can be arranged by contacting the site in advance; **Permits:** For special usage and commercial photography; **Fees:** Admission to the Constitution Museum is $2.50 for adults, $2 for seniors, and $1.50 for children 6 to 16; those under 6 are free. All other sites in the Navy Yard are free; **Visitor facilities:** Restrooms; **HANDICAPPED ACCESSIBILITY:** Rest-rooms; **Any limitations on vehicle usage:** Parking at the Navy Yard is limited, particularly for trailers or large vehicles; **Hiking trails:** The Charlestown Navy Yard is located along Bos-ton's historic Freedom Trail; **Camping:** No; **Overnight accommodations:** Hotels and motels are located throughout Boston; **First Aid available in park:** Yes; **Nearest Hospitals:** Massachusetts General, Bunker Hill Clinic; **Days/Hours:** The Navy Yard is open every day from 8 a.m. until 5 p.m. USS Constitution is open daily 9:30 a.m. until 3:50 p.m. The Con-stitution Museum is open daily 9 a.m. until 5 p.m. (until 6 p.m. in summer). The Boston Marine Society is open on weekdays from 9 a.m. until 3 p.m. The Commandant's House is open daily in the summer and on weekends in spring and fall; **Holiday Closings:** The USS Constitution is open every day. Other sites in the Navy Yard are closed on Thanksgiving, Dec. 25, and Jan. 1; **Visitor attractions closed for seasons:** The main deck of Cassin Young is open for casual visitation in spring, summer and fall. In winter the ship is open by guided tour only; **Weather:** Summer temperatures generally in the 80s; winter is windy with temper-atures down to the teens.

NEARBY FACILITIES & POINTS OF INTEREST: Adams, Saugus Iron Works,

John Fitzgerald Kennedy, Longfellow, Frederick Law Olmsted, and Salem Maritime National Historical Sites; Lowell and Minuteman National Historical Parks.

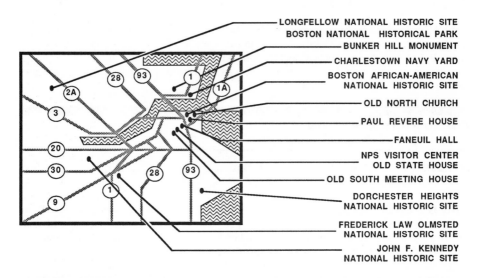

Dorchester Heights
Boston National Historical Park, Boston, MA

MAILING ADDRESS: Superintendent, Boston National Historical Park, Charlestown Navy Yard, Boston, MA 02129 **Telephone:** 617-242-5644

DIRECTIONS: Dorchester Heights is located in South Boston, approximately 2 miles (3.2 km) from downtown. By public transit take the subway (Red Line) to Broadway Station. From here board MBTA Bus #9 (City Point) and get off at "G" Street. It is a short walk to the Heights. By car from downtown Boston, cross into South Boston on the Congress Street Bridge. Turn right onto "A" Street, then left onto West Broadway. Follow Broadway to "G" Street and turn right to the monument.
     The colonial revival monument and small park mark the site of George Washington's 1776 fortifications. By placing men and artillery here the Americans forced the British evacuation of Boston on March 17, 1776. This bloodless victory was Washington's first military action as Commander-in-Chief of the new Continental Army.

VISITOR ACTIVITIES: The monument offers a magnificent view of Boston and her harbor. The surrounding park is a pleasant place for rest and passive recreation. Park Rangers are on duty during warmer weather to explain the significance of the site. Special tours of the monument and grounds for school or adult groups can be arranged by contacting the Park in advance; **Permits:** Only for special usage and commercial photography; **Fees:** No; **Visitor facilities:** There are no restrooms at the site; **Any limitations on vehicle usage:** Dorchester Heights is in a residential area of South Boston. Street parking around the monument is usually available; **Hiking trails:** No; **Camping:** No; **Food service:** There are restaurants on nearby Broadway and in downtown Boston; **Overnight accommodations:** Hotels and motels are located throughout Boston; **First Aid available in park:** Only when personnel are on duty; **Nearest Hospitals:** Massachusetts General, Tufts New England Medical Center; **Days/Hours:** Monument grounds are open daily until sunset; **Holiday Closings:** The grounds are open every day until sunset; **Visitor attractions closed for seasons:** The monument is open on a limited basis during the summer; **Weather:** Summer temperatures generally in the 80s; winter is windy with temperatures down to the teens.

NEARBY FACILITIES & POINTS OF INTEREST: Adams, Saugus Iron Works, John Fitzgerald Kennedy, Longfellow, Frederick Law Olmsted and Salem Maritime National Historical Sites; Lowell and Minute Man National Historical Parks.

Faneuil Hall
Boston National Historical Park, Boston, MA

MAILING ADDRESS: Superintendent, Boston National Historical Park, Charlestown Navy Yard, Boston, MA 02129 **Telephone:** 242-5644

DIRECTIONS: We recommend that you do not drive in downtown Boston; mass transit provides a good alternative. Faneuil Hall is located at Dock Square next to Quincy Market. The nearest subway stops are Government Center (Green and Blue subway lines) or State Street (Blue and Orange subway lines). From either station, it is a 5-minute walk to Faneuil Hall.

Faneuil Hall was built in 1742 to serve as the town meeting hall and as a public marketplace for colonial Boston. In the years before the American Revolution, meetings held here rallied public opposition to British rule. The "Cradle of Liberty" continues today to serve as a popular meeting place and assembly hall for Bostonians.

VISITOR ACTIVITIES: Faneuil Hall is owned by the City of Boston and is part of Boston National Historical Park. The National Park Service maintains the Hall and provides visitor services and interpretation of the site. The first floor of Faneuil Hall still serves as a marketplace. The meeting hall, located on the second floor, is open daily and staffed by Rangers who provide information and regularly scheduled talks throughout the day. A military museum and armory, maintained by the Ancient and Honorable Artillery Company, is located on the third floor; **Permits:** Faneuil Hall is still regularly used for gatherings and functions. Contact the Superintendent, Faneuil Hall, 1 Merchants Row, Boston, MA 02109. Telephone: 617-725-3105; **Fees:** No; **Visitor facilities:** Restrooms are available. **HANDICAPPED ACCESSIBILITY:** The second-floor meeting hall is accessible to the disabled; **Any limitations on vehicle usage:** Faneuil Hall is located in downtown Boston. Parking is very limited. Commercial parking lots are located on nearby Congress Street; **Hiking trails:** Yes. Faneuil Hall is located along Boston's historic Freedom Trail; **Camping:** No; **Food service:** Numerous restaurants are located in the vicinity; **Overnight accommodations:** Hotels and motels are located throughout Boston; **First Aid available in park:** Yes; **Nearest Hospital:** Massachusetts General; **Days/Hours:** Faneuil Hall is open daily from 9 a.m. until 5 p.m. The Museum and Armory of the Ancient and Honorable Artillery Company is open on weekdays from 10 a.m. until 4 p.m. Faneuil Hall is still frequently used as a meeting hall for various groups and organizations and may, at times, be closed to the public in preparation for or during these functions. For more information call the National Park Service Visitor Center at 617-242-5642; **Holiday Closings:** Thanksgiving, Dec. 25, and Jan. 1; **Visitor attractions closed for seasons:** No; **Weather:** Summer temperatures generally in the 80s; winter is windy with temperatures down to the teens.

NEARBY FACILITIES & POINTS OF INTEREST: Adams, Saugus Iron Works, John Fitzgerald Kennedy, Longfellow, Frederick Law Olmsted, and Salem Maritime National Historic Sites, Lowell and Minute Man National Historic Parks.

Frederick Law Olmsted National Historic Site
Brookline, Massachusetts

MAILING ADDRESS: 99 Warren Street, Brookline, MA 02146 **Telephone:** 617-566-1689

DIRECTIONS: From Rt. 128 (I-95), take exit for Rt. 9 East (toward Boston), follow past Brookline Reservoir, turn right on Warren Street to Site (2 blocks) to corner of Dudley and Warren Streets. From Southeast Expressway (I-93), go to Massachusetts Turnpike West and follow to Brighton-Harvard Street exit, stay on Harvard Street to Rt. 9 (Boylston Street), take right, go 2 traffic lights west to Warren Street and turn left and follow to site.

Historic home and office of the Founder of American landscape architecture, used by Frederick Law Olmsted, Sr., and his sons. Established December, 1979.

VISITOR ACTIVITIES: Guided tour of home with exhibits, guided tour of office and re-stored grounds, slide presentation; **Permits:** No; **Fees:** No; **Visitor facilities:** Restrooms and bookstore; **Any limitations on vehicle usage:** Very limited parking; **Hiking trails:** No; **Backcountry:** No; **Camping:** No; **Other overnight accommodations on site:** No; **Meals served in the park:** No; **Food and supplies obtainable in the park:** No; **Food and supplies obtainable nearby:** Yes, available in Brookline, 1½ miles (2.4 km), and Boston, 3 miles (4.8 km); **Overnight accommodations:** Available in Brookline and Boston; **First Aid available in park:** No; **Nearest Hospital:** Hospital with 1 mile (1.6 km); **Days/Hours:** Fri.-Sun. 10 a.m.-4:30 p.m. Groups at other times by reservation; **Holiday Closings:** Thanksgiving, Dec. 25, and Jan. 1; **Visitor attractions closed for seasons:** No.

TRAVEL ACCESS: Bus: MBTA; **Rail:** MBTA (Riverside) Rail, nearest terminal—Brookline Hills Stop; **Air:** Boston Terminals.

NEARBY FACILITIES & POINTS OF INTEREST: Hotel/Motel: Nearby in Boston; Campgrounds: Nearby; **Parks, other points of interest:** Boston Park System designed by Olmsted; Longfellow and John F. Kennedy National Historical Sites; Boston National Histor-ical Park; and John F. Kennedy Library.

John F. Kennedy National Historic Site
Brookline, Massachusetts

MAILING ADDRESS: Superintendent, John F. Kennedy National Historic Site, 83 Beals Street, Brookline, MA 02146 **Telephone:** 617-566-7937

DIRECTIONS: Take Allston, Brighton, Cambridge Exit from Mass. Turnpike Extension. Proceed towards Allston along Cambridge Street and turn left onto Harvard Street. Turn left from Harvard Street onto Beals Street. The Site is easily reached by public transportation.

This 9-room, 3-story structure is the birthplace and early childhood home (1917-1921) of the 35th President of the United States. Authorized for addition to the National Park System on May 26, 1967.

VISITOR ACTIVITIES: Ranger-guided with tape-recorded tour on the hour and ½ hour; Special School programs available for groups of students in K-3 by reservation only, Sept.-June; **Permits:** No; **Fees:** $1 for adults. Those under 16 and over 62 free. Golden Eagle and Golden Age Passports accepted and available; **Visitor facilities:** Small visitor reception area with exhibits and sales center; **Any limitations on vehicle usage:** Parking is available only on the street, which may be congested. Buses must not idle motors; **Meals served in the park:** No; **Food and supplies obtainable in the park:** No; **Food and supplies obtainable nearby:** Yes, about 2-4 blocks away; **Overnight accommodations:** Brookline, ½ mile (.8 km). Boston is 3 miles (4.8 km) distant; **First Aid available in park:** Yes; **Nearest Hospital:** Brookline, 1 mile (1.6 km); **Days/Hours:** Open daily from 10:00 a.m. to 4:30 p.m.; **Holiday Closings:** Thanksgiving, Dec. 25, and Jan. 1.

Longfellow National Historic Site
Cambridge, Massachusetts

MAILING ADDRESS: Superintendent, Longfellow National Historic Site, 105 Brattle Street, Cambridge, MA 02138 **Telephone:** 617-876-4491

DIRECTIONS: Cambridge is a historic city with both old and new buildings of interest. For visitors unfamiliar with the area the easiest way to see some of Cambridge's sights including the Longfellow House is to park in Boston under the Common and take the Red Line subway to Harvard Square. From there walk to Brattle Street and continue down Brattle about .6 mile (1 km) to Longfellow House. On your way you will pass 2 colonial mansions, the William Brattle House and the John Vassall, Sr. House. On your return to Harvard Square, you may wish to go via Mason Street and Cambridge Common. On the Common a bronze plaque marks the Site of the "Washington Elm" under whose branches George Washington took command of the Continental Army.

Poet Henry Wadsworth Longfellow lived here from 1837 to 1882. The house had been George Washington's headquarters during the siege of Boston, 1775-76. Authorized for addition to the National Park System on Oct. 9, 1972.

VISITOR ACTIVITIES: Guided tours, garden concerts on alternate Sundays during the summer beginning in mid-June; **Permits:** No; **Fees:** Entrance fee is $2 for adults. No charge for persons 12 and under or 62 and over. Golden Eagle and Golden Age Passports accepted and available; **Visitor facilities:** None on Site. A free brochure is available on request; **HANDICAPPED ACCESSIBILITY:** On-site parking may be arranged in advance. Telephone 617-876-4491; **Any limitations on vehicle usage:** No parking is available at the Site. Limited parking is .6 mile (1 km) distant; **Hiking trails:** No; **Meals served in the park:** No; **Food and supplies obtainable in the park:** No; **Food and supplies obtainable nearby:** Yes, in Cambridge (Harvard Square); **Overnight accommodations:** Cambridge, within walking distance, or Boston, 7 miles (11.2 km); **First Aid available in park:** No; **Nearest Hospital:** Mt. Auburn, .6 mile (1 km); **Days/Hours:** Open daily from 10 a.m. to 4:30 p.m.; **Holiday Closings:** Thanksgiving, Dec. 25, and Jan. 1; **Weather:** Moderately warm and humid summer, occasional inconvenience from snow and ice in winter.

GENERAL INFORMATION: Group tours are required to make reservations.

TRAVEL ACCESS: Bus: Trailways/Greyhound provide daily service to Boston; MBTA stops at Harvard Square; **Rail:** Amtrak provides daily service to Boston; **Air:** Major Airlines offer regular service into Boston; **Other:** Taxi service to the House is available from Harvard Square.

NEARBY FACILITIES & POINTS OF INTEREST: Hotel/Motel: Sheraton Commander, 16 Garden Street, Cambridge, 617-547-4800; **Parks, other points of interest:** Tory Row Houses; Harvard and Radcliffe Universities in Cambridge.

Lowell National Historical Park
Lowell, Massachusetts

MAILING ADDRESS: Superintendent, Lowell National Historical Park, 169 Merrimack St., Lowell, MA 01852 **Telephone:** 508-459-1000; TDD 508-459-1000

DIRECTIONS: Take the Lowell Connector from either Int. 495 or US 3. Exit on Thorndike Street North and proceed approximately ½ mile (.8 km) to Dutton Street. Take a right turn on Dutton Street. Follow Dutton to the marked parking lot. There is train access to Lowell from Boston's North Station. The Visitor Center is at 246 Market Street.

The park includes seven original mill complexes, a power canal system, and other early 19th-century structures of this planned city of the Industrial Revolution. Authorized for addition to the National Park System on June 5, 1978.

VISITOR ACTIVITIES: The Park offers guided tours daily by barge (July 1 - Columbus Day), aboard turn-of-the-century trolleys (Memorial Day - Columbus Day), and on foot (year-round). For reservations call 508-459-1000. Self-guided tours and exhibits available year-round; **Permits:** No, but tour reservations are required; **Fees:** Fees for boat and trolley tours are $2.00 Adults, $1.00 Senior Citizens, children 16 and under are free. **Visitor facilities:** Visitor Center, 246 Market St., open daily 8:30 a.m.-5 p.m. The "Working People Exhibit" at the Mogan Cultural Center open Mon.-Sat. 10 a.m.-4 p.m., July 1-Columbus Day; Wed.-Sun. 10 a.m.-4 p.m., the Boott Cotton Mills Museum, open daily, year-round, beginning Spring 1992, $2.00 Adults, $1.00 Senior Citizens, children 16 and under are free, parking, restrooms, Suffolk Mill Turbine Exhibit and Lowell Heritage State Park Water Power Exhibit, hours vary; **HANDICAPPED ACCESSIBILITY:** National and State Park Rangers provide access to many of the privately owned historic structures in downtown Lowell through interpretive programs and literature. Accessible buildings within the Parks presently include the National and State Parks Visitor Center and the Suffolk Mill Turbine Exhibit. Additional services include Braille and large-print literature, cassette tapes of park brochures, audio-visual and audio programs in printed format. More information on park programs and accessibility can be obtained by calling TTY 508-459-4030 or the Visitor Center at 508-459-1000 to access TDD. **Any limitations on vehicle usage:** Use of public transportation is recommended; **Hiking trails:** No; **Backcountry:** No; **Camping:** No; **Other overnight accommodations on site:** Lowell Hilton, 50 Warren Ave.; **Meals served in the park:** Yes; **Food and supplies obtainable in the park:** Yes; **Food and supplies obtainable nearby:** Yes; **Overnight accommodations:** On the periphery of Lowell, 2 miles (3.2 km); **First Aid available in park:** Yes; **Nearest Hospital:** St. John's, ¼ mile (.4 km); **Days/Hours:** Visitor Center open from 8:30 a.m. to 5 p.m. year-round; **Holiday Closings:** Thanksgiving, Dec. 25, and Jan. 1; **Visitor attractions closed for seasons:** Mill and canal tour from Memorial Day through Columbus Day only, trolley tours and walking tours year-round.

TRAVEL ACCESS: Bus: Trailways provides daily service into Lowell's New Industrial Ave. terminal; Lowell Regional Transit has regular service downtown; **Rail:** Boston & Maine RR provides regular service; **Air:** Access through Boston's Logan Airport.

NEARBY FACILITIES & POINTS OF INTEREST: Hotel/Motel: Town House Motor Inn, 850 Chelmsford St., Lowell, 508-454-5606, 2 miles (3.2 km); Radisson Heritage Hotel, 187 Chelmsford St., Chelmsford MA, 508-256-7511, 3 miles (4.8 km); Quality Inn, Rt. I-495 (Exit 34) and Rt. 110, Chelmsford, 508-256-0800, 3 miles (4.8 km); Holiday Inn, 95 Main St., Tewksbury, 508-640-9000, 3 miles (4.8 km); Lowell Courtyard by Marriott, 30 Industrial Ave., Lowell, 508-458-7575, 2 miles (3.2 km); **Campgrounds:** KOA Minuteman

Campground (508-772-0042); **Parks, other points of interest:** Tsongas Industrial History Center, New England Folklife Center of Lowell, Whistler House Museum of Art, Museum of American Textile History, Lowell-Dracut-Tyngsboro State Forest, Lawrence Heritage State Park.

Minute Man National Historical Park
Concord, Massachusetts

MAILING ADDRESS: Superintendent, Minute Man National Historical Park, P.O. Box 160, Concord, MA 01742 **Telephone:** 617-369-6993

DIRECTIONS: The North Bridge Visitor Center is located off Liberty Street in Concord. The Battle Road Visitor Center is located off Route 2A in Lexington. Information is available at both places.

This is the scene of the fighting on the opening day of the Revolutionary War, April 19, 1775. It includes The North Bridge, the Minute Man Statue, 4 miles (6.4 km) of Battle Road between Lexington and Concord, and "The Wayside," Nathaniel Hawthorne's Home. Authorized by act of Congress, September 21, 1959.

VISITOR ACTIVITIES: Interpretive exhibits and film, walking tours, interpretive talks, living history demonstrations. Sales and informational material are available; **Permits:** No; **Fees:** $1 admission fee at "The Wayside" for persons 16 and over. Golden Eagle and Golden Age Passports accepted and available; **Visitor facilities:** The North Bridge Unit (includes the famous Minute Man statue by Daniel Chester French), The Battle Road Visitor Center, the Wayside, Fiske Hill, parking, restrooms; **Any limitations on vehicle usage:** Use the parking facilities provided. Use caution on State Route 2A, a heavily traveled road; **Hiking trails:** Yes, a 1-mile (1.6-km) self-guiding trail is available at Fiske Hill on Route 2A in Lexington. A ⅔-mile (1.1-km) trail links the historic Hartwell Tavern and William Smith house. The restored battle road from the North Bridge leads to the North Bridge Visitor Center; **Backcountry:** No; **Camping:** No; **Other overnight accommodations on site:** No; **Meals served in the park:** No; **Food and supplies obtainable in the park:** No; **Food and supplies obtainable nearby:** Yes, in nearby towns: Concord, Lexington, Acton, and Bedford; **Overnight accommodations:** Concord, Lexington, Acton, and Bedford; **First Aid available in park:** Yes; **Nearest Hospital:** Emerson Hospital, Concord, 2 miles (3.2 km) from the Park; **Days/Hours:** North Bridge Visitor Center is open the year-round 8:30 a.m.-5 p.m. except Dec. 25, and Jan. 1. Call 617-369-6993 for hours and days of other facilities; **Weather:** New England climate: cold winters; warm summers.

GENERAL INFORMATION: Please respect the rights of private families living within the Park boundary. Visitors to the area can also see historic Sites relating to the lives of Henry David Thoreau, Louisa May Alcott, and Ralph Waldo Emerson.

Old North Church
Boston National Historical Park, Boston, MA

MAILING ADDRESS: Old North Church, 193 Salem Street, Boston, MA 02113 **Telephone:** 617-523-6676

DIRECTIONS: We recommend that you do not drive in downtown Boston; mass transit provides a good alternative. The closest subway stop is Haymarket Station (Orange or Green subway lines). From here cross under the elevated expressway into Boston's North End. At the tunnel entering the North End begin to follow the red line of the Freedom Trail. It is a 15-minute walk to the Old North Church.

The Old North Church, also known as Christ Church, was built in 1723 and remains an active Episcopal church today. It was from the steeple of Old North that two lanterns were hung on April 18th, 1775, warning colonials in Charlestown that the British were marching from Boston to Lexington and Concord to destroy colonial military supplies. On this night, Paul Revere made his famous "midnight ride" to warn the countryside that "the British are coming."

VISITOR ACTIVITIES: The Old North Church is a cooperative site of Boston National Historical Park. It remains an active Episcopal Church. Sunday services at 9 and 11 a.m. and 4 p.m. Old North Church is open every day. The site is maintained by the Church through donations. Staff are available to give historic talks on the Church throughout the day. A museum and gift shop are located on the grounds; **Permits:** Permits are required for special activities and commercial photography; **Fees:** Free; donations welcome; **HANDICAPPED ACCESSIBILITY:** Yes; **Any limitations on vehicle usage:** The Old North Church is in Boston's crowded North End. Street parking is limited to neighborhood residents; **Hiking trails:** Yes, Old North Church is located along Boston's historic Freedom Trail; **Camping:** No; **Food service:** There are numerous restaurants in the vicinity; **Overnight accommodations:** Hotels and motels are located throughout Boston; **First Aid available in park:** Yes, limited; **Nearest Hospital:** Massachusetts General; **Days/Hours:** Open every day from 9 a.m. until 5 p.m.; **Holiday Closings:** No; **Visitor attractions closed for season:** No; **Weather:** Summer temperatures generally in the 80s; winter is windy with temperatures down to the teens.

NEARBY FACILITIES & POINTS OF INTEREST: Adams, Saugus Iron Works, John Fitzgerald Kennedy, Longfellow, Frederick Law Olmsted, and Salem Maritime National Historical Sites; Lowell and Minute Man National Historical Parks.

Old South Meeting House
Boston National Historical Park, Boston, MA

MAILING ADDRESS: The Old South Meeting House, 310 Washington Street, Boston, MA 02108 **Telephone:** 617-482-6439

DIRECTIONS: We recommend that you do not drive in downtown Boston. Mass transit provides a good alternative. The closest subway stop is at State Street (Orange and Blue subway lines).

The Old South Meeting House, built as a Congregational place of worship in 1729, was the site of many meetings protesting British policies in the 1760s and 1770s, most notably the meeting preceding the Boston Tea Party. In 1877 the Old South Association was founded to save the property from demolition, one of the first instances of historic preservation in the nation.

VISITOR ACTIVITIES: The Old South Meeting House is a cooperative site in Boston National Historical Park. It is owned and operated by the Old South Association in Boston. Visitors are invited to tour this beautifully restored meeting hall that contains multi-media exhibits on the history of the site and life in 18th-century Boston. "Middays the Meeting House," a lecture and concert series, presents the issues, individuals, and music of America's past, every Tuesday at 12:15 p.m. from Oct. to March. "Town Meetings" pit Loyalists against Patriots in debates on "What's to be done with the obnoxious tea?" every Saturday at 2 p.m., mid-June through Labor Day. Old South is still used as a hall for concerts, meetings, and school activities throughout the year; **Permits:** Contact Old South Association Marketing Coordinator. Programs for school groups and others can be arranged in advance by contacting the Site. A featured program is "Tea Is Brewing," where school groups trace the events of the Boston Tea Party at Faneuil Hall, Old South, and the Boston Tea Party Ship. "Tea Is Brewing" is available by reservation and has a special fee; **Admission Fees:** $1.75 for adults, $1.25 for seniors and students with I.D., $.50 for children 6-16, free for those under 6; **Visitor facilities:** There are no restrooms at the site. **HANDICAPPED ACCESSIBILITY:** Accessible by wheelchair; **Any limitations on vehicle usage:** Old South is located in downtown Boston, convenient to all subway lines. Parking is very limited. Commercial parking lots are located on nearby Washington Street and the Boston Common; **Hiking trails:** Old South Meeting House is located along Boston's historic Freedom Trail; **Camping:** No; **Food service:** Numerous restaurants are located in the vicinity; **Overnight accommodations:** Hotels and motels are located throughout Boston; **First Aid available in park:** Yes, limited; **Nearest Hospital:** Massachusetts General, Tufts New England Medical Center; **Days/Hours:** April 1 through Oct. 31, 9:30 a.m.-4:45 p.m. daily. Nov. 1 through March 31, weekdays 10 a.m.-4 p.m., weekends 10 a.m.-5 p.m.; **Holiday Closings:** Thanksgiving, Dec. 24, Dec. 25, and Jan. 1; **Visitor attractions closed for seasons:** No; **Weather:** Summer temperatures generally in the 80s; winter is windy with temperatures down to the teens.

NEARBY FACILITIES & POINTS OF INTEREST: Adams, Saugus Iron Works, John Fitzgerald Kennedy, Longfellow, Frederick Law Olmsted, and Salem Maritime National Historical Sites; Lowell and Minute Man National Historical Parks.

Old State House
Boston National Historical Park, Boston, MA

MAILING ADDRESS: The Old State House, 206 Washington Street, Boston, MA 02109 **Telephone:** 617-720-1713

DIRECTIONS: We recommend that you do not drive in downtown Boston; mass transit provides a good alternative. The Old State House is located at the State Street stop on the subway (Blue or Orange subway lines).

The Old State House was built in 1712/13 and served as the seat of government for both colonial and later state government. The Boston Massacre took place outside the building on March 5, 1770. James Otis eloquently argued against the Writs of Assistance within its chambers in 1761. Because of the speech, John Adams later remarked, ''Here the child independence was born.''

VISITOR ACTIVITIES: The Old State House is owned by the City of Boston and is a part of Boston National Historical Park. It is managed by The Bostonian Society (the historical society for the city of Boston). The Old State House contains a gift shop and exhibits of Boston's colonial, revolutionary, and maritime history, as well as themes of current interest. Historical talks are offered hourly. Special activities are held throughout the year and announced in Boston newspapers. Programs for school groups can be arranged by contacting the site in advance; **Fees:** Admission fee $1.25 for adults, $.75 for students and older adults, $.50 for children under 16; children under 6 and Massachusetts school children admitted free; **Visitor facilities:** There are no restrooms on the site (restrooms are available at the National Park Service Visitor Center directly across from the site); **Any limitations on vehicle usage:** The Old State House is located in downtown Boston. Parking is limited. Commercial parking lots are located on nearby Congress and Washington Streets; **Hiking trails:** Yes. The Old State House is located on Boston's historic Freedom Trail; **Camping:** No; **Food service:** There are numerous restaurants in the vicinity; **Overnight accommodations:** Hotels and motels are located throughout Boston; **First Aid available in park:** Yes, at the National Park Service Visitor Center across from the Old State House; **Nearest Hospitals:** Massachusetts General, Tufts New England Medical Center; **Days/Hours:** April 1 through Oct. 31 open daily from 9:30 a.m. until 5 p.m. Nov. 1 through March 31 open Monday through Friday 10 a.m. until 4 p.m. Saturdays 9:30 a.m. until 5 p.m. and Sundays 11 a.m. until 5 p.m. **Holiday Closings:** Thanksgiving, Dec. 25, Jan. 1, and Easter Sunday; Please Note: The Old State House is scheduled for preservation work during 1990; the building will reopen in 1991; **Visitor attractions closed for seasons:** No; **Weather:** Summer temperatures generally in the 80s; winter is windy with temperatures down to the teens.

NEARBY FACILITIES & POINTS OF INTEREST: Adams, Saugus Iron Works, John Fitzgerald Kennedy, Longfellow, Frederick Law Olmsted, and Salem Maritime National Historical Sites; Lowell and Minute Man National Historical Parks.

Paul Revere House
Boston National Historical Park, Boston, MA

MAILING ADDRESS: Paul Revere House, 19 North Square, Boston, MA 02113 **Telephone:** 617-523-1676

DIRECTIONS: We recommend that you do not drive in downtown Boston; mass transit provides a good alternative. The closest subway stop is at Haymarket Station (Orange or Green subway lines). From here cross under the elevated expressway into Boston's North End. At the tunnel entering the North End begin to follow the red line of the Freedom Trail. It is a 10-minute walk from Haymarket to the Paul Revere House.

The Paul Revere House was built around 1680 and is the oldest surviving house in Boston. Paul Revere owned the house from 1770 until 1800. It was from here that he departed on his famous "midnight ride" to warn the colonials in Lexington and Concord of the approaching British.

VISITOR ACTIVITIES: The Paul Revere House is a cooperative site of Boston National Historical Park. It is owned and managed by the Paul Revere Memorial Association. Visitors may tour the 2-story colonial house throughout the year. Staff and exhibits tell the story of Paul Revere and life in colonial Boston; **Permits:** Only for special uses. Programs for school groups or other visiting organizations can be arranged by contacting the site in advance; **Fees:** Admission fee $2 for adults, $1.50 for senior citizens and students, $.50 for children under 17. Group rates are available by reservation only; **Visitor facilities:** There are no restrooms on the site. Foreign language folders are available in Japanese, French, German, Italian, and Spanish; **HANDICAPPED ACCESSIBILITY:** First floor is accessible by wheelchair; **Any limitations on vehicle usage:** The Paul Revere House is located in Boston's crowded North End. Street parking is limited to neighborhood residents; **Hiking trails:** Yes, the Paul Revere House is located along Boston's historic Freedom Trail; **Camping:** No; **Food Service:** There are numerous restaurants in the vicinity; **Overnight accommodations:** Hotels and motels are located throughout Boston; **First Aid available in park:** Yes, limited; **Nearest Hospitals:** The closest hospital is Massachusetts General; **Days/Hours:** April 15 through Oct. 31, 9:30 a.m. until 5:15 p.m. Nov. 1 through April 14, 9:30 a.m. until 4:15 p.m.; **Holiday Closings:** Thanksgiving, Dec. 25, and Jan. 1; **Visitor attractions closed for seasons:** Closed on Mondays in Jan., Feb., and March; **Weather:** Summer temperatures generally in the 80s; winter is windy with temperatures down to the teens.

NEARBY FACILITIES & POINTS OF INTEREST: Adams, Saugus Iron Works,

John Fitzgerald Kennedy, Longfellow, Frederick Law Olmsted, and Salem Maritime National Historical Sites; Lowell and Minute Man National Historical Parks.

Salem Maritime National Historic Site
Salem, Massachusetts

MAILING ADDRESS: Superintendent, Salem Maritime National Historic Site, Custom House, Derby Street, Salem, MA 01970 **Telephone:** 508-745-1470

DIRECTIONS: There are 2 visitor centers. One is across the street from Custom House, 178 Derby Street, Salem, 20 miles (32 km) northeast of Boston. A new visitor center is on Essex Street in Museum Place Mall.

This waterfront Site is a cross-section of the Port of Salem from the years when Salem ships were opening American trade with ports of the Far East. Nine acres of wharves and grounds provide public open space on the harbor, and ten historic buildings associated with port activities complete the historic scene. Area authorized for addition to the National Park System on Mar. 17, 1938.

VISITOR ACTIVITIES: Derby Wharf, Central Wharf, Hatch's Wharf, plus yards and gardens are normally open all day, as are the 1819 Custom House and c. 1800 West India Goods Store and Bonded Warehouse. Costumed interpretation, demonstrations, or Ranger-guided tours to additional historic buildings are scheduled on a seasonal basis. School programs available by reservation. **Permits:** No; **Fees:** No, except for concessioner services. Golden Age and Golden Eagle Passports available. **Visitor facilities:** Limited parking, restrooms, visitor information, interpretive exhibits, slide show; **HANDICAPPED ACCESSIBILITY:** Parking, public restrooms behind visitor centers accessible, Custom House; Derby Wharf Historic Trail; **Any limitations on vehicle usage:** Autos are prohibited on the historic roadway; **Hiking trails:** 1-mile (1.6-km) (round trip) Derby Wharf Historic Trail. **Backcountry:** No; **Camping:** No; **Other overnight accommodations on site:** No; **Meals served in the park:** No; **Food and supplies obtainable in the park:** No; **Food and supplies obtainable nearby:** Yes, in downtown Salem, within ½ mile (.8 km); **Overnight accommodations:** Downtown Salem, within ½ mile (.8 km); **First Aid available in park:** Yes; **Nearest Hospital:** Salem, 1½ mile (2.4 km); **Days/Hours:** Custom House open daily, 8:30 a.m.-5 p.m. Check here for hours of other structures; **Holiday Closings:** Thanksgiving, Dec. 25, and Jan. 1; **Visitor attractions closed for seasons:** Tour routes and structures visited may vary with season; **Weather:** There is a great weather and temperature range. Weather can be windy or snowy in winter, with temperatures from 0°F; sunny or rainy summer days and temperatures ranging as high as 90°F.

TRAVEL ACCESS: Bus: Mass. Bay Transit Authority provides service approximately hourly from Haymarket Square, Boston, to New Derby St., ¼ mi. (.4 km) west of Site; **Rail:** Mass. Bay Transit Authority provides service from North Station, Boston to Salem Depot, ½ mile (.8 km) east of Site; **Air:** Airlines serving Boston; **Other:** Taxis, available within city. Also rental cars within city. Private car: Traffic can be heavy and parking limited in City. Walking is best way to get around City. Bicycle travel is convenient, but traffic is heavy.

NEARBY FACILITIES & POINTS OF INTEREST: Hotel/Motel: Hawthorne Inn, 18 Washington Square, Salem, 617-744-4080, ¼ mile (.4 km) from Site; **Campgrounds:** Nearest State campgrounds: Harold Parker State Forest, North Reading, MA 617-686-3391, approximately 10 miles (16 km); **New information:** Special events for summer and school vacation include visitor participation.

Saugus Iron Works National Historic Site
Saugus, Massachusetts

MAILING ADDRESS: Superintendent, Saugus Iron Works National Historic Site, 244 Central Street, Saugus, MA 01906 **Telephone:** 617-233-0050

DIRECTIONS: Take the "Main Street Saugus" exit from Route 1, which brings you into Saugus Center. Park 2 blocks from Saugus Center: 244 Central Street.

This reconstruction of the first integrated iron works in North America, begun in 1646, includes the Iron Works House, furnace, forge, and rolling and slitting mill. Authorized for addition to the National Park System on April 5, 1968.

VISITOR ACTIVITIES: Photography, walking tours, exhibits, film; **Permits:** No; **Fees:** No; **Visitor facilities:** Visitors can tour the Site and museum and watch demonstrations of iron workings; **HANDICAPPED ACCESSIBILITY:** Restrooms, and Museum; **Any limitations on vehicle usage:** No; **Meals served in the park:** No; **Food and supplies obtainable in the park:** No; **Food and supplies obtainable nearby:** Yes, at Saugus Center, 2 blocks; **Overnight accommodations:** On Route 1, 1 mile (1.6 km) from the Site; **First Aid available in park:** Yes; **Nearest Hospital:** Wakefield, Lynn; **Days/Hours:** Open daily from 9 a.m. to 4 p.m. from Nov. 1 through March 31 and from 9 a.m. to 5 p.m. from April 1 to Oct. 31; **Holiday Closings:** Thanksgiving, Dec. 25, and Jan. 1; **Visitor attractions closed for season:** No; **Weather:** Humid in summer, cold in winter. This is an outdoor facility so visitors should dress for inclement weather.

GENERAL INFORMATION: *For Your Safety*—Be careful around the waterwheel pits and do not climb on the waterwheels or other historic structures. The slag can cause severe cuts.

Springfield Armory National Historic Site
Springfield, Massachusetts

MAILING ADDRESS: Superintendent, Springfield Armory National Historic Site, One Armory Square, Springfield, MA 01105 **Telephone:** 413-734-8551

DIRECTIONS: The Site is in downtown Springfield, MA, just off State Street. To reach the site from the Massachusetts Turnpike take exit 6 to Route I-291, then exit 3 to Armory Street south to Federal Street. From I-91, exit on I-291 eastbound (follow signs to Boston); take Armory St. exit; thereafter, same directions as above. The Site is entered through the gate on Federal Street.

Over a span of 200 years this small-arms manufacturing center produced weapons ranging from the 1795 flintlock to the 1903, M1 and M14 rifles. A large collection of small arms is maintained here. Authorized for addition to the National Park System on Oct. 26, 1974.

VISITOR ACTIVITIES: Self-guiding museum tours, guided tours by advance arrangement; **Permits:** No; **Fees:** No; **Visitor facilities:** Museum, restrooms; **HANDICAPPED ACCESSIBILITY:** Entire museum is wheelchair accessible, including restrooms; **Any limitations on vehicle usage:** No; **Hiking trails:** No; **Backcountry:** No; **Camping:** No; **Other overnight accommodations on site:** No; **Meals served in the park:** No; **Food and supplies obtainable in the park:** No; **Food and supplies obtainable nearby:** Yes, in Springfield; **Overnight accommodations:** Springfield, within walking distance; **First Aid available in park:** No; **Nearest Hospital:** Springfield, directly across from the museum; **Days/Hours:**

Open daily from 9:00 a.m. to 5:00 p.m. year-round; **Holiday Closings:** Thanksgiving, Dec. 25, and Jan. 1; **Weather:** Typical New England conditions prevail.

USS Constitution
Boston National Historical Park, Boston, MA

See Charlestown Navy Yard.

Visitor Center
Boston National Historical Park, Boston, MA

MAILING ADDRESS: Superintendent, Boston National Historical Park, Charlestown Navy Yard, Boston, MA 02129 **Telephone:** 617-242-5644

DIRECTIONS: The Visitor Center is located at 15 State Street in downtown Boston across from the Old State House. We recommend that you don't drive in downtown Boston; mass transit provides a good alternative. The Visitor Center is located at the State Street stop on the subway (Blue or Orange subway lines).

The Visitor Center provides information on the Boston area and beyond, as well as an orientation to the historic sites and services of Boston National Historical Park. The Park includes the Old South Meeting House, the Old State House, Faneuil Hall, the Paul Revere House, Old North Church, the Bunker Hill Monument, the Charlestown Navy Yard, and Dorchester Heights. The Center also provides information on Boston African American National Historic Site.

VISITOR ACTIVITIES: Park Rangers provide information on the park and facilities in the Boston area. A bookstore carries titles on Boston history, the American Revolution, U.S. maritime history, Black History, and travel in New England. A 7-minute slide program on Boston's historic Freedom Trail is available throughout the day. Ranger-led walks along the Freedom Trail originate from the Visitor Center. Walks, lasting 90 minutes, depart daily from mid-April through Nov.; **Permits:** Only for special usage. Special services for school or other visiting groups can be arranged by contacting the site in advance; **Fees:** No; **Visitor facilities:** Restrooms are available; **HANDICAPPED ACCESSIBILITY:** Completely accessible by wheelchair; **Any limitations on vehicle usage:** The Visitor Center is located in downtown Boston. Street parking is limited. Commercial parking lots are located on nearby Congress and Washington Streets; **Hiking trails:** The Visitor Center is located along Boston's historic Freedom Trail; **Camping:** No; **Food service:** There are numerous restaurants in the vicinity; **Overnight accommodations:** Hotels and motels are located throughout Boston; **First Aid available in park:** Yes; **Nearest Hospitals:** Massachusetts General, Tufts New England Medical Center; **Days/Hours:** Open daily from 9 a.m. until 5 p.m. on weekends, 8 a.m. until 5 p.m. on weekdays; **Holiday Closings:** Thanksgiving, Dec. 25, and Jan. 1; **Visitor attractions closed for seasons:** No; **Weather:** Summer temperatures generally in the 80s; winter is windy with temperatures down to the teens.

NEARBY FACILITIES & POINTS OF INTEREST: Adams, Saugus Iron Works, John Fitzgerald Kennedy, Longfellow, Frederick Law Olmsted, and Salem Maritime National Historical Sites; Lowell and Minute Man National Historical Parks.

Michigan

ISLE ROYALE NATIONAL PARK

PICTURED ROCKS NATIONAL LAKESHORE

FATHER MARQUETTE
NATIONAL MEMORIAL

SLEEPING BEAR DUNES
NATIONAL LAKESHORE

Detroit

Father Marquette National Memorial and Museum
St. Ignace, Michigan

MAILING ADDRESS: Straits State Park, 720 Church Street, St. Ignace, MI 49781 **Telephone:** 906-643-9394 or 906-643-8620

DIRECTIONS: The Memorial to Father Jacques Marquette, French priest and explorer, is in Straits State Park near St. Ignace, MI, where he founded a Jesuit mission in 1671 and was buried in 1678. A Memorial structure, restrooms, picnic area, parking lots, foottrails, overlook, and kiosks have been completed. The museum-theatre building and an amphitheatre are now completed and in use. This affiliated area was authorized for addition to the National Park System on Dec. 20, 1975.

Isle Royale National Park
Houghton, Michigan   **SEE CLIMATABLE NO. 21**

MAILING ADDRESS: Superintendent, Isle Royale National Park, 87 North Ripley St., Houghton, MI 49931 **Telephone:** 906-482-0984

DIRECTIONS: Transportation from the mainland to Isle Royale is by boat or float-plane. Reservations are recommended. Boats go from Houghton to Rock Harbor from June to Sept. For schedules, rates, and reservations for the National Park Service boat, *Ranger III*, contact the Superintendent, Isle Royale National Park, Houghton, MI 49931, phone 906-482-0984. From Copper Harbor to Rock Harbor (late June to late Sept.), contact Isle Royale Queen II,

Copper Harbor, MI 49918, phone 906-289-4437 (mid-June to Aug.) and 906-482-4950 (Sept. to mid-June). From Grand Portage, MN, to Windigo (late June to Labor Day) and Grand Portage to Rock Harbor via Windigo (May to Oct.), contact GPIR Transportation Lines, 1332 London Rd., Duluth, MN 55801, phone 218-728-1237 year-round. The *Voyageur II* circumnavigates Isle Royale and will discharge and pick up passengers at various points. Isle Royale Seaplane Service operates from Houghton, phone 906-482-8850 (summer).

The largest archipelago in Lake Superior, this forested "island" is distinguished for its wilderness character, timber wolves and moose, historic commercial fisheries, and pre-Columbian copper mines. Isle Royale was authorized for addition to the National Park System on Mar. 3, 1931.

VISITOR ACTIVITIES: Boating (rentals at Windigo and Rock Harbor Lodge), boat tours, hiking, scuba diving, camping, fishing, wildlife-watching, canoeing, big lake kayaking, interpretive programs; **Permits:** For camping, permits available at Rock Harbor and Windigo; **Fees:** No entrance fee; **Visitor facilities:** Boat tours, rental boats and motors, water taxi service, hiking trails, campgrounds, guided fishing trips, self-guiding trails, interpretive programs, full services and facilities available mid-June to Aug. 31, limited services and facilities at other times; **HANDICAPPED ACCESSIBILTY:** Contact park office for free brochure describing current accessibility; **Limitations on vehicle usage:** No vehicles of any type are allowed on the island as there are no roads; **Hiking trails:** 167 miles (267.2 km) of foot trails; **Backcountry:** 98% Federal Wilderness. A number of combination trips—boat one way and hike the other—can be arranged with commercial boat operators (note phone numbers above); **Camping:** Yes. Campsites cannot be reserved. All campers must obtain a camping permit, available at Rock Harbor or Windigo; **Other overnight accommodations on site:** Yes. Lodge and housekeeping facilities are available from late June through Labor Day. For reservations and rates during the seasons, contact Rock Harbor Lodge, P.O. Box 405, Houghton, MI 49931, phone 906-337-4993; out of season, contact National Park Concessions, Inc., Mammoth Cave, KY 42259, phone 502-773-2191; **Meals served in the park:** Yes. Restaurant service is available at Rock Harbor; **Food and supplies obtainable in the park:** Yes. (Limited) supplies at Rock Harbor and Windigo; **Food and supplies obtainable nearby:** Yes. Obtainable in Houghton, MI, and Grand Portage, MN; **Overnight accommodations:** Houghton, MI 60 miles (96 km) and Grand Portage, MN, 20 miles (32 km); **First Aid available in park:** Yes. Ranger Stations; **Nearest Hospital:** Houghton, MI. Note: Evacuation from the island is done at the cost of the visitor; **Days/Hours:** The Park is open to visitors from April 16 to Oct. 31, with full services offered mid June to Aug. 31. Call or write for current information prior to your visit; **Visitor attractions closed for seasons:** Park is closed Nov. 1-April 15; **Weather:** Mid-summer temperatures rarely exceed 80°; evenings are usually cool. Rain is frequent throughout the season.

GENERAL INFORMATION: Because Lake Superior is often rough, it is not safe to use boats of 20 feet or less to go to the island; however, such boats can be transported to Isle Royale on the *Ranger III*. The concession boat operators mentioned above will transport small runabouts and canoes. Fuel may be purchased at Rock Harbor and Windigo. Firearms, pets, and wheeled vehicles are prohibited in the Park.

Lake Survey Chart 14976, "Isle Royale," is recommended for anyone navigating the Park's waters. This chart and others can be purchased from the Park. A topographic map of Isle Royale can also be purchased at the Park.

North Country National Scenic Trail
For details see listing in New York

Pictured Rocks National Lakeshore
Munising, Michigan

MAILING ADDRESS: Superintendent, Pictured Rocks National Lakeshore, P.O. Box 40, Munising, MI 49862 **Telephone:** 906-387-3700 or 906-387-2607

DIRECTIONS: Pictured Rocks Cliffs are accessible by car at Miners Castle, 7 miles (11.2 km) east of Munising off County Road H-58. The Munising Information Center, located at the intersection of M-28 and H-58 in Munising, is operated jointly by the National Park Service and the U.S. Forest Service and is open year-round. The Interpretive Center is at Munising Falls, 2.5 miles (4 km) east of Munising; it is open daily in the summer. The headquarters building is at Sand Point, 2 miles (3.2 km) further and is open Monday through Friday, year-round. Grand Sable Visitor Center, 1 mile (1.6 km) west of Grand Marais, is open daily in summer. The Grand Marais Maritime Museum, located in Grand Marais on Coast Guard Point, is open daily in the summer and on an intermittent basis during the remainder of the year.

Multicolored sandstone cliffs, broad beaches, sand dunes, waterfalls, inland lakes, ponds, marshes, hardwood and coniferous forests, and numerous birds and animals comprise this scenic area on Lake Superior. This is the first national lakeshore, authorized for addition to the National Park System on Oct. 15, 1966.

VISITOR ACTIVITIES: Besides accessibility at the rock promontory called Miners Castle, the cliffs are visible from the Lakeshore Trail or by boat. Commercially operated scenic cruises are conducted daily in the summer from the city dock in Munising. Visitor activities include sightseeing, picnicking, scuba diving, camping, sunbathing, hiking, and photography. The water temperature of Lake Superior is normally too cold for all but the most hardy swimmers. Common throughout the area are inland lakes, ponds, streams, waterfalls and bogs, providing educational and recreational potential in the form of boating, fishing, hunting, and swimming. Winter activities include many miles of snowmobile trails and over 17 miles (27.2 km) of groomed and maintained cross-country ski trails in the Munising and Grand Marais areas. Snowshoeing and winter camping are also enjoyed in this winter wonderland. **Permits:** Backcountry camping permits required, available from visitor centers; **Fees:** Yes, there is a fee for privately operated scenic boat cruises on Lake Superior; fee for vehicle accessible campgrounds; **Visitor facilities:** Nature walks and campfire programs in summer; see schedule at camping areas and Ranger Stations; **HANDICAPPED ACCESSIBILITY:** Restrooms, parking, grills, and picnic tables; a half-mile (.8 km) handicapped accessible nature trail is located at Sand Point. Handicapped accessible campsites are available at the three campgrounds. They are held for use by handicapped persons until 6 p.m. each day. Additional campgrounds are in nearby Lake Superior State Forest and Hiawatha National Forest; **Any limitations on vehicle usage:** Vehicles and snowmobiles are restricted to designated roadways; **Hiking trails:** Yes, a 43 mile (68.8 km) lakeshore trail plus day use trails; **Backcountry camping:** Yes, permitted at backcountry campgrounds; **Camping:** Yes, camping areas accessible by auto at Hurricane River, Little Beaver Lake, and Twelvemile Beach; **Other overnight accommodations on site:** No; **Meals served in the park:** No; **Food and supplies obtainable in the park:** No; **Food and supplies obtainable nearby:** Yes, Munising and Grand Marais, MI; **Overnight accommodations:** Munising, County Road H-58; Grand Marais, State Highway M-77; **First Aid available in park:** Yes; **Nearest Hospital:** Munising, at west end of the park; **Days/Hours:** Open 24 hours a day, year-round; **Holiday Closings:** No; **Visitor attractions closed for seasons:** No; **Weather:** Over 200 inches of snow falls in winter. Summer is usually pleasant and warm.

GENERAL INFORMATION: *For Your Safety*—Hikers should be especially cautious when near the steep cliffs of the Pictured Rocks. Boaters should note that Lake Superior is always cold and frequently rough. Only boaters with proper equipment should venture on this lake. Summer visitors should be prepared for occasional cold, rainy weather and troublesome insects. Pets not permitted in backcountry; must be on leash in other areas.

TRAVEL ACCESS: Air: American Airlines and Mesaba Airlines provide service into Marquette, MI, and Escanaba, MI.

Sleeping Bear Dunes National Lakeshore
Empire, Michigan

MAILING ADDRESS: Superintendent, Sleeping Bear Dunes National Lakeshore. P.O. Box 277, Empire, MI 49630 **Telephone:** 616-326-5134

DIRECTIONS: The Visitor Center and Headquarters are located in a combined facility in Empire, MI. The facility is accessible by Hwy M-22 from Leland and Frankfort, MI, and M-72 from Traverse City, MI.
     Beaches, massive sand dunes, forests, and inland lakes are outstanding characteristics of the major mainland portion and the 2 offshore Manitou Islands. Authorized for addition to the National Park System on Oct. 21, 1970.

VISITOR ACTIVITIES: Bird- and wildlife-watching, fishing, camping, primitive camping, hiking, interpretive programs, canoeing, swimming, cross-country skiing; **Permits:** Michigan fishing and hunting license required; available at local outlets. Free backcountry camping permits required; available from local Rangers; **Fees:** $8 per night campground fee at Platte River and D.H. Day Campgrounds; **Visitor facilities:** Maritime museum, campgrounds, interpretive programs, canoe rentals, beaches, trails; **HANDICAPPED ACCESSIBILITY:** For mobility impaired: Parking and restrooms at Museum, Visitor Center, Pierce Stocking Scenic Drive; restrooms at Dune Climb and Great Lakes Picnic Area; ramp to one overlook at Lake Michigan overlook; dunes overlook and North Bar Lake overlook are accessible; station house exhibit at Maritime Museum not accessible; with assistance, wheelchair users can take ferry and motorized tour of South Manitou Island; Platte River and D.H. Day Campgrounds each have 1 accessible campsite and adjacent toilet. For visually impaired: Large relief map available; Ranger-led walks, guide dogs allowed everywhere; For hearing impaired: Maritime Museum has captioned video; captioning for slide program at Visitor Center; **Any limitations on vehicle usage:** All vehicles must remain on designated roads. Snowmobiles are restricted to county roads; **Hiking trails:** Yes, trails lead through forests and dune areas; **Backcountry:** Yes; **Camping:** Yes, no reservations are available for campsites; **Other overnight accommodations on site:** No; **Meals served in the park:** Yes, snacks at Dune Climb season; **Food and supplies obtainable in the park:** Yes; **Food and supplies obtainable nearby:** Yes, just outside the park and in Empire, Glen Arbor, and Platte River campground area; **Overnight accommodations:** Glen Arbor, MI 22, 1 mile (1.6 km); Empire, MI 22; Honor, US 31, 6 miles (9.6 km); Frankfort, MI 22, 12 miles (19.2 km); **First Aid available in park:** Yes; **Nearest Hospital:** Traverse City, MI 72, 30 miles (48 km); **Days/Hours:** Lakeshore open all year. Visitor Center open from 9 a.m. to 4 p.m. daily; **Holiday Closings:** Thanksgiving, Dec. 25; **Visitor attractions closed for seasons:** Maritime museum closed Nov.-Apr. Campgrounds are open year around with limited winter facilities (no water). **Weather:** Is tempered by Lake Michigan.

GENERAL INFORMATION: *A Safety Note:* Steep lakeshore bluffs are hazardous to climb and descend due to landslides and slumpage. On Lake Michigan, weather conditions can change drastically in a short time. If you are boating, be aware of the weather forecast and carry appropriate safety equipment. Avalanche conditions exist on steep, exposed slopes after heavy snows and/or strong winds. Hikers and cross-country skiers take caution.

TRAVEL ACCESS: Air: Simmons, Northwest Airlines, and Midstates Airlines service Traverse City.

Minnesota

VOYAGEURS NATIONAL PARK

GRAND PORTAGE
NATIONAL MONUMENT

SAINT CROIX
NATIONAL SCENIC RIVERWAY

LOWER ST.CROIX
NATIONAL SCENIC RIVERWAY

PIPESTONE
NATIONAL MONUMENT

Grand Portage National Monument
Grand Portage, Minnesota

MAILING ADDRESS: Superintendent, Grand Portage National Monument, P.O. Box 668, Grand Marais, MN 55604 **Telephone:** 218-387-2788

DIRECTIONS: The monument is located off US Highway 61, 36 miles (57.6 km) northeast of Grand Marais, MN, 145 miles (232 km) from Duluth, MN, and 45 miles (72 km) southwest of the Canadian city of Thunder Bay, Ontario. The Grand Portage bisects the reservation of the Grand Portage Band of the Minnesota Chippewa Tribe.

This 8.5 mile (13.6 km) portage was a rendezvous for traders and trappers on a principal route of Indians, explorers, missionaries, and fur traders into the Northwest. The fur trade depot and summer headquarters of the North West Company has been reconstructed here. Designated Sept. 15, 1951.

VISITOR ACTIVITIES: Reconstruction of historic buildings; guided tours, exhibits, demonstrations, audiovisual programs, hiking, cross-country skiing, primitive camping, picnicking; **Permits:** For backcountry, can be obtained at the Monument; **Fees:** Yes; **Visitor facilities:** Cultural Center, parking, picnic area, hiking/cross-country ski trail; **Any limitations on vehicle usage:** No; **Hiking trails:** Yes, Mount Rose Trail is ½ mile (.8 km) long. The Grand Portage leads to the Site of Fort Charlotte, 8.5 miles (13.6 km) away; **Backcountry:** Yes, information can be obtained at the Monument or at Headquarters; **Camping:** No, nearby; **Other overnight accommodations on site:** No; **Meals served in the park:** No, nearby; **Food and supplies obtainable in the park:** No; **Food and supplies obtainable nearby:** Yes, Grand Portage, Grand Marais, Thunder Bay; **Overnight accommodations:** Nearby lodge, and motels along Lake Superior shore. Contact the Park for a list of nearby accommodations; **First Aid available in park:** Yes; **Nearest Hospital:** Grand Marais, MN, US 61, 36 miles (57.6 km); **Days/Hours:** Open daily from 8 a.m. to 5 p.m., mid-May to mid-Oct.; **Holiday Closings:** No; **Visitor attractions closed for seasons:** Stockade closed from mid-Oct. through mid-May. Other areas open all year; **Weather:** Summer weather can be cool and windy along the shore.

GENERAL INFORMATION: The portage hike requires sturdy hiking shoes and a willingness to endure the discomforts of the trail, which include mud, rocks, mosquitoes and flies. Hikers should remember that emergency assistance is a long way off. A boat leaves daily from the dock for Isle Royale National Park, located 22 miles (35.2 km) offshore (see listing in this book). Beware of uneven ground and irregular steps while visiting Grand Portage. Watch your children near the water; Lake Superior is extremely cold.

TRAVEL ACCESS: Bus: Triangle Transportation provides daily service within 1 mile (1.6 km) of Park; **Rail:** No (Nearest U.S. service in Duluth); **Air:** No (Nearest U.S. service in Duluth); **Other:** Bicycle, hiking, boat, and canoe.

NEARBY FACILITIES & POINTS OF INTEREST: Hotel/Motel: Grand Portage Lodge, Grand Portage, MN 55605, 218-475-2401, 1 mile (1.6 km); **Food/Supplies:** Grand Portage Trading Post, Grand Portage, MN 55605, 218-475-2282, .2 mile (.3 km); **Campgrounds:** Grand Portage Campground, Grand Portage, MN 55605, 218-475-2249, 1 mile (1.6 km); **Parks, other points of interest:** Witch Tree, Mt. Josephine, High Falls.

Mississippi National River and Recreation Area
Omaha, Nebraska

MAILING ADDRESS: Mississippi National River and Recreation Area, c/o Midwest Region National Park Service, 1709 Jackson Street, Omaha, NE 68102. Contact: Alan Hutchings, Interim Site Manager **Telephone:** 402-221-3481

Now open to visitors.

This 69-mile segment of the Mississippi River and adjacent lands from **Dayton to Hastings, Minnesota, includes the entire Minneapolis-St. Paul** metropolitan critical area river corridor. The area encompasses natural and historical features, as well as modern industrial and commercial characteristics and a variety of cultural ethnic amenities, all of which combine to tell the story of the Mighty Mississippi.

Established: Nov. 18, 1988. Acreage: Approximately 50,000, all but about 60 acres are nonfederal.

Pipestone National Monument
Pipestone, Minnesota

MAILING ADDRESS: Superintendent, Pipestone National Monument, P.O. Box 727, Pipestone, MN 56154 **Telephone:** 507-825-5464

DIRECTIONS: The 283-acre park is adjacent to the north side of the city of Pipestone, in southwest Minnesota, near Sioux Falls, SD. Pipestone can be reached by US 75, and MN 23 and 30. A State Information Center is at Beaver Creek, directly off Interstate 90.

For at least three centuries Indians have obtained materials at this guarry for making ceremonial peace pipes. Established by act of Congress on August 25, 1937.

VISITOR ACTIVITIES: Besides the interesting geology, history, archaeology, and the pipestone crafts, the park offers an opportunity to observe and appreciate the natural environment. Picnicking is available; **Permits:** No; **Fees:** Entrance Fee $1 per person; **Visitor facilities:** Interpretive exhibits, audiovisual program, Indian Cultural Center, souvenir sales; **HANDI-CAPPED ACCESSIBILITY:** Parking, restrooms (main building and picnic area), trail, and Visitor Center exhibits. **Any limitations on vehicle usage:** No; **Hiking trails:** Yes, a ¾ mile (1.2 km) self-guiding trail leads past the quarries and other points of interest; **Backcountry:** No; **Camping:** No; **Other overnight accommodations on site:** No, overnight camping and recreational facilities are available nearby at Split Rock Creek State Park, Route 2, Jasper, MN 56144, phone 507-348-7908, located on MN 23, south of Pipestone; and at Blue Mounds State Park, Route 1, Luverne, MN 56144, phone 507-283-4892, located on US 75, south of Pipestone. No reservations are available for campsites, contact the Parks for further information. Check with Park Rangers at Pipestone for locations of private campgrounds and other overnight facilities; **Meals served in the park:** No; **Food and supplies obtainable in the park:** No; **Food and supplies obtainable nearby:** Yes, at Pipestone; **Overnight accommodations:** Pipestone, 1 mile (1.6 km); **First Aid available in park:** Yes; **Nearest Hospital:** Pipestone, 1 mile (1.6 km); **Days/Hours:** Visitor and Cultural Center are open from 8 a.m. to 6 p.m. Mon.-Thurs.: 8 a.m.-8 p.m. Fri.-Sun. Memorial Day to Labor Day and from 8 a.m. to 5 p.m. the rest of the year; **Holiday Closings:** Dec. 25 and Jan. 1; **Weather:** Summer is hot and humid; spring and fall are cool and pleasant; winter brings severe cold, strong winds and possible blizzards.

GENERAL INFORMATION: Visitors should see Winnewisa Falls, one of the stops on the scenic trail.

TRAVEL ACCESS: Rail: No; **Air:** United, NWA, Delta and TWA provide daily service to Sioux Falls, SD.

Voyageurs National Park
International Falls, Minnesota   **SEE CLIMATABLE NO. 22**

MAILING ADDRESS: Superintendent, Voyageurs National Park, HCR 9, Box 600, International Falls, MN 56649 **Telephone:** 218-283-9821

DIRECTIONS: The periphery of the Park is easily approached by surfaced roads from four points along US 53 when traveling from Duluth. County Rte. 23-24 from Orr leads to Crane Lake at the eastern end of the Park; County Rte. 129, or Ash River Trail, provides access to Namakan Lake; County Rte. 122, south of International Falls, provides access to the South shore of Lake Kabetogama; MN 11, from International Falls, approaches the Park area at Black Bay. There are no roads beyond the edge of the Park; access is by power-boat, canoe, or floatplane, hiking in summer and snowmobiling and cross-country skiing in winter.

Once the route of French-Canadian voyageurs, scenic northern lakes are surrounded by forest in this historic and geologically important area. Authorized for addition to the National Park System on Jan. 8, 1971; established on April 8, 1975.

VISITOR ACTIVITIES: Fishing, power boating, canoeing, camping, hiking, swimming, cross-country skiing, snowmobiling; **Permits:** No; **Fees:** No; **Visitor facilities:** Visitor Centers, naturalist-guided boat, canoe and hiking tours, campsites, boat ramps, boat and canoe rental, food, and lodging are available at nearby resorts outside of the park; **HANDICAPPED AC-CESSIBILITY:** Both Visitor Centers are accessible, including restrooms and parking; Rainy Lake Visitor Center's hiking trail is accessible for ½ mile (.8 km) of its 1-mile (1.6-km) length; **Any limitations on vehicle usage:** Yes, there are only 3 miles (4.8 km) of road in the Park. Access in the summer is by watercraft, floatplane, or hiking; in the winter, by ice road, snowmobile, ski plane, skiing, or snowshoeing; **Hiking trails:** Yes, there are about 25 miles (40 km) of trails, which must be reached by watercraft or floatplane; **Backcountry:** Yes, contact Headquarters for details; **Camping:** Yes, 100 primitive campsites (accessible only by boat or floatplane) are scattered throughout the Park, mostly on the major lakes; **Other overnight accommodations on site:** Yes, Kettle Falls Hotel; **Meals served in the park:** Yes, Kettle Falls Hotel; **Food and supplies obtainable in the park:** No; **Food and supplies obtainable nearby:** Yes, in International Falls, Rainy Lake, Kabetogama, Ash River, Orr, and Crane Lake; **Overnight accommodations:** International Falls, Rainy Lake, Kabetogama, Crane Lake, Ash River, Orr; **First Aid available in park:** Yes, Park Rangers on duty; **Nearest Hospital:** International Falls, Littlefork, Cook; **Days/Hours:** Park open year-round. Access is limited during lake freeze-up and ice-out periods, contact Headquarters for Visitor Center hours; **Holiday Closings:** No; **Weather:** Summer temperatures range from 50° to 90°F; winter, − 30° to 30°F.

GENERAL INFORMATION: Some of the land is privately owned, and there are many private cottages. Please respect the rights of these property holders. Boaters not familiar with the waters should obtain the services of a guide or use charts, both of which are available locally. The large lakes can suddenly become very rough. Keep informed about weather conditions. Users of small boats and canoes should be particularly cautious and should be prepared to wait out rough water. State boating regulations apply.

TRAVEL ACCESS: Bus: Triangle Transportation Company provides daily service to International Falls, Orr; **Rail:** Amtrak offers service to Duluth, MN; **Air:** Norhwest Airlines offers daily service to International Falls, MN; **Other:** Many resorts provide taxi service from bus or airline to their resort near the Park. Floatplanes provide access to the park from International Falls.

Mississippi

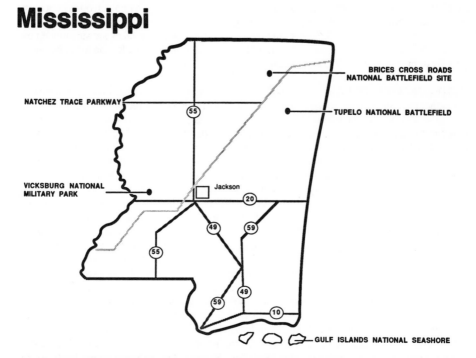

Brices Cross Roads National Battlefield Site
Baldwyn, Mississippi

MAILING ADDRESS: Superintendent, Natchez Trace Parkway, R.R. 1, NT-143, Tupelo, MS 38801 **Telephone:** 601-842-1572

DIRECTIONS: The Site is about 6 miles (9.6 km) west of Baldwyn on MS 370.

The Confederate cavalry, under Gen. Nathan Bedford Forrest, was employed with extraordinary skill here during the battle of June 10, 1864. One hundred and two known Confederate dead are buried in the adjacent Bethany Church cemetery. Established by act of Congress on Feb. 21, 1929.

VISITOR ACTIVITIES: The Park consists of one acre of land, but much of the scene of action is within view. Monuments and markers provide interpretation; **Permits:** No; **Fees:** No; **Visitor facilities:** No; **HANDICAPPED ACCESSIBILITY:** Area not accessible; **Any limitations on vehicle usage:** No; **Hiking trails:** No; **Meals served in the park:** No; **Food and supplies obtainable in the park:** No; **Food and supplies obtainable nearby:** Yes, in Tupelo; **Overnight accommodations:** Tupelo, US 45, 25 miles (40 km); Booneville, US 45, 13 miles (20.8 km); **First Aid available in park:** No, but nearby in Baldwyn, US 45; **Nearest Hospital:** Tupelo, South Gloster Street, 25 miles (40 km); **Days/Hours:** Open year-round; **Holiday Closings:** No.

Gulf Island National Seashore
For details see listing in Florida

Natchez National Historical Park
Natchez, Mississippi

MAILING ADDRESS: Superintendent, Natchez National Historical Park, P.O. Box 1208, Natchez, MS 39121 **Telephone:** 601-442-7047

DIRECTIONS: The park is within the city limits of Natchez, Mississippi and currently consists of two sites. Melrose a *ca.* 1845 antebellum estate, is located at 1 Melrose-Montebello Parkway off Sergeant Prentiss Drive (U.S. Hwy. 61 and 84). The William Johnson House complex, the *ca.* 1841 home of free black William Johnson, is located in downtown Natchez at 210 State Street.

The park, still in the very early stages of development, was created to "preserve and interpret the history of Natchez, Mississippi as a significant city in the history of the American South." In the decades leading up to the Civil War, Natchez became a commercial, cultural, and social center of the South's "cotton belt" with power and wealth unparalleled by other southern towns of comparable size. The city of Natchez today represents a well-preserved collection of significant antebellum properties. Established October 7, 1988.

VISITOR ACTIVITIES: Guided house tours, garden tours in season, interpretive walks and talks, school programs: **Permits:** No; **Fees:** Yes, for guided tours of Melrose mansion; **Visitor Facilities:** Restrooms, parking at Melrose, picnicking at Melrose, cooperating association bookstore; **HANDICAPPED ACCESSIBILITY:** Limited at present, but improvements are planned; **Any limitations on vehicle usage:** No; **Hiking Trails:** No; **Backcountry:** No; **Camping:** No; **Other overnight accommodations on site:** No; **Meals served in the park:** No; **Food and Supplies obtainable in the park:** No; **Food and supplies obtainable nearby:** Yes, at numerous locations in Natchez; **Overnight accommodations:** Natchez; **First Aid availble in park:** Basic only; **Nearest Hospital:** Jefferson Davis Memorial Hospital in Natchez, 1.5 miles (2.4 km); **Days/Hours:** Open daily from 8:30 a.m. to 5:00 p.m.; **Holiday Closings:** December 25; **Visitor attractions closed for seasons:** No; **Weather:** Spring—sunny and mild; summer—hot and humid; fall—sunny and mild; winter—mild with occasional subfreezing weather.

TRAVEL ACCESS: Bus: Greyhound; **Rail:** No; **Air:** No.

NEARBY FACILITIES & POINTS OF INTEREST. Natchez has numerous other historic homes, districts, and sites, many of which are open to the public. For additional information contact: Natchez Visitor and Convention Bureau: 1-800-647-6724.

Natchez Trace Parkway
Tupelo, Mississippi
(Also in Alabama and Tennesee)

MAILING ADDRESS: Superintendent, Natchez Trace Parkway, R.R. 1, NT-143, Tupelo, MS 38801 **Telephone:** 601-842-1572

DIRECTIONS: The Tupelo Visitor Center is 5 miles (8 km) north of Tupelo at the intersection of Natchez Trace Parkway and Bus. US 45 North.

This historic route generally follows the old Indian trace, or trail, between Nashville, TN, and Natchez, MS. 414 miles (662 km) of the planned 445 miles (712 km) are completed. Established by act of Congress on May 18, 1938.

VISITOR ACTIVITIES: Hiking, walking, auto tours, camping, swimming, boating, horseback riding, exhibits, biking, interpretive film, fishing, running and jogging, Ranger talks, crafts festival in fall; **Permits:** No; **Fees:** No; **Visitor facilities:** Visitor Center, interpretive film, hiking trails, campgrounds, picnic areas, boat ramp; **HANDICAPPED ACCESSIBILITY:** Most restrooms are accessible, as are all parking areas at Visitor/Contact stations. Trails are not accessible; **Any limitations on vehicle usage:** Hauling and commercial trucking are not permitted. Tent and trailer camping are permitted only at authorized campgrounds; **Hiking trails:** Yes, nature and hiking trails up to 4.6 miles (7.4 km) long; **Backcountry:** No; **Camping:** Yes, campgrounds are at Rocky Springs, Jeff Busby, and Meriwether Lewis. Campsites cannot be reserved; stays are limited to 15 days during periods of heavy visitation. You should bring insect netting and repellent. Contact the Park for detailed information on facilities at each camping area; **Other overnight accommodations on site:** No; **Meals served in the park:** No; **Food and supplies obtainable in the park:** No; **Food and supplies obtainable nearby:** Yes, at Natchez, Port Gibson, Jackson, Tupelo, Cherokee, and many other towns along the parkway; **Overnight accommodations:** Same as where food and supplies are available; **First Aid available in park:** Yes; **Nearest Hospital:** Natchez, Jackson, Kosciusko, Tupelo, Columbia, Florence; **Days/Hours:** Park open year-round, 24 hours a day. Tupelo Visitor Center open from 8 a.m. to 5 p.m. 364 days; **Holiday Closings:** Tupelo Visitor Center closed Dec. 25; **Visitor attractions closed for seasons:** No; **Weather:** Summer weather is generally hot and humid. Winter is usually cold and damp with occasional warm periods. Spring and autumn are mild and warm.

GENERAL INFORMATION: The only service station is at Jeff Busby. You can make the most of your visit by obtaining a brochure on Natchez Trace which is available by mail or at the Visitor Center. It provides detailed information of points of interest and facilities in different areas of the Parkway.

Tupelo National Battlefield
Tupelo, Mississippi

MAILING ADDRESS: Superintendent, Natchez Trace Parkway, R.R. 1, NT-143, Tupelo, MS 38801 **Telephone:** 601-842-1572

DIRECTIONS: The one-acre site is within the city limits of Tupelo, MS, on MS 6 about 1 mile (1.6 km) west of its intersection with US 45. It is 1.2 miles (1.9 km) east of the Natchez Trace Parkway.

Here, on July 13-14, 1864, Gen. Nathan Bedford Forrest's cavalry battled a Union force of 14,000 sent to keep Forrest from cutting the railroad supplying Major Gen. William T. Sherman's march on Atlanta. Created by Presidential Proclamation on Feb. 21, 1929.

VISITOR ACTIVITIES: Signs and markers provide interpretation. Information about the area is available at the Tupelo Visitor Center of the Natchez Trace Parkway; **Permits:** No; **Fees:** No; **Visitor facilities:** No; **HANDICAPPED ACCESSIBILITY:** Area not accessible; **Any limitations on vehicle usage:** No; **Hiking trails:** No; **Backcountry:** No; **Camping:** No; **Other overnight accommodations on site:** No; **Meals served in the park:** No; **Food and supplies obtainable in the park:** No; **Food and supplies obtainable nearby:** Yes, at Tupelo; **Overnight accommodations:** Tupelo; **First Aid available in park:** No; **Nearest Hospital:** Tupelo, South Gloster Street, 2 miles (3.2 km); **Days/Hours:** Park is always open.

Vicksburg National Military Park
Vicksburg, Mississippi

MAILING ADDRESS: Superintendent, Vicksburg National Military Park, 3201 Clay Street, Vicksburg, MS 39180 **Telephone:** 601-636-0583

DIRECTIONS: The Park is just inside Vicksburg on historic US 80 within 1 mile (1.6 km) of Interstate 20.
    Reconstructed fortifications of the 47-day siege of Vicksburg, which ended July 4, 1863, and 1,200 markers and monuments highlight a 16-mile (25.6 km) tour route. Victory gave the North control of the Mississippi River and cut the Confederacy in two. Vicksburg National Cemetery, containing about 17,000 Union graves, is within the Park. Confederate dead lie in the city cemetery. The restored ironclad gunboat, *U.S.S. Cairo* and the Cairo Museum, which features artifacts recovered from the boat, are located near the National Cemetery. Established by act of Congress on Feb. 21, 1899.

VISITOR ACTIVITIES: Interpretive audiovisual programs and exhibits, auto tours, guided and auto-tape tours; **Permits:** No; **Fees:** Yes; **Visitor facilities:** Parking and restrooms at Visitor Center; **HANDICAPPED ACCESSIBILITY:** Visitor Center and U.S.S. Cairo Museum are accessible, as is the main picnic area; **Any limitations on vehicle usage:** No; **Hiking trails:** No; **Backcountry:** No; **Camping:** No; **Other overnight accommodations on site:** No; **Meals served in the park:** No; **Food and supplies obtainable in the park:** No; **Food and supplies obtainable nearby:** Yes, at Vicksburg; **Overnight accommodations:** Vicksburg, from one block to 5 miles (8 km); **First Aid available in park:** Yes; **Nearest Hospital:** Vicksburg, less than 1 mile (1.6 km) from the Visitor Center; **Days/Hours:** Tour Road opens daily at 7 a.m. and closes at sunset. Visitor Center open daily from 8 a.m. to 5 p.m. Cairo Museum open daily from 8:30 a.m. until 5 p.m. Call for summer hours and programs conducted from June through mid-August; **Holiday Closings:** Dec. 25.

GENERAL INFORMATION: *For your safety*—Drive carefully on winding roads. Beware of poisonous plants, insects, and reptiles.

TRAVEL ACCESS: **Bus:** Trailways, Greyhound provide daily service to Vicksburg; **Rail:** No.

NEARBY FACILITIES & POINTS OF INTEREST: **Campgrounds:** Battlefield Campground, I-20 Frontage Rd., 601-636-9946; **Parks, other points of interest:** The Old Court House Museum in Vicksburg features an exhibit of relics from the siege.

Missouri

Kansas City

LEWIS AND CLARK NATIONAL
HISTORIC TRAIL

Saint Louis
JEFFERSON NATIONAL
EXPANSION MEMORIAL
NATIONAL HISTORIC SITE

OZARK NATIONAL
SCENIC RIVERWAYS

GEORGE WASHINGTON CARVER
NATIONAL MONUMENT

WILSON'S CREEK NATIONAL BATTLEFIELD

OREGON NATIONAL HISTORIC TRAIL

George Washington Carver National Monument
Diamond, Missouri

MAILING ADDRESS: Superintendent, George Washington Carver National Monument,
P.O. Box 38, Diamond, MO 64840 **Telephone:** 417-325-4151

DIRECTIONS: From either Neosho or Carthage take US 71 Alternate to the town of
Diamond. Go west 2 miles (3.2 km) on State Highway V and then south about 1 mile (1.6 km).
    Authorized by Congress in 1943, George Washington Carver National Monument is
both the Nation's first memorial to the achievements of a black man and the first such honor to
an individual other than a President. It preserves the birthplace Site and the natural environment which was instrumental in shaping the personality and ambitions of George Washington
Carver, a man who played an important role in the social and agricultural history of 20th-cen-

tury America. Included within the Park is a museum detailing the life and achievements of Carver and a Nature Trail that passes some of the natural and historic points within the Park.

VISITOR ACTIVITIES: Interpretive exhibits and film, guided tours, nature walks, picnicking; **Permits:** Yes; **Fees:** Yes; **Visitor facilities:** Visitor Center, parking, and picnic areas; **HANDICAPPED ACCESSIBILITY:** Nature Trail has slight inclines but is fully accessible; Drinking fountains, parking, ramps; displays are wheelchair viewable; subtitled film on boyhood of G.W. Carver; film of Nature Trail if unable to take trail; extra wheelchair available; **Any limitations on vehicle usage:** No; **Hiking trails:** Yes, a ¾ mile (1.2 km) nature trail; **Backcountry:** No; **Camping:** No; **Other overnight accommodations on site:** No; **Meals served in the park:** No; **Food and supplies obtainable in the park:** No; **Food and supplies obtainable nearby:** Yes, in Diamond; **Overnight accommodations:** Neosho, US 71 A, 10 miles (16 km), and Joplin, 14 miles (22.4 km) northwest on Interstate 44; **First Aid available in park:** Yes; **Nearest Hospital:** Joplin, 14 miles (22.4 km), Interstate 44; Neosho, US 71 A, 10 miles (16 km); **Days/Hours:** Open daily from 8:30 a.m. to 5 p.m. Memorial Day—Labor Day 8:30-7:00. Grounds open until dark; **Holiday Closings:** Dec. 25; **Visitor attractions closed for seasons:** No; **Weather:** Summer, hot with occasional thunderstorms; spring/fall cool, mostly dry.

GENERAL INFORMATION: Learn to identify and avoid poison ivy found along nature trail. Prairie restoration project in progress.

TRAVEL ACCESS: Bus: No, there are no regular bus routes to the Park, although a number of bus "tours" do stop by the Park; **Rail:** No; **Air:** The nearest airport is approximately 30 miles (48 km) west of the Park in the city of Joplin.

NEARBY FACILITIES & POINTS OF INTEREST: Parks, other points of interest: Within a 1- to 2-hour drive from Carver National Monument is Fort Scott National Historical Site and Wilson's Creek and Pea Ridge National Battlefields.

Harry S Truman National Historic Site
Independence, Missouri

MAILING ADDRESS: 223 North Main Street, Independence, MO 64050 **Telephone:** (816) 254-2720 (Administrative Offices) - 254-7199 (24-hour recording)

DIRECTIONS: East on Truman Road from I-435 or north on Noland Road from I-70. West on Truman Road from Noland Road.
    Established Dec. 8, 1982, the site interprets the home of President Harry S Truman.

VISITOR ACTIVITIES: Tickets for guided tours available *only* at Truman Home Ticket and Information Center at the corner of Truman Road and Main Street, adjacent to Independence Square; first-come, first-served ticket distribution; everyone must be present to pick up tickets; no advanced reservations; no special group accommodations; Walking tours of the Truman Neighborhood during summer season; **Permits:** No; **Fees:** Entrance fee is $1 per person. Golden Access, Golden Age, Golden Eagle, and Park Passports are accepted and available. Fee waived for visitors under 16 years of age; **Visitor facilities:** Information desk, audiovisual program, exhibits, restrooms at the ticket center; **HANDICAPPED ACCESSIBILITY:** Parking at Truman Home Ticket and Information Center and Truman Home; accessible restrooms only at Information Center. Ticket and Information Center is wheelchair accessible. Truman Home has stair-trac step-climbing device. Wheelchair is available. Scripts available for audiovisual program and Home tour for hearing impaired. Large-print script available for visually impaired; **Any limitations on vehicle usage:** Limited parking at the site; **Hiking trails:** No; **Backcountry:** No; **Camping:** No; **Other overnight accommodations on site:** No; **Meals served in the park:** No; **Food and supplies obtainable in the park:** No; **Food and supplies obtainable nearby:** Yes, in Independence; **Overnight accommodations:** Independence, MO, on U.S. Highway 24 and I-70 and Noland Road junction; **First Aid available in park:** Yes; also hospital 1 mile (1.6 km) west; **Days/Hours:** Ticket Center, 8:30 a.m. to 5:00 p.m.; guided tours from 9:00 a.m. to 4:45 p.m.; **Holiday Closings:** Thanksgiving, Dec. 25, and Jan. 1; **Visitor attractions closed for seasons:** No guided tours on Mondays after Labor Day until Memorial Day; ticket center open for audiovisual program; **Weather:** Hot humid summers, mild springs and falls, cold winters with snow and ice.

GENERAL INFORMATION: In the summer, tour tickets frequently are all distributed by 12:30 p.m.; come early in the day to avoid disappointment. Scripts available in French, German, Spanish, and Japanese.

TRAVEL ACCESS: Bus: Greyhound, 6 miles (9.6 km) south of ticket center; **Rail:** Amtrak, ½ mile (.8 km) southwest of site, morning/evening service; **Air:** TWA, American, Eastern 25 miles (40 km) northwest of site.

NEARBY FACILITIES & POINTS OF INTEREST: Hotel/Motel: Independence, 5 miles (8 km); **Food/Supplies:** Independence, 1 mile (1.6 km); **Campgrounds:** Lake Jacomo County Park, 11 miles (17.6 km); **Parks, other points of interest:** Harry S Truman Library; Jackson County Courthouse (30-minute audiovisual program about Truman); Truman Railroad Station; Vaile Mansion; Bingham-Waggoner Estate; 1859 Marshal's Home and Jail Museum in Independence; Harry S Truman Farm Home, Grandview, MO, 19 miles (30.4 km) south of site.

Jefferson National Expansion Memorial
St. Louis, Missouri

MAILING ADDRESS: Superintendent, Jefferson National Expansion Memorial, 11 North Fourth Street, St. Louis, MO 63102 **Telephone:** 314-425-4465

DIRECTIONS: The Park is within easy walking distance of downtown St. Louis. The Old Courthouse, with a varied program of exhibits and activities is open daily, as are the Gateway Arch and Museum of Westward Expansion.

The Park, located on the Mississippi riverfront in St. Louis, memorializes Thomas Jefferson and others who directed the territorial expansion of the United States. Eero Saarinen's prize-winning, stainless steel Gateway Arch commemorates westward pioneers. Visitors may ascend the 630-foot-high arch by elevator. In the nearby courthouse Dred Scott sued for freedom in the historic slavery case. Designated Dec. 20, 1935.

VISITOR ACTIVITIES: Interpretive exhibits, walking, photography, ascending the arch; **Permits:** No; **Fees:** Entrance fee: visitors between the ages of 17 and 61 pay $1 per person, with no more than $3 per family. The fee for the elevator ride to the top of the arch is $2.50 for adults and $.50 for children under 13; **Visitor facilities:** Museum, parking lot with fee, restrooms; **HANDICAPPED ACCESSIBILITY:** A 4-minute self-service video program for the physically disabled is available in the Arch visitor center and provides current information about access to the Park. A similar video is available at the Old Courthouse. Accessible restrooms are available in the Arch lobby and in the Museum of Westward Expansion; **Any limitations on vehicle usage:** No; **Meals served in the park:** No; **Food and supplies obtainable in the park:** No; **Food and supplies obtainable nearby:** Yes, in St. Louis, within 1 block of the Site; **Overnight accommodations:** in St. Louis, within walking distance; **First Aid available in park:** Yes; **Nearest Hospital:** St. Louis, within 8 miles (12.8 km); **Days/ Hours:** Open daily from 9 a.m. to 6 p.m., 8 a.m. to 10 p.m. from Memorial Day through Labor Day; **Holiday Closings:** Thanksgiving, Dec. 25, and Jan. 1; **Weather:** Winters are cold and snowy.

GENERAL INFORMATION: Use caution on walkways, stairways, and step-down wells. Be extra careful in the Old Courthouse, which has many steps and varying floor levels.

Oregon National Historic Trail
Missouri (also in Kansas, Nebraska, Wyoming, Idaho, Oregon, and Washington)

MAILING ADDRESS: Pacific Northwest Regional Office, National Park Service, 83 South King St., Seattle, WA 98104 **Telephone:** 206-553-5360

GENERAL INFORMATION: The Oregon Trail was the most important transportation route used by western emigrants during the years 1841-1848. These pioneers traveled 2,170 miles (3,200 km) from Independence, MO, across the plains and mountains of Kansas, Nebraska, Wyoming, Idaho, and Washington to Oregon's Willamette River Valley. The National Park Service Comprehensive Management and Use Plan describes the official Oregon National Historic Trail route, lists 125 historic sites and 7 cross-country segments, and makes recommendations for resource protection, trail management, and marking. Many of the sites and segments are on public lands and open to visitation. Others are located on private lands; please check with landowners before entry. For information about access and travel conditions along the cross-country segments, contact local offices of the Bureau of Land Management or the Forest Service. Agency addresses and phone numbers are listed in the trail brochure. General information and trail brochures are available from the National Park Service Pacific Northwest Regional Office.

Ozark National Scenic Riverways
Van Buren, Missouri

MAILING ADDRESS: Superintendent, Ozark National Scenic Riverways, P.O. Box 490, Van Buren, MO 63965 **Telephone:** 314-323-4236

DIRECTIONS: The Riverways is in Missouri, an easy day's drive from two large metropolitan centers—175 miles (280 km) south of St. Louis and 250 miles (400 km) southeast of Kansas City, MO.
    The Current and Jacks Fork Rivers flow for about 140 miles (224 km) through a quiet world of nature. Notable features include numerous caves, huge freshwater springs, and tall bluffs. Authorized for addition to the National Park System on Aug. 27, 1964.

VISITOR ACTIVITIES: Canoeing, camping, fishing, picnicking, float trips, boating, craft demonstrations, interpretive talks, cave tours, hunting, hiking, canoe demonstrations, swimming; **Permits:** No; **Fees:** Yes, for campsites, $7 per night per family per Site, $2 per person per night - cluster (10-20 people), $30 per Site for 15 persons and $2 additional per person per night up to 45, collected at Big Spring, Round Spring, Alley Spring, Akers, Pulltite, Powder Mill, and Two Rivers campgrounds year-round; **Visitor facilities:** Picnic and camping areas, restrooms, stores, canoe and John Boat rentals, showers, boat ramps and lodging; picnic shelters at some areas may be reserved April through Oct. $20 nonrefundable fee.

HANDICAPPED ACCESSIBILITY: Many of the facilities are considered wheelchair accessible with some assistance required. The three major areas in the park, Big Spring, Round Spring, and Alley Spring, are considered the most accessible; **Any limitations on vehicle usage:** All vehicles are restricted to designated roadways; **Hiking trails:** Yes, many miles of old logging roads available for hiking. Nine miles (14.4 km) of the Ozark Trail lie within the Riverways. This trail is being built in cooperation with other federal, state, and private conservation groups. When completed, the trail will extend from St. Louis County to the Arkansas border; **Backcountry:** Yes, contact Superintendent for more details. No reservations or permits are required; **Camping:** Yes, contact Park for reservations; **Other overnight accommodations on site:** Yes, rustic housekeeping cabins available at the Big Spring Unit; Rustic Motel at Alley Spring; Reservations can be made by contacting Big Spring Concessioner, P.O. Box 602, Van Buren, MO 63965, phone 314-323-4423, or Harvey's Alley Spring Canoe Rental, HCR 3, Box 18, Eminence, MO 65466, phone 314-226-3386; **Meals served in the park:** Yes, Big Spring Concessioner; **Food and supplies obtainable in the park:** Yes, at Akers, Pulltite, Round, Two Rivers and Alley Springs; **Food and supplies obtainable nearby:** Yes, in adjacent towns: Eminence, Van Buren, Salem, Ellington, Mountain View, Winona, and Birch Tree, MO; **Overnight accommodations:** Eminence, Van Buren, Salem, Ellington, Mountain View, Winona, and Birch Tree; **First Aid available in park:** Yes, small medical clinics also located in Van Buren and Winona, MO; **Nearest Hospital:** Ellington, MO, 21 miles (33.6 km) from Riverways headquarters in Van Buren via MO State Highway "D" and 21; **Days/Hours:** Open 24 hours a day; modern camping facilities open year-round; **Holiday Closings:** No; **Visitor attractions closed for seasons:** Mild winters allow year-round use of the Riverways.

GENERAL INFORMATION: Visitors should write for a pamphlet on the Riverways.

For Your Safety—Lifejackets or boat cushions must be carried for each person in the boat or canoe. Children under 7 are required to wear a PFD. Non-swimmers and weak swimmers should wear lifejackets at all times. Pick campsites well above river level. Flash flood warnings will be issued when possible. Extinguish campfires before leaving; fire is a great peril here. Know what to expect before launching. Talk to a Park Ranger or concessioner about river conditions and hazards. Carry first-aid kits, matches, billfolds and other valuables in waterproof containers. Stay out of caves until you check with a Park Ranger. The darkness may conceal mud pools, dropoffs, and harmful fungi.

Ulysses S. Grant National Historic Site
St. Louis County, Missouri

MAILING ADDRESS: Ulysses S. Grant National Historic Site, 7400 Grant Road, St. Louis, Missouri 63123. **Telephone:** 314-842-1867

Open to formal groups by appointment only.

This site preserves the home of Ulysses S. Grant and his wife Julia Dent. The Grants lived together at this home, White Haven, during the crucial pre-Civil War years. The estate has been set aside to pay tribute to Grant's heroic deeds and public service as a military leader and 18th President of the United States.

Authorized: Oct. 2, 1989. Acreage: 9.65, all federal property.

Wilson's Creek National Battlefield
Republic, Missouri

MAILING ADDRESS: Superintendent, Wilson's Creek National Battlefield, Route 2, Box 75, Republic, MO 65738 **Telephone:** 417-732-2662

DIRECTIONS: The Site is 3 miles (4.8 km) east of Republic, MO, and 10 miles (16 km) southwest of Springfield, MO. Take Int. 44 to MM Highway (Exit 70). Go south 6¾ miles (10.8 km) to Highway 60. Go straight on M Highway .7 miles to State Highway ZZ. Go south on ZZ 2 miles (3.2 km) to the Visitor Center. Highway signs are present to show the route.

VISITOR ACTIVITIES: Self-guided auto tour, interpretive exhibits at Visitor Center, living history programs on summer weekends; **Permits:** No; **Fees:** Adults $1 (up to $3/vehicle), Children under 17 and U.S. senior citizens over 62 are free; **Visitor facilities:** Visitor Center, 5-mile (8-km) tour road, trails, historic Ray House, picnic area, restrooms; **HANDICAPPED ACCESSIBILTY:** Visitor Center, restrooms, and tour road stops are accessible; **Any limitations on vehicle usage:** Vehicles are restricted to designated roadways; **Hiking trails:** Yes; **Backcountry:** No; **Camping:** No; **Other overnight accommodations on site:** No; **Meals served in the park:** No; **Food and supplies obtainable in the park:** No; **Food and supplies obtainable nearby:** Yes, at Republic; **Overnight accommodations:** Springfield, MO, 10 miles (16 km); **First Aid available in park:** Yes; **Nearest Hospital:** Springfield, 10 miles (16 km); **Days/Hours:** Summer 8 a.m. to 8 p.m., winter 8 a.m. to 5 p.m. Closing hours vary spring and fall. **Holiday Closings:** Dec. 25, Jan. 1; **Visitor attractions closed for seasons:** No; **Weather:** Hot, humid summer, cold with snow and ice in winter.

GENERAL INFORMATION: The Visitor Center offers a 13-minute film, a 6-minute fiber optic map display, museum area, and sales and display area. A picnic area is located next to the Visitor Center. The historic Ray House has been restored to its 1861 appearance. Historic Wire Road has been stabilized. Five-mile (8-km) tour road with exhibits, and biking lane.

TRAVEL ACCESS: Bus: No (except by charter in Springfield); **Rail:** No; **Air:** TWA and American service Springfield Regional Airport.

NEARBY FACILITIES & POINTS OF INTEREST: Campgrounds: KOA, Route 7, Box 215A, Springfield, MO, 417-831-3645; **Parks, other points of interest:** George Washington Carver National Monument, Fort Scott National Historical Site, Ozark National Scenic Riverways, Pea Ridge National Military Park, Buffalo National River.

Montana

LEWIS AND CLARK NATIONAL HISTORIC TRAIL

FORT UNION TRADING POST
NATIONAL HISTORIC SITE

GLACIER NATIONAL PARK

FORT BENTON

GRANT-KOHRS RANCH
NATIONAL HISTORIC SITE

Butte

BIG HOLE NATIONAL BATTLEFIELD

CUSTER BATTLEFIELD
NATIONAL MONUMENT

BIGHORN CANYON
NATIONAL RECREATION AREA

Big Hole National Battlefield
Wisdom, Montana

MAILING ADDRESS: Superintendent, Big Hole National Battlefield, P.O. Box 237, Wisdom, MT 59761 **Telephone:** 406-689-3155

DIRECTIONS: The Battlefield is 10 miles (16 km) west of Wisdom, MT, on MT 43. From Butte, take Interstate 15 southwest to Divide, then to Wisdom on MT 43; from the west, MT 43 intersects US 93 at the State line, between Salmon, ID, and Hamilton, MT. Stop first at the Visitor Center.

Nez Perce Indians and U.S. Army troops fought here in 1877—a dramatic episode in the long struggle to confine the Nez Perce, and other Indians, to reservations. Established by Presidential Proclamation on June 23, 1910.

VISITOR ACTIVITIES: Audiovisual and interpretive exhibits, self-guiding tours, picnicking, interpretive demonstrations, cross-country skiing, fishing; **Permits:** Montana fishing license can be obtained from local sporting goods dealers; **Fees:** Entrance fees May-Sept. $1 per person or $3 per carload; **Visitor facilities:** Restrooms, parking, and museum at Visitor Center, picnic tables; **Any limitations on vehicle usage:** No; **Hiking trails:** Yes, Big Hole Battlefield Trail follows the route of the Nez Perce War for 22.5 miles (36 km). It is a 2-day hiking and backpacking trail; **Backcountry:** No, obtain information from Headquarters; **Camping:** No; **Other overnight accommodations on site:** No, several nonreserved campsites are nearby. Check at Headquarters; **Meals served in the park:** No; **Food and supplies obtainable in the park:** No; **Food and supplies obtainable nearby:** Yes, in Wisdom (limited), Butte, and Hamilton, MT, Salmon, ID; **Overnight accommodations:** Wisdom, MT 43, 10 miles (16 km) west. Other accommodations are in Butte, MT, to the northeast, and Hamilton, MT, or Salmon, ID, to the West; **First Aid available in park:** Yes; **Nearest Hospital:** Hamilton, MT 93, 67 miles (107.2 km); **Days/Hours:** Open daily 8 a.m. to 5 p.m., until 8 p.m. from June 1 through Labor Day; **Visitor attractions closed for seasons:** Snow closes hiking trails; **Weather:** Winters are snowy, windy, and cold.

GENERAL INFORMATION: *For Your Protection*—animals native to the Park are dangerous when startled or approached too closely. Always keep a safe distance. Pets must be under physical control at all times.

NEARBY FACILITIES & POINTS OF INTEREST: Hotel/Motel: Nez Perce Lodge, Wisdom, MT., 406-689-3254, 10 miles (16 km) from Park; **Food/Supplies:** Wisdom Grocery, Wisdom, MT., 406-689-3271, 10 miles (16 km) from Park; **Campgrounds:** May Creek, US Forest Service area, 406-689-3243, 7 miles (11.2 km) from Park.

Bighorn Canyon National Recreation Area
Fort Smith, Montana and Lovell, Wyoming

MAILING ADDRESS: Superintendent, Bighorn Canyon National Recreation Area, P.O. Box 458, Fort Smith, MT 59035 **Telephone:** 406-666-2412 (MT) or 307-548-2251 (WY)

DIRECTIONS: North end accessible via MT 313 from Hardin, MT, 43 miles (68.8 km); south end via WY 14A, Wyoming State Road 37, from Lovell, WY, 13 miles (20.8 km).
Bighorn Lake, formed by Yellowtail Dam on the Bighorn River, extends 71 miles (113.6 km)), including a large section through scenic Bighorn Canyon. Much of the area borders on the Crow Indian Reservation. Established by act of Congress in 1966.

VISITOR ACTIVITIES: Year-round water activities (including winter ice fishing) and recreational activities, sightseeing, weekend visitor programs in summer; **Permits:** No; **Fees:** Yes, $3 per vehicle per night camping fee at Horseshoe Bend Campground; **Visitor facilities:** Campgrounds, boat ramps, Visitor Centers, concessioner services at Horseshoe Bend and OK-14-Beh; **Any limitations on vehicle usage:** All wheeled vehicles must stay on established roads; **Hiking trails:** Yes, short nature trails at both ends of the area; **Backcountry:** Yes, for information in Montana call 406-666-2412, in Wyoming, 307-548-2251; **Camping:** Yes, no reservations needed for campsites; **Other overnight accommodations on site:** No; **Meals served in the park:** Yes, at Horseshoe Bend and OK-14-Beh; **Food and supplies obtainable in the park:** Yes; **Food and supplies obtainable nearby:** Yes, in Fort Smith, MT, and Lovell, WY; **Overnight accommodations:** Hardin, MT, Hwy 313, 43 miles (68.8 km); Lovell, WY, Highway 14A, 13 miles (20.8 km), Ft. Smith, MT at North end; **First Aid available in park:** Yes; **Nearest Hospital:** Lovell, WY, Highway 14A, 13 miles (20.8 km); Hardin, MT 313, 43 miles (68.8 km); **Days/Hours:** Open year-round; **Holiday Closings:** Visitor Centers closed Thanksgiving, Dec. 25, and Jan. 1; **Weather:** Average summer temperature is in the 80s F; sub-zero temperatures with frequent snow in winter.

Custer Battlefield National Monument
Crow Agency, Montana

MAILING ADDRESS: Superintendent, Custer Battlefield National Monument, P.O. Box 39, Crow Agency, MT 59022 **Telephone:** 406-638-2621

DIRECTIONS: The Monument lies within the Crow Indian Reservation in southeastern Montana. US 87 (I-90) passes 1 mile (1.6 km) to the west; US 212 connects the Monument with the Black Hills and Yellowstone National Park. The Crow Agency is 2 miles (3.2 km) north, and Hardin, MT, is 18 miles (28.8 km) north. The nearest cities are Billings, MT, 65 miles (104 km) northwest, and Sheridan, WY, 70 miles (112 km) south.

The famous Battle of the Little Big Horn between the 7th U.S. Cavalry and the Sioux and Northern Cheyenne Indians was fought here on June 25-26, 1876. Lt. Col. George A. Custer and about 263 of his force were killed. Established as a national cemetery on Jan. 29, 1879; changed to Custer Battlefield National Monument by act of Congress on March 22, 1946.

VISITOR ACTIVITIES: Interpretive talks and exhibits at Visitor Center, guided bus tours, hiking; **Permits:** No; **Fees:** $3 per vehicle, 62 or older free; **Visitor facilities:** Parking and restrooms at Visitor Center, interpretive markers; **HANDICAPPED ACCESSIBILITY:** Visitor Center is accessible; reserved parking available; **Any limitations on vehicle usage:** All vehicles are restricted to designated roadways. Tour road has 8-ton limit. No commercial buses permitted beyond Visitor Center; **Hiking trails:** Yes, self-guiding walking trails; **Backcountry:** No; **Camping:** No; **Other overnight accommodations on site:** No; **Meals served in the park:** No; **Food and supplies obtainable in the park:** No; **Food and supplies obtainable nearby:** Yes, in Hardin, Crow Agency; **Overnight accommodations:** Hardin, MT, 15 miles (24 km) north on I-90; **First Aid available in park:** Yes; **Nearest Hospital:** Hardin, MT, 15 miles (24 km) north on I-90; **Days/Hours:** Visitor Center and Battlefield open from 8 a.m. to 7:45 p.m. from Memorial Day through Labor Day; from 8 a.m. to 4:30 p.m. from Labor Day to Memorial Day; until 6 p.m. during Daylight Savings Time; **Holiday Closings:** Thanksgiving, Dec. 25, and Jan. 1; **Visitor attractions closed for seasons:** No; **Weather:** Hot summers, mild spring and fall, cold winter.

GENERAL INFORMATION: *For Your Safety*—Beware of rattlesnakes. Stay on the pathways while walking on the battlefield.

TRAVEL ACCESS: Bus: Trailways provides daily service to Crow Agency ¼ mile (2 km) from Park; **Rail:** No; **Air:** Big Sky, Delta, Continental, Northwest, and United to Billings, MT, Aspen Air, Continental to Sheridan, WY.

Fort Benton
Fort Benton, Montana

MAILING ADDRESS: Fort Benton Museum, Box 69, Fort Benton, MT 59442 **Telephone:** None.

DIRECTIONS: Federal facilities are not yet open to the public. In summer, the community operates a museum, which is located in Old Fort Park. Telephone local newspaper for information, 406-622-3311.

Founded in 1846, this American Fur Trading Company trading post was an important river port from 1859 through the Montana gold rush of 1862-1869 until rail service surpassed river cargo transport. Authorized for addition to the National Park System on Oct. 16, 1976. The Bureau of Land Management will manage the Visitor Center at Fort Benton when construction is completed. Also the State of Montana now operates a State Museum of Agriculture, The Museum of the Northern Great Plains (handicapped accessible).

GENERAL INFORMATION: The community operates two museums in the summer. The Museum of the Upper Missouri is in Old Fort Park. Montana's museum of agriculture is located in the Museum of the Northern Great Plains at the Montana Agricultural Center.

TRAVEL ACCESS: Bus: Rimrock buses service to Riverview Greenhouse ½ block from park.

NEARBY FACILITIES & POINTS OF INTEREST: Parks, other points of interest: Old Fort Park, Montana Memorial to Lewis and Clark.

Fort Union Trading Post
For details see listing in North Dakota

Glacier National Park
West Glacier, Montana   **SEE CLIMATABLE NO. 23**

MAILING ADDRESS: Superintendent, Glacier National Park, West Glacier, MT 59936
Telephone: 406-888-5441

DIRECTIONS: The Park is on US 2 and 89 and near US 90 and 93. St. Mary Visitor Center is open mid-May through September; Apgar Information Center from mid-May through October (Apgar Visitor Center is also open on Saturday and Sunday all winter - November through April) and Logan Pass Visitor Center from mid-June through September. Opening and closing dates vary from year to year. For information on the Park, phone 406-888-5441.
     This ruggedly beautiful land includes more than 50 glaciers, countless lakes and streams, and a myriad of wildflowers and wildlife. Established May 11, 1910.

VISITOR ACTIVITIES: Hiking, backpacking, sightseeing, biking, horseback riding and tours, excursion boat cruises, non-fee fishing, cross-country skiing, snowshoeing, camping, auto, boat tours, picnicking, interpretive exhibits and programs; **Permits:** Free, required for overnight stays in the backcountry; can be obtained from Apgar Information Center, St. Mary Visitor Center, and most Ranger Stations; **Entrance fees:** $5 per vehicle entrance fee, $2 per person for those entering by means other than private non-commercial vehicles, $15 annual area pass also available; Persons under 16 years and 62 years or older are not charged. Golden Eagle and Golden Age Passports accepted and available. Campsites are $6 or $8 per night, depending on facilities. Group campsites are $2 per night per person; backcountry campsites are free with permit; **Visitor facilities:** Visitor Center, boat rentals, hiking trails, campgrounds, picnic areas, hotels, lodges, cabins, telephones, food service, saddle horse, lake cruises and tour buses; **HANDICAPPED ACCESSIBILITY:** Yes, contact Visitor Center for details. **Any limitations on vehicle usage:** On the Going-to-the-Sun Road. Vehicle units—July 1 to Sept. 1. Not to exceed 30 feet in length, 8-foot width. Before July or after Sept. length limit 35 feet, total width, including mirrors—8 feet. Vehicles, including bicycles, are not allowed on trails or off the roads. Bicycles not allowed on portions of Going-to-the-Sun Road during peak travel hours (June 15 through Labor Day); **Hiking trails:** Yes, there are more than 700 miles (1200 km) of maintained wilderness trails. Check at Visitor Centers for further information; **Backcountry:** Yes, 62 backcountry campsites, permit required for backcountry—check at any Ranger Station or Information Center; **Camping:** No reservations available for campsites; arrive early for best choice; **Other overnight accommodations on site:** Yes. Accommodations in the Park are available from Glacier Park, Inc.: May 17-Sept. 23 write East Glacier Park, MT 59434, phone 406-226-5551; Sept. 15-May 15 write Greyhound Tower, Station 1210 Phoenix, AZ 85077, phone 602-248-6000; Reservations are advised; deposits are required. Reservations for Granite Park and Sperry Chalets, accessible only by backcountry trails, are available from Belton Chalets, Inc., Box 188, West Glacier, MT 59936, phone 406-888-5511. Privately owned campgrounds are nearby; **Meals served in the park:** Yes, at Apgar, Swiftcurrent, Rising Sun, Many Glacier and Lake McDonald Hotels; **Food and supplies obtainable in the park:** Yes, Apgar, Lake McDonald, Swiftcurrent, Rising Sun, and Two Medicine have campers' stores; **Food and supplies obtainable nearby:** Yes, St. Mary, West Glacier, East Glacier; **Overnight accommodations:** St. Mary, West Glacier, East Glacier (adjacent to park entrances); **First Aid available in park:** Yes; **Nearest Hospital:** Cardston, Alberta, Canada, 35 miles (56 km) north of St. Mary on US 89 and in Whitefish, MT, 24 miles (38 km) west of West Glacier on US 93; **Days/Hours:** Park open 24 hours a day, 7 days a week, Park Offices M-F 8:00 a.m. to 4:30 p.m.; **Holiday Closings:** No; **Visitor attractions closed for seasons:** Going-to-the-Sun road is closed in winter, except between West Glacier and Lake McDonald Lodge and St. Mary to Rising Sun Road Road into Swift Current Valley is plowed, but status is weather dependent. Write the Park for detailed information on winter activities; **Weather:** Severe storms come quickly, even in summer, with attendant exposure to low temperatures, rain, snow, sleet, and lightning.

GENERAL INFORMATION: *For Your Safety*—Never climb alone. Register before and after the climb. However, climbing is not encouraged because of unstable sedimentary rock. Avoid steep snowfields. Keep your distance from all animals, and never try to approach or feed wildlife.

TRAVEL ACCESS: Rail: Amtrak provides service from major cities to Terminals in Belton (West Glacier) and East Glacier; **Air:** Glacier International Airport, 32 miles (51.2 km) west in Kalispell; Delta and Horizon Airlines, Great Falls International Airport (Gt. Falls), Western, NW Orient. Rental cars available in Kalispell, Cut Bank, East Glacier, and Great Falls. Bus service to Great Falls and Kalispell on Intermountain Transportation.

Grant-Kohrs Ranch National Historic Site
Deer Lodge, Montana

MAILING ADDRESS: Superintendent, Grant-Kohrs Ranch National Historic Site, P.O. Box 790, Deer Lodge, MT 59722 **Telephone:** 406-846-2070

DIRECTIONS: The ranch is located midway between Yellowstone and Glacier National Parks, ½ mile (.8 km) off Interstate 90 at Deer Lodge.

This was the headquarters of one of the largest and best known 19th-century range ranches in the country. Today the ranchhouse, bunkhouse, and outbuildings are much as they were from the 1860's through the 1950's. Authorized for addition to the National Park System on Aug. 25, 1972.

VISITOR ACTIVITIES: Guided tours of the house, self-guiding walks, and exhibits; **Permits:** No; **Fees:** $1 per person over age of 12. Maximum charge $3 per carload. Educational groups free; **Visitor facilities:** Visitor Center, restrooms, self-guiding trail, seasonal demonstrations of ranch activities; **HANDICAPPED ACCESSIBILITY:** Visitor Center and restrooms at ranch are accessible; wheelchair ramps available for bunkhouse row and blacksmith shop; guided tour of ranch house and wagon collection accessible; handicap parking reserved at ranch site; self-guided trail accessible; **Any limitations on vehicle usage:** Vehicles are left at the Visitor Center. The ranch is ¼ mile (.4 km) away by paved trail; **Hiking trails:** No; **Backcountry:** No; **Camping:** No; **Other overnight accommodations on site:** No; **Meals served in the park:** No; **Food and supplies obtainable in the park:** No; **Food and supplies obtainable nearby:** Yes, at Deer Lodge; **Overnight accommodations:** Deer Lodge, Int. 90, ¼ mile (.4 km); **First Aid available in park:** Yes; on emergency basis; **Nearest Hospital:** Deer Lodge, Interstate 90, 1½ miles (1.8 km); **Days/Hours:** Open daily from 9 a.m. to 4:30 p.m.; until 7:30 p.m. in summer; **Holiday Closings:** Thanksgiving, Dec. 25, and Jan. 1; **Visitor attractions closed for seasons:** No; **Weather:** Spring is short; summer, warm; fall, brisk; winter, cold.

GENERAL INFORMATION: Smoking is prohibited on the ranch site. Keep your distance from the animals. Pets are not allowed beyond the parking area.

Lewis and Clark Trail
For details see listing in Illinois

Nebraska

LEWIS AND CLARK NATIONAL HISTORIC TRAIL

AGATE FOSSIL BEDS NATIONAL MONUMENT

SCOTTS BLUFF NATIONAL MONUMENT

CHIMNEY ROCK NATIONAL HISTORIC SITE

Omaha

HOMESTEAD NATIONAL MONUMENT OF AMERICA

MORMON PIONEER NATIONAL HISTORIC TRAIL

OREGON NATIONAL HISTORIC TRAIL

Agate Fossil Beds National Monument
Gering, Nebraska

MAILING ADDRESS: Superintendent, Agate Fossil Beds National Monument and Scotts Bluff National Monument, P.O. Box 27, Gering, NE 69341 **Telephone:** 308-436-4340

DIRECTIONS: The Site is 34 miles (54.4 km) north of Mitchell on NE 29 and 3 miles (4.8 km) east on County Road; 22 miles (35.2 km) south of Harrison via NE 29 and 3 miles (4.8 km) east on County Road.

The Monument consists of 2,700 acres, including a 60-acre detached quarry Site. The quarries contain numerous concentrated, well-preserved Miocene mammal fossils, representing an important chapter in the evolution of mammals. Established by act of Congress on June 5, 1965.

VISITOR ACTIVITIES: Interpretive exhibits, self-guiding hikes; **Permits:** No; **Fees:** No; **Visitor facilities:** Visitor Center exhibits and nearby comfort stations, slide program, fishing, picnic tables and benches on trails; **Any limitations on vehicle usage:** Vehicles must stay on established roadways; **Hiking trails:** Yes, a 1-mile (1.6-km) paved trail leads to the fossil beds; a ½-mile (.8-km) mowed grass trail leads to the Daimonelix Fossil burrows area; **Backcountry:** No; **Camping:** No; **Other overnight accommodations on site:** No; **Meals served in the park:** No; **Food and supplies obtainable in the park:** No; **Food and supplies obtainable nearby:** Yes, in Harrison, NE, 25 miles (40 km) north; **Overnight accommodations:** Scottsbluff, Route 26, 45 miles (72 km) south, Harrison, NE 29, 25 miles (40 km) north, Mitchell, NE 29, 37 miles (59.2 km) south; **First Aid available in park:** Yes; **Nearest Hospital:** Scottsbluff, 45 miles (72 km); **Days/Hours:** Open daily from 8:30 a.m. to 5:30 p.m.; **Holiday Closings:** Dec. 25 and Jan. 1; **Visitor attractions closed for seasons:** Visitor Center open weekends only, 8:00 a.m.-5:00 p.m., Nov.-April.

GENERAL INFORMATION: *For Your Safety*—Watch for rattlesnakes while viewing the fossil areas or walking anywhere in the Park.

TRAVEL ACCESS: Bus: No; **Rail:** No; **Air:** Continental Express and G.P. Express Airlines daily service Scotts Bluff County Airport, Scotts Bluff, NE; **Other:** Hertz and National Car Rentals are available at the Scotts Bluff County Airport; **Parks, other points of interest:** Badlands, Devils Tower, Fort Laramie, Jewel Cave, Mount Rushmore, Scotts Bluff, Wind Cave, Chimney Rock.

Chimney Rock National Historic Site
Bayard, Nebraska

MAILING ADDRESS: Museum Director, Chimney Rock National Historic Site, Nebraska State Historical Society, Box 82554, Lincoln, NE 68501 **Telephone:** 402-471-4758 (Lincoln)

DIRECTIONS: The Site is 3½ miles (5.6 km) southwest of Bayard, on the south side of the North Platte River. From Bayard, US 26 intersects NE 92 at a point about 1½ miles (2.4 km) from the Site. Gravel roads lead from NE 92 to within ½ mile (.8 km) of the Site. Travel from there is by foot only, on unimproved path.

Pioneers camped near this famous landmark as they traveled west. It stands 500 feet above the Platte River along the Oregon Trail. Designated a National Historic Site on Aug. 9, 1956. Jointly administered by National Park Service, City of Bayard and the Nebraska State Historical Society.

VISITOR ACTIVITIES: Walking tours, picnicking, photography; **Permits:** No; **Fees:** No; **Visitor facilities:** Information trailer, groundbreaking for permanent Visitor Center 1992; expected completion date 1993, picnic area, pit toilets; **Any limitations on vehicle usage:** Vehicles are restricted to designated roadways; **Hiking trails:** Yes; **Backcountry:** No; **Camping:** No; **Other overnight accommodations on site:** No; **Meals served in the park:** No; **Food and supplies obtainable in the park:** No; **Food and supplies obtainable nearby:** Yes, Bayard; **Overnight accommodations:** Bayard, 4 miles (6.4 km); Bridgeport, 12 miles (19.2 km) east; **First Aid available in park:** No; **Nearest Hospital:** Scottsbluff, NE 92, approximately 25 miles (40 km); **Days/Hours:** Open during daylight hours, 365 days a year; **Visitor attractions closed for seasons:** Trailer #4 at the rest area on Neb. 92 operates from 9 a.m.-6 p.m. from Memorial Day through Labor Day; **Weather:** Expect violent storms in summer.

GENERAL INFORMATION: *For Your Safety*—Watch out for rattlesnakes, rough terrain, and yucca plants. Boots and hiking clothes are essential.

TRAVEL ACCESS: Air: Scottsbluff is nearest terminal.

NEARBY FACILITIES & POINTS OF INTEREST: Parks, other points of interest: Wild Cat Hills, and Scotts Bluff National Monument.

Homestead National Monument of America
Beatrice, Nebraska

MAILING ADDRESS: Superintendent, Homestead National Monument of America, Rt. 3 Box 47, Beatrice, NE 68310 **Telephone:** 402-223-3514

DIRECTIONS: The Monument is located in southeastern Nebraska, about 4.5 miles (7.2 km) northwest of Beatrice and about 40 miles (64 km) south of Lincoln. Take NE 4 from Beatrice to the Monument.

One of the first claims under the Homestead Act of 1862 was filed for this land. Authorized for addition to the National Park System on Mar. 19, 1936.

VISITOR ACTIVITIES: Audiovisual and interpretive exhibits, walking tours, living history demonstrations during special events in summer, hiking, cross-country skiing; **Permits:** No; **Fees:** No; **Visitor facilities:** Parking and restrooms at Visitor Center, parking available for larger vehicles/trailers, picnic area. **HANDICAPPED ACCESSIBILITY:** Parking and restrooms at Visitor Center; **Any limitations on vehicle usage:** Motorcycles, bicycles, and snowmobiles are not allowed on the trail or grounds; **Hiking trails:** Yes, a 2½-mile (4-km) trail around the Site; **Backcountry:** No; **Camping:** No; **Other overnight accommodations on site:** No, city-operated campsites are available in Beatrice. No reservations are accepted. For further information, write Beatrice Park and Recreation Department, City Auditorium, Beatrice, NE 68310, or phone 402-228-3649; **Meals served in the park:** No; **Food and supplies obtainable in the park:** No; **Food and supplies obtainable nearby:** Yes, in Beatrice; **Overnight accommodations:** Beatrice, NE 4, 5 miles (8 km); **First Aid available in park:** Yes; **Nearest Hospital:** Beatrice, NE 4, 5 miles (8 km); **Days/Hours:** Open 7 days a week: 8 a.m. to 6 p.m., Memorial Day-Labor Day; 8:30 a.m.-5 p.m. the rest of the year; **Holiday Closings:** Dec. 25; **Visitor attractions closed for seasons:** Freeman School open regularly only in summer; **Weather:** Summer is frequently hot with moderate humidity and the possibility of thundershowers. Winter is cold with occasional snow.

GENERAL INFORMATION: *For Your Safety*—Check carefully for ticks, which are most active from May through August. Do not smoke on the trail.

"Homestead Days" held in last week of June.

TRAVEL ACCESS: Bus: No; **Rail:** Amtrak provides daily service into Lincoln; **Air:** United Airlines, Continental Airline service to Lincoln.

Missouri National Recreational River
Omaha, Nebraska

MAILING ADDRESS: Midwest Region, National Park Service, 1709 Jackson Street, Omaha, NE 68102 **Telephone:** 402-221-4856

DIRECTIONS: If you are driving north of Omaha, NE, on I-29, exit west on South Dakota's Route U.S. 50 to Yankton. If you are driving south from Sioux Falls on I-29, exit west on South Dakota's Route U.S. 50 to Yankton.

VISITOR ACTIVITIES: No Federal landownership or development. State and local parks provide facilities and access to the 58-mile (92.8 km) river stretch. **Permits:** No permits required; **Fees:** Both the State of Nebraska and the State of South Dakota have entrance fees to use their facilities. **Visitor facilities:** None developed by the Federal Government; must use State and local access facilities; **Any limitations on vehicle usage:** No; **Hiking trails:** No; **Backcountry:** No; **Camping:** State and local parks in the area; **Other overnight accommodations on site:** Local motels; **Meals served in the park:** No; **Food and supplies obtainable in the park:** No; **Food and supplies obtainable nearby:** At local communities along this stretch of river; **Overnight accommodations:** Motels at Yankton, SD, and Sioux City, IA; **First Aid available in park:** No; **Nearest Hospital:** Yankton, SD, and Sioux City, IA; **Days/Hours:** None; **Holiday Closings:** No; **Visitor attractions closed for seasons:** State parks in area; **Weather:** Cool mornings and warm days in spring and fall. July and August daytime temperatures in mid to high 90s.

GENERAL INFORMATION: River is wide and current fast and carries a heavy silt load.

TRAVEL ACCESS: Bus: Yankton, SD, and Sioux City, IA; **Rail:** Yankton, SD, and Sioux City, IA; **Air:** Yankton, SD, and Sioux City, IA.

Mormon Pioneer Trail
For details see listing in Illinois

Oregon National Scenic Trail
For details see listing in Missouri

Scotts Bluff National Monument
Gering, Nebraska

MAILING ADDRESS: Superintendent, Scotts Bluff National Monument, P.O. Box 27, Gering, NE 69341 **Telephone:** 308-436-4340

DIRECTIONS: The Monument adjoins the south bank of the North Platte River 3 miles (4.8 km) west of Gering via NE 92, which bisects the area from east to west. From U.S. 26, travelers should connect with NE 71 south for 5 miles (8 km) to NE 92. From I-80, it is 45 miles (72 km) to the Monument via NE 71 and 92.

Rising 800 feet above the valley floor, this massive promontory was a landmark on the Oregon and California Trails, associated with the mass migration across the Great Plains between 1843 and 1869. Created by Presidential Proclamation on Dec. 12, 1919.

VISITOR ACTIVITIES: Museum, interpretive talks, nature trails, hiking, biking, living history programs; **Permits:** No; **Fees:** $3 per car entrance fee; Golden Eagle, Golden Access, and Golden Age Passports accepted and available; **Visitor facilities:** Museum, nature, hiking, and bicycle trails; **Any limitations on vehicle usage:** Vehicles must stay on established roads; trailers are not allowed to go to the top of the Summit Road; **Hiking trails:** Yes, 1.6-mile (2.6-km) Saddle Rock Trail from which visitors can view bluff formations, wildlife species, and the valley. On the Summit, 1 miles (1.6 km) of trails lead to overlooks from which visitors may look down on historic Mitchell Pass and the North Platte River Valley. From the Museum, a 200-yd (250-m) paved trail leads west from the parking lot and takes one to the Oregon and California Trail, at this location, a trough, worn down by the passage of thousands of emigrants; **Backcountry:** No; **Camping:** No; **Other overnight accommodations on site:** No; **Meals served in the park:** No; **Food and supplies obtainable in the park:** No; **Food and supplies obtainable nearby:** Yes, in Gering, 3 miles (4.8 km) east of Park Headquarters; **Overnight accommodations:** In Gering, NE 92, 4.5 miles (7.2 km) and Scottsbluff, NE 92 and 71, 7 miles (11.2 km); **First Aid available in park:** Yes; **Nearest Hospital:** Scottsbluff, 10 miles (16 km); **Days/Hours:** Open from 8 a.m. to 5 p.m. year-round; closed on off-season Federal holidays; Winter visitor activities include the museum, hiking trails, and on request walks and talks; The road to the top is closed intermittently by snow or rock slides in winter; **Weather:** Winter is snowy and windy; summer is hot and dry.

GENERAL INFORMATION: *For Your Safety*—Remain on the Park Trails; do not venture toward the cliff's edge; watch for rattlesnakes.

NEARBY FACILITIES & POINTS OF INTEREST: Parks, other points of interest: Chimney Rock, 23 miles (36.8 km) east; Fort Laramie National Historical Site, 55 miles (88 km) west; Agate Fossil Beds National Monument, 52 miles (83.2 km) north.

Nevada

GREAT BASIN NATIONAL PARK
LEHMAN CAVES NATIONAL MONUMENT

DEATH VALLEY NATIONAL MONUMENT

Las Vegas

LAKE MEAD NATIONAL RECREATION AREA

Great Basin National Park
Baker, Nevada   **SEE CLIMATABLE NO. 24**

MAILING ADDRESS: Superintendent, Great Basin National Park, Baker, NV 89311
Telephone: 702-234-7331

DIRECTIONS: (from N, S, E, W) Park headquarters is located 10 miles (16 km) from U.S.
6-50, near the Nevada-Utah boundary, and is reached via Nevada highways 487 and 488.
From Salt Lake City the park is 230 miles (368 km) via Interstate 15 and U.S. 6-50. From Las
Vegas the park is 286 miles (457.6 km) via Interstate 15, U.S. 93 and U.S. 6-50. From Reno
the park is 385 miles (616 km) via Interstate 80 and U.S. 50.

Great Basin National Park preserves 120 square miles (310 hectares) of the high Snake
Range, a prime example of the flora and fauna of the Great Basin Region. The park's diverse
environments range from high desert to alpine tundra and include stands of bristlecone pines
that are among the oldest known living things. The park also includes Lehman Caves, known
widely for its delicate dripstone formations. Created by Act of Congress on Oct. 27, 1986.
The former Lehman Caves National Monument was created on Jan. 24, 1922—the monument was absorbed into the new national park.

VISITOR ACTIVITIES: Interpretive walks and talks, scenic drive, hiking, camping, exhibits, audiovisual programs, picknicking, wildlife- and bird-watching, cave tours, photography, cross-country skiing, fishing, climbing, spelunking. Ranger-led tours of Lehman Caves are conducted daily on a ½-mile (.8-km) paved trail with stairways. About 1½ hours are required for the tour. The cave temperature averages a chilly 50°F (10°C), warm clothing is suggested. Tours are limited to a maximum of 30 people. Children under 16 must be accompanied by an adult. Ranger-led spelunking tours available through another cave in the park by reservation (from Memorial Day to Labor Day weekends only). This is a 3-hour tour and restrictions apply. Write ahead for reservation forms; **Permits:** Required for cave tours, available at Visitor Center. Spelunking Permit required for entry into any wild caves in the park. Voluntary registration for backcountry camping at Visitor Center. Nevada State fishing license and trout stamp required to fish the park streams; **Fees:** For Ranger-led cave tours: $3 for adults, $2 for children ages 6-15, $1.50 for Golden Age and Access Passport Holders, free for children under 6 years of age. For Ranger-led Spelunking Tours, $6 all participants. Dump station fee: $1. Camping fees $5 per night, $2.50 per night for Golden Age and Access Passport Holders; **Visitor facilities:** Visitor Center, exhibits, campgrounds, hiking trails, cafe and gift shop, picnic area, public telephone, trailer dump station; **HANDICAPPED ACCESSIBILITY:** Visitor Center and first room of cave are accessible. Some campsites accessible and may be reserved. **Any limitations on vehicle usage:** Wheeled vehicles are restricted to designated roadways, prohibited on hiking trails; **Hiking trails:** Yes, a nature trail at the Visitor Center and a system of trails on Wheeler Peak. Ask at Visitor Center for information on the many trails; **Backcountry:** Yes, extensive high elevation areas from 9,000 to 11,000 feet (2,700 to 3,300 m) accessible chiefly from May to Oct. Backcountry campers are asked to register at the Visitor Center upon their arrival in the Park. Knowledge of cross-country hiking skills recommended; **Camping:** Yes, 4 campgrounds, available on a first-come, first-served basis only; **Other overnight accommodations on site:** No; **Meals served in the park:** Yes, Easter weekend and Memorial Day weekend to the end of Oct. in a cafe adjacent to the Visitor Center; **Food and supplies obtainable in the park:** No; **Food and supplies obtainable nearby:** Yes, at Baker, NV 5 miles (8 km) east of Visitor Center, and Ely, NV 70 miles (112 km) west. Visitors traveling from the east should be aware that Delta, UT, 100 miles (160 km) east is the last stop for gas and supplies before reaching the vicinity of the Park; **Overnight accommodations:** Limited accommodations available in the Baker area, 5 miles (8 km). Additional accommodations available in Ely, NV 70 miles (112 km), or Delta, UT 100 miles (160 km). **First Aid available in park:** Yes; **Nearest Hospital:** Ely, NV 70 miles (112 km) via U.S. 6-50; **Days/Hours:** Park always open. Visitor Center open year-round from 8 a.m. to 5 p.m. Cave tours scheduled at least hourly in the summer; from Oct. to May tours at 9:00, 11:00, 2:00, and 4:00. Evening programs and guided walks on a varying schedule in the summer; **Holiday Closings:** Thanksgiving, Dec. 25, and Jan. 1; **Visitor attractions closed for seasons:** Cafe and Gift Shop closed Nov. through March. Wheeler Peak scenic drive inaccessible due to snow from approximately Oct. to May, above the 7500 foot (2200 m) level; **Weather:** Winters are cold with highs 30°F to 0°F. Summer temperatures reach 85° to 95°F during the daytime.

GENERAL INFORMATION: Visitors to the area should remain aware of the high elevation—7,000 to 13,000 feet (2,100 to 3,900 m)—those with a heart condition or difficulty breathing should adjust their activity accordingly. On the cave tours beware of low ceilings and slippery conditions; use the handrails and stay with your group at all times.

　　A Special Note: Great Basin National Park is one of America's newest National Parks, created by act of Congress on October 27, 1986. Currently a major planning effort is underway to determine levels of visitor use and development in the new park. As a result, facilities, permit requirements, and length of use limits may evolve over time. We suggest that you stop at the Visitor Center for up-to-the-minute information due to the changing situation at the Park or contact the Park by phone or mail in advance of your visit.

Death Valley National Monument
For details see listing in California

Lake Mead National Recreation Area
Boulder City, Nevada

MAILING ADDRESS: Superintendent, Lake Mead National Recreation Area, 601 Nevada Highway, Boulder City, NV 89005 **Telephone:** 702-293-8907

DIRECTIONS: The Alan Bible Visitor Center is near the west end of Lake Mead, on US Highway 93, 4 miles (6.4 km) east of Boulder City.

Lake Mead, formed by Hoover Dam, and Lake Mohave, formed by Davis Dam, dominate this first National Recreation Area. Both lakes are on the Colorado River and in the states of Nevada and Arizona. The Park was established by Congress on Oct. 8, 1964.

VISITOR ACTIVITIES: Swimming, fishing, boating, water skiing, dam tours, horseback riding, cruising, diving, backcountry hiking, hunting (in season only), camping; **Permits:** For fishing, an Arizona or a Nevada fishing license, available at most marinas, is required; **Fees:** $6 per night for developed campsites; **Visitor facilities:** Visitor Center, botanical garden, interpretive programs, camping and trailer sites, commercial boat trip, boat-mooring and marine supply rentals; **HANDICAPPED ACCESSIBILITY:** Many facilities are handicapped accessible. **Any limitations on vehicle usage:** Off-road vehicle travel is prohibited; **Hiking trails:** No, most hiking is cross-country; ask a Ranger about good routes; write for maps of approved roads. Carry plenty of water with you. In summer, the canyons heat up like furnaces. Hikers should have two or more quarts of water per person. There are no creeks or springs that have water suitable for drinking. Never enter abandoned mines or tunnels; shafts are deep and supporting timbers are old and rotten; **Backcountry:** Yes, check at the Visitor Center, see a Park Ranger; **Camping:** No reservations available for campsites. Nearly all developed areas have campgrounds equipped with individual campsites, fire grates, tables, water, restrooms, and sanitary disposal stations. Only at concessioner trailer courts are there utility hookups. To protect your gear, lock it when you leave camp and notify a Ranger if your campsite is left unattended for more than 24 hours. *Be alert for flash floods in stormy weather. Avoid wash bottoms, and never camp on low ground*; **Other overnight accommodations on site:** Yes, concession facilities are listed in a pamphlet available by mail from the Superintendent or at the Visitor Center; **Meals served in the park:** Yes, fast food available at each of the 9 developed areas; **Food and supplies obtainable in the park:** Yes, at concession facilities; **Food and supplies obtainable nearby:** Yes, in Boulder City, Searchlight, Bullhead City, Overton, Henderson; **Overnight accommodations:** Boulder City, 4 miles (6.4 km); Bullhead City, 6 miles (9.6 km); Henderson, 15 miles (24 km); Las Vegas, 25 miles (40 km); **First Aid available in park:** Yes; **Nearest Hospital:** Boulder City, 4 miles (6.4 km); **Days/Hours:** Park never closes; **Visitor attractions closed for seasons:** No; **Weather:** From late Sept. through late May, the weather is delightful. Even in July and August, when daytime temperatures may rise above 100°F, many visitors do not find the heat oppressive because of the low humidity. Summer nights are usually comfortable with low temperatures averaging 70°F. Be prepared for low temperatures on winter mornings and evenings. Bring warm clothing.

GENERAL INFORMATION: Safety Notes: For protection against brilliant sunshine, wear a hat and tinted glasses. When swimming, distances to the islands, buoys, and across coves are easily underestimated. Caution—air mattresses and blow-up toys, any inflatables, can blow away even on gentle wind, leaving you stranded far from shore. Never swim alone or from an unanchored boat. Remember, muscles tire quickly in cold water.

Always check the weather forecast and look for storm warning flags before going out boating or water skiing. If bad weather catches you on the water, put on your life jacket, head for the nearest sheltered cove, and wait it out. Call 702-736-3854 for a current forecast from the National Weather Service. Water skiers must wear a lifesaving device, and an observer must accompany the boat operator. Waters below Hoover Dam average in the low 50°s F, unsafe for swimming in Black Canyon. Beware of oleander bushes found in all campgrounds; they are poisonous. Do not let pets drink from the irrigation ditches. Do not use any part of this plant for firewood, or use its branches to roast marshmallows. Poison control phone 702-732-4989.

New Hampshire

APPALACHIAN NATIONAL SCENIC TRAIL

SAINT-GAUDENS NATIONAL HISTORIC SITE

Manchester

Appalachian National Scenic Trail
For details see listing in Maine

Saint-Gaudens National Historic Site
Cornish, New Hampshire

MAILING ADDRESS: Superintendent, Saint-Gaudens National Historic Site, R.R. 3, Box 73, Cornish, NH 03745 **Telephone:** 603-675-2175

DIRECTIONS: The Site is located on NH 12A in Cornish, NH, 9 miles (14.4 km) north of Claremont, NH, and 2 miles (3.2 km) from Windsor, VT. Visitors traveling via Int. 91 should use the Ascutney or Hartland, VT, exits; via 89, they should use the West Lebanon, NH, exit.

A memorial to the great American sculptor Augustus Saint-Gaudens (1848-1907), contains his home, "Aspet," and his studios and gardens. Authorized for addition to the National Park System on Aug. 31, 1964. Established in 1977.

VISITOR ACTIVITIES: Guided tours, Saint-Gaudens art works on exhibit, picnicking, fishing, concerts and art exhibitions in summer, snowshoe and cross-country skiing available on the grounds in winter; **Permits:** No; **Fees:** Entrance fee is $.50 per person, 16 and under free of charge (price is subject to change without notice; please call for current fee). Golden Eagle, Golden Age, and Golden Access Passports accepted and available; **Visitor facilities:** Parking, restrooms, picnic areas, museums, gardens and grounds; **Any limitations on vehicle usage:** No snowmobiles or other off-road vehicles are allowed; **Hiking trails:** 3½-mile (5.6-km) and nature trails; **Backcountry:** No; **Camping:** No; **Other overnight accommodations on site:** No; **Meals served in the park:** No; **Food and supplies obtainable in the park:** No; **Food and supplies obtainable nearby:** Yes, at Claremont, W. Lebanon, and Plainfield, NH, and Ascutney, Windsor, and Hartford, VT; **Overnight accommodations:** Claremont, W. Lebanon, NH, and Ascutney, Windsor, and Hartford, VT; **First Aid available in park:** No; **Nearest Hospital:** Windsor, VT, 2 miles (3.2 km); **Days/Hours:** Open Memorial Day weekend through Oct. from 8:30 a.m. to 4:30 p.m. daily; **Holiday Closings:** None (in season); **Visitor attractions closed for seasons:** House and studios are closed from Nov. through end of May; **Weather:** Temperatures range from 65-80°F in summer.

New Jersey

Appalachian National Scenic Trail
For details see listing in Maine

Delaware Water Gap National Recreation Area
For details see listing in Pennsylvania

Edison National Historic Site
West Orange, New Jersey

MAILING ADDRESS: Park Superintendent, Edison National Historic Site, Main Street at Lakeside Avenue, West Orange, NJ 07052 **Telephone:** 201-736-5050

DIRECTIONS: Site headquarters, on Main Street at Lakeside Avenue in West Orange, is 2 miles (3.2 km) west of Garden State Parkway (Exit 145) and ½ mile (.8 km) north of Interstate 280 (Exit 10—westbound, Exit 9—eastbound).
   Buildings and equipment used by Thomas A. Edison for many of his experiments are here, as are his library, papers, and models of some of his inventions. The Site also includes Glenmont, Edison's 15-acre estate and Victorian mansion, with original furnishings. Designated Dec. 6, 1955.

VISITOR ACTIVITIES: Guided tours, exhibits, audiovisual programs, school programs. **Permits:** For special uses and commercial photography only. **Fees:** $2 per person ages 17-61. Under 17 and over 61 are free. Golden Age/Access/Eagle Passports accepted and available. **Visitor facilities:** Parking, restrooms, sales area; **HANDICAPPED ACCESSIBILITY:** With assistance, the Laboratory Complex is accessible. Glenmont is not accessible. **Any limitations on vehicle usage:** Strollers not allowed on tour. Glenmont is located in a private residential community. Visitors are not permitted on private roads. Buses not permitted at Glenmont; **Hiking trails:** No; **Meals served in the park:** No; **Food and supplies obtainable in the park:** No; **Food and supplies obtainable nearby:** Yes, shops and restaurants within walking distance; **Overnight accommodations:** In the immediate area of West Orange, 1½ to 5 miles (2.4-8 km); **First Aid available in park:** Yes; **Nearest Hospital:** In Orange, 2 miles (3.2 km); **Days/Hours:** Visitor Center open daily, 9 a.m.-5 p.m. Laboratory tours daily 9:30 a.m.-3:30 p.m. Glenmont tours Wednesday through Sunday from April through September and again in December; otherwise, tours on Saturdays and Sundays. A pass for Glenmont must be obtained at the Laboratory Visitor Center. **Holiday Closings:** Thanksgiving, Dec. 25, and Jan. 1; **Visitor attractions closed for seasons:** Site is open year-round. Buildings are not air conditioned. Due to high heat and humidity in summer months portions of buildings may close. Tours go between buildings; inclement weather must be tolerated.

GENERAL INFORMATION: Interiors of both Glenmont and laboratory buildings can only be seen on guided tours. Tour reservations required for groups of 10 or more. Smoking food, and drink are not permitted on Site.

Gateway National Recreation Area
For details see listing in New York

Morristown National Historical Park
Morristown, New Jersey

MAILING ADDRESS: Superintendent, Morristown National Historical Park, Washington Place, Morristown, NJ 07960 **Telephone:** 201-539-2085

DIRECTIONS: The Park is most easily accessible by Int. 287. Southbound, use exit 32 for Washington's Headquarters and the Museum. Use exit 26B for the Jockey Hollow Area. Northbound, use exit 32A for the Headquarters and Museum, or for the Jockey Hollow Area use the exit for N. Maple Ave./Rte 202. Follow the brown directional signs. Morristown is also easily reached via US 202 or by NJ 24.

For two winters during the Revolution—1777 and 1779-80—the Continental Army established winter quarters here. The Park is divided into two main areas. The Jockey Hollow Area includes the Visitor Center, the Wick House, reconstructed soldier huts, hiking trails, and a tour loop road: Washington's Headquarters includes both the Museum and the Ford Mansion. Authorized for addition to the National Park System on Mar. 2, 1933.

VISITOR ACTIVITIES: Movies, exhibits, soldier life demonstrations, arts and crafts demonstrations, hiking, special events on weekends, wayside exhibits; **Permits:** No; **Fees:** Entrance fee is $1 for adults, under 17 and over 62 are free. Golden Eagle and Golden Age Passports accepted and available; **Visitor facilities:** Hiking trails, restrooms and sales areas throughout the Park; **HANDICAPPED ACCESSIBILITY:** Visitor Center in Jockey Hollow and Museum adjacent to Washington's Headquarters are wheelchair accessible. Historic buildings are *not* wheelchair accessible. **Any limitations on vehicle usage:** Park in designated areas only. Park roads are open from 8 a.m. to sunset; **Hiking trails:** Yes, Jockey Hollow has an extensive woodland trail system. Obtain maps at Visitor Center; **Backcountry:** No; **Camping:** No; **Other overnight accommodations on site:** No, within 30-40 miles (48-64 km) there are six State-run parks or forests that have camping facilities. In addition, there are several privately run campsites closer to Morristown. Contact the Park for further information; **Meals served in the park:** No, but picnic and eating facilities are available in the Lewis Morris County Park, which is adjacent to the Jockey Hollow Area; **Food and supplies obtainable in the park:** No; **Food and supplies obtainable nearby:** Yes, in Morristown, Bernardsville, Mendham; **Overnight accommodations:** About 5 miles (8 km) north of Morristown, near the intersection of Highways 10 and 202 East and West. Contact the Park for further information on nearby accommodations; **First Aid available in park:** Yes; **Nearest Hospital:** Morristown, Madison Avenue 1 mile (1.6 km) from HQ—5 miles (8 km) from Jockey Hollow area; **Days/Hours:** Park buildings open 9 a.m.-5 p.m.; Park roads open 8 a.m.-sunset, 7 days a week year-round; **Holiday Closings:** All Park buildings closed Thanksgiving, Dec. 25, and Jan. 1; **Visitor attractions closed for seasons:** Park is occasionally closed by snow or hazardous driving conditions. Some buildings closed during winter due to staff reductions.

GENERAL INFORMATION: Nearby points of interest include Edison National Historic Site (see listing in this book) and Great Swamp National Wildlife Refuge.

Pinelands National Reserve
New Jersey

DIRECTIONS: ONLY STATE PARK AREAS HAVE BEEN DEVELOPED AS YET. For further information, contact: State of New Jersey Department of Environmental Protection, Division of Parks and Forestry, State Park Service, CN 404, Trenton, NJ 08625, phone 609-292-2797.

Local, State, and Federal governments and the private sector combine in a new "reserve" policy to protect diversely owned lands from encroachment. This largest undeveloped tract on the Eastern seaboard has the equivalent of a 2,000 square-mile lake beneath the dwarfed pines and oaks of its shrubby, porous surface. Areas administered by N.J. Division of Parks and Forestry within Pinelands Reserve are Belleplain State Forest, Bass River State Forest, Double Trouble State Park, Island Beach State Park, Lebanon State Forest, Penn State Forest, and Wharton State Forest. Further information regarding Wildlife Management Areas may be obtained directly from the Division of Fish and Game and Wildlife, CN 400, Trenton, NJ 08625.

New Mexico

CAPULIN MOUNTAIN NATIONAL MONUMENT

AZTEC RUINS NATIONAL MONUMENT

FORT UNION NATIONAL MONUMENT

CHACO CULTURE NATIONAL HISTORICAL PARK

BANDELIER NATIONAL MONUMENT

PECOS NATIONAL MONUMENT

EL MALPAIS NATIONAL MONUMENT

EL MORRO NATIONAL MONUMENT

Albuquerque

SALINAS NATIONAL MONUMENT

GILA CLIFF DWELLINGS NATIONAL MONUMENT

WHITE SANDS NATIONAL MONUMENT

CARLSBAD CAVERNS NATIONAL PARK

Aztec Ruins National Monument
Aztec, New Mexico

MAILING ADDRESS: Superintendent, Aztec Ruins National Monument, P.O. Box 640, Aztec, NM 87410 **Telephone:** 505-334-6174, TDD: 334-6174

DIRECTIONS: The Monument is north of the city of Aztec, near the junction of US 550 and NM 544. You should stop first at the Visitor Center.

The 12th-century masonry and timber ruins of this Anasazi pueblo have been largely excavated and stabilized. The ruins, misnamed by early settlers, are unrelated to the Aztecs of Mexico. Created by Presidential Proclamation on Jan. 24, 1923.

VISITOR ACTIVITIES: Interpretive exhibits, picnicking, walking tours; **Permits:** No (subject to change); **Fees:** $1 per person 17 and older entrance fee. Golden Age, Golden Eagle, and Golden Access Passports accepted and available; **Visitor facilities:** Parking, restrooms, and exhibits at Visitor Center, picnic area; **HANDICAPPED ACCESSIBILITY:** Accessible restrooms, entrance, museum and sales area, and parking. TDD available. Sign language interpreter available on advance arrangement; **Any limitations on vehicle usage:** No (subject to change); **Hiking trails:** Yes, a self-guiding trail leads through the west ruin, the reconstructed Great Kiva, and the nearby Hubbard Ruin, a tri-walled structure; **Backcountry:** No; **Camping:** No; **Other overnight accommodations on site:** No; **Meals served in the park:** No; **Food and supplies obtainable in the park:** No; **Food and supplies obtainable nearby:** Yes, in Aztec; **Overnight accommodations:** Aztec, a short distance south on US 550 and NM 544; **First Aid available in park:** Yes, or nearby in Aztec; **Nearest Hospital:** Farmington, Maple Street, 15 miles (24 km); **Days/Hours:** Open daily from 8 a.m. to 5 p.m., longer hours from Memorial Day through Labor Day; **Holiday Closings:** Dec. 25 and Jan. 1; **Visitor attractions closed for seasons:** No; **Weather:** Summer: highs in the 90°'s, lows 40°s-50°s, thunderstorms late in the season. Fall and spring: highs 40°s to 80°s, lows often below 32°, spring is very windy. Winter: highs 20°s to 40°s, lows well below 32° with some snow.

GENERAL INFORMATION: The 800-year-old walls are fragile and will not tolerate people walking on them.

Bandelier National Monument
Los Alamos, New Mexico

MAILING ADDRESS: Superintendent, Bandelier National Monument, Los Alamos, NM 87544 **Telephone:** 505-672-3861

DIRECTIONS: The Monument is 46 miles (73.6 km) west of Santa Fe, NM, and is reached from Santa Fe north on US 285 to Pojoaque, then west on NM 502 to NM 4. Approach may also be made through the scenic Jemez country from Albuquerque via NM 44 and NM 4. Inquiry should be made during bad weather before attempting the latter trip. The Visitor Center, 3 miles (4.8 km) inside the Monument, is 10 miles (16 km) southwest of White Rock and 13 miles (20.8 km) south of Los Alamos, both on NM 4 (loop). The detached Tsankawi section of the Monument is 11 miles (17.6 km) north of Frijoles Canyon on NM 4.

Ruins of many cliff houses of 15th-century Pueblo Indians lie on the canyon-slashed slopes of the Pajarito Plateau. Created by Presidential Proclamation on Feb. 11, 1916.

VISITOR ACTIVITIES: Hiking, camping, interpretive and audiovisual exhibits, self-guiding walking tours, picnicking, campfire programs nightly in summer, printed ruins trail guides available in French, Spanish, Japanese, German; **Permits:** Required for backcountry travel, can be obtained from the Visitor Center; **Fees:** $5 per car entrance fee; $2 per person for individuals on buses, on foot, or traveling by other means. Golden Age, Golden Access, and Golden Eagle Passports accepted and available. $6 per night per site camping fee, ½ price for Golden Age Passport holders; **Visitor facilities:** Parking, restrooms, and exhibits at Visitor Center, campground is closed in December, January, February, picnic area, snack bar and gift shop are open all year; **HANDICAPPED ACCESSIBILITY:** Accessible restrooms in campground. First part of the ruins trail (Visitor Center to main ruin) wheelchair accessible. Wheelchair available for loan for use on ruins trail. Closed captioning available on audiovisual program. Braille guide to ruins available. **Any limitations on vehicle usage:** Vehicles are restricted to paved roads. Trail bikes are not allowed in the Monument; Trailers not allowed in canyon (all year, not just summer); parking on Mesa; **Hiking trails:** Yes, a 1-mile (1.6-km) round-trip trail from near the Visitor Center to the main ruin, and over 70 miles (112 km) of maintained backcountry trails; **Backcountry:** Yes, get information from a Park Ranger or by telephoning the Visitor Center; **Camping:** Yes, no reservations available for individual campsites. Group sites are reserved through the Visitor Center; **Other overnight accommodations on site:** No; **Meals served in the park:** Yes, at Frijoles Canyon snack bar; **Food and supplies obtainable in the park:** Yes; **Food and supplies obtainable nearby:** Yes, at White Rock, Los Alamos, Santa Fe; **Overnight accommodations:** White Rock, NM 4, 10 miles (16 km); Los Alamos, NM 4, 13 miles (20.8 km); Santa Fe, NM 4 to NM 502 at Pojoaque, US 285 to Santa Fe; **First Aid available in park:** Yes; **Nearest Hospital:** Los Alamos, NM 4, 13 miles (20.8 km); **Days/Hours:** Ruin trail open during daylight hours, Visitor Center 8 a.m.-4:30 p.m., longer hours in summer; **Holiday Closings:** Dec. 25; **Visitor attractions closed for seasons:** Trails are not cleared of snow in winter; **Weather:** From May-Sept., temperatures range from the low 50°sF at night to the high 80°sF in the daytime. The relative humidity is generally low. Thunderstorms, usually of short duration, are frequent in July and August.

GENERAL INFORMATION: Energy and endurance are required for longer hiking trips. You must be in good physical condition since trails lead into and out of deep, steep-walled canyons of the rough and broken country, and the altitude (about 7000 feet) places an additional burden on the heart and lungs. Dogs permitted in parking areas and campground only, must be on leash; not permitted on trails. No campfires in the backcountry.

TRAVEL ACCESS: Bus: Greyhound and Trailways provide daily service to Santa Fe; **Rail:** Amtrak serves Lamy (near Santa Fe); **Air:** Major airlines serve Albuquerque. Ross Airlines provides daily service to Los Alamos; **Other:** Taxi, charter tours available from Santa Fe, about 45 miles (72 km) away.

NEARBY FACILITIES & POINTS OF INTEREST: Campgrounds: Camel Rock Campground, north of Santa Fe on US 84-285; **Parks, other points of interest:** Pecos National Monument, Petroglyph National Monument in Albuquerque, the Los Alamos Science Museum and Los Alamos Historical Museum, Jemez State Monument (near Jemez Springs) and Coronado State Monument (in Bernalillo).

Capulin Volcano National Monument
Capulin, New Mexico

MAILING ADDRESS: Superintendent, Capulin Volcano National Monument, Capulin, NM 88414 **Telephone:** 505-278-2201

DIRECTIONS: The Monument is in the northeast corner of New Mexico. The entrance is on NM 325, 3 miles (4.8 km) north of the town of Capulin. From Clayton, Capulin is 54 miles (86.4 km) west on US 64/87; from Raton, 30 miles (48 km) east. The Visitor Center is ½ mile (.8 km) past the entrance.
   This symmetrical cinder cone is an interesting example of a geologically recent volcano. Created by Presidential Proclamation on Aug. 9, 1916.

VISITOR ACTIVITIES: Self-guiding trails, interpretive and audiovisual programs, picnicking; photography; flower-, bird-, and wildlife-watching; **Permits:** Yes, obtained at Visitor Center; **Fees:** $3 entrance fee per carload, $1 per person on commercial bus. Persons under 16 or over 62 are admitted free. Golden Age, Golden Eagle, and Golden Access Passports accepted and available; **Visitor facilities:** Parking, restrooms and water in the picnic area at the western base of the mountain; **HANDICAPPED ACCESSIBILITY:** Restroom and nature trail at Park Visitor Center. Parking at Visitor Center and in the picnic area and rim of the crater; **Any limitations on vehicle usage:** Vehicles are restricted to designated roadways; **Hiking trails:** Yes, trails lead around the rim and into the crater; **Backcountry:** No; **Camping:** No; **Other overnight accommodations on site:** No; **Meals served in the park:** No; **Food and supplies obtainable in the park:** No; **Food and supplies obtainable nearby:** Yes, in Capulin or Raton; **Overnight accommodations:** Raton, 30 miles (48 km) west on US 64-87, to Int. 25; **First Aid available in park:** Yes; **Nearest Hospital:** Raton, 30 miles (48 km) west on US 64-87, to Int. 25; **Days/Hours:** Park open all year. Visitor Center is open from 8 a.m.-4:30 p.m. Labor Day-Memorial Day; 8:00 a.m.-6:00 p.m. Memorial Day to Labor Day; Crater Rim Road closed at sunset; **Holiday Closings:** Dec. 25 and Jan. 1; **Visitor attractions closed for seasons:** The Monument is accessible throughout the year.

GENERAL INFORMATION: *For Your Safety*—The trails at Capulin Volcano are well-maintained but loose cinders on them can be hazardous. You should wear rubber-soled shoes on the hiking trails. Be on the lookout for rattlesnakes, which inhabit the area.

TRAVEL ACCESS: Bus: Greyhound provides service to Raton, NM, 30 miles (48 km) west of Park; **Rail:** Amtrak provides service to Raton, NM, 30 miles (48 km) west of Park; **Air:** Nearest air connections, Frontier flights to Pueblo, CO, 138 miles (220.8 km) northwest of Park; **Other:** Rental cars available in Raton.

NEARBY FACILITIES & POINTS OF INTEREST: Campgrounds: Capulin Camp, Capulin, NM, 505-278-2921, 3 miles (4.8 km) from Park. Sugarite State Park located in Raton.

Carlsbad Caverns National Park
Carlsbad, New Mexico   **SEE CLIMATABLE NO. 32**

MAILING ADDRESS: Superintendent, Carlsbad Caverns National Park, 3225 National Parks Highway, Carlsbad, NM 88220 Visitor Information No.: 505-785-2232

DIRECTIONS: The Park is just off US 62-180, 20 miles (32 km) southwest of Carlsbad, NM, and 150 miles (240 km) east of El Paso, TX. The Visitor Center is near the cavern entrance, which is 7 miles (11.2 km) west of Whites City, NM.

This series of connected caverns, one of the largest underground chambers yet discovered, has countless magnificent and unusual formations. Created by Presidential Proclamation on Oct. 25, 1923. Redesignated a national park May 14, 1930.

VISITOR ACTIVITIES: Picnicking, photography, cave tours, nature walks, exhibits, bat flight programs nightly in summer, primitive flashlight trips into New Cave; **Permits:** No; **Fees:** New Cave—$6 for adults, $3 for 15 and under; Carlsbad Cavern—$5 for adults, $3 for age 6 through 15, under 6 free; Golden Age and Access Passport holders 50% discount. **Visitor facilities:** Visitor Center, picnic areas, nature trails, restaurant, gift shop, nursery, kennel; **HANDICAPPED ACCESSIBILITY:** Parking, restrooms; reserved area for wheelchairs at amphitheater for Bat Flight Program; self-guiding nature trail is paved but has steep grades; in the cave, the RED TOUR is accessible, with some areas closed because of steep grades and narrow trails; the BLUE TOUR has stairs, steep grades and narrow tunnels; interpretive signs at pullouts along park entrance road; amplified radio receivers available for hearing impaired; Bat movie in theater captioned for heating impaired; **Any limitations on vehicle usage:** No, but be alert for deer and other animals bounding across the roadway; **Hiking trails:** Yes, hiking and backpacking opportunities in large, rugged backcountry but poorly marked trails. An adequate supply of water, good boots, and maps are essential; **Backcountry:** Yes, for safety, check with a Park Ranger before going into the backcountry; **Camping:** No; **Other overnight accommodations on site:** No; **Meals served in the park:** Yes, a restaurant is next to Visitor Center. Lunches and refreshments are also available underground; **Food and supplies obtainable in the park:** No; **Food and supplies obtainable nearby:** Yes, in Carlsbad and Whites City; **Overnight accommodations:** Carlsbad, 27 miles (43.2 km) and Whites City, 7 miles (11.2 km); **First Aid available in park:** Yes; **Nearest Hospital:** Carlsbad, 27 miles (43.2 km); **Days/Hours:** The Park and Visitor Center are open all year; **Holiday Closings:** Dec. 25; **Visitor attractions closed for seasons:** No; **Weather:** Summers are usually hot and winters mild. However, extreme changes can come at any time of the year. In spring, winds can be strong. In summer, thunderstorms accompanied by brief, but often heavy downpours, may bring flash floods to the canyon bottoms. In winter the normally mild weather may be broken by a short-lived snowstorm or a bone-chilling cold front sweeping through on gale force winds. In the caverns, the temperature remains a constant 56°F year-round.

GENERAL INFORMATION: *Precautions:* A light sweater or jacket is recommended and comfortable walking shoes with rubber soles and heels are a must for the cavern trip. Stay on cavern trails and do not run. If electrical power fails while you are underground, stop and remain quiet until emergency lights come on. Watch for rattlesnakes when hiking on the surface. Beware of the cactus and other desert plants; their spines can inflict painful injury.

Chaco Culture National Historical Park
Bloomfield, New Mexico

MAILING ADDRESS: Superintendent, Chaco Culture National Historical Park, Star Route 4, Box 6500, Bloomfield, NM 87413 **Telephone:** 505-988-6727

DIRECTIONS: The Park is in northwestern New Mexico. From the north, turn off NM 44 at Blanco Trading Post or Nageezi Trading Post, 7 miles (11.2 km) south of Blanco, and follow NM 57 for 29 miles (46.4 km) to park headquarters. This road is unpaved. From the south, turn north on NM 57 from I-40 at Thoreau and proceed 60 miles (96 km) to Chaco Canyon. A marked turnoff begins a 20-mile (32-km) stretch of unpaved NM Hwy 57, leading to the south entrance. The Visitor Center is just ahead. Because NM 57 is not paved into the Park, you should inquire locally regarding travel over this route in stormy weather.

The canyon, with hundreds of smaller ruins, contains 13 major Indian ruins unsurpassed in the United States, representing the highest point of Pueblo pre-Columbian civilization. Created by Presidential Proclamation on Mar. 11, 1907.

VISITOR ACTIVITIES: Guided tours and campfire talks in summer; exhibits, walking tours, picnicking, day hiking; Registration for the 4 Backcountry trails at trailhead. No overnight backpacking; **Fees:** An entrance fee is charged; $5 camping fee per night; **Visitor facilities:** Restrooms, campgrounds with firegrates, drinking water at Visitor Center, exhibits, interpretive programs; **HANDICAPPED ACCESSIBILITY:** Restrooms; several picnic tables adjusted for wheelchair use; two handicapped accessible campsites; handicapped accessible restroom in campground; **Any limitations on vehicle usage:** The Park's unpaved entrance roads are frequently rough, dusty and narrow; they are very slippery when wet. Do not drive off the graded roadway. Housetrailers longer than 30 feet in length are not allowed in the campground; **Hiking trails:** Yes, 5 self-guiding trails take you through several ruin complexes. Walking time for each is about 1 hour. There are 4 longer hikes as well. Inquire at Visitor Center; **Backcountry:** Day use only, by permit; **Camping:** Yes, no reservations accepted for the campsites, which are 1 mile (1.6 km) from the Visitor Center. Write to Chaco for group campsite reservations; **Other overnight accommodations on site:** No; **Meals served in the park:** No; **Food and supplies obtainable in the park:** No; **Food and supplies obtainable nearby:** At Blanco and Nageezi Trading Posts and in Crownpoint; **Overnight accommodations:** Thoreau, 60 miles (96 km); Bloomfield, 60 miles (96 km); Farmington, 80 miles (128 km); **First Aid available in park:** Yes; **Nearest Hospital:** Farmington, 80 miles (128 km); **Days/Hours:** 7 days a week from 8 a.m. to 5 p.m.; **Holiday Closings:** Visitor Center is closed Dec. 25 and Jan. 1; **Weather:** Although the climate is semi-arid, there is snow in winter, and thunderstorms are possible from June through September. Summers are usually hot and dry.

GENERAL INFORMATION: *For Your Safety*—Do not climb on the walls of the ruins, which are weak and dangerous. No collecting allowed of any artifacts, minerals, or plants. No telephone service available in the Park. Other points of interest in the vicinity are Mesa Verde National Park, 157 miles (251.8 km) north by road, El Morro National Monument, 96 miles (153.6 km) south and Aztec Ruins National Monument, 58 miles (92.8 km) (see listings in this book).

El Malpais National Monument
Grants, New Mexico

MAILING ADDRESS: El Malpais National Monument, Post Office Box 939, Grants, NM 87020. Contact: Doug Eury, Superintendent **Telephone:** 505-285-5406

Is now open to visitors.

El Malpais—"the badlands" in Spanish—is a spectacular volcanic area, partially formed as recently as 1,000 years ago, featuring spatter cones, a 17-mile-long lava tube system, and ice caves. The area is also rich in ancient Pueblo Indian history and features diverse ecosystems from high desert to subalpine forests.

Established: Dec. 31, 1987. Acreage: 114,886.68; Federal: 96,819.61; Nonfederal: 18,067.07.

El Morro National Monument
Ramah, New Mexico

MAILING ADDRESS: Superintendent, El Morro National Monument, Ramah, NM 87321 **Telephone:** 505-783-4226

DIRECTIONS: The Monument is 56 miles (89.6 km) southeast of Gallup via NM 602 and NM 53, and 42 miles (67.2 km) west of Grants via NM 53.

"Inscription Rock" is a soft sandstone monolith on which hundreds of inscriptions are carved, including those of 17th-century Spanish explorers and 19th-Century American emigrants and settlers. Pre-Columbian petroglyphs are also here. Created by Presidential Proclamation in 1906.

VISITOR ACTIVITIES: Hiking, camping, picnicking, campfire programs in summer; **Permits:** No; **Fees:** Yes, $1 per person, $3 per carload entrance fee. No charge for educational groups. Golden Age, Golden Eagle, and Golden Access Passports accepted and available; **Visitor facilities:** Self-guiding walk, campground and picnic area; **HANDICAPPED ACCESSIBILITY:** Hiking trails are surfaced with minimum inclines on the lower Inscription Rock Trail to make it suitable for guided wheelchair use; a wheelchair is available; **Any limitations on vehicle usage:** No off-road vehicles are allowed; vehicles are restricted to park roads; **Hiking trails:** Yes, 2 miles (3.2 km) of hiking trails; Mesa Top Trail rises 200 feet via switchbacks, a natural trail over the mesa top; **Backcountry:** No; **Camping:** Yes, no reservations accepted for campsites; **Other overnight accommodations on site:** No; **Meals served in the park:** No; **Food and supplies obtainable in the park:** No; **Food and supplies obtainable nearby:** Yes, limited supplies at Ramah, more extensive supplies at Grants and Gallup; **Overnight accommodations:** Grants, Int. 40, 42 miles (67.2 km); Gallup, Int. 40, 56 miles (89.6 km); **First Aid available in park:** Yes; **Nearest Hospital:** Grants, NM 53, 42 miles (67.2 km); Gallup, NM 53 and 32, 56 miles (89.6 km); **Days/Hours:** Open daily from 8 a.m to 5 p.m. year-round; until 7 p.m in summer, from approximately Memorial Day to Labor Day; **Holiday Closings:** Dec. 25; **Visitor attractions closed for seasons:** Mesa Top Trail closed during heavy snow accumulation; **Weather:** Warm sun (daytime) averaging 70s and 80s in summer; averaging 40s and 50s in winter; night-time average is 10s and 20s in winter with some -0 readings and 30s and 40s in summer. Usually a nice breeze in summer, average 16 to 18 inches of rain a year, and 4 to 12 inches of snow per storm.

GENERAL INFORMATION: Be cautious of soft terrain and high cliffs in this natural area. Dogs must be kept on a leash; hiking shoes or shoes with traction are recommended for the trails; children must be accompanied by an adult as the Mesa Top Trail is a natural trail climbing 200 feet. Advance notification is recommended to better accommodate groups.

Fort Union National Monument
Watrous, New Mexico

MAILING ADDRESS: Superintendent, Fort Union National Monument, Watrous, NM 87753 **Telephone:** 505-425-8025

DIRECTIONS: The Monument is 8 miles (12.8 km) north of I-25, at the end of NM 161. Watrous, NM, is ½ mile (.8 km) south of the intersection of these two highways.

Three successive U.S. Army forts were built on this site—a key defensive point on the Santa Fe Trail—and were occupied successively from 1851 to 1891. Ruins of the last fort, which was the largest military post in the Southwest, have been stabilized. Established by act of Congress on Apr. 5, 1956.

VISITOR ACTIVITIES: Interpretive exhibits, living history, walking tours, picnicking; **Permits:** No; **Fees:** Collected year-round, $1 per person or $3 per car; under 18 and over 62 free; **Visitor facilities:** Restrooms and parking at Visitor Center, picnic area, interpretive trail; **HANDICAPPED ACCESSIBILITY:** Parking, restrooms. Wheelchair is available at the Park for use on the trail; **Any limitations on vehicle usage:** All vehicles must park at the Visitor Center. No vehicles are allowed on the historic trail; **Hiking trails:** Yes, a 1½-mile (2.5-km) self-guiding trail; **Backcountry:** No; **Camping:** No; **Other overnight accommodations on site:** No; **Meals served in the park:** No; **Food and supplies obtainable in the park:** No; **Food and supplies obtainable nearby:** Yes, in Las Vegas, NM; **Overnight accommodations:** Las Vegas, NM, I-25, 28 miles (44.8 km) southwest; **First Aid available in park:** Yes; **Nearest Hospital:** Las Vegas, I-25, 28 miles (44.8 km) southwest; **Days/Hours:** Open daily from 8 a.m. to 5 p.m., longer hours in summer; **Holiday Closings:** Dec. 25 and Jan. 1; **Visitor attractions closed for seasons:** No; **Weather:** Summer is warm and windy with afternoon thundershowers. Winter is cold and windy with infrequent but sometimes heavy snowfalls.

GENERAL INFORMATION: *For Your Safety*—Do not climb on the walls or foundations of the ruins. Stay on the trail, because rattlesnakes can be found in the high grass. The third fort arsenal site is closed to the public.

Gila Cliff Dwellings National Monument
Silver City, New Mexico

MAILING ADDRESS: Gila Cliff Dwellings National Monument, Route 11, Box 100, Silver City, NM 88061 **Telephone:** 505-536-9461

DIRECTIONS: The Monument is 44 miles (70.4 km) north of Silver City at the end of NM 15, a steep and winding two-lane blacktop highway. The trip to the Dwellings through the mountains takes about 2 hours each way. Silver City is located on US 180, about 120 air miles (192 km) northwest of El Paso, TX. Due to road conditions, trailers over 20 feet are advised to use NM 35 through the scenic Mimbres Valley and by Lake Roberts, instead of NM 15. This is reached from NM 35, north from San Lorenzo, which is 19 miles (30.4 km) east of Silver City on Route 152.

These well-preserved cliff dwellings in natural alcoves on the face of a cliff were inhabited from about 1280 to the early 1300s. A.D. Created by Presidential Proclamation on Nov. 16, 1907.

VISITOR ACTIVITIES: Picnicking, fishing, exhibits, photography, walking; **Permits:** No; **Fees:** No; **Visitor facilities:** Self-guiding interpretive trail to the dwellings; Visitor Center with museum and bookstore; **Handicapped accessibility:** Parking and restrooms at Cliff Dwellings and Visitor Center. Contact Station and Visitor Center are accessible; **Any limitations on vehicle usage:** Restricted to pavement at Scorpion camping area; **Hiking trails:** Yes, a steep, 1 mile (1.6 km) trail leads to and through the Dwellings, situated about 180 feet above the canyon bottom. Plan about 1 hour for your visit; **Backcountry:** Yes, the Monument is surrounded by the Gila Wilderness; the trails are well-marked. Information at Gila Visitor Center. Wilderness permits are not required; **Camping:** No, but sites are available in Forest Service campgrounds nearby; **Other overnight accommodations on site:** No; **Meals served in the park:** No; **Food and supplies obtainable in the park:** No; **Food and supplies obtainable nearby:** Yes, Gila Hot Springs, about 3 miles (4.8 km) south of the Visitor Center; **Overnight accommodations:** Limited accommodations at Gila Hot Springs, NM 15, 3 miles (4.8 km); more extensive facilities at Silver City, NM 15, 44 miles (70.4 km); **First Aid available in park:** Yes; **Nearest Hospital:** Silver City, NM 15, 44 miles (70.4 km); **Days/ Hours:** Open daily from 8 a.m. to 6 p.m., Memorial Day through Labor Day; 9 a.m. to 4 p.m. the rest of the year. Visitor Center open daily from 8 a.m.-5 p.m. Memorial Day through Labor Day, and 8 a.m.-4:30 p.m. rest of year; **Holiday Closings:** Dec. 25 and Jan. 1; **Weather:** Summer daytime temperatures vary between 80 and 100°F; at night, from 45 to 55°F. Temperatures drop lower in the higher elevations. Spring and fall daytime temperatures range from 60 to 80°F, but nighttime temperatures require a selection of warm clothing. Warm bedding is a necessity, even in summer.

GENERAL INFORMATION: *For Your Safety*—Watch your step on the steep trails.

TRAVEL ACCESS: Bus: No; **Rail:** No; **Air:** No.

NEARBY FACILITIES & POINTS OF INTEREST: Camping, Food/Supplies, Hookups at Campbell's Vacation Center, Route 11, Box 80, Gila Cliff, NM; **Campgrounds:** Gila Cliff, NM, 505-536-9551, 3 miles (4.8 km) from Park.

Pecos National Historical Park
Pecos, New Mexico

MAILING ADDRESS: Superintendent, Pecos National Historical Park, Post Office Drawer 418, Pecos, NM 87552 **Telephone:** 505-757-6414 or 757-6032

DIRECTIONS: The park is 25 miles (40 km) southeast of Santa Fe by way of Int. 25 and may be reached from the interchanges at Glorieta, exit 299, via the town of Pecos, 2 miles (3.2 km) south, and Rowe, exit 307 miles, 5 miles (8 km) north.

Ruins of the ancient pueblo of Pecos (1350-1838) and two associated Spanish Colonial Missions built in the 17th and 18th centuries. The ruins later became a landmark on the Santa Fe Trail, ruts of which are still in existence. Authorized for addition to the National Park System on June 28, 1965.

VISITOR ACTIVITIES: Walking tours, picnicking; **Permits:** No; **Fees:** $1 per person, $3 per car; **Visitor facilities:** Visitor Center, picnic area, self-guiding interpretive trails; **HANDICAPPED ACCESSIBILTY:** Portions of the trail are handicap accessible, restrooms are accessible, and handicap parking is available both at the Visitor Center and picnic

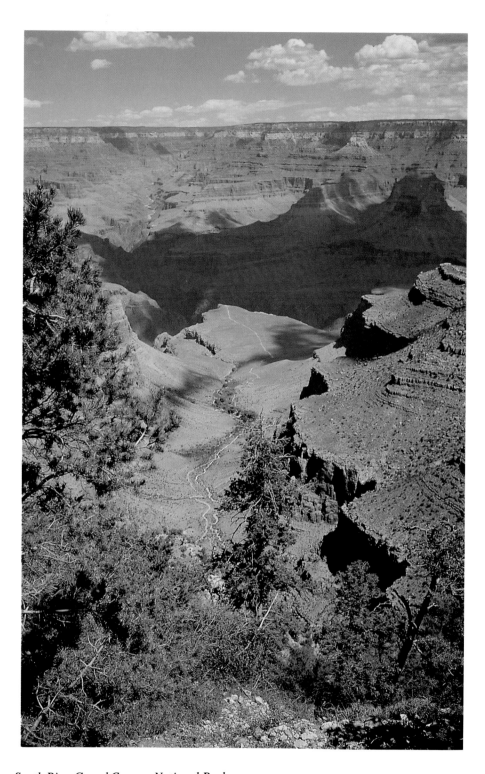

South Rim, Grand Canyon National Park

Halemaumau eruption, Hawaii Volcanoes National Park

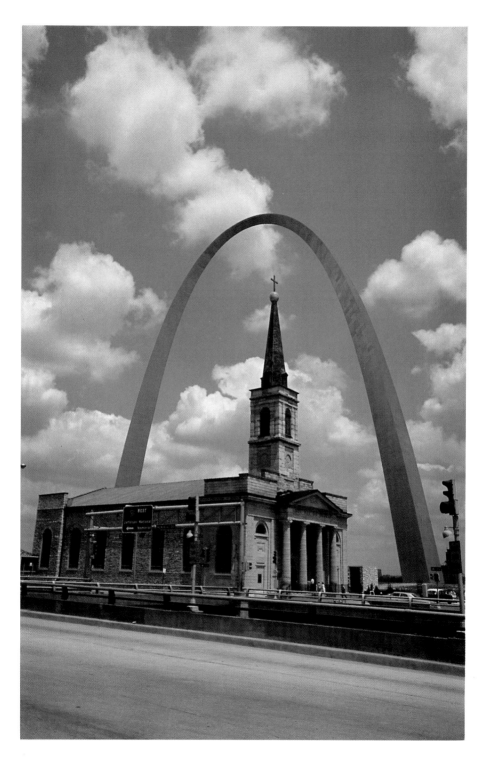

The Old Courthouse and Gateway Arch, Jefferson National Expansion Memorial

Birthplace of Martin Luther King, Jr.
Martin Luther King, Jr. National Historic Site and Preservation District

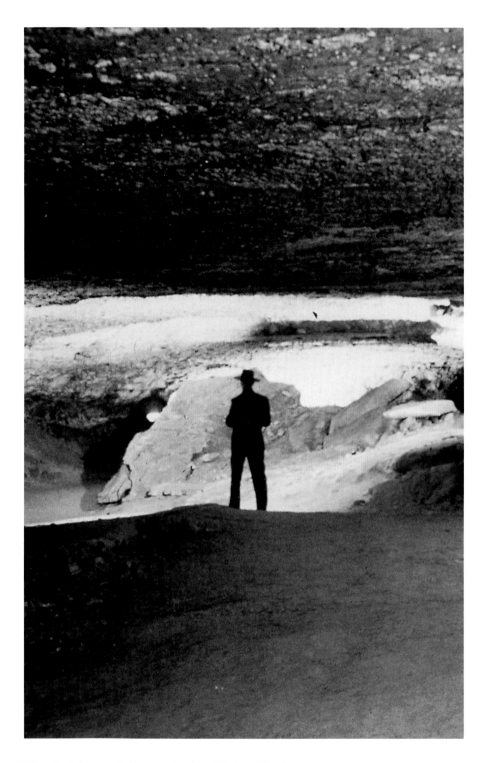

"Cleveland Avenue," Mammoth Cave National Park

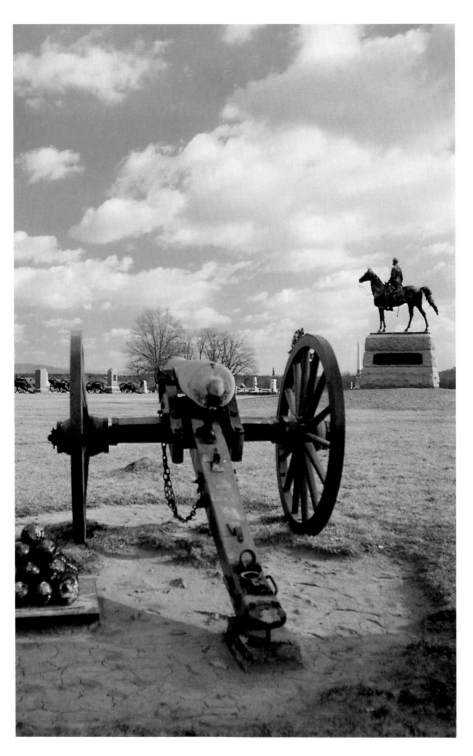

Cannon on battlefield, Gettysburg National Military Park

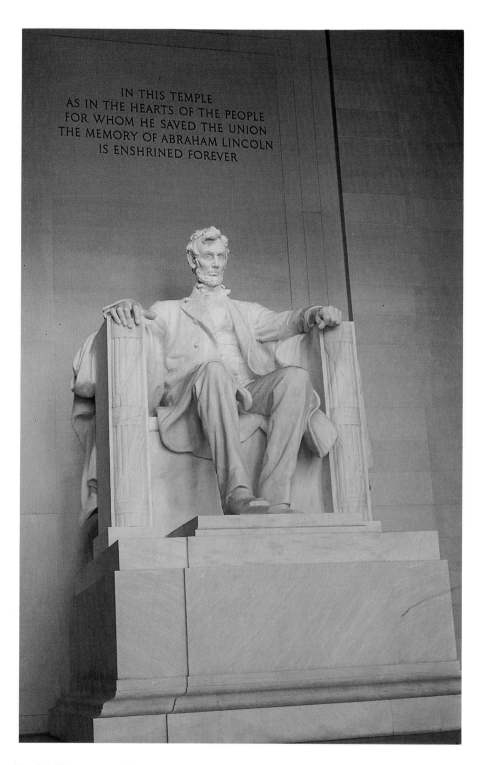

Daniel Chester French's statue of Abraham Lincoln, Lincoln Memorial

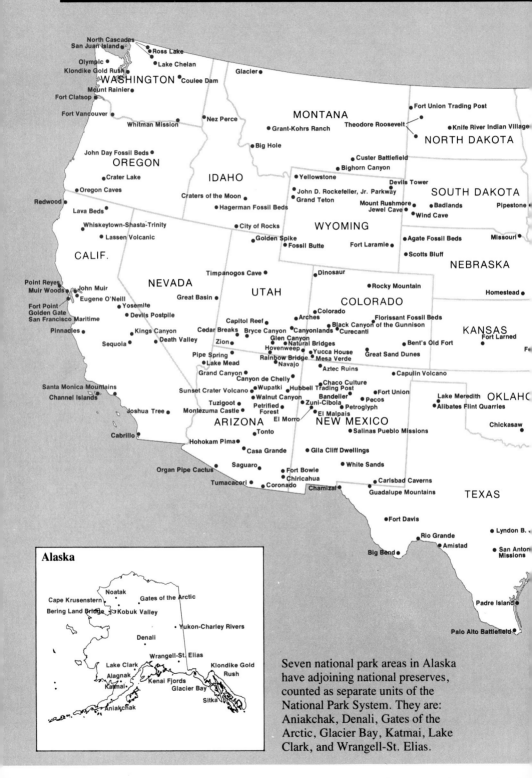

The National Park System

North Cascades
San Juan Island
Ross Lake
Olympic
Klondike Gold Rush
Lake Chelan
WASHINGTON
Coulee Dam
Glacier
Mount Rainier
Fort Clatsop
Fort Vancouver
Nez Perce
MONTANA
Fort Union Trading Post
Whitman Mission
Grant-Kohrs Ranch
Theodore Roosevelt
Knife River Indian Village
Big Hole
NORTH DAKOTA
John Day Fossil Beds
Custer Battlefield
OREGON
Bighorn Canyon
Crater Lake
IDAHO
Yellowstone
Devils Tower
Oregon Caves
Craters of the Moon
John D. Rockefeller, Jr. Parkway
SOUTH DAKOTA
Redwood
Hagerman Fossil Beds
Grand Teton
Mount Rushmore
Lava Beds
Jewel Cave
Badlands
Pipestone
Whiskeytown-Shasta-Trinity
City of Rocks
WYOMING
Wind Cave
Lassen Volcanic
Golden Spike
Fossil Butte
Fort Laramie
Agate Fossil Beds
Missouri
CALIF.
Scotts Bluff
NEBRASKA
Timpanogos Cave
Dinosaur
Point Reyes
Muir Woods
John Muir
NEVADA
Rocky Mountain
Homestead
Fort Point
Eugene O'Neill
Great Basin
UTAH
COLORADO
Golden Gate
San Francisco Maritime
Yosemite
Devils Postpile
Capitol Reef
Arches
Colorado
Florissant Fossil Beds
KANSAS
Pinnacles
Cedar Breaks
Bryce Canyon
Canyonlands
Black Canyon of the Gunnison
Curecanti
Fort Larned
Kings Canyon
Death Valley
Glen Canyon
Bent's Old Fort
Sequoia
Zion
Natural Bridges
Great Sand Dunes
Fe
Hovenweep
Yucca House
Pipe Spring
Rainbow Bridge
Mesa Verde
Lake Mead
Navajo
Aztec Ruins
Grand Canyon
Capulin Volcano
Santa Monica Mountains
Canyon de Chelly
Chaco Culture
Channel Islands
Sunset Crater Volcano
Wupatki
Hubbell Trading Post
Fort Union
Lake Meredith
OKLAHO
Walnut Canyon
Bandelier
Pecos
Tuzigoot
Zuni-Cibola
Petroglyph
Alibates Flint Quarries
Joshua Tree
Montezuma Castle
Petrified Forest
El Malpais
Chickasaw
ARIZONA
El Morro
NEW MEXICO
Cabrillo
Tonto
Hohokam Pima
Salinas Pueblo Missions
Casa Grande
Gila Cliff Dwellings
Saguaro
White Sands
Organ Pipe Cactus
Fort Bowie
TEXAS
Tumacacori
Chiricahua
Coronado
Chamizal
Carlsbad Caverns
Guadalupe Mountains
Fort Davis
Lyndon B.
Rio Grande
San Anton
Big Bend
Amistad
Missions

Alaska

Cape Krusenstern
Noatak
Gates of the Arctic
Bering Land Bridge
Kobuk Valley
Yukon-Charley Rivers
Denali
Wrangell-St. Elias
Lake Clark
Kliondike Gold Rush
Alagnak
Katmai
Kenai Fjords
Glacier Bay
Aniakchak
Sitka
Padre Island
Palo Alto Battlefield

Seven national park areas in Alaska have adjoining national preserves, counted as separate units of the National Park System. They are: Aniakchak, Denali, Gates of the Arctic, Glacier Bay, Katmai, Lake Clark, and Wrangell-St. Elias.

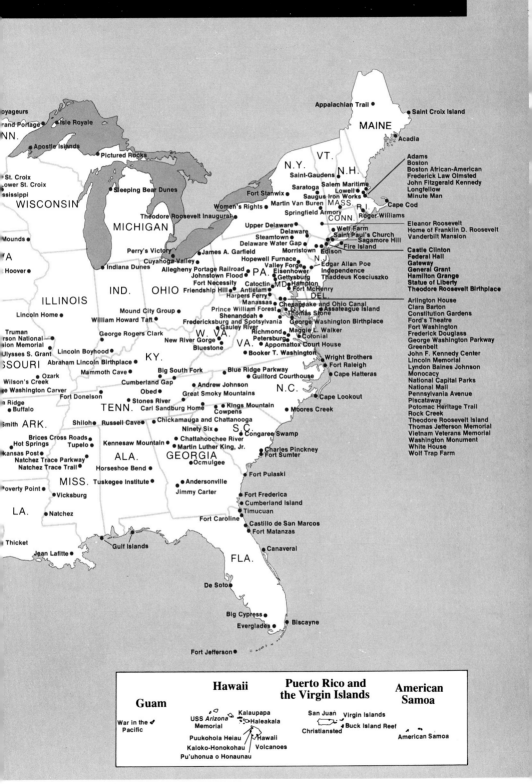

Voyageurs
Grand Portage
Isle Royale
MINN.
Apostle Islands
Pictured Rocks
St. Croix
Lower St. Croix
Mississippi
Sleeping Bear Dunes
WISCONSIN
Mounds
IOWA
Hoover
MICHIGAN
Theodore Roosevelt Inaugural
Perry's Victory
Cuyahoga Valley
James A. Garfield
Indiana Dunes
Allegheny Portage Railroad
Johnstown Flood
IND.   OHIO
Friendship Hill
ILLINOIS
Lincoln Home
Mound City Group
William Howard Taft
Truman
Jefferson National
Expansion Memorial
George Rogers Clark
Lincoln Boyhood
Ulysses S. Grant
Abraham Lincoln Birthplace
MISSOURI
Ozark
Wilson's Creek
George Washington Carver
Fort Donelson
KY.
Mammoth Cave
Big South Fork
Cumberland Gap
Andrew Johnson
Obed
Great Smoky Mountains
Ozark Ridge
Buffalo
Stones River
TENN.
Carl Sandburg Home
Smith ARK.
Shiloh   Russell Cave
Chickamauga and Chattanooga
Brices Cross Roads
Hot Springs   Tupelo
Ninety Six
Chattahoochee River
Kennesaw Mountain
Kansas Post
Natchez Trace Parkway
Natchez Trace Trail
Martin Luther King, Jr.
ALA.
GEORGIA
Ocmulgee
Horseshoe Bend
Poverty Point
MISS.
Tuskegee Institute
Andersonville
Vicksburg
Jimmy Carter
LA.
Natchez
Thicket
Jean Lafitte
Gulf Islands
FLA.
De Soto
Big Cypress
Everglades
Biscayne
Fort Jefferson

Appalachian Trail
Saint Croix Island
MAINE
Acadia
VT.
N.Y.
N.H.
Saint-Gaudens
Fort Stanwix
Saratoga
Salem Maritime
Lowell
Saugus Iron Works
MASS.
Women's Rights
Martin Van Buren
Springfield Armory
CONN.
Theodore Roosevelt Inaugural
R.I.
Cape Cod
Roger Williams
Upper Delaware
Delaware
Weir Farm
Steamtown
Saint Paul's Church
Delaware Water Gap
Sagamore Hill
Morristown
Fire Island
Hopewell Furnace
N.J.
Valley Forge
Edison
Eisenhower
Edgar Allan Poe
Gettysburg
Independence
PA.
MD.
Thaddeus Kosciuszko
Catoctin
Hampton
Antietam
Fort McHenry
Harpers Ferry
DEL.
Manassas
Chesapeake and Ohio Canal
Prince William Forest
Assateague Island
Shenandoah
Thomas Stone
Fredericksburg and Spotsylvania
George Washington Birthplace
Gauley River
Richmond
Maggie L. Walker
New River Gorge
W. VA.
Petersburg
Colonial
Bluestone
VA.
Appomattox Court House
Booker T. Washington
Wright Brothers
Fort Raleigh
Blue Ridge Parkway
Cape Hatteras
Guilford Courthouse
N.C.
Cape Lookout
Kings Mountain
Cowpens
Moores Creek
S.C.
Congaree Swamp
Charles Pinckney
Fort Sumter
Fort Pulaski
Fort Frederica
Cumberland Island
Timucuan
Fort Caroline
Castillo de San Marcos
Fort Matanzas
Canaveral

Adams
Boston
Boston African-American
Frederick Law Olmsted
John Fitzgerald Kennedy
Longfellow
Minute Man

Eleanor Roosevelt
Home of Franklin D. Roosevelt
Vanderbilt Mansion

Castle Clinton
Federal Hall
Gateway
General Grant
Hamilton Grange
Statue of Liberty
Theodore Roosevelt Birthplace

Arlington House
Clara Barton
Constitution Gardens
Ford's Theatre
Fort Washington
George Washington Parkway
Greenbelt
John F. Kennedy Center
Lincoln Memorial
Lyndon Baines Johnson
Monocacy
National Capital Parks
National Mall
Pennsylvania Avenue
Piscataway
Potomac Heritage Trail
Rock Creek
Theodore Roosevelt Island
Thomas Jefferson Memorial
Vietnam Veterans Memorial
Washington Monument
White House
Wolf Trap Farm

Guam
War in the
Pacific

Hawaii
USS Arizona
Memorial
Kalaupapa
Haleakala
Puukohola Heiau
Kaloko-Honokohau
Pu'uhonua o Honaunau
Hawaii
Volcanoes

Puerto Rico and
the Virgin Islands
San Juan
Virgin Islands
Christiansted
Buck Island Reef

American
Samoa
American Samoa

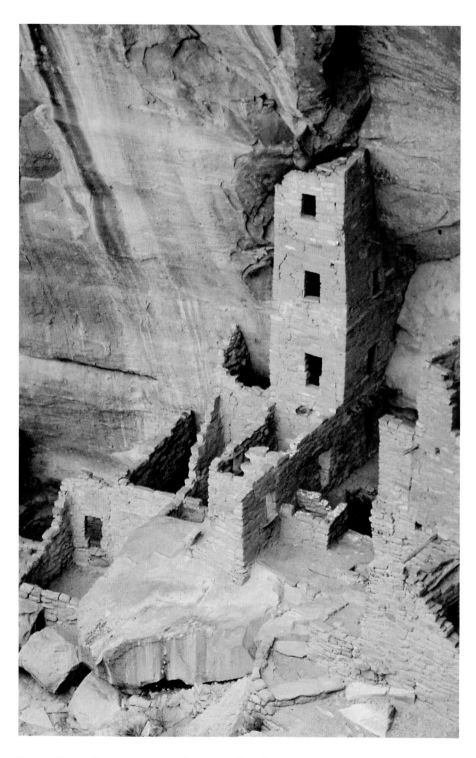

Square Tower House, Mesa Verde National Park

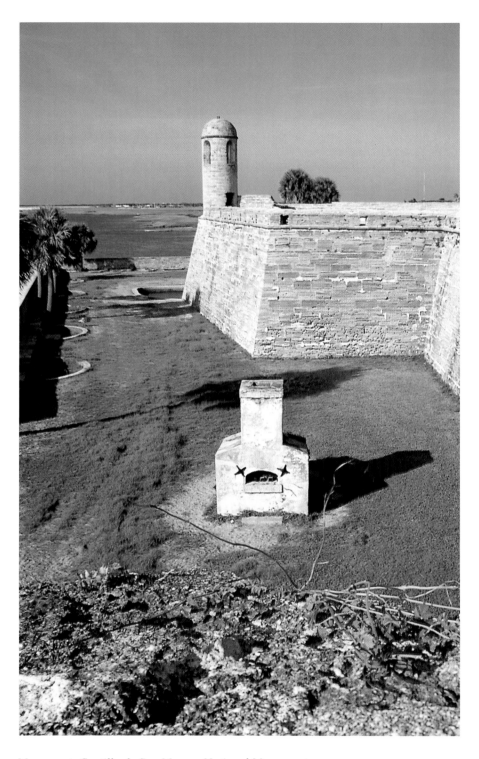

Monument, Castillo de San Marcos National Monument

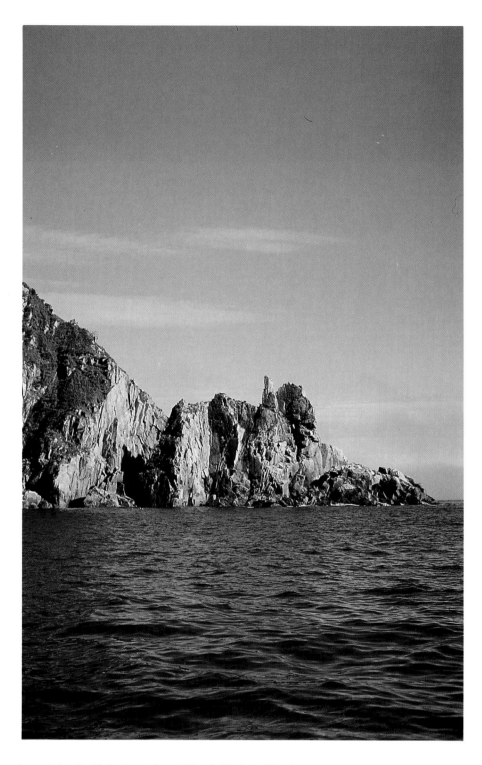

Outer Islands, Nuka Bay, Kenai Fjords National Park

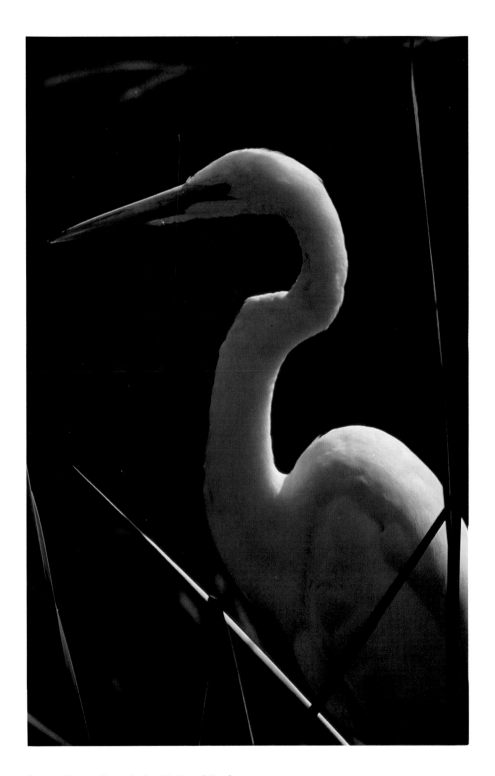

Snowy Egret, Everglades National Park

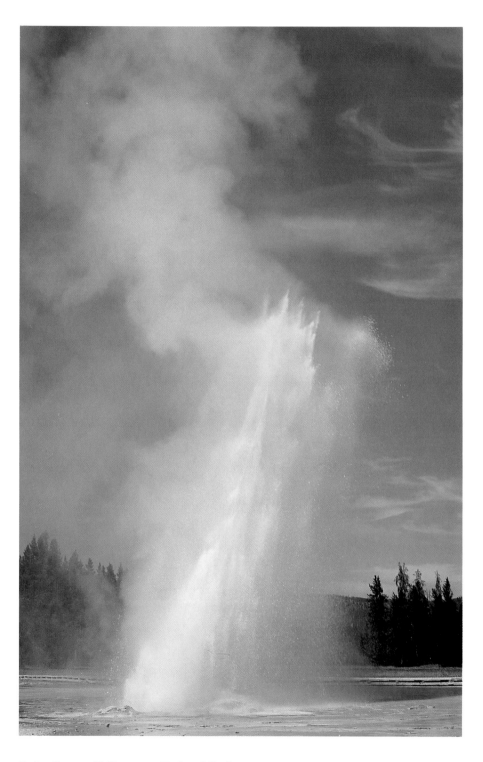

Daisy Geyser, Yellowstone National Park

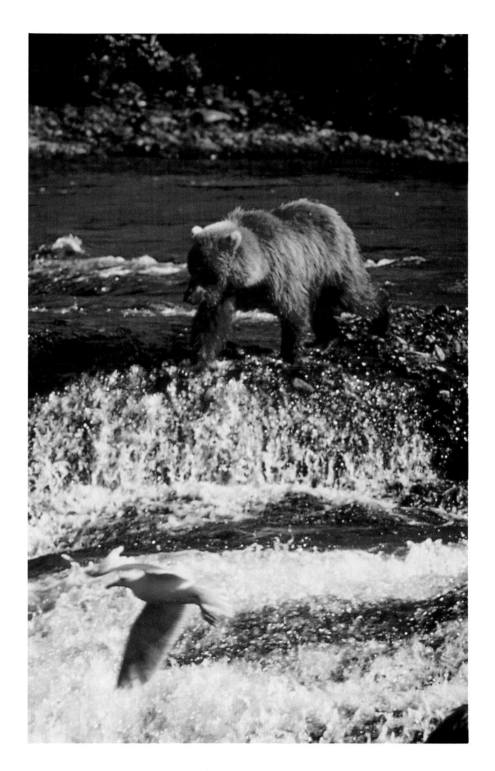

Bear on falls, Katmai National Park

Picnic area, Cuyahoga Valley National Recreation Area

area; **Any limitations on vehicle usage:** Vehicles are restricted to designated roadways; **Hiking trails:** Yes, a walking trail leads to the ruins; **Backcountry:** No; **Camping:** No; **Other overnight accommodations on site:** No, camping is available in the Santa Fe National Forest north of the village of Pecos, on State 63, and in other nearby areas. For further information, contact the Forest Supervisor, Santa Fe National Forest, P.O. Box 1689, Santa Fe, NM 98501, phone 505-988-6313; **Meals served in the park:** No, but in Pecos, NM, 2 miles (3.2 km) north of the park; **Food and supplies obtainable in the park:** No; **Food and supplies obtainable nearby:** Yes, in Pecos, 2 miles (3.2 km) north; **Overnight accommodations:** Pecos, adjacent to the Park; Santa Fe, 25 miles (40 km) northwest; Las Vegas, NM, 35 miles (56 km) east; **First Aid available in park:** Yes; **Nearest Hospital:** A small clinic is located in Pecos, NM, 2 miles (3.2 km) north of the park. A hospital is in Santa Fe, via I-25, 25 miles (40 km) distant; **Days/Hours:** Open daily from 8 a.m. to 5 p.m., until 6 p.m. in summer; **Holiday Closings:** Dec. 25 and Jan. 1; **Weather:** The elevation is 7000 feet. Summer daytime temperatures average in the 80s and 90s, with cool evenings. July and August are rainy. Winter temperatures are variable, ranging from 0° to the mid 40s; snowfall is heavy at times.

GENERAL INFORMATION: Visitors should use caution due to a few trail irregularities, an occasional prairie rattlesnake, and when using ladders into the restored kivas. Do not climb or stand on the fragile ruins.

Salinas Pueblo Missions National Monument
Mountainair, New Mexico

MAILING ADDRESS: Superintendent, Salinas Pueblo Missions National Monument, P.O. Box 496 Mountainair, NM 87036 **Telephone:** 505-847-2585

DIRECTIONS: Mountainair can be reached by taking I-25 south to Belen to NM 47 to U.S. 60 east 21 miles (33.6 km) to Mountainair. To travel the scenic route from the north, take I-40 east from Albuquerque to NM 337; turn south and drive 54 miles (86.4 km) to Mountainair. From U.S. 380 turn north at Carrizozo and drive 18 miles (28.8 km) via U.S. 54 to NM 55. Take NM 55 northwest and drive 61 miles (97.6 km) to U.S. 60. Area information is available at Salinas Pueblo Missions National Monument headquarters in Mountainair. Ruins of prehistoric Indian Pueblos and associated 17th-century Spanish Missions comprise the Abo', Quarai, and Gran Quivira units of Salinas Pueblo Missions National Monument. Established Dec. 19, 1980.

The Gran Quivira Unit is 26 miles (41.6 km) south on NM 55 from Mountainair; the Quarai Unit is 8 miles (12.8 km) north on NM 55, Abo' is 9 miles (14.4 km) west on U.S. 60 from Salinas headquarters.

VISITOR ACTIVITIES: Interpretive exhibits, a 30-minute self-guiding walking tour at Abo', Quarai, and Gran Quivira Ruins; picnicking at Abo', Gran Quivira, and Quarai Ruins; **Permits:** No; **Visitor facilities:** Visitor Center, parking, restrooms, picnic areas at Gran Quivira, Quarai, and Abo' Ruins; **HANDICAPPED ACCESSIBILITY:** Headquarters in Mountainair; Visitor Center, parking, restrooms, and picnic area; Quarai: Visitor Center, parking, picnic area, and trail when weather is good; Gran Quivira: Visitor Center, parking, and picnic area; Abo' is not handicapped accessible; Trails are accessible with some difficulty; **Any limitations on vehicle usage:** No; **Hiking trails:** Yes; ¼-mile (.4-km) trails around ruins at Abo', Quarai, and Gran Quivira Ruins; **Backcountry:** No; **Camping:** No; **Other overnight accommodations on site:** No; **Meals served in the park:** No; **Food and supplies obtainable nearby:** Yes, in Mountainair; **Overnight accommodations:** Mountainair; **First Aid available in park:** Yes, at Abo', Quarai, Gran Quivira Ruins and Park headquarters in Mountainair; **Nearest Hospital:** Albuquerque, I-25, 75 miles (120 km); **Days/Hours:** Headquarters in Mountainair, 8 a.m.-5 p.m.; Abo, Gran Quivira, Quarai, 9: a.m. - 6:00 p.m. MST; **Holiday Closings:** Dec. 25 and Jan. 1; **Visitor attractions closed for seasons:** No; **Weather:** Summer is warm with thundershowers likely; winter daytime temperatures range from 40° to 60°F.

NEARBY FACILITIES & POINTS OF INTEREST: Hotel/Motel: El Rancho Motel, and Trails End Motel, Mountainair, NM, 505-847-2577 and 505-847-2544, Shaffer Hotel, 505-847-2888; **Parks, other points of interest:** White Sands, Carlsbad Caverns, Pecos, Bandelier National Monument; **New information:** Gran Quivira National Monument became Salinas National Monument on Dec. 19, 1980. It also incorporated the former Abo' and Quarai State Monuments (Oct. 2, 1981). In Oct. 1988 Salinas National Monument changed its name to Salinas Pueblo Missions National Monument. A headquarters with visitor reception, exhibits, and an orientation slide show is located in Mountainair.

White Sands National Monument
Alamogordo, New Mexico

MAILING ADDRESS: Superintendent, White Sands National Monument, Box 458, Alamogordo, NM 88311-0458 **Telephone:** 505-479-6124 or 6125

DIRECTIONS: The Visitor Center is 15 miles (24 km) southwest of Alamogordo on US Highway 70-82.
Dunes of sparkling white gypsum sands 10 to 45 feet (3.05 to 13.71 m) high are home to small, light-colored animals that have adapted to this harsh environment. Created by Presidential Proclamation on Jan. 18, 1933.

VISITOR ACTIVITIES: Guided walks, illustrated evening programs, and star programs in summer; hiking; picnicking; backcountry; **Permits:** No; **Fees:** $3 per car entrance fee. Golden Eagle and Golden Age Passports accepted and available; **Visitor facilities:** Museum, gift shop, picnic areas, grills, comfort facilities, drinking water only at the Visitor Center; **HANDICAPPED ACCESSIBILITY:** Visitor's Center and comfort stations; **Any limitations on vehicle usage:** Vehicles are restricted to roads and parking areas; **Hiking trails:** Yes, self-guiding nature trails; **Backcountry:** No; **Camping:** No campgrounds, but primitive backcountry camping is available requiring registration and clearance at Headquarters. The nearest public camping facilities are in Lincoln National Forest, 35 miles (56 km) to the east and at Aguirre Springs, 30 miles (48 km) to the west. Information on National Forest camping can be obtained from the Forest Supervisor, Lincoln National Forest, Alamogordo, NM 88310. For information on Aguirre Springs, write the District Manager, Bureau of Land Management, P.O. Box 1420, Las Cruces, NM 88001. Several commercial campgrounds are open year-round in Alamogordo and Las Cruces. Oliver Lee Memorial State Park, 13 miles (20.8 km) south of Alamogordo, off Highway 54, has 44 sites, some with full hook-ups. Write Superintendent, Oliver Lee Memorial State Park, P.O. Box 1845, Alamogordo, NM 88310; **Meals served in the park:** No; **Food and supplies obtainable in the park:** Gift Shop has packaged sandwiches, snack food and drinks; **Food and supplies obtainable nearby:** Yes, at Alamogordo; **Overnight accommodations:** Alamogordo, Highway 70-82, 15 miles (24 km) northeast; **First Aid available in park:** Yes; **Nearest Hospital:** Alamogordo, Highway 70-82, 15 miles (24 km) northeast; **Days/Hours:** Visitor Center: Summers 8 a.m. to 7 p.m. Remainder of year 8 a.m. to 4:30 p.m. Dunes Drive: Summer 6:30 a.m. to 10 p.m.; Rest of year 7 a.m. to ½ hour after sunset; **Holiday Closings:** Dec. 25; **Weather:** Hot summers, with late summer thunderstorms. Mild, dry winters.

TRAVEL ACCESS: Bus: New Mexico Transportation provides regular transportation to Alamogordo, NM, and park area; **Rail:** Amtrak provides daily service to El Paso, TX, and Albuquerque, NM; **Air:** Airways of New Mexico provides service to Alamogordo, NM.

NEARBY FACILITIES & POINTS OF INTEREST: Hotel/Motel: Holiday Inn, Highway 54-70, 505-437-7100; Desert Aire Motor Hotel, Highway 54-70, 505-437-2110; **Campgrounds:** KOA campground, 412 24th St., Alamogordo, Breezy Point, Highway 82, 505-437-1761; **Parks, other points of interest:** New Tombaugh Omni Space Theater, International Space Hall of Fame in Alamogordo.

Zuni-Cibola National Historical Park
Sante Fe, New Mexico

MAILING ADDRESS: Zuni-Cibola National Historical Park, c/o Southwest Regional Office, National Park Service, Post Office Box 728, Sante Fe, NM 87504-0728

Will not be open in 1991-1992.
Established to preserve and protect the nationally significant historical, archeological, and cultural sites associated with the Zuni Tribe over its 1,700-year cultural continuum. Featured will be the Anasazi, Mogollon, and Hohokam roots of the Zuni people, the momentous encounter of the Zuni people with the 1540 Corondado Expedition seeking the "Seven Cities of Cibola," and the unique contribution represented by Zuni culture.
Established: Oct. 31, 1988. Establishment to become effective upon the development and approval of a leasehold agreement.

New York

SARATOGA NATIONAL HISTORIC PARK
FORT STANWIX NATIONAL MONUMENT

WOMEN'S RIGHTS NATIONAL
HISTORICAL PARK
THEODORE ROOSEVELT INAUGURAL
NATIONAL HISTORIC SITE

Buffalo

UPPER DELAWARE NATIONAL SCENIC RIVER
MARTIN VAN BUREN NATIONAL HISTORIC SITE
VANDERBILT MANSION NATIONAL HISTORIC SITE
HOME OF FRANKLIN DELANO ROOSEVELT
NATIONAL HISTORIC SITE
ELEANOR ROOSEVELT NATIONAL HISTORIC SITE
APPALACHIAN NATIONAL SCENIC TRAIL
SAINT PAUL'S CHURCH NATIONAL HISTORIC SITE
GATEWAY NATIONAL RECREATION AREA
SAGAMORE HILL NATIONAL HISTORIC SITE
FIRE ISLAND NATIONAL SEASHORE

New York

Appalachian National Scenic Trail
For details see listing in Maine

Castle Clinton National Monument
New York, New York

MAILING ADDRESS: Superintendent, Manhattan Sites, 26 Wall Street, New York, NY 10005 **Telephone:** 212-264-4456

DIRECTIONS: The Monument is located in Battery Park at the southern tip of Manhattan. Public transportation is recommended.

Built in 1807-11, this structure served successively as a defense for New York harbor, an entertainment center and opera house 1824-1855, an immigration depot 1855-1890, and the New York City Aquarium 1896-1941. The structure today resembles its original appearance as a fort during the War of 1812 period. Castle Clinton also serves as the N.P.S. Visitor Center for the New York area and ticket sales area for the ferry to the Statue of Liberty and Ellis Island scheduled to begin in 1990. Authorized for addition to the National Park System, Aug. 12, 1946.

VISITOR ACTIVITIES: Interpretive exhibits, tours, school programs; **Permits:** For special uses, commercial photography, public gatherings; **Fees:** For round-trip ferry to Statue of Liberty–Ellis Island tickets: Adults $6.00, Seniors $5.00, Children $3.00. Admission to Castle Clinton Museum is free; **Visitor facilities:** Museum, restrooms; **HANDICAPPED ACCESSIBILITY:** Museum, restrooms; **Any limitations on vehicle usage:** No vehicles are allowed in the park; **Meals served in the park:** No; **Food and supplies obtainable in the park:** No; **Food and supplies obtainable nearby:** Yes; **Overnight accommodations:** In New York City; **First Aid available in park:** Yes; **Nearest Hospital:** Beekman Downtown Hospital ½ mile (.8 km); **Visitor attractions closed for seasons:** Monument open 7 days a week; **Days/Hours:** 8:30 a.m. to 5 p.m. Call Circle Line at 212-563-3590 for current ferry schedules; **Holiday Closings:** Dec. 25; **Weather:** Windy and cold in winter, hot and humid in summer.

GENERAL INFORMATION: Castle Clinton is located in the northwest corner of Battery Park. Food and pets are prohibited inside the Monument.

TRAVEL ACCESS: Bus: New York City buses M1, M6, or M15 to South Ferry, Battery Park; **Other:** Subway: Lexington Avenue IRT express (#4,5) to Bowling Green; RR BMT to Whitehall Street; 7th Avenue IRT local (#1) to South Ferry.

NEARBY FACILITIES & POINTS OF INTEREST: Federal Hall, Statue of Liberty, and Ellis Island National Monuments (see listings in this book), Battery Park, Fraunces Tavern, South Street Seaport, Staten Island Ferry, Governors Island, New York Stock Exchange, and World Trade Center.

Eleanor Roosevelt National Historic Site
Hyde Park, New York

MAILING ADDRESS: Roosevelt-Vanderbilt National Historical Sites, 519 Albany Post Rd., Hyde Park, NY 12538 **Telephone:** Information: 914-229-7821, Reservations: 914-229-9115

DIRECTIONS: Two hours north of New York City - 2 miles due east on U.S. Rt. 9G (from the home of FDR, Vanderbilt Mansion NHS). Mrs. Roosevelt's home, known as Val-Kill, was authorized as a National Historic Site in 1977 "to commemorate for the education, inspiration, and benefit of present and future generations the life and work of an outstanding woman in American history." The site comprises several modest buildings in a setting of fields, woods, and wetlands.

VISITOR ACTIVITIES: Guided tours; **Permits:** No; **Fees:** No; **Visitor facilities:** Guided tour of Mrs. Roosevelt's home; **HANDICAPPED ACCESSIBILITY:** Restrooms first floor; **Hiking trails:** Yes, rough terrain, hiking boots needed; **Backcountry:** No; **Camping:** No; **Other overnight accommodations on site:** No; **Food and supplies obtainable in the park:** No; **Food and supplies obtainable nearby:** Yes, Town of Hyde Park; **Overnight accommodations:** In Town of Hyde Park; **First Aid available in park:** Yes; **Days/Hours:** Open 7 days a week May-Oct. 9 a.m.-5 p.m. Open Saturdays and Sundays in Nov., Dec., and March from 9 a.m.-5 p.m., access by private vehicle. Groups of 10 or more must make reservations all year except on Tuesdays and Wednesdays, Nov.-March; **Holiday Closings:** Thanksgiving Day, Dec. 25, and Jan. 1; **Visitor attractions closed for seasons:** No.

NEARBY FACILITIES & POINTS OF INTEREST: Hotel/Motels: Several in area; **Food/Supplies:** Several in area; **Campgrounds:** Norrie State Park, Staatsburg, phone 914-889-4100; **Parks, other points of interest:** Home of Franklin D. Roosevelt, Vanderbilt Mansion.

SAINT PAUL'S CHURCH NATIONAL HISTORIC SITE

HAMILTON GRANGE NATIONAL MEMORIAL

GENERAL GRANT NATIONAL MEMORIAL

THEODORE ROOSEVELT BIRTHPLACE
NATIONAL HISTORIC SITE

FEDERAL HALL NATIONAL MEMORIAL

CASTLE CLINTON NATIONAL MONUMENT

ELLIS ISLAND

STATUE OF LIBERTY NATIONAL MONUMENT

Ellis Island
New York, New York   **SEE CLIMATABLE NO. 25**

MAILING ADDRESS: Superintendent, Statue of Liberty National Monument, Liberty Island, New York, NY 10004 **Telephone:** 212-363-7770 or 7771

DIRECTIONS: Ellis Island is accessible only by ferry. Circle Line Ferries leave Battery Park in lower Manhattan and Liberty State Park in New Jersey. For schedule and group-rate information, call 212-269-5755.

More than half of the immigrants entering the United States between 1892 and 1924 passed through the gates of Ellis Island. Added by Presidential Proclamation to the Statue of Liberty National Monument on May 11, 1965.

VISITOR ACTIVITIES: Visitors can take advantage of guided tours, photographic tours, museum exhibits, library and movie theaters; **Permits:** Yes; **Fees:** $6 charge for adults and $3 for children under 17 for the round-trip ferry boat ride. No fees charged for admission to the Immigration Museum; **Visitor facilities:** Restrooms, public telephones, refreshments, souvenirs and books relating to Immigration are available; **Any limitations on vehicle usage:** No docking is permitted for private boats; **Hiking trails:** No; **Camping:** No; **Other overnight accommodations on site:** No; **Meals served in the park:** Yes, snacks available at refreshment stand; **Overnight accommodations:** New York City and nearby New Jersey; **First Aid available in park:** Yes; **Nearest Hospital:** New York—takes about 45 minutes to reach; **Days/Hours:** Open daily year-round from 9 a.m.-5 p.m., with extended hours in season; **Holiday Closings:** Dec. 25.

GENERAL INFORMATION: School groups should contact the school coordinator for pre-visit materials at 212-363-7620. Large groups should make reservations with the Circle Line Ferry, 212-269-5755.

TRAVEL ACCESS: Bus: Greyhound, Shortline, and other long-distance lines provide regular service to Port Authority Terminal; **Rail:** Amtrak, Conrail (Metropolitan Transit Authority intraregional lines) service both Pennsylvania Station and Grand Central Station; **Air:** Major and regional airlines provide regular service to Newark, La Guardia, and John F. Kennedy airports; **Other:**Metropolitan Transit Authority buses run frequently to South Ferry from Journal Square; Central Bus runs service morning and afternoon to Liberty State Park, Jersey City; Metropolitan Transit Authority provides subway service to South Ferry and Bowling Green Stations.

NEARBY FACILITIES & POINTS OF INTEREST: Parks, other points of interest: Liberty State Park, Jersey City, NJ.

Federal Hall National Memorial
New York, New York

MAILING ADDRESS: Superintendent, Manhattan Sites, 26 Wall Street, New York, NY 10005 **Telephone:** (212) 264-4456

DIRECTIONS: The Memorial is located at the corner of Wall and Nassau Streets, 1 block east of Broadway. Public transportation is recommended.

The building is on the site of the original City Hall where the trial of John Peter Zenger involving freedom of the press was held in 1735 and the Stamp Act Congress met in 1765. City Hall was remodeled into Federal Hall, the first capitol of the United States under the Constitution in 1788. George Washington was inaugurated and the Bill of Rights was written in Federal Hall in 1789. The present building was completed in 1842 as the U.S. Customs House. It also served as a Sub-Treasury, 1862-1920. Designated Federal Hall Memorial National Historic Site May 26, 1939, changed to Federal Hall National Memorial Aug. 11, 1955.

VISITOR ACTIVITIES: Interpretive exhibits, audiovisual programs, school programs, tours, Wednesday noontime classical concerts; **Permits:** For special uses, commercial photography, public gatherings; **Fees:** No; **Visitor facilities:** Museum, information center, restrooms, bookstore; **HANDICAPPED ACCESSIBILITY:** Yes, enter at 15 Pine Street; **Any limitations on vehicle usage:** On-street parking extremely limited; **Hiking trails:** No; **Meals served in the park:** No, but available nearby; **Food and supplies obtainable in the park:** No; **Food and supplies obtainable nearby:** Yes; **Overnight accommodations:** in New York City; **First Aid available in park:** Yes; **Nearest Hospital:** Beekman Downtown Hospital, ¼ mile (.4 km); **Days/Hours:** Open 9 a.m. to 5 p.m. Monday through Friday, year-round; **Holiday Closings:** Closed all major holidays except Washington's Birthday and July 4th; **Visitor attractions closed for seasons:** No; **Weather:** Windy and cold in winter, hot and humid in summer.

GENERAL INFORMATION: Special interpretive programs for George Washington's Birthday, the Anniversary of Washington's Inauguration April 30, and July 4th. The information desk has brochures and information on National Park Service sites and sites in New York City. Smoking, food and drink are prohibited in the building.

TRAVEL ACCESS: Bus: New York City, buses M1 and M6 to Wall Street and Broadway, M15 to Wall and Water Streets; **Other:** Subway: Lexington Avenue IRT express (#4,5) to Wall Street; "R" BMT to Rector Street; J,M BMT to Broad Street; 7th Avenue IRT express (#2,3) to Wall Street; 8th Avenue IND ("A") to Fulton Street.

NEARBY FACILITIES & POINTS OF INTEREST: Castle Clinton, Statue of Liberty, and Ellis Island National Monuments (see listings in this book), New York Stock Exchange, Trinity Church, Fraunces Tavern, South Street Seaport, Federal Reserve Bank, World Trade Center.

Fire Island National Seashore
Patchogue, New York

MAILING ADDRESS: Superintendent, Fire Island National Seashore, 120 Laurel Street, Patchogue, NY 11772 **Telephone:** 516-289- 4810

DIRECTIONS: By automobile you can reach the island via bridges at the state and county parks. Except for these two points, Fire Island is roadless. Several mainland ferryboat lines, operating from Bayshore, Sayville, and Patchogue, dock on the island. Sailors Haven and the Sunken Forest are served by the ferry terminal in Sayville, Watch Hill by the ferry terminal at Patchogue. All three mainland villages are serviced by the Long Island Rail Road. Public ferries run from May 15 to Oct. 15.

    This barrier island off the south shore of Long Island possesses opportunities for beach-oriented recreation and ecological observations. Authorized for addition to the National Park System on Sept. 11, 1964. Contains the only national wilderness area in New York State.

VISITOR ACTIVITIES: Fishing, clamming, swimming, walking, picnicking, guided nature walks and talks in summer, wildlife- and bird-watching, camping, interpretive exhibits, hiking, boating, hunting, special boardwalk nature trail for the handicapped at Smith Point. The William Floyd Estate is a detached area of the National Seashore, located on Washington Ave. in Mastic Beach on Long Island. This 612-acre estate is the home of a Signer of the Declaration of Independence. Free guided tour of house weekends, Apr. 1-Oct. 31, 10 a.m.-4:30 p.m. Self-guided grounds tour. Groups by appointment. No pets please. For street directions call 516-399-2030; **Permits:** For off-road vehicle travel, available at Smith Point only; **Fees:** No; **Visitor facilities:** Campground, marinas, guarded swimming beaches, snack bars, Visitor Center with exhibits, picnic areas, nature trails, restrooms, bathhouse, telephones, grocery stores; **HANDICAPPED ACCESSIBILITY:** Lighthouse Visitor Center is accessible to the physically handicapped. **Any limitations on vehicle usage:** Vehicle usage is regulated; **Hiking trails:** Yes, nature trails are at Smith Point West, Watch Hill, and Sailors Haven; **Backcountry:** There is a 7-mile (11.2-km) sand trail from Smith Point to Watch Hill in the National wilderness; **Camping:** Yes, reservations are required for the 25-site primitive campground at Watch Hill. Phone the number above; **Other overnight accommodations on site:** Yes, contact the park for further information on accommodations on the island; **Meals served in the park:** Yes, snacks are available at Watch Hill and Sailors Haven; **Food and supplies obtainable in the park:** Yes, Watch Hill and Sailors Haven; **Food and supplies obtainable nearby:** Yes, on mainland at Sayville, Patchogue and Bay Shore; **Overnight accommodations:** Motels are in most major communities on Long Island; **First Aid available in park:** Yes, **Nearest Hospital:** On mainland at Patchogue, Bay Shore; **Days/Hours:** Open 24 hours a day everyday; **Holiday Closings:** No; **Visitor attractions closed for seasons:** Marinas, Visitor Centers, and restrooms closed in winter.

GENERAL INFORMATION: *For Your Safety*—Swim at protected beaches. Wear footgear on all boardwalks. Splinters are a common first aid problem. Watch for poison ivy, which abounds on the island. Do not walk on the dunes; their fragile vegetation is easily destroyed by human feet. Ticks are common in grass and underbrush, and may carry disease.

Fort Stanwix National Monument
Rome, New York

MAILING ADDRESS: Superintendent, Fort Stanwix National Monument, 112 East Park Street, Rome, NY 13440 **Telephone:** 315-336-2090

DIRECTIONS: The Monument is in downtown Rome, NY, which may be reached by car, bus, train, or plane. State Routes 26, 46, 49, 69, and 365 pass within sight of the Fort. If you are traveling on the NY Thruway, take exits 32 or 33. A city parking garage is on North James Street, within ½ block of the Monument's entrance.

The American stand here in Aug., 1777, was a major factor in repulsing the British invasion from Canada. This was also the site of the Treaty of Fort Stanwix, negotiated with the Iroquois on Nov. 5, 1768. Also the site of the last treaty of the American Revolution, Oct. 22, 1784, between the Iroquois Nation and the new United States. Authorized for addition to the National Park System on Aug. 21, 1935.

VISITOR ACTIVITIES: Interpretive films and exhibits, guided tours, living history program from May-Sept. includes drill and occasional weapons-firing demonstrations; **Permits:** No; **Fees:** Yes, $1 per person, 17 years old and up; **Visitor facilities:** Restrooms inside the Fort; **HANDICAPPED ACCESSIBILITY:** A wheelchair ramp was installed in the park museum in March 1991, making this facility fully handicapped accessible. Restroom, parking in front of park; a wheelchair is available upon request; **Any limitations on vehicle usage:** No direct vehicle access to the park; **Hiking trails:** No; **Backcountry:** No; **Camping:** No; **Other overnight accommodations on site:** No; **Meals served in the park:** No; **Food and supplies obtainable in the park:** No; **Food and supplies obtainable nearby:** Yes, in Rome; **Overnight accommodations:** In and around Rome; **First Aid available in park:** Yes; **Nearest Hospital:** Rome Memorial, NY 49, 69, 365, 3 miles (4.8 km); **Days/Hours:** Open daily from 9 a.m. to 5 p.m.; **Holiday Closings:** Thanksgiving Day, Dec. 25; **Visitor attractions closed for seasons:** Closed from Jan. through March; **Weather:** Summers are generally cool.

GENERAL INFORMATION: *For Your Safety*—Follow the staff's instructions during weapon demonstrations. Do not smoke inside wooden buildings.

Gateway National Recreation Area
New York & New Jersey

MAILING ADDRESS: General Superintendent, Gateway National Recreation Area, Floyd Bennett Field, Brooklyn, NY 11234 **Telephone:** 718-338-3575

DIRECTIONS: Gateway National Recreation Area consists of four units. Three are in New York: Jamaica Bay Unit, in Brooklyn; Breezy Point Unit, located on the Rockaway Peninsula in Queens; and the Staten Island Unit, located on the Raritan Bay in Staten Island. The fourth area is the Sandy Hook Unit, situated on a peninsula in the northeast corner of New Jersey in Monmouth County. Detailed mass transit and auto directions are available from Headquarters.

The Park contains beaches, marshes, islands, and adjacent waters in the New York harbor area, and is one of the first major urban parks in the National Park System. Established by act of Congress on Oct. 27, 1972.

VISITOR ACTIVITIES: Swimming, picnicking, sunbathing, sports, interpretive programs, biking, fishing, boating, bird-watching, crabbing, horseback riding and during warmer months special events; **Permits:** A fishing permit is required at some locations. Permits are also required for baseball, softball, tennis, soccer, archery, football, and basketball facilities at Miller Field in the Staten Island Unit. Information and permits can be obtained by calling 718-351-8700 or by writing the Unit Manager, P.O. Box 37, Staten Island, NY 10306; **Fees:** For boat launching and mooring facilities at Great Kills Park in the Staten Island Unit, mooring facilities at Barren Island Marina, and a parking fee at the Riis Park parking lot, Breezy Point Unit; and summer beach parking at Sandy Hook, NJ Unit. **Visitor facilities:** Marina, boathouse, beaches, sports facilities, restrooms, parking areas, wildlife refuge, bicycle trail, picnic areas; **Any limitations on vehicle usage:** Off-road vehicles are not permitted on beaches and in certain natural areas; **Hiking trails:** Yes, nature trails, ocean and waterfront areas; **Backcountry:** No; **Camping:** Yes, primitive campsites are available for use by organized youth groups on a reservation basis. These reservations must be made through the Unit Manager's office at Sandy Hook Unit, P.O. Box 530, Sandy Hook, NJ 07732 or by calling 908-872-0115 and at Floyd Bennett Field, 718-338-3706; **Other overnight accommodations on site:** No; **Meals served in the park:** Yes, fast food available in summer at all 4 units; **Food and supplies obtainable in the park:** No; **Food and supplies obtainable nearby:** Yes, at Sandy Hook, Red Bank, Highlands, Staten Island, Jamaica Bay, Boroughs of Brooklyn and Queens, Breezy Point; **Overnight accommodations:** Sandy Hook, Red Bank, Highlands, Staten Island, Jamaica Bay, Brooklyn and Queens, Breezy Point; **First Aid available in park:** Yes, in all 4 units during the summer; **Nearest Hospital:** Sandy Hook: Patterson Army Hospital, River View Hospital; Staten Island: Staten Island Hospital; Jamacia Bay: Coney Island Hospital, Brookdale Hospital, Peninsula Hospital; **Days/Hours:** Open 7 days a week, 52 weeks a year. Full services are provided from Memorial Day through Sept. 30 from 9 a.m.-8:30 p.m.; **Holiday Closings:** Jamaica Bay Wildlife Refuge is closed Dec. 25, and Jan. 1; **Visitor attractions closed for seasons:** Beach closed for season; **Weather:** Excellent beach weather, with temperatures in the 90°'s in June, July, and August.

GENERAL INFORMATION: *For Your Safety*—Swim only where lifeguards are on duty. The ocean can be dangerous. Be alert for riptides. Do not take glass containers, rafts, rubber tubs, snorkels, and masks to any beach. Beware of sunburn. Some of the areas have large patches of poison ivy. Consult park personnel for locations of poison ivy. Write to Park Public Affairs Office, Floyd Bennett Field, Brooklyn, NY 11234 for free copy of Seasonal Program Guides.

TRAVEL ACCESS: Bus: NY, Keansburg and Long Branch Bus from Port Authority Terminal, NYC, to Sandy Hook, NJ, weekends on the hour. N.Y.C. Transit-Authority and Green Bus Lines to Riis Beach (summers), Jamaica Bay and Breezy Point units and TA bus to Staten Island Unit.

General Grant National Memorial
New York, New York

MAILING ADDRESS: Superintendent, Manhattan Sites, 26 Wall Street, New York, NY 10005 **Telephone:** 212-264-4456

DIRECTIONS: The Memorial is located in Riverside Park near the Intersection of Riverside Drive and West 122nd Street. You can reach the vicinity of the memorial by IRT #1 subway to 116th or 125th Street, or 125th Street crosstown bus. Riverside Drive is also accessible from the Henry Hudson Parkway at several points. Parking is permitted near the Memorial.

This Memorial to Ulysses S. Grant, the Union commander who brought the Civil War to an end, includes the sarcophagi of General and Mrs. Grant. As President of the United States (1869-1877), Grant signed the act establishing the first National Park, Yellowstone, on Mar. 1, 1872. Memorial dedicated on April 27, 1897.

VISITOR ACTIVITIES: Interpretive talks and exhibits; **Permits:** No; **Fees:** No; **Visitor facilities:** Exhibit rooms; **Any limitations on vehicle usage:** No; **Meals served in the park:** No; **Food and supplies obtainable in the park:** No; **Food and supplies obtainable nearby:** Yes, several blocks, in Manhattan; **Overnight accommodations:** New York City; **First Aid available in park:** Yes; **Nearest Hospital:** St. Luke's Amsterdam Ave., about 10 blocks;

Days/Hours: Open Wednesday through Sunday 9:00 a.m. to 4:30 p.m.; closed on Wednesdays that follow Federal holidays that are on Mondays and Tuesdays. **Holiday Closings:** Thanksgiving, Dec. 25, and Jan. 1; **Visitor attractions closed for seasons:** No; **Weather:** Cold winters with occasional snow; hot humid summers.

GENERAL INFORMATION: Please call to verify days and hours.

Hamilton Grange National Memorial
New York, NY

MAILING ADDRESS: Superintendent, Manhattan Sites, 26 Wall Street, New York, NY 10005 **Telephone:** 212-264-4456

DIRECTIONS: The Memorial is at Convent Avenue and West 141st Street. Access by public transportation is recommended. Take the 8th Avenue IND express subway to West 145th Street. You can also catch the Broadway Bus #4 to West 145th St. and Convent Avenue, or Convent Avenue bus #3 to 142nd Street.
   "The Grange," named after his grandfather's estate in Scotland, was the home of Alexander Hamilton, American Statesman and first Secretary of the U.S. Treasury. Authorized for addition to the National Park System on Apr. 27, 1962.

VISITOR ACTIVITIES: Exhibits, guided tours, audiovisual program; **Permits:** No; **Fees:** No; **Visitor facilities:** Restrooms available; **Any limitations on vehicle usage:** No vehicle usage in the park; **Hiking trails:** No; **Meals served in the park:** No; **Food and supplies obtainable in the park:** No; **Food and supplies obtainable nearby:** Yes, in New York City; **Overnight accommodations:** New York; **First Aid available in park:** Yes; **Nearest Hospital:** New York City; **Days/Hours:** Open Wed.-Sun. from 9 a.m. to 4:30 p.m.; **Holiday Closings:** Thanksgiving, Dec. 25, and Jan. 1, and Wednesdays following Federal Holidays which fall on Monday and Tuesday; **Visitor attractions closed for seasons:** No; **Weather:** Cold winters with snow; hot humid summers. Pleasantly mild spring and fall.

GENERAL INFORMATION: Be careful walking up and down stairs; they are quite slippery when wet.

Home of Franklin D. Roosevelt National Historic Site
Hyde Park, New York

MAILING ADDRESS: Superintendent, Roosevelt-Vanderbilt National Historic Sites, 519 Albany Post Rd., Hyde Park, NY 12538 **Information:** 914-229-7821, **Reservations:** 914-229-9115

DIRECTIONS: The Home is on Route 9 in Hyde Park, just north of Poughkeepsie, two hours north of New York City
   This was the birthplace, lifetime residence, and "Summer White House" of the 32nd President, who entertained many distinguished visitors here. The gravesites of President and Mrs. Roosevelt are in the Rose Garden. Accepted by the Secretary of the Interior, Nov. 21, 1945.

VISITOR ACTIVITIES: House tours, exhibits in the Franklin D. Roosevelt Library; **Permits:** No; **Fees:** $4.00 entrance fee permits access to Roosevelt Home and Library. Persons 16 and under are admitted free. $1.00 entry fee to FDR Library for seniors over 62.

Seniors over 62 are admitted free to the Park. Golden Eagle, Golden Access and Golden Age Passports accepted; **Visitor facilities:** Bookstore, Tourist Information Center, parking, restrooms, library; **HANDICAPPED ACCESSIBILITY:** Parking, restrooms, ramps with handrails; **Any limitations on vehicle usage:** No; **Hiking trails:** Yes; **Meals served in the park:** No; **Food and supplies obtainable in the park:** No; **Food and supplies obtainable nearby:** Yes, in town of Hyde Park; **Overnight accommodations:** Hyde Park and vicinity; **First Aid available in park:** Yes; **Nearest Hospital:** Poughkeepsie, US 9, 6 miles (9.6 km); **Days/Hours:** Open daily from 9 a.m. to 5 p.m. Closed Tuesday and Wednesday Nov. through March; **Holiday Closings:** Thanksgiving Day, Dec. 25, and Jan. 1.

GENERAL INFORMATION: For bus tour or large group reservations please write to Roosevelt-Vanderbilt National Historic Sites, 249 Albany Post Rd., Hyde Park, NY 12538 in advance.

TRAVEL ACCESS: Bus: Dutchess County Transportation, and Mountainview Coach Lines provide flag stop service daily to Poughkeepsie; **Rail:** Metro North service to Poughkeepsie, NY and Amtrak.

NEARBY FACILITIES & POINTS OF INTEREST: Parks, other points of interest: F.D.R. Library Museum, Vanderbilt Mansion, Eleanor Roosevelt National Historic Site.

Martin Van Buren National Historic Site
Kinderhook, New York

MAILING ADDRESS: Superintendent, Martin Van Buren National Historic Site, P.O. Box 545, Kinderhook, NY 12106 **Telephone:** 518-758-9689

DIRECTIONS: The Site is on route 9H in Kinderhook Township, 25 miles (40 km) south of Albany.
    Lindenwald estate, south of Albany, was the home of the 8th President for 21 years until his death in 1862. Authorized for addition to the National Park System on Oct. 26, 1974.

VISITOR ACTIVITIES: Guided tours, special events, interpretive audiovisual program and exhibits, off-site programs (slide shows) for community and professional organizations; **Permits:** No; **Fees:** Entrance fee is $1 for adults. No charge for persons 16 and younger or 62 and over. Golden Eagle and Golden Age Passports accepted and available; **Visitor facilities:** Limited parking and restroom facilities; **HANDICAPPED ACCESSIBILITY:** Parking adjacent to Mansion. **Any limitations on vehicle usage:** Vehicles restricted to roadways; **Hiking trails:** No; **Backcountry:** No; **Camping:** No; **Other overnight accommodations on site:** No; **Meals served in the park:** No; **Food and supplies obtainable in the park:** No; **Food and supplies obtainable nearby:** Yes, in Kinderhook, 1½ miles (2.4 km) north; **Overnight accommodations:** Kinderhook; **First Aid available in park:** Yes; **Nearest Hospital:** Hudson, NY, 12 miles (19.2 km) south; **Days/Hours:** Open daily 9 a.m. to 5 p.m. (mid-April to Oct.); open Wed.-Sun. 9 a.m. to 5 p.m. Nov. to Dec 5. Grounds open throughout the year; **Holiday Closings:** Thanksgiving; **Visitor attractions closed for seasons:** Mansion closed Dec. 6 through mid-April; **Weather:** Summer is warm, humid, and breezy. The average temperature is in the high 70s or low 80s.

GENERAL INFORMATION: Group tours are requested to make reservations.

TRAVEL ACCESS: Bus: Mt. View bus provides service Hudson-Albany, NY, 3 times daily; **Rail:** Amtrak provides service into Hudson; **Air:** U.S.Air, Delta, Northwest, United, American provide service to Albany, NY.

NEARBY FACILITIES & POINTS OF INTEREST: Hotel/Motel: Blue Spruce Motel, Rt. 9H, 518-758-9711, 5 miles (8 km) from Site; **Food/Supplies:** Grand Union, Valatie, NY, 3 miles (4.8 km); **Campgrounds:** Lake Taghkanic State Park, Ancram, NY 518-851-3631, 30 miles (48 km); **Parks, other points of interest:** Albany sites, 25 miles; American Museum of Firefighting, Hudson, NY, 12 miles 518-828-7695; DAR Museum, Hudson, NY, 12 miles 518-851-9049; Columbia County Historic Society Museum, Kinderhook, NY, 518-758-9265, 2 miles (3.2 km); The Shaker Museum, (Old) Chatham, NY, 518-794-9100, 11 miles (17.6 km); Olana State Historic Site, Hudson, NY, 518-828-0135, 12 miles (19.2 km).

North Country National Scenic Trail
New York, Pennsylvania, Ohio, Michigan, Wisconsin, Minnesota, North Dakota

MAILING ADDRESS: c/o Midwest Regional Office, National Park Service, 1709 Jackson Street, Omaha, NE 68102 **Telephone:** 402-221-3481

DIRECTIONS: When completed, the Scenic Trail will extend approximately 3,200 miles from the vicinity of Crown Point, New York, to Lake Sakakawea State Park on the Missouri River in North Dakota, the route of the Lewis and Clark National Historic Trail. Approximately 1,400 miles are presently available for public use. Established by an act of Congress on Mar. 5, 1980.

VISITOR ACTIVITIES: Hiking, backpacking, camping, nature study. Some trail segments are open to horseback riding, bicycling, cross-country skiing; **Permits:** Yes, for a few trail segments; **Fees:** Yes, for some developed campgrounds within the National Forests, State Parks, and similar areas along the trail; **Visitor facilities:** Various, as provided by the managing authority for a particular segment; **HANDICAPPED ACCESSIBILITY:** A few sections of the trail are accessible to the handicapped (wheelchair use). Restroom and other facilities at developed areas in many Federal and State parks along the trail are accessible. **Any limitations on vehicle usage:** Use of motorized vehicles by the public is prohibited along the trail; **Hiking trails:** Yes; **Backcountry:** Yes, for information, write to the above address; **Camping:** As permitted; **Other overnight accommodations on site:** No; **Meals served in the park:** No; **Food and supplies obtainable in the park:** Yes, in some parks along the trail; **Food and supplies obtainable nearby:** Yes, in many communities along or near the trail; **Overnight accommodations:** In many communities along or near the trail; **First Aid available in park:** No; **Days/Hours:** Open at all times, except as limited by regulations governing individual parks/forests through which the trail passes.

TRAVEL ACCESS: Many points on or near the trail are accessible by bus, rail, or air.

NEARBY FACILITIES & POINTS OF INTEREST: Scenic, historic, natural, and cultural interests are located along the trail. **Campsites:** Reservation system in use for some public and private campgrounds.

Theodore Roosevelt Birthplace National Historic Site
New York, New York

MAILING ADDRESS: Superintendent, Manhattan Sites, 26 Wall Street, New York, New York 10005. **Telephone:** 212-264-4456

DIRECTIONS: The Site can be reached from the 23rd Street or 14th Street stops of the IRT (Lexington Ave.) or BMT Subway. Parking space in the vicinity is scarce.

The 26th President of the United States was born in the original house on this site on Oct. 27, 1858. Authorized for addition to the National Park System on July 25, 1962.

VISITOR ACTIVITIES: Guided tours of Victorian-period rooms, museums, films, and Sat. afternoon concerts; **Permits:** No; **Fees:** $1 per adult, Seniors and children under 17 free; **Visitor facilities:** Restrooms; **HANDICAPPED ACCESSIBILITY:** No; **Any limitations on vehicle usage:** No; **Meals served in the park:** No; **Food and supplies obtainable in the park:** No; **Food and supplies obtainable nearby:** Yes, in the neighborhood; **Overnight accommodations:** No; **First Aid available in park:** Yes; **Nearest Hospital:** Cabrini Med. Center; **Days/Hours:** Open Wed.-Sun. 9 a.m.-5 p.m.; **Holiday Closings:** Closed on Federal holidays; **Visitor attractions closed for seasons:** No.

NEARBY FACILITIES & POINTS OF INTEREST: Hotel/Motel: Gramercy Park, 2 Lexington Ave., 212-475-4320.

Theodore Roosevelt Inaugural National Historic Site
Buffalo, New York

MAILING ADDRESS: Superintendent, Theodore Roosevelt Inaugural National Historic Site, 641 Delaware Ave., Buffalo, NY 14202 **Telephone:** 716-884-0095

DIRECTIONS: The entrance to the house is on Delaware Avenue near North Street. Parking at the rear of the house is accessible from Franklin Street, a one-way street leading north from downtown Buffalo. Buses from downtown Buffalo stop in front of the Site.

Here in the Ansley Wilcox House, Theodore Roosevelt took the oath of office as President of the United States on Sept. 14, 1901, shortly after the assassination of President William McKinley. Authorized for addition to the National Park System on Nov. 2, 1966. Site is operated by the Theodore Roosevelt Inaugural Site Foundation.

VISITOR ACTIVITIES: Guided tours, quilt show, Victorian Christmas display, art shows, self-directed (cassette) walking tours, August–Teddy Bear Picnic; **Permits:** No; **Fees:** $2 adults, $1 children, maximum family $5.50 entrance fee; **Visitor facilities:** Parking, off Franklin Street, one-way going north, restrooms, art gallery; **HANDICAPPED ACCESSIBILITY:** First floor only. Captioned slide presentation; Lower level is going to be rehabed with a chair lift and lavatory that will make it accessible for the handicapped; Completion date, 1991; **Any limitations on vehicle usage:** No; **Meals served in the park:** No; **Food and supplies obtainable in the park:** No; **Food and supplies obtainable nearby:** Yes, Buffalo, across the street; **Overnight accommodations:** Buffalo; **First Aid available in park:** Yes; **Nearest Hospital:** Buffalo, ½ mile (.8 km) from the site; **Days/Hours:** Open Mon.-Fri: 9 a.m.-5 p.m.; Sat.-Sun: Noon-5 p.m.; **Holiday Closings:** Closed on Federal holidays and Saturdays Jan.-Mar.; **Visitor attractions closed for seasons:** No.

NEARBY FACILITIES & POINTS OF INTEREST: Hotel/Motel: Site is in a preservation district; noteworthy architecture. Allentown area has many antique shops, boutiques, restaurants.

Sagamore Hill National Historic Site
Oyster Bay, New York

MAILING ADDRESS: Superintendent, Sagamore Hill National Historic Site, 20 Sagamore Hill Road, Oyster Bay, NY 11771-1899 **Telephone:** 516-922-4447

DIRECTIONS: Sagamore Hill is on Cove Neck Road, 3 miles (4.8 km) east of Oyster Bay, NY. It can be reached by the Long Island Rail Road from New York City's Pennsylvania Station at 7th Avenue and 33rd Street. Taxis meet all trains. If traveling by car, take either Exit 41N from the Long Island Expressway or Exit 35 North from the Northern State Parkway to Route 106 Northbound. Follow Route 106 to the Village of Oyster Bay. Turn right at the third traffic light in Oyster Bay onto East Main Street. Follow the green and white signs marked "Sagamore Hill."

This estate was the home of Theodore Roosevelt, the 26th President of the United States, from 1885 until his death in 1919. Authorized for addition to the National Park System on July 25, 1962.

VISITOR ACTIVITIES: Visitors can take self-guided tour of the Roosevelt home, the pet cemetery, and the Old Orchard Home, containing exhibits relating to Theodore Roosevelt's political career, family life at Sagamore Hill, and the lives of his six children. There is also a 26-minute film presentation; **Permits:** No; **Fees:** $1 between 16 and 62 years of age. Golden Eagle and Golden Age Passports are accepted and available; **Visitor facilities:** Souvenir and book sales, parking; **HANDICAPPED ACCESSIBILITY:** Restrooms and parking; **Any limitations on vehicle usage:** Vehicles are limited to the entrance road and visitor parking area; **Hiking trails:** No; **Meals served in the park:** Snack shop open during summer season; **Food and supplies obtainable in the park:** No; **Food and supplies obtainable nearby:** Yes, in Oyster Bay, 3 miles (4.8 km) west; **Overnight accommodations:** East Norwich and Oyster Bay, South Street, Rt. 25A, 5 miles (8 km); **First Aid available in park:** Yes, in all buildings; **Nearest Hospital:** Glen Cove, St. Andrews Lane, 7 miles (11.2 km); **Days/Hours:** Open every day 9:30 a.m. to 5 p.m. **Holiday Closings:** Thanksgiving, Dec. 25, and Jan. 1; **Visitor attractions closed for seasons:** No; **Weather:** Temperatures range from 65-90° in summer and 0-40° in winter.

GENERAL INFORMATION: Poison ivy and ticks are common in the area; please keep to the established paths and walkways. Pets must be leashed or carried. Heat exhaustion is common in the summer, so judge your limits. Park fences are historic and unsafe for climbing.

Saint Paul's National Historic Site with the Bill of Rights Museum
Mount Vernon, New York

MAILING ADDRESS: Superintendent, Manhattan Sites, 26 Wall Street, New York, New York 10005, **Telephone:** 212-264-4456

DIRECTIONS: Take New England Thruway North (Rte. 95) to Conner Street Exit. Make a left, go up one light, and make another left. Go straight and that road becomes Rte. 22 (a.k.a. S. Columbus Ave.). Follow to St. Paul's #897 on right. Or get off Hutchinson River Parkway North at US-1 Boston Post Road in Pelham Manor, NY. Turn left and go to Pelham Parkway. Make a right, follow to S. Columbus Avenue and make a left. Follow to site on left.

This 18th-century church is important because of its connection with the events leading to the John Peter Zenger trial involving freedom of the press, and because of its place in American history, especially the Revolution. It is a significant example of American Colonial Architecture. This affiliated area of the National Park System was designated on July 5, 1943. Lands were donated to National Park Service on Nov. 1, 1980, and July 4, 1981. Bill of Rights Museum opened October 28, 1984.

VISITOR ACTIVITIES: Walking tours of the church, museum, and cemetery; **Permits:** No; **Fees:** No; **Visitor facilities:** Parking and restrooms, Museum shop; **HANDICAPPED ACCESSIBILITY:** Museum accessible with ramp; has accessible bathrooms and limited parking. Access to other Site areas under development. Call for details; **Any limitations on vehicle usage:** No; **Meals served in the park:** No; **Food and supplies obtainable in the park:** No; **Food and supplies obtainable nearby:** Yes, in Mount Vernon and the immediate area; **Overnight accommodations:** Mount Vernon, Bronx, New Rochelle, or anywhere in metropolitan New York City; **First Aid available in park:** No; **Nearest Hospital:** Mount Vernon, N. 7th Ave., 2 miles (3.2 km); **Days/Hours:** Tues.-Fri. from 9 a.m.-5 p.m. by appointment, Sat. from 12 p.m.-4 p.m. without appointment. Groups over 5 are asked to call in advance for Saturday tours. Visitors services and Museum Shop available. **Visitor attractions closed for seasons:** Sundays, Mondays, and Saturdays prior to Federal holidays that fall on Mondays. Also Thanksgiving, Dec. 25, and Jan. 1; **Weather:** Typical New York weather, with seasonal snow or rain.

Saratoga National Historical Park
Stillwater, New York

MAILING ADDRESS: Superintendent, Saratoga National Historical Park, R.D. #2, Box 33 Stillwater, NY 12170 **Telephone:** 518-664-9821

DIRECTIONS: The Park entrance lies 30 miles (48 km) north of Albany, NY, on US 4 and NY 32. Exit 12 off Northway (I-87).

The American victory here over the British in 1777 was the turning point of the Revolution and one of the decisive battles in world history. Major General Philip Schuyler's country home and the Saratoga Monument both in Schuylerville are open during the summer months. Authorized for addition to the National Park System on June 1, 1938. Established by act of Congress on June 22, 1948.

VISITOR ACTIVITIES: Visual program, talks, and exhibits are available at the Visitor Center, which is open from 9:00 a.m. to 5:00 p.m. Craft and weapon demonstrations are given in summer. The Park is open all year for hiking and skiing; **Permits:** No; **Fees:** Yes; **Visitor facilities:** An interpretive tour starts at the Visitor Center; Saratoga Monument is closed for renovation; **HANDICAPPED ACCESSIBILITY:** Visitor Center parking, restrooms; tour stops; trails not accessible; **Any limitations on vehicle usage:** Snowmobiles are prohibited; **Hiking trails:** Yes, the historic 1777 road system is gradually being turned into hiking trails; includes Wm. Wilkinson National Historic Trail; **Backcountry:** No; **Camping:** No; **Other overnight accommodations on site:** No; **Meals served in the park:** No; **Food and supplies obtainable in the park:** No; **Food and supplies obtainable nearby:** Yes, in Stillwater and Schuylerville; **Overnight accommodations:** Schuylerville, 8 miles (12.8 km); **First Aid available in park:** Yes; **Nearest Hospital:** Saratoga Springs, Rte. 32 to 423 to 9P, 17 miles (27.2 km); **Days/Hours:** Park open from 9 a.m. to 5 p.m. daily. Park roads are open from about Apr. 15 to Nov. 30 as weather permits; **Holiday Closings:** Visitor Center is closed Thanksgiving, Dec. 25, and Jan. 1.

Statue of Liberty National Monument
New York, New York

MAILING ADDRESS: Superintendent, Statue of Liberty National Monument, Liberty Island, New York, NY 10004 **Telephone:** 212-363-7770

DIRECTIONS: Liberty Island is accessible only by ferry. Circle Line Ferries leave Battery Park in Lower Manhattan and Liberty State Park in New Jersey. For schedule and group-rate information, call 212-269-5755.

The famous 152-foot copper statue bearing the torch of freedom was a gift of the French people in 1886 to commemorate the alliance of the two nations during the American Revolution. The Monument includes The American Museum of Immigration, in the base of the statue. Created by Presidential Proclamation on Oct. 15, 1924.

VISITOR ACTIVITIES: Visitors can reach the top of the pedestal by elevator or stairs. The public is not permitted access to the torch itself. You can climb stairs to the statue's crown; **Permits:** No; **Fees:** No. Round-trip concession boat fee is $6 for adults; children under 17 years-$3; **Visitor facilities:** Restrooms, public telephones, refreshments, souvenirs and books relating to the Statue and to Immigration are available; **Any limitations on vehicle usage:** No vehicle access available; vehicle access available to Liberty State Park; **Hiking trails:** No; **Backcountry:** No; **Camping:** No; **Other overnight accommodations on site:** No; **Meals served in the park:** Yes, snacks available at refreshment stand; **Food and supplies obtainable in the park:** No; **Food and supplies obtainable nearby:** No; **Overnight accommodations:** New York City; **First Aid available in the park:** Yes; **Nearest Hospital:** New York—takes about 1 hour to reach; **Days/Hours:** Open daily year-round from 9 a.m.-5 p.m., with extended hours in season; **Holiday Closings:** Dec. 25.

GENERAL INFORMATION: Ascent to the Statue's crown from the top of the pedestal is by spiral staircase only. The climb is equivalent to 22 stories and those with physical difficulties are urged not to attempt it.

TRAVEL ACCESS: Bus: Greyhound, Shortline, and other long-distance lines provide regular service to Port Authority Terminal; **Rail:** Amtrak, Conrail (Metropolitan Transit Authority intraregional lines) service both Pennsylvania Station and Grand Central Station; **Air:** Major and regional airlines provide regular service to Newark, La Guardia, and John F. Kennedy airports; **Other:** Metropolitan Transit Authority buses run frequently to South Ferry from Journal Square; Central Bus runs service morning and afternoon to Liberty State Park, Jersey City; Metropolitan Transit Authority provides subway service to South Ferry. Public bus and subway transportation available.

NEARBY FACILITIES & POINTS OF INTEREST: Parks, other points of interest: Liberty State Park, Jersey City, NJ.

Upper Delaware Scenic & Recreational River
New York (also in Pennsylvania)

MAILING ADDRESS: Upper Delaware Scenic & Recreational River, P.O. Box C, Narrowsburg, NY 12764 **Telephone:** 717-729-8251

DIRECTIONS: Nearly 73 miles (116.8 km) of this free-flowing fishing and canoeing/rafting stream are protected from Hancock, NY, to the vicinity of Sparrow Bush, NY, Authorized for addition to the National Park System on Nov. 10, 1978.

VISITOR ACTIVITIES: Canoeing, kayaking, rafting, tubing, sightseeing, and fishing; **Permits:** New York or Pennsylvania fishing license required when fishing the Upper Delaware River; **Fees:** No; **Visitor facilities:** Information Center, 5 kiosks and Roebling Bridge Contact Station staffed during summer months for dispensing information. Zane Grey Museum open daily, Memorial Day to Labor Day, weekends, spring and fall, contains exhibits, audiovisual program, guided tours, and sales desk. Boat rentals and campgrounds are available in the vicinity. **HANDICAPPED ACCESSIBILITY:** Roebling Bridge, Information Center, Information Kiosks.

TRAVEL ACCESS: Bus: Short Line provides summer service to Narrowsburg, NY; **Rail:** N.J. Transit offers regular service to Port Jervis, NY.

NEARBY FACILITIES & POINTS OF INTEREST: Campgrounds: Contact area for directory of campgrounds; **Other points of interest:** Minisink Battleground Park, Fort Delaware; **Reservation system in use for campsites, other facilities:** Canoe rentals available at various locations along the Upper Delaware River, contact area for more information.

Vanderbilt Mansion National Historic Site
Hyde Park, New York

MAILING ADDRESS: Superintendent, Roosevelt-Vanderbilt National Historic Sites, 519 Albany Post Rd., Hyde Park, NY 12538 **Information:** 914-229-7821 **Reservations:** 914-229-9115

DIRECTIONS: The Site is on US 9 about 8 miles (12.8 km) north of Poughkeepsie, NY. Entrance to the grounds is by the main gate on US 9 north in the village of Hyde Park. The Visitor Center is in the Pavilion near the mansion. It is located 2 hours north of New York City on the east bank of the Hudson River.

This palatial mansion is a fine example of homes built by 19th-century financiers. Designated Dec. 18, 1940.

VISITOR ACTIVITIES: Tours available beginning at Visitor Center, interpretive exhibits and audiovisual program; **Permits:** No; **Fees:** Entrance fee is $2. Persons 16 and under and 62 and over admitted free. Golden Eagle, Golden Age and Golden Access Passports accepted and available; **Visitor facilities:** Parking, restrooms; **HANDICAPPED ACCESSIBILITY:** Posted parking, elevator in mansion; **Any limitations on vehicle usage:** No; **Hiking trails:** Yes; **Backcountry:** No; **Camping:** No; **Other overnight accommodations on site:** No; **Meals served in the park:** No; **Food and supplies obtainable in the park:** No; **Food and supplies obtainable nearby:** Yes, Town of Hyde Park; **Overnight accommodations:** Hyde Park and vicinity; **First Aid available in park:** Yes; **Nearest Hospital:** Poughkeepsie, US 9, 6 miles (9.6 km); **Days/Hours:** Open Thurs. through Mon. from 9 a.m. to 5 p.m. Nov.-Mar. Open daily from 9 a.m. to 5 p.m. Apr.-Oct.; **Holiday Closings:** Thanksgiving Day, Dec. 25, and Jan. 1.

TRAVEL ACCESS: Bus: Dutchess County Transportation provides service to Poughkeepsie 7 miles (11.2 km); **Rail:** Conrail and Metro North provide service to Poughkeepsie from New York City; **Air:** Commercial lines at Stewart Airport, Newburgh, NY 45 minutes north of Hyde Park.

NEARBY FACILITIES & POINTS OF INTEREST: Parks, other points of interest: F.D.R. Library Museum; Home of Franklin D. Roosevelt and Eleanor Roosevelt National Historic Site. **Reservation systems:** For groups or bus tour reservations please write to Roosevelt-Vanderbilt National Historic Sites, 519 Albany Post Rd., Hyde Park, NY 12538.

Women's Rights National Historical Park
Seneca Falls & Waterloo, New York

MAILING ADDRESS: Women's Rights National Historical Park, P.O. Box 70, Seneca Falls, NY 13148

DIRECTIONS: New York Thruway Exit 41 onto State Route 414 South, 4 miles (6.4 km), then east on State Routes 5 and 20, 3 miles (4.8 km). Established in December 1980. Visitor Center is at 116 Fall Street, downtown Seneca Falls.

VISITOR ACTIVITIES: Permits: No; **Fees:** No; **Visitor facilities:** Visitor Center located on Rtes. 5 and 20 in downtown Seneca Falls; exhibits, audiovisual programs, special events. Elizabeth Cady Stanton home restored and open to public for tours 9-5 daily, June 1-Sept. 30, rest of the year daily from 12-4, other hours by appointment. Remaining principal sites not open to public: Wesleyan Chapel, Hunt and M'Clintock houses. Self-guided walking tours available. Guided interpretive tours available May through Sept. and by appointment rest of year; **HANDICAPPED ACCESSIBILITY:** Visitor Center accessible via rear door; handicapped parking behind building; restrooms accessible. Scripts for audiovisual programs available, as well as taped recordings of exhibit label texts; **Any limitations on vehicle usage:** No; **Hiking trails:** No; **Backcountry:** No; **Camping:** No; **Other overnight accommodations on site:** No; **Meals served in the park:** No; **Food and supplies obtainable in the park:** No; **Food and supplies obtainable nearby:** Yes; **Overnight accommodations:** Cayuga Lake State Park, Private Motels; **First Aid available in park:** Yes; **Days/Hours:** Park Visitor Center open 9-5 daily, year-round; **Holiday Closings:** Closed Thanksgiving, Dec. 25, and Jan. 1; **Visitor attractions closed for seasons:** Limited winter programs; **Weather:** 80° in summer, 65° spring and fall, 30° in winter.

GENERAL INFORMATION: Call 315-568-2991 for more information or write for brochure for more information or write for brochure.

TRAVEL ACCESS: Bus: Onondaga Coach in Seneca Falls; **Rail:** Amtrak in Syracuse; **Air:** USAir, United, American, Delta in Syracuse, Rochester.

NEARBY FACILITIES & POINTS OF INTEREST: Hotel/Motel: Write Chamber of Commerce for listing; **Campgrounds:** Cayuga Lake State Park, Sampson State Park; **Parks, other points of interest:** National Women's Hall of Fame; Seneca Falls Historical Society, Montezuma National Wildlife Refuge 5 miles (8 km), Senaca Falls Urban Cultural Park Visitor Center; **Reservation Systems in Use for Campsites, other facilities:** Write State Park Office and/or Chamber of Commerce.

North Carolina

CAPE HATTERAS NATIONAL SEASHORE

CAPE LOOKOUT NATIONAL SEASHORE

GUILFORD COURTHOUSE
NATIONAL MILITARY PARK

APPALACHIAN NATIONAL SCENIC TRAIL

FORT RALEIGH NATIONAL HISTORIC SITE

WRIGHT BROTHERS NATIONAL MEMORIAL

Raleigh

Charlotte

GREAT SMOKY MOUNTAINS
NATIONAL PARK

CARL SANDBURG HOME
NATIONAL HISTORIC SITE

BLUE RIDGE PARKWAY

MOORES CREEK NATIONAL BATTLEFIELD

Appalachian National Scenic Trail
For details see listing in Maine

Blue Ridge Parkway
North Carolina and Virginia   **SEE CLIMATABLE NO. 26**

MAILING ADDRESS: Superintendent, Blue Ridge Parkway, 200 BB&T Building, 1 Pack Square, Asheville, NC 28801 **Telephone:** 704-259-0779

DIRECTIONS: The Parkway intersects many US and State highways, including Interstates 64, 77, 40, and 26. Obtain by mail or in person at any Visitor Center a copy of Blue Ridge Parkway Directory, which provides detailed maps and information.

The first national parkway follows the crest of the Blue Ridge and other mountain ranges and includes several large recreation areas. The Parkway is 470 miles (752 km) long and links Shenandoah National Park in Virginia with Great Smoky Mountains National Park in North Carolina. Established by act of Congress on June 30, 1936.

VISITOR ACTIVITIES: Auto tours, wildlife- and wildflower-watching, camping, exhibits, picnicking, hiking, fishing, interpretive walks and talks, craft sales and demonstrations; **Permits:** No; **Fees:** Campground fee charged at developed areas; **Visitor facilities:** Food service, gas, lodging, campgrounds, picnic areas, hiking trails, drinking water, restrooms; **HANDICAPPED ACCESSIBILITY:** Many facilities are wheelchair useable. Contact Parkway Access Coordinator, 704-259-0719; **Any limitations on vehicle usage:** Vehicles being used commercially are not allowed on the parkway unless they secure a special permit; **Hiking trails:** Yes, trails vary in length and difficulty; **Backcountry:** No, The Appalachian

Trail roughly parallels the parkway from Mile 0 at Rockfish Gap to Mile 103, where the trail takes a more westerly route toward the Great Smoky Mountains and Georgia. Shelters, usually 1 day's hike apart, are available on a first-come, first-served basis all along the trail. Information about the trail may be obtained from the Appalachian Trail Conference, P.O. Box 236, Harpers Ferry, WV 25425, phone 304-535-6331; **Camping:** Yes, the Parkway campgrounds are open from May through Oct. only, but limited camping facilities may be available in winter, depending on weather and other factors. Inquire in advance. Sites in each campground are designated for trailer use, but none are equipped for utility connections. Sanitary dumping facilities for trailers are provided at all campgrounds. Camping is limited to 14 days and campsites may not be reserved; **Other overnight accommodations on site:** Yes, Peaks of Otter Lodge, open all year, is operated by Virginia Peaks of Otter Co., Box 489, Bedford, VA 24523, phone 703-586-1081. To reserve at Rocky Knob Cabins, open June through Labor Day, write National Park Concessions, Inc., Meadows of Dan, VA 24120, phone 703-593-3503. For Bluffs Lodge (in Doughton Park), open May 1-Oct. 31, write National Park Concessions, Inc., Rt. 1, Box 266, Laurel Springs, NC 28644, phone 919-372-4499. For Pisgah Inn, open May 1-Oct. 31, contact Pisgah Inn, Inc., P.O. Drawer 749, Waynesville, NC 28786, phone 704-235-8228; **Meals served in the park:** Yes, at Whetstone Ridge, Otter Creek, Peaks of Otter, Mabry Mill, Doughton Park, Crabtree Meadows, Mount Pisgah; **Food and supplies obtainable in the park:** Yes, limited food and supplies at some Parkway gas stations and at campground stores; **Food and supplies obtainable nearby:** Yes, within a few miles of the Parkway in most of the larger communities; **Overnight accommodations:** At most nearby communities as well as Peaks of Otter, Rocky Knob, Doughton Park, and Mount Pisgah on the Parkway. For further information, obtain a copy of the pamphlet *Blue Ridge Parkway Directory* from any Visitor Center or by mail from the Superintendent; **First Aid available in park:** Yes, from Park Rangers; **Nearest Hospital:** Roanoke, Asheville, and many other cities near the Parkway; **Days/Hours:** Open all year. Some sections of the Parkway may be closed in winter due to snow and ice; **Holiday Closings:** No; **Visitor attractions closed for seasons:** Minerals Museum near Spruce Pine, NC, and The Folk Art Center near Asheville, NC, are open all year except Thanksgiving, Dec. 25, and Jan. 1; Campgrounds, picnic areas, and other visitor accommodations are open May 1 through Oct. Limited camping facilities may be available in winter; **Weather:** Because of its length and range in elevation, the entire Parkway seldom experiences the same weather at the same time. Most visitors come in summer and fall, but spring is pleasant, with fewer crowds. Winter brings snow and ice, which may cause temporary closing of sections of the Parkway.

GENERAL INFORMATION: See listings in this book for Great Smoky Mountains National Park at the southern end of Blue Ridge Parkway and Shenandoah National Park to the North.

OTTER CREEK VISITOR CENTER
PEEKS OF OTTER VISITOR CENTER
MABRY MILL VISITOR CENTER

HUMPBACK ROCKS VISITOR CENTER
SHENANDOAH NATIONAL PARK
SKYLINE DRIVE

ROCKY KNOB VISITOR CENTER
MOSES H. CONE MEMORIAL PARK
CRAGGY GARDENS VISITOR CENTER

GREAT SMOKY MOUNTAINS NATIONAL PARK

Cape Hatteras National Seashore
(Near) Manteo, North Carolina

MAILING ADDRESS: Superintendent, Cape Hatteras National Seashore, Route 1, Box 675, Manteo, NC 27954 **Telephone:** 919-473-2111/919-995-4474

DIRECTIONS: The Whalebone Junction Information Center, at the park entrance, is at the intersection of US 158 and NC 12 and US 64-264 at the town of Nags Head, southeast of Manteo. Information is also available at Hatteras Island Visitor Center in Buxton year-round, and at the Bodie Island Visitor Center (Nags Head) and Ocracoke Island Visitor Center (Ocracoke) late spring, summer, and early fall. Toll ferryboats operate between Ocracoke and Cedar Island (2¼ hours) connecting the park with the mainland. Visitors should check ferry schedules well in advance. Reservations are required. Call Ocracoke, 919-928-3841; Cedar Island, 919-225-3551.

Beaches, migratory waterfowl, fishing, and points of historical interest, including the Cape Hatteras Lighthouse overlooking the "graveyard of the Atlantic," are special features of the first national seashore. Authorized for addition to the National Park System on Aug. 17, 1937.

VISITOR ACTIVITIES: Interpretive exhibits, picnicking, swimming, fishing, guided walks and evening talks in summer, camping, exploring shipwrecks, biking, bird-watching, boating, hunting, surfing; **Permits:** No; **Fees:** Only for campsites—$10 per night per site plus reservation fee of $2 during summer, maximum of 6 people per site; **Visitor facilities:** Campgrounds, fishing piers, lifeguarded beaches in Summer, marina, nature trails, showers, restrooms, ferry service, wildlife refuge, picnic areas, boat ramps and rentals; **HANDICAPPED ACCESSIBILITY:** Vistor Centers, parking. All campgrounds have designated handicapped accessible sites/facilities on request. Many programs handicapped accessible; **Any limitations on vehicle usage:** Bicyclists should use extreme caution because there are no established bike trails within the park. Park your car only in the designated parking areas to avoid getting stuck in soft sands. Check with Rangers or at Visitor Centers for special regulations governing off-road vehicle travel; **Hiking trails:** Yes, self-guiding nature trail near Cape Hatteras Lighthouse, near Bodie Island Visitor Center, and near Ocracoke Campground; **Backcountry:** No; **Camping:** Yes, reservations for Ocracoke campground available through "Ticketron," approximately mid-May through mid-Sept. All other campgrounds first come-first served. Educational group camping special request. Sand and wind conditions require longer than normal tent stakes. Awnings for shade and netting for insect protection will make camping more enjoyable; **Other overnight accommodations on site:** No; **Meals served in the park:** Yes, Lunch counter at Oregon Inlet Marina; restaurants in various villages adjacent to the seashore; **Food and supplies obtainable in the park:** Yes, Oregon Inlet Marina; **Food and supplies obtainable nearby:** Yes, in Hatteras, NC, and various villages; **Overnight accommodations:** Hotels and motels in nearby communities. For a list, write Dare County Tourist Bureau, Manteo, NC 27954; **First Aid available in park:** Yes, or nearby in Manteo, Nags Head, and in Hatteras, NC; **Nearest Hospital:** Elizabeth City, NC, 80 miles (128 km); **Days/Hours:** Open 24 hours a day. All campgrounds closed approximately Nov.-Mar; Frisco and Salvo campgrounds close between Labor Day and approximately Mid-June; **Holiday Closings:** Hatteras Island Visitor Center closed Dec. 25; **Visitor attractions closed for seasons:** Bodie Island and Ocracoke Island Visitor Center closed Nov.-Apr. No organized interpretive programs offered during the off season; **Weather:** Summer is hot and humid; winter is humid and cold. Keep in mind that generally windy conditions make the temperatures feel cooler than they actually are.

GENERAL INFORMATION: *For Your Safety*—Strong littoral currents, rip currents, and shifting sand make swimming particularly dangerous. Tidal currents are hazardous near inlets. Offshore winds can quickly blow air mattresses and other flotation devices out to sea. Swim only where lifeguards are on duty. Sunburn can ruin your vacation. Short periods of exposure and the use of protective waterproof lotions are recommended. Hurricanes are not common but might occur in Aug. or Sept., and winter storms, called Northeasters, should not be taken lightly. Efforts will be made to warn you in time to leave low-lying areas should any of these storms occur. Be sure to walk—never drive—across the barrier dune to the sand beaches. Mosquitoes and other insect pests can make your trip an ordeal if you don't come prepared with repellent and suitable mosquito netting for camping. Lightweight clothing in summer should be adequate to protect you from the sun and keep you comfortable in the cool evenings. You should wear shoes when walking to the beach. Pets must be under physical restraint at all times.

TRAVEL ACCESS: Bus: Virginia Dare Transportation Co. (Trailways) operates into Manteo, NC, 15 miles (24 km), 3 trips daily to and from Elizabeth City, NC, and Norfolk, VA; **Rail:** Nearest passenger service Newsport News, VA 75 miles (120) km) and Rocky Mount, NC, 158 miles (252.8 km); **Air:** Dare County Regional Airport, Manteo, NC., commercial service at Norfolk, VA 80 miles (128 km).

NEARBY FACILITIES & POINTS OF INTEREST: Hotel/Motel: For hotels and campgrounds contact Dare County Tourist Bureau, Manteo, NC; **Parks, other points of interest:** Fort Raleigh National Historic Site, Wright Brothers National Memorial (see listings in this book); **Reservation system in use for Ocracoke campsite:** Ticketron Reservation System.

Cape Lookout National Seashore
Beaufort, North Carolina

MAILING ADDRESS: Superintendent, Cape Lookout National Seashore, 3601 Bridges Street, Suite F, Morehead City, NC 28557-2913 **Telephone:** 919-240-1409

DIRECTIONS: Park Headquarters is located as above. A District Office is located on Harkers Island, 26 miles (41.6 km) east of Morehead City. Ferry access to the Park is provided from Beaufort, Harkers Island, Davis, Atlantic, and Ocracoke. Ferry from Beaufort, Harkers Island, and Ocracoke transports passengers only. Others transport passengers and 4-wheel drive vehicles.
The Seashore embraces a series of barrier islands including 58 miles (92.8 km) of ocean beach, historic Portsmouth Village, and Cape Lookout lighthouse. Authorized for addition to the National Park System on Mar. 10, 1966.

VISITOR ACTIVITIES: Fishing, swimming, boating, shell collecting, photography, primitive camping, bird-watching; **Permits:** Yes, fee permit to leave vehicles in park, obtainable from Park Headquarters; **Fees:** Yes, for Concession and Charter Ferry; **Visitor facilities:** Interpretive programs offered in season. This is a developing park, and visitor facilities are limited; **Any limitations on vehicle usage:** No roads or bridges, 4-wheel drive vehicles only; **Hiking trails:** No; **Backcountry:** Yes, information from Park Headquarters; **Camping:** Yes, there are no developed campsites; **Other overnight accommodations on site:** Yes, concession-operated rustic cabins; **Meals served in the park:** No; **Food and supplies obtainable in the park:** No; **Food and supplies obtainable nearby:** Yes, at Harkers Island and Beaufort; **Overnight accommodations:** Harkers Island and Beaufort; **First Aid available in park:** No; physicians are in Harkers Island and Beaufort; **Nearest Hospital:** Morehead City and Sea Level; **Days/Hours:** Open 24 hours a day; **Holiday Closings:** No; **Visitor attractions closed for seasons:** Interpretive programs offered only in summer; **Weather:** Hot and humid in summer.

GENERAL INFORMATION: Be prepared to carry with you everything you need, particularly food and water. Don't go out without a shirt and a hat, because there is little shade or shelter on the islands. Make sure your tent is strong and able to withstand wind. It should have mosquito netting. Be prepared with repellent to combat many biting insects.

TRAVEL ACCESS: Bus: Trailways, Seashore Line, service Morehead City, NC; **Rail:** No; **Air:** No.

NEARBY FACILITIES & POINTS OF INTEREST: Hotel/Motel: several in the area; **Parks, other points of interest:** North Carolina Maritime Museum, Beaufort, NC; North Carolina Aquarium, Pine Knoll Shores, NC.

Carl Sandburg Home National Historic Site
Flat Rock, North Carolina

MAILING ADDRESS: Superintendent, Carl Sandburg Home National Historic Site,

1928 Little River Road, Flat Rock, NC 28731 **Telephone:** 704-693-4178

DIRECTIONS: The Site is 3 miles (4.8 km) south of Hendersonville. Turn off US 25 onto Little River Road at the Flat Rock Playhouse. The Park is 26 miles (41.6 km) south of Asheville via Int. 26.

"Connemara" was the home of the noted poet-author Carl Sandburg for the last 22 years of his life. Authorized for addition to the National Park System on Oct. 17, 1968.

VISITOR ACTIVITIES: Self-guiding tour, guided house tours, exhibits; **Permits:** No; **Fees:** $1; **Visitor facilities:** Restrooms at Information Center, parking; **HANDICAPPED ACCESSIBILITY:** Shuttle van available for getting from parking area to the home; **Any limitations on vehicle usage:** Visitors must park in the designated area and walk to the home or use shuttle van; **Hiking trails:** Yes, self-guiding paths and trails lead around the Site; **Backcountry:** No; **Camping:** No; **Other overnight accommodations on site:** No; **Meals served in the park:** No; **Food and supplies obtainable in the park:** No; **Food and supplies obtainable nearby:** Yes, Hendersonville; **Overnight accommodations:** Hendersonville, 3 miles (4.8 km) north on US 25; **First Aid available in park:** Yes; **Nearest Hospital:** Hendersonville, 4 miles (6.4 km); **Days/Hours:** Open daily 9 a.m. to 5 p.m. **Holiday Closings:** Dec. 25; **Weather:** Moderate summers, cool spring and fall, cold winters.

GENERAL INFORMATION: *For Your Safety*—Be cautious on trails, around ponds and lakes, and while standing on the rock face atop Big Glassy Mountain. Be wary of farm animals that can bite or kick. Stay on established walks and paths, do not climb fences, and be alert for snakes and poison ivy.

TRAVEL ACCESS: Bus: Trailway and Greyhound provide service to Hendersonville, NC; **Rail:** Southern Railway provides service to Spartanburg and Greenville, SC; **Air:** Piedmont, Wheeler, Atlantic Southeast, Sunbird, and Metro Airlines provide service to Asheville.

Fort Raleigh National Historic Site
Manteo, North Carolina

MAILING ADDRESS: Superintendent, Cape Hatteras National Seashore, Route 1, Box 675, Manteo, NC 27954 **Telephone:** 919- 473-5772

DIRECTIONS: The site is on US 64-264, 3 miles (4.8 km) north of Manteo, NC, 92 miles (147.2 km) southeast of Norfolk, VA, and 67 miles (107.2 km) southeast of Elizabeth City, NC.

The first English settlement was attempted here from 1585-87. The fate of Sir Walter Raleigh's "Lost Colony" remains a mystery. Designated Apr. 5, 1941.

VISITOR ACTIVITIES: Interpretive exhibits and film, walking tours. In summer, "Lost Colony," a symphonic-drama, is produced in the Waterside Theater; **Permits:** No; **Fees:** Only to see "Lost Colony"; **Visitor facilities:** Parking, restrooms, picnic area; **HANDI-CAPPED ACCESSIBILITY:** Visitor Center, exhibits, restrooms, historic trails, programs; **Any limitations on vehicle usage:** No; **Hiking trails:** Yes, nature trails around the Site; **Backcountry:** No; **Camping:** No; **Other overnight accommodations on site:** No; **Meals served in the park:** No; **Food and supplies obtainable in the park:** No; **Food and supplies obtainable nearby:** Yes, at Manteo; **Overnight accommodations:** Manteo, 4 miles (6.4 km) or on the Outer Banks, 14-18 miles (22.4-28.8 km); **First Aid available in park:** Yes, or nearby in Manteo and Nags Head; **Nearest Hospital:** Elizabeth City, NC, US 158, 80 miles

(128 km); **Days/Hours:** Open 9 a.m. to 8 p.m. in season, 9 a.m. to 6 p.m. on Sundays, 9 a.m. to 5 p.m. remainder of year; **Holiday Closings:** Dec. 25.

GENERAL INFORMATION: Adjacent to the Historic Site is the Elizabethan Garden, maintained by the Garden Club of North Carolina, Inc. The admission fee is set by that organization.

TRAVEL ACCESS: Bus: Virginia Dare Trans. Co. (Trailways) provides daily service into Manteo, NC, from Elizabeth City, NC, and Norfolk, VA; **Rail:** No, nearest passenger service is Rocky Mount, NC, 140 miles (224 km) and Newport News, VA, 93 miles (148.8 km); **Air:** Charter flights may be arranged from airport at Manteo; nearest commercial service at Norfolk, VA, 88 miles (140.8 km).

NEARBY FACILITIES & POINTS OF INTEREST: Campgrounds: NPS campgrounds on Cape Hatteras National Seashore, nearest at Oregon Inlet 17 miles (27.2 km); **Parks, other points of interest:** Cape Hatteras National Seashore, Wright Brothers National Memorial.

Great Smoky Mountains National Park
For details see listing in Tennessee

Guilford Courthouse National Military Park
Greensboro, North Carolina

MAILING ADDRESS: Superintendent, Guilford Courthouse National Military Park, P.O. Box 9806, Greensboro, NC 27429-0806 **Telephone:** 919-288-1776

DIRECTIONS: The Visitor Center is near the intersection of Old Battleground Road and New Garden Road, in northwest Greensboro.
The battle fought here on Mar. 15, 1781, opened the campaign that led to Yorktown and the end of the Revolution. Established by act of Congress on Mar. 2, 1917. This was the first Revolution battlefield to become part of the National Park System.

VISITOR ACTIVITIES: Interpretive film and exhibits; auto, bicycle, and walking tours, interpretive talks; **Permits:** No; **Fees:** No; **Visitor facilities:** Parking and restrooms at Visitor Center; Museum, bicycle and foot trails; **HANDICAPPED ACCESSIBILITY:** Yes; Auditorium film captioned; **Any limitations on vehicle usage:** 1-hour parking limits in most parking lots; **Hiking trails:** Yes, self-guiding foot trails; **Backcountry:** No; **Camping:** No; **Other overnight accommodations on site:** No; **Meals served in the park:** No; **Food and supplies obtainable in the park:** No; **Food and supplies obtainable nearby:** Yes, in Greensboro; **Overnight accommodations:** Greensboro, 2-10 miles (3.2-16 km); **First Aid available in park:** Yes; **Nearest Hospital:** Greensboro, 3 miles (4.8 km); **Days/Hours:** Open daily from 8:30 a.m. to 5 p.m. Tour road closes ½-hour earlier; **Holiday Closings:** Dec. 25 and Jan. 1; **Visitor attractions closed for seasons:** No; **Weather:** Hot, humid summer; cold moderate winter.

GENERAL INFORMATION: Watch out for traffic on New Garden Road and Old Battleground Road. Park has 28 monuments honoring men and women of the Revolutionary period, including the Nathanael Greene Monument and the Signers Monument, where two of North Carolina's three signers of the Declaration of Independence are buried.

Moores Creek National Battlefield
Currie, North Carolina

MAILING ADDRESS: Superintendent, Moores Creek National Battlefield, P.O. Box 69, Currie, NC 28435 **Telephone:** 919-283-5591

DIRECTIONS: The park is approximately 20 miles (32 km) northwest of Wilmington, NC, and can be reached via US 421 and NC 210. From Interstate 40, follow 210 west at the Rocky Point exit.

The brief, violent battle on Feb. 27, 1776, between North Carolina Patriots and Loyalists is commemorated here. The Patriot victory notably advanced the revolutionary cause in the South, ending Royal authority in the colony. This helped forestall a British invasion of the South and encouraged North Carolina to instruct its delegation to the Continental Congress, on Apr. 12, 1776, to support total independence—the first colony to so act. Established June 2, 1926.

VISITOR ACTIVITIES: Exhibits, walking tours, picnicking, wildflower-watching in season; **Permits:** No; **Fees:** No; **Visitor facilities:** Restrooms, museum, trails, and picnic areas; **HANDICAPPED ACCESSIBILITY:** Visitor Center, Visitor Center parking, and picnic area parking. Accessible restrooms at Visitor Center and picnic area; **Any limitations on vehicle usage:** No; **Hiking trails:** Yes, a 1 mile (1.6 km) History Trail and a .3 mile (.5 km) Tarheel Trail depicting the local naval stores industry during the Revolution; **Backcountry:** No; **Camping:** No; **Other overnight accommodations on site:** No; **Meals served in the park:** No; **Food and supplies obtainable in the park:** No; **Food and supplies obtainable nearby:** Yes, at Currie, Atkinson, Burgaw, or Wilmington; **Overnight accommodations:** Wilmington, 20 miles (32 km) southeast of Moores Creek; **First Aid available in park:** Usually, or nearby in Atkinson or at Hospital in Burgaw; **Nearest Hospital:** Pender Memorial Hospital in Burgaw, 14 miles (22.4 km) northeast of Moores Creek; **Days/Hours:** Open daily from 9 a.m. to 5 p.m.; 8 a.m. to 6 p.m. on Saturday and Sunday from Memorial Day to Labor Day; **Holiday Closings:** Dec. 25 and Jan. 1; **Visitor attractions closed for seasons:** No; **Weather:** Spring—sunny and mild; summer—hot and humid; fall—sunny and mild; winter—mild with infrequent subfreezing weather.

GENERAL INFORMATION: When near the creek, be sure to watch your children. Visitors should be aware of several species of poisonous snakes that live in the Park.

TRAVEL ACCESS: **Bus:** Greyhound provides regular service to Wilmington, NC; **Rail:** No; **Air:** Piedmont Airlines provides daily service to Wilmington, NC; no commercial transportation between park and Wilmington except by taxi.

Wright Brothers National Memorial
(in) Kill Devil Hills, North Carolina

MAILING ADDRESS: Superintendent, Wright Brothers National Memorial, c/o Cape Hatteras National Seashore, Rt. 1, Box 675, Manteo, NC 27954 **Telephone:** 919-441-7430

DIRECTIONS: The Memorial is located on the Outer Banks of North Carolina in the town of Kill Devil Hills. The Visitor Center is 15 miles (24 km) northeast of Manteo on US 158.

The first sustained flights in a heavier-than-air machine were made here by Wilbur and Orville Wright on Dec. 17, 1903. Authorized March 2, 1927.

VISITOR ACTIVITIES: Interpretive exhibits, including reproductions of the Wright Brothers' 1902 glider and 1903 flyer; walking tours, orientation talks year-round; **Permits:** No; **Fees:** Yes, $1 per person or $3 per car; **Visitor facilities:** Reconstruction of an airplane hangar and the Wright Brothers' workshop and residence, granite monuments mark the sites of glider experiments and the spot where the first plane left the ground; **HANDICAPPED ACCESSIBILITY:** Visitor Center, exhibits, restrooms, historic trail, most programs accessible. **Any limitations on vehicle usage:** No; **Hiking trails:** No; **Backcountry:** No; **Camping:** No; **Other overnight accommodations on site:** No; **Meals served in the park:** No; **Food and supplies obtainable in the park:** No; **Food and supplies obtainable nearby:** Yes, at Kitty Hawk, Kill Devil Hills, and Nags Head; **Overnight accommodations:** Kitty Hawk, Kill Devil Hills and Nags Head, within a 14-mile (22.4-km) radius; **First Aid available in park:** Yes, or nearby in Nags Head, NC; **Nearest Hospital:** Elizabeth City, NC, 66 miles (105.6 km); **Days/Hours:** Open daily from 9:00 a.m. to 5:00 p.m.; 9:00 a.m. to 7:00 p.m. in summer; **Holiday Closings:** Dec. 25; **Visitor attractions closed for seasons:** Reduced organized interpretive programs during off-season; **Weather:** Weather is generally moderate and windy.

GENERAL INFORMATION: *For Your Safety*—Keep in mind that the generally windy conditions make the temperatures feel cooler than they actually are. Even in relatively warm temperatures high winds can make hypothermia, the loss of body heat, a serious threat. From spring through early fall protect against sunburn, especially from 10 a.m. to 3 p.m.

Nearby points of interest include Cape Hatteras National Seashore, which is 10 miles (16 km) south of the Memorial and Fort Raleigh National Historic Site, located on Roanoke Island about 18 miles (28.8 km) southwest of the Memorial (see listing in this book). This is the site of what is known as the Lost Colony, England's unsuccessful first attempt to colonize the North American continent. It can be reached via U.S. 64-264.

TRAVEL ACCESS: Bus: Virginia Dare Transportation Co. (Trailways) operates into Manteo, NC, 15 miles (24 km), 3 trips daily to and from Elizabeth City, NC, and Norfolk, VA; **Rail:** Nearest passenger service Newport News, VA, 75 miles (120 km) and Rocky Mount, NC, 158 miles (252.8 km); **Air:** Yes, via private and charter flights to the Park's First Flight (3,000-foot) Airstrip. Nearest commercial service at Norfolk, VA, 70 miles (112 km). Commuter/Charter flights available from Dare County Regional Airport near Manteo.

NEARBY FACILITIES & POINTS OF INTEREST: Campgrounds: NPS Campgrounds on Cape Hatteras National Seashore; **Parks, other points of interest:** Cape Hatteras National Seashore, Fort Raleigh National Historic Site.

North Dakota

INTERNATIONAL
PEACE GARDEN

FORT UNION TRADING
POST NATIONAL HISTORIC SITE

THEODORE ROOSEVELT
NATIONAL PARK

Bismarck

LEWIS AND CLARK NATIONAL HISTORIC TRAIL

KNIFE RIVER INDIAN VILLAGES NATIONAL HISTORIC SITE

Fort Union Trading Post National Historic Site
North Dakota and Montana

MAILING ADDRESS: Superintendent, Fort Union Trading Post National Historic Site, RR 3, Box 71, Williston, ND 58801 **Telephone:** 701-572-9083

DIRECTIONS: The Site is on the border of North Dakota and Montana, and can be reached via US 2 and N.D. 1804 West from Williston, ND, which is 25 miles (40 km) to the northeast, or from Sidney, MT, 21 miles (33.6 km) south via ND58.

The trading post that stood here was the principal fur-trading depot in the Upper Missouri River region from 1829 to 1867. The National Park Service has partially reconstructed the fort. Authorized for addition to the National Park System on June 20, 1966.

VISITOR ACTIVITIES: Interpretive exhibits, living history programs, walking tours; **Permits:** No; **Fees:** No; **Visitor facilities:** A Visitor Center is located in the reconstructed 1851 Bourgeois House at the site. Guided tours of the fort site and a teepee display are provided; **HANDICAPPED ACCESSIBILITY:** All facilities; **Any limitations on vehicle usage:** Vehicles are limited to established roadways; **Hiking trails:** No; **Backcountry:** No; **Camping:** No; **Other overnight accommodations on site:** No; **Meals served in the park:** No; **Food and supplies obtainable in the park:** No; **Food and supplies obtainable nearby:** Yes, at Williston or Sidney, MT; **Overnight accommodations:** Williston, Sidney; **First Aid available in park:** Yes; **Nearest Hospital:** Williston, 25 miles (40 km); **Days/Hours:** Open daily from 9 a.m. to 5:30 p.m. in winter; 8 a.m. until 8 p.m. in summer; **Holiday Closings:** Dec. 25 and Jan. 1; **Visitor attractions closed for seasons:** Living history programs offered only from mid-May through mid-Oct.; **Weather:** Winters are cold with temperatures often below zero. Summers are warm and dry. Wet, cool springs and dry, cool falls are normal. Windy conditions may be expected during any season.

International Peace Garden
Dunseith, North Dakota

MAILING ADDRESS: Superintendent, International Peace Garden, P.O. Box 116, Dunseith, ND 58329 **Telephone:** 701-263-4390

DIRECTIONS: The Garden is 13 miles (20.8 km) north of Dunseith on US 281.

Peaceful relations between Canada and the United States are commemorated here. The Garden contains 2,339 acres (888 in North Dakota, 1,451 in Manitoba), which are administered by the International Peace Garden, Inc. The National Park Service has assisted in the master plan. This affiliated area of the National Park System was dedicated on July 14, 1932.

VISITOR ACTIVITIES: Walking, picnicking, camping, guided tours, snowshoeing; **Permits:** No; **Fees:** Yes, $5 per vehicle daily pass, $10 per vehicle season decal, $2 per person pedestrian pass; **Visitor facilities:** Landscaped gardens, amphitheatre, exhibits, picnic areas, campgrounds, food service, souvenir shops, chapel, bell tower, arboretum, International Music Camp, Canadian Legion Sports Camp, Masonic Auditorium, Peace Tower; **Any limitations on vehicle usage:** Vehicles are restricted to designated roadways; **Backcountry:** No; **Camping:** Yes, no reservations available for campsites; fee is $10 cement pad, electricity, water, $8 water, electricity, $6 unserviced, $2 overflow. Write or call the Garden for further information on camping facilities; **Other overnight accommodations on site:** No; **Meals served in the park:** Yes, at both American and Canadian concessions; **Food and supplies obtainable in the park:** Yes, at both American and Canadian concessions; **Food and supplies obtainable nearby:** Yes, in Dunseith and Boissevain; **Overnight accommodations:** Boissevain, Manitoba, 16 miles (25.6 km) north on Hwy 10; Dunseith, ND, 13 miles (20.8 km) south on Hwy 281; **First Aid available in park:** No; **Nearest Hospital:** Boissevain, Manitoba, Hwy 10, 16 miles (25.6 km); Bottineau, ND, US 281 to ND 5, 30 miles (48 km); **Days/Hours:** Open 24 hours a day year-round; **Holiday Closings:** No; **Visitor attractions closed for seasons:** Activities are curtailed in winter; **Weather:** Occasional rain and wind with dry, cool evenings. Temperatures range from 60-95°F.

NEARBY FACILITIES & POINTS OF INTEREST: Parks, other points of interest: Turtle Mountain Provincial Parks, 5 miles (8 km) north, Lake Metigoshe State Park 25 miles (40 km) west both have camping facilities.

Knife River Indian Villages National Historic Site
Stanton, North Dakota

MAILING ADDRESS: Superintendent, Knife River Indian Villages National Historic Site, R.R. 1, Stanton, ND 58571 **Telephone:** 701-745-3300

DIRECTIONS: From I-94 at Bismarck, north on US 83 to ND 200A at Washburn, 40 miles (64 km); west on ND 200A to ND 31, 22 miles (35.2 km); north on ND 31 to Stanton, 2 miles (3.2 km). The Visitor Center is .5 (.8 km) miles north of Stanton.

Remnants of three Mandan and Hidatsa villages are an archaeological treasure of the Plains Indians. Visitors to the area include Lewis and Clark, George Catlin, Karl Bodmer, Prince Maximilian, and John James Audubon. Authorized for addition to the National Park System on Oct. 16, 1974.

VISITOR ACTIVITIES: Summer programs are conducted daily June through August.

They include guided tours to village sites, museum exhibits, slide shows, cultural demonstrations, and guest speakers. Daily programs continue until Labor Day. Special tours and programs are arranged upon request. Open daily all year, closes Thanksgiving, Christmas and New Years Day. Summer hours 8:00 a.m.-8:00 p.m. MDT, winter hours 8:00 a.m.-4:30 p.m. MDT. Visitor Center, restroom facilities and trail to two village sites are handicapped accessible.

NEARBY FACILITIES & POINTS OF INTEREST: Hotel/Motel: Yes, Stanton, ND; ½ mile (.8 km) south of Park; **Food/Supplies:** Yes, ½ mile (.8 km) south of Park; **Parks, other points of interest:** Fort Clark State Historic Site, 7 miles (11.2 km) south; Garrison Dam National Fish Hatchery and Sakakawea State Park, 19 miles (30.4 km) north.

Lewis and Clark Trail
For details see listing in Illinois

North Country National Scenic Trail
For details see listing in New York

Theodore Roosevelt National Park
Medora, North Dakota   **SEE CLIMATABLE NO. 27**

MAILING ADDRESS: Superintendent, Theodore Roosevelt National Park, Medora, ND 58645 **Telephone:** 701-623-4466

DIRECTIONS: The North Unit is 15 miles (24 km) south of Watford City and 55 miles (88 km) north of Belfield, on Highway 85. A stop at the North Unit Visitor Center will help you plan and enjoy your visit. The South Unit Visitor Center is at Medora, 17 miles (27.2 km) west of Belfield and 63 miles (100.8 km) east of Glendive, off Highway I-94. A rough, poorly maintained dirt road of about 20 miles (32 km) leads from the South Unit to the site of Theodore Roosevelt's second ranch, the Elkhorn. Almost nothing of this ranch exists today. Inquiry should be made before attempting this trip.

The Park contains scenic badlands along the Little Missouri River, the cabin from Roosevelt's Maltese Cross Ranch, and the site of Roosevelt's Elkhorn Ranch, as well as bison and some of the original prairie.

VISITOR ACTIVITIES: Interpretive exhibits, guided walks, campfire programs, auto tours, hiking, camping, photography, backcountry, horseback riding, picnicking, birdwatching, float trips, cross-country skiing; **Permits:** For backcountry, free permits available at Visitor Center; **Fees:** Yes, entrance fee is $3, camping is $7, group camping is $1 South Unit, $2 North Unit, per person (subject to change). Golden Eagle, Golden Age Passports, and Golden Access Passports accepted and available; **Visitor facilities:** Visitor Centers, museum slide program, movie, campgrounds, scenic overlooks, picnic areas, guided trail rides, hiking trails, restrooms, parking; **HANDICAPPED ACCESSIBILITY:** All 3 Vistor Centers, both Cottonwood and Squaw Creek Campgrounds, the Maltese Cross Cabin, evening campfire programs, naturalist talks, some of the naturalist guided walks, sites in picnic areas, wayside exhibits, and Vistor Centers and campground restrooms; **Any limitations on vehicle usage:** Off-road and cross-country vehicular travel are prohibited; **Hiking trails:** Yes, information on the many trails is available at the Visitor Centers; **Backcountry:** Yes, backcountry use is regulated; for a backcountry camping permit and further information, check at Visitor Centers; **Camping:** Yes, no reservations available for individual campsites, but group camping requires a written reservation from the Park Superintendent. Other Federal and State-maintained campsites are nearby; **Other overnight accommodations on site:** No; **Meals served in the park:** No; **Food and supplies obtainable in the park:** No; **Food and supplies obtainable nearby:** Yes, near the South Unit, Medora, in summer; Belfield, year-round. Near the North Unit, Watford City, 15 miles (24 km) north of the park entrance; **Overnight accommodations:** Medora and Watford City; **First Aid available in park:** Yes; **Nearest Hospital:** Watford City and Dickinson; **Days/Hours:** The Park is open all year. Peak season is from May through Oct.; **Holiday Closings:** Visitor Centers closed Thanksgiving, Dec. 25, and Jan. 1; **Visitor attractions closed for seasons:** Portions of the park road may be closed during the winter months, depending on snow/ice conditions; trail ride concession closed from late Sept. to early May. Painted Canyon Visitor Contact Center closed from Oct. through March, North Unit Visitor Contact Center closed some weekdays from Oct. to May, and most attractions in Medora closed Labor Day to Memorial Day; **Weather:** Generally mild, warm to hot days, cool nights. Expect thunderstorms in summer and sudden blizzards in winter.

GENERAL INFORMATION: *WARNING: Wildlife is dangerous*—So keep your distance. Drinking water should be obtained from approved water sources. Most backcountry water is not fit for human use. The weather in the badlands is very harsh with extremes in temperature and sudden violent storms. Prepare yourself for a variety of conditions.

Visitors to the area should also see the Chateau de Mores State Historic Site, a 27-room chateau across the river from Medora. The chateau is open to visitors from May through early October.

No firewood available in campground and picnic area; gathering of wood is prohibited.

Ohio

Cuyahoga Valley National Recreation Area
Brecksville, Ohio

MAILING ADDRESS: Superintendent, Cuyahoga Valley National Recreation Area,

15610 Vaughn Road, Brecksville, OH 44141 **Telephone:** 216-650-4636

DIRECTIONS: Park Headquarters is at 15610 Vaughn Road Brecksville, OH, south of OH 82 on Riverview Road and east of OH 21 on Snowville Road. Happy Days Visitor Center (serving the south end of the park) is on OH 303 1 mile (1.6 km) west of OH 8 and 2 miles (3.2 km) east of Peninsula. Canal Visitor Center (serving the north end of the park) is on Canal Road at Hillside Road, south of Rockside Road in the Cleveland suburb of Valley View.

This recreation area links the urban centers of Cleveland and Akron and preserves the rural character of the Cuyahoga River Valley and the 150-year-old Ohio and Erie Canal system. Authorized for addition to the National Park System on Dec. 27, 1974.

VISITOR ACTIVITIES: Hiking, biking, picnicking, auto tours, interpretive programs and exhibits, special events, environmental education, horseback riding, fishing, xc-skiing, ice skating, sledding, tobogganning, etc. Cooperating organizations within the park also provide Blossom Music Center (summer home of the Cleveland Orchestra)—classical, pop, country and western concerts, and ballet; Porthouse Theater (summer stock theater of Kent State University)—plays, musicals, operetta, both classical and popular/contemporary; Boston Mills Ski Resort—downhill skiing in winter/art classes and festivals in summer; Brandywine Ski Center and Dover Lake Park—downhill skiing in winter/camping, swimming, water slides in summer; Brandywine, Astorhust, Sleepy Hollow, and Shawnee Hills Golf Courses—golf; Cuyahoga Valley Line—historic steam train excursions through the park in summer (June-Oct.) on weekends; Hale Farm and Village—historic village recreation with living history interpretation and traditional craft demonstrations of blacksmithing, glassblowing, pottery making, spinning and weaving, fireplace cooking, etc.; **Permits:** No; **Fees:** NPS facilities: $30 fee for reserving picnic shelters—No other NPS fee. Most Non-NPS facilities, Yes in varying amounts; **Visitor facilities:** Trails, picnic areas, reservable picnic shelters, ponds, open playfields, warming shelters, contact stations, two visitor centers, scenic overlooks, restrooms, historic sites (Indians, Ohio and Erie Canal, Western Reserve settlement and life, etc.), cultural attractions (Blossom Music Center, Porthouse Theater, etc.), commercial downhill ski areas, commercial golf courses, Boy and Girl Scout camps, environmental education center, scenic roads, commercial camping and swimming area, commercial steam train excursion, sledding hills; **HANDICAPPED ACCESSIBILITY:** Both Visitor Centers are accessible and can provide visitors with information about trails and other features within CVNRA that are also accessible. **Any limitations on vehicle usage:** No; **Hiking trails:** Yes, there are many foot trails throughout the Park; **Backcountry:** No; **Camping:** Commercial at Dover Lake Park; **Other overnight accommodations on site:** Stanford Farm Hostel operated by American Youth Hostels, Inc.; **Meals served in the park:** No; **Food and supplies obtainable in the park:** No; **Food and supplies obtainable nearby:** Yes, in any of the numerous communities surrounding the Park; **Overnight accommodations:** Motels on OH 8, in Brecksville on OH 21, and in Cleveland and Akron; **First Aid available in park:** Yes; **Nearest Hospital:** Cuyahoga Falls, OH, State Road, approximately 5 miles (8 km). Northern areas of the Park have some nearby hospitals in suburbs of Cleveland; **Days/Hours:** 7 days a week 8 a.m.-11 p.m., some areas closed at dusk; **Holiday Closings:** Thanksgiving, Dec. 25, and Jan. 1 for Visitor Centers; **Visitor attractions closed for seasons:** Blossom Music Center open in summer only: Hale Farm and Village open May-Oct. and in Dec.; Porthouse Theatre open in summer only; Cuyahoga Valley Line runs June-Oct.; Golf course open summer only; ski areas (downhill) winter only.

James A. Garfield National Historic Site
Mentor, Ohio

MAILING ADDRESS: Superintendent, James A. Garfield National Historic Site, Lawnfield, 8095 Mentor Avenue, Mentor, OH 44060 **Telephone:** 216-255-8722

DIRECTIONS: **From the east:** Take I-90 to the Mentor-Kirtland Rte. 306 exit. Turn right; take Rte. 306 for two miles north to Rte. 20 (Mentor Ave.) for two miles east. Lawnfield is on Rte. 20, on the north side of the road. **From the west:** Take I-90 to the Mentor-Kirtland Rte. 306 exit. Turn left; take Rte. 306 for two miles north to Rte. 20 (Mentor Ave.). Turn right; take Rte. 20 for two miles east. Lawnfield is on Rte. 20 on the north side of the road.

VISITOR ACTIVIITIES: This site preserves Lawnfield, home of 20th president James A. Garfield, in Mentor. This includes outbuildings; Carriage House, Pump House, and Campaign Office. The Site, added to the National Park system on December 28, 1980, is operated by the Western Reserve Historical Society. **Hours:** Tuesday-Saturday: 10:00 a.m. to 5:00 p.m.; Sunday, Noon to 5:00 p.m. **Admission charged:** Yes.

Mound City Group National Monument
Chillicothe, Ohio

MAILING ADDRESS: Superintendent, Mound City Group National Monument, 16062 State Route 104, Chillicothe, OH 45601 **Telephone:** 614-774-1125

DIRECTIONS: Mound City is on the west bank of the Scioto River, on OH 104, 2 miles (3.2 km) north of the US 35 intersection and 3 miles (4.8 km) north of Chillicothe, OH.
    Two thousand years ago (200 B.C.-500 A.D.), the Ohio River Valley was the focal point of the Hopewell Indian culture. The Hopewell Indians created some of the finest prehistoric art in North America, built vast geometrical earthworks, and constructed burial mounds. The largest known concentration of these mounds is preserved at this Monument. The burial mounds yield copper breastplates, tools, obsidian blades, shells, ornaments of grizzly bear teeth and stone pipes carved as birds and animals. Authorized for addition to the National Park System on Mar. 2, 1923.

VISITOR ACTIVITIES: Interpretive exhibits, walking, picnicking. Organized groups may receive special services; advance arrangements should be made with the Superintendent; **Permits:** No; **Fees:** Yes, at entrance; **Visitor facilities:** Visitor Center, restrooms, picnic area, interpretive trails; **HANDICAPPED ACCESSIBILITY:** Parking; most facilities are accessible; **Any limitations on vehicle usage:** Vehicles are restricted to designated roadways; **Hiking trails:** Yes, self-guiding interpretive trail; **Backcountry:** No; **Camping:** No, camping is available in Chillicothe and in nearby state parks. Contact the Monument for further information; **Other overnight accommodations on site:** No; **Meals served in the park:** No; **Food and supplies obtainable in the park:** No; **Food and supplies obtainable nearby:** Yes, in Chillicothe; **Overnight accommodations:** Chillicothe, 3 miles (4.8 km) south on OH 104; **First Aid available in park:** Yes; **Nearest Hospital:** Medical Center Hospital, US 23, 6 miles (9.6 km) north; **Days/Hours:** From Labor Day until mid-June the Visitor Center is open from 8 a.m. to 5 p.m.; extended hours from mid-June to Labor Day. The Park is always open during daylight hours; **Holiday Closings:** Thanksgiving, Dec. 25, and Jan. 1.

GENERAL INFORMATION: *For Your Safety*—Watch for ground squirrel holes and uneven ground; be extra cautious along the Scioto River trail as it can be very slippery. Keep children under control near the water's edge. Southern Ohio is very rich in prehistoric Indian sites. Among those set aside as State memorials under the custody of the Ohio Historical Society are Fort Ancient, Fort Hill, Miamisburg Mound, Newark Earthworks, Seip Mound and Serpent Mound. You can see historical and archaeological exhibits in the Ross County Historical Society Museum in Chillicothe and at the Ohio Historical Center in Columbus.

The outdoor drama "Tecumseh!" depicts the story of the Shawnee leader. It is held at 8:00 p.m. on Monday through Saturday from mid-June through Labor Day at Sugarloaf Mountain Amphitheatre, which is 5 miles (8 km) from Chillicothe. For further information, write The Scioto Society, Inc., P.O. Box 73, Chillicothe, OH 45601. Call 614-775-0700 after Mar. 1.

TRAVEL ACCESS: Bus: Greyhound provides daily service to Chillicothe, OH, 4 miles (64 km) south; **Rail:** No.

NEARBY FACILITIES & POINTS OF INTEREST: Parks, other points of interest: Adena State Memorial; Several Ross County museums; Outdoor Drama-"Tecumseh!"; 4 state parks nearby. Ross-Chillicothe Convention and Visitors Bureau provides information on entire area—write P.O. Box 73, Chillicothe, OH 45601, or phone 614-775-4100.

North Country National Scenic Trail
For details see listing in New York

Perry's Victory and International Peace Memorial
Put-in-Bay, Ohio

MAILING ADDRESS: Superintendent, Perry's Victory and International Peace Memorial, P.O. Box 549, Put-in-Bay, OH 43456 **Telephone:** 419-285-2184

DIRECTIONS: The Memorial is on South Bass Island in the village of Put-in-Bay. The island is about 3 miles (4.8 km) from Catawba, OH and 8 miles (12.8 km) from Port Clinton, OH. Ferry boats from both Catawba and Port Clinton to Put-in-Bay operate from mid-Apr. to mid-Nov. Airplanes provide passenger service year-round.

Commodore Oliver H. Perry won the greatest naval battle of the War of 1812 on Lake Erie. The Memorial (the World's most massive Doric Column) was constructed in 1912-15 "to inculcate the lessons of international peace by arbitration and disarmament." Established by act of Congress on June 2, 1936.

VISITOR ACTIVITIES: A Visitor Center Information Station is near the entrance to the park. An elevator carries visitors to the top of the Memorial. Interpretive programs are presented several times each day during the summer. Special arrangements may be made for interpretive talks at other times by writing or calling the Superintendent. Fishing is available; **Permits:** No; **Fees:** Elevator fee is $1 for persons over 16 years of age, 16 and under free, 62 and over free. No charge for educational or special groups upon request from administrative office. Golden Eagle and Golden Age Passports accepted; **HANDICAPPED ACCESSIBILITY:** Restrooms; **Camping:** No, for further information on nearby camping facilities, contact South Bass Island State Park, Put-in-Bay, OH 43456, phone 419-285-2112; **Other overnight accommodations on site:** No; **Meals served in the park:** No; **Food and supplies obtainable in the park:** No; **Food and supplies obtainable nearby:** Yes, grocery store in village of Put-in-Bay or on mainland in Catawba or Port Clinton; **Overnight accommodations:** Within several blocks of the Memorial. Reservations are advised, Contact the Put-in-Bay Chamber of Commerce for further information; **First Aid available in park:** Yes; **Nearest Hospital:** Port Clinton, OH 8 miles (12.8 km); **Days/Hours:** Mon.-Fri.: 10 a.m. to 5 p.m.; spring and fall; 9:00 a.m. to 6:00 p.m., summer; 7 days a week late Apr. to late Oct. **Holiday Closings:** No, during operating season; **Visitor attractions closed for seasons:** The Memorial is closed from the end of Oct. through mid-April.

TRAVEL ACCESS: Bus: No; **Air:** Island Airlines, 10 flights daily May 15-Labor Day 8:15 a.m.-7:30 p.m., more limited schedule during fall, winter, and early spring from Port Clinton, OH; **Other:** Miller Boat Line from Catawba, OH to island, 18-minute trip (docks 2 miles (3.2 km) from village of Put-in-Bay); Put-in Bay Boat Line a 25-minute trip from Port Clinton, OH to island, (docks downtown Village of Put-in-Bay); Bicycle rentals available near both boat lines; Golf cart rental near both boat lines; Tour train near boat dock or downtown terminal.

NEARBY FACILITIES & POINTS OF INTEREST: Campgrounds: South Bass Island State Park, Put-in-Bay, OH, 419-285-2184, 125 Class B campsites; **Parks, other points of interest:** Winery, caves, gift shops; For a complete listing of facilities available write Put-in-Bay Chamber of Commerce, P.O. Box 76, Put-in-Bay, OH 43456.

William Howard Taft National Historic Site
Cincinnati, Ohio

MAILING ADDRESS: Superintendent, William Howard Taft National Historic Site, 2038 Auburn Avenue, Cincinnati, OH 45219 **Telephone:** 513-684-3262

DIRECTIONS: The Site is at 2038 Auburn Avenue, 1 block north of near the intersection of Auburn and Dorchester Avenues.

This house was the birthplace and boyhood home of William Howard Taft, the only person to serve as President (1909-13) and Chief Justice of the United States (1921-30). Authorized for addition to the National Park System on Dec. 2, 1969.

VISITOR ACTIVITIES: Interpretive exhibits, house tours; advance reservations are requested for groups of 25 or more; **Permits:** No; **Fees:** No; **Visitor facilities:** Exhibits, restrooms, book sales; **HANDICAPPED ACCESSIBILITY:** Elevator; **Any limitations on vehicle usage:** Parking lot available; **Meals served in the park:** No; **Food and supplies obtainable in the park:** No; **Food and supplies obtainable nearby:** Yes, within several blocks; **Overnight accommodations:** Cincinnati and vicinity; **First Aid available in park:** Yes; **Nearest Hospital:** The Christ Hospital, 2 blocks north of Site; **Days/Hours:** Open daily 10 a.m.-4 p.m.; **Holiday Closings:** Thanksgiving, Dec. 25, and Jan. 1; **Visitor attractions closed for seasons:** No; **Weather:** Hot, humid summers; cold, snowy or icy winters; moderate spring and fall.

GENERAL INFORMATION: Visitors may also want to see the Taft Museum at 316 Pike Street in Cincinnati.

TRAVEL ACCESS: Bus: Queen City Metro; **Rail:** Amtrak to Cincinnati; **Air:** American, Delta, TWA, US Air, Conair, Piedmont, Republic.

Oklahoma

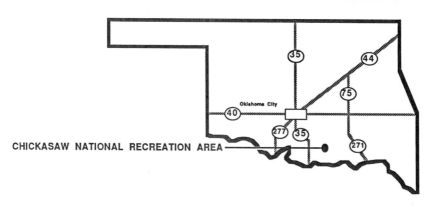

CHICKASAW NATIONAL RECREATION AREA

Chickasaw National Recreation Area
Sulphur, Oklahoma

MAILING ADDRESS: Superintendent, Chickasaw National Recreation Area, P.O. Box 201, Sulphur, OK 73086 **Telephone:** 405-622-3161

DIRECTIONS: Chickasaw lies near Sulphur, OK on Routes US 177 and OK 7, accessible from Oklahoma City and Dallas-Fort Worth via Int. 35.

Springs, streams, and lakes in the forested hills of south-central Oklahoma provide the setting for a wide range of outdoor recreation. The Travertine Nature Center provides opportunities for nature studies, and mineral water is available from springs and artesian wells. Established June 26, 1906, Platt National Park; 1976, Chickasaw National Recreation Area.

VISITOR ACTIVITIES: Interpretive exhibits, camping, picnicking, swimming, water skiing, fishing, boating, biking, walking, guided nature walks, hiking, hunting, campfire programs, and nature film; **Permits:** For camping; **Fees:** $6 nightly camping fee, Group camping $1 per person per night, minimum charge is $10 per night per site; **Visitor facilities:** Campgrounds, picnic areas, beach, boat launches, trailer dump station, Nature Center; **HANDI-CAPPED ACCESSIBILITY:** Travertine Nature Center, fishing docks, and most restrooms; **Any limitations on vehicle usage:** Bicycles are not allowed on trails east of the Nature Center or on Bromide Hill trail; **Hiking trails:** Yes; **Backcountry:** No; **Camping:** Yes, reservations are not accepted for individual campsites; all are on a first-come first-served basis. Reservations are accepted for group camping on a year-round basis by calling 405-622-6121 or writing the Superintendent at the above address; **Other overnight accommodations on site:** No; **Meals served in the park:** No; **Food and supplies obtainable in the park:** No; **Food and supplies obtainable nearby:** Yes, in Sulphur; **Overnight accommodations:** Sulphur; **First Aid available in park:** Yes; **Nearest Hospital:** Sulphur, 2 miles (3.2 km) west of the main entrance; **Days/Hours:** Park never closes; **Holiday Closings:** Travertine Nature Center closes on all holidays except Memorial Day, July 4, and Labor Day; **Weather:** Summers are hot and humid, with severe thunderstorms common in May and June. Tornadoes and thunderstorms are a threat in April through June. Temperatures above 100°F occur and humidity frequently exceeds 50%. Winters are generally mild and rarely subject to prolonged freezing temperatures.

GENERAL INFORMATION: Be cautious of poisonous snakes and poison ivy.

TRAVEL ACCESS: Bus: Trailways provides daily service to Davis, OK, 10 miles (16 km) from Park; **Rail:** No; **Air:** Nearest regular service is Oklahoma City, 92 miles (147.2 km) from Parks.

NEARBY FACILITIES & POINTS OF INTEREST: Hotel/Motel: Chickasaw Motel, Sulphur, outside north entrance to Park, Super 8 Motel, west edge of Sulphur; **Campgrounds:** Lake Murray State Park, 30 miles (48 km) south and Turner Falls, 15 miles (24 km) west.

Oregon

FORT CLATSOP NATIONAL MEMORIAL

McLOUGHLIN HOUSE NATIONAL HISTORIC SITE
OREGON NATIONAL HISTORIC TRAIL
JOHN DAY FOSSIL BEDS NATIONAL MONUMENT

CRATER LAKE NATIONAL PARK

OREGON CAVES NATIONAL MONUMENT

Crater Lake National Park
Crater Lake, Oregon   **SEE CLIMATABLE NO. 28**

MAILING ADDRESS: Superintendent, Crater Lake National Park, P.O. Box 7, Crater Lake, OR **Telephone:** 503-594-2211

DIRECTIONS: The south and west entrances on OR 62 are open all year. The north entrance off Hwy 138 and Rim Drive are open from mid-June to early Oct., weather permitting.
The Park's deep blue lake, formed by accumulated water from rain and snow, reaches 1,932 feet in depth. It lies in the heart of Mount Mazama, an ancient volcanic peak that collapsed centuries ago. Park established by act of Congress on May 22, 1902.

VISITOR ACTIVITIES: Summer (late-June through early-Sept.) Ranger programs at Mazama Campground, daily Ranger talks, interpretive walks, concession boat tours around Crater Lake, wildlife-watching, auto tours, fishing, hiking, picnicking, and camping. Movie shown throughout the day at Steel Center, snowmobile access to the Rim to the north side of the Park, cross-country skiing, snowshoeing, and other types of winter recreational activities; **Permits:** Backcountry permits obtained in summer at Steel Center, Rim Village Visitor Center or from a Park Ranger; in winter, at Steel Center or a Park Ranger; **Fees:** $5 entrance fee, $10 campground fee. Fees are collected from June through Sept., or later if weather permits. Golden Eagle and Golden Age Passports accepted and available; **Visitor facilities:** Picnic areas, restrooms, post office, are available throughout the summer. Campgrounds, lodging, food services, curio shop, groceries, gasoline service—all from mid-May through mid-October.

Hot meals and souvenirs at the cafeteria in Rim Village during winter. There are no overnight accommodations at Crater Lake during the winter months. Snowmobile and ungroomed ski trails are available; **Any limitations on vehicle usage:** All vehicles are restricted to designated roadways; chains or snow tires may be required in winter; **Hiking trails:** Yes; numerous scenic trails are described in the Park newspaper; **Backcountry:** Backcountry use permits are required for overnight stays in the backcountry. Information can be obtained by writing to the Park Superintendent or stopping at any Visitor Information Center; **Camping:** Yes, campsites are open from mid-June through mid-October, weather permitting. No reservations accepted for campsites; **Other overnight accommodations on site:** Yes, reservations for Mazama Cabins, open during the summer, can be made by contacting Crater Lake Lodge, Inc., Crater Lake, OR 97604, phone 503-594-2511; **Meals served in the park:** Yes, at Rim Village cafeteria; **Food and supplies obtainable in the park:** Yes, some groceries available at Mazama Village; **Food and supplies obtainable nearby:** Yes, at Fort Klamath, Union Creek; **Overnight accommodations:** Medford, 80 miles (128 km) from the west entrance on OR 62; Klamath Falls, 54 miles (86.4 km) from the south entrance on OR 62 and US 97. Union Creek and Fort Klamath on OR 62; **First Aid available in park:** Yes, as well as ambulance service in Chiloquin, OR, OR 62; **Nearest Hospital:** Medford, OR 62, 80 miles (128 km); or Klamath Falls, OR 62 and 97, 54 miles (86.4 km); **Days/Hours:** 24 hours a day everyday in summer. In winter, the south and west road on OR 62 to Park Headquarters is open 24 hours. The road from Park Headquarters to Rim Village is open from 8 a.m. to sunset; **Holiday Closings:** Park is open every day, but visitor facilities are closed on Dec. 25. The north entrance road and Rim Drive are closed from approximately mid-Oct. to late June, depending on snow conditions. The Park averages 45 feet of snowfall annually. In winter, overnight accommodations are available near the Park. Carry towrope, shovel, and tire chains, which may be necessary at any time.

GENERAL INFORMATION: *For Your Safety*—Stay on trails, especially along the caldera rim. Footing can be treacherous on this volcanic rock and soil. Descent to the lake is permitted only on the Cleetwood Trail.

Keep your distance from wildlife. Remember these animals are wild and can be dangerous. Do *not* feed any wildlife.

Fort Clatsop National Memorial
Astoria, Oregon

MAILING ADDRESS: Superintendent, Fort Clatsop National Memorial, Route 3, Box 604-FC, Astoria. OR 97103 **Telephone:** 503-861-2471

DIRECTIONS: The historic site is 6 miles (9.6 km) southwest of Astoria on US 101.
This is the site of the 1805-1806 winter encampment of the Lewis and Clark Expedition. Authorized for addition to the National Park System on May 29, 1958.

VISITOR ACTIVITIES: Interpretive exhibits, film and slide program, living history demonstrations in summer, walking, picnicking; **Permits:** No; **Fees:** Apr.-Sept. $1 ages 17-61, families $3 maximum, all others free; **Visitor facilities:** Parking, restrooms, bookstore at Visitor Center, picnic area; **HANDICAPPED ACCESSIBILITY:** Parking, restrooms, Visitor Center; **Any limitations on vehicle usage:** No; **Hiking trails:** Yes, walking trails around the fort; **Backcountry:** No; **Camping:** No; **Other overnight accommodations on site:** No, camping facilities are at Fort Stevens State Park, 5 miles (8 km) away. Reserve space by writing to Fort Stevens State Park, Hammond, OR 97121; **Meals served in the park:** No; **Food and supplies obtainable nearby:** Yes, at Astoria, Warrenton, and Seaside; **Overnight accom-**

modations: Astoria, US 101, 6 miles (9.6 km); Seaside, US 101, 13 miles (20.8 km); **First Aid available in park:** Yes; **Nearest Hospital:** Astoria, US 101, 6 miles (9.6 km); **Days/ Hours:** Open daily from 8 a.m. to 5 p.m., until 6 p.m. in summer; **Holiday Closings:** Dec. 25; **Visitor attractions closed for seasons:** Living history program mid-June to Labor Day; **Weather:** There is frequent rainfall.

GENERAL INFORMATION: Caution is necessary when at the canoe landing as the banks of the river and slough can be slippery. Other nearby Lewis and Clark sites are the Salt Works in Seaside, OR; the trail over Tillamook Head to Cannon Beach, OR; Campsite, McGowan, WA; and Lewis and Clark Interpretive Center at Ft. Canby State Park in Ilwaco, WA.

John Day Fossil Beds National Monument
John Day, Oregon

MAILING ADDRESS: Superintendent, John Day Fossil Beds National Monument, 420 West Main Street, John Day, OR 97845 **Telephone:** 503-575-0721

DIRECTIONS: The Monument Headquarters is in John Day. The Monument comprises three separate units: Sheep Rock Unit, 6 miles (9.6 km) west of Dayville; Painted Hills Unit, 10 miles (16 km) northwest of Mitchell; Clarno Unit, 20 miles (32 km) west of Fossil.

Plant and animal fossils show four epochs, from Eocene to the end of Pliocene, at this site in north central Oregon. Authorized for addition to the National Park System on Oct. 26, 1974.

VISITOR ACTIVITIES: Exhibits, interpretive talks, picnicking, wildlife- and wildflower-watching, hiking, fishing; **Permits:** No; **Fees:** No; **Visitor facilities:** Visitor Center, restrooms, picnic areas, hiking trails, drinking water; **HANDICAPPED ACCESSIBILITY:** Visitor Center, restrooms; **Any limitations on vehicle usage:** Off-road vehicles are prohibited; **Hiking trails:** Yes, 4 (2 self-guiding) at Painted Hills Unit; 4 (2 with exhibits) at Blue Basin in Sheep Rock Unit; 2 (1 self-guiding) at Clarno Unit; **Backcountry:** No; **Camping:** No; **Other overnight accommodations on site:** No, Federal and State-operated and private campgrounds are in the area. Camping information is posted in each unit; **Meals served in the park:** No; **Food and supplies obtainable in the park:** No; **Food and supplies obtainable nearby:** Yes, at John Day, Fossil, Dayville, Mt. Vernon and Mitchell; **Overnight accommodations:** John Day, Hwy 26, US 395 intersection; Mount Vernon, also 26-395; Fossil, Hwy 218-19; Mitchell, Hwy 26-207; **First Aid available in park:** Yes, or at clinic in Fossil; **Nearest Hospital:** John Day, Madras, and Prineville; **Days/Hours:** You can visit the formations year-round. Headquarters in John Day are open weekdays all year; **Visitor attractions closed for seasons:** Visitor Center at Sheep Rock Unit is open from 9 a.m. to 6 p.m. from Apr. 1 through Oct. 30 and most weekdays Nov. through Mar. **Weather:** Spring, wet and cool; summer, dry and hot; fall, warm and sunny.

GENERAL INFORMATION: *For Your Safety and the protection of the fragile fossil resource*—Do not climb on the geologic formations. Be on the lookout for rattlesnakes. Beware of deer unexpectedly crossing roads at night.

TRAVEL ACCESS: Bus: Trailways provides daily service into Burns, OR; **Rail:** No; **Air:** Air Oregon, Republic provide daily service into Redmond, OR.

Lewis and Clark Trail
For details see listing in Illinois

McLoughlin House National Historic Site
Oregon City, Oregon

MAILING ADDRESS: Superintendent, McLoughlin House National Historic Site, 713 Center Street, Oregon City, OR 97045 **Telephone:** 503-656-5146

DIRECTIONS: The McLoughlin House is in McLoughlin Park between 7th and 8th Streets, less than 4 blocks east of Pacific Hwy (US 99). Bus service is available from Portland, 13 miles (20.8 km) away.
    The house is one of the few remaining pioneer dwellings in the area once known as the "Oregon Country." Dr. John McLoughlin, often called the "Father of Oregon," who was prominent in the development of the Pacific Northwest as Superintendent of Fort Vancouver, built the house and lived here from 1846 to 1857. This affiliated area of the National Park System is owned and operated by the McLoughlin Memorial Association and was established by act of Congress in 1941.

VISITOR ACTIVITIES: Guided house tours; **Permits:** No; **Fees:** Adults $2.50, Seniors $2, Students 6-17 $1, under 6 free if with parents, group rates for 12 or more; **Visitor facilities:** House tours; **Any limitations on vehicle usage:** No; **Meals served in the park:** No; **Food and supplies obtainable in the park:** No; **Food and supplies obtainable nearby:** Yes, at Oregon City; **Overnight accommodations:** Portland, I-5 and/or Pacific Hwy (99 E), 13 miles (20.8 km); Oregon City, McLoughlin Blvd., .6 mile (1 km); **First Aid available in park:** No; **Nearest Hospital:** Oregon City, Division Street, 2.5 miles (4 km); **Days/Hours:** The house is open every Sunday, 1 p.m. to 4 p.m., weekday hours (Tues. through Sat.) are 10 a.m. to 4 p.m. The Site is closed in January and holidays; **Weather:** Winters are fairly mild. Summers are hot 105°-107° (unusual). Rainy periods—all seasons but usually not extreme.

GENERAL INFORMATION: The Park is more like the grounds of a private home (½ city block) and has no facilities. Convenience store 1 block away, several small restaurants within a few blocks.

NEARBY FACILITIES & POINTS OF INTEREST: Hotel/Motel: Value-Inn, 1900 Clackwater Dr., 503-655-7141, 1 mile (1.6 km) roughly (99E); Lewis Motel, 18710 S. Hwy. 99E, 503-656-7052, 2 miles (3.2 km); Poolside Motel, 19224 McLoughlin Bus. (99E), 503-656-1955, 3 miles (4.8 km); **Parks, other points of interest:** Viewpoint falls of the Willamette River within walking distance, Promenade along Cliff above original town. Clackamas County History Museum 2 blocks away, open Tues. through Sat. 10 a.m.-4 p.m., "End of the Oregon Trail" Interpretive Center 3 blocks from McLoughlin House, open Tues.-Sat. 10 a.m.-4 p.m. Sun. 12 p.m.-4 p.m.; Salmon fishing seasonally in the Willamette River. Swimming in the Clackamas River where it runs into Willamette at Clackamette Park. Museum at Rose Farm, built in 1847, the oldest American home in Oregon City, where Oregon's first Territorial Governor was inaugurated on the balcony of the house in 1849. Ermatinger House, 6th and John Adams, oldest home in Oregon City (1845). Frances Ermatinger was the manager of the HBC properties in Oregon City. Open Wed. through Sun. 12 a.m. - 4 p.m. Tours. Adm.; New Museum: Trails' End Heritage Center, 211 Tumwater Drive, Oregon City, 655-5574. Open: Monday through Friday, 10 a.m.-5 p.m. Saturday and Sunday 1 p.m.-5 p.m. The museum is run by the Clackamas County Historical Society and features the story of the early settlement of Oregon.

Oregon Caves National Monument
Cave Junction, Oregon

MAILING ADDRESS: Superintendent, Oregon Caves National Monument, 19000 Caves Highway, Cave Junction, OR 97523 **Telephone:** 503-592-2100

DIRECTIONS: The Monument is 20 miles (32 km) southeast of Cave Junction on OR 46 and can be reached by traveling either 50 miles (80 km) south of Grants Pass or 76 miles (121.6 km) north from Crescent City on US 199. The last 8 miles (12.8 km) of OR 46 are quite narrow and winding. Information is available on OR 46 just as you exit OR 199.

Ground water dissolving marble bedrock formed these cave passages and intricate flowstone formations. Created by Presidential Proclamation on July 12, 1909.

VISITOR ACTIVITIES: Cave tours, hiking, wildlife- and bird-watching, evening programs in summer; **Permits:** No; **Fees:** All visitors wishing to see the cave must do so on a guided tour provided by the Oregon Caves Company, a private concessioner, for a fee regulated by the U.S. Department of the Interior. Current fees are adults $6.75, children under 12 $3.75. Daily tours are frequent and hours vary with season. Check for tour schedule at the time of your visit; **Visitor facilities:** Parking, lodge, hiking trails, restrooms; **Any limitations on vehicle usage:** Towing trailers is not recommended due to narrow roads, infrequent turn-arounds, and lack of parking space; **Hiking trails:** Yes, a maintained and marked system of trails provides access to the park for day hikers. Connecting trails lead into the adjacent Siskiyou National Forest. Snowshoes are usually required in winter and spring; check trail conditions with Park Rangers before setting out; **Backcountry:** No; **Camping:** No, but the U.S. Forest Service operates 2 campgrounds in the adjacent Siskiyou National Forest from approximately mid-June through the first week of Sept. Cave Creek campground is 4 miles (6.4 km) from the park on OR 46. No trailers are permitted. Grayback campground is 8 miles (12.8 km) down OR 46. Trailers are permitted in the campground. Although the campgrounds are rarely filled, campsites are assigned on a first-come, first-served basis. There are no showers and no utility connections. For further information, call 503-592-2166; **Other overnight accommodations on site:** Yes, the Oregon Caves Company operates a lodge from approximately mid-June to the first week in Sept. For reservations and information, write to Oregon Caves Co., Oregon Caves, OR 97523, phone 503-592-3400; The Chateau operates as a bed and breakfast during the month of September; **Meals served in the park:** Yes, at the Chateau, summer season only; **Food and supplies obtainable in the park:** No; **Food and supplies obtainable nearby:** Yes, at Cave Junction, 20 miles (32 km); **Overnight accommodations:** Motel on OR 46, about 12 miles (19.2 km) from the park. Several motels available on OR 199 in and around Cave Junction; **First Aid available in park:** Yes, there is also a doctor and clinic in Cave Junction, OR 46; **Nearest Hospital:** Grants Pass, 50 miles (80 km); **Holiday Closings:** Dec. 25; **Visitor attractions closed for seasons:** Campfire and interpretive programs during the summer season only, excluding cave tours.

GENERAL INFORMATION: Because parking is quite limited, you should arrive at the park during the morning hours if you visit the park in summer. Parking for trailers is extremely limited. If you are hiking, stay on the marked trails. *For Your Safety*—Wear proper clothing, including a jacket and walking shoes. The cave temperature varies from 38 to 45°F. Cave passageways may be slippery. The cave tour is not recommended for anyone with heart, breathing, or walking difficulty. Stay with your guide. There is an emergency exit one-third of the way through the cave for those who do not wish to continue the tour. Do not touch any of the cave walls or formations. Canes, crutches, tripods, and sticks are not permitted within the cave. Special regulations apply to children under the age of 6 entering the cave. A childcare service is available at the concession.

Oregon National Scenic Trail
For details see listing in Missouri

Pennsylvania

JOHNSTOWN FLOOD NATIONAL MEMORIAL

ALLEGHENY PORTAGE RAILROAD NATIONAL HISTORIC SITE

APPALACHIAN NATIONAL SCENIC TRAIL

DELAWARE WATER GAP NATIONAL RECREATION AREA

MIDDLE DELAWARE NATIONAL SCENIC RIVER

INDEPENDENCE NATIONAL HISTORICAL PARK

THADDEUS KOSCIUSZKO NATIONAL MEMORIAL

BENJAMIN FRANKLIN NATIONAL MEMORIAL

EDGAR ALLAN POE NATIONAL HISTORIC SITE

GLORIA DEI CHURCH NATIONAL HISTORIC SITE

FRIENDSHIP HILL NATIONAL HISTORIC SITE

FORT NECESSITY NATIONAL BATTLEFIELD

VALLEY FORGE NATIONAL HISTORICAL PARK

HOPEWELL VILLAGE NATIONAL HISTORIC SITE

GETTYSBURG NATIONAL MILITARY PARK

EISENHOWER NATIONAL HISTORIC SITE

STEAMTOWN NATIONAL HISTORIC SITE

Allegheny Portage Railroad National Historic Site
Cresson, Pennsylvania

MAILING ADDRESS: Superintendent, Allegheny Portage Railroad National Historic Site, P.O. Box 247, Cresson, PA 16630 **Telephone:** 814-886-8176

DIRECTIONS: The new park Visitor Center is located off the Gallitzin Exit of U.S. Highway 22 between Altoona and Cresson, PA. The Site also features the Lemon House, built in 1831-32 near the summit of Allegheny Mountain as a rest stop and tavern.
      The Site preserves structures and trace of the 36-mile inclined railroad built between 1831-34 to carry passengers and freight over the Allegheny Mountains between canal basins at Hollidaysburg and Johnstown. Established by act of Congress on August 31, 1964.

VISITOR ACTIVITIES: Interpretive talks and costumed demonstrations near Visitor Center and Lemon House, interpretive exhibits and trails, hiking, picnicking; **Permits:** No; **Fees:** No; **Visitor facilities:** Visitor Center with restrooms, walking trails through quiet spots with benches, picnic facilities including water, tables, restrooms, and grills; **HANDICAPPED ACCESSIBILITY:** Visitor Center, restrooms, and Lemon House. A boardwalk and paved trail allow access to the remains of the Allegheny Portage Railroad; **Any limitations on vehicle usage:** Vehicles are restricted to the parking lot of the Visitor Center, park roads, and parking lot of the picnic areas; **Hiking trails:** Yes; boardwalk, wood-chipped and dirt trails through site; **Backcountry:** No; **Camping:** No; **Other overnight accommodations on site:** No; **Meals served in the park:** No; **Food and supplies obtainable in the park:** No; **Food and supplies obtainable nearby:** Yes, in Gallitzin or Cresson; **Overnight accommoda-**

tions: Altoona, US 220, 12 miles (19.2 km); Ebensburg, US 22, 12 miles (19.2 km); **First Aid available in park:** Yes, or nearby in Cresson, US 22; **Nearest Hospital:** Altoona, US 220, 12 miles (19.2 km); **Days/Hours:** Open 8:30 a.m. to 5 p.m. Sept. to May. Extended summer hours June-Aug. 8:30 a.m. to 6 p.m.; **Holiday Closings:** Thanksgiving, Dec. 25, and Jan. 1; **Visitor attractions closed for seasons:** No tours or demonstrations in winter; **Weather:** Warm days and cool nights in summer; cold, windy and snowy in winter.

GENERAL INFORMATION: Visitors to the area can also see the nearby Johnstown Flood National Memorial (see listing in this book), located along US 219 and PA 869 near St. Michael, PA.

TRAVEL ACCESS: Bus: Greyhound Bus stops at Cresson, PA twice daily: once in the morning, once in afternoon; **Rail:** Amtrak daily service to Altoona, PA; **Air:** Allegheny Airlines daily service to Martinsburg, PA; **Other:** Rental car available in Altoona and at airport in Martinsburg; Park accessible by bicycle; however, it is atop Allegheny Mountain 2,290 feet.

NEARBY FACILITIES & POINTS OF INTEREST: Hotel/Motel: Lodging in nearby Altoona, 12 miles (19.2 km) east and Ebensburg, 12 miles (19.2 km) west; **Campgrounds:** Prince Gallitzin State Park, 25 miles (40 km), Blue Knob State Park, 25 miles (40 km), Laurelwood, 3 miles (4.8 km) west; Woodland Park, 14 miles (22.4 km) west; **Parks, other points of interest:** Horseshow Curve, 7 miles (11.2 km) northeast; Railroaders Museum, Altoona, 12 miles (19.2 km) east.

Benjamin Franklin National Memorial
Philadelphia, Pennsylvania

MAILING ADDRESS: Executive Director, Benjamin Franklin National Memorial, 20th Street and Benjamin Franklin Parkway, Philadelphia, PA 19103 **Telephone:** 215-448-1329

DIRECTIONS: The Memorial is in the Franklin Institute Science Museum at 20th Street and Benjamin Franklin Parkway in Philadelphia.
     James Earle Fraser's monumental statue of Franklin honors the inventor-statesman. This affiliated area of the National Park System, owned and administered by The Franklin Institute, was designated on Oct. 25, 1972.

VISITOR ACTIVITIES: Exhibits of Franklin artifacts; **Permits:** No; **Fees:** Admission to the Memorial is free. There is a separate admission fee for the adjacent Science Museum; **Visitor facilities:** Parking, restrooms, snack bar in Science Museum; **HANDICAPPED ACCESSIBILITY:** The Science Museum is wheelchair accessible. The Memorial is surrounded by stair entrances only but a ramp is available with prior notice. **Any limitations on vehicle usage:** No; **Hiking trails:** No; **Backcountry:** No; **Camping:** No; **Other overnight accommodations on site:** No; **Meals served in the park:** No, but available at snack bar in the Science Museum; **Food and supplies obtainable in the park:** No; **Food and supplies obtainable nearby:** Yes, in Philadelphia; **Overnight accommodations:** Within walking distance in Philadelphia; **First Aid available in park:** No, but through local hospitals and doctors in Philadelphia area; **Nearest Hospital:** Hannemann Hospital, 314 North Broad St., about 9 blocks from the Memorial; **Days/Hours:** 9:30 a.m. to 4:30 p.m. weekdays, 10 a.m. to 5 p.m. weekends; 10 a.m. to 5 p.m. daily in the summer; **Holiday Closings:** Dec. 24 and 25, Jan. 1, July 4, Thanksgiving.

Delaware Water Gap National Recreation Area
Bushkill, Pennsylvania also in New Jersey

MAILING ADDRESS: Superintendent, Delaware Water Gap National Recreation Area, Bushkill, PA 18324 **Telephone:** 717-588-2435, 717-588-2455 (TDD)

DIRECTIONS: The Area extends from the Delaware Water Gap for 35 miles (56 km) to Milford, PA. Int. 80 crosses the Gap. On the Pennsylvania side follow US 209. The best place to begin your visit is at the Kittatinny Point Visitor Center, open year-round, located on Int. 80 in NJ. Dingmans Falls Visitor Center, open April through Oct., is off U.S. 209, in PA.

This scenic area preserves relatively unspoiled land on both the New Jersey and Pennsylvania sides of the Delaware River. Authorized for addition to the National Park System on Sept. 1, 1965.

VISITOR ACTIVITIES: Fishing, swimming, canoeing, hiking, hunting, auto tours, cross-country skiing, ice fishing, snowmobiling, picnicking, craft demonstrations, conducted walks, interpretive exhibits, wildlife-watching, rock climbing; **Permits:** State licenses are required for hunting and fishing. Obtain them at nearby sporting goods stores. License fees vary in length of validity and cost; **Fees:** No; **Visitor facilities:** Parking and restrooms at Visitor Center, picnic areas, interpretive and hiking trails, launching ramps, environmental study areas, canoe rentals outside the Park, lifeguarded swimming areas; **HANDICAPPED ACCESSIBILITY:** Both Visitor Centers have accessible parking, building and restrooms. Printed scripts are available for the slide shows. There are accessible picnic sites at Kittatinny and Depew Picnic Areas in NJ and at Tom's Creek and Childs Park picnic areas in PA. Resort Point and Point of Gap Overlooks have accessible parking and ramps. For more information, request a copy of the Park brochure and the Accessibility Guide from the Park Superintendent. **Any limitations on vehicle usage:** No; **Hiking trails:** Yes, 26¼ miles (42 km) of the Appalachian Trail run through the area. Shorter nature trails are available. Check at the Visitor Center or write the Superintendent for further information; **Backcountry:** Yes, information is available from the Visitor Center or the Superintendent; **Camping:** Canoe camping in designated areas, 2 group campgrounds and 1 concession-operated family campground; **Other overnight accommodations on site:** No; **Meals served in the park:** No; **Food and supplies obtainable in the park:** No; **Food and supplies obtainable nearby:** Yes, Bushkill, Stroudsburg, Milford, Portland, and Delaware Water Gap, PA; Newton, Blairstown, and Branchville, NJ, Port Jervis, NY; **Overnight accommodations:** Bushkill, Stroudsburg, Milford, Portland, and Delaware Water Gap, PA; Newton, Blairstown, and Branchville, NJ, Port Jervis, NY; **First Aid available in park:** Yes; **Nearest Hospital:** East Stroudsburg, PA, Int. 80; Newton, NJ, NJ 206; Port Jervis, NY, US 209; **Days/Hours:** The Park is always open. Kittatinny Point Visitor Center is open daily from 9 a.m. to 5 p.m. Apr. thru Oct., and 9 a.m. to 4:30 p.m. Sat.-Sun., Nov.-Mar.; **Holiday Closings:** Dec. 25 and Jan. 1; **Visitor attractions closed for seasons:** Some facilities are closed during winter, but the Park remains open for x-c skiing, ice fishing, and snowmobiling in designated areas. A park newspaper, available on request, is published 3 times a year and lists current activities.

GENERAL INFORMATION: Swim only at designated beaches. Climbers must register before climb and check out after completing with the Kittatinny Point Visitor Center.

TRAVEL ACCESS: **Bus:** Martz Trailways provides daily service to Stroudsburg; Greyhound services the Stroudsburg Terminal.

Edgar Allan Poe National Historic Site
Philadelphia, Pennsylvania

MAILING ADDRESS: Superintendent, Edgar Allan Poe National Historic Site, c/o Independence National Historical Park, 313 Walnut Street, Philadelphia, PA 19106 **Telephone:** 215-597-8780 (voice/TDD)

DIRECTIONS: The Site is located at 7th and Spring Garden Streets, Philadelphia, PA 19123.

Edgar Allan Poe, poet, writer, editor, and critic lived with his wife and mother-in-law in this small brick house in the 1840s. Authorized for addition to the National Park System on Nov. 10, 1978.

VISITOR ACTIVITIES: Interpretive exhibits, school sessions, special events, children's programs, house tours and audiovisual programs; **Permits:** No; **Fees:** No; **Visitor facilities:** Restrooms; **HANDICAPPED ACCESSIBILITY:** Wheelchair access; **Any limitations on vehicle usage:** Avoid driving in downtown Philadelphia. Try to use public transportation. On-street parking usually available. To conserve energy try to use public transportation (SEPTA buses #47 AND #43 stop nearby); **Meals served in the park:** No; **Food and supplies obtainable in the park:** No; **Food and supplies obtainable nearby:** Yes, in Philadelphia; **Overnight accommodations:** Philadelphia; **First Aid available in park:** Yes; **Nearest Hospital:** Philadelphia, within 4 blocks; **Days/Hours:** open daily from 9 a.m. to 5 p.m.; **Holiday Closings:** Thanksgiving Day, Dec. 25 and Jan. 1; **Visitor attractions closed for seasons:** No; **Weather:** Summers are hot and humid; some snow and sleet in winter.

TRAVEL ACCESS: Bus: Greyhound and Trailways provide regular service within 8 blocks of Park; **Rail:** Amtrak serves Philadelphia; **Air:** Major Airlines service Philadelphia International Airport about 5 miles (8 km) from Park.

Eisenhower National Historic Site
Gettysburg, Pennsylvania

MAILING ADDRESS: Superintendent, Eisenhower National Historic Site, Gettysburg, PA 17325 **Telephone:** 717-334-1124

DIRECTIONS: This was the retirement home and farm of President and Mrs. Dwight D. Eisenhower. Designated Nov. 27, 1967. Opened to the public June, 1980. You should begin your tour at the Eisenhower Tour Information Center, in the lower end of the Gettysburg National Military Park Visitor Center, located on PA 134 (Taneytown Road) near its intersection with Business US 15 (Emmitsburg Road).

VISITOR ACTIVITIES: Self-guided tours of house and grounds, Ranger-conducted programs; **Permits:** No; **Fees:** Yes, for shuttle bus transportation to the farm and entrance fee, $2.25 for adults and $1.25 for children 13 to 16 and $.70 for children 6 to 12. Fees subject to change; **Visitor facilities:** Visitors Center, limited restroom facilities; **HANDICAPPED ACCESSIBILITY:** For those unable to board the shuttle bus, arrangements can be made to drive to the site. Ask at the Eisenhower Tour Center. The first floor of the house is accessible with staff assistance. Restrooms are not accessible. Free wheelchair loans are available. The orientation video is captioned and a large print guide is available for the house tour; **Any limitations on vehicle usage:** All visits to the farm are via shuttle bus from the Tour Information Center. No private vehicle access except to handicapped parking area; **Hiking trails:** No;

Backcountry: No; **Camping:** No; **Other overnight accommodations on site:** No; **Meals served in the park:** No, in the town of Gettysburg; **Food and supplies obtainable in the park:** No; **Food and supplies obtainable nearby:** Yes, in Gettysburg, 1 mile (1.6 km); **Overnight accommodations:** Numerous motels are adjacent to the Park; **First Aid available in park:** Yes; **Nearest Hospital:** Gettysburg, 1/2 mile (.8 km) from Tour Information Center, 2 miles (3.2 km) from farm; **Days/Hours:** Open daily Apr.-Oct., Wed.-Sun. Nov.-March.; First and last shuttle bus runs 9 a.m. and 4 p.m.; **Visitor attractions closed for seasons:** Park may be closed in Jan.; **Holiday Closings:** Thanksgiving, Dec. 25, and January (the entire month); **Weather:** Summers are hot, 60°-90°F, winters are cold, 10°-50°F.

Fort Necessity National Battlefield
Farmington, Pennsylvania

MAILING ADDRESS: Superintendent, Fort Necessity National Battlefield, The National Pike, RD 2-Box 528, Farmington, PA 15437 **Telephone:** 412-329-5512

DIRECTIONS: The Battlefield is 11 miles (17.6 km) east of Uniontown on US 40.
   Colonial troops commanded by Lt. Col. George Washington, then 22 years old, were defeated here in the opening battle of the French and Indian War on July 3, 1754. The Park also includes Jumonville Glen, site of the first skirmish of the French and Indian War, Braddock's grave, and Mount Washington Tavern, an early 19th-century stage coach inn. Established by act of Congress on Mar. 4, 1931.

VISITOR ACTIVITIES: Interpretive exhibits and slide presentation, hiking, cross-country skiing, picnicking; **Permits:** No; **Fees:** $1 per person over 16 and under 62, $3 maximum per family; **Visitor facilities:** Parking, restrooms, picnic area; **HANDICAPPED ACCESSI-BILITY:** Visitor facilities all wheelchair accessible; **Any limitations on vehicle usage:** Established roadway and parking lots only; **Hiking trails:** Yes, trails lead through the forest and meadow around the Battlefield; **Backcountry:** No; **Camping:** Primitive group campground available with prior reservation; short service project required; **Other overnight accommodations on site:** No, private and public campgrounds are located nearby; **Meals served in the park:** No; **Food and supplies obtainable in the park:** No; **Food and supplies obtainable nearby:** Yes, at Uniontown; **Overnight accommodations:** Along U.S. Route 40 within 10 miles (16 km) of park, in each direction; **First Aid available in park:** Yes; **Nearest Hospital:** Uniontown, PA, US 40, 11 miles (17.6 km) west of the Park; **Days/Hours:** Fort area and Braddock's Grave open daylight hours year-round; Visitor Center core hours daily 10:30 a.m. to 5:00 p.m. year-round (extended hours in summer, depending on staffing); Tavern core hours daily 10:30 a.m. to 5:00 p.m. from mid-March through late Oct., weekends only other times; **Holiday Closings:** Thanksgiving, Dec. 25, and Jan. 1; **Visitor attractions closed for seasons:** Picnic area and Jumorville Glen Unit closed from Nov. 1-Apr. 15.

Friendship Hill National Historic Site
Point Marion, Pennsylvania

MAILING ADDRESS: c/o Fort Necessity National Battlefield, The National Pike, RD2, Box 528, Farmington, PA 15437 **Telephone:** 412-329-5512 Park Office 412-725-9190

DIRECTIONS: 3 miles (4.8 km) north of Point Marion along state route 166.
   This was the country estate of Albert Gallatin (1761-1849), a Swiss immigrant who served as U.S. Secretary of Treasury under Presidents Jefferson and Madison. The house is

situated on a bluff above the Monongahela River.

The house is curently undergoing restoration. Completion and grand opening is tentatively scheduled for mid-May 1992.

VISITOR ACTIVITIES: Ranger-led tours of house and grounds (summer season only), self-guided tours of the restored house and grounds, exhibit area featuring a holographic image of Gallatin, audio-visual program, ENP&MA sales outlet, hiking & cross-country ski trails, picnic area. FestiFall held annually on last Sunday of September. **Permits:** No; **Fees:** $1.00 per person (ages 17 through 61); $3.00 per family; **Visitor facilities:** Visitor center, exhibit area, and ENP&MA sales outlet in the Gallatin house; comfort station and picnic area near parking lot; **HANDICAPPED ACCESSIBILITY:** Gallatin house, comfort station, and picnic area are wheelchair accessible; **Any limitations on vehicle usage:** Established roadway and parking lots only; **Hiking trails:** 5 miles (8 km) of trails pass through woods and fields and along the Monongahela; Trail maps available; **Backcountry:** No; **Camping:** No; **Meals served in the park:** No; **Food and supplies obtainable in the park:** No; **Food and supplies obtainable nearby:** Point Marion 3 miles (4.8 km) south, Masontown 6 miles (9.6 km) northwest; **First Aid available in park:** Yes; **Nearest Hospital:** Morgantown, WV, 12 miles (19.2 km) south of park; **Days/Hours:** Open daily 9:00 a.m. to 5:00 p.m.; **Holiday Closings:** Christmas Day, New Years Day; **Visitor attractions closed for seasons:** Ranger led tours of the house and grounds available in season only. Traveler's Information station broadcasts current information on 1610 KHZ, AM.

Gettysburg National Military Park
Gettysburg, Pennsylvania

MAILING ADDRESS: Superintendent, P.O. Box 1080, Gettysburg National Military Park, Gettysburg, PA 17325 **Telephone:** 717-334-1124

DIRECTIONS: You should start your tour of Gettysburg at the Visitor Center, which is located on PA 134 (Taneytown Road) near its intersection with US 15 (Emmitsburg Road).

The decisive Civil War battle fought here July 1-3, 1863, repulsed the second Confederate invasion of the North. Gettysburg National Cemetery adjoins the Park. President Lincoln delivered his Gettysburg Address here in dedicating the cemetery on Nov. 19, 1863. The Park was established by act of Congress Feb. 11, 1895.

VISITOR ACTIVITIES: Auto tours, Ranger-conducted walks and talks, living history and campfire programs, hiking, biking, jogging, cross-country skiing, picnicking, Gettysburg Address is on loan from the Library of Congress and displayed during the summer months; **Permits:** No; **Fees:** Yes, for special programs, Electric map is $2 adults, children under 16 free. Senior Citizens (over 62) $1.50. Cyclorama is $2 for those 16 and older. Battlefield guide, $20 for a 2-hour tour per car; recreational vehicles, higher; **Visitor facilities:** Visitor Centers, restrooms, licensed battlefield guides; **HANDICAPPED ACCESSIBILITY:** The major program areas of the Visitor Center and Cyclorama are accessible along with the restroom facilities. Handicapped parking areas are marked at each building. Free wheelchair loans are available. Various brochures and audio tapes with players provide information for those with hearing or sight impairments; **Any limitations on vehicle usage:** Park only in designated areas or on the avenues but not on the grass; **Hiking trails:** Yes, trails vary in length and difficulty; **Backcountry:** No, an information brochure on the trails is available by mail or at the Visitor Center; **Camping:** Yes, but only for organized youth groups. Group sites available from mid-Apr. to mid-Oct. Fee varies with group size. Call 717-334-0909. Groups may wish to make advance reservations for bus tours with a licensed battlefield guide included

($50). Inquiry for both services should be made to the Park at the above address; **Other overnight accommodations on site:** No; **Meals served in the park:** No, in the town of Gettysburg; **Food and supplies obtainable in the park:** No; **Food and supplies obtainable nearby:** Yes, in Gettysburg, 1 mile (1.6 km); **Overnight accommodations:** Numerous motels are adjacent to the Park; **First Aid available in park:** Yes; **Nearest Hospital:** Gettysburg, ½ mile (.8 km) from the Visitor Center; **Days/Hours:** Cyclorama Center open 9:00 a.m. to 5 p.m.; Visitor Center 8:00 a.m. to 6 p.m. from mid-June to Labor Day; 8 a.m. to 5 p.m. the rest of the year; **Holiday Closings:** Visitor Center and Cyclorama closed Thanksgiving, Dec. 25, and Jan. 1; **Weather:** Summers are hot, 60°-90°F; winters are cold, 10°-50°F.

GENERAL INFORMATION: *For Your Safety*—Do not climb on cannons and monuments. Running and climbing youngsters frequently fall and injure themselves, so parents are urged to closely supervise their children. Please use extreme caution driving the Park roads, especially when they intersect with heavily traveled highways. Bicycle riders are here in ever-increasing numbers; be cautious on blind curves and on one-way roads. Bikers should keep to the right with the flow of auto traffic.

Gloria Dei (Old Swedes') Church National Historic Site
Philadelphia, Pennsylvania

MAILING ADDRESS: Superintendent, Independence National Historical Park, 313 Walnut Street, Philadelphia, PA 19106 **Telephone:** 215-597-8974 (Voice/TDD)

DIRECTIONS: Located on the Delaware River, on Delaware Avenue between Christian Street and Washington Avenue; the site is north of the Walt Whitman Bridge and south of the Ben Franklin Bridge and is on the east side of I-95 (take exit marked Delaware Avenue/Washington Avenue).

This fine example of early Swedish religious architecture was erected about 1700 by a Swedish Lutheran congregation which was founded in 1677 and in 1845 became part of the Episcopal Church. This affiliated area of the National Park System was designated on Nov. 17, 1942. Church site owned and administered by Corporation of Gloria Dei (Old Swedes') Church.

VISITOR ACTIVITIES: The church and grounds are open to the public; arrangements should be made in advance if a guided tour for a group is desired; **Permits:** No; **Fees:** No; **Visitor facilities:** Restrooms, church and grounds; **Any limitations on vehicle usage:** Vehicles not permitted on the church grounds; **Hiking trails:** No; **Backcountry:** No; **Camping:** No; **Other overnight accommodations on site:** No; **Meals served in the park:** No; **Food and supplies obtainable in the park:** No; **Food and supplies obtainable nearby:** Yes, in Philadelphia; **Overnight accommodations:** Philadelphia, 2 miles (3.2 km); **First Aid available in park:** No; **Nearest Hospital:** Philadelphia, 1½ miles (2.4 km); **Days/Hours:** Open daily from 9 a.m. to 5 p.m.; **Holiday Closings:** No; **Visitor attractions closed for seasons:** No.

Hopewell Furnace National Historic Site
Elverson, Pennsylvania

MAILING ADDRESS: Superintendent, Hopewell Furnace National Historic Site, R.D. 1, Box 345, Elverson, PA 19520 **Telephone:** 215-582-8773

DIRECTIONS: The Site is 5 miles (8 km) south of Birdsboro on PA 345. It is 10 miles (16 km) from the Morgantown interchange on the PA Turnpike, via PA 23 East, and 345 North.

This is the finest example of a rural American 19th-century ironmaking community restored to the 1820-1840 period. The buildings include the blast furnace and its auxiliary structures. Designated Aug. 3, 1938.

VISITOR ACTIVITIES: Interpretive programs and exhibits at Visitor Center, living history programs in summer, hiking, self-guiding walking tours; **Permits:** No; **Fees:** Yes, $2 per person, maximum of $5 per family, 16 and under, 62 and over are free; **Visitor facilities:** Parking and restrooms at Visitor Center; **HANDICAPPED ACCESSIBILITY:** The park's Visitor Center, the general historic area, and a public restroom are wheelchair accessible with assistance. There are, however, a few historic structures in the park that are not wheelchair accessible. The audiovisual programs at the Visitor Center are captioned for the hearing impaired. Large-print park guides and a tape-recorded tour are also available; **Any limitations on vehicle usage:** No; **Hiking trails:** Yes, a nature trail, and a number of other trails through the park; **Backcountry:** No; **Camping:** No; **Other overnight accommodations on site:** No, swimming, picnicking, and unreserved camping facilities are available in the adjacent French Creek State Park (215) 582-1514; **Meals served in the park:** No; **Food and supplies obtainable in the park:** No; **Food and supplies obtainable nearby:** Yes, 5 miles (8 km) away in Birdsboro and Elverson; **Overnight accommodations:** Morgantown, PA Turnpike, 10 miles (16 km); Pottstown, Rte 100, then 724 or 422, 13 miles (20.8 km); Reading, Rte 422, 15 miles (24 km); **First Aid available in park:** Yes, or at Birdsboro, PA 345 North; **Nearest Hospital:** Reading, 15 miles (24 km); **Days/Hours:** Open daily from 9 a.m. to 5 p.m.; **Holiday Closings:** Thanksgiving Day, Dec. 25 and Jan. 1; **Visitor attractions closed for seasons:** No; **Weather:** Hot, humid summers and cold, icy winters, moderate spring and fall.

GENERAL INFORMATION: *For Your Safety*—Stay on established tour routes and do not climb on the unstable anthracite furnace ruins, fences, and other historic structures. The sharp slag can cause severe, jagged cuts. Do not enter fenced areas or feed or handle livestock. Those allergic to bee and wasp stings should be especially cautious.

Independence National Historical Park
Philadelphia, Pennsylvania

MAILING ADDRESS: Superintendent, Independence National Historical Park, 313 Walnut Street, Philadelphia, PA 19106 **Telephone:** Recorded information—215-627-1776 Visitor Center—215-597-8974 (voice/TDD)

DIRECTIONS: The best place to begin your visit is at the Visitor Center, located at 3rd and Chestnut Streets. The Park includes structures and properties in old Philadelphia associated with the American Revolution and the founding and growth of the United States, including: Independence Hall, Congress Hall, the Second Bank of the United States, Franklin Court, The Liberty Bell Pavilion, and many other sites. Authorized for addition to the National Park System on June 28, 1948.

The Deshler-Morris House, a unit of Independence National Historical Park, is located at 5442 Germantown Avenue, Philadelphia, PA. It is about 7 miles (11.2 km) from Independence National Historical Park. The site can be reached either by automobile (metered parking) or by public transportation.

VISITOR ACTIVITIES: Talks and tours in historic buildings, self-guiding outdoor walking tours (summer programs); **Permits:** Yes; **Fees:** No; **Visitor facilities:** Visitor Center, audiovisual exhibits, films, interpretive displays, post office, various tours; **HANDICAPPED ACCESSIBILITY:** Information concerning the Park's accessibility for those with physical disabilities is available at the Visitor Center; **Any limitations on vehicle usage:** Park in nearby parking garages or use public transportation; **Hiking trails:** No; **Meals served in the park:** Yes, at City Tavern, 2nd and Walnut (concessioner); **Food and supplies obtainable in the park:** No; **Food and supplies obtainable nearby:** Yes, in Philadelphia; **Overnight accommodations:** Philadelphia; **First Aid available in the park:** Yes; **Nearest Hospital:** within 4 blocks; **Days/Hours:** Open 7 days a week, 9 a.m. to 5 p.m., with extended hours in summer. Call the Park for detailed information on hours of various sites; **Holiday Closings:** All buildings except Independence Hall and the Liberty Bell Pavilion are closed on Dec. 25 and Jan. 1; **Visitor attractions closed for seasons:** Some buildings may be closed Dec.- Mar.; **Weather:** Summers are hot and humid; some snow and sleet in winter.

GENERAL INFORMATION: The 18th-century brick sidewalks are sometimes rough and uneven. Walk with caution. Try to avoid the midday crowds in summer by arriving between 9 and 10 a.m. or after 2 p.m. Thursday and Friday in the spring are also particularly busy because of school visitation.

TRAVEL ACCESS: Bus: Greyhound and Trailways provide service within 8 blocks of Park; **Rail:** Amtrak provides regular service to Philadelphia—24 blocks from Park; **Air:** Major Airlines provide service to Philadelphia International Airport; **Other:** Airport rail line stops at Market East station, 5 blocks from the Park. Philadelphia mass transit system (SEPTA) also provides access through buses, subway trains, and trolleys. Municipal Parking Garage on 2nd Street between Chestnut and Walnut.

Johnstown Flood National Memorial
St. Michael, Pennsylvania

MAILING ADDRESS: Superintendent, Johnstown Flood National Memorial, c/o Allegheny Portage National Historic Site, P.O. Box 247, Cresson, PA 16630 **Telephone:** 814- 495-4643

DIRECTIONS: The area is located along US 219 and PA 869 at the South Fork Dam Site, 10 miles (16 km) northeast of Johnstown near St. Michael, PA.
Remnants of the earthen South Fork Dam on the Little Conemaugh River, which burst on May 31, 1889, causing the devastating flood of Johnstown and nearby communities, are preserved here. Authorized for addition to the National Park System on Aug. 31, 1964.

VISITOR ACTIVITIES: Picnicking, hiking, interpretive exhibits at Visitor Center; **Permits:** No; **Fees:** No; **Visitor facilities:** Picnic area, interpretive trails, comfort stations, Visitor Center at the dam site on North Abutment; **HANDICAPPED ACCESSIBILITY:** Restrooms, parking; Visitor Center is fully accessible for mobility impaired; 35-minute historical documentary motion picture is captioned for hearing impaired and has audio description of scenes available for visually impaired. Both short trails to north and south Abutment of Dam Site paved/accessible; **Any limitations on vehicle usage:** No; **Hiking trails:** Yes; **Backcountry:** No; **Camping:** No; **Other overnight accommodations on site:** No; **Meals served in the park:** No; **Food and supplies obtainable in the park:** No; **Food and supplies obtainable nearby:** Yes, at St. Michael (limited), Johnstown; **Overnight accommodations:** Johnstown US 219 and PA 56 10 miles (16 km); **First Aid available in park:** Yes, or nearby in St. Michael, Sidman PA 869; **Nearest Hospital:** Johnstown, US 219 and PA 56, 10 miles (16 km); **Days/Hours:** Open 9:00 a.m. to 5:00 p.m.; **Holiday Closings:** Thanksgiving, Dec.

25, and Jan. 1; **Visitor attractions closed for seasons:** None; **Weather:** Warm days and cool nights in summer; cold, windy winter with snow.

GENERAL INFORMATION: Twenty-four miles from the remains of the South Fork Dam is the Allegheny Portage Railroad National Historic Site.

TRAVEL ACCESS: Bus: Greyhound Bus provides daily service to Johnstown, PA; **Rail:** Amtrak provides daily service to Johnstown, PA; **Air:** Allegheny Airlines provides daily service to Johnstown, PA.

NEARBY FACILITIES & POINTS OF INTEREST: Hotel/Motel: U.S. Rt. 219 South to Richland Township is 8 miles (12.8 km), U.S. Rt. 219 North and U.S. Rt. 22 East to Ebensburg is 14 miles (22.4 km); **Food/Supplies:** Food Stores and Restaurants at Richland Mall area, 8 miles (12.8 km); Johnstown, 10 miles (16 km); **Campgrounds:** Blue Knob State Park, 26 miles (41.6 km), does not accept reservations; first come, first served; **Parks, other points of interest:** Allegheny Portage Railroad National Historic Site, Johnstown Flood Museum, Inclined Plane.

Steamtown National Historic Site
Scranton, Pennsylvania

MAILING ADDRESS: Steamtown National Historic Site, Post Office Box 1280, Scranton, PA 18501-1280. Contact: John Latschar, Superintendent **Telephone:** 717-343-0760

Is open to visitors.

The park consists of the former Delaware, Lackawanna & Western Railroad yard, including the remains of the historic roundhouse, switchyard and associated buildings. The yard, as well as approximately 30 miles of the railroad's mainline, preserve the story of early 20th century steam railroading in America.

Authorized: Oct. 30, 1986. Acreage: 500; Federal: 40; Nonfederal: 460.

Thaddeus Kosciuszko National Memorial
Philadelphia, Pennsylvania

MAILING ADDRESS: Superintendent, Thaddeus Kosciuszko National Memorial, c/o Independence National Historical Park, 313 Walnut Street, Philadelphia, PA 19106 **Telephone:** 215-597-8974 (Voice/TDD)

DIRECTIONS: The Memorial is located at 301 Pine Street, Philadelphia.

This small house, built in 1775, commemorates the life and work of General Thaddeus Kosciuszko, Polish-born patriot and hero of the American Revolution. Created by Presidential Proclamation on Oct. 21, 1972.

VISITOR ACTIVITIES: Interpretive exhibits and audiovisual programs; **Permits:** No; **Fees:** No; **Visitor facilities:** Restrooms; **Any limitations on vehicle usage:** Avoid driving in downtown Philadelphia. Try to walk or use public transportation; **Meals served in the park:** No; **Food and supplies obtainable in the park:** No; **Food and supplies obtainable nearby:** Yes, in Philadelphia; **Overnight accommodations:** Philadelphia; **First Aid available in park:** Yes; **Nearest Hospital:** Philadelphia, within 6 blocks; **Days/Hours:** Open daily from 9 a.m. to 5 p.m.; **Holiday Closings:** Dec. 25 and Jan. 1; **Visitor attractions closed for sea-**

sons: No; **Weather:** Summers are hot and humid; some snow and sleet in winter.

TRAVEL ACCESS: Bus: Greyhound, Trailways provide regular service to nearby terminal; **Rail:** Amtrak; **Air:** Major airlines service Philadelphia International Airport; **Other:** Philadelphia mass transit system (SEPTA) also provides access through buses, subway trains, and trolleys. New Municipal Parking Garage on 2nd Street between Chestnut and Walnut.

Valley Forge National Historical Park
Valley Forge, Pennsylvania

MAILING ADDRESS: Superintendent, Valley Forge National Historical Park, Box 953, Valley Forge, PA 19481 **Telephone:** 215-783-1077

DIRECTIONS: This park is about 20 miles (32 km) west of Philadelphia. Entrances to the Park from the major highways are well marked. Traveling eastbound or westbound via the Pennsylvania Turnpike, take Exit 24 (Valley Forge). Stay in the right lane for the toll booth and immediately take the next right onto North Gulf Road. This will take you to the Visitor Center located at the intersection of Valley Forge Road and 23. Begin your tour here.

Westbound travelers on the Schuykill Expressway (Interstate 76) should use Goddard Blvd. exit, make a right at the traffic light onto Goddard Blvd. Then make a right at the first traffic light onto N. Gulph Road. This will bring you to the Park. Travelers on US 202 should take the Rt. 422 West exit and proceed 2 miles (3.2 km) to the Valley Forge exit (PA 23 West), turn right at the exit, and follow PA 23 to entrance and Visitor Center.

This is the site of General Washington's Continental Army encampment in the winter of 1777-78 during the Revolutionary War. A scenic drive through the Park leads to many historical features including Washington's Headquarters and earthen fortifications. Transferred to National Park Service administration on March 31, 1977.

VISITOR ACTIVITIES: 15-minute film and exhibits, self-guiding auto tour, picnicking, hiking, horseback riding trails, boating, fishing, biking, auto tape tour June-Sept., interpretation of historic homes, soldier life demonstrations, guided walks; **Permits:** No; **Fees:** Presently, there is a fee for Washington's Headquarters. The fee is $1 for adults ages 17-61; Golden Age Passport accepted; **Visitor facilities:** Parking, hiking and bike trails, bus tours, picnic areas, boat ramp, snack bar; **HANDICAPPED ACCESSIBILITY:** Parking, restrooms, drinking fountains and telephones at Visitor Center, wayside exhibits, picnic area. 10-mile (16-km) self-guided tour can be done by car. A wheelchair is available. There is one 6-mile (9.6-km) paved multi-use path; hiking trails are uneven, natural earth terrrain. For hearing impaired: open-captioned 15-minute film; printed brochure. For visually impaired: audiotape of tour route available for purchase; some audio exhibits; **Any limitations on vehicle usage:** All vehicles must stay on the Park roads, which are narrow; **Hiking trails:** Yes, paved and unpaved trails lead to nearly all of the Park's historical features; **Backcountry:** No; **Camping:** No; **Other overnight accommodations on site:** No; **Meals served in the park:** No; **Food and supplies obtainable in the park:** No; **Food and supplies obtainable nearby:** Yes, in King of Prussia; **Overnight accommodations:** All major hotels are within 5 miles (8 km); **First Aid available in park:** Yes; **Nearest Hospital:** Phoenixville, 6 miles (9.6 km); **Days/Hours:** Open daily from 8:30 a.m. to 5 p.m. all year round; **Holiday Closings:** Dec. 25; **Visitor attractions closed for seasons:** No; **Weather:** Cold winters, pleasantly mild spring, summer and fall.

TRAVEL ACCESS: Bus: SEPTA Route #125, public transportation from Center City Philadelphia to Valley Forge Area, stops at all King of Prussia hotels, and return. Regular schedule Mon.-Fri. Not available Sat. and Sun. For schedule times, call: 215-734-1300 or 574-7800; **Air:** Nearest major airports are Philadelphia International and Northeast Philadelphia Airport; **Other:** Shuttle service from airport to hotel nearby Park is available. Taxi service from King of Prussia, PA, and other nearby communities.

NEARBY FACILITIES & POINTS OF INTEREST: Parks, other points of interest: Independence National Historical Park and Hopewell Village National Historic Site.

Rhode Island

Roger Williams National Memorial
Providence, Rhode Island

MAILING ADDRESS: Superintendent, Roger Williams National Memorial, 282 N. Main St., Providence, RI 02903 **Telephone:** 401-528-5385

DIRECTIONS: The Memorial is between Canal and North Main Streets, at the corner of Smith Street, in Providence.

This Memorial is in honor of the founder of the Rhode Island Colony and a pioneer in religious freedom. Authorized for addition to the National Park System on Oct. 22, 1965.

VISITOR ACTIVITIES: Interpretive exhibits; **Permits:** No; **Fees:** No; **Visitor facilities:** Park includes Visitor Center and over 4 acres of landscaped grounds; **HANDICAPPED ACCESSIBILITY:** Parking, Visitor Center displays and restrooms, paths through park; **Any limitations on vehicle usage:** No vehicle roads through park; **Hiking trails:** No; **Backcountry:** No; **Camping:** No; **Other overnight accommodations on site:** No; **Meals served in the park:** No; **Food and supplies obtainable in the park:** No; **Food and supplies obtainable nearby:** Yes, Providence; **Overnight accommodations:** Providence; **First Aid available in park:** Yes; **Nearest Hospital:** Within a 2-mile (3.2 km) radius; **Days/Hours:** Open daily

8:00 a.m. until 4:30 p.m. all year; **Holiday Closings:** Thanksgiving, Dec. 25, and Jan. 1; **Weather:** Summers are hot and humid.

GENERAL INFORMATION: Stop at the Visitor Center for a list of nearby points of interest in historic Providence.

TRAVEL ACCESS: Bus: Rhode Island Public Transit provides local bus service; **Rail:** Amtrak; **Air:** USAir, American, TWA, Eastern, National, Piedmont, United provides access into Providence.

Touro Synagogue National Historic Site
Newport, Rhode Island

MAILING ADDRESS: Touro Synagogue National Historic Site, 85 Touro Street, Newport, RI 02840 **Telephone:** 401-847-4794

DIRECTIONS: Touro Synagogue is on Touro Street in downtown Newport, RI, about 1-1/2 blocks east of the Old Colony on Washington Square.
    Touro Synagogue is one of the most significant buildings in Newport and the oldest existing synagogue in the United States. This affiliated area was authorized for addition to the National Park System on Mar. 5, 1946.

VISITOR ACTIVITIES: Guided tours offered from the last week of June until Labor Day; **Permits:** No; **Fees:** No; **Visitor facilities:** Souvenir stand; **Any limitations on vehicle usage:** No; **Hiking trails:** No; **Backcountry:** No; **Camping:** No; **Other overnight accommodations on site:** No; **Meals served in the park:** No; **Food and supplies obtainable in the park:** No; **Food and supplies obtainable nearby:** Yes, in Newport; **Overnight accommodations:** In the city of Newport, RI; **First Aid available in park:** No; **Nearest Hospital:** Newport Hospital is about 1 mile (1.6 km) from the Synagogue; **Days/Hours:** Hours during regular tourist season are now Sun. through Fri. from 10 a.m. to 5 p.m. The rest of the year from 1 p.m. to 3 p.m. on Sundays. Call for extended hours - spring and fall. Services are held on Fridays during the summer at 7:30 p.m. and during the rest of the year at sunset. Saturday services are at 9 a.m.

TRAVEL ACCESS: Bus: Bonanza and Greyhound; **Rail:** Amtrak; **Air:** via Providence, RI.

South Carolina

COWPENS NATIONAL BATTLEFIELD

KINGS MOUNTAIN
NATIONAL MILITARY PARK

NINETY SIX
NATIONAL HISTORIC SITE

CONGAREE SWAMP
NATIONAL MONUMENT

FORT SUMTER NATIONAL MONUMENT

Charles Pinckney National Historical Site
Mt. Pleasant, South Carolina

MAILING ADDRESS: Charles Pinckney National Historical Site, c/o Fort Sumter National Monument, 1214 Middle Street, Sullivans Island, SC 29482

DIRECTIONS: Follow U.S. 17 to Longpoint Road, ¼-mile (.4-km) to entrance opposite Boone Hall Plantation.

VISITOR ACTIVITIES: HANDICAPPED ACCESSIBILITY: Grounds and first floor of cottage accessible as well as restrooms.

GENERAL INFORMATION: Will open August 25, 1991.
     Charles Pinckney (1757–1824) fought in the Revolutionary War and became one of the principal framers of the Constitution. He served as Governor of South Carolina, a member of both the U.S. Senate and House of Representatives, and was President Jefferson's minister to Spain. His estate, known as Snee Farm, contains the remains of the Pickney country estate including brick foundations of the home and outbuildings and subsurface remnants of the Pickney gardens. Also, 1820 Tidewater cottage, unfurnished, remains in good condition.
     Authorized: Sept. 8, 1988. Acreage: 28.00 federal.

Congaree Swamp National Monument
Columbia, South Carolina

MAILING ADDRESS: Superintendent, Congaree Swamp National Monument, 200 Caroline Sims Road, Hopkins, SC 29061 **Telephone:** 803-776-4396; FAX 803-783-4241

DIRECTIONS: Off SC Highway 48 approximately 20 miles (32 km) southeast of Columbia, SC. Located on the alluvial floodplain of the Congaree River, the 22,200-acre Monument harbors the last significant tract of southern bottomland hardwood forest in the United States.
     The Monument was established on October 18, 1976, by an act of Congress, and is home to a diversity of plants and wildlife. Many trees are of record- or near-record size.

VISITOR ACTIVITIES: Hiking, canoeing, fishing, primitive camping, birdwatching, photography, picnicking, guided nature walks. **Permits:** required for camping; **Fees:** No; **Visitor facilities:** Visitor Center, restrooms, picnic area, hiking trails, two boardwalks; **HANDICAPPED ACCESSIBILITY:** Visitor Center, restrooms, one boardwalk; **Any limitations on vehicle usage:** Yes; **Hiking trails:** Yes, 18 miles (28.8 km) of marked trails; **Backcountry:** Yes; **Camping:** Yes, with permit; **Other overnight accommodations on site:** No; **Meals served in the park:** No; **Food and supplies obtainable in the park:** No; **Food and supplies obtainable nearby:** Yes, in Columbia, SC; **Overnight accommodations:** Columbia, SC; **First Aid available in park:** Yes; **Nearest Hospital:** Baptist Hospital, Columbia, SC.

Cowpens National Battlefield
Chesnee, South Carolina

MAILING ADDRESS: Cowpens National Battlefield, Superintendent, P.O. Box 308, Chesnee, SC 29323 **Telephone:** 803-461-2828

DIRECTIONS: The Battlefield is 11 miles (17.6 km) west of I-85 and Gaffney, SC and about 2 miles (3.2 km) east of US 221 and Chesnee, SC
     Brig. Gen. Daniel Morgan won a decisive Revolutionary War Victory here over British Lt. Col. Banastre Tarleton on Jan. 17, 1781. Established on Mar. 4, 1929. Additional lands acquired in 1972.

VISITOR ACTIVITIES: Ranger-conducted walking tours (if scheduled in advance), exhibits, and audiovisual slide presentation at the Visitor Center, Adults: $1, Children: $.50 each, Groups: $.50 each, auto tours; **Permits:** No; **Fees:** No; **Visitor facilities:** Restored 1830 log cabin, historic monuments, parking, tour road, walking trails, picnic area, information and exhibits; **HANDICAPPED ACCESSIBILITY:** All Visitor Center facilities, picnic tables, and main portion of battlefield trail; **Any limitations on vehicle usage:** Recreational vehicles are permitted; commercial vehicles are prohibited; **Hiking trails:** Yes, 1 mile (1.6 km) walking trail; **Backcountry:** No; **Camping:** No; **Other overnight accommodations on site:** No; **Meals served in the park:** No; **Food and supplies obtainable in the park:** No; **Food and supplies obtainable nearby:** Yes, in Chesnee, 2 miles (3.2 km). Limited food and gas stations within 3 miles (4.8 km) of the Park; **Overnight accommodations:** Gaffney, SC 11 and I-85, 11 miles (17.6 km) from the Park; **First Aid available in park:** Yes; **Nearest Hospital:** Gaffney, SC 11, 10 miles (16 km); **Days/Hours:** Open 7 days a week, 9 a.m. to 5 p.m.; **Holiday Closings:** Dec. 25; **Visitor attractions closed for seasons:** Weather conditions may limit access on roads and trails; **Weather:** Summers are hot and humid; winters are mild with occasional snow.

TRAVEL ACCESS: Bus: Trailways and Greyhound provide daily service to Spartanburg; **Rail:** Southern Railway provides daily service to Spartanburg; **Air:** American, Delta, Northwest, United, USAir.

NEARBY FACILITIES & POINTS OF INTEREST: Hotel/Motel: overnight lodging available in Gaffney and Spartanburg; **Campgrounds:** Several private and state camping facilities within 30 miles (48 km); **Parks, other points of interest:** Kings Mountain National Military Park 32 miles (51.2 km) north of Park, Walnut Grove Plantation 30 miles (48 km) south of Park.

Fort Sumter National Monument
Sullivan's Island, South Carolina

MAILING ADDRESS: Superintendent, Fort Sumter National Monument, 1214 Middle Street, Sullivan's Island, SC 29482 **Telephone:** 803-883-3123

DIRECTIONS: Fort Sumter is in Charleston Harbor and can be reached only by boat. Tour boats leave from the city boat marina on Lockwood Drive, just south of US 17 in Charleston. For boat schedules, phone Fort Sumter Tours, 803-722-1691, or write 17 Lockwood Dr., Charleston, SC 29401. Fort Moultrie, administered together with Fort Sumter, is on west Middle Street on Sullivan's Island. From US 17, take SC 703 to Middle Street. The Visitor Center is at Fort Moultrie.

The first engagement of the Civil War took place here on Apr. 12, 1861. The Park also includes Fort Moultrie, scene of the patriot victory of June 28, 1776, one of the early defeats of the British in the Revolutionary War. Fort Sumter was authorized for addition to the National Park System on Apr. 28, 1948. Fort Moultrie was added in 1960.

VISITOR ACTIVITIES: Interpretive exhibits, film program, walking tours; **Permits:** No; **Fees:** Yes, tour boat to Fort Sumter is $8.00 for adults, $4.00 for children under 12. Children under 6 free. There is no admission fee at Fort Moultrie; **Visitor facilities:** Restrooms at both forts, observation deck at Visitor Center and Fort Moultrie; **HANDICAPPED ACCESSIBILITY:** Ft. Sumter has a wheelchair lift that provides access to the restroom for the handicapped. Ft. Moultrie has parking for the handicapped and wheelchair ramps that provide access to the Visitor Center; **Any limitations on vehicle usage:** No; **Hiking trails:** No; **Backcountry:** No; **Camping:** No; **Other overnight accommodations on site:** No; **Meals served in the park:** No; **Food and supplies obtainable in the park:** No; **Food and supplies obtainable nearby:** Yes, Mt. Pleasant and Sullivan's Island and vicinity; **Overnight accommodations:** Hotels in Charleston and Mount Pleasant; **First Aid available in park:** Yes; **Nearest Hospital:** Mt. Pleasant, Hwy. 17 North, 5 miles (8 km); **Days/Hours:** Open daily from 9 a.m. to 5 p.m., until 6 p.m. in summer; **Holiday Closings:** Dec. 25; **Visitor attractions closed for seasons:** No; **Weather:** Summers are hot and humid; winters are moderately cool with occasional days of extreme cold.

GENERAL INFORMATION: *For Your Safety*—Be especially careful on uneven surfaces, stairways, and near the chain barriers.

TRAVEL ACCESS: **Bus:** Greyhound, Continental provide daily service to Charleston; **Rail:** Amtrak provides regular service to Charleston; **Air:** Delta, Eastern, Piedmont, and other airlines service Charleston.

NEARBY FACILITIES & POINTS OF INTEREST: Parks, other points of interest: Charles Pinckney National Historic Site.

Kings Mountain National Military Park
Kings Mountain, South Carolina

MAILING ADDRESS: Superintendent, Kings Mountain National Military Park, P.O.Box 40, Kings Mountain, NC 28086 **Telephone:** 803-936-7921

DIRECTIONS: The park is easily reached from Charlotte, NC, by Int. 85; from Spartanburg,

SC, by Int 85; and from York, SC, by SC 161. Kings Mountain is on SC Hwy 216, off I-85, about 10 miles (16 km) from Kings Mountain, NC, and about 15 miles (24 km) southwest of Gastonia, NC, and northeast of Gaffney, SC.

American frontiersmen defeated the British here on Oct. 7, 1780, at a critical point during the struggle for independence and the battle was considered by Thomas Jefferson to be the turning point of the American Revolution.

VISITOR ACTIVITIES: Interpretive exhibits and programs, walking tours, photography, horseback riding; **Permits:** No; **Fees:** No; **Visitor facilities:** Visitor Center, hiking trail, horseback riding trail; **HANDICAPPED ACCESSIBILITY:** Parking, restrooms. Trail is paved but steep in places. Edited script of 18-minute film available for hearing impaired. Tapes of wayside exhibits available for sight impaired; **Any limitations on vehicle usage:** Commercial vehicles are prohibited; drivers should be alert for pedestrians and hikers; **Hiking trails:** Yes, a foot trail leads from the Visitor Center to the chief features of the battlefield; **Backcountry:** Yes, information and brochure available at Visitor Center; **Camping:** Primitive campsite to accommodate backpackers; **Other overnight accommodations on site:** No, general camping is permitted only in Kings Mountain State Park, which adjoins the National Military Park on the east. You can also swim (in season) and picnic in the State Park; **Meals served in the park:** No; **Food and supplies obtainable in the park:** No; **Food and supplies obtainable nearby:** Yes, Kings Mountain, NC, Blacksburg, SC; York, SC; **Overnight accommodations:** Kings Mountain, NC, northeast of the park; **First Aid available in park:** Yes; **Nearest Hospital:** Kings Mountain, NC, 10 miles (16 km), SC-NC Hwy 216 to US 74 west; **Days/Hours:** Open daily from 9 a.m. to 5 p.m; until 6 p.m. in summer; **Holiday Closings:** Thanksgiving Day, Dec. 25, Jan. 1; **Visitor attractions closed for seasons:** No; **Weather:** Summer is warm and humid. Spring and fall are pleasantly mild. Winter is cold, but snow and ice are infrequent.

TRAVEL ACCESS: Bus: Trailways provides daily service to Kings Mountain; **Rail:** Amtrak provides daily service to Gastonia, NC; **Air:** Eastern, Delta, and USAir provide daily service to Charlotte, NC.

NEARBY FACILITIES & POINTS OF INTEREST: Hotel/Motel: Holiday Inn, I-85 and NC 161, 704-739-2544, 8 miles (12.8 km) from Park, Comfort Inn, 704-739-7070; **Camping:** Kings Mountain State Park (adjacent to Kings Mountain National Park); **Parks, other points of interest:** Cowpens National Battlefield, 30 miles (48 km) southwest.

Ninety Six National Historic Site
Ninety Six, South Carolina

MAILING ADDRESS: Superintendent, Ninety Six National Historic Site, P.O. Box 496, Ninety Six, SC 29666 **Telephone:** 803-543-4068

DIRECTIONS: The Visitor Center is 2 miles (3.2 km) south of Ninety Six, SC, off US 248 in Greenwood County.

This colonial trading village dates from the 1730s and became an important government seat after 1768. Held by the British during the Revolutionary War, this Site contains earthwork embankments of a 1780 fortification. Authorized for addition to the National Park System on Aug. 19, 1976.

VISITOR ACTIVITIES: Interpretive exhibits, walking, horseback riding, hiking, fishing; **Permits:** Required for special uses such as group camping, collecting natural specimens, etc.; Can be obtained from Visitor Center; **Fees:** No; **Visitor facilities:** Parking and restrooms at Visitor Center, interpretive trail; **HANDICAPPED ACCESSIBILITY:** Restrooms and Visitor Center; **Any limitations on vehicle usage:** No vehicular traffic is allowed in the Park; **Hiking trails:** Yes, a 1-mile (1.6-km) interpretive trail; **Backcountry:** Yes; **Camping:** No; **Other overnight accommodations on site:** No; **Meals served in the park:** No; **Food and supplies obtainable in the park:** No; **Food and supplies obtainable nearby:** Yes, Ninety Six, 2 miles (3.2 km) north; **Overnight accommodations:** Greenwood, SC 34, 10 miles (16 km) west; **First Aid available in park:** Yes; **Nearest Hospital:** Greenwood, SC 34, 9 miles (14.4 km); **Days/Hours:** Open daily from 8 a.m. to 5 p.m.; **Holiday Closings:** Dec. 25 and Jan. 1.

NEARBY FACILITIES & POINTS OF INTEREST: Parks, other points of interest: Greenwood Museum, Railway Museum in Greenwood, State Historical Markers nearby.

South Dakota

Badlands National Park
Interior, South Dakota   **SEE CLIMATABLE NO. 29**

MAILING ADDRESS: Superintendent, Badlands National Park, P.O. Box 6, Interior, SD 57750 **Telephone:** 605-433-5361

DIRECTIONS: The Ben Reifel Visitor Center, 2¾ miles (4.4 km) northeast of Interior on Route SH240, 28 miles (44.8 km) southwest of Kadoka and 29 miles (46.4 km) southeast of Wall—both on I-90.

This Park, carved by erosion, contains animal fossils from 37-23 million years ago. Prairie grasslands support bison, bighorn sheep, deer, antelope, and prairie dogs. Proclaimed a national monument on Jan. 25, 1939 it was redesignated a National Park by Congress on Nov. 10, 1978.

VISITOR ACTIVITIES: Ranger-conducted activities including nature walks, canyon climbs, evening programs, fossil preparation demonstrations in summer; camping, hiking, scenic drives, wildlife observation; **Permits:** No; **Fees:** $3 per vehicle entrance fee, $1 per person on commercial buses, $7 per campsite per night. Golden Eagle, Golden Age, and Golden Access Passports accepted and available; **Visitor facilities:** Campgrounds, nature trails, 2 visitor centers, picnic areas, lodging, restaurant, souvenirs; **HANDICAPPED AC-CESSIBILITY:** Visitor Centers and restrooms are accessible. Some campsites and restrooms in Cedar Pass Campground are accessible. Accessible trails are Fossil Exhibit Trail, Window Trail. Park orientation video at Ben Reifel Visitor Center is captioned on request. In the Touch Room, fossils, bones, rocks, and plants are accessible and may be handled; **Any limitations on vehicle usage:** No off-road driving. Be on the lookout for wild animals, especially at night; **Hiking trails:** Yes, self-guiding trails of varying degrees of difficulty lead from the Park road; **Backcountry:** Yes, write ahead for complete backcountry and/or trail information. Otherwise, check at Ben Reifel or White River Visitor Centers; **Camping:** Yes, camping available year-round; no campsite reservations except for groups. Commercial campgrounds available at or near Interior, Cactus Flat, Wall, or Kadoka; **Other overnight accommodations on site:** Yes, reservations for lodging should be made with Cedar Pass Lodge (open early May-early Oct.), phone 605-433-5460; **Meals served in the park:** Yes, at Cedar Pass Lodge, from mid-April to late October; **Food and supplies obtainable in the park:** Yes, at Cedar Pass Lodge; **Food and supplies obtainable nearby:** Yes, in Interior, Wall, and Kadoka; **Overnight accommodations:** Wall, I-90, 30 miles (48 km) northwest, Kadoka, 28 miles (44.8 km) northeast; **First Aid available in park:** Yes, at Ranger stations; doctors in Wall, Kadoka and Rapid City; **Nearest Hospital:** Phillip 35 miles (56 km) NE of Cedar Pass; **Days/Hours:** Open 24 hours a day, year-round. Ben Reifel Visitor Center open every day except winter holidays; White River Visitor Center open daily in summer, closed in off-season; **Holiday Closings:** Visitor Center closed Thanksgiving, Dec. 25, and Jan. 1; **Visitor attractions closed for seasons:** The most popular seasons are spring, summer, and autumn. Winter visits can also be rewarding but blizzards may temporarily block roads; **Weather:** Changes in the weather can be sudden and quite drastic in the Badlands. Summer is hot, with frequent storms bringing lightning, hail, and high winds. Even on mild days, prolonged exposure to a shower can lead to hypothermia, a potentially fatal reduction in body temperature. Dress adequately and avoid open areas during electrical storms.

GENERAL INFORMATION: *Warning!* Be alert for rattlesnakes, particularly during the warm months. Water should be carried on longer hikes. Drinking water should come from approved sources, such as those at designated campgrounds. Other backcountry water sources are for native wildlife only, and are not fit for human consumption. When afoot, keep a safe distance from buffalo, 100 yards or more.

Climbing is discouraged on the steep, barren slopes where slippery clays and soft sediments may suddenly yield under foot.

No open fires are allowed anywhere in the Park. Cooking stoves and charcoal grills are permitted in campgrounds.

Other points of interest in the Black Hills include Jewel Cave, Wind Cave, and Mount Rushmore (see listings in this book).

Jewel Cave National Monument
Custer, South Dakota   **SEE CLIMATABLE NO. 30**

MAILING ADDRESS: Superintendent, Jewel Cave National Monument, RR 1, Box 60AA, Custer, SD, 57730 **Telephone:** 605-673-2288

DIRECTIONS: The area is accessible by US 16, which crosses the northern part of the Park between Custer, SD, and Newcastle, WY. The Visitor Center is on US 16, 13 miles (20.8 km) west of Custer.

Limestone formation caverns consist of a series of chambers connected by narrow passages, with many side galleries and fine calcite crystal encrustations. Created by Presidential Proclamation on Feb. 7, 1908, Jewel Cave is currently the fourth longest cave in the world.

VISITOR ACTIVITIES: Interpretive exhibits, cave tours, picnicking; **Permits:** No; **Fees:** There is a guide fee for tours: ages 5 and under, free; 6 to 15, $2; 16 and over, $4; holders of Golden Age Passports, $2.00; Spelunking tours are $6; **Visitor facilities:** Exhibits, information, sales counter, picnic area, drinking water, restrooms; **Any limitations on vehicle usage:** Vehicles must stay on the roads or in the parking area; **Hiking trails:** Yes, a short trail leads from the parking area to the historic cave entrance; **Backcountry:** No; **Camping:** No; **Other overnight accommodations on site:** No, several campgrounds are near Newcastle, WY, and Custer, SD. Contact the monument for further information; **Meals served in the park:** No; **Food and supplies obtainable in the park:** No; **Food and supplies obtainable nearby:** Yes, in Newcastle, WY, or Custer, SD; **Overnight accommodations:** Yes, in Newcastle 25 miles (40 km) west of the Monument on US 16, or Custer, 13 miles (20.8 km) east on US 16; **First Aid available in park:** Yes; **Nearest Hospital:** Custer, 13 miles (20.8 km) east on US 16, or Newcastle 25 miles (40 km) west on US 16; **Days/Hours:** Visitor Center open daily year-round. Portions of the cave are open to the public, and interpretive tours are offered daily from May through Sept. Tour schedules, if any, during the rest of the year are irregular and subject to change without notice; **Holiday Closings:** Thanksgiving, Dec. 25, and Jan. 1; **Weather:** Days are warm and sunny; temperatures at night are moderate. There are occasional afternoon thundershowers.

GENERAL INFORMATION: Wear low-heeled walking shoes with non-slip soles while touring the cave. Do not wear sandals or shoes with leather or hard composition soles or with high heels. A light sweater or jacket is desirable—the cave temperature is about 47°F all year. Cave trails include numerous stairs. The tours are not recommended for individuals who have heart trouble or respiratory ailments, or for those who are recovering from a recent operation or hospitalization. Consider each tour description carefully before making a choice. Never leave a child or pet in a locked car. Due to the popularity of the scenic tour, lengthy waits of up to 2 hours may be encountered during mid-day. Reservations are required for the spelunking tour. Scenic tours are on a first-come, first-served basis.

TRAVEL ACCESS: Bus: Continental Trailways provides service into Custer, SD; **Rail:** Amtrak provides service into Cheyenne, WY; **Air:** Continental Express, Northwest, Delta, United Express provide service to Rapid City, SD.

NEARBY FACILITIES & POINTS OF INTEREST: Campgrounds: Nearest public campground is USFS Comanche Park Campground, 7 miles (11.2 km) east on US 16; **Parks, other points of interest:** Wind Cave National Park, 35 miles (56 km) southeast; Mt. Rushmore National Memorial, 35 miles (56 km) northeast; Custer State Park, 15 miles (24 km) east; Badlands National Park, 133 miles (212.8 km) east; Devils Tower National Monument, 96 miles (153.6 km) northwest (see listings).

Mount Rushmore National Memorial
Keystone, South Dakota   **SEE CLIMATABLE NO. 30**

MAILING ADDRESS: Superintendent, Mount Rushmore National Memorial, P.O. Box 268, Keystone, SD 57751 **Telephone:** 605-574-2523

DIRECTIONS: The Visitor Center is 2 miles (3.2 km) southwest of Keystone on SD 244 and 25 miles (40 km) south of Rapid City on US 16.

Monumental heads of Presidents George Washington, Thomas Jefferson, Abraham Lincoln, and Theodore Roosevelt were sculpted by Gutzon Borglum on the face of a granite mountain. Authorized for addition to the National Park System on Mar. 3, 1925.

VISITOR ACTIVITIES: Evening programs in summer, interpretive exhibits, audio-visual programs, wildlife- and bird-watching; **Permits:** Commercial film permits required; **Fees:** No; **Visitor facilities:** Visitor Center, restrooms, parking lot, feature-length film, floodlighted memorial, dining room, gift shop all year; **HANDICAPPED ACCESSIBILITY:** Programs for physically disadvantaged, hearing impaired, at Visitor Center; **Any limitations on vehicle usage:** No commercial vehicles allowed through the park. Leave your vehicle in gear and set your handbrake when parking; **Hiking trails:** Yes, short trails provide varied views of the sculpture; **Backcountry:** No; **Camping:** No; **Picniking;** No; **Other overnight accommodations on site:** No, many commercial, state park and U.S. Forest Service campgrounds exist in the surrounding Black Hills National Forest, Custer State Park, and nearby towns of Rapid City, Rockerville, Keystone, Custer, Hill City, and Hot Springs, SD. Most of these campgrounds can accommodate tents, trailers, and recreational vehicles. Contact U.S. Forest Service, Black Hills National Forest, P.O. Box 792, Custer, SD 57730, phone 605-673-2251; Custer State Park, Hermosa, SD 57744, phone 605-255-4515; South Dakota Division of Tourism, Pierre, SD 57501, phone 605-773-3301; **Meals served in the park:** Yes, complete dining service is available at the concession area during the summer season. Limited food service available during most of the rest of the year; **Food and supplies obtainable in the park:** No; **Food and supplies obtainable nearby:** Yes, at Keystone and Hill City; **Overnight accommodations:** Keystone, 2 miles (3.2 km) northeast; Hill City, 15 miles (24 km) southwest; For further information on accommodations in the vicinity contact the Chamber of Commerce, P.O. Box 747, Rapid City, SD 57701, phone 605-343-1744; **First Aid available in park:** Yes; **Nearest Hospital:** Rapid City, 25 miles (40 km) north on US 16; **Days/Hours:** Visitor Center open from 8 a.m. to 10 p.m. from mid-May through mid-Sept; from 8 a.m. to 5 p.m. the remainder of the year. Inquire locally to verify hours, which are subject to change; **Holiday Closings:** Park open, Visitor Center closed Dec. 25; **Visitor attractions closed for seasons:** No; **Weather:** Summer daytime temperatures range from 70-90°F, cool evenings; Winter temperatures range from 40°F to -20°F.

GENERAL INFORMATION: Climbing of Mount Rushmore is prohibited. Stay on trails and stairways. Do not run. Visitors who have heart problems or who have trouble breathing should be aware of the high elevation (5,250 feet). For information on tourist attractions in the Black Hills area, contact the South Dakota Division of Tourism, Pierre, SD 57501, phone 605-773-3301, Toll free 1-800-843-1930.

TRAVEL ACCESS: Bus: Gray Line of the Black Hills, 605-342-4461, Stagecoach West, 605-343-3113; Jack Rabbit Bus Lines, 605-348-3300, provide charter service for park tours; **Rail:** No; **Air:** Western Airlines, United Airlines, and Republic Airlines provide service to Rapid City Regional Airport.

NEARBY FACILITIES & POINTS OF INTEREST: Parks, other points of interest: Custer State Park, Wind Cave National Park, Jewel Cave National Monument, private attractions in Black Hills Region.

Wind Cave National Park
Hot Springs, South Dakota   **SEE CLIMATABLE NO. 30**

MAILING ADDRESS: Superintendent, Wind Cave National Park, Hot Springs, SD 57747 **Telephone:** 605-745-4600

DIRECTIONS: The Visitor Center is 11 miles (17.6 km) from the town of Hot Springs on US 385.

This limestone cavern in the scenic Black Hills contains boxwork and calcite crystal formations. Elk, deer, prairie dogs, and bison live in the park. Established by act of Congress on Jan. 9, 1903.

VISITOR ACTIVITIES: Guided cave tours, candlelight and spelunking tours, evening campfire programs, interpretive exhibits, picnicking, camping, cross-country hiking; **Permits:** No; **Fees:** Yes, for camping and cave tours. Camping is $8 per night per site. Cave tour format now consists of a Garden of Eden Tour, a Natural Entrance Tour, and a Fairgrounds Tour, as well as the Candlelight and Caving Tours. Costs: Garden of Eden, $2; Natural Entrance, $4; Fairgrounds, $5. Candlelight tours are $5 each, for 6-15 years old, Garden of Eden, $1, Natural Entrance, $2, Fairgrounds, $2.50, Candlelight, $2.50, under 6 free, ½ price for those holding Golden Age Passports. Spelunking tour, $6 (only 14 and over allowed); **Visitor facilities:** Parking and restrooms at Visitor Center, picnic area, food service from May-Sept.; **HANDICAPPED ACCESSIBILITY:** Visitor Center has accessible parking, is ramped; restrooms and snackbar and gift shop are accessible. An elevator is available in the Visitor Center for both floors. Campground has 2 accessible restrooms with modified campsites. The cave is accessible by informal arrangement made at the information desk. **Any limitations on vehicle usage:** Drive only on the roadways. Park at parking areas only; **Hiking trails:** Yes, 2 self-guiding nature trails; daytime cross-country hikes; **Backcountry:** Yes, an experimental backcountry camping plan went into effect in 1986. Check at the Visitor Center for permits and restrictions; **Camping:** Yes, no reservations accepted for campsites, which are open from about May 15 through Sept. Winter camping available, no water, no fee. There are many private campgrounds in the Black Hills. For further information, contact the South Dakota Division of Tourism, Pierre, SD 57501, phone 605-773-3301; **Other overnight accommodations on site:** No; **Meals served in the park:** Yes, complete lunch service at Visitor Center in summer; **Food and supplies obtainable in the park:** No; **Food and supplies obtainable nearby:** Yes, at Hot Springs and Custer; **Overnight accommodations:** Hot Springs, 11 miles (17.6 km) south on Hwy 385; **First Aid available in park:** Only for major injuries; **Nearest Hospital:** Southern General Hills Hospital, Hot Springs, Hwy 385, 11 miles (17.6 km); **Days/Hours:** Park always open, Cave tours offered daily, with a very limited schedule in winter; **Holiday Closings:** Cave closed Thanksgiving, Dec. 25, and Jan. 1; **Visitor attractions closed for seasons:** Many of the Black Hills attractions are open only from Memorial Day through Labor Day. Cave tours are not given as often in winter; **Weather:** Fall is generally warm and pleasant. Spring can be blustery and is occasionally marred by heavy snowfalls. Winter is moderately severe, but icy roads, lack of accommodations, and closed tourist attractions discourage visitors.

GENERAL INFORMATION: The cave trail is dimly lit, and the surface is paved but uneven. Be sure to wear low-heeled walking shoes with non-slip soles, not sandals or high heels. A light sweater or jacket is desirable, since the cave temperature is about 53°F all year. Beware of bison, which may attack if disturbed or annoyed. Prairie dogs can bite, and their burrows may harbor rattlesnakes. Poison ivy abounds in the park and elsewhere in the Black Hills. Learn to recognize and avoid it. If you wish to avoid crowds, plan your visit for spring or fall.

TRAVEL ACCESS: Bus: Trailways Bus operates service into Hot Springs, SD; **Rail:** Nearest Amtrak service into Cheyenne, WY, 380 miles (608 km) south of Park; **Air:** Major Airlines offer service into Rapid City, SD, 60 miles (36 km), north.

NEARBY FACILITIES & POINTS OF INTEREST: Campgrounds: Elk Mountain Campground; **Parks, other points of interest:** Mt. Rushmore, 50 miles (80 km) north; Custer State Park, 10 miles (16 km) north; Jewel Cave National Monument, 35 miles (56 km) northwest.

Tennessee

BIG SOUTH FORK NATIONAL
RIVER AND RECREATION AREA

CUMBERLAND GAP
NATIONAL HISTORICAL PARK

OBED WILD AND SCENIC RIVER

APPALACHIAN
NATIONAL SCENIC TRAIL

STONES RIVER NATIONAL
BATTLEFIELD AND CEMETERY

FORT DONELSON NATIONAL MILITARY PARK

ANDREW JOHNSON
NATIONAL HISTORIC SITE

GREAT SMOKY MOUNTAINS
NATIONAL PARK

SHILOH NATIONAL MILITARY PARK

NATCHEZ TRACE PARKWAY

CHICKAMAUGA AND CHATTANOOGA
NATIONAL MILITARY PARK

Andrew Johnson National Historic Site
Greeneville, Tennessee

MAILING ADDRESS: Superintendent, Andrew Johnson National Historic Site, P.O. Box 1088, Greeneville, TN 37744-1088 **Telephone:** 615-638-3551/1326

DIRECTIONS: From I-81 follow 11E North if traveling north or TN 172 if traveling south. Follow directional signs to the Visitor Center, located at the corner of College and Depot Streets. Rangers will direct visitors to the Homestead and National Cemetery.

This 16-acre Site was established by Presidential Proclamation on Apr. 27, 1942, and preserves two homes, the tailor shop and cemetery where President Andrew Johnson lived, worked, and is buried.

VISITOR ACTIVITIES: Interpretive exhibits and historic building tour, auto tours; **Permits:** No; **Fees:** Entrance fee at Homestead only for those 17 years or older, year-round. Golden Age, Golden Access, and Golden Eagle Passports accepted and available; **Visitor facilities:** Parking at the Visitor Center, Homestead, and National Cemetery. Restrooms at the Visitor Center; **Any limitations on vehicle usage:** Vehicles are restricted to tour roads and parking areas; **Hiking trails:** No; **Backcountry:** No; **Camping:** No; **Other overnight accommodations on site:** No; **Meals served in the park:** No; **Food and supplies obtainable in the park:** No; **Food and supplies obtainable nearby:** Yes, Greeneville; **Overnight accommodations:** Several motels in Greeneville; **First Aid available in park:** Yes; **Nearest Hospital:** Laughlin Memorial and Takoma Adventist Hospitals, both in Greeneville; **Days/Hours:** Open daily from 9 a.m. to 5 p.m.; **Holiday Closings:** Dec. 25; **Visitor attractions closed for seasons:** No.

GENERAL INFORMATION: Three parts of the Historic Site are open to visitors. A museum and Andrew Johnson's tailor shop are located within the Visitor Center. The Andrew Johnson Homestead, last home of the 17th President, has been completely restored. President Johnson is buried in the Andrew Johnson National Cemetery.

TRAVEL ACCESS: Bus: Continental Trailways provides service to Greeneville; **Rail:** No; **Air:** Tri-City Airport 45 miles (72 km) northeast of Greeneville. Knoxville's McGhee Tyson Airport 75 miles (120 km) southwest.

NEARBY FACILITIES & POINTS OF INTEREST: Historic Jonesborough, oldest town in Tennessee, is 25 miles (40 km) northeast on US 11E/321. Davy Crockett Birthplace State Historic Area is 15 miles (24 km) northeast via US 11E/321. Camping at Forest Service campgrounds, Davy Crockett Birthplace State Historic Area, and Kinser Park.

Big South Fork National River and Recreation Area
Tennessee and Kentucky

MAILING ADDRESS: Superintendent, Big South Fork National River and Recreation Area, Rt. 3, Box 401, Oneida, TN 37841 **Telephone:** 615-569-9778

DIRECTIONS: I-75 and I-40 are the major access routes to the Recreation Area. From I-75 proceed west via KY 80, 90, or 92 or TN 63 to US 27, and then via US 27 to Oneida, TN. The Visitor Center is located 12 miles (19.2 km) west off TN 297 in the Bandy Creek Campground. From I-40 proceed north via US 127 through Jamestown and then north on US 154 to TN 297. The Visitor Center is located 12 miles (19.2 km) east of US 154 off TN 297 in the Bandy Creek Campground.

The free-flowing Big South Fork of the Cumberland River and its tributaries pass through scenic gorges and valleys containing a wide range of natural and historic features. Authorized for addition to the National Park System in 1974.

VISITOR ACTIVITIES: Canoeing, raft trips, hiking, horseback riding, mountain bike riding, camping, interpretive walks, fishing, hunting, swimming, and picnicking; **Permits:** No; **Fees:** No; **Visitor facilities:** Exhibits at Visitor Center and Blue Heron Mining Community; interpretive trails, Bandy Creek Campground, Blue Heron Campground and Alum Fork Campground, interpretive program, hiking and horse trails; **HANDICAPPED ACCESSIBILITY:** Restrooms, parking; Bandy Creek and Blue Heron Campgrounds are handicapped accessible; **Any limitations on vehicle usage:** Vehicles restricted from river gorge and limited to established roads; **Hiking trails:** Yes, over 140 miles (224 km) completed; **Horse trails:** Yes, over 120 miles (192 km) completed; **Backcountry:** Yes, ask at Visitor Center for details; **Camping:** Yes, Alum Ford Campground has no water; Lodging at Charit Creek; **Other overnight accommodations on site:** Yes, camping at Charit Creek and backcountry camping allowed; **Meals served in the park:** No; **Food and supplies obtainable in the park:** No; **Food and supplies obtainable nearby:** Yes, at Oneida of Jamestown, TN, or Whitley City, KY; **Overnight accommodations:** Oneida of Jamestown, TN of Whitley City, KY; **First Aid available in park:** Yes; **Nearest Hospital:** Oneida of Jamestown, TN.

GENERAL INFORMATION: Developed by the U.S. Army Corps of Engineers, the Big South Fork NRRA has been transferred to the Dept. of the Interior and is now under management by the National Park Service. *For your safety*—Paddling can be a dangerous sport on certain sections of the Big South Fork's rivers. Select a stream that matches your experience and abilities. Coast Guard-approved life jackets must be carried, and should be worn, by all persons on the river.

Stay on designated hiking trails. Many trails pass close to high ledges and cliffs. Serious or fatal falls are possible. Carry a first aid kit at all times.

Steep grades (13%) and sharp hairpin turns will be encountered on highway 297 as it passes through the river gorge. Cars with trailers and large RVs are advised to use caution.

Fort Donelson National Battlefield
Dover, Tennessee

MAILING ADDRESS: Superintendent, Fort Donelson National Battlefield, P.O. Box 434, Dover, TN 37058 **Telephone:** Office 615-232-5348; Visitor Center, 615-232-5706

DIRECTIONS: The Park is 1 mile (1.6 km) west of Dover town square and 3 miles (4.8 km) east of Land Between the Lakes National Recreation Area on US 79.

The first major victory for the Union Army in the Civil War occurred here in February, 1862, under the leadership of Ulysses S. Grant. The Park was established by act of Congress on March 26, 1928. Fort Donelson National Cemetery (estab. 1867) adjoins the Park.

VISITOR ACTIVITIES: Interpretive and audiovisual programs at Visitor Center, museum and wayside exhibits, auto tour, fishing, picnicking, hiking; **Permits:** Tennessee fishing license available from local stores. Licenses vary in length of validity and cost; **Fees:** No; **Visitor facilities:** Visitor Centers, restrooms, picnic area, hiking trails; **HANDICAP-PED ACCESSIBILITY:** Visitor Center and Dover Hotel have accessible parking and are accessible to enter. The Dover Hotel has accessible restrooms; **Any limitations on vehicle usage:** Park only in pull-offs. Bikers should ride single-file in the direction of the traffic; **Hiking trails:** Yes, self-guiding walking tours of natural and historical areas; **Backcountry:** No; **Camping:** Primitive camping for organized youth groups only, group leader should contact the park; **Other overnight accommodations on site:** No; **Meals served in the park:** No; **Food and supplies obtainable in the park:** No; **Food and supplies obtainable nearby:** Yes, Dover; **Overnight accommodations:** Dover, Paris Landing State Park, 16 miles (25.6 km) southeast on US 79; Clarksville and Paris, TN both on US 79, 30 miles (48 km) in opposite directions; Murry, KY, 30 miles (48 km) on KY 121; **First Aid available in park:** Yes, nearby or in Dover; **Nearest Hospital:** Erin, TN 49, 20 miles (32 km); **Days/Hours:** Open daily 8 a.m. to 4:30 p.m.; **Holiday Closings:** Dec. 25; **Visitor attractions closed for seasons:** Living history program offered only in summer; **Weather:** Average summer high 95°F; average winter low 20°F; average rainfall 48″; average snowfall 5.6″.

GENERAL INFORMATION: *For Your Safety*—Be cautious near the Cumberland River; it is swift and deep. Watch for poison ivy and poisonous snakes. Hikers should walk facing traffic along Park roads.

NEARBY FACILITIES & POINTS OF INTEREST: Campgrounds: TVA Land Between the Lakes, Golden Pond, KY 42231; Paris Landing State Park, Buchanan, TN.

Great Smoky Mountains National Park
Gatlinburg, Tennessee (also in North Carolina)   **SEE CLIMATABLE NO. 26**

MAILING ADDRESS: Superintendent, Great Smoky Mountains National Park, Gatlinburg, TN 37738 **Telephone:** 615-436-1200

DIRECTIONS: The Park Headquarters and Sugarlands Visitor Center are on US 441, 2 miles (3.2 km) south of Gatlinburg, TN. The Oconaluftee Visitor Center is 2 miles (3.2 km) north of Cherokee, NC. There is also a Visitor Center in Cades Cove. Obtain a copy of the "Smokies Guide," a newspaper containing up-to-date information on activities, facilities, and medical services.

The loftiest range east of the Black Hills, and one of the oldest uplands on earth, the

Smokies have a diversified and luxuriant plantlife, with specimens often of extraordinary size. Authorized for full development as part of the National Park System on June 15, 1934.

VISITOR ACTIVITIES: Hiking, camping (available year-round), interpretive programs, nature walks, fishing, auto tours, horseback riding, wildflower- and bird-watching, picnicking; **Permits:** Backcountry camping permits available at any Ranger Station or Visitor Center. A TN or NC fishing permit, available locally, is required; **Fees:** $8 per night for developed campsites; $11 for reservation campgrounds (May 15-Oct. 31); No fee for backcountry campsites; **Visitor facilities:** Restrooms, developed campgrounds, picnic areas, trail shelters, horses for hire, lookout tower, nature and foot trails, limited lodging and supplies; **HANDICAPPED ACCESSIBILITY:** Parking, restrooms at Visitor Centers, Elkmont, Smokemont, Cades Cove, Cataloochee, Abrams Creek Campgrounds; audiotape available for sight-impaired; reading matter for hearing impaired. **Any limitations on vehicle usage:** Motorists should be alert for hazards caused by changing natural conditions. Some secondary roads closed to buses and recreational vehicles; **Hiking trails:** Yes, short, self-guiding nature trails, and more than 900 miles (1,440 km) of foot and horse trails. Trails are open all year (no pets allowed); **Backcountry:** Yes, backcountry permit is required; available at Ranger Stations and Visitor Centers. Pick up a Trail Map and Guide when you obtain your permit; Because of overcrowding, it is necessary to ration several backcountry sites. Check the Trail Map and Guide for specifics; **Camping:** Yes, you must bring your own tent and other camping equipment. Backcountry shelters are located at 13 points along the Appalachian Trail and at Mt. LeConte, Laurel Gap, Kephart Prong, Scott Gap, and Rich Mountain. There are no showers or hookups for trailers. Three developed campgrounds are on the Ticketron reservation system from May 15 through Oct. 31; write Park Superintendent for information. Seven other campgrounds are on a first-come, first-served basis. **Other overnight accommodations on site:** Yes, LeConte Lodge is accessible only by trail, and offers accommodations within the park from late March to early Nov. Allow ½ day to hike up a mountain trail to this secluded retreat. Reservations are necessary; call or write LeConte Lodge, Gatlinburg, TN 37738, 615-436-4473; Wonderland Club Hotel is accessible by car and offers accommodations from late May through October. For rates call or write Wonderland Club Hotel, Route 2, Gatlinburg, TN 37738, 615-436-5490. **Meals served in the park:** Yes, at Wonderland Hotel and LeConte Lodge; **Food and supplies obtainable in the park:** Yes, at Cades Cove Campground; **Food and supplies obtainable nearby:** Yes, at Gatlinburg, Cosby, and Townsend, TN, and Cherokee, and Bryson City, NC; **First Aid available in park:** Yes; **Nearest Hospital:** The Park is served by numerous clinics, medical centers, and hospitals; **Days/Hours:** Open daily year-round; **Holiday Closings:** Visitor Centers closed Dec. 25; **Visitor attractions closed for seasons:** Some picnic areas, campgrounds, roads and other facilities close in winter. See "Smokies Guide" for further information; **Weather:** Wildflowers and migrating birds attract many visitors in late April and early May. If you intend to hike or camp in the Spring, bring warm clothing and be prepared for a variety of weather conditions including frequent rainstorms. Summer days are warm, and nights are usually cool. At higher elevations, temperatures may range from 15-20 degrees lower than those in the valleys. During June and July, the blooming of rhododendrons and azaleas is the outstanding natural event. July and August usually bring the heaviest rainfall, and thunderstorms sometimes come without warning. For greatest comfort on summer hikes, carry a raincoat and insect repellent. Autumn days are cool and clear—ideal for hiking. Winter is the most unpredictable season; yet you shouldn't discount it as a time to visit the Smokies. A quiet peace pervades the park. Be prepared, however, for sudden snowstorms and icy road conditions.

GENERAL INFORMATION: Hikers must be prepared to meet nature on its own terms. *For Your Safety*—Don't travel alone, let someone know your schedule, have proper clothes and equipment, boil all drinking water, and observe park regulations. Stay on the trails, keep off waterfalls and cliff faces, and closely watch and control children. From Nov. through

March, winter gear and clothing suitable for survival in deep snow and -20°F temperatures is necessary. *Bears* may appear tame, but they are dangerous wild animals and should not be approached or fed.

TRAVEL ACCESS: **Air:** Several major airlines provide service to Knoxville, TN, and Asheville, NC.

Obed Wild and Scenic River
Wartburg, Tennessee

MAILING ADDRESS: Unit Manager, Obed Wild and Scenic River, P.O. Box 429, Wartburg, TN 37887 **Telephone:** 615-346-6294

DIRECTIONS: U.S. 27 or State Rt. 62 to Wartburg, TN.
    The Obed Wild and Scenic River consists of a portion of the Emory River, the Obed River, and their two main tributaries, Clear Creek and Daddy's Creek. These fast-flowing rivers have cut into the Cumberland Plateau of East Tennessee, providing some of the most rugged scenery and outstanding whitewater in the Southeast. Authorized for addition to the National Park System on Oct. 12, 1976. **HANDICAPPED ACCESSIBILITY:** The Visitor Center is handicapped accessible. Development within the park is very limited making access difficult for all. No handicapped accessible areas within the park. Minimal access by automobile.

TRAVEL ACCESS: **Bus:** No; **Rail:** No; **Air:** closest commercial terminal is Knoxville/Maryville.

NEARBY FACILITIES & POINTS OF INTEREST: **Hotel/Motel:** Hub Motel, Wartburg, TN, 615-346-3213, 10 miles (16 km); White Oak Lodge, Sunbright, TN, 615-628-2259, 22 miles (35.2 km); **Campgrounds:** Primitive Campground, Frozen Head State Park, Wartburg, TN, 615-346-3318.

Shiloh National Military Park
Shiloh, Tennessee

MAILING ADDRESS: Superintendent, Shiloh National Military Park, Shiloh, TN 38376 **Telephone:** 901-689-5275

DIRECTIONS: The Park is about 10 miles (16 km) south of Savannah and Adamsville, TN, via US 64 and State Route 22 and 23 miles (36.8 km) north of Corinth, MS, via MS 2 and TN 22.
    The fierce battle fought here April 6-7, 1862 prepared the way for Major Gen. U.S. Grant's successful siege of Vicksburg. Well-preserved prehistoric Indian mounds overlook the river. Established by act of Congress on Dec. 27, 1894.

VISITOR ACTIVITIES: Interpretive film and exhibits at Visitor Center, auto tours, hiking, biking, picnicking; **Permits:** No; **Fees:** Yes, $1 ages 17 to 61; **Visitor facilities:** The Visitor Center is 12 miles (19.2 km) south of Savannah, via TN 22 and US 64; **HANDICAPPED ACCESSIBILITY:** Yes; **Any limitations on vehicle usage:** Vehicles must stay on designated roadways; **Hiking trails:** Yes, interpretive military trail and environmental trail; **Backcountry:** No; **Camping:** No; **Other overnight accommodations on site:** No; **Meals served in the park:** No; **Food and supplies obtainable in the park:** No; **Food and supplies obtainable nearby:** Yes, in Shiloh, TN, TN 22; Adamsville and Savannah, TN, US 64; **Overnight**

accommodations: Adamsville, TN, 10 miles (16 km) Savannah, TN, 12 miles (19.2 km); Selmer, TN, 15 miles (24 km), Pickwick Landing, TN, 15 miles (24 km), Corinth, MS, 22 miles (35.2 km); **First Aid available in park:** Yes; **Nearest Hospital:** Savannah, TN, US 64, 12 miles (19.2 km); **Days/Hours:** The Visitor Center is open every day from 8 a.m. to 5 p.m.; **Holiday Closings:** Dec. 25; **Visitor attractions closed for seasons:** No.

GENERAL INFORMATION: You will be sharing the park roads with others. All motorists, hikers, and cyclists should use caution. Be extra careful near the river banks.

TRAVEL ACCESS: Bus: No; **Rail:** ICG, Southern offer service into Memphis, TN; **Air:** Atlantic Southeast provides daily service to Muscle Shoals, AL.

NEARBY FACILITIES & POINTS OF INTEREST: Hotel/Motel: Pickwick Inn, Pickwick Landing State Park, 901-689-3135, 15 miles (24 km); **Campgrounds:** Battlefield Campground, Shiloh, TN, 3 miles (4.8 km); **Parks, other points of interest:** Pickwick Landing State Park.

Stones River National Battlefield and Cemetery
Murfreesboro, Tennessee

MAILING ADDRESS: Superintendent, Stones River National Battlefield and Cemetery, 3501 Old Nashville Highway, Murfreesboro, TN 37129 **Telephone:** 615-893-9501

DIRECTIONS: The Park is in the northwest corner of Murfreesboro, 27 miles (43.2 km) southeast of Nashville on US 41/70S. The Visitor Center should be your first stop, since orientation is necessary.

A fierce midwinter Civil War battle which began the Federal offensive to trisect the Confederacy took place here between Dec. 31, 1862, and Jan. 2, 1863. National Cemetery established June 26, 1865, and National Military Park established March 3, 1927.

VISITOR ACTIVITIES: Slide program, museum, reference library, publication sales, auto tape tours and Visitor Center, self-guiding auto tours, living history weapon demonstrations from mid-June to Aug. on weekends only, biking; **Permits:** No; **Admission:** Free; **Visitor facilities:** Parking, restrooms, picnic area at Visitor Center, hiking trails, interpretive trails; **HANDICAPPED ACCESSIBILITY:** Parking, yes; restrooms, yes. Trails, no. Captioned slide program available on request. Braille guide to Park available; **Any limitations on vehicle**

usage: All motorized vehicles must use existing paved roads and parking areas only; **Hiking trails:** Yes, 2- and 5-mile (3.2- and 8-km) hiking trails, shorter interpretive trails along auto tour; **Backcountry:** No; **Camping:** No; **Other overnight accommodations on site:** No, public campgrounds and motels abound within a 10-mile (16-km) radius of the park; **Meals served in the park:** No, within 2 miles (3.2 km) of the park in Murfreesboro; **Food and supplies obtainable in the park:** No; **Food and supplies obtainable nearby:** Yes, in Murfreesboro; **Overnight accommodations:** Murfreesboro, US 41/70S, TN 96, US 231, and 124. Motels are within 5 miles (8 km) of the park; **First Aid available in park:** Yes; **Nearest Hospital:** In the center of Murfreesboro; **Days/Hours:** Park, Cemetery, and Visitor Center open daily 8 a.m. to 5 p.m.; **Holiday Closings:** Park closed Dec. 25; **Visitor attractions closed for seasons:** Living history programs only offered mid-June-Aug. on weekends only; **Weather:** Temperatures range from 80°-95°F and dry June-Aug.; 45°-75°F, occasional rain (mostly pleasant) Sept.-Nov. and Mar.-May; 20°-40°F, frequent rain, some snow Dec.-Feb.

GENERAL INFORMATION: The oldest Civil War memorial, The Hazen Brigade Monument, is at tour stop 8.

Texas

ALIBATES
NATIONAL MONUMENT

FORT DAVIS NATIONAL
HISTORIC SITE

GUADALUPE MOUNTAINS
NATIONAL PARK

LAKE MEREDITH
NATIONAL RECREATION AREA

LYNDON B. JOHNSON
NATIONAL HISTORICAL PARK

BIG THICKET NATIONAL PRESERVE

CHAMIZAL
NATIONAL MEMORIAL

BIG BEND NATIONAL PARK

RIO GRANDE WILD
AND SCENIC RIVER

AMISTAD NATIONAL
RECREATION AREA

SAN ANTONIO MISSIONS
NATIONAL HISTORICAL PARK

SAN JOSE MISSION
NATIONAL HISTORIC SITE

PADRE ISLAND
NATIONAL SEASHORE

PALO ALTO BATTLEFIELD
NATIONAL HISTORIC SITE

Alibates Flint Quarries National Monument
Fritch, Texas

MAILING ADDRESS: Superintendent, Lake Meredith National Recreation Area, P.O. Box 1438, Fritch, TX 79036 **Telephone:** 806-857-3151

DIRECTIONS: On Rte. 136, 6 miles (9.6 km) south of Fritch, take Alibates Road 5 miles (8 km) to Bates Canyon Information Station at Lake Meredith. Access to Alibates Flint quarries is available only by Ranger-guided tours from Bates Canyon Information Station.

Undeveloped area authorized for addition to the National Park System on Aug. 31, 1965, preserves site where for more than 10,000 years pre-Columbian Indians dug agatized dolomite at these quarries to make projectile points, knives, scrapers, and other tools.

VISITOR ACTIVITIES: Ranger-guided tours given twice daily from Bates Canyon Information Station at Lake Meredith National Recreation Area, exhibits; **Permits:** No; **Fees:** No; **Visitor facilities:** No; **Any limitations on vehicle usage:** No vehicles permitted; **Hiking trails:** Yes, for Ranger-guided tours only; **Backcountry:** No; **Camping:** No; **Other overnight accommodations on site:** No; **Meals served in the park:** No; **Food and supplies obtainable in the park:** No; **Food and supplies obtainable nearby:** Yes, in Fritch, Borger, Dumas, Amarillo; **Overnight accommodations:** Fritch, Borger, Dumas, Amarillo; **First Aid available in park:** No; **Nearest Hospital:** Borger, TX 136, 21 miles (33.6 km); **Days/Hours:** Open 9:30 a.m.-4:30 p.m. from Memorial Day through Labor Day. Tours are generally given at 10 a.m. and 2 p.m. more frequently if need be. Off-season tours are by appointment only; **Holiday Closings:** None in season; **Visitor attractions closed for seasons:** From Labor Day to Memorial Day, except by appointment; **Weather:** Hot in summer, cold in winter, with winds especially high in spring.

GENERAL INFORMATION: The Panhandle Plains Historical Museum, on the campus of West Texas State University, has several exhibits of archaeological material from this region and a model of what a Plains Village structure might look like. The Museum is in Canyon, TX, 16 miles (25.6 km) south of Amarillo.

Amistad National Recreation Area
Del Rio, Texas

MAILING ADDRESS: Superintendent, Amistad Recreation Area, P.O. Box 420367, Del Rio, TX 78842-0367 **Telephone:** 512-775-7491

DIRECTIONS: Park Headquarters and Information Center are located just west of Del Rio on Highway 90.

Amistad (meaning "friendship" in Spanish) offers outstanding opportunities for water recreation. Located at the confluence of the Rio Grande, Devil's, and Pecos River, this international reservoir was created by the construction of Amistad Dam. Established by Congress November 28, 1990; originally managed by National Park Service under a cooperative international agreement.

VISITOR ACTIVITIES: Boating, water skiing, swimming, fishing, hunting and camping on land and from boat, picnicking, hiking; **Permits:** *For fishing*—A Texas fishing license, available at marinas, local hardware and fishing supply shops is required for fishing only on the United States side of the lake. A Mexican fishing license is required to fish in Mexican waters. Mexican licenses are sold at several fishing supply shops in Del Rio, TX and across from Mexican Customs in Cuidad Acuña, Mexico. The license is $20.00 and is good for one year. **Fees:** No; **Visitor facilities:** Ten major boat ramps, designated swim beaches, primitive camping facilities, boat rentals, rental slips, fuel, bait, ice, snacks, and beverages. Gasoline and store facilities are available in nearby towns; **HANDICAPPED ACCESSIBILITY:** Handicapped accessible toilets are available at park headquarters, at the Diablo East, Pecos, and Rough Canyon Areas, in the campgrounds, and at Black Brush launch ramp. Park Headquarters and Governor's Landing amphitheaters are handicapped accessible. Handicapped parking is available at park headquarters, the Diablo East and Pecos launch ramps, and in the campgrounds and picnic areas; **Any limitations on vehicle usage:** Designated areas for driving to the water's edge and boat launching from vehicles permitted only at those sites; **Hiking trails:** No; **Backcountry:** Yes; **Camping:** Yes, 4 campgrounds: 277 North and South, San Pedro Flats, and Governor's Landing. Picnic tables, firegrills, ramadas, and chemical toilets. No water or electricity; **Other overnight accommodations on site:** No; **Meals served in the park:** No; **Food and supplies obtainable in the park:** Yes; **Food and supplies obtainable nearby:** Yes, some supplies at Diablo East and Rough Canyon marinas; **Overnight accommodations:** Commercial campsites are available near Diablo East, Rough Canyon, and Pecos. Motels, travel trailer parks, hotels, restaurant, service stations are in Del Rio and along US 90; **First Aid available in park:** Yes; **Nearest Hospital:** Del Rio, 7 miles (11.2 km); **Days/Hours:** Open daily from 8 a.m.-5 p.m.; **Holiday Closings:** Thanksgiving, Dec. 25, and Jan. 1; **Visitor attractions closed for seasons:** No; **Weather:** Weather is suitable for swimming and water sports for 9 months of the year. December, January, and February will occasionally have low temperatures in the low 30°'sF.

GENERAL INFORMATION: *For Your Safety*—Strong winds can make boating extremely hazardous—and in a very short time. Find a sheltered cove and wait until severe winds subside. It is not safe to stay on the lake during lightning storms. Winters are usually not severe, but extended exposure to wind and water can induce hypothermia. Always watch the weather and dress accordingly. Call 512-775-2115 for a current National Weather Service forecast. Water skiers must wear an approved life-saving device, and an observer must accompany the boat operator. The National Park Service offers free boat safety inspections; check with any Park Ranger.

NEARBY FACILITIES & POINTS OF INTEREST: Hotel/Motel: Amistad Lodge Highway 90 West 512-775-8591 on the Lake (boat ramp approximately 1 mile (1.6 km); Anglers Lodge, Highway 90 West, 512-775-1586, on the Lake (boat ramp approximately 2 miles (3.2 km); **Food/Supplies:** Fina Service Station, Highway 90 West, 512-775-8156, 1 mile (1.6 km) to Diablo East Boat Ramp & Marina; **Campgrounds:** Amistad American, Highway 90 West, 512-775-6484, 3 miles (4.8 km) to Diablo East Boat Ramp & Marina; Amistad Park Campground, Highway 90 West, 512-775-6491, 3 miles (4.8 km) to Diablo East Boat Ramp & Marina; Holiday Trav-L-Park, Highway 90 West, 512-775-7784, 3 miles (4.8 km) to Diablo East Boat Ramp & Marina; **Parks, other points of interest:** Seminole Canyon State Historical Park, Box 806, Comstock, TX 512-292-4464; **Reservation systems in use for campsites; other facilities:** No.

Big Bend National Park
Big Bend National Park, Texas   **SEE CLIMATABLE NO. 31**

MAILING ADDRESS: Superintendent, Big Bend National Park, Big Bend National Park, TX 79834 **Telephone:** 915-477-2251

DIRECTIONS: From San Antonio, it is 410 miles (656 km) to Park headquarters at Panther Junction via US 90 to Marathon and south via US 385. From El Paso, it is 323 miles (516.8

km) to Panther Junction via Int. 10 to Van Horn, US 90 to Alpine, and south via TX 118; or it is 353 miles (564.8 km) via US 67 to Presidio and Texas Ranch Road 170—the "Camino del Rio." The Headquarters building is 27 miles (43.5 km) off Hwy 385, 70 miles (112 km) south of Marathon or 25 miles east of Study Butte.

Mountain scenery contrasts with Chihuahuan Desert in this great bend of the Rio Grande, where a variety of unusual geological structures are found. Authorized for addition to the National Park System on June 20, 1935.

VISITOR ACTIVITIES: Interpretive programs, camping, hiking, horseback riding, picnicking, fishing, walking and auto tours, boating, biking, bird-watching; **Permits:** For backcountry camping and boating on the Rio Grande available from Headquarters; **Fees:** Yes, entrance fee, and fees are charged for camping at developed campsites and concessioner-operated trailer sites; **Visitor facilities:** Campgrounds, hiking trails, evening talks, lodge, food service, trailer parks, picnic tables, showers, stores, service stations, public telephones, post office, rental saddle horses and pack animals, laundry, restrooms; **Any limitations on vehicle usage:** No off-road travel permitted; take the numerous road dips slowly, trailers over 20 feet are not advised to try to enter the Basin, or the 5 miles (8 km) continuous grade out of Castolon; **Hiking trails:** Yes, check at Headquarters for information on the many trails; **Backcountry:** Yes, information can be obtained from Headquarters; **Camping:** Yes, no reservations available for individual campsites; **Other overnight accommodations on site:** Yes, trailer parks and lodge. For reservations at Chisos Mountain Lodge, write to National Park Concessions, Inc., Big Bend National Park, TX 79834, phone 915-477-2291; **Meals served in the park:** Yes, at Chisos Mountain Lodge; **Food and supplies obtainable in the park:** Yes, limited supplies available at the Basin, Rio Grande Village, Castolon, and Panther Junction; **Food and supplies obtainable nearby:** Yes, at Alpine and Study Butte; **Overnight accommodations:** Terlingua, TX 118, 23 miles (36.8 km), Lajitas, TX 118 and TX Ranch Road 170, 39 miles (62.4 km) and in Marathon at the junction of US 385 and US 90, 70 miles (112 km) from Headquarters; **First Aid available in park:** Yes; **Nearest Hospital:** Alpine, 108 miles (172.8 km) from Headquarters; **Days/Hours:** Park is always open. Information desk open from 8 a.m. to 6 p.m. with extended hours during busy periods; **Holiday Closings:** No; **Visitor attractions closed for seasons:** No; **Weather:** Winter is nippy in the mountains and comfortably warm during the day in the lowlands. Once or twice a year snow falls in the mountains. Spring weather arrives early. Midsummer temperatures in desert and river valley are likely to hover above 100° during the day. This is the best time to go to the mountains. In the Basin (5400-foot elevation), daytime temperatures average a comfortable 85°F, and nights are cool. Autumn is usually warm.

GENERAL INFORMATION: Be sure to obtain a pamphlet describing regulations and precautions, available at Headquarters. Carry your own first-aid supplies, including tweezers to extract cactus spines. Carry drinking water on the trail and in the desert. Check with a Park Ranger before traveling on any of the primitive roads. Wear stout shoes and tough clothing while you are hiking. Stay on the trails.

Big Thicket National Preserve
Beaumont, Texas

MAILING ADDRESS: Superintendent, Big Thicket National Preserve, 3785 Milam, Beaumont, TX 77701 **Telephone:** 409-839-2689

DIRECTIONS: The Preserve is located in southeastern Texas. The 12 separate units are bounded by US 96 on the east, US 90 on the south, US 59 on the west and US 190 on the north. Write or call in advance for a map of the area and information on facilities and activities in each area. The Preserve's headquarters is at 3785 Milam, Beaumont. A small Visitor Station is in the southern end of the Turkey Creek Unit, on FM 420, 2½ miles (4 km) off the Hwy 69, phone 409-246-2337. Reservations are required for all naturalist-led programs and can be made at the Information Station.

The Preserve contains 86,000 acres composed of 12 units of various sizes spread over 3,600 square miles. It is an area of great plant diversity caused by the convergence of several major plant communities. Plants and animals representing southeastern swamps, Appalachians, eastern forests, central plains, and southwest deserts can be found in the Preserve. Established by act of Congress on October 11, 1974.

VISITOR ACTIVITIES: Due to the Preserve status, development of visitor facilities will be minimal. There are hiking and nature trails in four Preserve units. Nearly 1,000 flowering plants, including four types of carnivorous plants, bloom in the Preserve with spring being peak wildflower season. Birding is a favorite activity, especially during spring and fall. From late March to early May many bird species pass through on their way to northern nesting grounds. Fall migrations occur in October and November. There are picnic sites, some with barbecue grills, in many of the units; contained charcoal grills (hibachi-type) are also allowed. Collecting wood and open fires are prohibited. Boating is popular on the Neches River, Pine Island Bayou, and along Village Creek. Few water access points have been developed, but you can launch at most road crossings. Some boat ramps located on private property charge a launch fee. A self-guided canoe trip is available that travels through an open bayou to a backwater slough. Fishing is allowed in all waters. A Texas fishing license is required and State laws apply. Hunting and trapping are allowed only in specific areas at certain dates and times. A permit from the Superintendent is required. Please write or call Preserve headquarters for details. Naturalist programs include guided hikes, talks, and guided boat tours and canoe trips. Individuals and groups can call (409) 246-2337 for information and reservations. The Roy E. Larson Sandyland Sanctuary is a privately-owned area that protects some of the best examples of arid sandylands found in the Big Thicket region. A hiking trail is open to the public. Special tours may be arranged by contacting Caretaker, Roy E. Larson Sandyland Sanctuary, P.O. Box 909, Silsbee, TX 77656. **Permits:** A backcountry camping permit is required for overnight camping, available at Information Station; **Fees:** No; **Visitor facilities:** A Visitor Information Station is located in the Turkey Creek Unit on FM420. Hiking trails and picnic areas are available; **HANDICAPPED ACCESSIBILITY:** Picnic tables, parking, and restrooms are available at the Information Station and Sundew Trail. Parking and restrooms are available at Pitcher Plant Trail. The Pitcher Plant and Sundew Trails are handicapped accessible. **Any limitations on vehicle usage:** Vehicles must stay on public roads. No motorized vehicles of any kind are permitted on Preserve trails. **Hiking trails:** Yes, Kirby Nature Trail, 2½ miles (4 km); Turkey Creek Trail, 15 miles (24 km), Pitcher Plant, ¼ mile (.4 km); Sundew Trail, 1 mile (1.6 km); Woodlands Trail, 6 miles (9.6 km); Beech Woods Trail, 1 mile (1.6 km); Beaver Slide Trail, 1.5 miles (2.4 km); Big Sandy Horse Trail, 18 miles (28.8 km) round trip. Horses and all-terrain bicycles are permitted only on the Big Sandy Horse Trail. **Backcountry:** Yes, write the Superintendent for information; **Camping:** There are no developed campgrounds. Several private and public campgrounds nearby offer tent and recreational vehicle sites. Primitive backcountry camping with permit, for groups up to 8 persons, is available in certain areas of the Preserve. Permits are free and good up to 5 nights. Open fires are not allowed in the backcountry. **Other overnight accommodations on site:** No; **Meals served in the park;** No; **Food and supplies obtainable in the park:** No; **Food and supplies obtainable nearby:** Yes, at Beaumont, Kountze, Woodville, Silsbee; **Overnight accommodations:** Beaumont, Woodville, Kountze, Silsbee; **First Aid available in park:** Yes; **Nearest Hospital:** Beaumont, Woodville, Silsbee; **Days/Hours:** 24 hours a day, 364 days a year. Information Station is open 9 a.m. to 5 p.m., seven days a week; **Holiday Closings:** Dec. 25; **Visitor attractions closed for season:** No; **Weather:** Summers are hot and humid;

temperature and humidity combined often make it feel over 100 degrees; winters are cool and wet.

GENERAL INFORMATION: *For Your Safety*—Wear clothing suitable for weather extremes. Carry plenty of drinking water and do not drink from any creeks or ponds. To avoid becoming disoriented in the woods, especially on cloudy days, carry a good compass, a map, and stay on the established trails. If you canoe or boat, wear a life jacket, take a partner and a first aid kit, let someone know where you are going, and don't overload the boat. Beware of snakes, four types of poisonous snakes are found in the Preserve. Do not kill any snake, they are protected here as part of the natural scene. Watch out for poison ivy, ticks, wasps, hornets, chiggers, mosquitoes, and fire ants. Use plenty of repellent and watch where where you sit or stand.

Pets must be on a leash or otherwise restrained at all times. Pets are not allowed on trails or in backcountry. Plants and animals must not be disturbed or removed. All of the lands adjoining the Preserve units are in private ownership. If in doubt, don't trespass.

Chamizal National Memorial
El Paso, Texas

MAILING ADDRESS: Superintendent, Chamizal National Memorial, 800 S. San Marcial, El Paso, TX 79905 **Telephone:** 915-532-7273

DIRECTIONS: The Memorial is in south-central metropolitan El Paso immediately adjacent to the international boundary. Entrances to the park are from San Marcial Street and Delta Drive.

The Memorial commemorates the Chamizal Settlement of 1963, which ended a bitter century-long territorial dispute between the United States and Mexico. It also presents the history of the 2,000 mile border since 1848, and the diplomatic problems created by natural river processes. An amphitheater and a 500 seat theater are used for musical, dance, and theatrical presentations from the United States and abroad. Authorized for addition to the National Park System June 30, 1966.

VISITOR ACTIVITIES: Picnicking, interpretive exhibits, arts and crafts presentations and film, guided tours, theatrical performances; Border Folk Festival the first weekend in October, Classic Spanish Drama Festival in March, Border Jazz Festival Memorial Day Weekend, Zarzuela Festival July-August; **Permits:** No; **Fees:** No entrance fee is charged, but tickets are sold for some special theatrical performances; **Visitor facilities:** Parking and picnic areas, auditorium, restrooms; **Any limitations on vehicle usage:** No; **Hiking trails:** No; **Backcountry:** No; **Camping:** No; **Other overnight accommodations on site:** No; **Meals served in the park:** No; **Food and supplies obtainable in the park:** No; **Food and supplies obtainable nearby:** Yes, downtown El Paso, west of the park; **Overnight accommodations:** El Paso; **First Aid available in park:** Yes; **Nearest Hospital:** El Paso, North Stanton, 3 miles (4.8 km); **Days/Hours:** 8 a.m. to 5 p.m. (to 11 p.m. on evenings of cultural events) year-round; **Holiday Closings:** No; **Visitor attractions closed for seasons:** No.

GENERAL INFORMATION: Directly across the Rio Grande, the Republic of the United Mexican States has established a companion park on a portion of Mexico's Chamizal land. You are encouraged to visit the park, which includes formal gardens, outstanding architectural structures, a museum of art and history, an outdoor archeological museum, and statuary.

TRAVEL ACCESS: Bus: Local bus transportation to Park entrance hourly; **Rail:** Amtrak provides service to El Paso; **Air:** American, Continental, America West, Delta, United, Southwest, and other carriers service El Paso.

NEARBY FACILITIES & POINTS OF INTEREST: Campgrounds: KOA, commercial camps, 6-8 miles (9.6-12.8 km) from Memorial; **Parks, other points of interest:** Chamizal Park of Mexico, 19 museums, 3 State Parks; Call 915-534-6668 or 532-7273 for information on programs (about 225 different programs per year, multi-lingual and multi-cultural, in the fine arts and folk arts, of Chamizal).

Fort Davis National Historic Site
Fort Davis, Texas

MAILING ADDRESS: Superintendent, Fort Davis National Historic Site, P.O. Box 1456, Fort Davis, TX 79734 **Telephone:** 915-426-3225/4

DIRECTIONS: The Site is on the northern edge of the town of Fort Davis, TX. It can be reached from Interstate 10 on the north, US 90 on the south by Texas 17 and 118, and US 90 on the east by Texas 505, 166, and 17. Marfa is 21 miles (33.6 km) to the southeast.

A key post in the West Texas defensive system, the fort guarded emigrants on the San Antonio-El Paso road from 1854 to 1891. Authorized for addition to the National Park System on Sept. 8, 1961.

VISITOR ACTIVITIES: Self-guiding tours of buildings and grounds. During June, July, and August refurnished Commanding Officer's Quarters, Enlisted Men's barracks, and Officer's Kitchen and Servant's Quarters open to public with interpreters dressed in styles of the 1880s; Post Hospital, Lieutenant's Quarters, and Commissary open for self-guided tour; picnicking, interpretive exhibits, audiovisual programs, hiking; **Permits:** Yes, obtainable at the Visitor Center; **Fees:** Entrance fee is $1 per person; Golden Age, Golden Access, and Golden Eagle Passports are accepted and available; **Visitor facilities:** Parking, restrooms at Visitor Center, hiking trails; **HANDICAPPED ACCESSIBILITY:** Parking, water fountain, free electric cart available at Visitor Center, ramps to other buildings, paved ramp to level, grassy picnic area; restrooms at Visitor Center being made accessible—call to check; written script and explanations available for hearing impaired, TTY-TDD available—call 915-426-3224; interpreters available for visually impaired; some refurbished buildings have objects that may be handled; **Any limitations on vehicle usage:** No driving tours in the park. Electric golf cart is available for handicapped persons only; **Hiking trails:** Yes, 3 miles (4.8 km) of moderately strenuous hiking trails; **Backcountry:** No; **Camping:** No; **Other overnight accommodations on site:** No; **Meals served in the park:** No, but there are several restaurants in the Fort Davis area; **Food and supplies obtainable in the park:** No; **Food and supplies obtainable nearby:** Yes, in the Fort Davis area and at "Indian Lodge" in the Davis Mountain State Park, 4 miles (6.4 km) west on TX 118; **Overnight accommodations:** In Fort Davis and at nearby Davis Mountain State Park. The telephone number for reservations is 915-426-3254; **First Aid available in park:** Yes, Fort Davis Volunteer Ambulance Service available; **Nearest Hospital:** Alpine, TX 26 miles (41.6 km); **Days/Hours:** Open daily from 8 a.m. to 5 p.m., until 6 p.m. in summer; **Holiday Closings:** Dec. 25; **Visitor attractions closed for seasons:** Living history programs offered in summer; **Weather:** Average annual temperature is 63°, summer 60°-90°, winter 20°-60°.

GENERAL INFORMATION: Carlsbad Caverns, Guadalupe Mountains, and Big Bend National Parks are within easy drive (see listings in this book).

TRAVEL ACCESS: Bus: Trailways Bus System provides service to Marfa, 21 miles

(33.6 km) from Park; **Rail:** Southern Pacific/Amtrak provide service to Alpine 26 miles (41.6 km) from Park; **Air:** Nearest commercial air terminals in El Paso, 200 miles (320 km) or Midland-Odessa, 170 miles (272 km).

NEARBY FACILITIES & POINTS OF INTEREST: Hotel/Motel: In Fort Davis: Limpia Hotel and Stone Village Motel, in Davis Mountain State Park: Indian Lodge; **Parks, other points of interest:** McDonald Observatory, 17 miles (27.2 km) northwest of Park.

Guadalupe Mountains National Park
Texas   **SEE CLIMATABLE NO. 32**

MAILING ADDRESS: Superintendent, Guadalupe Mountains National Park, HC 60, Box 400, Salt Flat, TX 79847-9400 **Telephone:** 915-828-3251 (Visitor Information and Administration)

DIRECTIONS: The Park is in western Texas, on Hwy 62-180, 55 miles (88 km) southwest of Carlsbad, NM, and 110 miles (176 km) east of El Paso, TX. Van Horn, TX, is 65 miles (104 km) south on Hwy 54. Stop first at the new Headquarters Visitor Center at Pine Springs on Hwy 62-180.

Rising abruptly from the desert, this mountain mass exposes portions of one of the world's most extensive and significant Permian limestone fossil reefs. Also noted for a tremendous earth fault, lofty peaks, rugged canyons, unusual flora and fauna. Authorized for addition to the National Park System on Oct. 15, 1966, established Sept. 30, 1972.

VISITOR ACTIVITIES: Mainly hiking and backpacking. Two drive-in campgrounds, horseback riding (bring your own horse), guided tours, and evening programs in summer; **Permits:** For overnight backcountry trips; obtained free at Visitor Center; **Fees:** $5 per site camping fee at Pine Springs Campground and at Dog Canyon Campground; no fee for backcountry permit; **Visitor facilities:** Visitor Center provides book store, information, exhibits, Orientation Program, restrooms, and water. Pine Springs Campground, vehicle campground, tent and RV sites (no hookups), offers flush toilets, picnic tables; located 1/4 (.4 km) west of Visitor Center. Limited road access to areas of park. Picnic area, exhibits, book sales at McKittrick Canyon; **HANDICAPPED ACCESSIBILITY:** Pine Springs Campground: 1 site designated for handicapped; restrooms accessible; New Visitor Center at Pine Springs: Fully accessible—exhibit area, theater, restroom, plans for accessible 1/4-1/2 mile (.4-.8 km) nature loop; McKittrick Canyon Visitor Center: Parking, restrooms, and display area; **Any limitations on vehicle usage:** Existing roads are limited: approximately 4 miles (6.4 km) of Hwy 62-180 travels through the park, 5 miles (8 km) paved road provides access from Hwy 62-180 to the mouth of McKittrick Canyon, and a 7-mile (11.2-km) 4-wheel drive road to Williams Ranch Historic Site requires permission to travel and a key to a locked gate (obtained at Visitor Center). No off-road vehicle use, no vehicles allowed on foot trails. NM State 137 and County Road 414 lead to Dog Canyon (northern side of the Park) all but 1 mile (1.6 km) paved; **Hiking trails:** Yes, over 80 miles (128 km) of hiking trails, in rugged mountainous terrain. **Backcountry:** Yes, contact Visitor Center. Hikers must sign in and out at trail registers and obtain free permits before starting overnight hikes. Hikers must carry all water. Topographic maps are for sale at Visitor Center; **Camping:** Yes, vehicle campgrounds at Pine Springs and Dog Canyon, also designated backcountry campsites, all on a first-come, first-served basis. No overnight lodging available in or near the park; **Other overnight accommodations on site:** No; **Meals served in the park:** No; **Food and supplies obtainable in the park:** Yes, *limited* supply at Pine Spring Cafe (Hwy 62-180); **Food and supplies obtainable nearby:** Yes, Nearest food service: Carlsbad, NM, and Van Horn 62/180 Junction, Van Horn

Jct, Nickel Creek, and El Paso, Van Horn, and Dell City, TX; **Overnight accommodations:** Whites City, NM (34 miles, 54.4 km), Carlsbad, NM US 62-180, 55 miles (88 km); Van Horn, TX, 65 miles (104 km); and El Paso, TX, US 62-180, 110 miles (176 km); **First Aid available in park:** Limited; **Nearest Hospital:** Carlsbad, NM, US 62-180, 55 miles (88 km); **Days/Hours:** Visitor Center open daily (including holidays and weekends, except Dec. 25) 8 a.m to 4:30 p.m., later in summer, campground open daily. McKittrick Canyon hiking area open only during daylight hours, gate closes at night; **Holiday Closings:** Visitor Center closed Dec. 25; **Visitor attractions closed for seasons:** Visitor use areas open all year except during occasional emergency situations caused by bad weather conditions; **Weather:** Anticipate storms and sudden weather changes. Thunderstorms are common in summer; freezing rain and occasional snowstorms in winter. Violent winds in spring and winter. Summer temperatures are extreme and winter temperatures usually mild but can suddenly drop to lows below freezing. Potential backpackers can call Visitor Center, 915-828-3251, for current weather conditions and forecasts.

GENERAL INFORMATION: *Safety Precautions:* Check with Park Ranger before hiking. Do not climb cliffs; rocks are unstable and considered unsuitable for technical climbing. Beware of cactus and spiny plants. Watch for and respect rattlesnakes during warmer months of the year. If planning a hike or backpack trip, come prepared; sturdy broken-in boots, a tent, tough clothing, cold-weather gear in winter, water repellent clothing for winter and summer, and capability to carry all your own water (one gallon per person per day is recommended).

Important regulations: Before bringing your pet, remember pets are not allowed on hiking trails and high summer and low winter temperatures make leaving your pet in a vehicle dangerous for the animal. The display or use of firearms is prohibited.

Lake Meredith National Recreation Area
Fritch, Texas

MAILING ADDRESS: Superintendent, Lake Meredith National Recreation Area, P.O. Box 1438, Fritch, TX 79036 **Telephone:** 806-857-3151

DIRECTIONS: The Park Headquarters building is on Hwy 136 in Fritch. Information about facilities at the various recreation sites is available here.

Man-made Lake Meredith on the Canadian River is a popular water-activity center in the southwest. On the south side of the lake, Alibates Flint Quarries National Monument can be seen by free guided tours in summer and by prior appointment at other times of the year. See Alibates listing in this book. Lake Meredith National Recreation Area established by act of Congress on Mar. 15, 1965.

VISITOR ACTIVITIES: Boating, water skiing, canoeing, fishing, picnicking, swimming, camping, hunting, scuba diving, sailing, motorcycling, interpretive exhibits; **Permits:** Texas hunting and fishing licenses available from Texas Parks and Wildlife Department or at local sporting goods stores; **Fees:** No entrance or camping fees; **Visitor facilities:** Marinas, restrooms, drinking water, beaches, launching ramps, picnic and camping areas, snack bar; **Any limitations on vehicle usage:** Boats are subject to Federal and State regulations; **Hiking trails:** No; **Backcountry:** Yes, topographic maps and information available from park Headquarters; **Camping:** Yes, no reservations available for campsites. Campers may stay up to 14 days. No camping is allowed in the launching areas or parking lots. Private campgrounds with hookups are located in nearby towns; **Other overnight accommodations on site:** No; **Meals served in the park:** Yes, snacks available at Sanford-Yake marina; **Food and supplies obtainable in the park:** Yes, limited picnic supplies at Sanford-Yake marina; **Food and**

supplies obtainable nearby: Yes, in Fritch, Sanford, Borger, Amarillo, Dumas; **Overnight accommodations:** Fritch, Borger, Amarillo, Dumas; **First Aid available in park:** No; **Nearest Hospital:** Borger, Hwy 136, 15 miles (24 km); Dumas, Hwy 13-19 to 19-13 to 152, 20 miles (32 km); Amarillo, Hwy 136, 25-45 miles (40-72 km); **Days/Hours:** Park never closes; **Holiday Closings:** No; **Visitor attractions closed for seasons:** Activities are curtailed and many areas closed due to inclement weather in winter; **Weather:** Summers are hot, with temperatures above 100°F on some days. Winters are cold; high winds in spring.

GENERAL INFORMATION: Boaters should be familiar with Federal and State boating regulations, which can be obtained from Park Rangers or from Lake Meredith headquarters. Listen for storm warnings! A sudden storm wind can reach 80 mph so fast that boats may have trouble getting off the lake. Get your boat to shore in a sheltered area and wait out the storm if ramps cannot be reached safely.

Lyndon B. Johnson National Historical Park
Johnson City, and Stonewall, Texas

MAILING ADDRESS: Superintendent, Lyndon B. Johnson National Historical Park, P.O. Box 329, Johnson City, TX 78636 **Telephone:** 512-868-7128

DIRECTIONS: There are 2 units to the park, 1 in Johnson City and 1 near Stonewall. Johnson City and Stonewall are about 50 miles (80 km) west of Austin and 60 miles (96 km) north of San Antonio. Both are located on US 290, an east-west highway connecting Austin and Fredericksburg. North-South US 281 connects San Antonio and Wichita Falls. In Johnson City, stop first at the Visitor Center in the center of town. Near Stonewall, begin your visit at the Visitor Center of the LBJ State Historical Park.

The Park includes the birthplace, boyhood home, grandfather's settlement, ranch, and gravesite of the 36th President of the United States. Authorized for addition to the National Park System on Dec. 2, 1969.

VISITOR ACTIVITIES: Johnson City has guided tours of the boyhood home and the pioneer settlement of his grandparents. Stonewall: Free tour buses to Johnson's school, birthplace, family cemetery, gravesite, and the LBJ Ranch. All bus tours are about 90 minutes long; **Permits:** No; **Fees:** No; **Visitor facilities:** Parking, restrooms, interpretive activities. A full range of facilities is available in the surrounding area; **HANDICAPPED ACCESSIBILITY:** Parking, restrooms, interpretive activities; **Any limitations on vehicle usage:** Access to the LBJ Ranch is by tour bus only. Access to the Johnson Settlement is by 1/4-mile (.4 km) walking trail; **Hiking trails:** No; **Backcountry:** No; **Camping:** No, but camping is available in Lady Bird Johnson Municipal Park in Fredericksburg, Pedernales Falls State Park, and Blanco State Park. There are a number of other state and commercial facilities in the immediate area. Contact the Park for further information; **Other overnight accommodations on site:** No; **Meals served in the park:** No; **Food and supplies obtainable in the park:** No; **Food and supplies obtainable nearby:** Yes, in Johnson City, Stonewall, and Fredericksburg, TX; **Overnight accommodations:** Johnson City, Stonewall, Blanco, and Fredericksburg; **First Aid available in park:** Yes; **Nearest Hospital:** Fredericksburg, 30 miles (48 km) west of Johnson City and 17 miles (27.2 km) west of LBJ Ranch; **Days/Hours:** Johnson City: 9 a.m. to 5 p.m. every day; Stonewall: By tour bus only, 10 a.m. to 4:00 p.m. daily; **Holiday Closings:** Dec. 25 LBJ Ranch, and Dec. 25 and Jan. 1 at Boyhood Home and Settlement; **Visitor attractions closed for seasons:** No; **Weather:** Moderate weather. Summer temperatures are in the mid to upper 90°sF but there is usually a light breeze. Winters average about 40°F with occasional showers. It rarely snows; rain occasionally freezes on the roads. Summer tours may be shortened when temperature and humidity criteria exceed predetermined comfort levels.

GENERAL INFORMATION: Advance reservations are required for assured group tours. Groups arriving without reservations may experience long delays prior to being accommodated. Arrangements may be made by calling 512-868-7128.

Padre Island National Seashore
Corpus Christi, Texas

MAILING ADDRESS: Superintendent, Padre Island National Seashore, 9405 S. Padre Island Dr., Corpus Christi, TX 78418-5597 **Telephone:** 512-937-2621

DIRECTIONS: The only motor vehicle access to the National Seashore is from the north end. There are two approaches: The first leads over a causeway from Corpus Christi to North Padre Island (Park Road 22), the other leads from Port Aransas down Mustang Island via Park Road 53. The Visitor Center is approximately 10 miles (16 km) south of the junction of Park Roads 53 and 22.

Noted for its wide sand beaches, excellent fishing, outstanding sailboarding, and abundant bird and marine life, this barrier island stretches along the Gulf Coast for 66 miles (105.6 km). Authorized for addition to the National Park System on Sept. 28, 1962.

VISITOR ACTIVITIES: Beach driving, fishing, swimming, wind surfing, sailing, boating, surfing bird- and wildlife-watching, hiking, shelling, water-skiing, interpretive exhibits and programs; **Permits:** Texas State fishing license required for those between 17 and 65 years of age, salt water fishing stamp required; **Fees:** $3 per vehicle entrance fee, 7 day stay, or $10 Annual Pass; $5 camping fee ($2.50 with Golden Age Passports) at Malaquite Beach Campground; **Visitor facilities:** Nature trails; A Visitor Center with information, exhibits and a small book store is open 7 days a week. Rangers are on duty to answer questions and provide information. The Padre Island Park Company operates a concessions store. The store provides snacks, ice and beach items. A boat ramp is available at Bird Island Basin; **HANDICAPPED ACCESSIBILITY:** The Malaquite Beach Visitor Center, Bath House, and the Padre Island Park Company are fully accessible. Handicapped accessible restrooms are available throughout the park; **Any limitations on vehicle usage:** Valid state drivers license. Vehicles must remain on the roads and the beach. Driving on the beach in front of the campground is prohibited; **Hiking trails:** Yes, self-guiding nature trail; **Backcountry:** No; **Camping:** Yes, no reservations available for campsites; open camping permitted on 7-1/2 miles (12 km) of beach accessible by all 2-wheel-drive vehicles. Open camping on 50 miles (80 km) of beach accessible by 4-wheel-drive vehicles. **Other overnight accommodations on site:** No, a paved campground with 42 sites, located south of the Ranger Station on the beach, can be used by trailers and recreational vehicles. Hookups are not provided. Rinse-off showers and flush toilets are provided. Hook-ups are available at Padre Balli County Park, and at Mustang Island State Park north of the National Seashore boundary. For information on camping rates and facilities, write Nueces County Parks, 10901 South Padre Island Dr., Box 3G, Corpus Christi, TX 78418; **Snacks served in the park:** Snacks are available; **Food and supplies obtainable in the park:** Padre Island Park Company provides snacks and beach supplies; **Food and supplies obtainable nearby:** Full service at Corpus Christi, about 16 miles (25.6 km) north of the seashore boundary, on the Park Road 22; **Overnight accommodations:** Corpus Christi and North Padre Island; **First Aid available in park:** Yes, year-round at Gulf District Ranger Station and at the Malaquite Visitor Center; **Nearest Hospital:** Take crosstown freeway to Morgan Exit. Memorial Medical Center has emergency services; **Days/Hours:** Park always open; **Holiday Closings:** No; **Visitor attractions closed for seasons:** No; **Weather:** Summer is usually quite humid, hot, and windy. Late fall is temperate and mild. Late winter has many northers; cold and rainy spring.

GENERAL INFORMATION: *Beware of the following hazards:* —overexposure to the sun, swimming alone, rattlesnakes, Portuguese man-of-war jellyfish, small stingrays, fishing lines, broken glass and boards with nails, getting your car stuck in the sand, vehicle traffic on the beach, medical waste, toxic waste in mislabeled or unmarked drums washed up on beach. Always wear shoes when hiking. Phone 512-949-8175 for a recorded informational message on beach condition. Visitor Center open at Malaquite Beach, 512-949-8068.

TRAVEL ACCESS: Air: American, Southwest, Eastern, Continental, and others service Corpus Christi, TX.

NEARBY FACILITIES & POINTS OF INTEREST: Hotel/Motel: For full information, contact Corpus Christi Chamber of Commerce, 512-882-6161, 1201 N. Shoreline, Corpus Christi, TX 78401.

Palo Alto Battlefield National Historic Site
Brownsville, Texas

MAILING ADDRESS: Palo Alto Battlefield National Historic Site, c/o Padre Island National Seashore, 9405 South Padre Island Dr., Corpus Christi, TX 78418 **Telephone:** 512-937-2621

DIRECTIONS: NOT YET OPEN TO PUBLIC. NO VISITOR FACILITIES.
This area commemorates the site of one of two Mexican war battles fought on U.S. soil. Authorized for addition to the National Park Service on Nov. 10, 1978.

Rio Grande Wild and Scenic River
Texas

MAILING ADDRESS: c/o Superintendent, Big Bend National Park, TX 79834 **Telephone:** (915) 477-2251 or for River Information (915) 477-2393

DIRECTIONS: This is an undeveloped area administered by Big Bend National Park. It extends from Mariscal Canyon in Big Bend National Park to the Terrell/Val Verde County line. See Big Bend National Park for directions.
Authorized for addition to the National Park System on Nov. 10, 1978, to preserve a 191-mile (305.6-km) segment of the Rio Grande from above Mariscal Canyon in Big Bend National Park to Terrell/Val Verde County line in Texas.

VISITOR ACTIVITIES: Canoeing and rafting year-round; **Permits:** Required for floating. May be obtained at Persimmon Gap Visitor Center at the North Entrance of Big Bend National Park and any Ranger Station in the park; **Fees:** Entrance fee applicable; **Visitor facilities:** Visitor Centers at Persimmon Gap and Rio Grande Village. Developed campground, store, trailer village, amphitheater at Rio Grande Village. No visitor facilities in the Lower Canyons outside of Big Bend National Park; **Any limitations on vehicle usage:** All vehicles must stay on developed roads. Little or no access to the Lower Canyons; **Hiking trails:** Only in Big Bend National Park; **Backcountry:** Primitive roadside camping in Big Bend National Park; **Camping:** Backcounty camping in Lower Canyons, developed campgrounds in Big Bend; **Other overnight accommodations on site:** None near the Lower Canyons. See Big Bend National Park; **Meals served in the park:** See Big Bend; **Food and supplies obtainable in the park:** See Big Bend; **Food and supplies obtainable nearby:** See Big Bend; **First**

Aid available in park: At any Ranger Station; **Nearest Hospital:** Alpine TX, 100 miles (160 km) from park headquarters; **Days/Hours:** N/A; **Holiday Closings:** No; **Visitor attractions closed for seasons:** Rio Grande Village Visitor Center closed June to Oct.; **Weather:** Summer is hot; mild the rest of the year.

GENERAL INFORMATION: Floating the Lower Canyons requires approximately 7 days. There are no take-out points between La Linda Mexico and Dryden Crossing, 83 miles (132.8 km). In an emergency parties should be prepared to evacuate themselves, rescue is difficult and patrols infrequent. Within the park there are 2 canyons (Mariscal and Boquillas) that are relatively easy and numerous put-in points. Write to park for equipment requirements.

TRAVEL ACCESS: See Big Bend National Park.

San Antonio Missions National Historical Park
San Antonio, Texas

MAILING ADDRESS: 2202 Roosevelt Avenue, San Antonio, TX 78210-4919 **Telephone:** 512-229-5701

DIRECTIONS: The Park preserves Missions Concepcion, San Jose, San Juan, and Espada, which represent, along with the Alamo, the country's greatest concentration of 18th-Century Spanish Colonial missions. The Alamo (Mission San Antonio de Valero) is not included in the Park. The Park also preserves Mission Espada's irrigation system, which consists of a stone dam and aqueduct and about 5 miles (8 km) of irrigation ditch (acequia). It is the country's best preserved Spanish Colonial irrigation system. This affiliated area was authorized for addition to the National Park System on Nov. 10, 1978, and began operation on Apr. 1, 1983.

VISITOR ACTIVITIES: Walking tours; **Permits:** No; **Fees:** No; **Visitor facilities:** Parking and restrooms; **HANDICAPPED ACCESSIBILITY:** Missions San Jose and Concepcion are accessible for individuals with impaired mobility. At Missions San Juan and Espada, the walks are graveled and challenging for individuals with mobile difficulty. **Any limitations on vehicle usage:** No; **Hiking trails:** No; **Backcountry:** No; **Camping:** No; **Other overnight accommodations on site:** No; **Meals served in the park:** No; **Food and supplies obtainable in the park:** No; **Food and supplies obtainable nearby:** Yes, in San Antonio; **Overnight accommodations:** San Antonio; **First Aid available in park:** Yes; **Nearest Hospital:** San Antonio; **Days/Hours:** Open daily from 9 a.m. to 6 p.m., during Daylight Savings Time and 8 a.m. to 5 p.m., during Standard Time; **Holiday Closings:** Dec. 25, Jan. 1; **Visitor attractions closed for seasons:** No.

GENERAL INFORMATION: There is a short .3 mile (.48 km) Nature Trail located at Mission San Juan.

Utah

GOLDEN SPIKE HISTORIC SITE

MORMON PIONEER
NATIONAL HISTORIC TRAIL

DINOSAUR NATIONAL MONUMENT

TIMPANOGOS CAVE NATIONAL MONUMENT

ARCHES NATIONAL PARK
CANYONLANDS NATIONAL PARK
CAPITOL REEF NATIONAL PARK

NATURAL BRIDGES NATIONAL MONUMENT
HOVENWEEP NATIONAL MONUMENT

RAINBOW BRIDGE NATIONAL MONUMENT

ZION
NATIONAL PARK

GLEN CANYON NATIONAL RECREATION AREA

CEDAR BREAKS
NATIONAL MONUMENT

BRYCE CANYON NATIONAL PARK

Salt Lake City

Arches National Park
Moab, Utah   **SEE CLIMATABLE NO. 33**

MAILING ADDRESS: Superintendent, Arches National Park, P.O. Box 907, Moab, UT 84532 **Telephone:** 801-259-8161

DIRECTIONS: The Visitor Center is 5 miles (8 km) northwest of Moab on US 191.
Extraordinary products of erosion in the form of giant arches, windows, pinnacles, and pedestals change color constantly in the sunlight. Arches National Monument created by Presidential Proclamation on Apr. 12, 1929, designated Arches National Park in 1971.

VISITOR ACTIVITIES: Interpretive exhibits, walks and talks, auto tours, wildlife-watching, picnicking, backcountry, camping; **Permits:** Required for overnight backcountry use. They can be obtained from the Visitor Center; **Fees:** $3/vehicle, $10/annual/reciprocal at CANY, $1 walking or commercial, $5 camping per night, $7 camping fee (March through Oct.). Golden Age and Golden Eagle Passports accepted and available; **Visitor facilities:** Parking and restrooms at Visitor Center, foot trails, campground (no water-pit toilets in winter), picnic area, self-guiding trails; **HANDICAPPED ACCESSIBILITY:** Restroom at Visitor Center, toilets in campground, at Devils Garden Picnic Area and Windows Trailhead. Wheelchair accessible short trail at South Park Avenue. One accessible campsite at Devils Garden Campground, available on first-come first-served basis for disabled visitors. Site is level with accessible picnic table, adjacent to accessible restroom; **Any limitations on vehicle usage:** All vehicles must stay on established roads; **Hiking trails:** Yes, obtain brochures describing self-guiding walking tours at the Visitor Center; **Backcountry:** Yes, backcountry hikers must obtain backcountry permits at the Visitor Center; **Camping:** Yes; individual campsites cannot be reserved, but group sites are on a reservation system. Write the park for reservations; **Other overnight accommodations on site:** No; **Meals served in the park:** No; **Food and supplies obtainable in the park:** No; **Food and supplies obtainable nearby:** Yes, in Moab; **Overnight accommodations:** Moab, US 191, 5 miles (8 km); **First Aid available in park:** Yes; **Nearest Hospital:** Moab, US 191, 5 miles (8 km); **Days/Hours:** Open 24 hours a day, 7 days a week year-round; **Holiday Closings:** Visitor Center closes Dec. 25; Park remains open; **Visitor attractions closed for seasons:** No; **Weather:** Spring and fall are the best times to visit Arches. Winters are mild and summers are warm, with temperatures frequently above 100°.

GENERAL INFORMATION: *For Your Safety*—You should carry plenty of water, because daytime temperatures here can reach 110°F. Always hike or climb in the company of others. Don't leave your car with children or pets locked inside—the heat of the direct sun can harm them. When hiking, stay on trails; climbing on sandstone can be hazardous. Pets not allowed on any trails. Mountain bikes are considered wheeled vehicles and must stay on maintained roads. They are *not* allowed on any trails. Water available year round at Visitor Center.

Bryce Canyon National Park
Bryce Canyon, UT   **SEE CLIMATABLE NO. 34**

MAILING ADDRESS: Superintendent, Bryce Canyon National Park, Bryce Canyon, UT 84717 **Telephone:** 801-834-5322

DIRECTIONS: The Park is in southwestern Utah within a 5-hour drive of 10 other units of the National Park System. Take Utah 12 east from US 89. The park entrance is 4 miles (6.4 km) off Route 12 on Utah 63. Utah 12 continues through Boulder to Capitol Reef National Park.

Pinnacles, walls, and spires form amphitheaters whose colors are everchanging with light and weather. High-altitude overlooks, spectacular scenery, and clean air combine in some of the world's finest views. Set aside by Presidential Proclamation June 8, 1923.

VISITOR ACTIVITIES: Information, slide program, exhibits and sales publications at the Visitor Center. Sightseeing, photography, wildlife watching, hiking and camping year round. Guided walks, horse back rides, van tours, and evening campfire programs during the summer. Cross-country skiing and snow-shoeing in winter; **Permits:** Free permits are required for overnight backpack camping. Snowshoes are available for loan with security. Both are available at the Visitor Center; **Fees:** $5 per private vehicle; $2 per person on bus or non-motor vehicle; Golden Eagle, Golden Age and Golden Access available and accepted; $6 campsite fee (first come, first served); **Visitor facilities:** Parking, restrooms at Visitor Center and Sunset Point year round (other areas seasonally); campgrounds; overlooks for viewing and photography; trails; picnic areas; conducted activities in summer; **HANDICAPPED ACCESSIBILITY:** Visitor Center, 2 sites north campground, lodge, General Store laundry/showers; overlooks are paved; Sunset to Sunrise Point Trail (may require assistance near Sunrise); **Any limitations on vehicle usage:** Trailers not allowed beyond Sunset Campground—can be left at Visitor Center parking. All vehicles restricted to paved roads and designated overlooks. Vehicles over 25' prohibited at Bryce/Paria Points from noon to 5 p.m., May-Sept. Speed limits vary with conditions, and are established for scenic viewing. Be prepared to stop for wildlife and other visitors; **Hiking trails:** Most trails descend into the canyons and are moderate to steep. High elevation requires extra exertion. Wear good shoes and watch your footing. You should carry water; **Backcountry:** Required permits, information, and maps available at Sunrise Nature Center from Memorial Day to Labor Day; Permits available at

Visitor Center remainder of year; **Camping:** 200 + campsites, first come, first served. Arrive early. Only one loop open for winter camping; **Other overnight accommodations on site:** Bryce Canyon Lodge, motel units and historical cabins, open mid-May through Sept. Reservations available from TW Recreational Services, 451 Main, P.O. Box 400, Cedar City, UT 84720, phone 801-586-7686; **Meals served in the park:** Bryce Canyon Lodge Dining Room; **Food and supplies obtainable nearby:** At stores and shops along routes into park and in nearby communities; **Overnight accommodations nearby:** At motels and campgrounds along routes into park and in nearby communities—seasonal and year round; **First Aid available in park:** At park Visitor Center year round. Also at Lodge in summer; **Nearest Hospital:** Panguitch, Utah Route 63 and Route 12 to US 89, then north to Panguitch—26 miles (41.6 km) ; **Days/Hours:** Park always open. Visitor Center open 8 a.m. to 4:30 p.m. with longer spring, summer, and fall hours; **Holiday Closings:** Visitor Center closed Dec. 25; **Visitor attractions closed for seasons:** Main park road open all year. Some spurs closed in winter to permit cross country ski access. Road and overlooks plowed when weather permits after winter snows; **Weather:** Pleasant days and cool nights from May through Oct.; July and Aug. thundershowers common. Snow from Nov. through March at higher elevations. Bright, crisp winter days afford best views of year.

GENERAL INFORMATION: *For Your Safety*—Be aware of the extra needs at high altitude where there is less oxygen. Know your physical limits. Summer storms are accompanied by lightning strikes in open areas and along the rim—seek shelter in your car. Animals are wild and should not be fed or handled for your sake as well as theirs.

TRAVEL ACCESS: Bus: Color Country Tours provides service from Cedar City, UT; **Rail:** No; **Air:** Closest commercial airport is in Cedar City. Private planes are permitted at the Bryce Canyon Airport, 4 miles (6.4 km) from the park. Air Nevada offers flights 3 times weekly between Las Vegas and Bryce Canyon. Rental cars are available in Cedar City.

NEARBY FACILITIES & POINTS OF INTEREST: Campgrounds: US Forest Service, State, and private campgrounds are located throughout southern Utah. Scenic Utah 12 offers local, state and Federal lands for a variety of recreational experiences. Contact the Scenic 12 Chamber of Commerce, P.O. Box 157, Tropic, UT 84776 for information.

Canyonlands National Park
Moab, Utah   **SEE CLIMATABLE NO. 33**

MAILING ADDRESS: Superintendent, Canyonlands National Park, 125 W. 2nd South, Moab, UT 84532 **Telephone:** 801-259-7164

DIRECTIONS: The Park is 35 miles (56 km) southwest of Moab. The Needles district is on UT 211, 34 miles (54.4 km) west of US 191. Island in the Sky is on UT 313, 30 miles (48 km) southwest of US 191. Maze district is 80 miles (128 km) east of UT 24 via dirt road, most of which is difficult four-wheel drive.

The geological area includes rocks, spires, and mesas that rise to 7,100 (2,158 km) and petroglyphs left by Indians 400-2500 years ago. Established by act of Congress on Sept. 12, 1964.

VISITOR ACTIVITIES: Hiking, four-wheel driving, mountain biking, picnicking, camping, boating, rafting, backcountry, auto and guided tours, interpretive exhibits and programs, horseback riding, bird-watching. Concession-operated tours and rentals are available nearby; **Permits:** For backcountry issued at districts; boating permits are mandatory (whitewater permits are available by application through the Chief Ranger's office; overnight flat-water permits are available at any Ranger Station prior to launching); **Fees:** $3 per private vehicle; $1 per person on commercial tour, bicycle, motorcycle, or on foot. Golden Age, Golden Access, and Golden Eagle passports available and accepted. Campground fee for the Needles district is $6 per night (collected March-October when water available in campground); **Visitor facilities:** Visitor Centers/Ranger Station, vault toilets, picnic areas, campgrounds, hiking trails. Limited concession facilities available seasonally at Needles Outpost adjacent to Needles District. Gas, general store, camping, showers, firewood. Be certain you have ample gas, water, tools, emergency supplies, etc. **HANDICAPPED ACCESSIBILITY:** Park offices in Moab and Monticello, the Visitor Centers located in the Needles and Island in the sky districts are accessible with restrooms nearby designed to accommodate wheelchairs. Both campgrounds have accessible restrooms. Grandview Point and Buck Canyon Overlooks are accessible with assistance. **Any limitations on vehicle usage:** All vehicles must stay on established roads and four-wheel-drive routes. Bicycles are considered vehicles. Trail bikes must be "street-legal" licensed, muffled, and operated by a licensed driver. Three-or-four-wheeler ATV use is prohibited; **Hiking trails:** Yes, check with a Ranger for information on the many miles of hiking trails; **Backcountry:** Yes, information can be obtained from a Park Ranger. Free backcountry permit is mandatory and available at any Ranger Station. You must provide your own water for backcountry travel; **Camping:** Yes, first come, first served, for individual frontcountry campsites. Campers must bring their own water for camping in the Island in the Sky and Maze Districts, and their own fuel for all districts. For group site reservations, (Needles District only), phone 801-259-7164; backcountry campsites along the popular White Rim four-wheel-drive route in the Island in the Sky District should be reserved by writing the White Rim Reservation Office, Canyonlands NP, 125 West Second South, Moab, UT 84532. Other backcountry four-wheel-drive campsites available first come, first served. Backcountry permit required; **Other overnight accommodations on site:** No; **Meals served in the park:** No; **Food and supplies obtainable in the park:** No; **Food and supplies obtainable nearby:** Yes, in Monticello, Moab, Green River, Hanksville; **Overnight accommodations:** Monticello, US 191, 50 miles (80 km) ; Moab, US 191, 35 miles (56 km); Green River, I-70 to 191, 60 miles (96 km); **First Aid available in park:** Yes; **Nearest Hospital:** Moab, Hwy 191, 35 miles (56 km); **Days/Hours:** Park Headquarters (in Moab) and information office (Monticello) is open from 8 a.m. to 4:30 p.m. weekdays except holidays. The park is open year-round; **Visitor attractions closed for seasons:** No; **Weather:** This is desert country. Winter is usually short, and cold, with little snow. Spring and autumn are long and pleasant, except for the high winds, sometimes accompanied by blowing sand. Summers are hot and temperatures frequently exceed 100°F.

GENERAL INFORMATION: Piped water is available in the Needles District, but nowhere else in the park. Information also available at Visitor Centers and Ranger Station in the districts and at Arches National Park Visitor Center daily.

Capitol Reef National Park
Torrey, Utah   **SEE CLIMATABLE NO. 33**

MAILING ADDRESS: Superintendent, Capitol Reef National Park, Torrey, UT 84775 **Telephone:** 801-425-3791

DIRECTIONS: The Visitor Center is 11 miles (17.6 km) east of Torrey on UT 24.
Narrow high-walled gorges cut through 75 (120 km) miles of the Waterpocket Fold uplift of colorful sedimentary formations. Dome-shaped white sandstone formations along the Fremont River account for the name. Created by act of Congress, 1971.

VISITOR ACTIVITIES: Auto tours, interpretive exhibits, camping, picnicking, interpretive programs, hiking, backcountry; **Permits:** For backcountry, available at Visitor Center; **Fees:** Entrance fee, $3, $6 camping fee per vehicle per night, except at Cedar Mesa and Cathedral Valley campgrounds, where there is no charge for camping; **Visitor facilities:** Scenic drive, campgrounds, picnic areas, hiking trails, drinking water; **HANDICAPPED ACCESSIBILITY:** Partially accessible Visitor Center and a handicapped accessible restroom a mile (1.6 km) from the Visitor Center; **Any limitations on vehicle usage:** Vehicles and mountain bikes are restricted to established roads; **Hiking trails:** Yes, trails vary in length and difficulty; **Backcountry:** Yes, information is available from Visitor Center or by contacting the Superintendent; **Camping:** Yes, no reservations available for individual campsites. Group sites can be reserved in advance by writing the Superintendent. A complete list of nearby accommodations and services is available at the Visitor Center; **Other overnight accommodations on site:** No; **Meals served in the park:** No; **Food and supplies obtainable in the park:** No; **Food and supplies obtainable nearby:** Yes, Torrey, Bicknell, Loa, Hanksville; **Overnight accommodations:** In communities west of the park and at Hanksville to the east; **First Aid available in park:** Yes; **Nearest Hospital:** Richfield; Utah 24 to 119 to 89, 72 miles (115.2 km); **Days/Hours:** Park open 24 hours a day year-round; Visitor Center hours vary with the seasons; **Holiday Closings:** Closed Federal holidays, Nov. through Apr.; **Visitor attractions closed for seasons:** Weather conditions occasionally prohibit access to areas served by dirt and gravel roads; **Weather:** The elevation and desert climate make the area prone to temperature extremes. July and August are the hottest months, with midday temperatures in the upper 90°sF common. Summer evenings cool to the 50°-60°F range. Thunderstorms can bring flash floods from July through Sept. Spring and fall are usually mild, with warm days and cool nights. Spring has the most unpredictable weather. Winter daytime temperatures average below 50°F, dropping below freezing at night. Bitter cold comes occasionally during the winter, but snowfall is usually light. The average annual precipitation is about 18 cm (7 inches) with low relative humidity.

GENERAL INFORMATION: *For Your Safety*—Be sure to carry water with you even on short hikes. Most water in Capitol Reef is contaminated with minerals or by animals. Keep pets under physical restraint.

NEARBY FACILITIES & POINTS OF INTEREST: Hotel/Motel: Rim Rock Motel & Restaurant, U-24, 8 miles (12.8 km) west, 801-425-3843; Capitol Reef Inn, 801-425-3271, Chuck Wagon, 801-425-3288, (both in Torrey, 11 miles (17.6) west of Visitor Center), Sunglow Motel & Cafe, 801-425-3821, and Aquarius Inn, 801-425-3835 (both in Bicknell, about 20 miles (32 km) west of Visitor Center); **Campgrounds:** U.S. Forest Service Campgrounds; Sunglow, 22 miles (35.2 km) off U-24; Singletree 22 miles (35.2 km) , off U-12; Pleasant Creek, 27 miles (43.2 km) off U-12; and Oak Creek 28 miles (44.8 km) off U-12; also private camping at Rim Rock Motel & Restaurant, 8 miles (12.8 km) 801-425-3843, and Chuck Wagon in Torrey, 11 miles (17.6 km) west, 801-425-3288.

Cedar Breaks National Monument
Cedar City, Utah

MAILING ADDRESS: Superintendent, Cedar Breaks National Monument, P.O. Box 749 Cedar City, UT 84720; **Telephone:** 801-586-9451

DIRECTIONS: The Monument is reached via UT 14, 27 miles (43.2 km) from US 89 at Long Valley Junction, and 23 miles (36.8 km) from Int. 15 at Cedar City via UT 14. It can also be reached via UT 143, 14 miles (22.4 km) from Parowan. The Visitor Center is on the rim 1 mile (1.6 km) from the south entrance.

A huge natural amphitheater has eroded into the variegated Pink Cliffs (Wasatch Formation), which are 2000 feet (607 m) thick at this point. Created by Presidential Proclamation on Aug. 23, 1933.

VISITOR ACTIVITIES: Camping, picnicking, interpretive talks, snowmobiling, wildflower-watching; **Permits:** No; **Fees:** Entrance fee $3 per vehicle, Campground fee is $6 per night; **Visitor facilities:** Restrooms at Visitor Center, campground; **HANDICAPPED ACCESSIBILITY:** Restrooms, campground, picnic area, Visitor Center, and overlooks; **Any limitations on vehicle usage:** Drive only on established roads. Do not drive on meadows; **Hiking trails:** Yes, trails vary in length and difficulty. Amphitheater is largely inaccessible; **Backcountry:** No; **Camping:** Yes, no reservations available for campgrounds; **Other overnight accommodations on site:** No; **Meals served in the park:** No; **Food and supplies obtainable in the park:** No; **Food and supplies obtainable nearby:** Yes, in Cedar City, Parowan, Panguitch; **Overnight accommodations:** Cedar City, Parowan, Panguitch, or Brian Head 8 miles (12.8 km) from Visitor Center; **First Aid available in park:** Yes; **Nearest Hospital:** Cedar City via UT 143-UT 14, 23 miles (36.8 km); **Days/Hours:** Visitor Center is open 8 a.m. to 6 p.m. from Memorial Day through late Sept.; road open June through Oct. depending on the weather; **Holiday Closings:** None in season; **Visitor attractions closed for seasons:** The travel season extends from early June to late Oct., depending on the weather. At other times, check road conditions before driving to the Monument; **Weather:** Usually permits comfortable camping from late June to Labor Day; at other times, freezing temperatures are common at night.

GENERAL INFORMATION: Nearby points of interest include Zion National Park, 79 miles (126.4 km) away via Cedar City and Int. 15, or 73 miles (116.8 km) via Long Valley Junction and US 89; Bryce Canyon National Park, 65 miles (104 km) away (see listings in this book).

TRAVEL ACCESS: Bus: Greyhound provides daily service to Cedar City about 23 miles (36.8 km) from park; **Rail:** Amtrak provides regular service to Milford, UT; **Air:** Skywest Airlines provides daily service to Cedar City; **Other:** Color Country Touring Vans provide access directly to park from Cedar City.

NEARBY FACILITIES & POINTS OF INTEREST: Campgrounds: KOA Campground Main Street, Cedar City, UT, several U.S. Forest Service campgrounds nearby; **Parks, other points of interest:** Bryce Canyon National Park, Zion National Park, Navajo Lake (USFS), Duck Creek (USFS).

Dinosaur National Monument
For details see listing in Colorado

Glen Canyon National Recreation Area
For details see listing in Arizona

Golden Spike National Historic Site
Brigham City, Utah

MAILING ADDRESS: Superintendent, Golden Spike National Historic Site, P.O. Box 897, Brigham City, UT 84302 **Telephone:** 801-471-2209

DIRECTIONS: The Site is about 30 miles (48 km) west of Brigham City. To reach the Site, drive 23 miles (36.8 km) westward on UT 13/83 to the Promontory Junctions; turn left and go 2 miles (3.2 km) to the next junction; then turn right and go 5 miles (8 km). Roads are well-marked.

Completion of the first transcontinental railroad in the United States was celebrated here when the Central Pacific and Union Pacific Railroads met in 1869. Authorized July 30, 1965.

VISITOR ACTIVITIES: Interpretive exhibits, audiovisual programs, picnicking, history programs in summer, working replica steam locomotives exhibited May through Oct. 2 auto tours on historic RR grade; **Permits:** No; **Fees:** $1 per adult up to $3 per vehicle, $1 per bus passenger; **Visitor facilities:** Visitor Center, parking, restrooms, picnic area; **Any limitations on vehicle usage:** Drive only on established roads; **Hiking trails:** Yes, trails follow the historic railroads; **Backcountry:** No; **Camping:** No; **Other overnight accommodations on site:** No; **Meals served in the park:** No; **Food and supplies obtainable in the park:** Soda pop and snack vending machines; **Food and supplies obtainable nearby:** Yes, Brigham City or Tremonton, UT; **Overnight accommodations:** Brigham City, 30 miles (48 km) east on UT 83, or Tremonton, 30 miles (48 km) northeast on UT 83 and 102; **First Aid available in park:** Yes; **Nearest Hospital:** Brigham City, 30 miles (48 km) east; **Days/Hours:** Open daily from 8 a.m. to 4:30 p.m.; until 6 p.m. in summer; **Holiday Closings:** Thanksgiving, Dec. 25, and Jan. 1; **Visitor attractions closed for seasons:** Self-guided auto tours are not available in winter.

TRAVEL ACCESS: Bus: Service into Brigham City, UT; **Rail:** Service into Salt Lake City, and Ogden, UT; **Air:** Service into Salt Lake City, UT.

Hovenweep National Monument
For details see listing in Colorado

Mormon Pioneer Trail
For details see listing in Illinois

Natural Bridges National Monument
(near) Blanding, Utah

MAILING ADDRESS: Superintendent, Natural Bridges National Monument, Box 1, Lake Powell, UT 84533 **Telephone:** 801-259-5174

DIRECTIONS: The Visitor Center is 120 miles (192 km) south of Moab on US 191 and State 95, and 42 miles (67.2 km) west of Blanding on State 95. It is 26 miles (41.6 km) east of Fry Canyon on Utah 95 and 44 miles (70.4 km) north of Mexican Hat on Route 261.

Three natural bridges carved out of sandstone are protected here. The highest is 220 feet (67 m) above the streambed, with a span of 268 feet. Created by Presidential Proclamation on Apr. 16, 1908, the first National Park Service area in Utah.

VISITOR ACTIVITIES: Interpretive exhibits, camping, picnicking, auto tours, hiking; **Permits:** No; **Fees:** $3 per vehicle entrance fee, Golden Eagle and Golden Age Passports accepted and available; **Visitor facilities:** Visitor Center, campground, picnic area, parking lot, loop road; **HANDICAPPED ACCESSIBILITY:** Parking spaces are available; Visitor Center and restrooms are accessible; should check with Ranger on trail accessibility. **Any limitations on**

vehicle usage: Camping limited to 21-foot vehicles; **Hiking trails:** Yes, dirt trails lead to the three bridges. Short paved trails go to viewpoints at each bridge; **Backcountry:** No; **Camping:** Yes, no reservations available for the 13 campsites (21-foot length limit); **Other overnight accommodations on site:** No; **Meals served in the park:** No; **Food and supplies obtainable in the park:** No; **Food and supplies obtainable nearby:** Yes, Fry Canyon and Blanding; **Overnight accommodations:** Yes, Blanding, US 191 and State 95, 42 miles (67.2 km); Mexican Hat, Route 261, 44 miles (70.4 km); **First Aid available in park:** Yes, or nearby in Blanding, US 191; **Nearest Hospital:** Monticello, US 191, 64 miles (102.4 km) from the park; **Days/Hours:** Visitor Center is open 8 a.m. to 4:30 p.m.; **Holiday Closings:** Thanksgiving, Dec. 25, and Jan. 1; **Visitor attractions closed for seasons:** Hiking trails into the canyons may be closed in winter due to snow and ice; **Weather:** Best from late Apr. through Oct.

GENERAL INFORMATION: Visitors can see other points of interest in the area. They include Canyonlands and Arches National Park (see listings in this book), Lake Powell and Monument Valley. *Warning:* There is hazardous terrain throughout the area; lightning may strike overlooks and viewpoints during storms. Do not enter any ruins you may come across. If these or artifacts are disturbed in any way, a priceless archaeological story could be destroyed forever. The nearest source of gasoline is Blanding, 40 miles (64 km) east.

Rainbow Bridge National Monument
Utah

MAILING ADDRESS: Superintendent, c/o Glen Canyon National Recreation Area, P.O. Box 1507, Page, AZ 86040 **Telephone:** 602-645-2471

DIRECTIONS: You can reach Rainbow Bridge on foot or on horseback (contact 602-672-3852) on the trail from Navajo Mountain Trading Post 15 miles (24 km) or on a trail that begins at the abandoned Rainbow Lodge on foot 13 miles (20.8 km). But the most commonly used approach is by boat on Lake Powell. Many visitors now take the water route of 50 miles (80 km) from Wahweap, Bullfrog, or Halls Crossing to the landing at Bridge Canyon and then walk up the Canyon to the bridge (1/4 to 1 mile depending on lake elevation).

Greatest of the world's known natural bridges, this symmetrical arch of salmon-pink sandstone rises 290 feet above the floor of Bridge Canyon. Created by Presidential Proclamation on May 30, 1910.

VISITOR ACTIVITIES: Hiking, walking trails; **Permits:** Yes, obtain through the Navajo Tribe, Window Rock, AZ; **Fees:** No; **Visitor facilities:** For people who bring their own boats, there are launching ramps at Wahweap, Halls Crossing, Bullfrog, and Hite. Concessioners at these places sell boating and camping supplies, and they will provide guided boat tours from Wahweap and Bullfrog. Closest marina facilities are at Dangling Rope Marina, 7 miles (11.2 km) west (accessible by boat only); **Any limitations on vehicle usage:** No road access to Monument; **Hiking trails:** Yes; **Backcountry:** No; **Camping:** No; **Other overnight accommodations on site:** No; **Meals served in the park:** No; **Food and supplies obtainable in the park:** No; **Food and supplies obtainable nearby:** No; **Overnight accommodations:** Page, AZ, on US 89, near Glen Canyon Dam, 50 miles (80 km) Wahweap and Bullfrog, also 50 miles (80 km) away by water; **First Aid available in park:** Yes, at Dangling Rope Marina, 7 miles (11.2 km) west, (accessible only by boat); **Days/Hours:** Park never closes; **Holiday Closings:** No; **Visitor attractions closed for seasons:** No; **Weather:** Extremely hot, sunny summers. Winter temperatures 40's.

GENERAL INFORMATION: Before beginning a trail trip, be sure to call Navajo Mountain Trading Post, Tuba City, AZ 86045 602-672-2852, about the following: the condition of the trails, whether or not trading posts are open, and places at which water and supplies are available. Summer visitors should wear cool clothing and thick-soled shoes. Bring a hat, sunglasses, and protective lotion. Hikers should carry 1 gallon of water per person per day in summer. Many hikers arrange for one-way transportation by boat after hiking from Navajo Mountain.

NEARBY FACILITIES & POINTS OF INTEREST: Parks, other points of interest: Lake Powell, Glen Canyon National Recreation Area, Navajo National Monument, Grand Canyon National Park.

Timpanogos Cave National Monument
American Fork, Utah

MAILING ADDRESS: Superintendent, Timpanogos Cave National Monument, Rural Route 3, Box 200, American Fork, UT 84003 **Telephone:** 801-756-5238

DIRECTIONS: If you are driving south from Salt Lake City on I-15, turn east at UT 92, the Alpine exit #287. If you are driving north from Provo, turn east at Pleasant Grove exit #273 or American Fork exit #277. Timpanogos Cave is 7 miles (11.2 km) from either town via UT 146 or UT 74.

This series of three limestone caverns on the side of Mt. Timpanogos is noted for its colorful water-created formations and geological history. The first cave was discovered in 1887 and the Monument was created by Presidential Proclamation on Oct. 14, 1922.

VISITOR ACTIVITIES: Visitors follow a 1.5 mile (2.4 km) trail from the Visitor Center up to the cave entrance rising 1,065 feet in elevation. Picnicking, hiking, fishing, and nature walks are available; **Permits:** No; **Fees:** Purchase tickets for cave tours at the Visitor Center. A user fee of $4 is charged for persons 16 and over, $3 for 6 to 16, under 6 is free. Golden Age Passport holders are admitted for half the price; **Visitor facilities:** Picnic area, snacks, and souvenirs in summer; **HANDICAPPED ACCESSIBILITY:** Visitor Center, concession, picnic areas; restrooms. Cave trail closed to wheeled conveyances. All facilities open to visually and hearing disabled; **Any limitations on vehicle usage:** Vehicles confined to UT 92 and authorized parking areas; **Hiking trails:** Yes, 2 short trails on site; other hiking trails and backcountry available nearby at Uinta National Forest, U.S. Forest Service, 88 West 100 North, Provo, UT 84601, phone, 801-377-5780; **Camping:** No; **Other overnight accommodations on site:** No, reserved and non-reserved campsites are available nearby at Uinta National Forest. Contact the forest for reservations and further information; **Meals served in the park:** Yes, snacks at the concession stand from mid-May to mid-Sept.; **Food and supplies obtainable in the park:** No; **Food and supplies obtainable nearby:** Yes, in Highland, American Fork, and Pleasant Grove; **Overnight accommodations:** Minimal accommodations at American Fork, 7 miles (11.2 km) west of the cave on UT 92 and Pleasant Grove 10 miles (16 km) southeast of the cave on US 89 or I-15; **First Aid available in park:** Yes; **Nearest Hospital:** American Fork, UT 92, 7 miles (11.2 km); **Days/Hours:** The cave is open daily from about mid-May through mid-Oct. depending on weather. Visitor Center is open year-round; **Holiday Closings:** All holidays during winter; **Visitor attractions closed for seasons:** Snow and ice make the trail to the cave impassable from late Oct.-Apr.; **Weather:** Cool mornings and warm days in spring and fall. July and August daytime temperatures in mid to high 90°sF. Occasional summer rains close the cave trail temporarily. Winter months are cold with considerable snow accumulation.

GENERAL INFORMATION: About 3 hours are required for the hike and tour of the cave. Because tour sizes are limited, frequently it is not possible to accommodate all visitors who wish to tour the cave. It is advisable to call for current conditions before coming, 801-756-5238. **Advanced Ticket Sales:** Advanced ticket sales can be purchased by writing or calling the park at least two weeks ahead of your visit. They may also be purchased at the visitor center up to the day before the tour. Tickets may be purchased the day of the tour if still available. Temperature within the cave is a damp, chilly 43°F. A warm jacket or sweater and comfortable walking shoes with gripping soles are advised.

Zion National Park
Springdale, Utah   **SEE CLIMATABLE NO. 35**

MAILING ADDRESS: Superintendent, Zion National Park, Springdale, UT 84767 **Telephone:** 801-772-3256

DIRECTIONS: Visitor Center at Kolob Canyons exit 40 from I-15. I-15 passes west of Zion and connects with UT 9 and 17 to the park. US 89 passes east and connects with UT 9 to the Park. The Zion Canyon Visitor Center is a short distance from the Park's South Entrance.
Colorful canyon and mesa scenery includes erosion and rockfault patterns and evidence of former volcanic activity. Established by act of Congress on Nov. 19, 1919.

VISITOR ACTIVITIES: Interpretive films, exhibits, and programs (schedules posted throughout the park), driving, walking and hiking, mountain climbing, wading, camping, biking, horseback trips (make arrangements at Zion Lodge), 1½-hour tram tour of major points of interest leaves from Zion Lodge in summer, wildlife- and bird-watching; **Permits:** Required for backcountry, available at Visitor Centers; **Fees:** $5 per vehicle or $2 per person on commercial vehicles is the entrance fee for persons 12 and over. Camping fee is $6 per night per site. Golden Eagle and Golden Age Passports are accepted and available; **Visitor facilities:** Visitor Center, Nature Center for children 6 through 12, Memorial Day to Labor Day, campgrounds, tap water, fire grates, tables, sanitary disposal station, telephones, picnic sites, religious services (May-Sept.), lodging and food service year-round; **HANDICAPPED ACCESSIBILITY:** The Zion Canyon and Kolob Canyons Visitor Centers and the Zion Lodge are handicapped accessible. There are campsites in the South Campground specifically adapted for use by individuals in wheelchairs. Many interpretive talks are accessible. Inquire at the Zion Canyon Visitor Center for details. The 1-mile (1.6-km) Gateway to the Narrows Trail, which begins at the north end of Zion Canyon Drive, is paved and accessible with assistance; **Any limitations on vehicle usage:** Do not park on curves. Watch for deer. Your car's lights must be in good working order; they are essential when traveling through the tunnel on East Entrance Road; There are special restrictions on large vehicles passing through the 1.1 mile (1.76 km) tunnel on the Zion-Mt. Carmel Highway (Rt. 9) in the park. RV drivers should note the tunnel height at the East entrance is 11'4". A fee may be required for escort service through this narrow tunnel. During the summer, regulations restrict the parking of large vehicles in parts of Zion Canyon; **Hiking trails:** Yes, a wide variety of trails is available; **Backcountry:** Backcountry permits are required for overnight trips and for day trips through the Narrows; **Camping:** Yes, camping is permitted only in designated campsites and is limited to 14 days. Campgrounds are run on a first-come, first-served basis; **Other overnight accommodations on site:** Zion Lodge is operated by the Utah Parks Division of TWRS (451 North Main Street, Cedar City, UT 84720). Zion Lodge has cabin and motel accommodations within the Park. Reservations are advisable. Call 801-586-7686. Communities in the vicinity offer year-round accommodations; **Meals served in the park:** Yes, Zion Lodge has a dining room and a soda fountain; **Food and supplies obtainable in the park:** No; **Food and supplies obtainable nearby:** Yes, at Springdale; **Overnight accommodations:** Springdale and other nearby communities; **First Aid available in park:** Yes, at the Visitor Center year-round. Physician's assistant in Springdale in summer. A physician is in Hurricane, 24 miles (38.4 km) west of the Park; **Nearest Hospital:** St. George, 45 miles (72 km) west of the Park, Cedar City, 60 miles (96 km) north, and Kanab, 42 miles (67.2 km) east; **Days/Hours:** Open 24 hours a day year-round; **Holiday Closings:** No; **Visitor attractions closed for seasons:** Higher hiking trails are closed by snow in winter. The Virgin River Narrows hike is closed typically from mid to late Oct. to mid-May (closed due to cold water and air temperatures and high river levels). During the open season, trips through the Narrows are permitted when the weather allows a sufficient level of safety. The danger of flash floods exists during thunderstorms (July, Aug., and early Sept.). It is important to check with the park for current weather conditions. Best times for the trip are late June, late Sept., and early Oct. Then, go only after thorough preparation. Permits are required for all through Virgin River Narrows hikes (short trips from the bottom no longer require a permit); **Weather:** Snow may fall intermittently from Dec. to March; average winter maximum and minimum temperatures are 53°F and 30°F. May to Oct. daytime temperatures range from 72°F to 103°F; nighttime, from 45°F to 73°F.

GENERAL INFORMATION: *For Your Safety*—All hikers should take precautions. Obtain detailed information from a Park Ranger before attempting backcountry trails; tell someone where you plan to go and when you plan to return. Do not hike alone. Stay on established trails; taking shortcuts may endanger yourself and others. Stay out of drainage areas during thunderstorms as dry washes can become raging torrents in minutes. Watch your step if taking pictures or hiking near cliffs. Many trails have long dropoffs. Be alert for rockfalls and landslides.

The town of Springdale is situated within easy commuting distance of Bryce Canyon, the North Rim of the Grand Canyon, and other well-known attractions. Zion Campgrounds have become very crowded, filling on many days. It would be better not to encourage people to use Zion as a base for visiting other areas.) Other nearby attractions include "Ghost Towns" in Washington County and the Shakespearean Festival in Cedar City, which runs from mid-July to mid-Aug.

TRAVEL ACCESS: Bus: Greyhound provides service to Hurricane, UT, and Trailways serves Kanab, UT; **Rail:** No; **Air:** Sky West Airlines provides service to St. George and Cedar City, UT; **Other:** Color Country Tours operate from Cedar City, UT, and St. George, Tues., Thurs. and Sat. in season. UT Toll-free 1-800-634-3905.

NEARBY FACILITIES & POINTS OF INTEREST: Campgrounds: Zion Canyon Campground, Springdale, UT 84767, 801-772-3237; **Parks, other points of interest:** Bryce, 2-hour drive; Pipe Spring, 1½-hour drive; Cedar Breaks, 1½-hour drive, north rim of Grand Canyon, 2½ hour drive.

Virginia

CHESAPEAKE AND OHIO CANAL NATIONAL HISTORICAL PARK

MANASSAS NATIONAL BATTLEFIELD PARK

PRINCE WILLIAM FOREST PARK

GEORGE WASHINGTON BIRTHPLACE NATIONAL MONUMENT

FREDERICKSBURG AND SPOTSYLVANIA COUNTY BATTLEFIELDS NATIONAL MILITARY PARK

YORKTOWN BATTLEFIELD PARK

SHENANDOAH NATIONAL PARK

APPALACHIAN NATIONAL SCENIC TRAIL

TURKEY RUN FARM

GREAT FALLS PARK

WOLF TRAP FARM PARK FOR THE PERFORMING ARTS

ASSATEAGUE ISLAND NATIONAL SEASHORE

Richmond

Norfolk

CUMBERLAND GAP NATIONAL HISTORICAL PARK

BLUE RIDGE PARKWAY

BOOKER T. WASHINGTON NATIONAL MONUMENT

COLONIAL NATIONAL HISTORICAL PARK

JAMESTOWN NATIONAL HISTORIC SITE

PETERSBURG NATIONAL BATTLEFIELD

RICHMOND NATIONAL BATTLEFIELD PARK

MAGGIE L. WALKER NATIONAL HISTORIC SITE

APPOMATTOX COURT HOUSE NATIONAL HISTORICAL PARK

Appalachian National Scenic Trail
For details see listing in Maine

Appomattox Court House National Historical Park
Appomattox, Virginia

MAILING ADDRESS: Superintendent, Appomattox Court House National Historical Park, P.O. Box 218, Appomattox, VA 24522 **Telephone:** 804-352-8987

DIRECTIONS: The Visitor Center is in the reconstructed Courthouse on VA 24, 3 miles (4.8 km) northeast of the town of Appomattox, VA.
General Robert E. Lee surrendered the Confederacy's largest field army to Lt. Gen. Ulysses S. Grant here on Apr. 9, 1865. The village has been restored. Authorized for addition to the National Park System on June 18, 1930.

VISITOR ACTIVITIES: Walking tours (pamphlet available at the Visitor Center), living history talks in summer, interpretive exhibits; **Permits:** No; **Fees:** $2 per person, ages 17 through 61, entrance fee is charged year round; **Visitor facilities:** Parking areas and restrooms, interpretive exhibits, furnished historic buildings; **HANDICAPPED ACCESSIBILITY:** Parking, restrooms (Tavern Slave quarters) drinking fountain; wheelchair available; ramps at parking lot, Visitor Center, Book Store Tavern Slave Quarters, Tavern Guest House (exhibits); wheelchair lift at McLean House. Audiovisual programs on first floor of Visitor Center. Living

History Interpretive Program by soldiers at Clover Hill Tavern (June-Aug.). For visually impaired: Braille and large print brochures, table model Braille map of village, Braille Audioguide. For hearing impaired: captioned slide program; **Any limitations on vehicle usage:** No vehicles are permitted in the village area; **Hiking trails:** Yes, self-guiding trails throughout the Park; **Backcountry:** No; **Camping:** No, but picnic areas and camping facilities are nearby; **Other overnight accommodations on site:** No; **Meals served in the park:** No; **Food and supplies obtainable in the park:** No; **Food and supplies obtainable nearby:** Yes, town of Appomattox; **Overnight accommodations:** Appomattox, VA 24, 3 miles (4.8 km); **First Aid available in park:** Yes, Rescue squad in Appomattox, VA; **Nearest Hospital:** Lynchburg, US 460, 25 miles (40 km); **Days/Hours:** Open daily 9:00 a.m. to 5 p.m.; **Holiday Closings:** Washington's Birthday, Martin Luther King, Jr.'s Birthday, Veteran's Day, Thanksgiving, Dec. 25, and Jan. 1; **Visitor attractions closed for seasons:** Living history talks are only offered during the summer months; **Weather:** Warm, humid summers; cool, humid winters.

GENERAL INFORMATION: All pets must be kept on a leash while in the Park. Pets not allowed in public buildings.

TRAVEL ACCESS: Bus: Greyhound Bus Lines 804-846-6614; **Rail:** Amtrak provides daily service to Lynchburg, VA, 804-847-8247; **Air:** Lynchburg Municipal Airport, Lynchburg, VA; **Other:** Lynchburg Taxi Cab Service available at Lynchburg Municipal Airport, Amtrak Station, or Bus Terminal; Avis Rent-a-car, 804-239-3622, and Hertz Rent-a-car, 804-239-3251, both at Lynchburg Municipal Airport.

NEARBY FACILITIES & POINTS OF INTEREST: Hotel/Motel: Traveler's Inn Motel, 7 West Confederate Avenue, Appomattox, VA 24552, 804-352-7451, 2 miles (3.2 km) south of Park; Lee-Grant Motel—Hwy. 460, Appomattox, VA 24522, 804-352-5234, 5 miles (8 km), Super 8, 804-352-2339 (same location as Lee-Grant); **Campgrounds:** Jellystone Park Campground, Highway 460 west, Appomattox, VA 24522, 804-993-3332, 9 miles (14.4 km) west of Park; **Parks, other points of interest:** Holiday Lake State Park, Appomattox, VA 24522, 804-248-6308, 10 miles (16 km) north of Park.

Arlington House, The Robert E. Lee Memorial
Arlington, Virginia

MAILING ADDRESS: Site Supervisor, Arlington House, c/o George Washington Memorial Parkway, Turkey Run Park, McLean, VA 22101 **Telephone:** 703-557-0613

DIRECTIONS: Access from Washington is via the Memorial Bridge. In Virginia access is from the George Washington Memorial Parkway. Parking available at the Arlington National Cemetery Visitor Center. No vehicles allowed in cemetery. House is a 10-minute walk from Visitors Center. Tourmobile available.

This was the home of Robert E. Lee, 1831-1866, when he left to take command of the military forces of Virginia during the Civil War. It is located in Arlington National Cemetery, overlooking the Potomac River and the city of Washington. Established by Act of Congress on Mar. 4, 1925.

VISITOR ACTIVITIES: Interpretive exhibits, guided and self-guiding tours of the house; **Permits:** No; **Fees:** No; **Visitor facilities:** Parking at Visitors Center, restrooms and bookstore on site; **HANDICAPPED ACCESSIBILITY:** Wheelchair lift to 1st floor, 2nd floor not accessible. **Any limitations on vehicle usage:** No vehicles are allowed on House grounds; **Hiking trails:** No; **Backcountry:** No; **Camping:** No; **Other overnight accommo-**

dations on site: No; **Meals served in the park:** No; **Food and supplies obtainable in the park:** No; **Food and supplies obtainable nearby:** Yes, Arlington, VA, or Washington, DC; **Overnight accommodations:** In Washington metropolitan area; **First Aid available in park:** Yes; **Nearest Hospital:** Arlington, VA, and Washington, DC; **Days/Hours:** Open daily from 9:30 a.m. to 4:30 p.m. Oct.-Mar. Until 6 p.m. Apr.-Sept.; **Holiday Closings:** Dec. 25, Jan. 1; **Visitor attractions closed for seasons:** No.

Blue Ridge Parkway
For details see listing in North Carolina

Booker T. Washington National Monument
Hardy, Virginia

MAILING ADDRESS: Superintendent, Booker T. Washington National Monument, Route 3, Box 310, Hardy, VA 24101 **Telephone:** 703-721-2094

DIRECTIONS: The Monument is 16 miles (25.6 km) northeast of Rocky Mount, VA, via VA 122N, 20 miles (32 km) southeast of Roanoke, VA, via VA 116S and 122N; 21 miles (33.6 km) south of Bedford, VA, via Rt 122.

This was the birthplace and early childhood home of the famous black leader and educator. Authorized for addition to the National Park System on Apr. 2, 1956.

VISITOR ACTIVITIES: Audiovisual programs, conducted tours, craft demonstrations from mid-June through Labor Day, picnicking, photography; **Permits:** No; **Fees:** There is in entrance fee for visitors to the park. The charge is $1 for those 17 to 61 years of age; children are admitted free. Free Golden Age Passports are available for anyone over the age of 61. Free Golden Access Passports are available for anyone permanently disabled. In addition, Golden Eagle, Family, and Booker T. Washington National Monument Passports are for sale; **Visitor facilities:** Visitor Center and Environmental Education and Cultural Center, picnic area, parking, sales area, restrooms; **HANDICAPPED ACCESSIBILITY:** Parking and Visitor Center facilities; limited accessibility: restrooms and trail; **Any limitations on vehicle usage:** No; **Hiking trails:** Yes, walking and nature trails; **Backcountry:** No; **Camping:** No; **Other overnight accommodations on site:** No; **Meals served in the park:** No; **Food and supplies obtainable in the park:** No; **Food and supplies obtainable nearby:** Yes, within a 10-mile (16-km) radius; more extensive facilities are at Roanoke, Rocky Mount, and Bedford; **Overnight accommodations:** Roanoke, VA, 122S and 116N, 20 miles (32 km); Rocky Mount, VA, 122S, 16 miles (25.6 km); Beford, VA, VA 122N, 21 miles (33.6 km); **First Aid available in park:** Yes; **Nearest Hospital:** Roanoke, VA 122S and 116N, 20 miles (32 km); Rocky Mount, VA 122S, 16 miles (25.6 km); **Days/Hours:** The park grounds and Visitor Center are open 8:30 a.m. to 5 p.m. daily; **Holiday Closings:** Thanksgiving, Dec. 25, and Jan. 1; **Visitor attractions closed for seasons:** No; **Weather:** Spring is warm and mild; summer is warm to hot; fall is mild, cool and pleasant; winter is generally mild with a few light snowfalls.

GENERAL INFORMATION: *For Your Safety*—Keep your distance from the animals. Do not enter the pastures or pens.

NEARBY FACILITIES & POINTS OF INTEREST: For Hotel and campground information phone 703-721-2094 or write to the Park; **Parks, other points of interest:** Blue Ridge Parkway, Fairy Stone State Park, and Smith Mountain Lake.

Colonial National Historical Park
Yorktown, Virginia

MAILING ADDRESS: Superintendent, Colonial National Historical Park, P.O. Box 210, Yorktown, VA 23690 **Telephone:** 804-898-3400

DIRECTIONS: Both Jamestown and Yorktown are located off major highways: Rte. 17 and I-64. Both sites are accessible via the Colonial Parkway, which joins Jamestown, Williamsburg, and Yorktown.
    The Park encompasses most of Jamestown Island, site of the first permanent English settlement in America in 1607; Yorktown, scene of the culminating battle of the American Revolution in 1781; the 23 miles (36.8 km) Colonial Parkway connecting these and other colonial sites including Williamsburg; and Cape Henry Memorial, which marks the approximate site of the first landing of Jamestown's colonists in 1607. Authorized for addition to the National Park System on July 3, 1930.

VISITOR ACTIVITIES: Self-guided auto and walking tours, guided walking tours, interpretive exhibits, living history and children's programs; **Permits:** Yes, a $3 bus permit is required for Colonial Parkway, available at Jamestown Entrance Station and Yorktown Visitor Center; **Fees:** Yes, Jamestown Entrance Station fee is $5 per vehicle or $2 per person for those 16 and over who arrive by bus or bicycle. Educational groups and holders of Golden Age, Golden Access, and Golden Eagle Passports are admitted free; **Visitor facilities:** Souvenirs, exhibits, and audiovisual programs are offered at Jamestown and Yorktown (see listings in this book); **Any limitations on vehicle usage:** Park only in designated areas. There are no service stations, and the road is closed to commercial traffic except buses, for which permits are required; **Hiking trails:** No; **Backcountry:** No; **Camping:** No; **Other overnight accommodations on site:** No, City- and privately-operated campgrounds are nearby. Contact the Park for further information on directions and facilities; **Meals served in the park:** No, there are picnic areas along the Colonial parkway and at Yorktown Beach; **Food and supplies obtainable in the park:** No; **Food and supplies obtainable nearby:** Yes, at Yorktown and Williamsburg; **Overnight accommodations:** Restaurant and Motel Facilities are available in Yorktown and nearby along Rte. 17, and in Williamsburg; **First Aid available in park:** Yes; **Nearest Hospital:** Mary Immaculate Hospital, Newport News, 5 miles (8 km) from Yorktown; Williamsburg Community Hospital is 9½ miles (15.2 km) from Jamestown; **Days/Hours:** Jamestown Entrance Station open daily from 8:30 a.m. to 4:30 p.m. with extended hours from Apr. through Oct.; Yorktown Visitor Center open daily from 8:30 a.m. to 5 p.m. with extended hours from Apr.-Oct.; **Holiday Closings:** Dec. 25; **Visitor attractions closed for seasons:** Moore House, Nelson House, and picnic areas are closed in winter.

NEARBY FACILITIES & POINTS OF INTEREST: Campgrounds: Newport News City Park is the closest campground to Yorktown, but there are many others nearby. There are also many campgrounds along Route 31 near Jamestown Island.

Cumberland Gap National Historical Park
For details see listing in Kentucky

Chesapeake and Ohio Canal National Historical Park
For details see listing in Maryland

Fredericksburg and Spotsylvania County Battlefields Memorial National Military Park
Fredericksburg, Virginia

MAILING ADDRESS: Superintendent, Fredericksburg and Spotsylvania County Battlefields Memorial National Military Park, P.O. Box 679, Fredericksburg, VA 22404 **Telephone:** 703-373-4461

DIRECTIONS: The Visitor Center is in Fredericksburg on US 1 at the foot of Marye's Heights. Another Visitor Center is on the Chancellorsville Battlefield 10 miles (16 km) west of Fredericksburg on VA 3.
   Portions of four major Civil War Battlefields—Fredericksburg, Chancellorsville, the Wilderness, Spotsylvania Court House—and several smaller historic sites comprise the Park. The battles occurred during 1862, 1863, and 1864. Established by act of Congress on Feb. 14, 1927.

VISITOR ACTIVITIES: Museums, interpretive exhibits, living history demonstrations in summer, biking, hiking, picnicking; **Permits:** No; **Fees:** No; **Visitor facilities:** Museums, historic houses, trails, picnic sites; **HANDICAPPED ACCESSIBILITY:** Both Visitor Centers and Jackson Shrine are accessible to wheelchairs; however, Fredericksburg Battlefield Visitor Center has limited accessibility—ground floor only. Handicapped restrooms are available at both Visitor Centers and Chatham Manor. Audiotape tours may be rented or bought covering each of the battlefield tour roads. The trails are covered by wood chips or are natural terrain, which may be difficult for wheelchairs. Special features: audio programs at Chancellorsville Visitor Center, scripts available for slide shows, and scrapbooks covering exhibits on the lower floor of Fredericksburg Battlefield Visitor Center and the interior of Chatham Manor are available at the respective sites. **Any limitations on vehicle usage:** All motorized vehicles must stay on established roadways that are open to the public; **Hiking trails:** Yes, along historic traces and to historic sites; **Backcountry:** No; **Camping:** No; **Other overnight accommodations on site:** No, camping is available at Prince William Forest Park (see listings in this book), 20 miles (32 km) north on Int. 95; **Meals served in the park:** No; **Food and supplies obtainable in the park:** No; **Food and supplies obtainable nearby:** Yes, in Fredericksburg; **Overnight accommodations:** Fredericksburg; **First Aid available in park:** Yes; **Nearest Hospital:** Fredericksburg, Jefferson Davis Hwy (Rte. 1 bypass); **Days/Hours:** Park roads open during daylight hours; Visitor Centers open daily, 9 a.m. to 5 p.m. generally until 6 p.m. in summer; **Holiday Closings:** Dec. 25 and Jan. 1.

GENERAL INFORMATION: *For Your Safety*—Auto tours require turning onto and off of heavily traveled roadways. Beware of poisonous insects, plants, and reptiles which may be encountered during your visit. Watch your footing while on the trails. Physically handicapped visitors are encouraged to start their visits at the Chancellorsville Visitor Center, which is best equipped for access needs.

TRAVEL ACCESS: **Bus:** Greyhound and Trailways Bus Systems provide daily service to Washington, Richmond, and other cities; **Rail:** Amtrak provides service to Washington and Richmond within 1 mile (1.6 km) of Park; **Air:** Byrd Airport in Richmond, 60 miles (96 km); Washington's Dulles Airport, 55 miles (88 km); Washington's National Airport, 45 miles (72 km); **Other:** Groome Transportation runs shuttle buses and limousines between Byrd and National Airports with an intermediate stop in Fredericksburg. It is even possible to rent a bicycle at several downtown locations.

NEARBY FACILITIES & POINTS OF INTEREST: Hotel/Motel: Sheraton, Interstate 95 off Route 3, 703-786-8321, 4 miles (6.4 km) from Park.

George Washington Birthplace National Monument
Washington's Birthplace, Virginia

MAILING ADDRESS: Superintendent, George Washington Birthplace National Monument, RR 1, Box 717, Washington's Birthplace, VA 22443 **Telephone:** 804-224-1732

DIRECTIONS: The Monument is on the Potomac River, 38 miles (60.8 km) east of Fredericksburg, VA, and is accessible over VA 3 and VA 204.
    Birthplace of the first U.S. President, the park includes a Visitor Center, memorial mansion, colonial farm, gardens, and a family burial ground containing memorial tablets of his father, grandfather, and great-grandfather. Established by act of Congress on Jan. 23, 1930.

VISITOR ACTIVITIES: Picnicking, interpretive exhibits and film, guided tours of memorial house, self-guided nature walks; **Permits:** No; **Fees:** Yes, $1 for persons 17 to 61; **Visitor facilities:** Restrooms and parking area, Visitor Center, historic mansion, colonial farm, burial ground, picnic areas; **HANDICAPPED ACCESSIBILITY:** Parking, restrooms, trails, and buildings; **Any limitations on vehicle usage:** Yes, no off-road travel; **Hiking trails:** No; **Backcountry:** No; **Camping:** No; **Other overnight accommodations on site:** No; **Meals served in the park:** No; **Food and supplies obtainable in the park:** No; **Food and supplies obtainable nearby:** Yes, in Montross and Colonial Beach; **Overnight accommodations:** Fredericksburg, 38 miles (60.8 km); Montross, 12 miles (19.2 km); Colonial Beach, 10 miles (16 km); **First Aid available in park:** Yes; **Nearest Hospital:** Fredericksburg, 38 miles (60.8 km); **Days/Hours:** Open daily from 9 a.m. to 5 p.m.; **Holiday Closings:** Dec. 25 and Jan. 1.

GENERAL INFORMATION: Visitors to the area can also see the birthplace of Robert E. Lee, Stratford Hall, which is several miles south of Washington's Birthplace. *For Your Safety*—Do not feed or tease the animals or enter the pastures or pens. Poisonous plants are common in the area.

George Washington Memorial Parkway
McLean, Virginia

MAILING ADDRESS: Superintendent, George Washington Memorial Parkway, Turkey Run Park, McLean, VA 22101 **Telephone:** 703-285-2598

DIRECTIONS: Access to the Parkway is from Exit 14 of the Capital Beltway (Int. 495) from Chain Bridge on Rte. 123, or from Washington via the 14th Street, Memorial, or Theodore Roosevelt Bridges.
    The Parkway is a landscape scenic road which parallels the Potomac River for much of its route. There are several places for recreation along the Parkway. Established by act of Congress on May 29, 1930.

VISITOR ACTIVITIES: Areas assigned to the Parkway's administration such as Arlington House, Great Falls Park, Clara Barton National Historic Site, Glen Echo Park, and Theodore Roosevelt Island offer opportunities for interpretive talks, exhibits, picnicking, hiking, climbing, biking, and fishing; **Permits:** Yes, fishing permits required, picnic permit,

Ft. Hunt Park, Apr.-Oct.; **Fees:** User fee for 6 areas, $50-$300 weekends, half price Mon.-Thurs.; **Other Visitor facilities:** Picnic tables, restrooms, parking, boat ramp, bike/pedestrian trail; **HANDICAPPED ACCESSIBILITY:** Areas under jurisdiction of the George Washington Parkway: Arlington House, the Robert E. Lee Memorial: first floor, museum, grounds, and parking; restrooms available at Arlington National Cemetery Visitor Center. Great Falls Park; main interpretive trail, Overlook 2, and parking lot. Mount Vernon Trail: an 18.5-mile (29.6-km) multi-use trail paralleling the Potomac River, paved with varying degrees of slope, *however,* some sections very steep—user discretion advised, dependent on skill level. Accessible parking for trail at Theodore Roosevelt Island, Belle Haven, and Riverside; **Any limitations on vehicle usage:** All vehicles are restricted to paved roads; **Hiking trails:** Yes, trails vary in slope and difficulty; **Backcountry:** No; **Camping:** No; **Other overnight accommodations on site:** No; **Meals served in the park:** Yes, in Great Falls Park, VA, Mount Vernon, Dangerfield Island, Lady Bird Johnson Park; **Food and supplies obtainable in the park:** No; **Food and supplies obtainable nearby:** Yes, in all local towns; **Overnight accommodations:** In the Washington, D.C., metropolitan area; **First Aid available in park:** Yes; **Nearest Hospital:** Virginia suburbs; **Days/Hours;** Open during daylight hours; the parks close at dark; **Holiday Closings:** Dec. 25; Theodore Roosevelt Island remains open; **Visitor attractions closed for seasons:** Glen Echo Carousel, Oct.-Apr.; **Weather:** Hot and humid in summer, very pleasant and mild spring and fall. Moderate winters.

GENERAL INFORMATION: Visitor use areas managed by the Parkway also include U.S. Navy Marine Memorial, Mount Vernon Pedestrian/Bike Trail, Riverside Park, Fort Hunt Park, Fort Marcy, and Dyke Marsh.

Great Falls Park
Great Falls, Virginia

MAILING ADDRESS: Site Manager, Great Falls Park, P.O. Box 66, Great Falls, VA 22066 **Telephone:** 703-285-2966

DIRECTIONS: The Park is about 15 miles (24 km) from Washington, DC, at the intersection of VA 193 (Georgetown Pike) and VA 738 (Old Dominion Drive) in Great Falls, VA. Beltway exit #13.
   The Park provides a fine view of the Great Falls of the Potomac from the Virginia side of the river. Authorized for addition to the National Park System in 1968.

VISITOR ACTIVITIES: Tours, hiking, fishing, picnicking, horseback riding, rock climbing (registration at Visitor Center is required) cross-country skiing in winter; **Permits:** A VA or MD fishing license is required, available at local sporting goods stores; **Fees:** $3 per vehicle, $10 annual park pass, $25 Golden Eagle, 62 and over free; **Visitor facilities:** Interpretive tours and hikes, picnic tables, no grills are provided, you may bring your own, horse trails, snack bar; **HANDICAPPED ACCESSIBILITY:** With assistance; **Any limitations on vehicle usage:** Motor vehicles are not allowed on trails or in the picnic area. Park only in designated areas; **Hiking trails:** Yes, novice and expert hikers will find suitably enjoyable trails within the Park; **Backcountry:** No; **Camping:** No; **Other overnight accommodations on site:** No, information on campgrounds in the Washington area is available at the Visitor Center or on request to the Site Manager; **Meals served in the park:** Yes, snacks are available at the Visitor Center; **Food and supplies obtainable in the park:** No; **Food and supplies obtainable nearby:** Yes, in Great Falls, 2 miles (3.2 km); **Overnight accommodations:** In Virginia or the Washington, DC, metropolitan area; **First Aid available in park:** Yes, or nearby in Great Falls and McLean, VA; **Nearest Hospital:** Reston, VA, 7 miles (11.2 km); **Days/Hours:** Visitor Center open 9 a.m. to 5 p.m. Park open 7 a.m. to dark; **Holiday Clos-**

ings: Dec. 25; **Visitor attractions closed for seasons:** No; **Weather:** Summers are hot and humid. Temperatures range from 65-95°; Winters are mild to cold, 25-45°.

GENERAL INFORMATION: These warnings must be heeded for a safe visit: Strong currents are extremely hazardous at *all* places along the banks of the Potomac River in the park. Fish from the shoreline only. NO SWIMMING OR WADING; no alcoholic beverages permitted. This prohibition is strictly enforced. STAY OFF ROCKS AT WATER'S EDGE. Check in with Ranger Station before boating the Potomac.

Jamestown Island
Jamestown, Virginia

MAILING ADDRESS: Superintendent, Colonial National Historical Park, P.O. Box 210, Yorktown, VA 23690 **Telephone:** 804-898-3400

DIRECTIONS: Follow I-64 to Hwy 199 West and take the Colonial Parkway to Jamestown Island.

Jamestown Island is the site of the first permanent English-speaking settlement in North America, dating to 1607. As the first capital of Virginia from 1607-1699 it was the location of the first meeting of a representative legislative assembly on July 30, 1619. In 1893 the Association for the Preservation of Virginia Antiquities (APVA) acquired 22½ acres on Jamestown Island. The remainder of the 1,500-acre area became part of the Colonial National Historical Park in 1934. Jamestown has been jointly administered by the National Park Service, U.S. Department of Interior, and the APVA since 1940.

VISITOR ACTIVITIES: Auto and foot tours, 15-minute orientation film, exhibits of artifacts, foundations of 17th- century structures, glassmaking demonstrations at the Jamestown Glasshouse, Pottery demonstrations at the Dale House; **Permits:** $3 bus permit is required for Colonial Parkway, available at Jamestown Entrance Station and Yorktown Visitor Center; **Fees:** Jamestown Entrance Station fee is $5 per vehicle or $2 per person for those 16 and over who arrive by bus or bicycle. Educational groups and holders of Golden Age and Golden Eagle Passports are admitted free; **Visitor facilities:** Post office, gift shop, interpretive signs, rental tapes of audio tours available for the town site and island loop drive, loop drive, glasshouse, wayside exhibits; **HANDICAPPED ACCESSIBILITY:** Theater; wheelchairs and strollers available for use at visitor center; **Any limitations on vehicle usage:** Park only in designated areas; **Hiking trails:** No; **Backcountry:** No; **Camping:** No, campgrounds are located nearby in Williamsburg, Newport News, and James City County. Contact the park for further information on directions and facilities; **Other overnight accommodations on site:** No; **Meals served in the park:** No; **Food and supplies obtainable in the park:** No; **Food and supplies obtainable nearby:** Yes, at Yorktown and Williamsburg; **Overnight accommodations:** Motel facilities available in Yorktown and nearby along Rt. 17, and in Williamsburg; **First Aid available in park:** Yes; **Nearest Hospital:** Williamsburg, 9½ miles (15.2 km); **Days/Hours:** Jamestown Entrance Station open daily from 8:30 a.m. to 4:30 p.m. with extended hours from Apr. through Oct.; **Holiday Closings:** Dec. 25; **Visitor attractions closed for seasons:** No; **Weather:** Temperate.

GENERAL INFORMATION: *For Your Safety*—Keep on the paths and watch your children. Stay off the ruins and away from the river, which is deep here.

TRAVEL ACCESS: Jamestown does not receive direct airline, bus, or rail service. Transportation to either site is limited to taxi or limousine service from Williamsburg, Fort Eustis,

Newport News/Williamsburg International, Norfolk International Airport and Byrd International Airport in Richmond. **Bus:** Daily direct service by Greyhound to Williamsburg and Fort Eustis; Trailways to Richmond and Norfolk; **Rail:** Direct service by Amtrak to Williamsburg, Lee Hall, and Newport News from New York, Philadelphia, Baltimore, and Washington once a day. **Air:** Approximately 15 miles (24 km) from Newport News/Williamsburg International Airport in Newport News and 45 miles (72 km) from Norfolk International Airport and Byrd International Airport in Richmond. **Other:** The Virginia Division of Tourism, under the Department of Conservation and Economic Development of the Commonwealth of Virginia, in New York, Washington, and Richmond can provide further information and reservations. The Colonial Williamsburg Foundation can also be called toll free from anywhere in the Continental United States by dialing 1-800-HISTORY.

Maggie L. Walker National Historic Site
Richmond, Virginia

MAILING ADDRESS: c/o Richmond National Battlefield Park, 3215 East Broad Street, Richmond, VA 23223 **Telephone:** 804-780-1380

DIRECTIONS: Maggie L. Walker, black leader, became the first American woman to establish a bank, the St. Luke Penny Savings Bank, in her native Richmond in 1903, presently known as the Consolidated Bank and Trust Co. Later she lived here in this large house of Victorian-Italianate Style with a Colonial Revival porch located at 110½ East Leigh Street. Authorized for addition to the National Park System on Nov. 10, 1978.

VISITOR ACTIVITIES: Guided tours through house museum; **Fees:** No; **Visitor facilities:** Restrooms; **HANDICAPPED ACCESSIBILITY:** Exterior ramp provides access to first floor. **Food and supplies obtainable nearby:** Yes, in downtown Richmond; **Days/Hours:** Open only during daylight hours. Maggie Walker house open 9:00 a.m. to 5:00 p.m. Wed. through Sun.; **Holiday Closing:** Dec. 25 and Jan. 1, Thanksgiving; **Weather:** Hot and humid summers, mild spring and fall, and moderate winters.

TRAVEL ACCESS: Bus: Greyhound, Trailways provide access to Richmond, Greater Richmond Transit services Site; **Rail:** Amtrak provides service to Richmond; **Air:** Eastern, Piedmont, United, American, USAir provide service to Richmond's Byrd International Airport.

Manassas National Battlefield Park
Manassas, Virginia

MAILING ADDRESS: Superintendent, Manassas National Battlefield Park, Manassas, VA 22110 **Telephone:** 703-361-1865

DIRECTIONS: The Park is 26 miles (41.6 km) southwest of Washington, DC, near the intersection of Int. 66 and VA 234. The Visitor Center is on VA 234, ¾ mile (1.2 km) north of the intersection of I-66 and VA 234.

Gen. Thomas J. ("Stonewall") Jackson figured prominently in two Confederate victories here. Also called "Bull Run" the First Battle of Manassas, July 21, 1861, ended any illusion of a short war. The Second Battle of Manassas, Aug. 28-30, 1862, brought Southern forces to the height of their military power. Designated May 10, 1940.

VISITOR ACTIVITIES: Interpretive exhibits, slide programs, conducted tours in season, auto tours, hiking, horseback riding, picnicking; **Permits:** For certain group activities. Inquire of superintendent at Visitor Center; **Fees:** Yes, $1 for ages 17-61. Those under/over—free; **Visitor facilities:** Parking, hiking, and bridle trails, sales, picnic area; **HANDICAPPED ACCESSIBILITY:** Parking, Visitor Center, restrooms; slide show; **Any limitations on vehicle usage:** Parking is not allowed on the road shoulders. All motorized vehicles must stay on established roadways and may not stop on grassy areas or trails; **Hiking trails:** Yes, there are self-guiding walking tours of Henry Hill and unfinished railroad; **Backcountry:** No; **Camping:** No; **Other overnight accommodations on site:** No; **Meals served in the park:** No; **Food and supplies obtainable in the park:** No; **Food and supplies obtainable nearby:** Yes, Manassas, south on VA 234; **Overnight accommodations:** Manassas, south on VA 234; **First Aid available in park:** Yes; **Nearest Hospital:** Manassas, VA 234, 4 miles (6.4 km); **Days/Hours:** Park open daily from sunrise to sunset. Visitor Center open daily from 8:30 a.m to 5 p.m. and until 6 p.m. in summer; **Holiday Closings:** Park and Visitor Center closed Dec. 25; **Visitor attractions closed for seasons:** Stone House is closed in winter; **Weather:** Winters are mild to moderate; summers are moderate.

GENERAL INFORMATION: *CAUTION:* Two heavily traveled roadways divide the Park. Use extreme caution while driving across or turning onto and off these highways.

Petersburg National Battlefield
Petersburg, Virginia

MAILING ADDRESS: Superintendent, Petersburg National Battlefield, P.O. Box 549, Petersburg, VA 23804 **Telephone:** 804-732-3531

DIRECTIONS: The Main Park Visitor Center is 2½ miles (4 km) east of the center of Petersburg on State Route 36.

The Union Army waged a 10-month campaign here in 1864-65 to seize Petersburg, center of the railroads supplying Richmond and the Confederate Army of Northern Virginia. Established by act of Congress on July 3, 1926.

The City Point Unit in the City of Hopewell, at the corner of Pecan Avenue and Cedar Lane, was the location of Grant's Headquarters throughout the siege. Here also the Union army organized the largest supply base and supply operation of the Civil War. Visitor service facilities are being developed for this site. Appomattox Manor, ancestral home of the Eppes family, is on the grounds and open to the public. U.S. Grant's Headquarters cabin is on the grounds.

VISITOR ACTIVITIES: A 17-minute map presentation is offered hourly at the Visitor Center. In summer, demonstrations of mortar and cannon, with actual firings, and soldier life may be seen. Biking, picnicking, hiking, self-guiding auto tours; **Permits:** No; **Fees:** Yes, $1; $3 per car; **Visitor facilities:** Bike trails, parking, restrooms, picnic area; **Any limitations on vehicle usage:** The Park tour roads are often congested, so drive slowly and carefully; **Hiking trails:** Yes; **Backcountry:** No; **Camping:** No; **Other overnight accommodations on site:** No, reservations for campsites can be made at Holiday Inn Travel Park which is 7 miles (11.2 km) from the Battlefield. Contact the Park at Route 4, Box 500, Petersburg, VA 23803, phone 804-861-2616; **Meals served in the park:** No; **Food and supplies obtainable in the park:** No; **Food and supplies obtainable nearby:** Yes, ½ mile (.8 km) west on Route 36; **Overnight accommodations:** Petersburg, VA, via Route 36, 2½ miles (4 km) west; Hopewell, VA, via Route 36, 2 miles (3.2 km) east; **First Aid available in park:** Yes; **Nearest Hospital:** Petersburg, VA, Rte. 36 to Washington St. to Sycamore St., 3½ miles (5.6 km); **Days/Hours:** Battlefield open 8 a.m. to dark year-round; Visitor Center open from

8 a.m. to 5 p.m., until 7 p.m. in summer; **Holiday Closings:** Dec. 25 and Jan. 1; **Visitor attractions closed for seasons:** Living history program operates only from mid-June through late Aug.; **Weather:** Spring and fall are generally mild. Summers are very hot and humid. Winters are moderately cold and humid.

GENERAL INFORMATION: Visitors to the area can also see the nearby Poplar Grove National Cemetery, which contains the graves of more than 6,000 soldiers. It is on VA 675, 3 miles (4.8 km) south of Petersburg.

TRAVEL ACCESS: Bus: Greyhound, Trailways provide regular service to Petersburg; **Rail:** Amtrak serves Richmond, VA; **Air:** Piedmont, Eastern, United provide service to Byrd International, 30 miles (48 km) north.

NEARBY FACILITIES & POINTS OF INTEREST: Hotel/Motel: Petersburg, VA. **Points of Interest:** Old town in Petersburg and Quartermaster Museum in nearby Fort Lee, VA. Hopewell and Vicinity: Weston Manor and numerous historic James River Plantations nearby.

Prince William Forest Park
Triangle, Virginia

MAILING ADDRESS: Superintendent, Prince William Forest Park, P.O. Box 209, Triangle, VA 22172 **Visitor Center Telephone:** 703-221-7181 (Concession operated-Travel Trailer Village 703-221-2474.)

DIRECTIONS: The Park is about 32 miles (51.2 km) south of Washington, DC. The main entrance is west on VA 619, just ¼ mile (.4 km) beyond I-95, Exit 50B. The Visitor Center is less than 1 mile (1.6 km) from the main entrance. If you are arriving in a travel trailer and desire hookups, take the VA 234 west exit from I-95. Follow signs to Travel Trailer Village.
   The park's 17,000 acres are an example of a mature eastern deciduous Piedmont forest on the fall line. Authorized for addition to the National Park System in 1936.

VISITOR ACTIVITIES: Biking, camping, fishing, hiking, wildlife-watching, interpretive exhibits, naturalist programs, picnicking, backcountry camping, bicycling; **Permits:** State of Virginia fishing license required; **Fees:** Entrance fee is $3 per vehicle good for 7 days, or $10 for an annual pass; family camping fee is $7 per night per site; **Visitor facilities:** Park information and exhibits at the Visitor Center, nature trails, picnic areas, concessioner trailer village, backcountry campsites, individual family, and group campgrounds, group cabins by reservation only; **HANDICAPPED ACCESSIBILITY:** Pine Grove Nature Trail is wheelchair accessible, as are several campground sites and restrooms. See park brochure or contact park Visitor Center. All visitor areas have marked parking areas for the physically challenged; **Any limitations on vehicle usage:** All vehicles are restricted to designated roadways and parking areas. No off-road use; **Hiking trails:** Yes, the Park has approximately 35 miles (56 km) of trails and fire roads; **Backcountry:** Yes. Backcountry permits are required, free of charge, and available in person or by writing to Visitor Center; **Camping:** Yes. No reservations are available for family tent camping, only for group tent camping and cabin camping. Backcountry permits are available in advance. Contact the park for further information; **Other overnight accommodations on site:** No; **Meals served in the park:** No; **Food and supplies obtainable in the park:** No; **Food and supplies obtainable nearby:** Yes, Triangle or Dumfries; **Overnight accommodations:** Triangle or Dumfries, Rte. 234 and I-95, within a 1- to 5-mile (1.6- to 8-km) radius; **First Aid available in park:** Yes; **Nearest Hospital:** Potomac Hospital, Woodbridge, 9 miles (14.4 km) from the park; **Days/Hours:** Park open during daylight hours;

campgrounds always open; **Holiday Closings:** No; **Visitor attractions closed for seasons:** No. Offices closed Thanksgiving and Christmas.

TRAVEL ACCESS: Bus: Greyhound provides service to Triangle, VA; **Rail:** Amtrak provides service to Quantico, VA, call 800-872-7245; **Air:** Access through Washington, DC airports; **Other:** Radio Cab Co. Greyhound Bus Terminal, Triangle, VA, 703-491-2222; Prince William County Yellow Cab Co., 703-640-6464.

NEARBY FACILITIES & POINTS OF INTEREST: Hotel/Motel: Econo Lodge, 17005 Dumfries Road, Dumfries, VA, 703-221-4176, 1-3/4 miles (2.8 km); Quality Inn, 17133 Dumfries Road, Dumfries, VA, 703-221-1141, 1-1/2 miles (2.4 km); Toll-free 800-228-5151; **Parks, other points of interest:** Manassas National Battlefield, Fredericksburg National Battlefield, Historic Fredericksburg, Potomac Mills Mall, Washington, DC; **Reservation systems in use for group campsites, Travel Trailer Village, and other facilities:** Required for group cabins and tenting areas. Permits available for backcountry camping. Contact Park Visitor Center at 703-221-7181; P.O. Box 209, Triangle, VA 22172.

Richmond National Battlefield Park
Richmond, Virginia

MAILING ADDRESS: Superintendent, Richmond National Battlefield Park, 3215 East Broad St., Richmond, VA 23223 **Telephone:** 804-226-1981

DIRECTIONS: You should begin your tour at Chimborazo Visitor Center, 3215 East Broad Street, Richmond. A small Visitor Center with exhibits is available at the Fort Harrison unit, and an exhibit shelter with exhibits and an electronic battlemap is available at Cold Harbor.

The Park commemorates the numerous battles and campaigns designed to capture Richmond, which was the Confederate Capital during the Civil War. Chimborazo Visitor Center occupies the site of one of the Confederacy's largest hospitals. Extensive remains of Union and Confederate earthworks are preserved in several park areas.

VISITOR ACTIVITIES: Interpretive exhibits and audiovisual programs, self-guided auto tours, picnicking, environmental program, living history programs in season; **Permits:** No; **Fees:** No; **Visitor facilities:** Parking, restrooms, sales area, picnic facilities, information desk, small museum, interpretive trails with exhibits, historic houses; **HANDICAPPED ACCESSIBILITY:** Slide program is captioned. Restrooms at Chimborazo and Fort Harrison Visitor Centers are accessible; all parking areas have reserved spaces and ramps or curb cuts; Chimborazo Visitor Center has exterior ramp and interior chair lifts to all levels. Brochure is also on audio tape; **Any limitations on vehicle usage:** Park only in designated areas; **Hiking trails:** Trails at four battle sites totaling 3½ miles (5.6 km); **Backcountry:** No; **Camping:** No; **Other overnight accommodations on site:** No; **Meals served in the park:** No; **Food and supplies obtainable in the park:** No; **Food and supplies obtainable nearby:** Yes, along the tour route and in Richmond; **Overnight accommodations:** Along the tour route and in Richmond; **First Aid available in park:** Yes; **Nearest Hospital:** Medical College of VA, Broad Street, 12 blocks west of Chimborazo Visitor Center; **Days/Hours:** Open only during daylight hours. Chimborazo Visitor Center is open 9 a.m to 5 p.m. daily year-round; **Holiday Closings:** Dec. 25 and Jan. 1; **Visitor attractions closed for seasons:** Fort Harrison Visitor Center is open daily June through Aug. from 9 a.m. to 5 p.m.; **Weather:** Hot and humid summers, mild spring and fall, moderate winters.

GENERAL INFORMATION: Whenever possible, spend some time walking in each area; it is the best way to gain a real understanding of its significance.

Shenandoah National Park
Luray, Virginia

MAILING ADDRESS: Superintendent, Shenandoah National Park, Rt. 4, Box 348, Luray, VA 22835 **Telephone:** 703-999-2243

DIRECTIONS: The Headquarters of Shenandoah National Park is 4 miles (6.4 km) west of Thornton Gap and 4 miles (6.4 km) east of Luray on US 211. Visitor Centers are at Dickey Ridge and Big Meadows. Skyline Drive winds through hardwood forest along the crest of the Blue Ridge Mountains. Authorized for addition to the National Park System on May 26, 1926; fully established Dec. 26, 1935.

VISITOR ACTIVITIES: Driving, horseback riding, picnicking, camping, field trips, campfire programs, nature walks. Pick up a Park newspaper from any Visitor Center, entrance station, or concession lodge; **Visitor facilities:** Food service, gift shops, service stations, grocery and camping supply stores, showers and laundry buildings, ice and wood sales, 2 lodges, riding stables, self-guiding nature trails; **HANDICAPPED ACCESSIBILITY:** Lodges, campgrounds, picnic grounds, most public buildings are accessible with parking and comfort stations. A variety of Park interpretive activities and literature are also accessible. Further information may be obtained by writing the Park Superintendent. **Any limitations on vehicle usage:** Vehicles must stay on public roads. Commercial trucking is restricted to park business only. Bicycles and other vehicles are prohibited on trails. Chains and snow tires may be required in winter; **Hiking trails:** Yes, about 500 miles (800 km) of trails including self-guiding nature trails can be enjoyed year-round; **Backcountry:** Yes, information available at Visitors Centers and Park Headquarters or by mail from the Superintendent; **Camping:** Yes, advance reservations are accepted for organized groups at Dundo campground. For camping at Big Meadows May through October reservations are recommended. Contact Ticketron, P.O. Box 617516, Chicago, IL 60661-7516 or call 1-800-452-1111. Other campgrounds are on a first-come, first-served basis; **Other overnight accommodations on site:** Yes, for lodging information and reservations, contact ARA-Virginia Sky-Line Company, Box 727, Luray, VA 22835, phone: 1-800-999-4714; **Meals served in the park:** Yes, at Elkwallow, Panorama, Skyland, Big Meadows, Loft Mountain; **Food and supplies obtainable in the park:** Yes, at Elkwallow, Big Meadows, Lewis Mountain, Loft Mountain; **Food and supplies obtainable nearby:** Yes, in towns along Highways 340, 211, 33. Some of these are within 10 miles (16 km); **First Aid available in park:** Yes; **Nearest Hospital:** Front Royal, Highway 340, 6 miles (9.6 km); Luray, Highway 211, 10 miles (16 km); Harrisonburg, Highway 33; Waynesboro, 250; **Days/Hours:** Park always open. Sections of the drive may be closed due to weather or for resource management; **Holiday Closings:** No; **Visitor attractions closed for seasons:** All facilities are operated in summer; some are available in spring and autumn; **Weather:** Temperate.

GENERAL INFORMATION: *For Your Safety*—wear proper footwear when walking on trails. Most visitor injuries are caused by falls. Do your sightseeing from overlooks and trails, not while driving. Do not feed or approach park animals. Bears roam the park, so safeguard all food to protect yourself and your property. Know where your children are at all times. Always plan where to meet if you become separated. Stay on trails.

TRAVEL ACCESS: Bus: Trailways provides regular service to Waynesboro, VA; **Rail:** No; **Air:** No.

The Claude Moore Colonial Farm at Turkey Run
McLean, Virginia

MAILING ADDRESS: The Claude Moore Colonial Farm at Turkey Run, 6310 Georgetown Pike, McLean, VA 22101 **Telephone:** 703-442-7557

DIRECTIONS: From the Capital Beltway (Int. 495), take Exit 13, Route 193 east toward Langley; drive 2.3 miles (3.7 km); and turn left at Claude Moore Colonial Farm sign onto access road; the parking lot is ½ mile (.8 km) on the left. From Washington, DC, take the George Washington Memorial Parkway north to the exit for Route 123 toward McLean; drive almost 1 mile (1.6 km) and turn right on to Route 193; make the first right at Claude Moore Colonial Farm sign and follow access road ½ mile (.8 km) to parking lot on the left.

The day-to-day operations of a small-scale, low-income colonial farm of the 18th century are re-enacted in this wooded setting. Established by act of Congress in 1973.

The Farm is operated by "Friends of The Claude Moore Colonial Farm at Turkey Run, Inc.," a private, non-profit organization, in cooperation with the National Park Service.

VISITOR ACTIVITIES: Living history demonstrations, self-guided walks, picnicking; **Permits:** No; **Fees:** $2 for adults, $1 for children 3-12 years, members free; **Visitor facilities:** Parking, restrooms, picnic tables; **HANDICAPPED ACCESSIBILTY:** Please call in advance to make special arrangements: 703-442-7557, Mon.-Fri., 9 a.m.-5 p.m.; **Any limitations on vehicle usage:** No vehicles; visitors must walk from the parking lot; **Hiking trails:** No; **Backcountry:** No; **Camping:** No; **Other overnight accommodations on site:** No; **Meals served in the park:** No; **Food and supplies obtainable in the park:** No; **Food and supplies obtainable nearby:** Yes, McLean, VA; **Overnight accommodations:** McLean, VA, or metropolitan Washington, DC; **First Aid available in park:** No; **Nearest Hospital:** Fairfax Hospital, Falls Church, VA; **Days/Hours:** April-mid-Dec.: Wed.-Sun. 10 a.m.-4:30 p.m.; **Holiday Closings:** Thanksgiving; **Visitor attractions closed for seasons:** Closed mid-Dec.-Mar.; **Weather:** The farm is an outdoor experience. Remember to dress for the weather.

GENERAL INFORMATION: The need to preserve the 18th-century atmosphere of the site precludes the use of guided tours by park staff. Visitors are invited to observe the "farm family's" activities and ask questions.

U.S. Marine Corps War Memorial and Netherlands Carillon
Arlington, Virginia

MAILING ADDRESS: Superintendent, George Washington Memorial Parkway, Turkey Run Park, McLean, VA 22101 **Telephone:** 703-285-2598

DIRECTIONS: The Memorial and Carillon are located in Arlington, VA, off US 50, and can be reached from Washington, DC, via Memorial Bridge or Key Bridge.

Also known as the Iwo Jima Memorial, this monumental sculpture is dedicated to all Marines who have died for their country. Authorized for addition to the National Park System on Nov. 10, 1954. The 49-bell Netherlands Carillon symbolizes the gratitude of the Dutch people for U.S. aid given during and after World War II. Carillon dedicated on May 5, 1960.

VISITOR ACTIVITIES: Sunset parades by the U.S. Marine Drum and Bugle Corps and the Silent Drill Team are held at the Memorial on Tues. evenings, June, July, Aug.; Carillon concerts Saturday afternoons, Apr., May, Sept. 2-4 p.m.; June through Aug. 6:30-8:30 p.m.;

Permits: No; **Fees:** No; **Visitor facilities:** Parking area; **HANDICAPPED ACCESSIBILITY:** Parking and trails; restrooms not accessible; **Any limitations on vehicle usage:** Vehicles are restricted to paved roads; **Hiking trails:** No; **Backcountry:** No; **Camping:** No; **Other overnight accommodations on site:** No; **Meals served in the park:** No; **Food and supplies obtainable in the park:** No; **Food and supplies obtainable nearby:** Yes, Arlington, VA, or Washington, DC; **Overnight accommodations:** Arlington, VA, or metropolitan Washington, DC; **First Aid available in park:** No; **Nearest Hospital:** Arlington, VA; **Days/Hours:** Memorial never closes; **Holiday Closings:** No; **Visitor attractions closed for seasons:** No; **Weather:** Hot, humid summers; cold, snowy winters.

Wolf Trap Farm Park
Vienna, Virginia

MAILING ADDRESS: Director, Wolf Trap Farm Park, 1551 Trap Road, Vienna, VA 22182 **Telephone:** 703-255-1800

DIRECTIONS: From downtown Washington, DC: Take the George Washington Memorial Parkway to Capital Beltway (I-495) heading south into Virginia. Exit I-495 at Exit 11-S (Tyson's Corner—VA Rte. 123). Follow Rte. 123 briefly to U.S. Route 7 (Leesburg Pike) and turn right. Travel west on Route 7 to Towlston Road. Turn left on Towlston Road at Wolf Trap Farm Park sign. The Park entrance is 1 mile (1.6 km) from this turn and is well marked. Driving time from downtown Washington, DC, is 30 minutes in nonrush-hour traffic, where you will find free parking. Cars may also enter from the Dulles Toll Road up to 2 hours before performance time ONLY. Take exit 12B (from I-495) or exit 20 (from Rte. 66) and follow to the Wolf Trap exit.

Established by an act of Congress on Oct. 15, 1966, as the Nation's only Park for the performing arts, the Filene Center can accommodate an audience of 6,786 including 3,000 on the sloping lawn in a setting of rolling hills and woods.

VISITOR ACTIVITIES: Attending performance ranging from ballet to pop; free performance previews; free children's programs; picnicking; walking tours of the Filene Center; interpretive programs; **Permits:** Yes; **Fees:** Yes, tickets are required for most performances. See local newspaper or call the box office at 703-255-1860 for information on events; **Visitor facilities:** Refreshment bar, food service during Filene Center performances; parking; restrooms; picnic areas; **HANDICAPPED ACCESSIBIITY:** Special arrangements for the handicapped can be made in advance by calling 703-255-1820 (TDD). The park will also furnish wheelchairs upon request. Free transportation from the parking lots to the Filene Center is available by Ranger-operated carts for those who need it. FM loop amplification headsets are available upon request for the hearing impaired during Filene Center performances; **Any limitations on vehicle usage:** Park only in designated areas; **Hiking trails:** No; **Backcountry:** No; **Camping:** No; **Other overnight accommodations on site:** No; **Meals served in the park:** Yes, during June, July, and Aug. The Meadows Restaurant & Lounge adjacent to the Filene Center offers a choice of meal services beginning 2 hours before each performance. A buffet dinner is available, or a variety of picnic box suppers may be ordered in advance. Reservations are required by 1 p.m. on the day of the performance. Telephone 703-281-4256. Snack bars serve sandwiches, soft drinks, and assorted snacks prior to each performance and at intermission; **Food and supplies obtainable in the park:** No; **Food and supplies obtainable nearby:** Yes, Vienna, VA, and Tyson's Corner, where you can prepare your own picnic; **Overnight accommodations:** In suburban Virginia or Washington, DC; **First Aid available in park:** Yes, physician in attendance at most performances; **Nearest Hospital:** Reston Hospital Center, Reston, VA; **Days/Hours:** Park open year-round from 7:00 a.m. to dusk. The

Filene Center is open for performances from June through Labor Day; **Holiday Closings:** Dec. 25; **Visitor attractions closed for seasons:** The Filene Center, the free children's programs and nature walks are in operation only in summer.

Yorktown Battlefield
Yorktown, Virginia

MAILING ADDRESS: Superintendent, Colonial National Historical Park, P.O. Box 210, Yorktown, VA 23690 **Telephone:** 804-898-3400

DIRECTIONS: Follow I-64 to Hwy 199 East, then Colonial Parkway to Yorktown.
Yorktown was the scene of the culminating battle of the American Revolution when Washington triumphed over Cornwallis in 1781. Authorized for addition to the National Park System on July 3, 1930.

VISITOR ACTIVITIES: Interpretive exhibits, artifact displays, 16-minute film, rooftop overlook, self-guiding auto tour, bookstore, tape player rentals for tours. Theatrical presentation on Thomas Nelson, Jr., a signer of the Declaration of Independence and the commander of the Virginia militia at the Siege of Yorktown, is offered at the Nelson House during the summer season; **Permits:** $3 bus permit is required for Colonial Parkway, available at Jamestown Entrance Station and Yorktown Visitor Center; **Fees:** No; **Visitor facilities:** Interpretive exhibits, Visitor Center, orientation map, film, overlook, bookstore, encampment and battlefield drives, theatrical presentations at Moore House and Nelson House during the summer season, picnic area at Yorktown Beach; **HANDICAPPED ACCESSIBILITY:** Visitor Center parking lot and restrooms. Descriptive tape recording for the blind is available at the Visitor Center information desk. The Nelson House is wheelchair accessible by stairwalking machine with prior notice (contact the Visitor Center); **Any limitations on vehicle usage:** Park only in designated areas; **Hiking trails:** No; **Backcountry:** No; **Camping:** No; **Other overnight accommodations on site:** No, campgrounds are located nearby in Williamsburg, Newport News, and James City County. Contact the park for further information on directions and facilities; **Meals served in the park:** No; **Food and supplies obtainable in the park:** No; **Food and supplies obtainable nearby:** Yes, Yorktown and Williamsburg; **Overnight accommodations:** Along Rte. 17 in Yorktown and vicinity and in Williamsburg; **First Aid available in park:** Yes; **Nearest Hospital:** Mary Immaculate Hospital, 5 miles (8 km); **Days/Hours:** Daily from 8:30 a.m. to 5:00 p.m., with extended hours from Apr.-Oct.; **Holiday Closings:** Dec. 25; **Visitor attractions closed for seasons:** Moore House, Nelson House, and picnic areas closed in winter.

TRAVEL ACCESS: Yorktown does not receive direct airline, bus, or rail service. Transportation to either site is limited to taxi or limousine service from Williamsburg, Fort Eustis, Patrick Henry International Airport in Newport News, Norfolk International Airport, and Byrd International Airport in Richmond. **Bus:** Daily direct service by Greyhound to Williamsburg and Fort Eustis; Trailways to Richmond and Norfolk; **Rail:** Direct service by Amtrak to Williamsburg, Lee Hall, and Newport News from New York, Philadelphia, Baltimore and Washington, DC, once a day. **Air:** Approximately 5 miles (8 km) from Patrick Henry International Airport in Newport News and 45 miles (72 km) from Norfolk International Airport and Byrd International Airport in Richmond. **Other:** The Virginia Division of Tourism, under the Department of Conservation and Economic Development of the Commonwealth of Virginia, in New York, Washington, DC, and Richmond can provide further information and reservations. The Colonial Williamsburg Foundation can also be called toll free from anywhere in the Continental United Stated by dialing 1-800-446-8956 (1-800-446-8976).

Washington

ROSS LAKE NATIONAL
RECREATION AREA

LAKE CHELAN NATIONAL
RECREATION AREA

NORTH CASCADES NATIONAL PARK

SAN JUAN ISLAND
NATIONAL HISTORICAL PARK

EBEY'S LANDING NATIONAL
HISTORICAL RESERVE

OLYMPIC NATIONAL PARK

KLONDIKE GOLD RUSH
NATIONAL HISTORICAL PARK

MOUNT RAINIER NATIONAL PARK

FORT VANCOUVER NATIONAL HISTORIC SITE

COULEE DAM NATIONAL RECREATION AREA

Seattle

WHITMAN MISSION
NATIONAL HISTORIC SITE

LEWIS AND CLARK NATIONAL HISTORIC TRAIL

Coulee Dam National Recreational Area
Coulee Dam, Washington

MAILING ADDRESS: Superintendent, Coulee Dam National Recreation Area, P.O. Box 37, Coulee Dam, WA 99116 **Telephone:** 509-633-9441

DIRECTIONS: Information about access to the entire area is available from the National Recreation Area Headquarters in Coulee Dam. There are Visitor Centers at Fort Spokane and Kettle Falls, and at the Grand Coulee Dam.

Formed by the Grand Coulee Dam (part of the Columbia River Basin project), the 150-mile (241-km)-long Franklin D. Roosevelt Lake is the principal recreation feature here. Admitted to the National Park System on Dec. 18, 1946.

VISITOR ACTIVITIES: Water skiing, boating, swimming, camping, bird-watching, picnicking, audiovisual programs, interpretive talks and exhibits, fishing, hunting; **Permits:** For fishing and hunting, available at local sporting goods stores. Licenses vary in length of validity and cost; **Fees:** $7 camping fee at the following sites: Kettle Falls, Evans, Ft. Spokane, Spring Canyon, Keller Ferry, Hunters, Marcus Island, Gifford, Porcupine Bay; **Visitor facilities:** Picnic areas, boat ramps, individual and group campsites, boat and trailer dump stations, drinking water, bathhouse, ferry service; **Any limitations on vehicle usage:** Off-road vehicle use is prohibited; **Hiking trails:** Yes, 4 short, 1-mile (1.6-km) nature trails; **Backcountry:** No; **Rental Boats:** Houseboats, run-abouts, and skiff rentals at Keller Ferry and Kettle Falls concessioners; **Camping:** Yes, no reservations available for campsites; **Other overnight accommodations on site:** No, for further information on lodging in the vicinity, contact Chamber of Commerce, Grand Coulee, WA 99133, phone 509-633-0361; **Meals served in the park:** Yes, during summer at Spring Canyon Campground and Seven Bays

Marina; **Food and supplies obtainable in the park:** Yes, at various marinas; **Food and supplies obtainable nearby:** Yes, in Grand Coulee, Coulee Dam, Colville, Kettle Falls, Northport; **Overnight accommodations:** Grand Coulee, Coulee Dam, Colville, Kettle Falls, Northport; **First Aid available in park:** Yes; **Nearest Hospitals:** Grand Coulee, 5 miles (8 km) from Spring Canyon campground; Davenport, 25 miles (40 km) from Fort Spokane campground; and Colville, 10 miles (16 km) from Kettle Falls campground; **Days/Hours:** Park always open. Visitor Centers are open daily during summer months and intermittently the remainder of the year; **Holiday Closings:** Visitor Center at the Grand Coulee Dam closed Thanksgiving, Dec. 25, and Jan. 1; **Visitor attractions closed for seasons:** The recreation season is May through Oct.; **Weather:** The west arm of the lake is usually quite warm and sunny, while the north arm, influenced by the mountains, tends to be cooler and have more clouds and precipitation. Summer temperatures range from 75°-100°F during the day and between 50°and 60° at night. It is somewhat cooler in spring and autumn. Bring a light jacket for chilly evenings. Occasional foggy and cloudy days occur in winter and spring.

GENERAL INFORMATION: *For Your Safety*—Be alert to avoid floating logs and debris. Be sure to drown your campfires.

TRAVEL ACCESS: Bus: Empire Lines provides twice-daily service to Coulee Dam; **Rail:** No; **Air: No.**

Fort Vancouver National Historic Site
Vancouver, Washington

MAILING ADDRESS: Superintendent, Fort Vancouver National Historic Site, 612 E. Reserve St., Vancouver, WA 98661 **Telephone:** 206-696-7655

DIRECTIONS: To reach the site, turn off I-5 at the Mill Plain Boulevard interchange and then follow signs to the Visitor Center on East Evergreen Boulevard.

Fort Vancouver was a fur-trade depot for the Hudson's Bay Company from 1825 to 1860. From the fort, John McLoughlin, chief factor from 1825 to 1845, administered the company's fur operations in what is now British Columbia, Washington, Oregon, Idaho, and western Montana.

In 1849, the U.S. Army established a post near Fort Vancouver. The site of the Hudson's Bay Company fort was purchased by the Army in the late 1860s. A portion of Vancouver Barracks still remains active today. The site of the historic trading post was authorized for addition to the National Park Service on June 19, 1948.

VISITOR ACTIVITIES: Interpretive exhibits and tours of reconstructed buildings at the fort site; **Permits:** No; **Fees:** Yes, entrance fee at fort site, $1 for adults, $3 per family, 16 and under free; **Visitor facilities:** Parking and restrooms at the Visitor Center and at the fort site, information and sales desk; **HANDICAPPED ACCESSIBILITY:** Visitor Center and 3 buildings, restrooms at fort site; **Any limitations on vehicle usage:** No; **Hiking trails:** No; **Backcountry:** No; **Camping:** No; **Other overnight accommodations on site:** No; **Meals served in the park:** No; **Food and supplies obtainable in the park:** No; **Food and supplies obtainable nearby:** Yes, in Vancouver; **Overnight accommodations:** Vancouver; **First Aid available in park:** Yes; **Nearest Hospital:** Vancouver Memorial Hospital, 2 miles (3.2 km); **Days/Hours:** Open daily from 9:00 a.m.-5:00 p.m. with shortened hours during the winter; **Holiday Closings:** Thanksgiving, Dec. 25, and Jan. 1; **Visitor attractions closed for seasons:** Living history demonstrations are limited from Oct. through May; **Weather:** Rain is common from Oct. through May; cold weather from Nov. through Feb. Summers are warm.

GENERAL INFORMATION: *For Your Safety*—Watch your step at the fort because ground is uneven. **Special Events:** Queen Victoria's Birthday, Waterloo Day, Brigade Encampment, Candle Lantern Tour, Christmas Open House; Dates: May, June, July, Oct., and Dec. respectively.

TRAVEL ACCESS: **Bus:** Local transportation via Vancouver Transit runs regularly within 1 block of site, Greyhound provides inter-city service to terminal 1½ miles (2.4 km) away; **Rail:** Amtrak (Burlington Northern) provides regular service to terminal 2 miles (3.2 km) away; **Air:** Major airlines access through Portland International Airport, 6 miles (9.6 km) away.

NEARBY FACILITIES & POINTS OF INTEREST: Parks, other points of interest: McLoughlin House National Historical Site, Oregon City, OR.

Klondike Gold Rush National Historical Park
For details see listing in Alaska

Lewis and Clark Trail
For details see listing in Illinois

Lake Chelan National Recreation Area
Chelan, Washington   **SEE CLIMATABLE NO. 36**

MAILING ADDRESS: District Manager, Lake Chelan National Recreation Area, P.O. Box 7, Stehekin, WA 98852

DIRECTIONS: The main access to Stehekin in Lake Chelan National Recreation Area is by boat or float plane from the town of Chelan on Hwy 97. There is no road access into Stehekin. Service is provided by Lake Chelan Boat Co., Chelan, WA 98816, phone 509-682-2224. Daily boat service from Stehekin to Chelan is maintained from Apr. 15 to Oct. 15. From Oct. 16 to Apr. 14 the boats go on Sun., Mon., Wed., and Fri. There is no Sun. boat from Jan. 1-Feb. 14. Air service is available for charter year-round, weather permitting, from Chelan Airways, Chelan, WA 98816, phone 509-682-5555.
    Here the scenic Stehekin Valley, with a portion of fjordlike Lake Chelan, adjoins the southern unit of North Cascades National Park. Established by act of Congress Oct. 2, 1968.

VISITOR ACTIVITIES: Interpretive exhibits, guided and self-guiding tours, picnicking, camping, hiking, mountain climbing, horseback riding, boating, fishing, hunting, commercial river rafting; **Permits:** Required for backcountry, are available at Ranger Stations at Stehekin, Chelan, and Marblemount; **Fees:** No; **Visitor facilities:** Picnic area, campground, backcountry, boat and bicycle rentals, restaurant, lodging, supplies, post office, shuttle bus; **Any limitations on vehicle usage:** The Area is inaccessible to vehicles; **Hiking trails:** Yes, a variety from low land day hikes to elevation gains of 6,000 feet; **Backcountry:** Yes; **Camping:** Yes, no permits are required for boat camps. Reservations required by mail, filled on first-come first-served basis only for campsites. Backcountry, cross-country, and trail camps require a permit. Group camp-grounds are available by mail reservation; Write for information on reservation system for wilderness sites: North Cascades National Park Service Complex, Wilderness District Office, 728 Ranger Station Road, Marblemount, WA 98267; **Other**

overnight accommodations on site: Yes, Lodge rooms and housekeeping facilities available on a seasonal basis. Write or call North Cascades Lodge, Stehekin, WA 98852, 509-682-4711. Various private cabins for rent also; **Meals served in the park:** Yes, at North Cascades Lodge and other facilities; **Food and supplies obtainable in the park:** Yes, at North Cascades Lodge; **Food and supplies obtainable nearby:** Yes, Chelan; **Overnight accommodations:** Chelan, 50 miles (80 km); **First Aid available in park:** Yes, at Ranger Station; **Nearest Hospital:** Chelan, 50 miles (80 km); **Days/Hours:** Open 24 hours a day everyday; **Holiday Closings:** No; **Visitor attractions closed for seasons:** Guided walks and programs from late June to early Sept. Shuttle bus from May 15 to Oct. 15; **Weather:** Outdoor recreation can be enjoyed year-round. The lower levels of the valley are snow free from early Apr. to mid-Nov.

GENERAL INFORMATION: See listing in this book for North Cascades National Park and Ross Lake National Recreation Area, the 2 other areas of the North Cascades National Park Service Complex. For your safety in the backcountry: Hang all food out of the reach of bears. Stream crossings can be hazardous during periods of high water. Check conditions with a Park Ranger before starting out. Snow may linger in higher places. Crossing snowfields may require special equipment. Pelletized feed required in the backcountry; no unprocessed hay permitted. Grazing permitted in the NRA only. A camping permit is required for livestock use.

Mount Rainier National Park
Ashford, Washington   **SEE CLIMATABLE NO. 37**

MAILING ADDRESS: Superintendent, Mount Rainier National Park, Tahoma Woods, Star Route, Ashford, WA 98304 **Telephone:** 206-569-2211

DIRECTIONS: The Paradise Visitor Center is 74 miles (118.4 km) southeast of Tacoma on Route 7 to Elbe, then Route 706 to Longmire. It is 98 miles (156.8 km) southeast of Seattle and 87 miles (139.2 km) west of Yakima.
    This greatest single-peak glacial system in the contiguous U.S. radiates from the summit and slopes of an ancient dormant volcano, with dense forests and sub-alpine flowered meadows below. Established by act of Congress on Mar. 2, 1899.

VISITOR ACTIVITIES: Backcountry hiking and mountain climbing, snowshoeing, camping, cross-country skiing, picnicking, winter sports, interpretive programs, wildlife-watching; **Permits:** Permits for backcountry camping required year-round, available at Ranger Stations and Visitor Centers; **Fees:** $5; Golden Age, Golden Access, and Golden Eagle Passports are accepted and available; **Visitor facilities:** Exhibits at Visitor Centers, restrooms, lodging, hiking trails, picnic areas, cross-country ski lessons and rentals, mountain climbing, equipment rentals, food service, nature trails; **HANDICAPPED ACCESSIBILITY:** Longmire Museum, Visitor Centers accessible by inclined walkways. The National Park Inn at Longmire is accessible by ramp; dining room, restrooms, and gift shop are on main level; limited number of rooms are accessible. The Paradise Inn is accessible by outside walkway. The Sunrise Lodge accessible by ramp; restrooms are in a separate building that has limited access. Visitor Centers at Paradise and Paradise Plaza are fully accessible. Those at Longmire Plaza, Ohanapecosh Visitor Center and Sunrise Plaza have limited access. Cougar Rock Campground has limited accessible campsite and restroom. All campgrounds except Ipsut Creek have paved roadways. Self-guiding trails have limited access. Wheelchairs are available for short-time use at Visitor Centers. Texts available for audiovisual programs; **Any limitations on vehicle usage:** Vehicles must stay on public automobile roads, no commercial vehicles (other than buses); **Hiking trails:** Yes, self-guiding nature trails in different areas of the Park; **Backcountry:** Yes, permit required; inquire at Ranger Stations or Visitor Centers; **Camping:** Yes, no reservations available for campsites; **Other overnight accommodations on site:** Yes, accommodations are available at National Park Inn at Longmire open year-round and at Paradise Inn (late May through early Oct.). For information on schedule and rates, write or call Mount Rainier Guest Service, Star Route, Ashford, WA 98304, phone 206-569-2275; **Meals served in the park:** Yes, Longmire, Paradise Inn, Paradise Visitor Center, and Sunrise; **Food and supplies obtainable in the park:** Yes, at Longmire and Sunrise; **Food and supplies obtainable nearby:** Yes, at Ashford, Elbe, Packwood, Enumclaw; **Overnight accommodations:** Ashford, Hwy 706, Alder and Elbe, Hwy 7 immediately adjacent to the Park; **First Aid available in park:** Yes; **Nearest Hospital:** Enumclaw, Hwy 410, 45 miles (72 km); Morton, Hwy 12, 40 miles (64 km), Good Samaritan Hospital, Puyallup, WA 40 miles (64 km); **Days/Hours:** Open 24 hours a day year-round; **Holiday Closings:** No; **Visitor attractions closed for seasons:** Snow closes roads for short periods. Chains may be required for winter driving. Except for the roads from Nisqually Entrance to Paradise (WA 706), many park roads are usually closed from late Nov. through June or July.

GENERAL INFORMATION: *For Your Safety*—In the backcountry, hike only in the company of others; remember your limitations. Be prepared for sudden and extreme weather changes. Bring your own shelter. Conducted climbs are given by Rainier Mountaineering, Inc., 201 St. Helens, Tacoma, WA 98042, 206-627-6242. From June to Sept., Paradise, WA 98398, 206-569-2227.

North Cascades National Park
Sedro Woolley, Washington

MAILING ADDRESS: Superintendent, North Cascades National Park, 2105 Highway 20, Sedro Woolley, WA 98284 **Telephone:** 206-856-5700

DIRECTIONS: Access to the North Cascades area from Burlington on the west and Twisp on the east follows WA 20 with branch routes to Baker Lake and Cascade River. Hiking access and roadside views of the northwest corner are available from WA 542 east from Bellingham. Access to Stehekin Valley is by boat, float-plane, or trail. Vehicle access to Ross Lake is by unimproved road from Canada.

High jagged peaks intercept moisture-laden winds, producing glaciers, icefalls, waterfalls, and other water phenomena in this wild alpine region, with varied plant and animal communities in the valleys. Established by act of Congress on Oct. 2, 1968.

VISITOR ACTIVITIES: Camping, backcountry, viewing scenery, hiking, mountain climbing, horseback riding, fishing, auto tours, boating, wildlife- and bird-watching; **Permits:** For backcountry, available without charge at Park Offices or Ranger Stations and by mail through the Wilderness District Office in Marblemount. Call 206/873-4500 for permit information. A Washington State fishing license, available locally, is required; **Fees:** Yes, fees are charged in the developed road access campgrounds in Ross Lake National Recreation Area; **Visitor facilities:** Campgrounds, launching ramps, resorts, hiking trails, horse and mule rentals nearby, professional guide and packtrain services; **HANDICAPPED ACCESSIBILITY:** Sedro Woolley Headquarters: Office and restrooms; some overlooks and campgrounds; **Any limitations on vehicle usage:** Vehicles are restricted to maintained roads; **Hiking trails:** Yes, about 360 miles (576 km) of hiking and horse trails throughout the 4 North Cascades units; **Backcountry:** Yes, information can be obtained from Park Offices or Ranger Stations; **Camping:** Yes, no reservations available for campsites. All vehicle accessible campgrounds available on a first come-first served basis; **Other overnight accommodations on site:** Yes, for information on lodging, contact North Cascades Lodge, Stehekin, WA 98852; Diablo Lake Resort, P.O. Box 176, Rockport, WA 98283; Ross Lake Resort, Rockport, WA 98283. See listings in this book for two other units of the North Cascades National Park Complex: the Ross Lake and Lake Chelan National Recreation Areas for accommodations available; **Meals served in the park:** No; **Food and supplies obtainable in the park:** No; **Food and supplies obtainable nearby:** Yes, Marblemount, Newhalem and Stehekin area. (Also see listings in this book for Ross Lake and Lake Chelan National Recreation Area.); **Overnight accommodations:** The larger cities and towns near the North Cascades group have the usual tourist accommodations, but are 2-to-3 hour drives from park boundaries. Small communities within or adjacent to the areas have limited guest accommodations. The Chambers of Commerce for each of the counties and towns surrounding the North Cascades group have information on accommodations, packers, guides, and other outdoor services; **First Aid available in park:** Yes, at Ranger Stations; **Nearest Hospital:** Sedro Woolley; **Days/Hours:** Park open all year, but snow conditions prevent access during the winter. Highway 20, the North Cascades Highway, closes to through vehicle traffic during winter months. Exact time of closure depends on snow and avalanche conditions; **Holiday Closings:** No; **Visitor attractions closed for seasons:** Restricted access to most areas in winter; **Weather:** Outdoor recreation can be enjoyed year-round. The lower elevations and the big lakes are accessible from early Apr. to mid-Oct., but at higher elevations the season is from mid-July to mid-Sept. The western side of the North Cascades gets more rain, has more lakes and streams, and more abundant vegetation. Consequently, it has less sunshine and cooler days than the eastern side of the mountains, where more sunshine, warm rock surfaces, and sparse vegetation afford warm days and cool nights typical of a dry climate.

GENERAL INFORMATION: The new North Cascades National Park Visitor Center, located at Newhalem, will open in the fall of 1992. See listings in this book for 2 other units of the North Cascades Group: Lake Chelan and Ross Lake National Recreation Areas. *For Your Safety in the backcountry:* Hang all food out of the reach of bears. Stream crossings can be hazardous during periods of high water. Check conditions with a Park Ranger before starting out. Snow may linger in higher places. Crossing snowfields may require special equipment. Adequate feed should be carried for horses. Forage is scarce in most of the park. Grazing not permitted in the Park. A special permit is required for livestock use.

Olympic National Park
Port Angeles, Washington   **SEE CLIMATABLE NO. 38**

MAILING ADDRESS: Superintendent, Olympic National Park, 600 East Park Avenue, Port Angeles, WA 98362 **Telephone:** 206-452-4501, extension 230

DIRECTIONS: Visitor Centers at Port Angeles and Hoh Rain Forest are open year-around. Kalaloch and Storm King Visitor Centers are open only in the summer.

This mountain wilderness contains the finest remnant of Pacific Northwest rain forest (the only temperate zone rain forest in North America), active glaciers, rare Roosevelt elk, and 57 miles (91.2 km) of wild, scenic ocean shore. Proclaimed a national monument on Mar. 2, 1909; established as a national park on June 29, 1938. Olympic is a World Heritage Park and Biosphere Reserve.

VISITOR ACTIVITIES: Interpretive and audiovisual programs, camping, auto tours, bird- and wildlife-watching, picnicking, nature walks, hiking, horseback riding, mountain climbing, fishing, backcountry, swimming, skiing, snowshoeing; **Permits:** For backcountry, available at Ranger Stations; **Fees:** Entrance fees (good for 7 days) will be collected at Elwha, Heart O' the Hills/Hurricane Ridge, Hoh, and Soleduck entrance stations from Memorial Day through Labor Day or later. Year-round for camping in developed "class A" campgrounds; **Visitor facilities:** Nature trails, parking, restrooms, campgrounds, fireplaces, picnic area, beaches, bathhouse, ski and snowshoe trails, lodging; **HANDICAPPED ACCESSIBILITY:** Most restrooms. Accessible trails: Madison Falls, Hall of Mosses, and Spruce Nature trails. Trails accessible with assistance: Hurricane Hill, Meadow Loop, Marymere Falls, Rialto Beach and parts of Hall of Mosses and Spruce Nature trails. **Any limitations on vehicle usage:** Vehicles are restricted to designated roadways; **Hiking trails:** Yes, trails vary from those requiring a day or less to wilderness pathways taking up to a week or more. Trails open year-round with higher elevations accessible normally between July 15-Oct. 1. Trail condition reports are available at Visitor Centers and Ranger Stations; **Backcountry:** Yes, information available at Ranger Stations and Visitor Centers; **Camping:** Yes, reservations for groups only at Kalaloch, Mora, Ozette, or Quinault Ranger Stations; **Other overnight accommodations on site:** Yes, reserve lodging by the lodging facility; Kalaloch Lodge, Inc., HC-80, Box 1100, Forks, WA 98331, phone 206-962-2271; Log Cabin Resort, 6540 E. Beach Road, Port Angeles, WA 98362, phone 206-928-3245; Lake Crescent Lodge, HC-62, Box 11, Port Angeles, WA 98362, phone 206-928-3211; Sol Duc Hot Springs Resort, P.O. Box 2169, Port Angeles, WA 98362, phone 206-327-3583; **Meals served in the park:** Yes, at Hurricane Ridge, Sol Duc, Fairholm, Kalaloch, Lake Crescent; **Food and supplies obtainable in the park:** Yes, at small grocery at some lodges; **Food and supplies obtainable nearby:** Yes, at supermarkets at Sequim, Port Angeles, Forks, Shelton, and Aberdeen; **Overnight accommodations:** Port Angeles, Aberdeen, Forks, Sequim and Shelton. For information on facilities near the park, write the Olympic Peninsula Resort and Hotel Association, Coleman Ferry Terminal, Seattle, WA 98104; **First Aid available in park:** Yes, at most Ranger Stations; **Nearest Hospital:** Port Angeles, Forks, Shelton, Aberdeen-Hoquiam; **Days/Hours:** Park open year-round. Only Visitor Centers and Ranger Stations have closing hours. Most Ranger Stations open 8 a.m.-5 p.m. Hoh Visitor Center: 9 a.m.-4 p.m. Port Angeles Visitor Center: 8 a.m.-4 p.m.; **Holiday Closings:** Buildings closed Dec. 25, and Jan. 1; **Visitor attractions closed for seasons:** Some lodges are open only in summer. All roads in high elevations are usually open June 1-Oct. 1; high elevation trails normally open July 15-Oct. 1.

GENERAL INFORMATION: *For your safety*—Stay on trails. Backcountry campers should include a tent and a backpacker's stove in their equipment. Keep your distance from animals. When hiking on the beach, round the headlands only on the outgoing tide to avoid being trapped against the headland cliffs by the incoming tide. The tide and cliffs permit no escape.

Ross Lake National Recreation Area
Sedro Woolley, Washington   **SEE CLIMATABLE NO. 36**

MAILING ADDRESS: Superintendent, Ross Lake National Recreation Area, c/o North Cascades National Park, 2105 Highway 20, Sedro Woolley, WA 98284 **Telephone:** 206-856-5700

DIRECTIONS: Access to the Park is via WA 20 from Burlington on the west and Winthrop on the east. The north end of Ross Lake is reached by a 38 mile (60.8 km) gravel road exiting from the Trans-Canada Highway near Hope, British Columbia. *Note:* There is no road access from Highway 20 to the south end of Ross Lake.

Ringed by mountains, this recreation area in the Skagit River drainage separates the north and south units of North Cascades National Park. Established by act of Congress on Oct. 2, 1968.

VISITOR ACTIVITIES: Hiking, boating, canoeing, viewing scenery, rock climbing, camping, wildlife- and bird-watching, auto tours, backcountry, horseback riding; **Permits:** Required for backcountry, can be obtained at all Ranger Stations and by mail through the Wilderness District Office in Marblemount. Call 206-873-4500 for permit information. *Note:* A Washington State Fishing license, available locally, is required for fishing; **Fees:** Camping fee is $7 per night per site at Colonial Creek and Newhalem Creek Campgrounds, $5 per night at Goodell Creek Campground (camping fees subject to change); **Visitor facilities:** Boat rentals, campgrounds, lodging, boat launching ramps, wayside exhibits; **HANDICAPPED ACCESSIBILITY:** Call for details; **Any limitations on vehicle usage:** Only 1 vehicle is allowed at each campsite. Vehicles are restricted to maintained roads; **Hiking trails:** Yes, 7 major trails lead outward from Ross Lake into the backcountry; **Backcountry:** Yes, information can be obtained by writing the Superintendent or visiting park offices in Sedro Woolley, Chelan, or Marblemount; **Camping:** Yes, no reservations available for campsites. All vehicle accessible campgrounds available on a first come-first served basis; **Other overnight accommodations on site:** Yes, for information on lodging, contact: Diablo Lake Resort, Rockport, WA 98283, phone 206-386-4429; Ross Lake Resort, Rockport, WA 98283, phone 206-386-4437; **Meals served in the park:** Yes, Diablo Lake Resort; **Food and supplies obtainable in the park:** Yes, at Diablo Lake Resort and Newhalem, WA; **Food and supplies obtainable nearby:** Yes, at Marblemount, WA, and Concrete, WA; **Overnight accommodations:** Marblemount, WA, 8 miles (12.8 km); Concrete, WA, 28 miles (44.8 km); **First Aid available in park:** Yes, or nearby in Diablo and Newhalem, WA; **Nearest Hospital:** Sedro Woolley, WA 20, 50 miles (80 km); **Days/Hours:** Park open year-round; **Holiday Closings:** Office closed Dec. 25, and Jan. 1; **Visitor attractions closed for seasons:** Hwy 20 and all campgrounds except Goodell Creek are closed in winter; **Weather:** Summer is warm and sometimes quite hot with temperatures sometimes reaching the high 90°sF. Fall has warm days and cool nights. Hazardous strong winds and whitecaps on lake waters occur frequently and without warning.

GENERAL INFORMATION: See listings in this book for other units of the North Cascades Group: Lake Chelan National Recreation Area and North Cascades National Park. Seattle City Light offers tours of their hydro-electric projects. For tour reservations and year-round information, contact the Skagit Tour desk at Seattle City Light, 1015 Third Avenue, Seattle, Washington. Telephone: 206-684-3030. The new North Cascades National Park Visitor Center, located at Newhalem, will be open in the fall of 1992. *For Your Safety in the backcountry:* Hang all food out of the reach of bears. Stream crossings can be hazardous during periods of high water. Check conditions with the Park Ranger before starting out. Snow may linger in higher places. Crossing snowfields may require special equipment. Adequate feed should be carried for horses. Forage is scarce in most of the park. Grazing not permitted in the park. A special permit is required for livestock use.

San Juan Island National Historical Park
Friday Harbor, Washington

MAILING ADDRESS: Superintendent, San Juan Island National Historical Park, Box 429, Friday Harbor, WA 98250 **Telephone:** 206-378-2240

DIRECTIONS: San Juan Island is reached by Washington State Ferries from Anacortes, WA, 83 miles (132.8 km) north of Seattle; or from Sidney, British Columbia, 15 miles (24 km) north of Victoria. The island is also accessible by private boats. There are good docking facilities at Friday and Roche Harbors. Commercial air flights are scheduled regularly from Bellingham and Seattle, WA, to Friday Harbor. Private 1- and 2-engine planes can land at airstrips at Friday and Roche Harbors.

The park commemorates the peaceful settlement reached through arbitration by the United States and Great Britain in the 1859 boundary dispute over the ownership of the San Juan Islands. British and American military campsites are included. Authorized for addition to the National Park System on Sept. 9, 1966.

VISITOR ACTIVITIES: Picnicking, hiking, interpretive exhibits—no camping is allowed at either American or British Camps; **Permits:** No; **Fees:** No; **Visitor facilities:** Park headquarters and information center is located in Friday Harbor at 125 Spring Street. It is open 8 a.m. to 4:30 p.m. Mon. through Fri. in fall, winter, and spring and 8 a.m. to 6 p.m. daily in summer. **Visitor facilities:** Rangers are on duty during the summer to answer questions and explain points of interest. Picnic areas are available at both camps but water is only available at the American Camp. Facilities for small fires are provided at American Camp; **Any limitations on vehicle usage:** Off-road vehicle travel is not allowed within the park; **Hiking trails:** Yes, American and British Camps have historic trails; **Backcountry:** No; **Camping:** No; **Other overnight accommodations on site:** No; **Meals served in the park:** No, but, nearby at Friday and Roche Harbors; **Food and supplies obtainable in the park:** No; **Food and supplies obtainable nearby:** Yes, Friday Harbor (year-round); **Overnight accommodations:** Friday Harbor, 6 miles (9.6 km) from American Camp, and 11 miles (17.6 km) from British Camp; **First Aid available in park:** Yes; **Nearest Hospital:** Friday Harbor, 6 miles (9.6 km) from American Camp, and 11 miles (17.6 km) from British Camp; **Days/Hours:** The roads through the park are open year-round. The buildings are open about 9 a.m. to 6 p.m. daily during the summer and on weekends during spring and fall; **Holiday Closings:** Thanksgiving, Dec. 25, and Jan. 1; **Visitor attractions closed for seasons:** Buildings and exhibits at British Camp are closed for the winter; **Weather:** Winters can be cold, windy and rainy; summers are warm, but never hot.

GENERAL INFORMATION: *For your safety*—Watch your step, especially in the vicinity of the American Camp. The San Juan rabbit digs many holes that can cause sprained ankles and broken bones. Swimming is discouraged because the water temperature remains below 50° all year. Try beachcombing instead. Tree climbing is dangerous for you and harmful to the trees. Look out for insecure footing on the primitive trails and watch for overhanging branches and downed limbs.

Whitman Mission National Historic Site
Walla Walla, Washington

MAILING ADDRESS: Superintendent, Whitman Mission National Historic Site, Route 2, Box 247, Walla Walla, WA 99362 **Telephone:** 509-529-2761

DIRECTIONS: The Visitor Center is 7 miles (11.2 km) west of Walla Walla on US 12. It is 3 miles (4.8 km) west of College Place.
   Dr. and Mrs. Marcus Whitman founded a mission among the Cayuse Indians in 1836 until slain in an uprising in 1847. The Mission was a landmark on the Oregon Trail. Authorized for addition to the National Park System in 1936.

VISITOR ACTIVITIES: Interpretive exhibits, picnicking, cultural demonstrations; **Permits:** No; **Fees:** Yes, $1 per adult, $3 maximum per family; **Visitor facilities:** Self-guiding foot trails, wayside exhibits, museum with audiovisual program, picnic area; **HANDICAPPED ACCESSIBILITY:** All facilities; **Any limitations on vehicle usage:** No; **Hiking trails:** No, there are 9/10 mile (1.4 km) of foot trails; **Backcountry:** No; **Camping:** No; **Other overnight accommodations on site:** No; **Meals served in the park:** No; **Food and supplies ob-**

tainable in the park: No; **Food and supplies obtainable nearby:** Yes, College Place and Walla Walla; **Overnight accommodations:** Walla Walla and College Place, 6-8 miles (9.6-12.8 km) east of the park; **First Aid available in park:** Yes, in the Visitor Center; **Nearest Hospital:** Walla Walla, 8 miles (12.8 km) east of the park; **Days/Hours:** Open daily from 8 a.m. to 4:30 p.m., with extended hours in summer; **Holiday Closings:** Thanksgiving, Dec. 25, and Jan 1; **Visitor attractions closed for seasons:** Cultural demonstrations are only offered in summer; **Weather:** Summer is hot and dry; winter is cold and dry.

West Virginia

Bluestone National Scenic River
Glen Jean, West Virginia

MAILING ADDRESS: New River Gorge NR, Post Office Box 246, Glen Jean, WV 25846. Contact: Superintendent of New River Gorge NR, Joseph Kennedy **Telephone:** 304-465-0508

Is now open to visitors.
This scenic river preserves relatively unspoiled land in southwest West Virginia. It contains both natural and historic features of the Appalachian plateau. The 11 river miles of the lower Bluestone offer excellent warm water fishing, hiking, boating, and scenic drives.
Authorized: Oct. 26, 1988. Land surveys being conducted.

Gauley River National Recreation Area
Glen Jean, West Virginia

MAILING ADDRESS: Gauley River National Recreation Area, c/o New River Gorge National River, Post Office Box 246, Glen Jean, WV 25846. Contact: Superintendent of New River Gorge NR, Joseph Kennedy **Telephone:** 304-465-0508

The 25 miles of free-flowing Gauley River and the 6 miles of the Meadow River pass through scenic gorges and valleys containing a wide variety of natural and cultural features. The Gauley River contains several stretches of Class VI rapids, making it one of the most adventurous whitewater boating rivers in the eastern U.S. Both rivers provide excellent fishing and hiking.

Authorized: Oct. 26, 1988. Land surveys are being conducted.

Appalachian National Scenic Trail
For details see listing in Maine

Harpers Ferry National Historical Park
Harpers Ferry, West Virginia   **SEE CLIMATABLE NO. 68**

MAILING ADDRESS: Superintendent, Harpers Ferry National Historical Park, P.O. Box 65, Harpers Ferry, WV 25425 **Telephone:** 304-535-6371, ext. 6222

DIRECTIONS: The Park is 20 miles (32.2 km) southwest of Frederick, MD, via US 340. Signs along US 340 direct visitors to the Visitor Center and parking facility by turning at the signal light on US 340.

A Federal Armory was established at Harpers Ferry in the late 1700s. John Brown's raid took place here in 1859. Because of its strategic location at the confluence of the Shenandoah and Potomac Rivers, the town changed hands many times during the Civil War. Authorized for addition to the National Park System on June 20, 1944.

VISITOR ACTIVITIES: Interpretive audiovisual progam, walking tours, mountain climbing, hiking, fishing, living history demonstrations, wildflower-watching, Christmas festival on the first weekend in December; **Permits:** Yes, permit for climbing, must be obtained at Park Ranger's office; **Fees:** Yes; **Visitor facilities:** Parking, restrooms, picnic area, restored sites. Campgrounds are in the immediate area, but not in the park itself; **Any limitations on vehicle usage:** Drive carefully; automobile traffic on the narrow streets is often quite heavy; **Hiking trails:** Yes, variety of hiking trails are located nearby; **Backcountry:** No; **Camping:** No; **Other overnight accommodations on site:** No, but several are located nearby, see Nearby Facilities Section. **Meals served in the park:** No; **Food and supplies obtainable in the park:** No; **Food and supplies obtainable nearby:** Yes, in the towns of Harpers Ferry, Boliver, Charles Town, and other nearby communities; **Overnight accommodations:** Harpers Ferry, Charles Town, on US 340, 7 miles (11.2 km); **First Aid available in park:** Yes, at the Ranger Office; **Nearest Hospital:** Charles Town, US 340, 7 miles (11.2 km); **Days/Hours:** The Visitor Center and National Park Service sites are open daily all year, from 8 a.m. to 5 p.m.; **Holiday Closings:** Dec. 25; **Visitor attractions closed for seasons:** Most of the activities in the park are centered around the spring and summer months. In the fall and spring, park activities are usually restricted to weekends, but the Visitor Center and several of the historic buildings do remain open. Wildflowers abound in late spring, and fall colors are striking.

GENERAL INFORMATION: Brick and natural stone walkways and steps are sometimes uneven or slippery. Pedestrians, especially children, should be cautious, as automobile traffic is often quite heavy. Mountain climbers must register at the Ranger Station before climbing the cliffs on Maryland Heights. Beware of the rivers. At low water they appear calm and peaceful. This is deceptive, however, as deep holes and swift undercurrents make them treacherous at any time of the year. There are no frequent checks on pollutants. Swimming is not advised. Fishermen and boaters should wear life jackets.

TRAVEL ACCESS: **Bus:** No; **Rail:** Call 1-800-325-RAIL, or 304-535-6346; **Air:** No.

NEARBY FACILITIES & POINTS OF INTEREST: **Hotel/Motel:** Comfort Inn, Harpers Ferry, WV 25425, 304-535-6391, ½ mile (.8 km) from park; Hilltop House Hotel, Harpers Ferry, WV 25425, 304-535-6321, ½ mile (.8 km) from park; Cliffside Motor Inn, Harpers Ferry, WV 25425, 304-535-6302, 1 mile (1.6 km) from park. 8 km) from park; **Food/Supplies:** A variety of restaurants are within walking distance of the park; **Campgrounds:** Camp Resort - ½ mile (.8 km) from park, 304-535-6869; Canal Campground - 4 miles (6.4 km) from park, 301-834-9240. **Parks, other points of interest:** Antietam National Battlefield, 16 miles (25.6 km), Gettysburg 60 miles (96 km).

New River Gorge National River
West Virginia

MAILING ADDRESS: New River Gorge National River, P.O. Box 246, Glen Jean, WV 25846 **Telephone:** 304-465-0508

DIRECTIONS: The Canyon Rim Visitor Center is open year-round and located on U.S. Route 19 near Fayetteville at the north end of the New River Gorge Bridge. The Hinton Visitor Center, located on State Route 3 By-Pass at Hinton, West Virginia, is open seasonally. The Grandview Visitor Contact Station is located six miles off Interstate 64 on State Route 9 and open seasonally. The Old Glen Jean Bank Visitor Contact Station is located one-half mile off U.S. Route 19 at Glen Jean, West Virginia, and is open seasonally. All visitor contact stations are handicapped accessible. Special interpretive programs are scheduled throughout the year at each of the visitor contact areas.

Eastern National Park and Monument Association provides sales literature for more in-depth information about the Park.

New River Gorge National River preserves 53 miles (84.8 km) of the New River in West Virginia, from Hinton to Fayetteville, as a free-flowing stream abundant in natural, scenic, historic, and recreational values. It was authorized for addition to the National Park System on November 10, 1978.

HANDICAPPED ACCESSIBILITY: Canyon Rim Visitor Center, Kaymoor and Bridge Overlooks; Boardwalk Overlook not accessible.

TRAVEL ACCESS: **Bus:** Greyhound provides service to Beckley, WV; **Rail:** Amtrak service at Prince and Hinton, WV, with Thurmond, WV, as a summer seasons flagstop; **Air:** Service to Charleston (1-hour drive away) and Beckley. **Other:** Taxicab service available from Oak Hill, Beckley, and Hinton.

NEARBY FACILITIES & POINTS OF INTEREST: **Hotel/Motel:** Towns close to the park provide lodging. Chain motels include the Holiday Inn, Ramada Inn, Best Western, Beckley, WV; Holiday Inn and Comfort Inn located in Oak Hill and Fayetteville, respectively; **Campgrounds:** Babcock State Park is located within the National River boundary; Private campgrounds and other state park campgrounds are located throughout the National River vicinity; **Parks, other points of interest:** Nearby state parks offer a variety of recreational attractions. Theater West Virginia performs three outdoor dramas at Grandview during the summer months. An exhibition coal mine is at Beckley, WV. The longest single, steel arch bridge in the world is located at Fayetteville.

Wisconsin

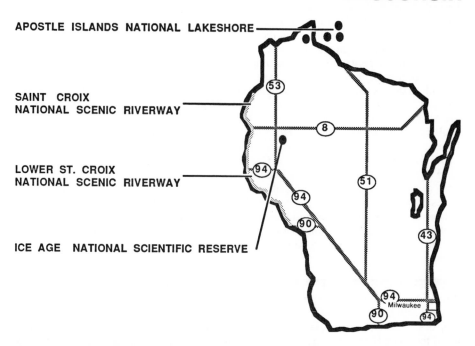

APOSTLE ISLANDS NATIONAL LAKESHORE

SAINT CROIX
NATIONAL SCENIC RIVERWAY

LOWER ST. CROIX
NATIONAL SCENIC RIVERWAY

ICE AGE NATIONAL SCIENTIFIC RESERVE

Apostle Islands National Lakeshore
Bayfield, Wisconsin

MAILING ADDRESS: Superintendent, Apostle Islands National Lakeshore, Route 1, Box 4, Bayfield, WI 54814 **Telephone:** 715-779-3397

DIRECTIONS: East of Duluth from US 2, WI 13 leads north up the east shore of Bayfield Peninsula to Bayfield, site of the Park Headquarters and Visitor Center.

The Lakeshore comprises 21 picturesque wooded islands and an 11-mile (17.6-km) strip of adjacent Bayfield Peninsula in the southwestern portion of Lake Superior characterized by sand beaches, high clay banks, and sandstone cliffs. Established by act of Congress on Sept. 26, 1970.

VISITOR ACTIVITIES: Island camping, hiking, picnicking, swimming, boating, excursion boats, sea kayaking and scuba diving, water taxi service, chartered fishing trips, rental sail boats and outstanding sport fishing are available; **Permits:** Yes, Wisconsin State fishing license is available locally. Free backcountry permits available at Visitor Centers. Free dive permit (available at Visitor Centers) required for scuba diving in the National Lakeshore; **Fees:** No; **Visitor facilities:** Interpretive exhibits and audiovisual programs at Visitor Center and in summer, evening programs and nature walks are presented at various mainland and island locations. Tours of lighthouse and historic commercial fisheries conducted during summer months. Campgrounds in numerous designated areas, concessioners provide shuttle trips between islands and excursion trips. Sailboat rental, charter fishing trips, marina, launch ramps, parking and showers also available in the area; **HANDICAPPED ACCESSIBILITY:** The Park Headquarters Visitor Center in Bayfield is accessible to the handicapped. The Apostle Islands Cruise Service excursion boat is also accessible. Handicapped visitors travelling through the islands by boat will find the Visitor Center on Stockton Island and the grounds of the Manitou Island Fish Camp to be accessible. **Any limitations on vehicle usage:** No motor vehicles permitted on islands within the park; **Hiking trails:** Yes, wide range from maintained trails to old logging and railroad trails overgrown with underbrush or rocky trails, which may be slippery or loose; **Backcountry:** Yes, on islands; **Camping:** Yes; **Other overnight accommodations on site:** No; **Meals served in the park:** No; **Food and supplies obtainable in the park:** No; **Food and supplies obtainable nearby:** Yes, at Bayfield, Cornucopia, Ashland, Washburn, and Madeline Island; **Overnight accommodations:** Bayfield, Washburn, Ashland, Cornucopia, and the nearby Chequamegon National Forest; **First Aid available in park:** Yes; **Nearest Hospital:** Ashland, Hwy 13, 23 miles (36.8 km); **Days/ Hours:** 8 a.m. to 6 p.m. Memorial Day through Labor Day; daily 8:00 a.m. to 4:30 p.m. Labor Day through the last weekend in Oct., and Mon. through Fri., 8 a.m. to 4:30 p.m., the remainder of the year; **Holiday Closings:** Thanksgiving, Dec. 25, and Jan. 1; **Visitor attractions closed for seasons:** Yes, tours offered summer months only; **Weather:** Winter temperatures of -30°F and wind chill factors of -60°F are not uncommon. Nearly 100 inches of snow falls each year. Winter ice conditions vary with temperature, snowfall, and wind. Extreme caution is required for traveling across ice, as shifting winds may cause cracks and floes. Summer temperatures average 80°F during the day and 55°F at night. Thundershowers are common.

GENERAL INFORMATION: Biting insects are common from early May to mid-Aug. When hiking or camping, be prepared. Insect repellents are useful, but clothing that covers exposed skin is the best protection. Black bears can be found on several of the islands. To keep bears out of a campsite, keep it clean and store food in plastic bags suspended at least 10 ft. off the ground between two trees. Hiking near cliffs can be dangerous! Wet rocks are slippery and loose rocks may cause falls. Beware of dangerous waters. Even in summer, Lake Superior's waters are dangerously cold, and sudden storms break its surface. The temperature of the water a meter or so from shore may be 50°F or less—cold enough to cause a strong swimmer to drown in 15 minutes.

About 3 miles (4.8 km) north of Bayfield is the Red Cliff Indian Reservation, the home of approximately 600 Chippewa Indians. Madeline Island, the largest Apostle Island, is not in the National Lakeshore. It can be reached by a 20 minute car ferry ride from Bayfield. Big Bay State Park and the Madeline Island Museum are two of the island's attractions.

TRAVEL ACCESS: **Other:** Mainland Visitor Centers accessible by car. Islands in the park accessible by private boat (sea kayak, power and sail) and through the Apostle Islands Cruise Service and the Apostle Islands Water-Taxi, Inc.

Ice Age National Scientific Reserve
Wisconsin

MAILING ADDRESS: Wisconsin Department of Natural Resources, P.O. Box 7921, Madison, WI 53707 **Telephone:** 608-266-2181

DIRECTIONS: Devils Lake and Mill Bluff are accessible from Int. 90-94. Kettle Moraine is accessible from WI 67, which runs through the unit. Access to Interstate Unit is from US 8 and WI 35.

This first national scientific reserve contains significant features of continental glaciation. There are nine separate units located across the State from Lake Michigan on the east to the St. Croix River on the Minnesota-Wisconsin border. Five of the nine units are operational: The Kettle Moraine State Forest, Devils Lake, Mill Bluff, Interstate Parks, and the Horicon Marsh Wildlife Area. Authorized for addition to the National Park System on Oct. 13, 1964.

VISITOR ACTIVITIES: Interpretive exhibits, auto tours, camping, hiking, fishing, swimming, picnicking, naturalist services, cross-country skiing; **Permits:** Wisconsin fishing licenses, available from local sporting goods stores or from the Department of Natural Resources, are required; **Fees:** Vehicle use fees are $3.50 per day or $14 annually for residents of Wisconsin, $6 per day or $30 annually for non-residents. Camping fees vary from $4 to $10 per site, depending on facilities. Golden Eagle, Golden Age, and Golden Access Passports accepted for admission and available; **Visitor facilities:** Scenic drives, hiking trails, beaches, campgrounds, picnic areas, restrooms, ski trails; Visitor Centers at Kettle Moraine and Interstate; Nature Center at Devils Lake; **HANDICAPPED ACCESSIBILITY:** Camping, picnicking, Kettle Moraine, Devils Lake, Interstate, Mill Bluff; **Any limitations on vehicle usage:** Motor vehicles should be operated only where permitted; **Hiking trails:** Yes, trails vary from nature walks to a 30-mile (48-km) hiking trail at Kettle Moraine, which offers reserved shelters; **Backcountry:** Yes, by contacting Kettle Moraine, phone 414-626-2116; **Camping:** Yes, information by contacting the following units: Devils Lake, phone 608-356-8301; Northern Kettle Moraine, phone 414-626-2116; Interstate, phone 715-483-3747, Mill Bluff, phone 608-427-6692; **Other overnight accommodations on site:** No; **Meals served in the park:** No; **Food and supplies obtainable in the park:** Yes, at Kettle Moraine and Devils Lake; **Food and supplies obtainable nearby:** Yes, Baraboo, Campbellsport, St. Croix Falls, Horicon, and other nearby towns; **Overnight accommodations:** Baraboo, Campbellsport, St. Croix Falls, and other towns near the Ice Age Units; **First Aid available in park:** Yes; **Nearest Hospital:** Fond du Lac, Baraboo, Campbellsport, St. Croix Falls, and other nearby communities; **Days/Hours:** Most parks open from 6 a.m. to 11 p.m.; **Holiday Closings:** No; **Visitor attractions closed for seasons:** Naturalist activities are curtailed at Mill Bluff during the off-season, but are offered year-round at Kettle Moraine, Devils Lake, Interstate, and Horicon.

GENERAL INFORMATION: *For Your Safety*—When hiking, stay on designated trails. Swim only in authorized areas when lifeguards are on duty.

Ice Age National Scenic Trail
Wisconsin

MAILING ADDRESS: National Park Service, 700 Rayovac Drive, Suite 100, Madison, WI 53711 **Telephone:** 608-264-5610

DIRECTIONS: When completed, this scenic Trail will meander approximately 1,000 miles (1,600 km) across Wisconsin following a chain of glacial landscape features—moraines, eskers, kames, kettles, potholes, and erratics. Six of the nine units of the Ice Age National Scientific Reserve are linked together by the trail. Four hundred miles (640 km) of the trail are presently available for public use.

Designated by an act of Congress on October 3, 1980.

VISITOR ACTIVITIES: Hiking, backpacking, camping, nature study. Some trail segments are open to bicycling, cross-country skiing, and limited snowmobiling; **Permits:** Yes, for a few trail segments; **Fees:** Yes, for some developed campgrounds within the National Forest and State Parks along the trail; **Visitor facilities:** Various, as provided by the managing authority for a particular segment; **HANDICAPPED ACCESSIBILITY:** Restrooms, Visitor

Centers, and other facilities are accessible in *some* park and forest areas along the trail. Few segments of the trail itself are accessible. **Any limitations on vehicle usage:** Except for certain segments open to snowmobiling, use of motorized vehicles by the public is prohibited along the trail; **Hiking trails:** Yes; **Backcountry:** Yes, for information, write to the above address; **Camping:** As permitted; **Other overnight accommodations on site:** No; **Meals served in the park:** No; **Food and supplies obtainable in the park:** Yes, in some parks along the trail; **Food and supplies obtainable nearby:** Yes, in many communities along the trail; **Overnight accommodations:** In many communities along/near the trail; **First Aid available in park:** No; **Days/Hours:** Open at all times, except as limited by regulations governing individual parks/forests or private lands through which the trail passes.

TRAVEL ACCESS: Many points on or near the trail are accessible by bus, rail, or air.

NEARBY FACILITIES & POINTS OF INTEREST: Scenic, historic, natural, and cultural interests are located along the trail. The main theme of the trail is Wisconsin's glacial features. **Campsites:** Reservation systems in use for some public and private campgrounds.

Lower St. Croix National Scenic Riverway
Wisconsin (also in Minnesota)

MAILING ADDRESS: Superintendent, Lower Saint Croix River, c/o Saint Croix National Scenic River, P.O. Box 708, St. Croix Falls, WI 54024 **Telephone:** 715-483-3284

DIRECTIONS: Park Headquarters located at the corner of Hamilton and Massachusetts Streets in St. Croix Falls, WI.
Recreational opportunities for much of the upper Midwest are provided here along this 52-mile (83.2-km) segment of the St. Croix River, a component of the Wild and Scenic River System. Authorized for addition to the National Park System on Oct. 25, 1972; 27 miles (43.2 km) of this segment are administered by the National Park Service with the remaining 25 miles (40 km) administered by the states of Wisconsin and Minnesota.

VISITOR ACTIVITIES: Boating, fishing, camping, interpretive exhibits, swimming, hunting, and hiking within state parks located along the Riverway, commercial boat trips; **Permits:** No; **Fees:** No; **Visitor facilities:** Visitor Center with exhibits and auditorium at Stillwater, MN. Campgrounds, boat ramps, canoe rentals, commercial guided boat trip available on the river at Taylor's Falls and Stillwater, MN; **HANDICAPPED ACCESSIBILITY:** Restrooms, exhibit area, and auditorium in Visitor Center at Riverway Headquarters in St. Croix Falls, WI; restrooms, picnic sites, and vault toilets at Osceola Landing day use area. There are also handicapped facilities within each of the State Parks found along the Riverway. **Any limitations on vehicle usage:** Recreational vehicle use discouraged at designated canoe landings with road access; **Hiking trails:** No, but hiking trails are within state parks located along Riverway; **Backcountry:** No; **Camping:** Yes, no reservations for campsites on Federal lands. For information and reservations in state parks write the Departments of Natural Resources in either St. Paul, MN 55155, phone 612-296-6157, or Madison, WI 53702, phone 608-266-2621; **Other overnight accommodations on site:** No; **Meals served in the park:** No; **Food and supplies obtainable in the park:** No; **Food and supplies obtainable nearby:** Yes, Marine on St. Croix, Osceola, Stillwater, **Overnight accommodations:** Hudson, Stillwater and other towns along the riverway; **First Aid available in park:** Yes, at Park Headquarters or State Park Ranger Stations; **Nearest Hospital:** Osceola, Hudson, and St. Croix Falls, WI, and Stillwater, MN; **Days/Hours:** Riverway open year-round but normal season is from Memorial Day through Labor Day with most activities available from about Apr.

through Oct.; **Holiday Closings:** Park Headquarters closed Thanksgiving, Dec. 25 and Jan. 1; **Visitor attractions closed for seasons:** Visitor Center at Headquarter's open Mon.-Fri. in winter. Visitor Center at Stillwater open Fri.-Sun. in winter. Commercial boat trips closed in winter.

GENERAL INFORMATION: Before setting out for canoeing, make sure you have a life preserver for each person, an extra paddle, insect repellent, a small gasoline stove, and drinking water. Firewood is very scarce in the vicinity of the campsites, and the cutting of trees or brush is prohibited. Drinking water is available at only a few places along the river.

TRAVEL ACCESS: Bus: Greyhound Lines provides daily service to Hudson, WI; **Rail:** Rail Service to Minneapolis/St. Paul; **Air:** Major airlines to Minneapolis/St. Paul Airport; **Other:** People arriving by bus, rail, or air need to make special transportation arrangements to visit most of the Riverway.

Saint Croix National Scenic Riverway
Wisconsin (also in Minnesota)

MAILING ADDRESS: Superintendent, Saint Croix National Scenic Riverway, P.O. Box 708, Saint Croix Falls, WI 54024 **Telephone:** 715-483-3284

DIRECTIONS: Park Headquarters is at the corner of Hamilton and Massachusetts Streets in St. Croix Falls. Interpretive pamphlets and maps are available here.

Over 200 miles (320 km) of the scenic St. Croix River and its Namekagon tributary make up this area, an initial component of the National Wild and Scenic River System. Authorized for addition to the National Park System on Oct. 2, 1968.

VISITOR ACTIVITIES: Fishing, canoeing, wildlife- and bird-watching, swimming, boating, interpretive exhibits, camping, hiking in nearby state forests and parks, hunting, cross-country skiing; **Permits:** No; **Fees:** No; **Visitor facilities:** Campsites, boat launching sites, light outfitting services, and canoe rentals. There are limited Federal facilities along the riverway; **HANDICAPPED ACCESSIBILITY:** Restrooms, exhibit area, and auditorium in Visitor Center at Riverway Headquarters in St. Croix Falls, WI; restrooms, exhibit area, and auditorium in Visitor Center on Highway 70 near Grantsburg, WI; restrooms, exhibit area, and auditorium in Visitor Center near Trego, WI; vault toilets and picnic sites in Earl Park day use area near Trego, WI; exhibit area and auditorium at Visitor Center in Stillwater, MN; **Any limitations on vehicle usage:** Recreational vehicle use is discouraged at designated canoe landings with road access; **Hiking trails:** No, hiking trails available in nearby state forests and parks; **Backcountry:** No; **Camping:** Type B campsites and state campgrounds are available nearby. For information, contact State Departments of Natural Resources, St. Paul, MN 55155, phone 612-296-6157, and Madison, WI 53702, phone 608-266-2621; **Meals served in the park:** No; **Food and supplies obtainable in the park:** No; **Food and supplies obtainable nearby:** Yes, at Cable, Hayward, Trego, Grantsberg, Saint Croix Falls, Taylor's Falls, Stillwater; **Overnight accommodations:** Hayward, Trego, Saint Croix Falls, Taylor's Falls, and other communities near the riverway; **First Aid available in park:** Yes, at Ranger Stations on the Riverway; **Nearest Hospital:** Hayward, Spooner, Grantsburg, and St. Croix Falls, WI, all of which are within 10 miles (16 km) of the Riverway; **Days/Hours:** Riverway open year-round but normal season is from Memorial Day to Labor Day with most activities available from about Apr. through Oct. Information Stations closed in winter; **Holiday Closings:** Park Headquarters closed on Thanksgiving, Dec. 25, and Jan. 1; **Visitor attractions closed for seasons:** Trego and Grantsburg Visitor Information Stations closed in winter months. The uppermost sections of the St. Croix and Namekagon may become too shallow for canoeing during periods of low water, usually in late summer and autumn.

GENERAL INFORMATION: Before setting out for canoeing, make sure you have a life preserver for each person, an extra paddle, insect repellent, a small gasoline stove, and drinking water. Firewood is very scarce in the vicinity of the campsites, and the cutting of trees or brush is prohibited. Drinking water is available at only a few places along the River.

TRAVEL ACCESS: Rail: No; **Other:** People arriving by air or bus must arrange for shuttle to other areas on Riverway by private canoe outfitters located along or near the Riverway.

Wyoming

BIGHORN CANYON NATIONAL RECREATION AREA

DEVIL'S TOWER NATIONAL MONUMENT

YELLOWSTONE NATIONAL PARK

JOHN D. ROCKEFELLER, JR. MEMORIAL PARKWAY

GRAND TETON NATIONAL PARK

MORMON PIONEER NATIONAL HISTORIC TRAIL

FOSSIL BUTTE NATIONAL MONUMENT

OREGON NATIONAL HISTORIC TRAIL

FORT LARAMIE NATIONAL HISTORIC SITE

North Country National Scenic Trail
For details see listing in New York

Bighorn Canyon National Recreation Area
For details see listing in Montana

Devils Tower National Monument
Devils Tower, Wyoming

MAILING ADDRESS: Superintendent, Devils Tower National Monument, P.O. Box 8, Devils Tower, WY 82714 **Telephone:** 307-467-5370

DIRECTIONS: The monument entrance, off WY 24, is 7 miles (11.2 km) north of US 14; 28 miles (44.8 km) northwest of Sundance, WY; 33 miles (52.8 km) northeast of Moorcroft, WY; and 52 miles (83.2 km) southwest of Belle Fourche, SD. The Visitor Center is about 3 miles (4.8 km) from the Monument's entrance and close to the Tower.

This 865-foot tower of columnar rock, the remains of a volcanic intrusion, is the Nation's first national monument. Created by Presidential Proclamation on Sept. 24, 1906.

VISITOR ACTIVITIES: Interpretive exhibits, photography, walking, camping, hiking, mountain climbing, picnicking, fishing, bird- and wildlife-watching; **Permits:** Yes, climbing; **Fees:** Entrance fee is $3 per vehicle, $1 for each bus passenger, $1 for individual (biker, hiker, etc.); those under 17 or 62 and over—U.S. citizens—are admitted free. Golden Eagle and Golden Age Passports accepted and available; **Visitor facilities:** Parking and restrooms at the Visitor Center, picnic area, Administration office, campground; **HANDICAPPED AC- CESSIBILITY:** Restrooms in picnic area, Campground Loop "B" and Administration Building are accessible. Campground Loop "B" has one fully accessible campsite. Several other campsites have picnic tables that will accommodate wheelchairs. Visitor Center is accessible but restrooms are not. Trails are steep and narrow. **Any limitations on vehicle usage:** Vehicles are restricted to designated roadways; **Hiking trails:** Yes, self-guiding nature trails of varying lengths; **Backcountry:** No; **Camping:** Yes, no reservations accepted for campsites. Fee is $7 per site per night (camping), with a 14-day limit during summer; **Other overnight accommodations on site:** No; **Meals served in the park:** No; **Food and supplies obtainable in the park:** No; **Food and supplies obtainable nearby:** Yes, within 2 miles (3.2 km) of the campground; **Overnight accommodations:** Sundance, WY 24 and US 14, 28 miles (44.8 km); Hulett, 11 miles (17.6 km) north, Moorcroft, WY 24 and US 14, 34 miles (54.4 km); **First Aid available in park:** Yes; **Nearest Hospital:** Sundance, via WY 24 and US 14, 28 miles (44.8 km); **Days/Hours:** The Monument is open all year. Visitor Center is open from May through Oct.; **Holiday Closings:** No; **Visitor attractions closed for seasons:** Campground is closed by snow in winter; **Weather:** In summer, the days are generally sunny, but when the sun sets or during storms you will need a sweater or light jacket.

GENERAL INFORMATION: Be cautious of rattlesnakes, which seldom bite humans unless disturbed or mistreated. Stay clear of prairie dogs, which carry fleas and can bite.

Fort Laramie National Historic Site
Fort Laramie, Wyoming

MAILING ADDRESS: Superintendent, Fort Laramie National Historic Site, Fort Laramie, WY 82212 **Telephone:** 307-837-2221

DIRECTIONS: The site is about 3.1 miles (5 km) southwest of the town of Fort Laramie, WY, on State Rt. 160.

A fur-trade post once stood here, but the surviving buildings are those of a major military post that served the high plains, 1849-90. Created by Presidential Proclamation on July 16, 1938.

VISITOR ACTIVITIES: Walking tours, interpretive exhibits, picnicking, living history programs in summer; **Permits:** No; **Fees:** Yes; **Visitor facilities:** Parking at Visitor Center, self-guided tours, picnic area and audiovisual program; **HANDICAPPED ACCESSIBILITY:** Parking, restrooms, drinking fountain. Transportation around site for mobility impaired individuals may be available, depending on staffing—check at Visitor Center; **Any limitations on vehicle usage:** No; **Hiking trails:** No; **Backcountry:** No; **Camping:** No; **Other overnight accom- modations on site:** No; **Meals served in the park:** No, but cold drinks available in summer; **Food and supplies obtainable in the park:** No; **Food and supplies obtainable nearby:** Yes, in towns of Fort Laramie, Guernsey, Lingle or Torrington; **Overnight accommoda- tions:** Fort Laramie, 3.1 miles (5 km) northeast on Hwy 160; Guernsey, 13 miles (20.8 km) northwest of Fort Laramie; or in Torrington, 20 miles (32 km) southeast of Fort Laramie; both on US 26; **First Aid available in park:** Yes; **Nearest Hospital:** Torrington 20 miles (32 km) southeast of Fort Laramie by US 26; **Days/Hours:** From mid-June through August, 8 a.m. to 7 p.m.; 8 a.m. to 4:30 p. m. the remainder of the year; **Holiday Closings:** Thanksgiving Day, Dec. 25, and Jan. 1; **Visitor attractions closed for seasons:** No living history programs are offered between mid-August and June; **Weather:** Winters can be severe. Summer temperatures can reach 100°F with low humidity. Summer nights are usually cool.

Fossil Butte National Monument
Kemmerer, Wyoming

MAILING ADDRESS: Superintendent, Fossil Butte National Monument, P.O. Box 592, Kemmerer, WY 83101 **Telephone:** 307-877-4455

DIRECTIONS: The Monument is in southwest Wyoming, about 14 miles (22.4 km) west of Kemmerer. The Butte is located just north of US 30 N and the Union Pacific Railroad, both of which traverse the valley.

An abundance of rare fish fossils, 48-52 million years old, is evidence of former habitation of this now semiarid region. Established by act of Congress on Oct. 23, 1972.

VISITOR ACTIVITIES: Picnicking, fossil displays, auto tours, wildlife- and bird-watching, hiking; **Permits:** No; **Fees:** No; **Visitor facilities:** Interpretive exhibits, restrooms. **HANDICAPPED ACCESSIBILITY:** Parking, Visitor Center, restrooms; picnic site has short trail with 5% grade; **Any limitations on vehicle usage:** Rain or snow may make travel difficult or impossible. Check with Administrative offices at monument. Mon.-Fri., 8:30 to 4:30; **Hiking trails:** Yes, 2½ mile (4 km) interpretive trail, 1.5 (2.4 km) trail; **Backcountry:** No; **Camping:** No; **Other overnight accommodations on site:** No; **Meals served in the park:** No; **Food and supplies obtainable in the park:** No; **Food and supplies obtainable nearby:** Yes, Kemmerer and Cokeville; **Overnight accommodations:** Kemmerer, 14 miles (22.4 km) east on US 30 N, and Cokeville, 33 miles (52.8 km) west on US 30 N; **First Aid available in park:** Yes, when employees are available. The park is routinely patrolled; **Nearest Hospital:** Kemmerer; **Days/Hours:** The Visitor Center is open 8 a.m. to 7 p.m. from June-August, 8 a.m. to 4:30 p.m. Sept.-May, daily; **Holiday Closings:** No; **Visitor attractions closed for seasons:** Park roads north of Visitor Center usually closed by snow from November to early May; **Weather:** The climate is semiarid and cool-temperate.

GENERAL INFORMATION: Reservations for accommodations in the area should be made well in advance of the visit. Contact the Monument for further information on local lodging.

Grand Teton National Park
Moose, Wyoming   **SEE CLIMATABLE NO. 39**

MAILING ADDRESS: Superintendent, Grand Teton National Park, P.O. Drawer 170, Moose, WY 83012 **Telephone:** 307-733-2880

DIRECTIONS: Park Headquarters and a Visitor Center are at Moose, 13 miles (20.8 km) north of Jackson on US 26, 89, and 191.

This scenic area of mountain peaks, alpine lakes, and sagebrush flats is filled with moose, elk, trumpeter swans and other wildlife. It offers a great variety of recreational opportunities to the visitor. Much of the Teton Range was protected as a National Park on Feb. 26, 1929, and expanded in 1950 to include most of the valley called Jackson Hole.

VISITOR ACTIVITIES: Exhibits, Ranger-led activities, picnicking, camping, backcountry hiking, mountain climbing, horseback riding, boating, fishing, biking, snowmobiling, cross-country skiing, animal- and bird-watching; **Permits:** Required for fishing (state license), backcountry camping, boating and oversnow travel; **Fees:** $10 for motorboats, $5 for non-motorized boats and snowmobiles. $10 entrance fee good for 1 week in both Yellowstone and Grand Teton National Parks. Golden Eagle, Golden Age, and Golden Access Passports accepted and available; **Visitor facilities:** Visitor Centers, campgrounds, trails, picnic areas, boat rentals and ramps, snowmobile route, cross-country ski trails, lodging, meals, gas, groceries, post office, religious services, restrooms, telephones; **HANDICAPPED ACCESSIBILITY:** Yes, contact Visitor Center for brochure on handicapped access; **Any limitations on vehicle usage:** Drive only on established roadways. Keep motor vehicles off bikelanes; **Hiking trails:** Yes, over 200 miles (320 km) of maintained park trails; **Backcountry:** Yes, information can be obtained at Visitor Centers or Jenny Lake Ranger Station; **Camping:** Yes, no reservations available for individual campsites. Reservations for the trailer village with all hookups at Colter Bay can be made by contacting the Grand Teton Lodge Company, P.O. Box 240, Moran, WY 83013, phone 307-543-2855. Group campsites are reserved in advance by writing the Chief Ranger between Jan. 1 and June 1. More than a dozen Forest Service and commercial campgrounds are located near the park; **Other overnight accommodations on site:** Yes, for information and reservations at other accommodations, contact the Grand Teton Lodge Company, Reservations Dept., P.O. Box 240, Moran, WY 83013, phone 307-543-2855, or Signal Mountain Lodge, Moran, WY 83013, phone 307-543-2831; **Meals served in the park:** Yes, at Dornans, Colter Bay, Jackson Lake, Jenny Lake, and Signal Mountain Lodges; **Food and supplies obtainable in the park:** Yes, at Colter Bay Village, Jackson Lake Lodge, Jenny Lake, Signal Mountain, Moose, and Kelly; **Food and supplies obtainable nearby:** Yes, at Jackson; **Overnight accommodations:** Nearby at Jackson; **First Aid available in park:** at Visitor Centers, Ranger Stations, and Jackson Lake Lodge; **Nearest Hospital:** St. John's Hospital in Jackson, south of Park; **Days/Hours:** The Park is open year-round, 24 hours a day; **Holiday Closings:** Moose Visitor Center closed Dec. 25; **Visitor attractions closed for seasons:** Most facilities are closed during the winter (Oct. through May); Colter Bay Visitor Center closed Oct. 1 through mid-May; **Weather:** Latitude and elevation are the main factors producing cool summers and cold winters. Despite frequent rains and cool temperatures, spring visitors may enjoy wildflowers, moose, elk, and migrating birds. Be prepared for a variety of weather conditions. It snows even in May and June. Raingear and warm clothing (layers work best) are essential. Spring temperatures can range from below zero to 70°F. Summer days during July and Aug. are generally warm and occasionally hot. Afternoon thundershowers are possible. Daytime temperatures average near 80°F, dropping to 40°F at night. Summer visitation exceeds two million. Most campgrounds usually fill by early afternoon. The Cascade Canyon Trail is often crowded.

Autumn color is best about the second or third week of September. Days are generally cool and clear during Sept. and Oct.—many visitors feel this is the best time to visit. Most park facilities are open in Sept. when it's easy to find space in lodges and campgrounds. During late Oct. and Nov., elk migrate through the Park to their winter range. Expect frosty nights warming to about 65°F during the day in early autumn.

Winter lasts from Nov. through Apr. with an average 16 feet of snowfall. Blizzards may last for several days, making travel hazardous. Carry tire chains.

GENERAL INFORMATION: A recorded information service is available on a 24-hour basis all year. Phone 307-733-2220. To talk with park personnel, call 307-733-2880. For State of Wyoming travel information, contact the Wyoming Travel Commission, Cheyenne,

WY 82001; phone 307-777-7777.

For Your Safety—Register at Jenny Lake Ranger Station in summer and at Park Headquarters during other seasons before starting any off-trail hike or climb. Do not feed or touch any park animal. Lightning-caused fires are allowed to burn in some parts of the Park. If one is in progress, check with a Ranger before planning a trip to the burn area.

Dogs are prohibited on all hiking trails and in the backcountry. Bicycles are not allowed on any trail.

John D. Rockefeller, Jr. Memorial Parkway
Wyoming

MAILING ADDRESS: Superintendent, Grand Teton National Park, P.O. Drawer 170, Moose, WY 83012 **Telephone:** 307-733-2880

DIRECTIONS: The Parkway Ranger Station is located just north of Flagg Ranch Village on US 89. Information on the parkway is available through Dial-A-Park in Grand Teton: 307-733-2220.

This 7-mile (11.2-km) long area linking Yellowstone and Grand Teton National Parks commemorates Mr. Rockefeller's role in aiding the establishment of many parks, including Grand Teton. Authorized for addition to the National Park System on Aug. 25, 1972.

VISITOR ACTIVITIES: Information and self-guiding trails are provided through the Parkway. River float trips, horseback riding, snowmobiling, and cross-country skiing are available; **Permits:** Required for snowmobiling, boating, backcountry camping and fishing (state license). Available (except fishing) from Moose Visitor Center in Grand Teton National Park; **Fees:** $10 for motorboat, $5 for nonmotorized boat and snowmobile permits; **Visitor facilities:** At Flagg Ranch Village, gasoline is available during the summer and winter seasons. From May 15-Oct. 15: lodging, food store, float trips, horseback riding, trailer park with and without full hookups. From Dec. 15-Mar. 15: lodging, food store, snowmobile and cross-country ski rentals and snowcoach rides. **Any limitations on vehicle usage:** Drive only on established roadways; **Hiking trails:** Yes, 3 miles (4.8 km); **Backcountry:** Yes, information available at Ranger Station on Parkway or Visitor Centers or Ranger Stations in Grand Teton National Park; **Camping:** Yes, Flagg Ranch Village; **Other overnight accommodations on**

site: Yes, Flagg Ranch Village, Moran, WY 83103, phone 307-543-2861. Both camping and lodge are open in season; inquire about exact dates of operation; **Meals served in the park:** Yes, at Flagg Ranch Village; **Food and supplies obtainable in the park:** Yes, at Flagg Ranch Village in season; **Food and supplies obtainable nearby:** Yes, during the summer at Colter Bay Village 18 miles (28.8 km) south and Grant Village in Yellowstone; **Overnight accommodations:** Jackson, 55 miles (88 km) south, Colter Bay Village, 18 miles (28.8 km) south, Jackson Lake Lodge, 23 miles (36.8 km) south, Signal Mountain Lodge, 27 miles (43.2 km) south, Jenny Lake Lodge, 35 miles (56 km) south, or Yellowstone to the north; **First Aid available in park:** Yes, emergency first aid at Ranger Station, Medical Clinic at Jackson Lake Lodge 23 miles (36.8 km) south during summer; **Nearest Hospital:** St. John's Hospital, Jackson, WY, 55 miles (88 km) south; **Days/Hours:** Park is open year-round, 24 hours a day; **Holiday Closings:** No; **Visitor attractions closed for seasons:** Normal seasonal closings affect appropriate activities.

GENERAL INFORMATION: Visitors to the area can also see Yellowstone and Grand Teton National Parks (see listings in this book).

Mormon Pioneer Trail
For details see listing in Illinois

Oregon National Scenic Trail
For details see listing in Missouri

Yellowstone National Park
Yellowstone National Park, Wyoming   **SEE CLIMATABLE NO. 39**

MAILING ADDRESS: National Park Service, P.O. Box 168, Yellowstone National Park, WY 82190 **Telephone:** 307-344-7381

DIRECTIONS: The Park can be reached from many directions: from the north, US 89; from the northeast, US 212; from the east through Cody, US 20, 14, and 16, merged; from the south, via the John D. Rockefeller, Jr. Memorial Parkway, US 89 and US 26; and from the west via West Yellowstone, US 191 and 20.

This is the world's greatest geyser area, with Old Faithful and some 10,000 other geysers and hot springs. Here, too, are lakes, waterfalls, high mountains, and the Grand Canyon of the Yellowstone—all set apart in 1872 as the world's first national park. Yellowstone is the largest Park in the lower 48 states. Established Mar. 1, 1872.

VISITOR ACTIVITIES: Fishing, camping, boating, driving, hiking, horseback riding, bird- and wildlife-watching, biking, stagecoach rides, boat and bus tours, snowmobiling, cross-country skiing, snowshoeing, interpretive and campfire programs; **Permits:** Required for fishing, boating, and backcountry camping and can be obtained at any Visitor Center or Ranger Station; **Fees:** Yes, fees for campsites vary from free backcountry sites to $6-$10 for well-developed campsites. Fee for Bridge Bay is $10. A $5 fee is charged for all non-motorized boating permits and a $10 fee is required for all motorized boating permits for recreational use within the park. Fees are also charged for horseback riding, stagecoach rides, boat and bus tours, and trailer park with utilities. There is a combination entrance fee to both Yellowstone and Grand Teton National Parks—$10 per vehicle, which is valid for 7 days. Persons entering on foot, motorcycle, bicycle, or by bus will be charged $4. All entrance fees are valid for 7 days. Golden Eagle, Golden Access, and Golden Age passports are accepted and available; **Visitor facilities:** Roadside radio interpretation, interpretive display boards, hotels, cabins, amphitheatres, boat rentals, campgrounds, church services, food service, gasoline stations, horse rental, laundries, photo shops, post offices, sewage dump stations, showers, tour buses, fee trailer park with utilities, Visitor Centers, marina, bike trails; **HANDICAPPED ACCESSIBILITY:** Accessible showers are available at Grant Village lodging units and Old Faithful Lodge. Accessible showers are available for guests at the Lake Yellowstone Hotel. Bridge Bay has accessible store, restroom at picnic area on Marina entrance road, amphitheater (with assistance); Canyon has accessible food service, stores, restroom, laundry, amphitheater, visitor center, and post office; Fishing Bridge has accessible camping (at the private R.V. park), food service, store, restroom, visitor center, laundry, and amphitheater; Grant Village has accessible lodging, food service, stores, restrooms, shower, laundry, amphitheater, visitor center, and post office; Lake has accessible lodging, food service, stores, restroom, medical, and post office; Madison has accessible camping and amphitheater; Mammoth has accessible lodging, food service, store, restrooms, medical, and visitor center (access in rear with assistance); Norris has accessible restroom, visitor center, and amphitheater; Old Faithful has accessible lodging, food service, stores, medical, restrooms, shower, and visitor center; Tower-Roosevelt has accessible food service, store, and restroom; **Any limitations on vehicle usage:** Motor vehicles are restricted to designated roads. Bicycles are restricted to roads and designated bicycle trails. Visitors may encounter snow and hazardous driving conditions during spring and fall, with temporary road closures. Oversnow vehicles are subject to park rules and regulations; **Hiking trails:** Yes, about 1,200 miles (1920 km) of trails lead to remote sections of the Park. Some offer easy part-day trips over gentle terrain; others require strength and endurance because of their elevation, length, and ruggedness. Good topographic maps, which can be purchased at any Visitor Center, are highly recommended. Always check trail conditions and possible closures with a Ranger before setting out on overnight or long hike; **Backcountry:** Permits are required for some day hikes and *all* overnight trips. Permits must be obtained in person and no more than 48 hours in advance. There is no charge for the permit.**Camping:** There are 11 NPS campgrounds in Yellowstone National Park. Campsites are available on a first-come, first-served basis with the exception of Bridge Bay campground which as a partial reservation system operated by Ticketron. Camping or overnight vehicle parking in pullouts, parking areas, picnic grounds, or any place other than a designated campground is not permitted, and there are no overflow camping facilities. Campsites do fill early in the day, and we recommend visitors secure their campsite early in the day (campgrounds fill by noon during the busy summer season). **Other overnight accommodations on site:** Yes, reservations for hotels, lodges, cabins, and a trailer park, all open from mid-June through Labor Day, can be made by writing the TW Services, Inc., Yellowstone National Park, WY 82190, phone 307-344-7311. Reservations are advised, especially during July and Aug. Those visitors already in Yellowstone may make advance room reservations at any hotel or lodge anywhere in the Park; **Meals served in the park:** Yes, Lake, Canyon, Tower-Roosevelt, Mammoth Hot Springs, Old Faithful, Grant Village; **Food and supplies obtainable in the park:** Yes, at Lake, Fishing Bridge, Canyon, Tower-Roosevelt, Tower Fall, Mammoth Hot Springs, Grant Village, Old Faithful; **Food and supplies obtainable nearby:** Yes, at each community near the 5 park entrances: Livingston, Bozeman, Gardiner, MT, West Yellowstone, Red Lodge, Cooke City/Silver Gate, MT; Cody and Jackson, WY; **Overnight accommodations:** Gardiner, Cooke City/Silver Gate, Livingston, Bozeman, West Yellowstone, and Red Lodge, MT; Cody and Jackson, WY; **First Aid available in park:** Yes; **Nearest Hospital:** Lake Medical, Mammoth Clinic, Old Faithful Clinic hours vary; **Days/Hours:** Open 24 hours a day, every day; **Holiday Closings:** No; **Visitor attractions closed for seasons:** Park roads and entrances, except the North Entrance to Cooke City, MT, are ordinarily closed by snow to auto traffic between Oct. 31 and May 1. Most park campgrounds do not open before June, except at Mammoth, where camping is available all year.

Wintertime activities abound. In recent years, thousands of visitors have entered the Park by oversnow vehicle. Heated snow coaches are operated by concessioners from West Yellowstone, Mammoth Hot Springs, and South Entrance. Private snowmobiles may also use groomed roads, but no cross-country vehicle use is permitted. Ski and snowshoe touring are also on the increase. The Albright Visitor Center and Museum in Mammoth is open year-round, with interpretive activities scheduled. The Old Faithful Visitor Center is open during the winter from about mid-Dec. to mid-Mar., providing information, evening programs, and winter walks. Meals and overnight lodging are available through the winter at Old Faithful. Mammoth Hot Springs Hotel offers overnight lodging, as well as snowmobile and cross-country ski rental, restaurant, and gift shop. The only roads open for auto traffic are Gardiner to Mammoth and from there to the Northeast Entrance and Cooke City. This drive offers an excellent opportunity to see wildlife. Special information on winter activities and services may be obtained by writing to the Park. Reservations for winter facilities may be made by writing to the TW Services, Inc., Yellowstone National Park, WY 82190. Reservations may also be made by telephoning 307-344-7311, and are advised, especially during the holidays.

GENERAL INFORMATION: Assistance for any emergency in the park can be obtained anytime by calling Park Headquarters at 307-344-7381. 911 is available for emergency assistance. Write the above address for informative pamphlets and a map. Five national forests providing recreational opportunites border on Yellowstone. To the south lies Grand Teton National Park, with many concessioner and Federal facilities (see listing in this book).

TRAVEL ACCESS: Bus: Greyhound serves Billings, Bozeman, Livingston, and West Yellowstone in Montana; Idaho Falls in Idaho. TW Services, Inc., the park concessioner, has a connecting bus service into the Park from Bozeman, Livingston, and West Yellowstone, in the summer season; **Rail:** There is no easy or convenient train service to Yellowstone. Amtrak provides service to Shelby, Whitefish, and Havre, MT. Both routes are far to the north of the Park; **Air:** Airline service is available to Billings, Bozeman, West Yellowstone, in Montana; and Jackson Hole and Cody, WY. The airports at West Yellowstone are limited to the summer season. **Other:** The only in-park public transportation is via TW Services, Inc., tour buses. There is no shuttle-bus system, other than TW.

NEARBY FACILITIES & POINTS OF INTEREST: Parks, other points of interest: Grand Teton National Park, WY; **Reservation systems in use for other facilities.** Reservations must be made for all overnight accommodations within the Park, and for Fishing

Bridge Recreational Vehicle Park, through TW Services Inc., Reservations Dept., Yellowstone National Park, WY 82190, 307-344-7311. Campsites cannot be reserved in advance, except for the Bridge Bay (campground tents) through the Ticketron System: 1-800-452-1111.

Roosevelt Campobello International Park
New Brunswick, Canada

MAILING ADDRESS: Executive Secretary, Roosevelt Campobello International Park Commission, P.O. Box 97, Lubec, ME 04652 **Telephone:** 506-752-2922

DIRECTIONS: Follow Maine Route 1 to 189. Cross Roosevelt Memorial Bridge at Lubec, ME, to New Brunswick Route 774. The Park is about 1½ miles (2.4 km) from Canadian Customs.
     At the age of 39, President Franklin D. Roosevelt was striken by poliomyelitis here at his summer home. The Park has scenic vistas in a 2,800-acre natural area. This is the first international park to be administered by a joint commission. Established by act of Congress in 1964.

VISITOR ACTIVITIES: Tours of the Roosevelt Cottage, orientation film, visual aid displays, picnicking, beach activities; **Permits:** No; **Fees:** No; **Visitor facilities:** Parking and restrooms at the Reception Center, exhibits; **HANDICAPPED ACCESSIBILITY:** Restrooms in Visitor Center. The first floor of the Roosevelt Cottage is accessible (ramps have been installed), as well as the Hubbard Cottage when it is open and not being used for the conference program; **Any limitations on vehicle usage:** Cars must be parked at the Reception Center in the cottage area; **Hiking trails:** Yes, trails are located in the natural area. Obtain maps at the Reception Center; **Backcountry:** No; **Camping:** No; **Other overnight accommodations on site:** No, tourist facilities are at Welshpool and Wilson's Beach, just north of the park. The Province of New Brunswick maintains a Park with tent and trailer sites and picnic areas at the northern end of Herring Cove. There are also tourist facilities in and near Lubec. The State of Maine has 2 parks in the area, with tenting and trailer facilities at Cobscook Bay Park in the Moosehorn Game Refuge at Whiting and picnic areas at Quoddy Head State Park; **Meals served in the park:** No; **Food and supplies obtainable in the park:** No; **Food and supplies obtainable nearby:** Yes, Wilson's Beach, NB, and Lubec, ME; **Overnight accommodations:** On the Island, within 5 miles (8 km); **First Aid available in park:** No, nearby at Welshpool Health Center, 2 miles (3.2 km); **Nearest Hospital:** Machias, ME, US Rt. 1, 30 miles (48 km); **Days/Hours:** Open 7 days per week, 9 a.m. to 5 p.m. The Park opens the Saturday before U.S. Memorial Day and is open 20 consecutive weeks from that date. **Holiday Closings:** No; **Visitor attractions closed for seasons:** Park is closed from mid-Oct. through May; **Weather:** July and August are warm months. September has warm days and cool nights.

North Mariana Islands

Guam

American Memorial Park
Saipan, Northern Mariana Islands

MAILING ADDRESS: P.O. Box 198 CHRB, Saipan, MP 96950

DIRECTIONS: The Park lies just north of Garapan Village and consists of 133 acres of partially developed memorial and recreation facilities. Established on Aug. 18, 1978.

VISITOR ACTIVITIES: Swimming, picnicking, boating, other recreation; **Permits:** No; **Fees:** No; **Visitor facilities:** Picnic facilities, monument, tour boats, launching ramp, jogging path, and sports fields. Excellent beach. **HANDICAPPED ACCESSIBILITY:** No; **Any limitations on vehicle usage:** Not allowed on beach; **Hiking trails:** No; **Backcountry:** No; **Camping:** No; **Other overnight accommodations on site:** No; **Meals served in the park:** No; **Food and supplies obtainable in the park:** No; **Food and supplies obtainable nearby:** Yes, in Garapan; **Overnight accommodations:** Several hotels within 1 mile (1.6 km) of park; **First Aid available in park:** Yes; **Nearest Hospital:** Adjacent to park; **Days/Hours:** Park open year-round; **Holiday Closings:** No; **Visitor attractions closed for seasons:** No; **Weather:** Humid tropical climate year round. Rainy season June-Nov. Subject to typhoons.

GENERAL INFORMATION: Park is dedicated as a "living" memorial to those who died in the Marianas Campaign of World War II.

TRAVEL ACCESS: Bus: No; **Rail:** No; **Air:** Continental Air Micronesia, Northwest Airlines, Japan Airlines; **Other:** Direct flights to Saipan from Guam and Japan; Cruise ships: Various, from Honolulu and Japan.

NEARBY FACILITIES & POINTS OF INTEREST: Hotel/Motel: Hyatt Regency,

Intercontinental, Hafa Dai, Saipan Beach, Nikko, Saipan Diamond, P.I.C. (Pacific Islands Club), Pacific Gardenia; **Food/Supplies:** Several stores and restaurants near park; **Parks, other points of interest:** Invasion Beaches, Mt. Takpochao, Suicide Cliff, Bonzai Cliff, Grotto, Bird Island, Kalabera Cave, Command Post, Managaha Island, and Sugar King.

War in the Pacific National Historical Park
Agana, Guam

MAILING ADDRESS: Superintendent, War in the Pacific National Historical Park, Marine Dr., Asan P.O. Box FA, Agana, Guam 96910 **Telephone:** Guam: 671-477-9362 or 472-7240. Fax: 671-472-7241. Guam is 15 hours ahead of Eastern Standard Time. Guam does not observe Daylight Savings Time.

DIRECTIONS: Guam is in the Western Pacific and is the southernmost island of the Mariana Islands. Guam is approximately 1,500 miles (2,500 km) south of Tokyo and 6,100 miles (9,900 km) west of San Francisco. The park consists of 7 separate units, all located on the Philippine Sea (west) side of the island. The Visitor Information Centre and Park Headquarters are located on the beach side of Marine Drive in the village of Asan.

Portions of the Park are open, including a Visitor Information Center with various museum and audiovisual programs available in Japanese and English. The park was established to honor the bravery and sacrifices of all people from all nations who were involved in the Pacific Theatre of World War II. There are numerous features from the Pacific Theatre that are scattered in the 7 units. There are several sites of underwater World War II wreckage that are open to certified scuba divers. Authorized for addition to the National Park Service on Aug. 18, 1978.

VISITOR ACTIVITIES: Interpretive programs and exhibits at the Visitor Center, walking trails in 2 of the units, scuba diving in 2 units; **Permits:** No; **Fees:** No; **Visitors facilities:** Restrooms in Visitor Center and southern unit, swimming beaches, picnic sites; **Any limitations on vehicle usage:** Vehicles are not permitted off paved road surfaces; **Hiking trails;** Yes; **Backcountry:** No; **Camping:** No; **Other overnight accommodations on site:** No; **Meals served in park:** No; **Food and supplies obtainable nearby:** Yes, in Agana and Tamuning; **Overnight accommodations:** Yes, in Tumon; **First Aid available in park:** Yes; **Nearest Hospital:** Naval Regional Medical Center and Guam Memorial Hospital, 1 mile (1.6 km); **Days/Hours:** 7:30 a.m. to 3:30 p.m. Mon. through Fri. and 8:30 a.m. to 2:00 p.m. Sat., Sun., and Federal holidays; **Holiday Closings;** Thanksgiving, Dec. 25, and Jan. 1; **Visitor attractions closed for seasons:** No; **Weather:** Guam's climate makes it an ideal place for outdoor activities. The year-round average temperature is 80° and the ocean temperature averages a pleasant 81°F. May to Nov. is the rainy season and you can expect wet, hot, and humid days. Temperatures cool down from Nov. through Apr., the dry season, and tropical trade winds are common. Typhoons can occur in any month, but they are more common during the rainy season.

GENERAL INFORMATION: *For Your Safety*—Please stay off all historic structures and guns, and do not disturb any of the historic ground features, such as foxholes and bomb craters. Do not enter any of the caves. Some may contain hidden explosives. You are especially cautioned not to try to open sealed caves.

Do not trespass on private property. Some lands in the park are privately owned. Please respect these property rights.

Use caution when swimming, snorkeling, or diving along the reefs. Strong currents and heavy winds may be present at any time. There are also several species of poisonous fish on the reef; you should make an effort to recognize them. Dangerous military explosives are found in the water—leave them alone!

Most important of all; Please do not disturb or remove any ammunition that you may find on or off shore. To do so is extremely dangerous!

TRAVEL ACCESS: Air: Japan Airlines, All Nippon Airways, Northwest Orient Airlines, and Continental/Air Micronesia provide daily direct service to Guam International Airport from Tokyo, Japan. Continental/Air Micronesia and Hawaiian Airlines provide direct daily service from Honolulu. Continental Airlines provides direct, weekly service to Sydney, Australia, and Bali, Indonesia. Direct air service from Manila, Philippines, is provided by Continental/Air Micronesia. From Guam, air service is available to Saipan and the Northern Marianas, Hong Kong, and Seoul, Korea.

TRAVEL INFORMATION: No passport or visa are required of U.S. citizens coming drectly from Honolulu. A passport is required for travel to Guam via Japan. Non-U.S. citizens must conform to U.S. passport and visa requirements. Although Guam is a duty-free port and outside the U.S. Customs Zone, expect to have your baggage inspected on arrival by local customs inspectors to help keep plant and animal pests and diseases out of the Territory. Tourists from the U.S. can purchase up to $800, instead of the normal $400, of non-U.S.-made goods and be exempt from duty on returning home.

NEARBY FACILITIES AND POINTS OF INTEREST: Outstanding scuba diving is available in the islands of Truk and Belau (Palau). Both are about a 2-hour flight from Guam. American Memorial Park is located on the island of Saipan and is about a 30-minute flight from Guam. Other areas of interest include Japan, Hong Kong, Philippines, China, Taiwan, Australia, and the islands of Micronesia and Melanesia.

Hawaii

OAHU

KALAUPAPA NATIONAL HISTORIC SITE

U.S.S. ARIZONA MEMORIAL

Honolulu

MAUI

HALEAKALA NATIONAL PARK

PUUKOHOLA HEIAU NATIONAL HISTORIC SITE

HAWAII

KALOKO-HONOKOHAU NATIONAL HISTORIC PARK

PU'UHONUA O HONAUNAU NATIONAL HISTORICAL PARK

HAWAII VOLCANOES NATIONAL PARK

The National Park of American Samoa
Honolulu, Hawaii

MAILING ADDRESS: The National Park of American Samoa, c/o Pacific Area Office, Post Office Box 50165, Honolulu, HI 96850

Will not be open in 1990.

Two rainforest preserves and a coral reef are home to unique tropical animals including the Flying Fox, Pacific Boa, tortoises, and an array of birds and fish. The only paleotropical rainforests in the U.S. are on American Samoa. The park includes several thousand acres on the islands of Tutuila and Ta'u as well as the pristine coral reef and magnificent white sand beach on the Island of Ofu. NO FEDERAL FACILITIES.

Authorized: Oct. 31, 1988. Acreage: Approximately 7,000 to be leased from landowners through the Territorial government.

Puerto Rico

SAN JUAN NATIONAL HISTORIC SITE

San Juan National Historic Site
Old San Juan, Puerto Rico

MAILING ADDRESS: Superintendent, San Juan National Historic Site, P.O. Box 712, Old San Juan, PR 00902 **Telephone:** 809-729-6960

DIRECTIONS: The Site's information desk and other visitor facilities are on the entry plaza levels of forts El Morro and San Cristobal. The site includes the Spanish-built forts of El Morro, San Cristobal, El Cañuelo, and the city walls.

These massive masonry fortifications, the oldest in the territorial limits of the United States, were begun by the Spanish in the 16th Century to protect a strategic harbor guarding the sea lanes to the New World. Designated Feb. 14, 1949.

VISITOR ACTIVITIES: Exhibits; **Permits:** No; **Fees:** No; **Visitor facilities:** Restrooms, drinking fountains, museums; **HANDICAPPED ACCESSIBILITY:** Yes; **Any limitations on vehicle usage:** Limited parking available at Fort San Cristobal; ample parking at El Morro; **Hiking trails:** No; **Backcountry:** No; **Camping:** No; **Other overnight accommodations on site:** No; **Meals served in the park:** No; **Food and supplies obtainable in the park:** No; **Food and supplies obtainable nearby:** Yes, the city of San Juan; **Overnight accommodations:** San Juan, within walking distance; **First Aid available in park:** Yes; **Nearest Hospital:** San Juan, within 5 miles (8 km); **Days/Hours:** Open 7 days a week from 9:15 a.m. to 6 p.m.; **Holiday Closings:** No; **Visitor attractions closed for seasons:** No; **Weather:** Warm to hot all year with no change of seasons.

GENERAL INFORMATION: Walking shoes with rubber soles and low heels are recommended.

TRAVEL ACCESS: Bus: Metro Bus Authority provides regular service to Plaza Colon; **Rail:** No; **Air:** Eastern, Delta, American, Avianca, BWIA provide service to San Juan. City of San Juan mini-bus stops near El Morro Grounds main gate.

NEARBY FACILITIES & POINTS OF INTEREST: Hotel/Motel: Caribe Hilton,

Muñoz Rivera Ave., San Juan, PR, phone 809 721-0303, 2½ miles (4 km) from Site; El Convento Restaurant and Hotel, 100 Cristo St., San Juan, PR, 723-9621; **Food/Supplies:** La Mallorca Restaurant, La Mallorquina Restaurant, Siglo Veinte Resturant, Pueblo Supermarket (all in old San Juan) within walking distance; **Parks, other points of interest:** San Jose church, San Juan Cathedral, La Fortaleza, Cristo Chapel, and Casablanca.

Virgin Islands

SAN JUAN NATIONAL HISTORIC SITE

Charlotte Amalie

San Juan

ST.JOHN

ST.THOMAS

VIRGIN ISLANDS NATIONAL PARK

BUCK ISLAND REEF NATIONAL MONUMENT

CHRISTIANSTED NATIONAL HISTORIC SITE

ST.CROIX

Buck Island Reef National Monument
Saint Croix, Virgin Islands

MAILING ADDRESS: Superintendent, Christiansted National Historic Site, P.O. Box 160, Christiansted, Saint Croix, Virgin Islands 00820 **Telephone:** 809-773-1460

DIRECTIONS: Access to the Monument is by National Park Service Concessioners or private boat. Concession boats are available at Christainsted Wharf. The Monument is a 5½ mile (8.8 km) sail from Christiansted.

Coral, grottoes, sea fans, gorgonias, and tropical fishes—along an underwater trail—make this one of the finest marine gardens in the Caribbean. The Island is a rookery for frigate birds and pelicans and the habitat of green turtles. Created by Presidential Proclamation on Dec. 28, 1961.

VISITOR ACTIVITIES: Swimming, snorkeling, boat trips, hiking, bird-watching, picnicking; **Permits:** No; **Fees:** Concession boat fees; **Visitor facilities:** Picnic tables, charcoal grilles, changing house (no showers), a sheltered picnic pavilion, restrooms, nature trail; **Any limitations on vehicle usage:** Boats should be maneuvered slowly through park waters. Water skiing, speeding, and reckless boating are prohibited; **Hiking trails:** Yes, nature trail; **Backcountry:** No; **Camping:** No, but you may camp on your boat; **Other overnight accommodations on site:** No; **Meals served in the park:** No; **Food and supplies obtainable in the park:** No; **Food and supplies obtainable nearby:** No; **Overnight accommodations:** St. Croix; **First Aid available in park:** Yes; **Nearest Hospital:** 6½ miles (10.4 km) from downtown Christiansted; **Days/Hours:** 24 hrs.; **Holiday Closings:** No; **Visitor attractions closed for seasons:** No; **Weather:** Temperatures range from 75° in winter to 90° in summer.

GENERAL INFORMATION: *For Your Safety*—Avoid sunburn. Short periods in the sun and the use of protective waterproof lotions are recommended. Use caution in the water. Cuts from coral can inflict painful wounds that may be slow to heal. The common spiny sea urchins are a particularly sharp hazard. Jellyfish, the Portuguese man-of-war, and fire corals can sting and burn, some severely. Treat all underwater creatures with respect. If you haven't snorkeled before, be sure to practice in shallow water before daring the reef. Make sure your face mask fits snugly.

Christiansted National Historic Site
Christiansted, Virgin Islands

MAILING ADDRESS: Superintendent, Christiansted National Historic Site, P.O. Box 160, Christiansted, Virgin Islands 00820 **Telephone:** 809-773-1460

DIRECTIONS: National Park Service Headquarters is in The Old Customs House in downtown Christiansted. Begin your tour at the Fort.

Christiansted is one of the most picturesque towns in the West Indies because of its harbor setting and the dignity and charm of its 18th-and 19th-century architecture, which developed during the years it was the capital of the Danish West Indies. Christiansted National Historic Site allows you to step back two centuries as you visit the old Danish Fort, the Scale House, the Customs House, and the Steeple Building Museum. The Danish West Indies were purchased from Denmark in 1917. Designated on March 4, 1952.

VISITOR ACTIVITIES: Self-guided walking tours, interpretive exhibits; **Permits:** No; **Fees:** Yes, $1 entrance fee for persons between 12 and 62, for Fort and Steeple Building Museum; **Visitor facilities:** Restrooms, museum (open 8 a.m. to 5 p.m., Mon. through Fri., and 9 a.m. to 5 p.m. Sat. and Sun.); **Any limitations on vehicle usage:** No; **Hiking trails:** No; **Backcountry:** No; **Camping:** No; **Other overnight accommodations on site:** No; **Meals served in the park:** No; **Food and supplies obtainable in the park:** No; **Food and supplies obtainable nearby:** Yes, Christiansted; **Overnight accommodations:** Christiansted; **First Aid available in park:** Yes; **Nearest Hospital:** St. Croix, 6 miles (9.6 km) from the downtown area; **Days/Hours:** 8 a.m. to 5:00 p.m.; **Holiday Closings:** No; **Visitor attractions closed for seasons:** No; **Weather:** Average temperatures are 75° in winter and 90° in summer.

GENERAL INFORMATION: Beware of uneven walkways and stairs.

Virgin Islands National Park
St. John, Virgin Islands   **SEE CLIMATABLE NO. 40**

MAILING ADDRESS: Superintendent, Virgin Islands National Park, P.O. Box 7789, Charlotte Amalie, St. Thomas, Virgin Islands 00801 **Telephone:** Cruz Bay Visitor Center: 809-776-6201 or Headquarters: 809-775-6238

DIRECTIONS: Park headquarters and Visitor Center are in Red Hook at the National Park Service Dock on St. Thomas. A Visitor Center is at Cruz Bay on St. John. You can fly directly to Charlotte Amalie, St. Thomas, or via San Juan, or travel by ship. Taxis and buses run between Charlotte Amalie and Red Hook. A ferry operates hourly 7 a.m. to 11 p.m. across Pillsbury Sound from Red Hook to Cruz Bay. Water taxi service is available after hours. A special boat for guests at Caneel Bay Plantation runs between the Red Hook Visitor Station and Caneel Bay. Very popular with those who can stay only a day are the package vehicle tours and scenic boat charters that leave from St. Thomas with all transportation arranged. See a travel agent or make arrangements in advance. Taxi service is available on St. John.

The Park covers about two-thirds of St. John and includes quiet coves, blue-green waters, and white sandy beaches fringed by lush green hills. The remains of Danish colonial sugar plantations are found in the Park, several of which have been restored. Authorized for addition to the National Park System on Aug. 2, 1956.

VISITOR ACTIVITIES: Interpretive walks, talks, and exhibits, hiking, camping, guided snorkel trips, cultural demonstrations, picnicking, swimming, snorkeling, fishing, auto tours; **Permits:** Persons returning to the U.S. mainland from the Virgin Islands must go through Customs and Immigration at San Juan, Puerto Rico, St. Thomas, or other U.S. ports of entry. A special permit from the Department of Agriculture is required to exit with fruits, vegetables, plant cuttings, and seeds; **Fees:** No; **Visitor facilities:** Self-guiding walking and underwater trails, picnic areas, beaches, campgrounds, boat rentals, rental vehicles (make reservations in Cruz Bay well in advance); **HANDICAPPED ACCESSIBILITY:** Some beach areas are easier to access by wheelchair than others. Check with park staff in Cruz Bay. Annaberg Sugar Mill is wheelchair accessible with assistance, though trails are steep and caution is advised. Cruz Bay visitor center is accessible and will have new exhibits installed by 1900 which interpret the park. Ferry travel between St. Thomas and St. John poses the major barrier, but can be negotiated with assistance; **Any limitations on vehicle usage:** Speed limit is 20 miles (32 km) per hour. Remember to drive on the left. Sound your horn at blind curves; **Hiking trails:** Yes, trails range from easy walks to difficult climbs. Bring tennis or hiking shoes and cool clothing. Small knapsacks and belt canteens are also handy. Water is not available along hiking trails; **Backcountry:** No; **Camping:** Yes; **Other overnight accommodations on site:** Yes, cottage and tent site reservations must be made well in advance, but not more than 8 months prior to the visit. Primitive, unequipped campsites can also be reserved. Contact the Concessioner, Cinnamon Bay Campground, P.O. Box 720, St. John, V.I. 00830, phone 809-776-6330, or see a travel agent; **Meals served in the park:** Yes, at Cruz Bay, Trunk Bay, Cinnamon Bay; **Food and supplies obtainable in the park:** Yes, at Cruz Bay; **Food and supplies obtainable nearby:** Yes, at St. Thomas; **Overnight accommodations:** St. Thomas, 4 miles (6.4 km) by water; **First Aid available in park:** Yes; **Nearest Hospital:** The clinic at Cruz Bay is open Mon.-Fri. from 7 a.m. to 11 p.m.; Sat. and Sun., 8 a.m. to 11 p.m., phone 809-776-6400. A nurse and doctor are on 24-hour call daily; you can reach them by phoning the Dept. of Public Safety, 809-776-6471; **Days/Hours:** The Park is open every day. Park Headquarters and Visitor Center in Red Hook open from 8:30 a.m. to 5 p.m.; Cruz Bay Visitor Center open from 8 a.m. to 4:30 p.m.; **Holiday Closings:** No; **Visitor attractions closed for seasons:** No; **Weather:** The yearly temperature averages 79°F and varies little between winter and summer. Temperatures rarely exceed 98°F or fall below 65°F. Rainfall averages approximately 40 inches per year, coming mostly in brief night showers.

GENERAL INFORMATION: *For Your Safety*—Insect repellent may be useful because of mosquitoes and sand flies. While snorkeling and swimming, use lifeguard-posted beaches and avoid touching or standing on corals, which are fragile and can cause nasty cuts and scrapes. Protect yourself from sunburn. Avoid heavy surf and never go out alone. While hiking, avoid long and strenuous hikes in the heat of the day (10 a.m. to 3 p.m.). Bring drinking water. Avoid eating unidentified plants. Stay on the trails—do not shortcut. Do not climb around or over ruins. Wear sturdy hiking shoes or boots. Tell someone of your plans and *do not hike alone*.

Climatables™

Weather Charts for the Park Areas

CLIMATABLE NO. 1

Katmai NP, Lake Clark NP, Alagnak Wild River

WEATHER PARAMETERS	J	F	M	A	M	J	J	A	S	O	N	D
TEMPERATURE												
Normal Daily Maximum	24	26	31	41	55	63	67	64	57	41	32	22
Normal Daily Minimum	3	4	8	22	32	40	45	45	38	25	15	5
Extreme High	54	54	56	63	78	86	90	88	75	66	53	53
Extreme Low	−42	−50	−50	−11	13	24	25	22	11	−5	−20	−48
Days Above 70°	0	0	0	0	1	4	10	4	0	0	0	0
Days Below 32°	29	26	29	25	16	3	2	2	5	24	27	28
PRECIPITATION												
Normal	2.1	1.4	1.9	2.4	1.5	1.8	2.2	4.2	3.5	3.1	2.4	2.5
Maximum	3.0	3.0	2.4	3.0	3.0	3.9	4.9	11.2	6.6	6.4	3.4	3.6
Maximum 24 Hr. Precipitation	1.0	0.8	0.8	1.0	0.6	1.3	1.3	3.5	1.9	2.4	1.1	1.2
Maximum Snowfall	21	24	36	30	10	1	0	0	1	15	28	17
Days With Measurable Precip.	10	8	10	10	11	12	14	16	15	13	11	11
Average No. Thunderstorms	0	0	0	0	0	0	0	0	0	0	0	0
SUNSHINE/CLOUDINESS												
No. Clear Days	8	8	7	4	3	1	1	1	2	4	6	7
No. Partly Cloudy Days	5	5	6	6	6	5	5	5	6	7	5	6
No. Cloudy Days	18	15	18	20	22	24	25	25	22	20	19	18
% Possible Sunshine	NA	NA	NA	NA	NA	NA	NA	NA	NA	NA	NA	NA

TEMPERATURE NORMALS AND EXTREMES

% OF SUNNY/PTLY CLOUDY/CLOUDY DAYS

□ Clear ▦ Ptly Cloudy ■ Cloudy

etc.

- Wide variations in weather are experienced in the Parks due to differences in terrain and exposure to prevailing wind.
- Precipitation is highest on the windward or eastern slopes and sharply decreases on the leeward sides.
- In the area of the glaciers, total annual precipitation is 100 to 200".

CLIMATABLE NO. 2

TEMPERATURE NORMALS AND EXTREMES

% OF SUNNY/PTLY CLOUDY/CLOUDY DAYS

☐ Clear   ▥ Ptly Cloudy   ■ Cloudy

WEATHER PARAMETERS	J	F	M	A	M	J	J	A	S	O	N	D
TEMPERATURE												
Normal Daily Maximum	29	31	35	42	49	57	61	60	54	44	35	30
Normal Daily Minimum	14	19	21	28	34	42	46	45	41	33	24	17
Extreme High	58	55	59	67	82	84	86	86	72	64	58	54
Extreme Low	-30	-21	-24	-9	6	29	32	30	20	-1	-8	-23
Days Above 70°	0	0	0	0	0	1	1	1	0	0	0	0
Days Below 32°	28	24	28	22	10	1	0	0	3	16	23	27
PRECIPITATION												
Normal	6.1	6.8	5.4	5.7	5.8	4.7	6.2	6.8	13.1	14.5	10.4	9.5
Maximum	15.8	19.0	12.4	12.2	13.6	13.2	17.8	18.3	27.7	26.6	30.6	19.8
Maximum 24 Hr. Precipitation	3.2	4.1	2.4	4.4	3.6	3.0	4.6	4.4	4.7	5.0	4.6	4.5
Maximum Snowfall	46	80	89	61	16	0	0	0	T	15	48	71
Days With Measurable Precip.	17	16	16	15	16	15	15	14	15	16	17	17
Average No. Thunderstorms	0	0	0	0	0	0	0	0	0	0	0	0
SUNSHINE/CLOUDINESS												
No. Clear Days	5	6	7	5	3	3	3	4	5	7	6	6
No. Partly Cloudy Days	4	4	5	5	6	6	6	6	5	5	5	4
No. Cloudy Days	22	18	19	20	22	21	22	21	19	19	19	21
% Possible Sunshine	NA	NA	NA	NA	NA	NA	NA	NA	NA	NA	NA	NA

etc.

- As evidenced by the glaciers, precipitation is greater at higher elevations.
- Record annual precipitation for Alaska of 332.29" was recorded on Montague Island in 1976.
- At Thompson Pass just north of Valdez, a seasonal snowfall of 974.5" was recorded in 1952-53.

CLIMATABLE NO. 3

**Bering Land Bridge NP, Kobuk Valley NP, Noatak NP
Gates of the Arctic NP, Cape Krusenstern NM**

TEMPERATURE NORMALS AND EXTREMES

WEATHER PARAMETERS	MONTH											
	J	F	M	A	M	J	J	A	S	O	N	D
TEMPERATURE												
Normal Daily Maximum	-2	0	10	28	46	65	66	61	48	27	10	0
Normal Daily Minimum	-20	-17	-9	7	28	42	48	44	33	15	-2	-15
Extreme High	39	40	42	59	79	90	86	84	70	54	39	40
Extreme Low	-58	-64	-55	-44	-18	19	30	19	-1	-20	-50	-58
Days Above 70°	0	0	0	0	1	11	15	6	0	0	0	0
Days Below 32°	31	28	31	28	11	1	0	1	13	26	30	31
PRECIPITATION												
Normal	0.7	0.6	0.8	0.8	0.9	1.2	2.7	2.7	0.9	0.9	1.2	0.8
Maximum	2.6	2.9	3.6	1.9	1.4	3.6	5.4	5.9	3.8	3.8	3.8	2.0
Maximum 24 Hr. Precipitation	0.9	0.6	0.8	1.0	0.9	1.2	2.0	2.1	1.4	0.9	0.7	0.5
Maximum Snowfall	24	14	22	18	12	2	1	1	7	18	29	22
Days With Measurable Precip.	8	7	8	6	6	8	11	14	12	10	10	9
Average No. Thunderstorms	0	0	0	0	0	1	2	0	0	0	0	0
SUNSHINE/CLOUDINESS												
No. Clear Days	13	11	11	9	7	4	3	3	6	7	8	10
No. Partly Cloudy Days	4	4	5	8	10	12	9	7	6	5	5	5
No. Cloudy Days	14	13	15	13	14	14	19	21	18	19	17	16
% Possible Sunshine	44	46	48	53	51	48	32	26	34	35	36	30

% OF SUNNY/PTLY CLOUDY/CLOUDY DAYS

☐ Clear   ▤ Ptly Cloudy   ▧ Cloudy

etc.

- The "Land of the "Midnight Sun"! The sun remains continuously above the horizon from the beginning of June until the middle of July.
- On the Seward Peninsula, temperatures are more moderate and precipitation totals are less than in the remaining areas represented by this table.

CLIMATABLE NO. 4

TEMPERATURE NORMALS AND EXTREMES

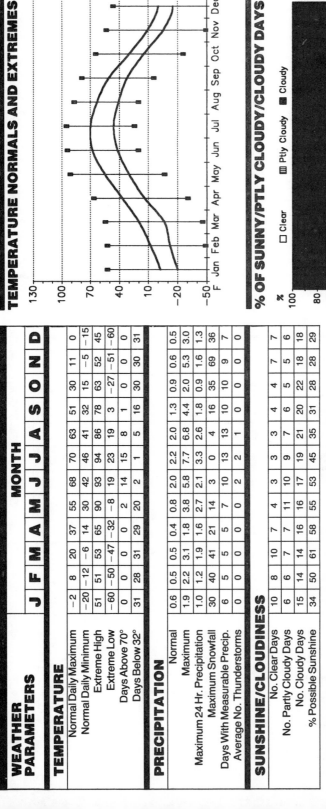

% OF SUNNY/PTLY CLOUDY/CLOUDY DAYS

☐ Clear   ⊞ Ptly Cloudy   ■ Cloudy

WEATHER PARAMETERS	J	F	M	A	M	J	J	A	S	O	N	D
TEMPERATURE												
Normal Daily Maximum	-2	8	20	37	55	68	70	63	51	30	11	0
Normal Daily Minimum	-20	-12	-6	14	30	42	46	41	32	15	-5	-15
Extreme High	51	51	53	65	90	93	94	86	78	63	52	45
Extreme Low	-60	-50	-47	-32	-8	19	23	19	3	-27	-51	-60
Days Above 70°	0	0	0	0	2	14	15	8	1	0	0	0
Days Below 32°	31	28	31	29	20	2	1	5	16	30	30	31
PRECIPITATION												
Normal	0.6	0.5	0.5	0.4	0.8	2.0	2.2	2.0	1.3	0.9	0.6	0.5
Maximum	1.9	2.2	3.1	1.8	3.8	5.8	7.7	6.8	4.4	2.0	5.3	3.0
Maximum 24 Hr. Precipitation	1.0	1.2	1.9	1.6	2.7	2.1	3.3	2.6	1.8	0.9	1.6	1.3
Maximum Snowfall	30	40	41	21	14	3	0	4	16	35	69	36
Days With Measurable Precip.	6	5	5	5	7	10	13	13	10	10	9	7
Average No. Thunderstorms	0	0	0	0	0	2	2	1	0	0	0	0
SUNSHINE/CLOUDINESS												
No. Clear Days	10	8	10	7	4	3	3	3	4	4	7	7
No. Partly Cloudy Days	6	6	7	7	11	10	9	7	6	5	5	6
No. Cloudy Days	15	14	14	16	16	17	19	21	20	22	18	18
% Possible Sunshine	34	50	61	58	55	53	45	35	31	28	28	29

etc.

- In June, length of day ranges from 19 to 23 hours; in December, duration of daylight is 3 to 5 hours.
- Yukon-Charley NP has colder winters and warmer summers than Denali NP, but weather is more variable in Denali NP.
- Alaska's record high temperature of 100 degrees was recorded at Fort Yukon in June, 1915.

CLIMATABLE NO. 5

Sitka NHP, Glacier Bay NP, Klondike Gold Rush NHP

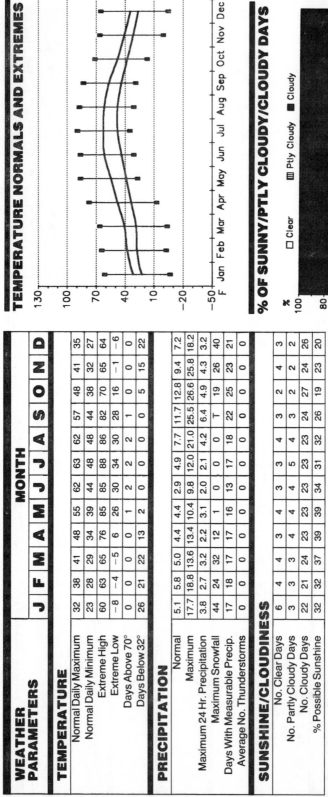

WEATHER PARAMETERS	MONTH											
	J	F	M	A	M	J	J	A	S	O	N	D
TEMPERATURE												
Normal Daily Maximum	32	38	41	48	55	62	63	62	57	48	41	35
Normal Daily Minimum	23	28	29	34	39	44	48	48	44	38	32	27
Extreme High	60	63	65	76	85	85	88	86	82	70	65	64
Extreme Low	-8	-4	-5	6	26	30	34	30	28	16	-1	-6
Days Above 70°	0	0	0	0	1	2	2	2	1	0	0	0
Days Below 32°	26	21	22	13	2	0	0	0	0	5	15	22
PRECIPITATION												
Normal	5.1	5.8	5.0	4.4	4.4	2.9	4.9	7.7	11.7	12.8	9.4	7.2
Maximum	17.7	18.8	13.6	13.4	10.4	9.8	12.0	21.0	25.5	26.6	25.8	18.2
Maximum 24 Hr. Precipitation	3.8	2.7	3.2	2.2	3.1	2.0	2.1	4.2	6.4	4.9	4.3	3.2
Maximum Snowfall	44	24	32	12	1	0	0	0	T	19	26	40
Days With Measurable Precip.	17	18	17	17	16	13	17	18	22	25	23	21
Average No. Thunderstorms	0	0	0	0	0	0	0	0	0	0	0	0
SUNSHINE/CLOUDINESS												
No. Clear Days	6	4	4	3	3	3	3	4	3	2	4	3
No. Partly Cloudy Days	3	3	3	4	4	5	4	3	3	2	2	2
No. Cloudy Days	22	21	24	23	23	23	23	23	24	27	24	26
% Possible Sunshine	32	32	37	39	34	31	32	26	26	19	23	20

etc.

- Climate moderated by warm Alaska current flowing northward along the coast.
- In higher elevation areas, temperatures are lower and precipitation is greater than shown in the table.
- Wind speeds greater than 50 mph are often experienced in winter; watch the wind chill temperature!

CLIMATABLE NO. 6

Glen Canyon NRA, Grand Canyon NP

TEMPERATURE NORMALS AND EXTREMES

% OF SUNNY/PTLY CLOUDY/CLOUDY DAYS

□ Clear ▤ Ptlycldy ■ Cloudy

WEATHER PARAMETERS	MONTH											
	J	F	M	A	M	J	J	A	S	O	N	D
TEMPERATURE												
Normal Daily Maximum	42	48	59	69	79	88	94	91	85	68	54	44
Normal Daily Minimum	21	26	31	37	49	58	65	63	57	42	31	23
Extreme High	72	75	84	90	98	109	107	106	104	94	80	73
Extreme Low	−16	−14	−3	9	13	28	31	30	25	3	−1	−13
Days Above 90°	0	0	0	0	4	17	28	24	9	0	0	0
Days Below 32°	26	18	13	4	1	0	0	0	0	1	11	26
PRECIPITATION												
Normal	1.2	1.1	1.3	0.9	0.5	0.5	1.4	2.1	1.0	0.9	0.8	1.4
Maximum	NA	NA	NA	NA	NA	NA	NA	NA	NA	NA	NA	NA
Maximum 24 Hr. Precipitation	1.7	1.8	4.0	1.1	1.2	2.2	2.6	2.2	2.7	1.8	1.3	2.2
Maximum Snowfall	60	33	44	46	19	0	0	0	0	12	22	32
Days With Measurable Precip.	6	6	7	5	4	4	7	9	5	5	5	6
Average No. Thunderstorms	0	0	0	1	4	5	13	14	7	2	0	0
SUNSHINE/CLOUDINESS												
No. Clear Days	12	11	12	13	16	19	9	10	16	17	16	14
No. Partly Cloudy Days	6	6	8	8	9	7	13	13	10	7	6	6
No. Cloudy Days	13	11	11	9	6	4	9	8	4	7	8	11
% Possible Sunshine	77	72	72	81	88	84	70	73	78	76	73	71

etc.

- There is a strong temperature contrast between the floor and the rim of the Grand Canyon. The summer climate of the Canyon floor is torrid! Temperatures can become dangerously high. The Canyon floor is considerably drier than the rim.
- The Glen Canyon area is even drier than the Grand Canyon.

CLIMATABLE NO. 7   Hot Springs NP

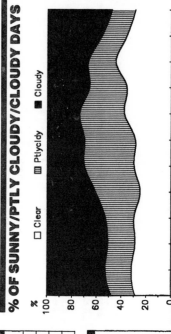

TEMPERATURE NORMALS AND EXTREMES

% OF SUNNY/PTLY CLOUDY/CLOUDY DAYS

☐ Clear   ▦ Ptlycldy   ■ Cloudy

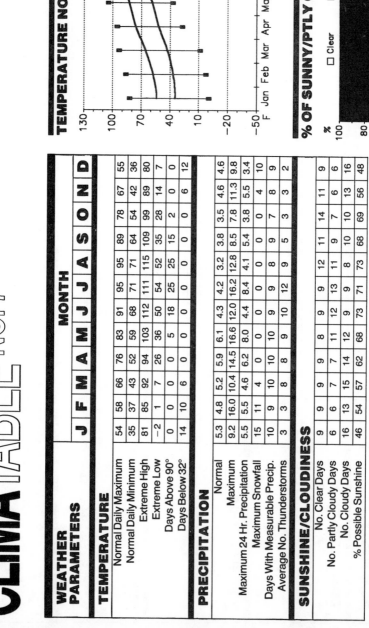

WEATHER PARAMETERS	J	F	M	A	M	J	J	A	S	O	N	D
TEMPERATURE												
Normal Daily Maximum	54	58	66	76	83	91	95	95	89	78	67	55
Normal Daily Minimum	35	37	43	52	59	68	71	71	64	54	42	36
Extreme High	81	85	92	94	103	112	111	115	109	99	89	80
Extreme Low	-2	1	7	26	36	50	54	52	35	28	14	7
Days Above 90°	0	0	0	0	5	18	25	25	15	2	0	0
Days Below 32°	14	10	6	0	0	0	0	0	0	0	6	12
PRECIPITATION												
Normal	5.3	4.8	5.2	5.9	6.1	4.3	4.2	3.2	3.8	3.5	4.6	4.6
Maximum	9.2	16.0	10.4	14.5	16.6	12.0	16.2	12.8	8.5	7.8	11.3	9.8
Maximum 24 Hr. Precipitation	5.5	5.5	4.6	6.2	8.0	4.4	8.4	4.1	5.4	3.8	5.5	3.4
Maximum Snowfall	15	11	4	0	0	0	0	0	0	0	4	10
Days With Measurable Precip.	10	9	10	10	10	9	9	8	7	8	8	9
Average No. Thunderstorms	3	3	8	8	9	10	12	9	5	3	3	2
SUNSHINE/CLOUDINESS												
No. Clear Days	9	9	9	9	8	9	9	11	11	11	9	9
No. Partly Cloudy Days	6	6	7	7	11	12	13	9	7	6	6	6
No. Cloudy Days	16	13	15	14	12	9	9	8	10	13	13	16
% Possible Sunshine	46	54	57	62	68	73	71	73	68	69	56	48

etc.

• Summers are warm and humid . . . watch the Heat Index.
• Summer rain falls as scattered showers and thunderstorms, often brief but locally heavy.
• Winters are relatively mild; warm spells with temperatures in the 60's and 70's are not uncommon.

CLIMATABLE NO. 8

Cabrillo NM, Channel Islands NP, Santa Monica Mts. NRA

TEMPERATURE NORMALS AND EXTREMES

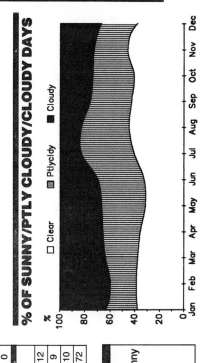

% OF SUNNY/PTLY CLOUDY/CLOUDY DAYS

☐ Clear   ⊞ Ptlycldy   ■ Cloudy

WEATHER PARAMETERS	MONTH											
	J	F	M	A	M	J	J	A	S	O	N	D
TEMPERATURE												
Normal Daily Maximum	63	64	63	64	65	68	70	72	72	70	68	65
Normal Daily Minimum	47	48	49	51	55	58	61	62	61	56	51	47
Extreme High	85	87	91	88	94	93	91	89	104	99	100	89
Extreme Low	24	31	32	39	43	45	51	52	44	36	34	30
Days Above 90°	0	0	0	0	0	0	0	0	0	0	0	0
Days Below 32°	0	0	0	0	0	0	0	0	0	0	0	0
PRECIPITATION												
Normal	3.3	3.0	2.1	1.0	0.2	0.0	0.0	0.2	0.1	0.2	1.7	1.9
Maximum	13.9	14.1	9.8	5.5	2.9	0.2	0.4	3.1	1.1	1.8	8.7	6.5
Maximum 24 Hr. Precipitation	5.3	4.2	4.1	2.1	1.5	1.1	0.4	2.8	1.9	0.9	4.2	5.3
Maximum Snowfall	0	0	0	0	0	0	0	0	0	0	0	0
Days With Measurable Precip.	6	6	6	3	1	0	0	0	1	2	4	5
Average No. Thunderstorms	0	0	0	0	0	0	0	0	0	0	0	0
SUNSHINE/CLOUDINESS												
No. Clear Days	12	11	12	11	10	10	13	14	13	13	14	12
No. Partly Cloudy Days	8	6	8	9	11	11	13	12	10	10	8	9
No. Cloudy Days	11	11	11	10	10	9	5	5	7	8	8	10
% Possible Sunshine	72	72	70	67	58	57	69	70	68	68	74	72

etc.
- Summer is very distinctly the dry season; little or no precipitation occurs.
- Spring and summer are characterized by morning low cloudiness and sunny afternoons.
- In winter, fog can be expected on one day in four.
- In the spring, seas of 5' or higher are observed 30% to 40% of the time.

CLIMATABLE NO. 9

Yosemite NP, Devil's Postpile NM

TEMPERATURE NORMALS AND EXTREMES

% OF SUNNY/PTLY CLOUDY/CLOUDY DAYS

Legend: ☐ Clear ▦ Ptlycldy ■ Cloudy

WEATHER PARAMETERS	J	F	M	A	M	J	J	A	S	O	N	D
TEMPERATURE												
Normal Daily Maximum	47	55	59	66	73	82	90	90	85	74	58	46
Normal Daily Minimum	26	29	31	35	42	48	53	52	47	39	31	26
Extreme High	69	79	89	90	91	102	104	104	102	98	86	65
Extreme Low	7	10	10	20	26	30	38	32	28	16	0	−1
Days Above 90°	0	0	0	0	1	6	18	18	9	1	0	0
Days Below 32°	27	22	21	11	2	0	0	0	0	5	21	27
PRECIPITATION												
Normal	6.6	5.0	4.6	3.5	1.5	0.6	0.4	0.3	0.7	1.4	4.7	6.9
Maximum	22.3	17.2	11.5	12.1	4.8	1.6	1.6	1.3	5.2	4.6	13.0	29.8
Maximum 24 Hr. Precipitation	5.8	4.6	2.9	2.9	1.9	1.0	1.0	0.7	3.2	2.3	3.4	6.9
Maximum Snowfall	49	89	67	81	7	0	0	0	0	T	21	51
Days With Measurable Precip.	12	10	11	9	6	3	1	1	2	5	9	11
Average No. Thunderstorms	0	0	1	2	3	4	5	3	2	0	0	0
SUNSHINE/CLOUDINESS												
No. Clear Days	9	8	9	10	12	19	26	25	23	16	10	9
No. Partly Cloudy Days	5	5	5	7	8	5	3	4	4	6	5	5
No. Cloudy Days	17	15	17	13	11	6	2	2	3	9	15	17
% Possible Sunshine	60	60	70	75	80	90	90	90	90	80	70	60

etc.

- Temperature and precipitation, especially snowfall, vary considerably with elevation, the higher elevation areas being cooler and wetter.
- Summer evenings can be quite chilly.

CLIMA TABLE NO. 10

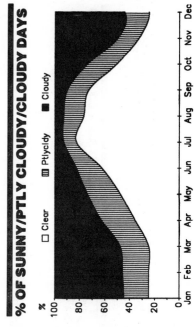

TEMPERATURE NORMALS AND EXTREMES

% OF SUNNY/PTLY CLOUDY/CLOUDY DAYS

☐ Clear   ▥ Ptlycldy   ■ Cloudy

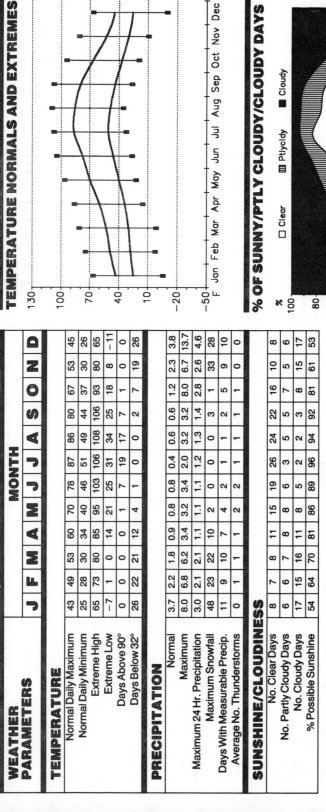

WEATHER PARAMETERS	MONTH											
	J	F	M	A	M	J	J	A	S	O	N	D
TEMPERATURE												
Normal Daily Maximum	43	49	53	60	70	78	87	86	80	67	53	45
Normal Daily Minimum	25	28	30	34	40	46	51	49	44	37	30	26
Extreme High	65	73	80	85	95	103	106	108	106	93	80	65
Extreme Low	-7	1	0	14	21	25	31	34	25	18	8	-11
Days Above 90°	0	0	0	0	1	7	19	17	7	1	0	0
Days Below 32°	26	22	21	12	4	1	0	0	2	7	19	26
PRECIPITATION												
Normal	3.7	2.2	1.8	0.9	0.8	0.8	0.4	0.6	0.6	1.2	2.3	3.8
Maximum	8.0	6.8	6.2	3.4	3.2	3.4	2.0	3.2	3.2	8.0	6.7	13.7
Maximum 24 Hr. Precipitation	3.0	2.1	2.1	1.1	1.1	1.1	1.2	1.3	1.4	2.8	2.6	4.6
Maximum Snowfall	48	23	22	10	2	0	0	0	0	1	33	28
Days With Measurable Precip.	11	9	10	7	4	2	0	1	2	5	9	10
Average No. Thunderstorms	0	1	1	1	2	2	1	1	1	1	0	0
SUNSHINE/CLOUDINESS												
No. Clear Days	8	7	8	11	15	19	26	24	22	16	10	8
No. Partly Cloudy Days	6	6	7	8	8	6	3	5	5	7	5	6
No. Cloudy Days	17	15	16	11	8	5	2	2	3	8	15	17
% Possible Sunshine	54	64	70	81	86	89	96	94	92	81	61	53

etc.

- Precipitation is a maximum in winter; heavy, persistent rains over periods of 7-10 days may be experienced.
- Near Mt. Shasta, North America's record snowfall of 189" for a single snowstorm, occurred.
- Precipitation amounts are markedly less on the eastern slopes of the mountains.

CLIMATABLE NO. 11

Redwood NP, Lava Beds NM

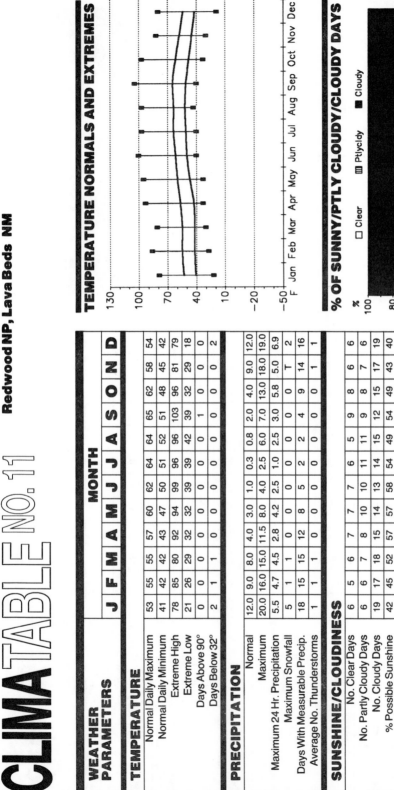

TEMPERATURE NORMALS AND EXTREMES

WEATHER PARAMETERS	MONTH											
	J	F	M	A	M	J	J	A	S	O	N	D
TEMPERATURE												
Normal Daily Maximum	53	55	55	57	60	62	64	64	65	62	58	54
Normal Daily Minimum	41	42	42	43	47	50	51	52	51	48	45	42
Extreme High	78	85	80	92	94	99	96	96	103	96	81	79
Extreme Low	21	26	29	32	32	39	39	42	39	32	29	18
Days Above 90°	0	0	0	0	0	0	0	0	1	0	0	0
Days Below 32°	2	1	1	0	0	0	0	0	0	0	0	2
PRECIPITATION												
Normal	12.0	8.0	8.0	4.0	3.0	1.0	0.3	0.8	2.0	4.0	9.0	12.0
Maximum	20.0	16.0	15.0	11.5	8.0	4.0	2.5	6.0	7.0	13.0	18.0	19.0
Maximum 24 Hr. Precipitation	5.5	4.7	4.5	2.8	4.2	2.5	1.0	2.5	3.0	5.8	5.0	6.9
Maximum Snowfall	5	1	1	0	0	0	0	0	0	0	T	2
Days With Measurable Precip.	18	15	15	12	8	5	2	2	4	9	14	16
Average No. Thunderstorms	1	1	1	0	0	0	0	0	0	0	1	1
SUNSHINE/CLOUDINESS												
No. Clear Days	6	5	6	7	7	7	6	5	9	8	6	6
No. Partly Cloudy Days	6	6	7	8	10	10	11	11	9	8	7	6
No. Cloudy Days	19	17	18	15	14	13	14	15	12	15	17	19
% Possible Sunshine	42	45	52	57	57	58	54	49	54	49	43	40

% OF SUNNY/PTLY CLOUDY/CLOUDY DAYS

☐ Clear   ▦ Ptlycldy   ■ Cloudy

etc.

- Usually over 90% of the annual precipitation falls in the period October through April; the total wintertime precipitation increases with distance north of Eureka.
- With extended periods of heavy winter precipitation, some flooding can be expected along the Klamath River.

CLIMATABLE NO. 12

Sequoia & Kings Canyon NP's

TEMPERATURE NORMALS AND EXTREMES

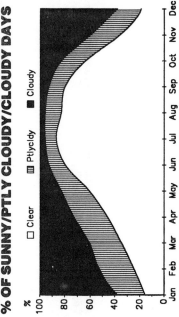

WEATHER PARAMETERS	J	F	M	A	M	J	J	A	S	O	N	D
TEMPERATURE												
Normal Daily Maximum	43	44	45	49	57	66	75	74	69	60	50	44
Normal Daily Minimum	24	25	25	29	36	44	50	49	45	38	30	26
Extreme High	65	70	72	75	82	87	90	86	87	79	72	70
Extreme Low	−5	−2	0	8	17	23	35	28	26	11	9	−4
Days Above 90°	0	0	0	0	0	0	0	0	0	0	0	0
Days Below 32°	28	24	26	20	10	1	0	0	1	7	20	26
PRECIPITATION												
Normal	8.8	6.4	6.0	4.5	1.5	0.5	0.1	0.1	0.6	1.3	4.9	7.8
Maximum	38.2	23.6	16.5	14.9	8.3	2.2	0.6	0.5	2.2	3.4	14.0	28.3
Maximum 24 Hr. Precipitation	7.5	6.8	4.6	4.0	5.1	1.2	0.4	0.4	1.4	2.7	3.9	10.1
Maximum Snowfall	101	154	168	143	31	8	0	0	4	11	57	80
Days With Measurable Precip.	10	9	10	8	5	2	1	1	2	3	7	10
Average No. Thunderstorms	0	0	0	2	2	2	1	1	2	0	0	0
SUNSHINE/CLOUDINESS												
No. Clear Days	5	7	11	14	19	24	27	26	24	20	11	6
No. Partly Cloudy Days	7	8	8	8	7	4	3	4	4	6	7	6
No. Cloudy Days	19	13	12	8	5	2	1	1	2	5	12	19
% Possible Sunshine	47	65	77	85	90	94	96	96	93	88	65	45

MONTH

% OF SUNNY/PTLY CLOUDY/CLOUDY DAYS

□ Clear   ▨ Ptlycldy   ■ Cloudy

etc.

- The distinct summer dry season is typical of California.
- Winter precipitation and snowfall can be extremely heavy along the western slopes of the Sierra Nevada mountains.

CLIMATABLE NO. 13

Hovenweep NM, Yucca House NM, Mesa Verde NP

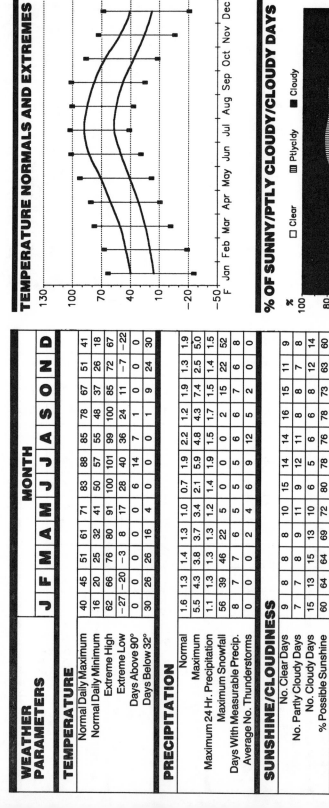

TEMPERATURE NORMALS AND EXTREMES

% OF SUNNY/PTLY CLOUDY/CLOUDY DAYS

□ Clear   ▦ Ptlycldy   ■ Cloudy

WEATHER PARAMETERS	J	F	M	A	M	J	J	A	S	O	N	D
TEMPERATURE												
Normal Daily Maximum	40	45	51	61	71	83	88	85	78	67	51	41
Normal Daily Minimum	16	20	25	32	41	50	57	55	48	37	26	18
Extreme High	62	66	76	80	91	100	101	99	100	85	72	67
Extreme Low	−27	−20	−3	8	17	28	40	36	24	11	−7	−22
Days Above 90°	0	0	0	0	0	6	14	7	1	0	0	0
Days Below 32°	30	26	26	16	4	0	0	0	1	9	24	30
PRECIPITATION												
Normal	1.6	1.3	1.4	1.3	1.0	0.7	1.9	2.2	1.2	1.9	1.3	1.9
Maximum	5.5	4.3	3.8	3.7	3.4	2.1	5.9	4.8	4.3	7.4	2.5	5.0
Maximum 24 Hr. Precipitation	1.1	1.3	1.3	1.3	1.2	1.4	1.9	1.5	1.7	1.5	1.4	1.5
Maximum Snowfall	56	39	46	22	5	0	0	0	2	15	22	52
Days With Measurable Precip.	8	7	7	6	5	5	5	6	6	7	6	8
Average No. Thunderstorms	0	0	0	2	4	6	9	12	5	2	0	0
SUNSHINE/CLOUDINESS												
No. Clear Days	9	8	8	8	10	15	14	14	16	15	11	9
No. Partly Cloudy Days	7	7	8	9	11	9	12	11	8	8	7	8
No. Cloudy Days	15	13	15	13	10	6	5	6	6	8	12	14
% Possible Sunshine	60	64	64	69	72	80	78	76	78	73	63	60

etc.

- Precipitation is fairly evenly distributed throughout the year. There is a slight maximum of precipitation in winter while June tends to be the driest month.

CLIMATABLE NO. 14

TEMPERATURE NORMALS AND EXTREMES

% OF SUNNY/PTLY CLOUDY/CLOUDY DAYS

□ Clear ▥ Ptlycldy ■ Cloudy

WEATHER PARAMETERS

WEATHER PARAMETERS	J	F	M	A	M	J	J	A	S	O	N	D
TEMPERATURE												
Normal Daily Maximum	27	30	36	47	50	61	75	72	66	55	40	29
Normal Daily Minimum	1	2	8	21	30	36	42	41	33	25	15	6
Extreme High	47	55	57	69	76	88	86	83	81	71	58	47
Extreme Low	−46	−41	−30	−13	12	23	29	27	14	10	−20	−30
Days Above 90°	0	0	0	0	0	0	0	0	0	0	0	0
Days Below 32°	31	28	31	29	24	7	1	2	14	28	29	31
PRECIPITATION												
Normal	1.1	0.9	1.1	1.0	1.3	1.4	1.5	1.0	1.3	0.9	0.8	1.2
Maximum	2.1	1.6	2.0	2.7	3.2	4.3	3.2	3.0	5.4	3.7	1.9	4.0
Maximum 24 Hr. Precipitation	0.8	0.6	0.7	0.6	1.4	1.0	0.9	0.8	1.2	1.4	0.6	1.3
Maximum Snowfall	29	32	26	23	12	T	T	T	38	39	22	32
Days With Measurable Precip.	7	5	7	7	7	9	9	9	7	6	5	6
Average No. Thunderstorms	0	0	0	2	8	10	16	14	6	1	0	0
SUNSHINE/CLOUDINESS												
No. Clear Days	10	8	8	7	6	10	9	9	13	13	10	11
No. Partly Cloudy Days	9	9	10	11	12	12	16	15	9	9	10	10
No. Cloudy Days	12	11	13	12	13	8	6	7	8	9	10	10
% Possible Sunshine	71	71	70	68	65	71	72	74	74	72	64	67

etc.

- Pleasantly cool summers and bitterly cold winters; below-freezing temperatures have been observed in every month of the year.
- Snow has fallen in every month of the year; near the National Park, a 24-hour snowfall of 76", the record for North America, was recorded.

CLIMATABLE NO. 15

All District of Columbia sites, Arlington House, Robert E. Lee Memorial, George Washington Memorial Parkway, U.S. Marine Corps War Memorial and Netherlands Carillon

TEMPERATURE NORMALS AND EXTREMES

% OF SUNNY/PTLY CLOUDY/CLOUDY DAYS

☐ Clear   ▥ Ptlycldy   ■ Cloudy

WEATHER PARAMETERS	MONTH											
	J	F	M	A	M	J	J	A	S	O	N	D
TEMPERATURE												
Normal Daily Maximum	43	46	55	67	76	84	88	86	80	69	57	46
Normal Daily Minimum	28	29	37	46	56	65	70	69	62	50	40	31
Extreme High	79	82	89	95	97	101	103	101	101	94	86	75
Extreme Low	−5	4	11	24	34	47	55	49	39	29	16	1
Days Above 90°	0	0	0	0	2	8	13	10	4	0	0	0
Days Below 32°	23	19	8	1	0	0	0	0	0	0	4	16
PRECIPITATION												
Normal	2.8	2.6	3.5	2.9	3.5	3.4	3.9	4.4	3.2	2.9	2.8	3.2
Maximum	7.1	5.7	7.4	6.9	10.7	11.5	11.1	14.3	12.4	8.2	6.7	6.5
Maximum 24 Hr. Precipitation	2.2	1.9	3.4	3.1	4.3	7.2	4.7	6.4	5.3	5.0	2.6	2.9
Maximum Snowfall	21	31	17	1	T	0	0	0	0	T	7	16
Days With Measurable Precip.	10	9	11	9	11	10	10	9	8	7	8	9
Average No. Thunderstorms	0	0	1	3	6	7	8	8	3	1	0	0
SUNSHINE/CLOUDINESS												
No. Clear Days	8	8	8	7	7	8	8	9	10	11	8	9
No. Partly Cloudy Days	7	6	8	9	10	11	12	10	8	7	8	6
No. Cloudy Days	16	14	15	14	14	11	11	12	13	14	14	16
% Possible Sunshine	48	51	55	57	59	64	63	63	62	58	51	47

etc.
- Summer days can be hot, humid and very oppressive . . . watch the Heat Index.
- Winters are cold, but rarely severe. The normal total seasonal snowfall is less than 18".
- Freezing temperatures normally occur until April 1st.

CLIMATABLE NO. 16

TEMPERATURE NORMALS AND EXTREMES

% OF SUNNY/PTLY CLOUDY/CLOUDY DAYS

☐ Clear   ▨ Ptlycldy   ■ Cloudy

WEATHER PARAMETERS	J	F	M	A	M	J	J	A	S	O	N	D
TEMPERATURE												
Normal Daily Maximum	76	76	80	83	86	88	90	90	89	85	81	77
Normal Daily Minimum	56	57	61	65	69	73	75	75	74	70	63	58
Extreme High	88	89	92	96	98	98	99	98	99	95	90	88
Extreme Low	28	30	32	43	53	60	65	64	65	49	33	29
Days Above 90°	0	0	0	1	9	15	22	24	20	6	0	0
Days Below 32°	0	0	0	0	0	0	0	0	0	0	0	0
PRECIPITATION												
Normal	2.1	2.0	1.9	3.1	6.5	9.2	6.0	7.0	8.1	7.1	2.7	1.9
Maximum	6.8	8.1	10.6	17.3	18.5	23.5	17.4	16.9	24.4	21.1	13.2	6.4
Maximum 24 Hr. Precipitation	2.7	6.0	7.1	16.2	11.6	10.1	4.6	6.9	7.6	10.0	7.9	4.4
Maximum Snowfall	0	0	0	0	0	0	0	0	0	0	0	0
Days With Measurable Precip.	6	6	6	6	10	15	16	17	17	14	8	7
Average No. Thunderstorms	1	1	2	4	11	19	22	24	16	6	1	1
SUNSHINE/CLOUDINESS												
No. Clear Days	10	9	9	8	6	3	3	2	2	6	8	9
No. Partly Cloudy Days	13	12	14	15	15	14	17	18	15	14	14	13
No. Cloudy Days	8	7	8	7	10	13	11	13	13	11	8	9
% Possible Sunshine	69	68	77	78	71	74	76	75	72	72	67	65

etc.

- Summers are hot and humid; frequent daytime thunderstorms are often accompanied by rapid drops in temperature that persist for the remainder of the day.
- Summer showers are typically short; rainfall generally extends over less than 10% of the day.

CLIMATABLE NO. 17   Biscayne NP

WEATHER PARAMETERS

MONTH

WEATHER PARAMETERS	J	F	M	A	M	J	J	A	S	O	N	D
TEMPERATURE												
Normal Daily Maximum	74	74	77	80	83	86	87	88	86	83	79	75
Normal Daily Minimum	63	63	66	71	74	76	78	78	77	74	69	64
Extreme High	86	88	91	94	95	97	98	98	96	93	90	85
Extreme Low	34	38	41	48	61	65	68	68	68	55	39	35
Days Above 90°	0	0	0	1	1	2	3	5	2	0	0	0
Days Below 32°	0	0	0	0	0	0	0	0	0	0	0	0
PRECIPITATION												
Normal	2.0	2.1	1.6	2.4	4.3	7.0	4.4	4.3	7.1	6.1	2.5	1.7
Maximum	6.3	7.3	4.3	10.4	11.7	18.9	8.0	14.0	16.0	18.0	10.9	7.8
Maximum 24 Hr. Precipitation	3.1	2.5	1.6	6.9	5.9	6.3	4.9	5.8	8.4	5.3	6.7	3.2
Maximum Snowfall	0	0	0	0	0	0	0	0	0	0	0	0
Days With Measurable Precip.	6	6	6	6	9	12	11	11	12	12	7	6
Average No. Thunderstorms	1	1	2	4	9	17	20	22	14	6	1	1
SUNSHINE/CLOUDINESS												
No. Clear Days	10	9	9	8	6	3	3	2	2	6	8	9
No. Partly Cloudy Days	13	12	14	15	15	14	17	18	15	14	14	13
No. Cloudy Days	8	7	8	7	10	13	11	11	13	11	8	9
% Possible Sunshine	69	68	77	78	71	74	76	75	72	72	67	65

etc.

- The intensity of the sunshine in summer can be distressing!
- Daily summer showers are most frequent in the morning; in nearby inland areas, they are more frequent in the afternoon. Total annual rainfall is significantly less along the coast.
- No freezing temperatures have ever been recorded.

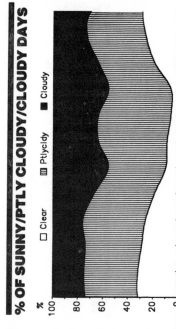

TEMPERATURE NORMALS AND EXTREMES

(130, 100, 70, 40, 10, −20, −50 °F; months Jan Feb Mar Apr May Jun Jul Aug Sep Oct Nov Dec)

% OF SUNNY/PTLY CLOUDY/CLOUDY DAYS

□ Clear   ▥ Ptlycldy   ■ Cloudy

(% 100, 80, 60, 40, 20, 0)

CLIMATABLE NO. 18

Hawaii Volcanoes NP

WEATHER PARAMETERS

TEMPERATURE

	J	F	M	A	M	J	J	A	S	O	N	D
Normal Daily Maximum	66	65	66	66	68	69	70	71	71	71	68	66
Normal Daily Minimum	50	50	50	52	53	54	55	55	54	54	53	51
Extreme High	77	81	77	76	83	83	85	81	85	80	79	75
Extreme Low	39	37	38	42	44	46	48	44	45	45	44	40
Days Above 90°	0	0	0	0	0	0	0	0	0	0	0	0
Days Below 32°	0	0	0	0	0	0	0	0	0	0	0	0

PRECIPITATION

	J	F	M	A	M	J	J	A	S	O	N	D
Normal	12.1	10.3	11.9	10.9	8.0	4.2	4.9	7.2	4.5	6.5	12.9	12.3
Maximum	34.6	28.4	28.4	33.8	23.4	8.7	9.4	17.2	7.5	24.2	26.1	34.3
Maximum 24 Hr. Precipitation	10.5	4.8	5.2	7.4	4.8	3.6	3.7	11.0	4.2	10.0	11.7	9.4
Maximum Snowfall	0	0	0	0	0	0	0	0	0	0	0	0
Days With Measurable Precip.	17	18	24	25	25	24	27	26	23	24	23	21
Average No. Thunderstorms	1	1	2	1	1	0	0	0	0	1	1	1

SUNSHINE/CLOUDINESS

	J	F	M	A	M	J	J	A	S	O	N	D
No. Clear Days	7	5	3	3	1	2	1	1	3	3	3	5
No. Partly Cloudy Days	11	10	10	8	10	11	12	12	12	12	11	11
No. Cloudy Days	13	13	18	21	20	17	18	15	16	16	15	15
% Possible Sunshine	47	45	40	35	37	43	42	44	39	35		38

etc.

- Precipitation amounts are very sensitive to elevation and exposure to the trade winds.
- Maximum precipitation on the windward slopes occurs at elevations between 2000 and 4000 feet. Near the peaks, rainfall is scarce, humidity is very low, and below-freezing temperatures are common.

TEMPERATURE NORMALS AND EXTREMES

% OF SUNNY/PTLY CLOUDY/CLOUDY DAYS

☐ Clear   ▤ Ptlycldy   ▨ Cloudy

CLIMATABLE NO. 19

Abraham Lincoln Birthplace NHS, Mammoth Cave NP

TEMPERATURE NORMALS AND EXTREMES

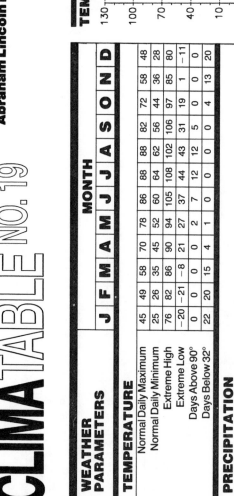

WEATHER PARAMETERS	J	F	M	A	M	J	J	A	S	O	N	D
TEMPERATURE												
Normal Daily Maximum	45	49	58	70	78	86	88	88	82	72	58	48
Normal Daily Minimum	25	26	35	45	52	60	64	62	56	44	36	28
Extreme High	76	82	86	90	94	105	108	102	106	97	85	80
Extreme Low	-20	-21	-8	21	27	37	44	43	31	19	1	-11
Days Above 90°	0	0	0	0	2	7	12	12	5	0	0	0
Days Below 32°	22	20	15	4	1	0	0	0	0	4	13	20
PRECIPITATION												
Normal	4.2	3.8	5.1	4.4	4.5	4.6	4.7	3.4	3.6	2.6	4.0	4.5
Maximum	10.7	10.3	13.8	13.3	10.5	9.0	10.2	8.5	12.2	5.6	13.1	11.7
Maximum 24 Hr. Precipitation	3.9	3.2	4.3	5.0	4.2	3.6	4.0	3.7	4.8	3.2	6.7	3.1
Maximum Snowfall	22	15	24	2	0	0	0	0	0	0	15	11
Days With Measurable Precip.	11	11	13	12	12	10	10	9	8	8	10	11
Average No. Thunderstorms	2	2	6	8	10	12	15	10	5	3	2	1
SUNSHINE/CLOUDINESS												
No. Clear Days	6	6	6	6	8	8	8	10	11	10	7	6
No. Partly Cloudy Days	6	6	8	9	9	11	13	12	9	8	6	6
No. Cloudy Days	19	16	17	15	14	11	10	9	11	12	17	19
% Possible Sunshine	42	47	50	55	61	66	67	65	61	61	46	40

% OF SUNNY/PTLY CLOUDY/CLOUDY DAYS

☐ Clear   ▦ Ptlycldy   ■ Cloudy

etc.

- In general, winters are moderately cold and summers are quite warm.
- The duration of periods of very cold weather in winter is usually short.
- On occasion, extended periods of hot, sultry weather are experienced in summer....see the Heat Index chart.
- Autumn is the driest season.

CLIMATABLE NO. 20

Acadia NP, Roosevelt Campobello International Park, Saint Croix Island NM

TEMPERATURE NORMALS AND EXTREMES

% OF SUNNY/PTLY CLOUDY/CLOUDY DAYS

☐ Clear   ▦ Ptlycldy   ■ Cloudy

WEATHER PARAMETERS	J	F	M	A	M	J	J	A	S	O	N	D
TEMPERATURE												
Normal Daily Maximum	31	32	39	50	61	70	76	74	66	57	46	35
Normal Daily Minimum	15	16	24	34	42	50	54	54	49	42	33	20
Extreme High	57	54	63	82	88	93	96	94	92	81	71	61
Extreme Low	-16	-16	-3	10	25	35	41	35	30	21	6	-11
Days Above 90°	0	0	0	0	0	0	1	0	0	0	0	0
Days Below 32°	29	27	26	14	2	0	0	0	0	4	16	26
PRECIPITATION												
Normal	4.4	4.1	3.8	3.8	3.9	2.9	3.0	3.0	3.8	4.2	5.5	5.2
Maximum	12.0	9.9	10.7	8.1	11.0	8.2	7.2	6.1	6.0	9.2	9.6	10.3
Maximum 24 Hr. Precipitation	3.5	2.8	3.3	2.8	6.3	2.6	2.9	3.4	3.8	3.5	3.5	4.5
Maximum Snowfall	54	43	44	18	6	0	0	0	0	3	16	53
Days With Measurable Precip.	11	10	11	12	13	11	10	10	8	9	12	12
Average No. Thunderstorms	0	0	1	1	2	5	6	5	2	1	0	0
SUNSHINE/CLOUDINESS												
No. Clear Days	10	9	8	8	6	7	8	9	10	10	8	9
No. Partly Cloudy Days	7	7	7	7	10	10	11	11	8	8	7	7
No. Cloudy Days	14	12	15	15	15	13	12	11	12	13	15	15
% Possible Sunshine	56	59	56	55	55	59	64	63	62	58	48	52

etc.

- In winter, "northeasters" bring considerable rain, freezing rain, wet snow and high tides to these coastal areas; inland precipitation is mostly snow.
- Lies in the foggiest area of the U.S. east coast; heavy fog occurs on the average of 60 days/year. Over 1500 hours per year are foggy.

CLIMATABLE NO. 21

Isle Royale NP

TEMPERATURE NORMALS AND EXTREMES

WEATHER PARAMETERS	J	F	M	A	M	J	J	A	S	O	N	D
TEMPERATURE												
Normal Daily Maximum	11	20	32	45	54	62	68	69	60	52	33	18
Normal Daily Minimum	-11	-5	9	25	36	43	50	54	47	39	17	-1
Extreme High	48	53	66	70	79	87	89	86	82	72	65	57
Extreme Low	-46	-44	-38	-5	19	32	37	34	29	12	-32	-41
Days Above 90°	0	0	0	0	0	0	0	0	0	0	0	0
Days Below 32°	31	28	30	22	8	0	0	0	1	6	28	31
PRECIPITATION												
Normal	1.2	0.9	1.8	2.2	2.5	3.1	2.5	3.2	3.4	2.1	1.7	1.3
Maximum	4.7	2.4	5.1	5.8	7.7	8.0	8.5	10.3	6.6	7.5	5.0	3.7
Maximum 24 Hr. Precipitation	1.7	1.4	2.4	2.3	2.6	2.5	2.3	1.8	4.5	1.8	2.6	2.1
Maximum Snowfall	47	32	46	32	8	0	0	0	4	9	38	44
Days With Measurable Precip.	12	10	11	11	12	13	11	11	12	10	11	12
Average No. Thunderstorms	0	0	0	0	1	2	2	2	2	1	0	0
SUNSHINE/CLOUDINESS												
No. Clear Days	7	7	7	6	6	5	7	7	6	6	4	6
No. Partly Cloudy Days	7	6	7	8	9	11	13	12	9	8	6	6
No. Cloudy Days	17	15	17	16	16	14	11	12	15	17	20	19
% Possible Sunshine	49	52	55	55	56	58	65	60	51	46	35	40

% OF SUNNY/PTLY CLOUDY/CLOUDY DAYS

☐ Clear ▦ Ptlycldy ■ Cloudy

etc.
- Summers are cool and winters are very cold; periods of warm summer temperatures rarely exceed 2 to 3 days in length.
- Day to day temperature changes are strongly moderated by the surrounding waters of Lake Superior, the coldest of the Great Lakes.

CLIMATABLE NO. 22

TEMPERATURE NORMALS AND EXTREMES

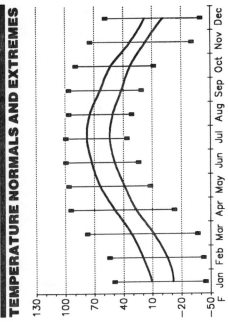

% OF SUNNY/PTLY CLOUDY/CLOUDY DAYS

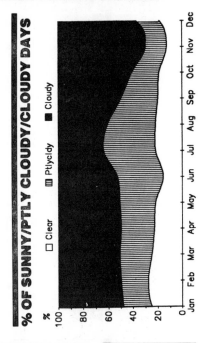

□ Clear   ▥ Ptlycldy   ■ Cloudy

WEATHER PARAMETERS	MONTH											
	J	F	M	A	M	J	J	A	S	O	N	D
TEMPERATURE												
Normal Daily Maximum	11	20	32	49	64	73	78	75	64	53	33	18
Normal Daily Minimum	-11	-5	9	27	39	49	54	51	42	33	17	-1
Extreme High	48	53	76	93	95	98	98	95	95	88	73	57
Extreme Low	-46	-44	-38	-14	11	23	35	30	20	7	-32	-41
Days Above 90°	0	0	0	0	0	1	2	1	0	0	0	0
Days Below 32°	31	28	30	22	8	0	0	0	5	15	28	31
PRECIPITATION												
Normal	0.9	0.7	1.1	1.6	2.4	3.7	3.8	3.0	3.2	1.8	1.3	0.9
Maximum	3.0	1.8	3.1	3.3	6.7	8.2	9.5	11.3	7.4	4.8	3.5	1.7
Maximum 24 Hr. Precipitation	1.5	1.1	1.8	1.6	2.5	3.8	4.9	4.8	3.4	2.6	1.6	1.2
Maximum Snowfall	43	26	32	23	13	T	0	T	2	8	30	23
Days With Measurable Precip.	12	9	10	9	11	13	11	12	12	10	11	12
Average No. Thunderstorms	0	0	0	1	5	10	12	9	4	1	0	0
SUNSHINE/CLOUDINESS												
No. Clear Days	8	8	8	7	7	5	7	7	6	6	4	6
No. Partly Cloudy Days	7	6	8	8	9	11	13	12	9	7	5	6
No. Cloudy Days	16	14	15	15	15	14	11	12	15	18	21	19
% Possible Sunshine	NA	NA	NA	NA	NA	NA	NA	NA	NA	NA	NA	NA

etc.

- From December through February, the temperature falls below zero on most days and occasionally remains below zero for a week or more.
- Winter can bring some heavy snowfalls with blizzard conditions and severely drifting snow.

CLIMATABLE NO. 23   Glacier NP

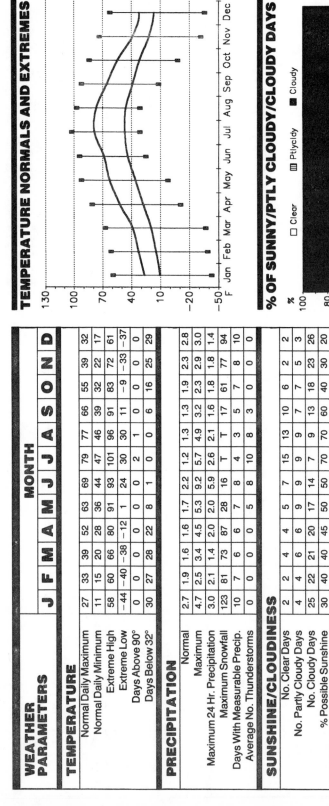

TEMPERATURE NORMALS AND EXTREMES

% OF SUNNY/PTLY CLOUDY/CLOUDY DAYS

Clear   Ptlycldy   Cloudy

WEATHER PARAMETERS	J	F	M	A	M	J	J	A	S	O	N	D
TEMPERATURE												
Normal Daily Maximum	27	33	39	52	63	69	79	77	66	55	39	32
Normal Daily Minimum	11	15	20	28	36	44	47	46	39	32	22	17
Extreme High	58	60	66	80	91	93	101	96	91	83	72	61
Extreme Low	-44	-40	-38	-12	1	24	30	30	11	-9	-33	-37
Days Above 90°	0	0	0	0	0	0	2	1	0	0	0	0
Days Below 32°	30	27	28	22	8	1	0	0	6	16	25	29
PRECIPITATION												
Normal	2.7	1.9	1.6	1.6	1.7	2.2	1.2	1.3	1.3	1.9	2.3	2.8
Maximum	4.7	2.5	3.4	4.5	5.3	9.2	5.7	4.9	3.2	2.3	2.9	3.0
Maximum 24 Hr. Precipitation	3.0	2.1	1.4	2.0	2.0	5.9	2.6	2.1	1.6	1.8	1.8	1.4
Maximum Snowfall	123	81	73	87	28	16	T	T	17	61	77	94
Days With Measurable Precip.	10	7	6	6	7	8	4	3	5	7	8	10
Average No. Thunderstorms	0	0	0	0	5	8	8	10	3	0	0	0
SUNSHINE/CLOUDINESS												
No. Clear Days	2	2	4	4	5	7	15	13	10	6	2	2
No. Partly Cloudy Days	4	4	6	6	9	9	9	9	7	7	5	3
No. Cloudy Days	25	22	21	20	17	14	7	9	13	18	23	26
% Possible Sunshine	30	40	40	45	50	50	70	70	60	40	30	20

etc.

• Annual precipitation varies within the Park from from 20" to nearly 200" at the higher elevations of the windward slopes. The seasonal snowfall may exceed 1000" in some areas. Near the eastern border of the Park, the record 24-hour drop in temperature for the U.S. of 100 degrees was recorded.

CLIMATABLE NO. 24

Great Basin NP

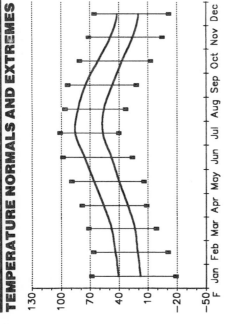

TEMPERATURE NORMALS AND EXTREMES

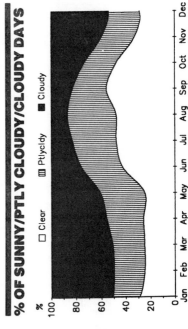

% OF SUNNY/PTLY CLOUDY/CLOUDY DAYS

Clear   Ptlycldy   Cloudy

WEATHER PARAMETERS	J	F	M	A	M	J	J	A	S	O	N	D
MONTH												
TEMPERATURE												
Normal Daily Maximum	41	44	48	56	66	76	86	83	75	62	49	42
Normal Daily Minimum	18	21	24	31	40	48	57	56	47	37	26	20
Extreme High	67	65	70	77	88	97	100	95	92	80	70	64
Extreme Low	-20	-12	0	10	13	25	39	32	21	6	-6	-13
Days Above 90°	0	0	0	0	0	1	7	3	0	0	0	0
Days Below 32°	29	25	26	18	7	1	0	0	2	10	23	29
PRECIPITATION												
Normal	0.9	1.0	1.4	1.3	1.1	0.9	0.9	1.1	0.9	1.0	1.2	1.2
Maximum	3.2	3.6	5.0	3.0	4.7	3.4	2.1	3.7	2.7	3.0	3.4	3.4
Maximum 24 Hr. Precipitation	2.2	1.6	1.5	1.6	1.6	1.4	1.1	0.8	2.4	1.1	1.5	1.6
Maximum Snowfall	34	39	52	35	23	8	0	0	2	42	48	46
Days With Measurable Precip.	7	7	8	8	7	5	6	5	4	5	5	6
Average No. Thunderstorms	0	0	0	1	5	7	12	12	4	1	0	0
SUNSHINE/CLOUDINESS												
No. Clear Days	9	7	8	8	8	13	15	15	17	15	10	9
No. Partly Cloudy Days	7	7	8	9	11	10	11	12	8	8	8	8
No. Cloudy Days	15	14	15	13	12	7	5	4	5	8	12	14
% Possible Sunshine	67	67	70	69	72	80	80	81	82	75	66	65

etc.

- This is a fairly arid area with a slight maximum of precipitation in the spring.
- Thunderstorms are relatively infrequent and, for the most part, are not severe.
- Local mountain and valley winds noticeably influence temperatures throughout the year.

CLIMATABLE NO. 25

Ellis Island, Statue of Liberty NM and all New York City sites, St. Paul's NHS, Theodore Roosevelt Birthplace NHS

WEATHER PARAMETERS	J	F	M	A	M	J	J	A	S	O	N	D
TEMPERATURE												
Normal Daily Maximum	38	40	49	61	72	80	85	84	76	66	54	42
Normal Daily Minimum	26	27	34	44	53	63	68	67	60	50	41	30
Extreme High	72	75	86	96	99	101	106	104	102	94	84	72
Extreme Low	-6	-15	3	12	32	44	52	50	39	28	5	-13
Days Above 90°	0	0	0	0	0	1	3	4	2	0	0	0
Days Below 32°	23	20	12	2	0	0	0	0	0	0	5	18
PRECIPITATION												
Normal	3.2	3.1	4.2	3.8	3.2	3.2	3.8	4.0	3.7	3.4	4.2	3.8
Maximum	10.5	6.9	10.4	8.8	9.7	9.8	11.9	10.9	16.8	13.3	12.4	10.0
Maximum 24 Hr. Precipitation	3.9	3.0	4.2	4.9	4.7	3.6	5.8	8.3	11.2	8.1	3.2	
Maximum Snowfall	27	28	30	14	T	0	0	0	0	1	19	30
Days With Measurable Precip.	11	10	12	11	10	11	10	8	8	9	9	10
Average No. Thunderstorms	0	0	1	2	4	6	7	7	3	1	1	0
SUNSHINE/CLOUDINESS												
No. Clear Days	8	8	9	8	8	8	8	9	11	12	9	9
No. Partly Cloudy Days	9	9	10	10	12	12	13	12	10	10	9	9
No. Cloudy Days	14	11	12	12	11	10	10	10	9	9	12	13
% Possible Sunshine	50	55	56	59	61	64	65	64	62	61	52	49

TEMPERATURE NORMALS AND EXTREMES

(Temperatures in °F: 130, 100, 70, 40, 10, -20, -50; Months: Jan Feb Mar Apr May Jun Jul Aug Sep Oct Nov Dec)

% OF SUNNY/PTLY CLOUDY/CLOUDY DAYS

(% scale: 100, 80, 60, 40, 20, 0)

☐ Clear ▦ Ptlycldy ■ Cloudy

etc.

- City exhibits a very definite "heat island" effect; overnight temperatures are often distinctly warmer in both winter and summer as compared to surrounding suburban areas.
- Some summer days can be very hot and humid; however, both warm and cold spells tend not to be prolonged.

CLIMATABLE NO. 26

Appalachian NST

TEMPERATURE NORMALS AND EXTREMES

WEATHER PARAMETERS	MONTH											
	J	F	M	A	M	J	J	A	S	O	N	D
TEMPERATURE												
Normal Daily Maximum	48	51	60	70	76	82	84	84	78	70	59	51
Normal Daily Minimum	25	26	33	42	48	56	60	59	53	41	32	27
Extreme High	81	84	89	93	98	106	105	100	102	94	85	80
Extreme Low	-16	-16	-6	15	25	31	42	39	27	12	0	-12
Days Above 90°	0	0	0	0	1	5	8	7	3	0	0	0
Days Below 32°	22	20	17	7	1	0	0	0	0	6	17	22
PRECIPITATION												
Normal	4.5	4.2	5.6	4.5	4.4	4.6	5.1	4.5	3.7	3.0	3.7	4.2
Maximum	12.2	9.4	11.3	8.5	8.7	11.0	14.8	12.6	8.8	7.4	8.7	9.3
Maximum 24 Hr. Precipitation	3.4	3.3	4.5	3.3	3.1	4.6	4.4	3.6	3.0	3.7	2.8	3.1
Maximum Snowfall	26	19	25	2	0	0	0	0	0	8	7	15
Days With Measurable Precip.	11	10	12	10	12	11	11	11	9	8	10	10
Average No. Thunderstorms	1	1	4	6	10	12	13	11	4	1	1	1
SUNSHINE/CLOUDINESS												
No. Clear Days	8	8	8	9	8	7	6	7	7	12	9	8
No. Partly Cloudy Days	7	6	8	9	10	12	13	13	10	8	7	7
No. Cloudy Days	16	14	15	12	13	11	12	11	13	11	14	16
% Possible Sunshine	48	54	58	64	62	64	60	58	58	60	53	49

% OF SUNNY/PTLY CLOUDY/CLOUDY DAYS

☐ Clear   �255 Ptlycldy   ■ Cloudy

etc.

- Temperature and precipitation vary markedly with location depending on exposure and elevation. Precipitation is highest and temperature lowest along the ridge tops.
- In winter, precipitation falls mostly as rain in the valleys and snow or rain on the ridges; snowfall amounts are quite variable.

CLIMATABLE NO. 27

Theodore Roosevelt NP

TEMPERATURE NORMALS AND EXTREMES

% OF SUNNY/PTLY CLOUDY/CLOUDY DAYS

☐ Clear   ▓ Ptlycldy   ■ Cloudy

WEATHER PARAMETERS	J	F	M	A	M	J	J	A	S	O	N	D
TEMPERATURE												
Normal Daily Maximum	20	27	36	54	67	76	84	82	70	58	39	27
Normal Daily Minimum	-2	6	15	30	42	50	56	54	43	32	18	6
Extreme High	58	66	78	94	106	104	109	107	104	94	79	67
Extreme Low	-40	-41	-28	-15	4	30	34	35	17	0	-24	-50
Days Above 90°	0	0	0	0	1	2	8	9	2	0	0	0
Days Below 32°	31	28	29	18	4	0	0	0	3	15	28	31
PRECIPITATION												
Normal	0.5	0.6	1.5	2.1	3.0	2.0	1.5	1.5	0.8	0.5	0.5	0.5
Maximum	1.4	1.5	2.5	4.8	7.4	7.7	6.2	5.6	3.6	1.6	1.4	1.4
Maximum 24 Hr. Precipitation	0.5	1.0	2.0	2.7	3.1	5.0	2.8	2.2	2.2	0.8	0.9	0.9
Maximum Snowfall	24	16	31	22	16	4	0	0	4	14	17	16
Days With Measurable Precip.	8	7	8	8	10	10	9	7	7	5	6	8
Average No. Thunderstorms	0	0	0	1	5	12	12	9	3	0	0	0
SUNSHINE/CLOUDINESS												
No. Clear Days	5	5	7	6	6	7	11	12	9	9	7	6
No. Partly Cloudy Days	9	7	8	9	11	12	13	11	8	8	7	8
No. Cloudy Days	17	16	16	15	14	11	7	8	13	14	16	17
% Possible Sunshine	52	57	61	61	63	67	76	75	64	59	43	49

etc.

- Winters are long and cold with periods of bitterly cold temperatures. Occasionally, blizzard conditions with dangerous wind chill temperatures can be expected.
- Summers are punctuated with prolonged periods of high temperatures, though low humidity minimizes discomfort; nights are usually cool.

CLIMATABLE NO. 28

TEMPERATURE NORMALS AND EXTREMES

% OF SUNNY/PTLY CLOUDY/CLOUDY DAYS

☐ Clear   ▦ Ptlycldy   ■ Cloudy

WEATHER PARAMETERS	MONTH											
	J	F	M	A	M	J	J	A	S	O	N	D
TEMPERATURE												
Normal Daily Maximum	36	39	42	50	56	66	77	75	68	56	44	36
Normal Daily Minimum	17	18	20	24	30	35	40	39	34	29	24	19
Extreme High	58	66	69	82	86	98	97	101	96	87	72	58
Extreme Low	-26	-26	-15	0	5	11	18	15	9	0	-26	-30
Days Above 90°	0	0	0	0	0	0	2	1	0	0	0	0
Days Below 32°	31	28	30	27	20	11	5	6	13	22	26	30
PRECIPITATION												
Normal	10.8	8.7	8.2	4.3	3.3	2.5	0.6	0.6	2.0	6.4	8.0	11.7
Maximum	20.9	19.7	15.2	11.6	8.7	9.2	2.9	5.3	6.9	19.1	17.2	38.5
Maximum 24 Hr. Precipitation	3.8	3.5	2.3	4.2	1.9	2.0	1.5	1.1	2.6	3.2	2.6	5.1
Maximum Snowfall	313	248	194	144	103	14	T	5	20	88	128	196
Days With Measurable Precip.	17	15	16	12	10	7	3	3	5	10	13	16
Average No. Thunderstorms	0	0	0	1	2	3	3	2	1	0	0	0
SUNSHINE/CLOUDINESS												
No. Clear Days	2	3	5	6	9	13	23	21	18	10	3	2
No. Partly Cloudy Days	5	6	7	8	9	8	5	6	6	8	6	4
No. Cloudy Days	24	19	19	16	13	9	3	4	6	13	21	25
% Possible Sunshine	30	40	50	60	60	70	90	80	80	60	35	30

etc.

- Freezing temperatures may be encountered throughout the year.
- Prodigious amounts of snow fall in the Park, the greatest amounts on the western slopes; seasonal totals range between 275" and nearly 900".
- Snow depths can reach 20'.
- Summers are sunny with only brief, infrequent showers.

CLIMATABLE NO. 29

Badlands NP

TEMPERATURE NORMALS AND EXTREMES

% OF SUNNY/PTLY CLOUDY/CLOUDY DAYS

☐ Clear   ▦ Ptlycldy   ■ Cloudy

WEATHER PARAMETERS	J	F	M	A	M	J	J	A	S	O	N	D
TEMPERATURE												
Normal Daily Maximum	32	36	46	61	71	81	91	89	78	66	48	36
Normal Daily Minimum	6	9	19	32	42	53	59	56	46	33	20	10
Extreme High	75	74	88	92	105	114	116	113	108	98	81	77
Extreme Low	−42	−41	−28	−12	13	31	36	27	10	−7	−29	−41
Days Above 90°	0	0	0	0	1	6	17	16	5	0	0	0
Days Below 32°	30	27	27	16	4	0	0	0	2	14	27	30
PRECIPITATION												
Normal	0.4	0.4	0.8	1.8	2.8	3.0	1.8	1.6	1.1	0.9	0.4	0.4
Maximum	3.1	1.8	2.7	5.5	6.9	9.5	6.5	7.8	3.9	4.0	2.7	1.8
Maximum 24 Hr. Precipitation	2.3	1.0	1.7	2.0	4.0	3.0	2.5	5.2	3.3	2.4	1.4	0.8
Maximum Snowfall	19	16	24	28	8	0	0	T	12	21	17
Days With Measurable Precip.	3	3	4	7	9	10	7	6	5	4	2	3
Average No. Thunderstorms	0	0	0	2	7	15	15	11	4	0	0	0
SUNSHINE/CLOUDINESS												
No. Clear Days	7	6	6	6	7	9	13	14	13	12	8	8
No. Partly Cloudy Days	8	8	9	9	11	11	13	12	9	8	8	8
No. Cloudy Days	16	14	16	15	13	10	5	5	8	11	14	15
% Possible Sunshine	55	59	61	60	58	63	72	73	68	65	54	54

etc.

- Summer days are quite hot, but low humidity keeps the heat from feeling oppressive.
- Rainfall from late summer thunderstorms often evaporates before reaching the ground.
- Winters are bitterly cold; temperatures of 20 degrees below zero can be expected several times each winter.

CLIMATABLE NO. 30

Mount Rushmore NM, Jewel Cave NM ; Wind Cave NM

TEMPERATURE NORMALS AND EXTREMES

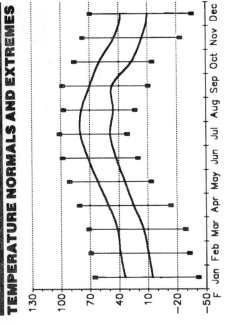

% OF SUNNY/PTLY CLOUDY/CLOUDY DAYS

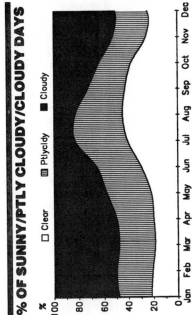

☐ Clear   ☷ Ptlycldy   ■ Cloudy

WEATHER PARAMETERS	MONTH											
	J	F	M	A	M	J	J	A	S	O	N	D
TEMPERATURE												
Normal Daily Maximum	34	39	42	51	62	72	80	79	70	60	45	38
Normal Daily Minimum	6	10	15	25	34	43	49	46	37	27	16	10
Extreme High	64	68	70	80	90	97	100	96	97	85	76	68
Extreme Low	-43	-34	-30	-15	5	19	30	22	8	4	-25	-37
Days Above 90°	0	0	0	0	0	1	3	2	1	0	0	0
Days Below 32°	31	28	30	26	13	2	0	1	10	24	29	30
PRECIPITATION												
Normal	0.4	0.5	0.9	1.9	3.1	3.5	3.0	2.0	1.2	0.7	0.5	0.5
Maximum	1.0	1.8	2.1	3.9	8.8	6.4	7.6	4.1	3.5	2.4	1.5	1.6
Maximum 24 Hr. Precipitation	0.5	0.6	1.0	2.0	4.0	3.4	2.0	2.4	1.3	1.6	0.4	0.6
Maximum Snowfall	26	29	38	49	26	13	0	0	15	22	27	46
Days With Measurable Precip.	7	7	9	9	12	12	9	8	7	5	6	6
Average No. Thunderstorms	0	0	0	2	7	15	15	11	4	0	0	0
SUNSHINE/CLOUDINESS												
No. Clear Days	7	6	6	6	7	9	13	14	13	12	8	8
No. Partly Cloudy Days	8	8	9	9	11	11	13	12	9	8	8	8
No. Cloudy Days	16	14	16	15	13	10	5	5	8	11	14	15
% Possible Sunshine	55	59	61	60	58	63	72	73	68	65	54	54

etc.

• Summer days range from warm to hot; nights are cool and comfortable.
• Sunny skies, the frequent occurrence of a warm, downslope wind or "chinook", and the tendency for cold, arctic air masses to stay east of the Black Hills, makes this region the warmest part of South Dakota in winter.

CLIMATABLE NO. 31 Big Bend NP

TEMPERATURE NORMALS AND EXTREMES

% OF SUNNY/PTLY CLOUDY/CLOUDY DAYS

□ Clear | ▦ Ptlycldy | ■ Cloudy

WEATHER PARAMETERS	J	F	M	A	M	J	J	A	S	O	N	D
TEMPERATURE												
Normal Daily Maximum	59	64	70	78	85	90	88	87	83	76	67	61
Normal Daily Minimum	36	38	43	50	58	64	64	63	58	52	42	37
Extreme High	82	85	91	97	101	105	104	103	99	93	89	81
Extreme Low	−3	3	10	21	32	38	53	49	36	26	8	1
Days Above 90°	0	0	0	1	8	15	14	11	5	0	0	0
Days Below 32°	14	10	6	1	0	0	0	0	0	1	4	12
PRECIPITATION												
Normal	0.8	0.4	0.3	0.6	1.5	2.3	2.9	2.4	1.9	1.4	0.4	0.6
Maximum	1.9	3.1	1.7	2.8	3.0	5.4	7.6	7.4	11.1	4.8	3.2	2.3
Maximum 24 Hr. Precipitation	1.3	1.3	0.8	1.2	1.7	2.6	3.3	2.9	2.4	4.3	1.4	1.1
Maximum Snowfall	26	7	2	2	0	0	0	0	0	T	4	9
Days With Measurable Precip.	4	3	2	2	2	3	8	8	5	4	3	4
Average No. Thunderstorms	0	0	1	1	3	5	13	11	4	2	0	0
SUNSHINE/CLOUDINESS												
No. Clear Days	14	14	15	16	19	20	12	14	18	19	17	15
No. Partly Cloudy Days	7	7	8	8	8	7	13	12	7	7	6	7
No. Cloudy Days	10	7	8	6	4	3	6	5	5	5	7	9
% Possible Sunshine	77	82	85	87	89	89	80	81	82	83	82	78

etc.

- Marked variations in weather are experienced over short distances due to changes in elevation and exposure.
- Summer is the "rainy" season with showers and thunderstorms. Even more precipitation occurs on the high mountains, especially on the windward slopes.

Guadalupe Mountains NP, Carlsbad Caverns NP

CLIMATABLE NO. 32

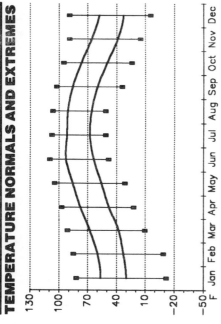

TEMPERATURE NORMALS AND EXTREMES

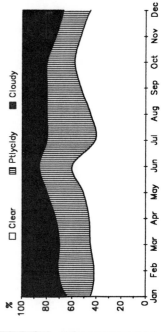

% OF SUNNY/PTLY CLOUDY/CLOUDY DAYS

☐ Clear   ▦ Ptlycldy   ▪ Cloudy

WEATHER PARAMETERS	MONTH											
	J	F	M	A	M	J	J	A	S	O	N	D
TEMPERATURE												
Normal Daily Maximum	57	60	68	78	86	93	92	91	86	77	66	58
Normal Daily Minimum	30	33	38	48	56	64	68	66	60	50	39	33
Extreme High	81	84	90	96	103	108	106	105	101	94	88	88
Extreme Low	−13	−10	9	21	30	47	50	50	33	23	14	3
Days Above 90°	0	0	0	2	10	23	24	22	11	1	0	0
Days Below 32°	18	15	8	1	0	0	0	0	0	1	6	16
PRECIPITATION												
Normal	0.4	0.3	0.4	0.6	0.9	1.3	1.8	2.0	1.9	1.3	0.4	0.5
Maximum	2.4	2.0	3.6	5.8	10.9	4.0	6.0	5.7	12.3	5.1	1.6	2.6
Maximum 24 Hr. Precipitation	1.1	1.0	1.2	4.6	3.0	2.5	3.1	2.7	3.9	3.6	1.1	0.8
Maximum Snowfall	13	10	8	T	0	0	0	0	0	T	18	18
Days With Measurable Precip.	4	3	2	2	4	4	8	8	6	4	3	4
Average No. Thunderstorms	0	0	1	2	5	7	13	11	4	2	0	0
SUNSHINE/CLOUDINESS												
No. Clear Days	14	12	14	14	16	18	13	14	16	18	16	14
No. Partly Cloudy Days	6	8	8	8	9	8	12	11	8	7	6	7
No. Cloudy Days	11	8	9	8	6	4	6	6	6	8	8	10
% Possible Sunshine	73	76	79	82	84	83	84	79	80	74	77	71

etc.

- Spring is a comfortable season with mild sunny days and cool nights; an occasional dust storm can be expected.
- Summer days are hot and nights are pleasantly cool.
- In the high mountain areas, temperatures are 10 to 20 degrees colder and the precipitation is double that shown in the table.

CLIMATABLE NO. 33

Canyonlands NP, Capitol Reef NP, Arches NP

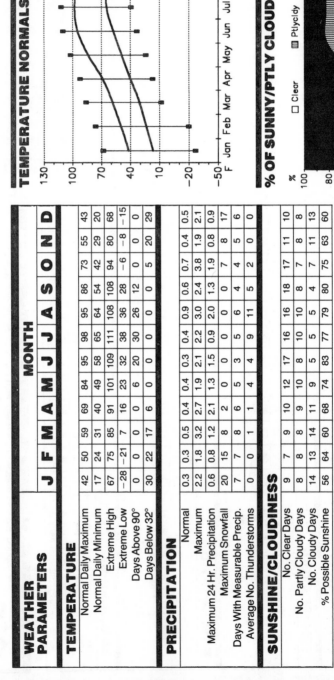

TEMPERATURE NORMALS AND EXTREMES

% OF SUNNY/PTLY CLOUDY/CLOUDY DAYS

☐ Clear   ▨ Ptlycldy   ■ Cloudy

WEATHER PARAMETERS	MONTH											
	J	F	M	A	M	J	J	A	S	O	N	D
TEMPERATURE												
Normal Daily Maximum	42	50	59	69	84	95	98	95	86	73	55	43
Normal Daily Minimum	17	24	31	40	49	58	65	64	54	42	29	20
Extreme High	67	75	85	91	101	109	111	108	108	94	80	68
Extreme Low	−28	−21	7	16	23	32	38	36	28	−6	−8	−15
Days Above 90°	0	0	0	0	6	20	30	26	12	0	0	0
Days Below 32°	30	22	17	6	0	0	0	0	0	5	20	29
PRECIPITATION												
Normal	0.3	0.3	0.5	0.4	0.4	0.3	0.4	0.9	0.6	0.7	0.4	0.5
Maximum	2.2	1.8	3.2	2.7	1.9	2.1	2.2	3.0	2.4	3.8	1.9	2.1
Maximum 24 Hr. Precipitation	0.6	0.8	1.2	2.1	1.3	1.5	0.9	2.0	1.3	1.9	0.8	0.9
Maximum Snowfall	20	15	8	2	0	0	0	0	0	7	8	17
Days With Measurable Precip.	7	7	8	6	5	3	5	6	4	4	5	6
Average No. Thunderstorms	0	0	1	1	4	4	9	11	5	2	0	0
SUNSHINE/CLOUDINESS												
No. Clear Days	9	7	9	10	12	17	16	16	18	17	11	10
No. Partly Cloudy Days	8	8	8	9	10	8	10	10	8	7	8	8
No. Cloudy Days	14	13	14	11	9	5	5	5	4	7	11	13
% Possible Sunshine	56	64	60	68	74	83	77	79	80	75	63	60

etc.

- This is a fairly arid region, lying in the rain shadow of the mountains to the west.
- Winters are quite cold, though below-zero temperatures are not common. On clear, still nights, cold air drainage keeps the valley bottoms significantly colder than the adjoining high elevation areas.

CLIMATABLE NO. 34

Bryce Canyon NP

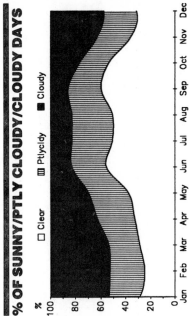

TEMPERATURE NORMALS AND EXTREMES

% OF SUNNY/PTLY CLOUDY/CLOUDY DAYS

☐ Clear   ▦ Ptlycldy   ■ Cloudy

WEATHER PARAMETERS	MONTH											
	J	F	M	A	M	J	J	A	S	O	N	D
TEMPERATURE												
Normal Daily Maximum	39	41	46	56	66	76	83	80	74	63	51	42
Normal Daily Minimum	9	13	17	25	31	38	47	45	37	29	19	11
Extreme High	62	66	76	82	89	96	97	94	91	85	75	67
Extreme Low	-30	-29	-13	-5	5	20	25	23	17	-2	-20	-23
Days Above 90°	0	0	0	0	0	1	4	2	0	0	0	0
Days Below 32°	31	28	31	27	20	6	0	1	9	22	29	31
PRECIPITATION												
Normal	1.7	1.4	1.4	1.2	0.8	0.6	1.4	2.2	1.4	1.4	1.2	1.6
Maximum	9.2	6.8	3.6	3.8	2.3	2.7	3.8	4.8	4.2	4.5	5.4	6.2
Maximum 24 Hr. Precipitation	2.3	1.5	1.1	1.8	1.2	1.7	1.8	3.8	3.4	1.7	1.5	3.2
Maximum Snowfall	63	75	75	62	18	6	T	T	4	22	22	49
Days With Measurable Precip.	7	7	8	6	5	3	5	6	4	4	5	6
Average No. Thunderstorms	0	0	0	1	5	6	14	19	7	2	0	0
SUNSHINE/CLOUDINESS												
No. Clear Days	9	7	9	10	12	17	16	18	17	11	11	10
No. Partly Cloudy Days	8	8	8	9	10	8	10	8	7	8	8	8
No. Cloudy Days	14	13	14	11	9	5	5	4	7	11	11	13
% Possible Sunshine	56	64	60	68	74	83	77	79	80	75	63	60

etc.

- Winters are very cold; below-zero readings occur often.
- Snowfall amounts vary with elevation; near the rim of Bryce Canyon, winter snowfall averages over 100".
- Summers are delightfully cool with pleasant days and quite chilly nights. Temperatures reach 90 degrees on just a few days a year.

CLIMATABLE NO. 35   Zion NP

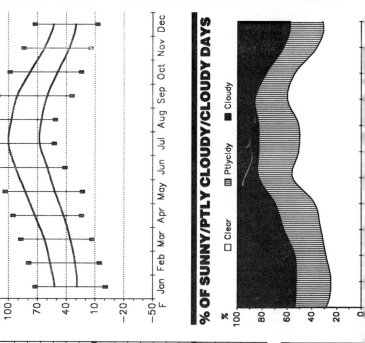

TEMPERATURE NORMALS AND EXTREMES

% OF SUNNY/PTLY CLOUDY/CLOUDY DAYS

☐ Clear   ▦ Ptlycldy   ■ Cloudy

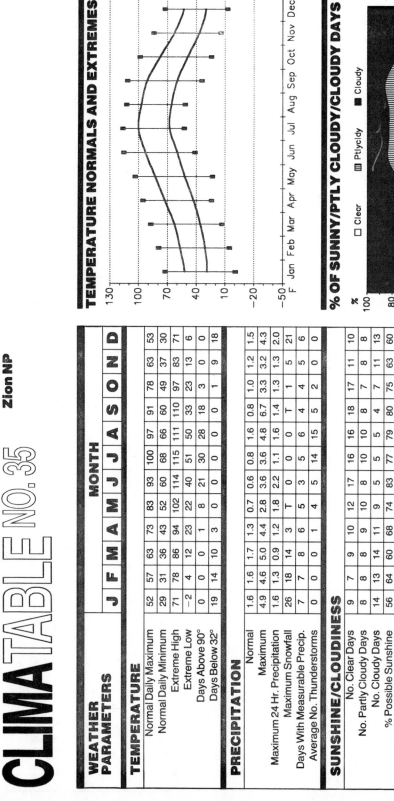

WEATHER PARAMETERS	J	F	M	A	M	J	J	A	S	O	N	D
TEMPERATURE												
Normal Daily Maximum	52	57	63	73	83	93	100	97	91	78	63	53
Normal Daily Minimum	29	31	36	43	52	60	68	66	60	49	37	30
Extreme High	71	78	86	94	102	114	115	111	110	97	83	71
Extreme Low	-2	4	12	23	22	40	51	50	33	23	13	6
Days Above 90°	0	0	0	0	8	21	30	28	18	3	0	0
Days Below 32°	19	14	10	3	0	0	0	0	0	1	9	18
PRECIPITATION												
Normal	1.6	1.6	1.7	1.3	0.7	0.6	0.8	1.6	0.8	1.0	1.2	1.5
Maximum	4.9	4.6	5.0	4.4	2.8	3.6	3.6	4.8	6.7	3.3	3.2	4.3
Maximum 24 Hr. Precipitation	1.6	1.3	0.9	1.2	1.8	2.2	1.1	1.6	1.4	1.3	1.3	2.0
Maximum Snowfall	26	18	14	3	T	0	0	0	T	1	5	21
Days With Measurable Precip.	7	7	8	6	5	3	5	6	4	4	5	6
Average No. Thunderstorms	0	0	0	1	4	5	14	15	5	2	0	0
SUNSHINE/CLOUDINESS												
No. Clear Days	9	9	10	12	17	16	16	18	17	11	11	10
No. Partly Cloudy Days	8	8	9	10	8	10	10	8	7	8	8	8
No. Cloudy Days	14	14	11	9	5	5	5	4	7	7	11	13
% Possible Sunshine	56	60	68	74	83	77	79	80	75	63	63	60

etc.

• Sharp changes in weather occur within the park due to the rugged topography and range of elevations.
• Seasonal snowfall averages 13", but much heavier snows accumulate in the high mountain areas.
• Summer days are hot, but mountain breezes keep evenings cool especially in lower elevation areas.

C IMATABLE NO. 36

Ross Lake NRA, Lake Chelan NRA

TEMPERATURE NORMALS AND EXTREMES

% OF SUNNY/PTLY CLOUDY/CLOUDY DAYS

□ Clear   ▨ Ptlycldy   ▣ Cloudy

WEATHER PARAMETERS	MONTH											
	J	F	M	A	M	J	J	A	S	O	N	D
TEMPERATURE												
Normal Daily Maximum	37	42	48	57	66	70	78	77	70	58	45	40
Normal Daily Minimum	26	29	32	37	43	48	52	52	48	41	34	31
Extreme High	62	60	73	85	94	99	106	100	100	83	65	57
Extreme Low	-8	-10	3	0	0	1	3	3	1	0	0	8
Days Above 90°	0	0	0	0	1	1	3	3	1	0	0	0
Days Below 32°	23	19	16	4	0	0	0	0	0	1	11	19
PRECIPITATION												
Normal	10.3	8.6	6.8	4.4	2.5	2.1	1.2	1.3	3.5	8.0	10.5	12.3
Maximum	26.5	20.4	12.8	14.0	5.1	5.3	2.5	3.8	10.8	18.0	19.5	18.6
Maximum 24 Hr. Precipitation	4.1	6.2	3.0	3.3	1.6	1.4	1.8	1.9	2.5	6.5	4.0	3.8
Maximum Snowfall	81	69	34	10	0	0	0	0	0	1	25	78
Days With Measurable Precip.	19	17	18	15	12	10	8	9	12	16	20	21
Average No. Thunderstorms	0	0	0	0	1	2	1	2	1	0	0	0
SUNSHINE/CLOUDINESS												
No. Clear Days	3	2	3	3	4	6	13	12	10	6	3	2
No. Partly Cloudy Days	2	3	4	5	6	5	7	8	6	5	3	2
No. Cloudy Days	26	23	24	22	21	19	11	11	14	20	24	27
% Possible Sunshine	28	35	42	50	52	55	65	65	55	45	30	20

etc.

- The table typifies the lower western slopes of the North Cascades.
- Temperatures are considerably colder and precipitation considerably greater in the high mountain areas to the east. In these areas, winter season snowfall ranges from 400' to 600'; snow depths can exceed 20'.

CLIMATABLE NO. 37   Mount Rainier NP

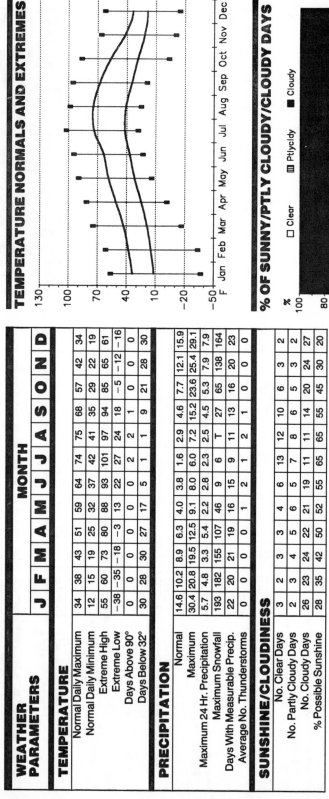

TEMPERATURE NORMALS AND EXTREMES

% OF SUNNY/PTLY CLOUDY/CLOUDY DAYS

□ Clear   ▦ Ptlycldy   ■ Cloudy

WEATHER PARAMETERS	MONTH											
	J	F	M	A	M	J	J	A	S	O	N	D
TEMPERATURE												
Normal Daily Maximum	34	38	43	51	59	64	74	75	68	57	42	34
Normal Daily Minimum	12	15	19	25	32	37	42	41	35	29	22	19
Extreme High	55	60	73	80	88	93	101	97	94	85	65	61
Extreme Low	-38	-35	-18	-3	13	22	27	24	18	-5	-12	-16
Days Above 90°	0	0	0	0	0	0	2	2	1	0	0	0
Days Below 32°	30	28	30	27	17	5	1	1	9	21	28	30
PRECIPITATION												
Normal	14.6	10.2	8.9	6.3	4.0	3.8	1.6	2.9	4.6	7.7	12.1	15.9
Maximum	30.4	20.8	19.5	12.5	9.1	8.0	6.0	7.2	15.2	23.6	25.4	29.1
Maximum 24 Hr. Precipitation	5.7	4.8	3.3	5.4	2.2	2.8	2.5	2.3	4.5	5.3	7.9	7.9
Maximum Snowfall	193	182	155	107	46	9	6	T	27	65	138	164
Days With Measurable Precip.	22	20	21	19	16	15	9	11	13	16	20	23
Average No. Thunderstorms	0	0	0	0	1	2	1	2	1	0	0	0
SUNSHINE/CLOUDINESS												
No. Clear Days	3	2	3	3	4	6	13	12	10	6	3	2
No. Partly Cloudy Days	2	3	4	5	6	5	7	8	6	5	3	2
No. Cloudy Days	26	23	24	22	21	19	11	11	14	20	24	27
% Possible Sunshine	28	35	42	50	52	55	65	65	55	45	30	20

etc.

- The temperature data shown typify the moderate elevation areas; the precipitation data typify the higher elevations.
- Winter season snowfall along the summit of the Cascades is 300"–500"; snow depths range from 10' to 25'. The record single season snowfall for North America of 1122" was set here.

CLIMATABLE NO. 38

Olympic N.

TEMPERATURE NORMALS AND EXTREMES

% OF SUNNY/PTLY CLOUDY/CLOUDY DAYS

☐ Clear   ▤ Ptlycldy   ■ Cloudy

WEATHER PARAMETERS	MONTH											
	J	F	M	A	M	J	J	A	S	O	N	D
TEMPERATURE												
Normal Daily Maximum	45	48	50	55	60	64	69	69	67	59	51	46
Normal Daily Minimum	33	35	34	37	42	46	49	50	47	42	37	35
Extreme High	65	72	70	79	90	96	95	99	92	81	69	64
Extreme Low	7	15	19	24	29	33	38	36	28	24	5	7
Days Above 90°	0	0	0	0	0	0	0	0	0	0	0	0
Days Below 32°	14	10	11	6	1	0	0	0	0	4	8	13
PRECIPITATION												
Normal	15.1	12.1	11.3	7.1	4.7	3.1	2.3	2.8	5.3	10.5	13.9	16.3
Maximum	23.3	20.6	21.9	13.9	12.4	8.5	11.0	10.1	10.9	27.2	29.1	27.8
Maximum 24 Hr. Precipitation	8.3	5.1	4.2	2.8	3.5	2.0	6.4	3.1	4.1	5.5	5.4	6.8
Maximum Snowfall	40	13	10	3	T	T	0	0	T	T	16	12
Days With Measurable Precip.	22	20	21	20	16	14	12	11	13	18	22	23
Average No. Thunderstorms	0	0	1	0	0	0	0	0	1	1	1	1
SUNSHINE/CLOUDINESS												
No. Clear Days	3	3	3	3	3	3	6	6	7	5	3	4
No. Partly Cloudy Days	3	3	6	6	8	7	8	9	8	7	5	4
No. Cloudy Days	25	22	22	21	20	20	17	16	15	19	22	23
% Possible Sunshine	21	27	31	35	36	35	42	43	43	33	21	18

etc.

- The data shown are for the Pacific shore segment of the Park. In the high mountain areas of the Olympic Peninsula, temperatures are lower and total precipitation exceeds 200".
- Winter is the rainy season; it rains often and moderately hard. Both gale force winds and fog are not unusual here.

CLIMATABLE NO. 39

Yellowstone NP, Grand Teton NP

TEMPERATURE NORMALS AND EXTREMES

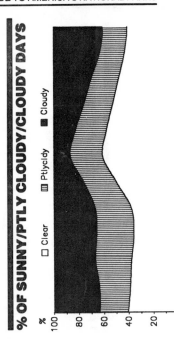

WEATHER PARAMETERS	MONTH											
	J	F	M	A	M	J	J	A	S	O	N	D
TEMPERATURE												
Normal Daily Maximum	26	32	38	48	60	70	80	78	68	56	38	28
Normal Daily Minimum	5	8	10	24	31	38	42	41	34	26	16	7
Extreme High	55	60	64	75	85	98	95	96	93	84	65	58
Extreme Low	-60	-63	-43	-28	0	18	24	18	7	-20	-36	-52
Days Above 90°	0	0	0	0	0	0	2	1	0	0	0	0
Days Below 32°	31	27	30	26	19	6	2	4	14	26	28	31
PRECIPITATION												
Normal	1.4	0.8	1.1	1.3	1.9	2.2	1.2	1.4	1.3	1.0	1.1	1.2
Maximum	3.8	1.8	3.0	2.8	2.9	4.0	2.2	3.9	3.7	2.6	2.5	4.1
Maximum 24 Hr. Precipitation	0.9	0.7	1.2	0.9	1.2	0.9	0.9	0.9	1.5	0.7	0.9	1.7
Maximum Snowfall	42	30	32	24	14	6	6	2	8	18	23	31
Days With Measurable Precip.	14	12	12	10	10	10	7	8	8	9	10	13
Average No. Thunderstorms	0	0	0	1	5	11	14	12	2	0	0	0
SUNSHINE/CLOUDINESS												
No. Clear Days	13	12	12	11	12	15	19	18	16	15	13	13
No. Partly Cloudy Days	7	7	9	9	9	8	8	8	7	7	6	6
No. Cloudy Days	11	10	10	10	10	7	4	5	7	9	11	12
% Possible Sunshine	46	53	60	59	61	63	78	75	66	60	44	41

% OF SUNNY/PTLY CLOUDY/CLOUDY DAYS

☐ Clear   ▦ Ptlycldy   ■ Cloudy

- The table characterizes the lower elevation areas of the Parks. Most of the park area is at higher elevations and, as such, temperatures will average at least 5 degrees colder. Precipitation will be much greater; the precipitation on the high windward slopes can be expected to be twice that shown here.

etc.

CLIMATABLE NO. 40

TEMPERATURE NORMALS AND EXTREMES

% OF SUNNY/PTLY CLOUDY/CLOUDY DAYS

☐ Clear   ▦ Ptlycldy   ■ Cloudy

WEATHER PARAMETERS	MONTH											
	J	F	M	A	M	J	J	A	S	O	N	D
TEMPERATURE												
Normal Daily Maximum	82	83	84	85	86	87	88	88	88	87	86	84
Normal Daily Minimum	71	71	72	74	75	77	77	77	76	76	74	73
Extreme High	86	87	88	90	90	91	92	92	92	91	90	88
Extreme Low	63	65	66	65	69	69	71	67	71	68	67	64
Days Above 90°	0	0	0	0	0	2	6	8	4	1	0	0
Days Below 32°	0	0	0	0	0	0	0	0	0	0	0	0
PRECIPITATION												
Normal	2.4	1.9	1.7	2.2	4.6	3.2	3.3	4.1	6.9	5.6	3.9	3.9
Maximum	NA	NA	NA	NA	NA	NA	NA	NA	NA	NA	NA	NA
Maximum 24 Hr. Precipitation	NA	NA	NA	NA	NA	NA	NA	NA	NA	NA	NA	NA
Maximum Snowfall	0	0	0	0	0	0	0	0	0	0	0	0
Days With Measurable Precip.	13	11	10	12	13	13	14	14	15	14	14	13
Average No. Thunderstorms	0	0	0	0	1	2	2	2	2	2	1	0
SUNSHINE/CLOUDINESS												
No. Clear Days	8	7	9	7	3	4	4	4	3	4	5	5
No. Partly Cloudy Days	19	17	18	17	16	16	18	18	17	17	18	19
No. Cloudy Days	4	4	4	6	12	10	9	9	10	10	7	7
% Possible Sunshine	67	70	74	69	61	62	67	67	61	61	59	60

etc.

- The dominant weather features are the consistent temperatures, the steady northeast trade winds, the daytime sea breezes and the afternoon showers.
- Tropical storms and disturbances can bring high winds and heavy rains, most commonly in the summer or fall.

WINDCHILL

The wind chill temperature is a measure of how cold a person is made to feel under the combined effects of temperature and wind. At temperatures below 50° F, increasing wind speeds result in a greater transfer of heat and a greater evaporation rate from the body. The result is an increased feeling of "cold." This chilling effect of the wind can be expressed as the temperature at which a person would feel equivalently cold in just a light breeze (actually, 4 mph is assumed).

To determine the wind chill temperature in the accompanying table, find the column corresponding to the air temperature in F and move down to the line corresponding to the wind speed. Along the left side of the chart, the wind speed is given in miles per hour; along the right side of the chart, you will find the wind speed in knots. For example, at a temperature of 16° F and a wind speed of 12 mph (10 knots), to the average person it would feel as if the temperature were –5 F.

WIND SPEED / KNOTS — TEMPERATURE °F — WIND SPEED / M.P.H.

M.P.H.	KNOTS	40	38	36	34	32	30	28	26	24	22	20	18	16	14	12	10	8	6	4	2	0	-2	-4	-6	-8	-10
4	3.5	40	38	36	34	32	30	28	26	24	22	20	18	16	14	12	10	8	6	4	2	0	-2	-4	-6	-8	-10
6	5	35	33	31	29	26	24	22	20	18	15	13	11	9	7	5	2	0	-2	-4	-6	-9	-11	-13	-15	-17	-20
8	7	31	29	27	24	22	20	17	15	13	10	8	6	3	1	-1	-4	-6	-8	-11	-13	-15	-18	-20	-22	-25	-27
10	9	28	26	23	21	18	16	13	11	9	6	4	1	-1	-4	-6	-9	-11	-14	-16	-18	-21	-23	-26	-28	-31	-33
12	10	26	23	21	18	15	13	10	8	5	3	0	-3	-5	-8	-10	-13	-15	-18	-20	-23	-26	-28	-31	-33	-36	-38
14	12	23	21	18	15	13	10	7	5	2	0	-3	-6	-8	-11	-14	-16	-19	-22	-24	-27	-30	-32	-35	-38	-40	-43
16	14	21	19	16	13	11	8	6	2	0	-3	-6	-9	-11	-14	-17	-19	-22	-25	-28	-30	-33	-36	-38	-41	-44	-47
18	16	20	17	14	12	9	6	3	0	-3	-5	-8	-11	-14	-17	-19	-22	-25	-28	-30	-33	-36	-39	-42	-44	-47	-50
20	17	18	15	13	10	7	4	2	-2	-5	-7	-10	-13	-16	-19	-22	-24	-27	-30	-33	-36	-39	-42	-44	-47	-50	-53
22	19	16	14	11	8	5	2	0	-3	-6	-9	-12	-15	-18	-21	-23	-25	-29	-32	-35	-38	-41	-44	-47	-50	-53	-56
24	21	15	13	10	7	4	1	-2	-5	-8	-11	-14	-17	-20	-23	-25	-28	-31	-34	-37	-40	-43	-46	-49	-52	-55	-58
26	23	14	12	9	6	3	0	-3	-6	-9	-12	-15	-18	-21	-24	-27	-30	-33	-36	-39	-42	-45	-48	-51	-54	-57	-60
28	24	13	11	8	5	2	-1	-4	-7	-10	-13	-16	-19	-22	-25	-28	-31	-35	-38	-41	-44	-47	-50	-53	-56	-59	-62
30	26	12	10	7	4	1	-2	-5	-8	-11	-14	-18	-21	-24	-27	-30	-33	-36	-39	-42	-45	-48	-51	-54	-57	-60	-63
32	28	12	9	6	3	0	-3	-6	-9	-12	-15	-19	-22	-25	-28	-31	-34	-37	-40	-43	-46	-49	-52	-55	-59	-62	-65
34	30	11	9	6	2	-1	-4	-7	-10	-13	-16	-19	-22	-26	-29	-32	-35	-38	-41	-44	-47	-50	-54	-57	-60	-63	-66
36	31	11	8	5	2	-1	-5	-8	-11	-14	-17	-20	-23	-26	-30	-33	-36	-39	-42	-45	-48	-51	-55	-58	-61	-64	-67
38	33	11	8	5	1	-2	-5	-8	-11	-15	-18	-21	-24	-27	-30	-33	-37	-40	-43	-46	-49	-52	-55	-59	-62	-65	-68
40	35	10	7	4	1	-2	-6	-9	-12	-15	-18	-21	-25	-28	-31	-34	-37	-40	-43	-47	-50	-53	-56	-59	-62	-66	-69

COOL — COLD — VERY COLD — BITTER — EXPOSED FLESH FREEZES

HEAT INDEX

The heat stress felt in hot weather is influenced by the air temperature, the humidity, the wind and exposure to direct sunshine. In direct sunlight, heat is added to the body and you feel warmer than in the shade. At temperatures higher than the normal temperature of the body (98.6°F), winds above 10 mph also add heat to the body. These factors aside, the air temperature and the humidity are the key elements affecting discomfort. The National Weather Service uses heat index to measure discomfort and the potential danger of sunstroke and heat exhaustion. The heat index is expressed as an "apparent temperature". It expresses what any combination of temperature and relative humidity feels like to a person standing in the shade with a light breeze.

To determine the heat index or "apparent temperature", find the column closest to the air temperature and move down that column to the line corresponding to the closest value of the relative humidity. For example, if the temperature were 90°F with a relative humidity of 60%, to a person standing in the shade, it would feel as if it were 100°F. CAUTION: In direct sunlight, it would feel 5 to 10 degrees warmer!

RELATIVE HUMIDITY %

RH % \ Temp °F	70	72	74	76	78	80	82	84	86	88	90	92	94	96	98	100	102	104	106	108	110	112	114	116	118	120
0	64	66	68	70	71	72	75	77	78	80	83	84	86	88	90	91	93	95	96	98	99	101	103	105	106	107
5	64	66	68	70	72	73	75	77	79	80	84	86	87	89	91	93	95	97	98	100	102	104	106	108	110	111
10	65	67	69	71	72	74	76	79	81	82	85	87	88	91	93	95	97	99	101	104	105	107	109	112	115	117
15	65	68	70	71	73	75	77	80	82	83	86	88	90	93	95	97	99	102	105	107	108	110	115	117	120	123
20	66	68	71	72	74	76	78	81	83	84	87	89	92	95	97	99	102	105	107	110	112	115	120	124	127	130
25	67	69	72	73	75	77	79	82	85	86	88	91	94	96	98	101	105	108	110	114	117	121	125	130	135	139
30	67	70	72	74	76	78	80	83	86	88	90	93	95	98	101	104	107	110	115	120	124	129	134	139	143	148
35	68	70	73	75	77	79	82	84	86	89	91	96	97	100	104	107	111	116	120	126	130	135	139			
40	68	71	73	76	77	79	82	85	87	90	93	98	99	103	107	110	116	121	127	132	137	143				
45	69	72	74	76	78	80	84	86	88	91	95	100	101	106	110	115	121	127	132	138	143					
50	69	72	74	76	79	81	84	87	90	93	96	100	105	109	115	120	127	134	138							
55	70	72	75	77	79	82	85	88	91	95	98	103	107	114	120	126	133	138								
60	70	73	76	78	80	83	86	89	93	96	100	106	110	118	125	132	139									
65	70	73	76	79	81	84	87	90	95	99	103	109	115	124	131	138										
70	70	74	77	79	82	85	89	93	97	101	106	113	120	129	138	144										
75	70	74	77	80	82	86	90	95	99	105	110	118	125	132	140											
80	71	74	78	81	83	86	91	96	101	107	114	122	130	140												
85	71	75	78	82	85	87	94	98	105	111	117	127	135													
90	71	75	79	82	85	89	95	100	107	115	122	131														
95	72	75	79	83	86	90	97	103	110	118	125	135														
100	72	76	79	83	87	91	98	106	115	121	130	140														

APPARENT TEMPERATURES CONTINUE TO RISE WITH INCREASING RELATIVE HUMIDITY

A — Very warm; fatigue possible with prolonged exposure

B — Hot; Sunstroke, Heat Cramps & Heat Exhaustion possible with prolonged exposure

C — Very Hot; Danger: Sunstroke, Heat Cramps, or Heat Exhaustion likely with prolonged exposure

D — Extreme Danger: Heat/Sunstroke highly likely with continued exposure

Peak Visitation

While a visit to one of our National Park areas is almost always enjoyable and enriching, the experience can be all the more relaxing if you can avoid making the visit during the heaviest visitor season. As the crowds disappear, your opportunities to explore more thoroughly, to ask questions, or simply to pause and reflect in an area of spectacular natural beauty or lasting historic significance, all increase. The frustrations of traffic, crowded facilities, and lodging or camping difficulties will be reduced.

The National Park Service does maintain records of peak visitation, indicating the relative peak times when more visitors are present. How significant these peak periods should be to you in planning your visit depend on many factors. You should not necessarily be discouraged from planning your visit, simply because you would be travelling during the particular park's peak visitation month. For example, some parks are not overcrowded, even during the peak visitation period. Conversely, for other parks, visitation may be constantly high, nearing the point of overcrowding for *several* months, so that while visitation is *heaviest* in one month, it may not be that much greater during the peak month than it is in one or more other months. From the visitor's standpoint, you may only be able to visit during the peak period. Your willingness to visit under less ideal climate conditions and the extent to which you are seeking solitude will influence your plans as well. Nonetheless, as a possible aid in your planning we are including a listing of the month in which each park area is the most crowded–the month of peak visitation.

Abraham Lincoln BPL NHS (*July*)
Acadia NP (*August*)
Adams NHS (*July*)
Agate Fossil Beds NM (*July*)
Alibates NM (*July*)
Allegheny Portage RR NHS (*July*)
Amistad NRA (*May*)
Andersonville NHS (*May*)
Andrew Johnson NHS (*May*)
Antietam NB (*September*)
Apostle Islands NL (*August*)
Appomattox Crt Hse NHP (*July*)
Arches NP (*August*)

Arkansas Post NMEM (*May*)
Arlington Hse RELee NMEM (*July*)
Assateague Island NS (*August*)
Aztec Ruins NM (*August*)

Badlands NM (*August*)
Bandelier NM (*July*)
Bent's Old Fort NHS (*July*)
Big Bend NP (*April*)
Big Cypress NPRES (*March*)
Big Hole NB (*July*)
Big Thicket NPRES (*May*)
Bighorn Canyon NRA (*July*)
Biscayne NP (*August*)
Black Canyon OTG NM (*August*)
Blue Ridge Parkway (*August*)
Booker T. Washington NM (*August*)
Boston NHP (*August*)
Brices Cross Roads NBS (*August*)
Bryce Canyon NP (*August*)
Buck Island Reef NM (*February*)
Buffalo NR (*June*)

C&O Canal NHP (*July*)
Cabrillo NM (*January*)
Canaveral NS (*July*)
Canyon de Chelly NM (*May*)
Canyonlands NP (*May*)
Cape Cod NS (*August*)
Cape Hatteras NS (*July*)
Cape Krusenstern NM (*September*)
Cape Lookout NS (*July*)
Capitol Reef NP (*May*)
Capulin Mountain NM (*July*)
Carl Sandburg Home NHS (*August*)
Carlsbad Caverns NP (*July*)
Casa Grande NM (*March*)
Castillo De San Marcos NM (*July*)
Castle Clinton NM (*August*)
Catoctin Mtn Park (*August*)
Cedar Breaks NM (*July*)
Chaco Culture NHP (*August*)
Chamizal NMEM (*July*)
Channel Islands NP (*August*)
Chickamauga and Chattanooga NMP (*July*)
Chickasaw NRA (*June*)
Chiricahua NM (*May*)
Christiansted NHS (*January*)
Clara Barton NHS (*August*)
Colonial NHP (*July*)
Colorado NM (*August*)
Coronado NMEM (*April*)

Coulee Dam NRA (*August*)
Cowpens NM (*June*)
Crater Lake NP (*July*)
Craters of the Moon NM (*July*)
Cumberland Gap NHP (*July*)
Cumberland Islands NS (*April*)
Curecanti NRA (*July*)
Custer Battlefield NM (*July*)
Cuyahoga Valley NRA (*July*)

DeSoto NMEM (*March*)
Death Valley NM (*April*)
Delaware Water Gap NRA (*July*)
Denali NP (*August*)
Devils Postpile NM (*August*)
Devils Tower NM (*August*)
Dinosaur NM (*July*)

Edgar Allen Poe NHS (*August*)
Edison NHS (*August*)
Effigy Mounds NM (*July*)
Eisenhower NHS (*July*)
El Morro NM (*August*)
Everglades NP (*March*)

Federal Hall NMEM (*July*)
Fire Island NS (*August*)
Florissant Fossil Beds NM (*August*)
Ford's Theatre NHS (*May*)
Fort Bowie NHS (*March*)
Fort Caroline NMEM (*July*)
Fort Clatsop NMEM (*August*)
Fort Davis NHS (*March*)
Fort Donelson NMP (*February*)
Fort Frederica NM (*March*)
Fort Jefferson NM (*July*)
Fort Laramie NHS (*July*)
Fort Larned NHS (*August*)
Fort Matanzas NM (*July*)
Fort McHenry NM&HS (*June*)
Fort Necessity NB (*July*)
Fort Point NHS (*May*)
Fort Pulaski NM (*June*)
Fort Raleigh NHS (*August*)
Fort Scott NHS (*June*)
Fort Smith NHS (*July*)
Fort Stanwix NM (*July*)
Fort Sumter NM (*July*)
Fort Union NM (*July*)
Fort Union Trad Post NHS (*July*)
Fort Vancouver NHS (*July*)
Fort Washington Park (*May*)
Fossil Butte NM (*July*)
Fredericksburg & Spotsylvania NMP
    (*August*)
Fredrk Douglass Home NM (*February*)

Gates of the Arctic NP & PRES (*August*)

Gateway NRA (*July*)
General Grant NMEM (*May*)
Geo Wash Birthplace NM (*May*)
Geo Wash Carver NM (*July*)
Geo Wash Mem Pkwy (*July*)
George Rogers Clark NHP (*May*)
Gettysburg NMP (*July*)
Gila Cliff Dwellings NM (*August*)
Glacier Bay NP & PRES (*August*)
Glacier NP (*July*)
Glen Canyon NRA (*August*)
Golden Gate NRA (*August*)
Golden Spike NHS (*July*)
Grand Canyon NP (*August*)
Grand Portage NM (*August*)
Grand Teton NP (*July*)
Grant-Kohrs NHS (*July*)
Great Basin NP (*August*)
Great Sand Dunes NM (*July*)
Great Smoky Mtns NP (*July*)
Greenbelt Park (*May*)
Guadalupe Mountains NP (*May*)
Guilford Courthouse NMP (*March*)
Gulf Islands NS (*June*)

Haleakala NP (*July*)
Hamilton Grange NMEM (*August*)
Hampton NHS (*September*)
Harpers Ferry NHP (*May*)
Harry S Truman NHS (*July*)
Hawaii Volcanoes NP (*September*)
Herbert Hoover NHS (*July*)
Home of FDR NHS (*August*)
Homestead NM of America (*June*)
Hopewell Furnace NHS (*August*)
Horseshoe Bend NMP (*April*)
Hot Springs NP (*July*)
Hovenweep NM (*July*)
Hubbell Trad Post NHS (*May*)

Independence NHP (*July*)
Indiana Dunes NL (*June*)
Isle Royale NP (*August*)

Jean Lafitte NHP (*March*)
Jefferson NEM NHS (*August*)
Jewel Cave NM (*July*)
JFK Ctr Perf Arts (*April*)
John D. Rockefeller Pkwy (*July*)
John Day Fossil Beds NM (*July*)
John F. Kennedy NHS (*August*)
John Muir NHS (*April*)
Johnstown Flood NMEM (*July*)
Joshua Tree NM (*April*)

Katmai NM (*July*)
Kenai Fjords NP (*July*)
Kennesaw Mountain NBP (*April*)

Kings Canyon NP (*August*)
Kings Mountain NMP (*July*)
Klondike Gold Rush NHP (*July*)
Knife River NHS (*July*)
Kobuk Valley NP (*July*)

Lake Clark NP & Pres (*August*)
Lake Mead NRA (*June*)
Lake Meredith NRA (*May*)
Lassen Volcanic NP (*September*)
Lava Beds NM (*August*)
Lincoln Boyhood NMEM (*August*)
Lincoln Home NHS (*July*)
Lincoln Memorial (*July*)
Longfellow NHS (*August*)
Lowell NHP (*July*)
Lyndon B. Johnson NHS (*March*)

Mammoth Cave NP (*July*)
Manassas NBP (*May*)
Martin L. King, Jr. NHS (*January*)
Mesa Verde NP (*July*)
Minute Man NHP (*July*)
Montezuma Castle NM (*April*)
Moores Creek NMP (*July*)
Morristown NHP (*August*)
Mound City Group NM (*August*)
Mount Rainier NP (*August*)
Mount Rushmore NMEM (*July*)
Muir Woods NM (*August*)

Natchez Trace Parkway (*July*)
National Capital Parks (*May*)
Natural Bridges NM (*June*)
Navajo NM (*August*)
New River Gorge NR(*July*)
Nez Perce NHP (*August*)
Noatah NPRES (*August*)
North Cascades NP (*August*)

Ocmulgee NM (*March*)
Olympic NP (*August*)
Oregon Caves NM (*August*)
Organ Pipe Cactus NM (*March*)
Ozark NSR (*July*)

Padre Island NS (*August*)
Pea Ridge NMP (*July*)
Pecos NM (*August*)
Perry's Victory & IPM (*July*)
Petersburg NB (*March*)
Petrified Forest NP (*July*)
Pictured Rocks NL (*August*)
Pinnacles NM (*April*)
Pipe Spring NM (*June*)
Pipestone NM (*July*)
Piscataway Park (*May*)
Point Reyes NS (*July*)
Prince William For Pk (*May*)

Pu'uhonua O Honaunau NHP (*July*)
Puukohola Heiau NHS (*August*)

Rainbow Bridge NM (*August*)
Redwood NP (*July*)
Richmond NBP (*July*)
Rock Creek Park (*August*)
Rocky Mountain NP (*August*)
Roger Williams NM (*August*)
Russel Cave NM (*July*)

Sagamore Hill NHS (*July*)
Saguaro NM (*February*)
Saint Croix NSR (*July*)
Saint-Gaudens NHS (*July*)
Salem Maritime NHS (*July*)
Salinas NM (*July*)
San Antonio Missions NHP (*May*)
San Juan Island NHP (*August*)
San Juan NHS (*March*)
Santa Monica Mtns. NRA (*May*)
Saratoga NHP (*August*)
Saugus Iron Works NHS (*August*)
Scott's Bluff NM (*June*)
Sequoia NP (*August*)
Shadow Mountain NRA (*July*)
Shenandoah NP (*August*)
Shiloh NMP (*April*)
Sitka NHP (*August*)
Sleeping Bear Dunes NL (*August*)
Springfield Armory NHS (*August*)
Statue of Liberty NM (*August*)
Steamtown NHS (*not yet open to public*)
Stones River NB (*July*)
Sunset Crater NM (*July*)

Theo Roosevelt Inaug NHS (*June*)
Theo Roosevelt Bpl NHS (*May*)
Theo Roosevelt Is (*May*)
Theo Roosevelt NP (*June*)
Thomas Jefferson Memorial (*April*)
Timpanogos Cave NM (*July*)
Tonto NM (*March*)
Tumacacori NM (*March*)
Tupelo NB (*August*)
Tuskegee Institute NHS (*September*)
Tuzigoot NM (*April*)

U.S.S. Arizona MEM (*July*)
Upper Delaware NSR (*July*)

Valley Forge NHP (*May*)
Vanderbilt Mansions NHS (*July*)
Vicksburg NMP (*August*)
Virgin Islands NP (*April*)
Voyageurs NP (*June*)

Walnut Canyon NM (*August*)
Washington Monument (*May*)

Whiskeytown NRA (*August*)
White House (*April*)
White Sands NM (*July*)
Whitman Mission NHS (*June*)
William Howard Taft NHS (*May*)
Wilson's Creek NB (*June*)
Wind Cave NP (*August*)
Wolf Trap Farm Park (*July*)
Women's Rights NHP (*July*)

Wrangell-St. Elais NP & PRES (*August*)
Wright Brothers NMEM (*August*)
Wupatki NM (*July*)

Yellowstone NP (*July*)
Yosemite NP (*August*)
Yukon Charley Rivers NPRES (*September*)

Zion NP (*August*)

Index

Explanation of Abbreviations:

MEM PKWY
Memorial Parkway
NB
National Battlefield
NBS
National Battlefield Site
NHP
National Historical Park
NHS
National Historic Site
NHT
National Historic Trail
NL
National Lakeshore
NM
National Monument
N MEM
National Memorial
NMP
National Military Park
NP
National Park
N PRES
National Preserve
NR
National River or Riverway
NRA
National Recreation Area
NS
National Seashore
NSR
National Scenic River or Riverway
NST
National Scenic Trail
PKWY
Parkway

Abraham Lincoln Birthplace NHS,
    KY **128**
Abraham Lincoln Memorial, DC (See
    Lincoln Memorial)
Acadia NP, ME **133**
Adams NHS, MA **148**
Agate Fossil Beds NM, NE **190**
Alagnak Wild River, AK **4**

Alexander Hamilton (See Hamilton
    Grange NM)
Alibates NM, TX **280**
Allegheny Portage Railroad NHS,
    PA **251**
American Memorial Park, Northern
    Mariana Islands **345**
Amistad NRA, TX **280**
Andersonville NHS, GA **99**
Andrew Johnson NHS, TN **273**
Aniakchak N PRES, AK **5**
Antietam NB, MD **137**
Apostle Islands NL, WI **331**
Appalachian NST, ME-NH-VT-MA-CT-
    NY-NJ-PA-MD-VA-TN-NC-GA **135**
Appomattox Court House NHP, VA **303**
Arches NP, UT **292**
Arkansas Post N MEM, AR **40**
Arlington House, The Robert E. Lee
    Memorial, VA **304**
Assateague Islands NS, MD-VA **138**
Aztec Ruins NM, NM **201**
Badlands NP, SD **268**
Bandelier NM, NM **202**
Barton, Clara (See Clara Barton)
Benjamin Franklin N MEM, PA **252**
Bent's Old Fort NHS, CO **64**
Bering Land Bridge N PRES, AK **6**
Big Bend NP, TX **281**
Big Cypress N PRES, FL **89**
Big Hole NB, MT **184**
Bighorn Canyon NRA, MT-WY **185**
Big South Fork NR and Recreation Area,
    TN-KY **274**
Big Thicket N PRES, TX **282**
Biscayne NP, FL **90**
Black Canyon of the Gunnison NM, CO **65**
Blue Ridge PKWY, NC-VA **228**
Bluestone NSR, WV **328**
Booker T. Washington NM, VA **305**
Boston African-American NHS, MA **149**
Boston NHP, MA **150**
Brices Cross Roads NBS, MS **174**
Bryce Canyon NP, UT **293**
Buck Island Reef NM, VI **350**
Buffalo NR, AR **41**
Bunker Hill Battlefield & Monument,
    MA **151**
Cabrillo NM, CA **45**

Canaveral NS, FL **91**
Canyon de Chelly NM, AZ **20**
Canyonlands NP, UT **294**
Cape Cod NS, MA **152**
Cape Hatteras NS, NC **230**
Cape Krusenstern NM, AK **7**
Cape Lookout NS, NC **232**
Capitol Reef NP, UT **295**
Capulin Mountain NM, NM **203**
Carl Sandburg Home NHS, NC **232**
Carlsbad Caverns NP, NM **204**
Carter, Jimmy (See Jimmy Carter)
Carver, George Washington (See George
    Washington Carver)
Casa Grande NM, AZ **22**
Castillo de San Marcos NM, FL **92**
Castle Clinton NM, NY **212**
Catoctin Mountain Park, MD **139**
Cedar Breaks NM, UT **296**
Chaco Culture NHP, NM **205**
Chamizal N MEM, TX **284**
Channel Islands NP, CA **45**
Charles Pinckney NHS, SC **264**
Charlestown Navy Yard, MA **153**
Chattahoochee River NRA, GA **100**
Chesapeake and Ohio Canal NHP, MD-
    VA-DC **140**
Chicago Portage NHP, IL **118**
Chickamauga and Chattanooga NMP,
    GA-TN **101**
Chickasaw NRA, OK **245**
Chimney Rock NHS, NE **191**
Chiricahua NM, AZ **22**
Christiansted NHS, VI **351**
City of Refuge NHP (See Pu'uhonua o
    Honaunau NHP)
City of Rocks N PRES, ID **115**
Clara Barton NHS, MD **142**
Clark, George Rogers (See George Rogers
    Clark)
Colonial NHP, VA **306**
Colorado NM, CO **66**
Congaree Swamp NM, SC **264**
Constitution Gardens, DC **76**
Coronado N MEM, AZ **23**
Coulee Dam NRA, WA **319**
Cowpens NB, SC **265**
Crater Lake NP, OR **246**
Craters of the Moon NM, ID **116**
Cumberland Gap NHP, KY-TN-VA **129**
Cumberland Island NS, GA **102**
Curecanti NRA, CO **67**

Custer Battlefield NM, MT **185**
Cuyahoga Valley NRA, OH **240**
Death Valley NM, CA-NV **47**
Delaware Water Gap NRA, PA-NJ **253**
Denali NP & PRES, AK **7**
De Soto N MEM, FL **93**
Devils Postpile NM, CA **48**
Devils Tower NM, WY **336**
Dinosaur NM, CO **68**
Dorchester Heights NHS, MA **154**
Douglass, Frederick, DC (See Frederick
    Douglass)
Edgar Allan Poe NHS, PA **254**
Edison NHS, NJ **199**
Effigy Mounds NM, IA **124**
Eisenhower NHS, PA **254**
Eleanor Roosevelt NHS, NY **213**
Ellis Island, NY **214**
El Malpais NM, NM **206**
El Morro NM, NM **206**
Eugene O'Neill NHS, CA **48**
Everglades NP, FL **93**
Faneuil Hall, MA **155**
Father Marquette N MEM, MI **166**
Federal Hall NM, NY **215**
Fire Island NS, NY **216**
Florissant Fossil Beds NM, CO **69**
Ford's Theatre NHS, DC **77**
Fort Benton, MT **186**
Fort Bowie NHS, AZ **24**
Fort Caroline N MEM, FL **95**
Fort Clatsop N MEM, OR **247**
Fort Davis NHS, TX **285**
Fort Donelson NMP, TN **275**
Fort Dupont Park and Activity Center,
    DC **78**
Fort Frederica NM, GA **103**
Fort Jefferson NM, FL **95**
Fort Laramie NHS, WY **337**
Fort Larned NHS, KS **126**
Fort Matanzas NM, FL **96**
Fort McHenry NM and Historic Shrine,
    MD **142**
Fort Moultrie, SC (See Fort Sumter
    NM)
Fort Necessity NB, PA **255**
Fort Point NHS, CA **49**
Fort Pulaski NM, GA **104**
Fort Raleigh NHS, NC **233**
Fort Scott NHS, KS **127**
Fort Smith NHS, AR **42**
Fort Stanwix NM, NY **216**

Fort Sumter NM, SC **266**
Fort Union NM, NM **207**
Fort Union Trading Post NHS, ND-MT **237**
Fort Vancouver NHS, WA **320**
Fort Washington Park, MD **143**
Fossil Butte NM, WY **338**
Franklin, Benjamin (See Benjamin Franklin)
Frederick Douglass NHS, DC **79**
Frederick Law Olmsted NHS, MA **156**
Fredericksburg and Spotsylvania County Battlefields Memorial NMP, VA **307**
Friendship Hill NHS, PA **255**
Gates of the Arctic NP & PRES, AK **8**
Gateway Arch, MO (See Jefferson National Expansion Memorial NHS)
Gateway NRA, NY-NJ **217**
Gauley River NRA, WV **328**
General Grant N MEM, NY **218**
George Rogers Clark NHP, IN **121**
George Washington Birthplace NM, VA **308**
George Washington Carver NM, MO **178**
George Washington MEM PKWY, VA-MD **308**
Gettysburg NMP, PA **256**
Gila Cliff Dwellings NM, NM **207**
Glacier Bay NP & PRES, AK **10**
Glacier NP, MT **187**
Glen Canyon NRA, UT-AZ **25**
Glen Echo Park, MD **144**
Gloria Dei (Old Swedes') Church NHS, PA **257**
Golden Gate NRA, CA **50**
Golden Spike NHS, UT **297**
Grand Canyon NP, AZ **26**
Grand Portage NM, MN **170**
Grand Teton NP, WY **338**
Grant, U.S. (See General Grant NM)
Grant-Kohrs Ranch NHS, MT **188**
Great Basin NP, NV **194**
Great Falls Park, VA **309**
Great Sand Dunes NM, CO **70**
Great Smoky Mountains NP, TN-NC **275**
Greenbelt Park, MD **144**
Guadalupe Mountains NP, TX **286**
Guilford Courthouse NMP, NC **234**
Gulf Islands NS, FL-MS **97**
Hagerman Fossil Beds NM, ID **116**
Haleakala NP, HI **108**
Hamilton, Alexander (See Hamilton Grange N MEM)
Hamilton Grange N MEM, NY **219**
Hampton NHS, MD **145**
Harpers Ferry NHP, WV-MD **329**
Harry S. Truman NHS, MO **179**
Hawaii Volcanoes NP, HI **110**
Herbert Hoover NHS, IA **125**
Hohokam Pima NM, AZ **28**
Home of Franklin D. Roosevelt NHS, NY **219**
Homestead NM of America, NE **191**
Hoover, Herbert (See Herbert Hoover)
Hopewell Furnace NHS, PA **257**
Horseshoe Bend NMP, AL **1**
Hot Springs NP, AR **42**
Hovenweep NM, CO-UT **71**
Hubbell Trading Post NHS, AZ **28**
Ice Age NST, WI **333**
Ice Age National Scientific Reserve, WI **332**
Independence NHP, PA **258**
Indiana Dunes NL, IN **122**
International Peace Garden, ND **238**
Isle Royale NP, MI **166**
J. Alden Weir Home, CT **88**
James A. Garfield NHS, OH **242**
Jamestown NHS, VA **310**
Jean Lafitte NHP, LA **131**
Jefferson Memorial, DC (See Thomas Jefferson Memorial)
Jefferson National Expansion Memorial NHS, MO **180**
Jewel Cave NM, SD **269**
Jimmy Carter NHS, GA **105**
John D. Rockefeller, Jr. MEM PKWY, WY **340**
John Day Fossil Beds NM, OR **248**
John F. Kennedy Center for the Performing Arts, DC **79**
John Fitzgerald Kennedy NHS, MA **156**
John Muir NHS, CA **51**
Johnson, Andrew (See Andrew Johnson)
Johnson, Lyndon B. (See Lyndon B. Johnson)
Johnstown Flood N MEM, PA **259**
Joshua Tree NM, CA **52**
Kalaupapa NHP, HI **111**
Kaloko-Honokohau NHP, HI **111**
Katmai NP & PRES, AK **11**
Kenai Fjords NP, AK **12**
Kennedy Center, DC (See John F. Kennedy Center)

Kennedy, John F. (See John F. Kennedy)
Kennesaw Mountain NBP, GA **266**
Kings Canyon NP, CA (See Sequoia and Kings Canyon NP)
Kings Mountain NMP, SC **266**
Klondike Gold Rush NHP, AK-WA **13**
Knife River Indian Village NHS, ND **238**
Kobuk Valley NP, AK **14**
Kosciuszko, Thaddeus (See Thaddeus Kosciuszko)
Lake Chelan NRA, WA **321**
Lake Clark NP & PRES, AK **15**
Lake Mead NRA, NV **196**
Lake Meredith NRA, TX **287**
Lassen Volcanic NP, CA **52**
Lava Beds NM, CA **54**
Lee, Robert E. (See Arlington House, The Robert E. Lee Memorial)
Lewis and Clark NHT, IL-MO-KS-NE-IA-SD-ND-MT-ID-OR-WA **119**
Lincoln Boyhood NM, IN **123**
Lincoln Home NHS, IL **119**
Lincoln Memorial, DC **80**
Longfellow NHS, MA **157**
Lowell NHP, MA **158**
Lower St. Croix NSR, WI-MN **334**
Lyndon B. Johnson NHP, TX **288**
Lyndon Baines Johnson Memorial Grove on the Potomac, DC **81**
McLoughlin House NHS, OR **249**
Maggie L. Walker NHS, VA **311**
Mammoth Cave NP, KY **130**
Manassas NBP, VA **311**
Martin Luther King, Jr. NHS, GA **106**
Martin Van Buren NHS, NY **220**
Mesa Verde NP, CO **72**
Minute Man NHP, MA **159**
Mississippi NR, MN **170**
Missouri National Recreational River, NE **192**
Monocacy NB, MD **146**
Montezuma Castle NM, AZ **29**
Moores Creek NB, NC **235**
Mormon Pioneer NHT, IL-IA-NE-WY-UT **120**
Morristown NHP, NJ **199**
Mound City Group NM, OH **242**
Mount Rainier NP, WA **322**
Mount Rushmore NM, SD **270**
Muir Woods NM, CA **55**
Natchez NHP, MS **175**
Natchez Trace PKWY, MS-AL-TN **175**

National Capital Region, DC-MD-VA **81**
National Mall, DC **82**
National Park of American Samoa **348**
Natural Bridges NM, UT **298**
Navajo NM, AZ **29**
New River Gorge NR, WV **330**
Nez Perce NHP, ID **117**
Ninety Six NHS, SC **267**
Noatak NP, AK **16**
North Cascades NP, WA **323**
North Country NST, NY **221**
Obed Wild and Scenic River, TN **277**
Ocmulgee NM, GA **107**
Old North Church, MA **159**
Old South Meeting House, MA **160**
Old State House, MA **161**
Old Stone House, DC **82**
Olympic NP, WA **324**
O'Neill, Eugene (See Eugene O'Neill)
Organ Pipe Cactus NM, AZ **31**
Oregon Caves NM, OR **250**
Oregon NHT, MO-KS-NE-WY-ID-OR-WA **181**
Oxon Hill Farm, MD **146**
Ozark NSR, MO **181**
Padre Island NS, TX **289**
Palo Alto Battlefield, NHS, TX **290**
Paul Revere House, MA **162**
Pea Ridge NMP, AR **43**
Pecos NM, NM **208**
Pennsylvania Avenue NHS, DC **82**
Perry's Victory and International Peace Memorial, OH **243**
Petersburg NB, VA **312**
Petrified Forest NP, AZ **32**
Pictured Rocks NL, MI **168**
Pinelands National Reserve, NJ **200**
Pinnacles NM, CA **55**
Pipe Spring NM, AZ **33**
Pipestone NM, MN **172**
Piscataway Park, MD **147**
Poe, Edgar Allan (See Edgar Allan Poe)
Point Reyes NS, CA **57**
Potomac Heritage NST, DC **83**
Poverty Point NM, LA **132**
Prince William Forest Park, VA **313**
Pu'uhonua o Honaunau NHP, HI **112**
Puukohola Heiau NHS, HI **113**
Rainbow Bridge NM, UT **299**
Redwood NP, CA **58**
Richmond NBP, VA **314**

Rio Grande Wild and Scenic River, TX **290**

Robert E. Lee Memorial (See Arlington House)

Rock Creek Park, DC **84**

Rockefeller, John D., Jr. (See John D. Rockefeller, Jr.)

Rocky Mountain NP, CO **73**

Roger Williams NM, RI **262**

Roosevelt Campobello International Park, Canada **344**

Roosevelt, Eleanor (See Eleanor Roosevelt)

Roosevelt, Franklin D. (See Home of Franklin D. Roosevelt; Roosevelt Campobello)

Roosevelt, Theodore (See Sagamore Hill; Theodore Roosevelt)

Ross Lake NRA, WA **325**

Russell Cave NM, AL **2**

Sagamore Hill NHS, NY **223**

Saguaro NM, AZ **33**

Saint Croix Island International Historic Site, ME **136**

St. Croix National Scenic Riverway, MN-WI **334**

Saint-Gaudens NHS, NH **197**

Saint Paul's NHS, NY **223**

Salem Maritime NHS, MA **163**

Salinas NM, NM **209**

Sandburg, Carl (See Carl Sandburg)

San Antonio Missions NHP, TX **291**

San Francisco Maritime NHP, CA **59**

San Juan Island NHP, WA **326**

San Juan NHS, Puerto Rico **349**

Santa Monica Mountains NRA, CA **59**

Saratoga NHP, NY **224**

Saugus Iron Works NHS, MA **164**

Scott's Bluff NM, NE **193**

Sequoia and Kings Canyon National Parks, CA **60**

Sewall-Belmont House NHS, DC **85**

Shenandoah NP, VA **315**

Shiloh NMP, TN **277**

Sitka NHP, AK **17**

Skyline Drive, VA (See Shenandoah NP)

Sleeping Bear Dunes NL, MI **169**

Springfield Armory NHS, MA **164**

Statue of Liberty NM, NY **225**

Steamtown NHS, PA **260**

Stones River NB and Cemetery, TN **278**

Sunset Crater NM, AZ **35**

Taft, W.H. (See William Howard Taft)

Thaddeus Kosciuszko NM, PA **260**

The Claude Moore Colonial Farm at Turkey Run, VA **316**

Theodore Roosevelt Birthplace NHS, NY **222**

Theodore Roosevelt Inaugural NHS, NY **222**

Theodore Roosevelt Island, DC **85**

Theodore Roosevelt NP, ND **239**

Thomas Jefferson Memorial, DC **86**

Thomas Stone NHS, MD **147**

Timpanogos Cave NM, UT **300**

Timucuan Ecological Historic Preserve, FL **98**

Tonto NM, AZ **35**

Touro Synagogue NHS, RI **263**

Tumacacori NM, AZ **36**

Tupelo NB, MS **176**

Tuskegee Institute NHS, AL **3**

Tuzigoot NM, AZ **37**

Ulysses S. Grant NHS, MO **182**

Upper Delaware Wild and Scenic River, NY **225**

U.S. Marine Corps Memorial and Netherlands Carillon, VA **316**

USS Arizona Memorial, HI **114**

USS Constitution, MA (See Charlestown Navy Yard)

Valley Forge NHP, PA **261**

Van Buren, Martin (See Martin Van Buren)

Vanderbilt Mansion NHS, NY **226**

Vicksburg NMP, MS **177**

Vietnam Veterans Memorial, DC **86**

Virgin Islands NP, VI **351**

Visitor Center, Boston NHP, MA **165**

Voyageurs NP, MN **172**

Walker, Maggie L. (See Maggie L. Walker

Walnut Canyon NM, AZ **38**

War in the Pacific NHP, Guam **346**

Washington, Booker T. (See Booker T. Washington; Tuskegee Institute NHS)

Washington Monument, DC **87**

Whiskeytown-Shasta-Trinity NRA, CA **61**

The White House, DC **88**

White Sands NM, NM **210**

Whitman Mission NHS, WA **327**

William Howard Taft NHS, OH **244**

Williams, Roger (See Roger Williams)

Wilson's Creek NB, MO **183**

Wind Cave NP, SD **271**

Wolf Trap Farm Park, VA **317**

Women's Rights NHP, NY **227**

Wrangell-Saint Elias NP & PRES, AK **17**
Wright Brothers N MEM, NC **235**
Wupatki NM, AZ **39**
Yellowstone NP, WY-MT-ID **341**
Yorktown Battlefield, VA **318**

Yosemite NP, CA **62**
Yucca House NM, CO **76**
Yukon-Charley Rivers NPRES, AK **19**
Zion NP, UT **301**
Zuni-Cibola NHP, NM **211**

EASY ACCESS NATIONAL PARKS

A half-hour video by Michael Tompane and Wendy Roth

**An inspiring video experience to selected opportunities
for people with disabilities, seniors and families with young children
to nine national parks across the United States.**

Everyone will enjoy these evocative journeys through rainforests, geyser basins, high mountain lakes, and seashores. The "tour guides" are park rangers and visitors with different disabilities. Some have mobility problems and use wheelchairs, some are blind and some are deaf. EASY ACCESS NATIONAL PARKS visits Yosemite, Olympic, Yellowstone, Rocky Mountain, Mesa Verde, Chaco Culture, Everglades, Shenandoah and Acadia national parks. Proceeds go to support the EASY ACCESS CHALLENGE, a National Park Foundation project to enhance access for people with disabilities in the national parks.

Narrated by DANIEL J. TRAVANTI

Music from "THE NARADA WILDERNESS COLLECTION"

EASY ACCESS
NATIONAL PARKS

A half-hour video by Michael Tompane and Wendy Roth

**An inspiring video experience to selected opportunities
for people with disabilities, seniors and families with young children
to nine national parks across the United States.**

Everyone will enjoy these evocative journeys through rainforests, geyser basins, high mountain lakes, and seashores. The "tour guides" are park rangers and visitors with different disabilities. Some have mobility problems and use wheelchairs, some are blind and some are deaf. EASY ACCESS NATIONAL PARKS visits Yosemite, Olympic, Yellowstone, Rocky Mountain, Mesa Verde, Chaco Culture, Everglades, Shenandoah and Acadia national parks. Proceeds go to support the EASY ACCESS CHALLENGE, a National Park Foundation project to enhance access for people with disabilities in the national parks.

Narrated by DANIEL J. TRAVANTI

Music from "THE NARADA WILDERNESS COLLECTION"

GIVE THE **NEW GUIDE** TO A FRIEND— AND BE A FRIEND OF THE PARKS!

By buying this book you helped to support our National Parks. And you can do it again. Send copies to friends or relatives who love the Parks as much as you do.

The National Park Foundation uses proceeds from sales of the *Guide* to support Park programs such as—

- new audio-visual programs for visitor centers
- environmental education programs for school children
- recruiting new volunteers
- providing professional training for park employees . . . and more.

The National Park Foundation was chartered by Congress as a nonprofit organization to provide a means for all of us to help support our Parks. You can help by ordering this book—and also by enclosing a tax-deductible contribution.

_____ **YES. I WANT TO BE A FRIEND OF THE PARKS!**

I want to order copies of this book.
(Also available at your local bookstore.)

QUANTITY	PRICE	TOTAL
_____	$15.95	_____
	(includes shipping and handling)	

Please add my tax deductible contribution
to help the National Parks.   _____

TOTAL ENCLOSED   _____

Send books to:

Name _____

Street _____

City _____ State _____ Zip _____

Make check or money order payable (in U.S. dollars) to the **National Park Foundation**, 1101 17th Street, N.W., Washington, D.C. 20036.

GIVE THE **NEW GUIDE** TO A FRIEND–
AND BE A FRIEND OF THE PARKS!

By buying this book you helped to support our National Parks.
And you can do it again. Send copies to friends or relatives who
love the Parks as much as you do.

The National Park Foundation uses proceeds from sales of the
Guide to support Park programs such as—

- new audio-visual programs for visitor centers
- environmental education programs for school children
- recruiting new volunteers
- providing professional training for park employees . . .
  and more.

The National Park Foundation was chartered by Congress as a
nonprofit organization to provide a means for all of us to help
support our Parks. You can help by ordering this book—and also
by enclosing a tax-deductible contribution.

_____ **YES.** I WANT TO BE A FRIEND OF THE PARKS!

I want to order copies of this book.
(Also available at your local bookstore.)

QUANTITY	PRICE	TOTAL
_____	$15.95	_____
	(includes shipping and handling)	

Please add my tax deductible contribution
to help the National Parks.   _____

TOTAL ENCLOSED _____

Send books to:

Name _____

Street _____

City _____ State _____ Zip _____

Make check or money order payable (in U.S. dollars) to the **National
Park Foundation**, 1101 17th Street, N.W., Washington, D.C.
20036.

GIVE THE **NEW GUIDE** TO A FRIEND– AND BE A FRIEND OF THE PARKS!

By buying this book you helped to support our National Parks. And you can do it again. Send copies to friends or relatives who love the Parks as much as you do.

The National Park Foundation uses proceeds from sales of the *Guide* to support Park programs such as—
- new audio-visual programs for visitor centers
- environmental education programs for school children
- recruiting new volunteers
- providing professional training for park employees . . . and more.

The National Park Foundation was chartered by Congress as a nonprofit organization to provide a means for all of us to help support our Parks. You can help by ordering this book—and also by enclosing a tax-deductible contribution.

_____ **YES. I WANT TO BE A FRIEND OF THE PARKS!**

I want to order copies of this book.
(Also available at your local bookstore.)

QUANTITY   **PRICE**   **TOTAL**

_____ $15.95   _____
(includes shipping and handling)

Please add my tax deductible contribution
to help the National Parks.   _____

TOTAL ENCLOSED   _____

Send books to:

Name _____

Street _____

City _____ State _____ Zip _____

Make check or money order payable (in U.S. dollars) to the **National Park Foundation**, 1101 17th Street, N.W., Washington, D.C. 20036.

GIVE THE **NEW GUIDE** TO A FRIEND—AND BE A FRIEND OF THE PARKS!

By buying this book you helped to support our National Parks. And you can do it again. Send copies to friends or relatives who love the Parks as much as you do.

The National Park Foundation uses proceeds from sales of the *Guide* to support Park programs such as—

- new audio-visual programs for visitor centers
- environmental education programs for school children
- recruiting new volunteers
- providing professional training for park employees . . . and more.

The National Park Foundation was chartered by Congress as a nonprofit organization to provide a means for all of us to help support our Parks. You can help by ordering this book—and also by enclosing a tax-deductible contribution.

_____ **YES.** I WANT TO BE A FRIEND OF THE PARKS!

I want to order copies of this book.
(Also available at your local bookstore.)

QUANTITY	PRICE	TOTAL
_____	$15.95	_____
	(includes shipping and handling)	

Please add my tax deductible contribution
to help the National Parks.   _____

TOTAL ENCLOSED   _____

Send books to:

Name _____

Street _____

City _____ State _____ Zip _____

Make check or money order payable (in U.S. dollars) to the **National Park Foundation**, 1101 17th Street, N.W., Washington, D.C. 20036.

GIVE THE **NEW GUIDE** TO A FRIEND– AND BE A FRIEND OF THE PARKS!

By buying this book you helped to support our National Parks. And you can do it again. Send copies to friends or relatives who love the Parks as much as you do.

The National Park Foundation uses proceeds from sales of the *Guide* to support Park programs such as—

- new audio-visual programs for visitor centers
- environmental education programs for school children
- recruiting new volunteers
- providing professional training for park employees . . . and more.

The National Park Foundation was chartered by Congress as a nonprofit organization to provide a means for all of us to help support our Parks. You can help by ordering this book—and also by enclosing a tax-deductible contribution.

_____ **YES. I WANT TO BE A FRIEND OF THE PARKS!**

I want to order copies of this book.
(Also available at your local bookstore.)

QUANTITY	PRICE	TOTAL
_____	$15.95 (includes shipping and handling)	_____

Please add my tax deductible contribution
to help the National Parks.   _____

TOTAL ENCLOSED   _____

Send books to:

Name _____

Street _____

City _____ State _____ Zip _____

Make check or money order payable (in U.S. dollars) to the **National Park Foundation**, 1101 17th Street, N.W., Washington, D.C. 20036.

GIVE THE **NEW GUIDE** TO A FRIEND—
AND BE A FRIEND OF THE PARKS!

By buying this book you helped to support our National Parks. And you can do it again. Send copies to friends or relatives who love the Parks as much as you do.

The National Park Foundation uses proceeds from sales of the *Guide* to support Park programs such as—
- new audio-visual programs for visitor centers
- environmental education programs for school children
- recruiting new volunteers
- providing professional training for park employees . . . and more.

The National Park Foundation was chartered by Congress as a nonprofit organization to provide a means for all of us to help support our Parks. You can help by ordering this book—and also by enclosing a tax-deductible contribution.

_____ **YES.** I WANT TO BE A FRIEND OF THE PARKS!

I want to order copies of this book.
(Also available at your local bookstore.)

QUANTITY	PRICE	TOTAL
_____	$15.95 (includes shipping and handling)	_____

Please add my tax deductible contribution
to help the National Parks.   _____

TOTAL ENCLOSED   _____

Send books to:

Name _____

Street _____

City _____ State _____ Zip _____

Make check or money order payable (in U.S. dollars) to the **National Park Foundation**, 1101 17th Street, N.W., Washington, D.C. 20036.